HUMAN DEVELOPMENT REPORT 1997

Published
for the United Nations
Development Programme
(UNDP)

New York   Oxford
Oxford University Press
1997

Oxford University Press
Oxford   New York
Athens   Auckland   Bangkok   Bombay
Calcutta   Cape Town   Dar es Salaam   Delhi
Florence   Hong Kong   Istanbul   Karachi
Kuala Lumpur   Madras   Madrid   Melbourne
Mexico City   Nairobi   Paris   Singapore
Taipei   Tokyo   Toronto

and associated companies in
Berlin   Ibadan

ISBN 0-19-511996-7 (cloth)
ISBN 0-19-511997-5 (paper)

9 8 7 6 5 4 3 2 1
Printed in the United States of America on acid-free, recycled paper.

Cover and design: Gerald Quinn, Quinn Information Design, Cabin John, Maryland

Editing, desktop composition and production management: American Writing division of Communications Development Incorporated,
Washington, DC, and New York

Foreword

The 1990s began with a great surge of hope. With the cold war over, the world could harness its enormous resources for development and prosperity. During the first six years of the 1990s world conferences and summit meetings emphasized the urgency of eradicating poverty. The World Summit for Social Development in Copenhagen—attended by representatives of 185 governments and an unprecedented 117 heads of state and government—sharpened this focus. Countries committed themselves to the goal of eradicating poverty "as an ethical, social, political and moral imperative of human-kind" and recognized people-centred development as the key to achieving it.

In parallel, poverty eradication has become an overarching goal of international action—and of the United Nations system's work in the followup to the UN conferences and summits. The social development summit's programme of action calls on the United Nations Development Programme "to undertake efforts to support the implementation of social development programmes". UNDP has made the eradication of poverty its overriding priority. As the principal antipoverty arm of the United Nations, it is well placed to work with other parts of the UN system, especially its sister organizations and agencies at the country level, to assist states in their programmes to eradicate poverty. Already UNDP is working with more than 70 countries to follow up on the commitment made at Copenhagen.

This year's *Human Development Report* builds on that commitment. Its most important message is that poverty is no longer inevitable. The world has the material and natural resources, the know-how and the people to make a poverty-free world a reality in less than a generation. This is not woolly idealism but a practical and achievable goal. Over the past three decades a dozen or more developing countries have shown that it is possible to eliminate absolute poverty. And most industrial countries had largely eradicated absolute poverty by the 1970s, although some have slipped in the past decade.

Poverty is not to be suffered in silence by the poor. Nor can it be tolerated by those with the power to change it. The challenge now is to mobilize action—state by state, organization by organization, individual by individual.

Poverty has many faces. It is much more than low income. It also reflects poor health and education, deprivation in knowledge and communication, inability to exercise human and political rights and the absence of dignity, confidence and self-respect. There is also environmental impoverishment and the impoverishment of entire nations, where essentially everyone lives in poverty. Behind these faces of poverty lies the grim reality of desperate lives without choices and, often, governments that lack the capacity to cope.

This year's Report offers ideas for eradicating absolute poverty. The agenda includes but goes beyond income, encompassing gender, pro-poor growth, globalization and governance.

As in previous years, this year's *Human Development Report* is the fruit of a collaborative effort by a team of eminent consultants and the Human Development Report team. Richard Jolly, my Special Adviser, together with Sakiko Fukuda-Parr, Director, Human Development Report Office, led the effort.

The analysis and policy recommendations in this Report do not necessarily reflect the views of UNDP, its Executive Board or its Member States. The independence of views and the professional integrity of its authors ensure that the conclusions and recommendations will have the greatest possible audience.

As always, this is an innovative and thought-provoking report. I welcome the publication of *Human Development Report 1997* as an important contribution to the international momentum for eradicating absolute poverty. Some 160 years ago the world launched a successful campaign against slavery. Today we must all help to lead a similar campaign against poverty.

James Gustave Speth

New York
May 1997

Team for the preparation of
Human Development Report 1997

Principal Coordinator
Richard Jolly

UNDP team
Director: Sakiko Fukuda-Parr
Deputy Director: Selim Jahan
Members: Håkan Björkman, Moez Saad Doraid, Laura Mourino-Casas, Caterina Ruggeri Laderchi, Ewa Ruminska-Zimny, A. K. Shiva Kumar, Gül Tanghe-Güllüova, Ozer Babakol, Mourad Wahba and Amei Zhang
Editors: Peter Stalker and Bruce Ross-Larson

Panel of consultants
Oscar Altimir, Sudhir Anand, Albert Berry, Meghnad Desai, Yuji Genda, Kenneth Hill, Susan Horton, Alfred Kahn, Sheila Kamerman, Michel Lavollay, Michael Lipton, Jacky Mathonnat, Dipak Mazumdar, Valentine Moghadam, Jyoti Parikh, Eul Yong Park, J. D. von Pischke, Amartya K. Sen, Gita Sen, Timothy Smeeding, Paul Streeten, Eimi Watanabe and Kevin Watkins

Acknowledgements

The preparation of the Report would not have been possible without the support and valuable contributions of a large number of individuals and organizations.

Several international institutions generously shared their experience, research materials and data with the authors. The Report drew from the databases and material of the Food and Agriculture Organization, International Fund for Agricultural Development, International Institute for Strategic Studies, International Labour Organisation, International Monetary Fund, International Telecommunication Union, Inter-Parliamentary Union, Joint United Nations Programme on HIV/AIDS, Office of the United Nations High Commissioner for Refugees, Organisation for Economic Co-operation and Development, Population and Statistical Divisions of the United Nations Department of Economic and Social Information and Policy Analysis, Statistical Office of the European Union, Stockholm International Peace Research Institute, Transparency International, United Nations Centre for Human Rights, United Nations Centre for Social Development and Humanitarian Affairs, United Nations Children's Fund, United Nations Division for the Advancement of Women, United Nations Economic Commission for Europe, United Nations Economic Commission for Latin America and the Caribbean, United Nations Educational, Scientific and Cultural Organization, United Nations Office at Vienna, United Nations Population Fund, United Nations Research Institute for Social Development, University of Pennsylvania, World Bank, World Food Programme and World Health Organization.

The Report drew from background research, statistical analysis or special contributions prepared by Bill Angel, Heidi Attwood, Ottar Brox, Lincoln Chen and staff of the Harvard Center for Population and Development Studies, Christopher Colclough, Elaine Darbellay, Ingrid Eide, Tim Evans, Gourishankar Ghosh, Arjan de Haan, Eva Jespersen, Ivar Lødemel, Wangari Maathai, Yasuyuki Matsunaga, Lars Mjøset, Harald Munthe-Kaas, Else Øyen, Alejandro Ramirez, Sethuramiah L. N. Rao, Leslie Roberts and her colleagues at the World Resources Institute, Douglas Roche, Pedro Sainz, Tom Scialfa, Anne Lise Seip, Kavita Sethuraman, Vivienne Taylor, Jamie Van Leeuwen, Denis Warner, Shahin Yaqub and Naisu Zhu.

The Report benefited greatly from intellectual advice and guidance provided by the external Advisory Panel of eminent experts, which included Bina Agarwal, Lourdes Arizpe, Lourdes Beneria, Robert Chambers, Nazli Choucri, Christian Comeliau, Susanna Davies, Carlos Fortin, Jacques van der Gaag, Ishrat Hussain, Devaki Jain, Jacques Loup, Wangari Maathai, Jim MacNeill, John Mason, Santosh Mehrotra, Solita Monsod, Caroline Moser, Jun Nishikawa, Arjun Sengupta, Vivienne Taylor, and Jan Vandermortele.

The Report also benefited greatly from discussions with, and kind contributions from, Sahid Ahmad, Sanjaya Baru, Yonas Biru, Thorsten Block, Nancy Chen, Shaohua Chen, Kevin Cleaver, Sonia Correa, Elizabeth Crayford, Herman Daly, Nitin Desai, Leandro Despouy, Clarence Dias, Teresita Escotto-Quesada, Shaukat Fareed, Anwar Fazal, Peter Hazell, Barry Herman, Alan Heston, Karl Hochgesand,

Tsuneo Ishikawa, Gareth Jones, John Langmore, Juan Luis Londoño, Chris McCormick, Michael McPeak, Geraldo Nascimento, Roger Normand, Peter Ohram, Saeed Ordoubadi, William Prince, Purificacion Quisumbing, Martin Ravallion, Lora Sabin, Nafis Sadik, Juan Somovìa, Lawrence Summers, Abram de Swaan, Peter Townsend, Tessa Wardlow, Yin Yan, Toru Yanagihara and Sarah Zaidi.

Colleagues in UNDP provided extremely useful comments, suggestions and inputs during the drafting of the Report. In particular, the authors would like to express their gratitude to Fikret Akcura, Saad Alfarargi, William Andrianasolo, Marcia de Castro, Georges Chapelier, Shabbir Cheema, Desmond Cohen, Angela Cropper, Djibril Diallo, Sissel Ekaas, Juliette El-Hage, Peter Gilruth, Noeleen Heyzer, Nadia Hijab, Nay Htun, Tijan Jallow, Ellen Johnson Sirleaf, Mbaya Kankwenda, Soheir Kansouh-Habib, Inge Kaul, Anton Kruiderink, John Lawrence, Normand Lauzon, Thierry Lemaresquier, Roberto Lenton, Carlos Lopes, Khalid Malik, Terry McKinley, Saraswathi Menon, Omar Noman, John Ohiorhenuan, Minh Pham, Elizabeth Reid, Jordan Ryan, Antonio Vigilante, David Whaley, Anders Wijkman and Fernando Zumbado.

Several offices in UNDP provided support and information, including UNDP country offices, UNDP's Regional Bureaux and the Bureau for Policy and Programme Support. The United Nations Office for Project Services provided the team with critical administrative support. Particular thanks go to Ingolf Schuetz-Mueller, Serene Ong and Barry Boehm.

Secretarial and administrative support for the Report's preparation were provided by Oscar Bernal, Renuka Corea, Chato Ledonio-Buckley, U Thiha and Marjorie Victor. And as in previous years, the Report benefited from the design of Gerald Quinn and the editing and pre-press production by American Writing's Bruce Ross-Larson, with Alison Strong, Kim Bieler, Donna Allen, Kelli Ashley, Mark Bock, Andrea Brunholzl, Sandra Cutshall, Meta de Coquereaumont, Heidi Gifford, Wendy Guyette, Paul Holtz, Damon Iacovelli, Barbara Karni, Megan Klose, Wendi Maloney, Vince McCullough, Glenn McGrath, Heidi Manley, Laurel Morais, Christian Perez and Erika Schelble.

The team was assisted in background research, statistics and other contributions by Kojo Acquaise, Ariana Donalds, Marlen Marroquin, Than Kyaw Nyi Nyi, Nadia Rasheed and Lea Salmon.

Special thanks go to Mahbub ul Haq, the originator of the very idea of the *Human Development Report*. He continues to inspire this Report with his vision of human development.

The team also expresses sincere appreciation to the peer reviewers, Nancy Folbre and Dharam Ghai.

The authors also wish to acknowledge their great debt to James Gustave Speth, UNDP Administrator. His deep commitment to and support for an independent and stimulating Report have inspired us all.

Thankful for all the support that they have received, the authors assume full responsibility for the opinions expressed.

Contents

CHAPTER FIVE

The politics of poverty eradication 94

CHAPTER SIX

Eradicating human poverty worldwide—an agenda for the 21st century 106

BOXES

TABLES

FIGURES

ABBREVIATIONS

AIDS	Acquired immunodeficiency syndrome
ASEAN	Association of Southeast Asian Nations
CARICOM	Caribbean Community
CIS	Commonwealth of Independent States
EU	European Union
FAO	Food and Agriculture Organization
FDI	Foreign direct investment
GDI	Gender-related development index
GEM	Gender empowerment measure
HDI	Human development index
HIV	Human immunodeficiency virus
HPI	Human poverty index
IFAD	International Fund for Agricultural Development
ILO	International Labour Organisation
IMF	International Monetary Fund
NGO	Non-governmental organization
OECD	Organisation for Economic Co-operation and Development
PPP	Purchasing power parity
UNCHS	United Nations Centre for Human Settlements
UNCTAD	United Nations Conference on Trade and Development
UNDP	United Nations Development Programme
UNEP	United Nations Environment Programme
UNESCO	United Nations Educational, Scientific and Cultural Organization
UNFPA	United Nations Population Fund
UNHCR	Office of the United Nations High Commissioner for Refugees
UNICEF	United Nations Children's Fund
UNIFEM	United Nations Development Fund for Women
WHO	World Health Organization
WTO	World Trade Organization

Human development to eradicate poverty

Human poverty is more than income poverty—it is the denial of choices and opportunities for living a tolerable life

The great success in reducing poverty in the 20th century shows that eradicating severe poverty in the first decades of the 21st century is feasible. This may seem an extraordinary ambition, but it is well within our grasp. Almost all countries committed themselves to this goal at the World Summit for Social Development in 1995. And many, including some of the largest, have embarked with all the seriousness necessary to achieve it.

Although poverty has been dramatically reduced in many parts of the world, a quarter of the world's people remain in severe poverty. In a global economy of $25 trillion, this is a scandal—reflecting shameful inequalities and inexcusable failures of national and international policy.

Human Development Report 1997 reviews the challenge to eradicate poverty from a human development perspective. It focuses not just on poverty of income but on poverty from a human development perspective—on poverty as a denial of choices and opportunities for living a tolerable life.

The progress in reducing poverty over the 20th century is remarkable and unprecedented . . .

Few people realize the great advances already made. In the past 50 years poverty has fallen more than in the previous 500. And it has been reduced in some respects in almost all countries.

The key indicators of human development have advanced strongly in the past few decades. Since 1960, in little more than a generation, child death rates in developing countries have been more than halved. Malnutrition rates have declined by almost

a third. The proportion of children out of primary school has fallen from more than half to less than a quarter. And the share of rural families without access to safe water has fallen from nine-tenths to about a quarter.

These advances are found in all regions of the world (figure 1). China, and another 14 countries or states with populations that add up to more than 1.6 billion, have halved the proportion of their people living below the national income poverty line in less than 20 years. Ten more countries, with almost another billion people, have reduced the proportion of their people in income poverty by a quarter or more. Beyond mere advances in income, there has been great progress in all these countries in life expectancy and access to basic social services.

The accelerated progress in reducing poverty in the 20th century began in Europe and North America in the 19th century—in what can now be seen as the first Great Ascent from poverty and human deprivation. The ascent started in the foothills of the industrial revolution, with rising incomes, improvements in public health and education and eventually programmes of social security. By the 1950s most of Europe and North America enjoyed full employment and welfare states.

The second Great Ascent started in the 1950s in the developing countries. The end of colonialism was followed by improvements in education and health and accelerated economic development that led to dramatic declines in poverty. By the end of the 20th century some 3–4 billion of the world's people will have experienced substantial improvements in their standard of living, and about 4–5 billion will have access to basic education and health care. It is precisely these gains that make eradicating poverty not some distant ideal—but a true possibility.

... but the advances have been uneven and marred by setbacks—and poverty remains pervasive.

Some stark figures summarize the balance sheet of poverty towards the end of the 20th century:
• More than a quarter of the developing world's people still live in poverty as measured by the human poverty index introduced in this Report. About a third—1.3 billion people—live on incomes of less than $1 a day.
• South Asia has the most people affected by human poverty. And it has the largest number of people in income poverty: 515 million. Together, South Asia, East Asia and South-East Asia and the Pacific have more than 950 million of the 1.3 billion people who are income-poor.
• Sub-Saharan Africa has the highest proportion of people in—and the fastest growth in—human poverty. Some 220 million people in the region are income-poor. Indeed, the Sub-Saharan and other least developed countries are poverty stricken—and it is estimated that by 2000 half the people in Sub-Saharan Africa will be in income poverty.
• In Latin America and the Caribbean income poverty is more pervasive than human poverty—affecting 110 million people—and it continues to grow.
• Eastern Europe and the countries of the Commonwealth of Independent States (CIS) have seen the greatest deterioration in the past decade. Income poverty has spread from a a small part of their population to about a third—120 million people below a poverty line of $4 a day.
• And in industrial countries more than 100 million people live below the income poverty line, set at half the individual median income. Thirty-seven million are jobless.

Within these broad groups some people suffer more than others—particularly children, women and the aged.

Children are especially vulnerable—hit by malnutrition and illness just when their brains and bodies are forming. Some 160 million children are moderately or severely malnourished. Some 110 million are out of school.

Women are disproportionately poor—and too often disempowered and burdened by the strains of productive work, the birth and care of children and other household and community responsibilities. And their lack of access to land, credit and better employment opportunities handicaps their ability to fend off poverty for themselves and their families—or to rise out of it. Women are particularly at risk in poor communities. Half a million women die each year in childbirth—at rates 10–100 times those in industrial countries.

The aged, a growing group in all regions, often live their twilight years in poverty and neglect.

Just when the possibilities for advance should be greater than ever, new global pressures are creating or threatening further increases in poverty.

Some danger signs:
• Slow economic growth, stagnation and even decline in some 100 developing and transition countries.
• Continuing conflict in 30 countries, most in Africa.
• Slowing advance in such key areas as nutrition.
• The rise of such threats as HIV/AIDS.

The latest data show that the human development index declined in the past year in 30 countries, more than in any year since the *Human Development Report* was first issued in 1990. Between 1987 and 1993 the number of people with incomes of less than $1 a day increased by almost 100 million to 1.3 billion—and the number appears to be still growing in every region except South-East Asia and the Pacific.

The transition from socialism to democracy and market economies has proved more difficult and costly than anyone imagined. The costs have been not only economic, from the dramatic decline in GDP. They have also been human, from falling wages, growing crime and loss of social pro-

New global pressures are creating or threatening further increases in poverty

FIGURE 1

Under-five mortality rate (per 1,000 live births)

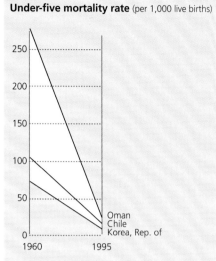

10 largest reductions	1970	1995	% decline
Oman	280	25	91
Korea, Rep. of	71	9	87
Chile	105	15	86
Saudi Arabia	185	34	82
Cuba	54	10	81
Barbados	54	10	81
Singapore	30	6	80
Tunisia	184	37	80
Jordan	123	25	80
Iran, Islamic Rep. of	196	40	80

Adult illiteracy rate (percent)

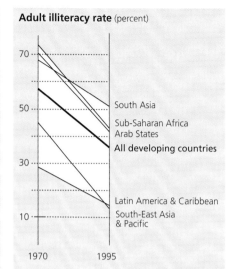

10 largest reductions	1970	1995	% decline
Korea, Rep. of	12	2	83
Lebanon	31	8	75
Jordan	53	13	75
Thailand	21	6	70
Philippines	17	5	68
Kenya	68	22	68
Cuba	13	4	67
Zimbabwe	45	15	67
Ecuador	28	10	65
Indonesia	46	16	65

Income poverty incidence
(percentage based on the $1-a-day poverty line)

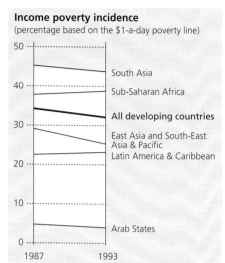

10 largest reductions	Period	First year	Last year	% change
China	1978–94	33	7	79
Tunisia	1967–90	33	7	79
Korea, Rep. of	1970–90	23	5	78
Malaysia	1970–93	60	14	77
Indonesia	1970–90	60	15	75
Singapore	1972–82	31	10	68
Morocco	1984–91	6	2	67
Indian states				
Kerala	1974–94	59	26	56
Punjab	1974–94	28	13	54
Haryana	1974–88	34	16	53

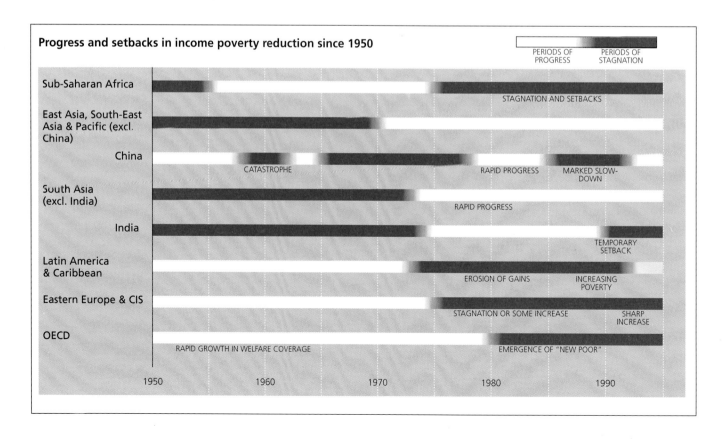

Progress and setbacks in income poverty reduction since 1950

tection. In some countries life expectancy has fallen by five years or more.

In many industrial countries unemployment is rising, and the traditional protections against poverty are being undermined by pressures on public spending and the welfare state. In some industrial countries, such as the United Kingdom and the United States, poverty has risen considerably.

None of these depressing developments was inevitable. And all can be reversed, if countries take more seriously the commitments already made to giving poverty reduction high priority, nationally and internationally.

From a human development perspective, poverty means the denial of choices and opportunities for a tolerable life.

It is in the deprivation of the lives people lead that poverty manifests itself. Poverty can mean more than a lack of what is necessary for material well-being. It can also mean the denial of opportunities and choices most basic to human development—to lead a long, healthy, creative life and to enjoy a decent standard of living, freedom, dignity, self-esteem and the respect of others.

For policy-makers, the poverty of choices and opportunities is often more relevant than the poverty of income, for it focuses on the causes of poverty and leads directly to strategies of empowerment and other actions to enhance opportunities for everyone.

Poverty must be addressed in all its dimensions, not income alone. The needs are great. An estimated 1.3 billion people survive on less than the equivalent of $1 a day. But there are other needs, equally basic and sometimes even more so (figure 2). Nearly a billion people are illiterate. Well over a billion lack access to safe water. Some 840 million go hungry or face food insecurity. And nearly a third of the people in the least developed countries—most of which are in Sub-Saharan Africa—are not expected to survive to age 40.

The human poverty index combines basic dimensions of poverty and reveals interesting contrasts with income poverty. This Report introduces a human poverty index (HPI). Rather than measure poverty by income, it uses indicators of the most basic dimensions of deprivation: a short life, lack of basic education and lack of access to public and private resources. Like all measures the HPI has weaknesses—in data and in concept. Like all measures it cannot capture the totality of human poverty. But by combining in a single poverty index the concerns that often get pushed aside when the focus is on income alone, the HPI makes a useful addition to the measures of poverty.

Among 78 developing countries ranked by the HPI, Trinidad and Tobago comes out on top, followed by Cuba, Chile, Singapore and Costa Rica. Human poverty has been

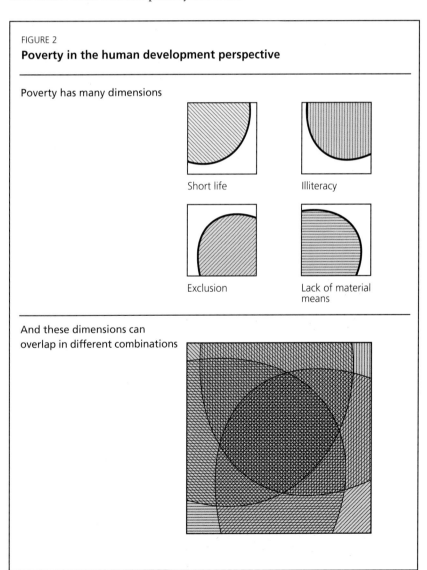

FIGURE 2

Poverty in the human development perspective

Poverty has many dimensions

Short life

Illiteracy

Exclusion

Lack of material means

And these dimensions can overlap in different combinations

reduced in these countries and now affects less than 10% of their people.

Where is human poverty most pervasive? The HPI exceeds 50% in seven countries—Niger, Sierra Leone, Burkina Faso, Ethiopia, Mali, Cambodia and Mozambique—implying that more than half their people suffer several forms of human poverty. Altogether, 35 of the 78 developing countries for which the HPI was calculated have HPIs exceeding 33%.

Comparing the HPI with income measures of poverty based on a $1-a-day poverty line reveals interesting contrasts:
• Both income poverty and human poverty are pervasive, affecting a quarter to a third of the people in the developing world.
• Sub-Saharan Africa and South Asia have the highest incidence of both income and human poverty—at about 40%.
• Most of the Arab States have made remarkable progress in reducing income poverty, now a mere 4%, but face a large backlog of human poverty (32%).
• Latin America and the Caribbean, with an HPI of 15%, has reduced human poverty in many countries, but income poverty is still 24%.
• In Egypt, Guinea, Morocco, Pakistan and 10 other countries the proportion of people in human poverty exceeds the proportion in income poverty.
• In Guinea-Bissau, Honduras, Kenya, Peru and Zimbabwe the proportion of people in income poverty exceeds the proportion in human poverty.

The scale of poverty is daunting, but we should take heart from what's already been achieved—and focus on six priorities for action to eradicate poverty.

Every country—developing and developed—needs policies and strategies for "substantially reducing overall poverty in the shortest time possible, reducing inequalities and eradicating absolute poverty by a target date to be specified by each country in its national context"—goals set at the World Summit for Social Development. This process needs to be undertaken in partnership by government and civil society, including the private sector.

The strategy for poverty reduction will naturally differ from country to country, but there are six priorities for action.

1. Everywhere the starting point is to empower women and men—and to ensure their participation in decisions that affect their lives and enable them to build their strengths and assets.

Poor people and poor communities rely primarily on their own energy, creativity and assets. Such assets are not just economic. They are also social, political, environmental and personal—both for women and for men.

A people-centred strategy for eradicating poverty should start by building the assets of the poor—and empowering the poor to win their fight against poverty. What does such a strategy entail?
• Political commitments to securing and protecting the political, economic, social and civil rights of poor people.
• Policy reforms and actions to enable poor people to gain access to assets that make them less vulnerable. Security of tenure for housing and land is as important as access to credit and other financial services.
• Education and health care for all, along with reproductive health services, family planning and safe water and sanitation. This needs to be achieved soon—not postponed for another generation.
• Social safety nets to prevent people from falling into destitution and to rescue them from disaster.

2. Gender equality is essential for empowering women—and for eradicating poverty.

Already women are on the front line of household and community efforts to escape poverty and cope with its impact. But too often they do not have a voice in decision-making—in the household, in the community or in national and international arenas.

A people-centred strategy for eradicating poverty should start by building the assets of the poor

Gender equality needs to be part of each country's strategy for eradicating poverty, both as an end and as a means to eradicating other forms of human poverty. This means:

• Focusing clearly on ending discrimination against girls in all aspects of health, education and upbringing—starting with survival.

• Empowering women by ensuring equal rights and access to land, credit and job opportunities.

• Taking more action to end violence against women, the all-too-pervasive hidden side of human poverty.

A creative commitment to gender equality will strengthen every area of action to reduce poverty—because women can bring new energy, new insights and a new basis for organization.

If development is not engendered, it is endangered. And if poverty reduction strategies fail to empower women, they will fail to empower society.

3. Sustained poverty reduction requires pro-poor growth in all countries— and faster growth in the 100 or so developing and transition countries where growth has been failing.

In the past 15–20 years more than 100 developing and transition countries have suffered disastrous failures in growth and deeper and more prolonged cuts in living standards than anything experienced in the industrial countries during the Great Depression of the 1930s. As a result of these setbacks, the incomes of more than a billion people have fallen below levels first reached 10, 20 and sometimes 30 years ago.

Economic growth can be a powerful means of reducing poverty, but its benefits are not automatic. Argentina grew 2% per capita a year in the 1950s, yet saw income poverty rise. Honduras grew 2% a year in 1986–89 and saw income poverty double. New Zealand, the United Kingdom and the United States all experienced good average growth during 1975–95, yet the proportion in poverty increased. That is why the policies for growth must be pro-poor.

Pro-poor growth

What makes growth pro-poor? Several key elements:

Restoring full employment as a high priority of economic policy. Economic growth contributes most to poverty reduction when it expands the employment, productivity and wages of poor people—and when public resources are channelled to promoting human development. *Human Development Report 1996* showed how a virtuous cycle of economic growth and human development arises when growth is labour-using and employment-generating—and when human skills and health improve rapidly.

Lessening inequality and moderating its extremes. If poverty is to be reduced, policy-makers must avoid "ruthless" growth that leads to increasing income inequality. Contrary to some perceptions, inequality usually hinders growth. In 29 of the 68 developing countries with data, the ratio of the incomes of the richest 20% to those of the poorest 20% exceeds 10 to 1; in 17, 15 to 1; and in 9, 20 to 1. In Latin America and the Caribbean the richest 20% have average incomes of more than $17,000, the poorest 20%, $930. Such inequalities undermine the whole process of development and slow poverty reduction.

Accelerating growth in poor countries. Poor countries urgently need to accelerate economic growth—to at least 3% per capita a year. This growth, if the right kind and if equitably distributed, would double incomes in a generation or even sooner. Under the right circumstances it could halve income poverty in a decade.

Something else is needed—mainstreaming the commitment to eradicate poverty. For macroeconomic policy this means much more than promoting economic growth. Poverty eradication must be a core priority of national economic policy, as it was in many countries that have successfully reduced poverty, such as Malaysia and Norway.

Actions for the rural poor

About three-quarters of the world's poorest people live in rural areas, dependent on

A creative commitment to gender equality will strengthen every area of action to reduce poverty

agricultural activities for their livelihoods. For these people pro-poor growth means raising agricultural productivity and incomes.

Key priorities include:

Creating an enabling environment for small-scale agriculture, microenterprises and the informal sector. These are the sectors on which most poor people depend for their livelihoods. They also contribute to growth, since they generate incomes and employment at low cost, with few imported inputs and low management requirements.

Raising the productivity of small-scale agriculture does more than benefit farmers. It also creates employment on the farm and off—and reduces food prices. The poor benefit most, because about 70% of their consumption is food, mostly staples, and regular supplies and stable prices can greatly reduce the vulnerability of the poor. Strong support to small-scale agriculture was at the core of the most successful cases of poverty reduction—such as China in 1978–85, Malaysia since 1971 and India in the early 1980s.

Fostering technological progress. The first green revolution helped millions of small farmers and urban food buyers escape poverty with technological breakthroughs in wheat, maize and rice farming in high-potential areas. A second green revolution is needed for poor farmers in resource-poor areas, dependent on such crops as millet and cassava.

Reversing environmental decline in marginal regions. About half of the poorest people in the world—more than 500 million—earn their livelihoods in ecologically fragile and low-productivity areas. Here, efforts to reduce poverty need to go hand in hand with efforts to protect the environment. Securing sustainable energy sources and protecting biodiversity should be part of building environmental sustainability.

Speeding the demographic transition. Poverty reduction is closely linked with slower population growth—poor families may have more children precisely because they need their labour to collect ever more distant supplies of fuel or water.

Education and health for all

As the experience of the fast-growing countries attests, basic education and health care are among the most powerful forces for growth. Studies have repeatedly shown the high rates of return to these investments, especially for girls. True, such investments in people yield rich dividends only over a long period. But no policy-maker should sacrifice those dividends as a short-run expedient.

Accelerated action to reduce human deprivation in education and health is a near-universal need and should not wait for growth to resume. In the past 15 years, despite disastrous declines in per capita income, many countries have made significant advances in reducing some aspects of poverty.

• During 1980–95 Burkina Faso, Gambia, Senegal and Zimbabwe cut child mortality by a third to a half—despite declines in income for much of this period.

• Also during 1980–95 Algeria, Jordan, Peru, Syria and Trinidad and Tobago reduced child mortality by a half to two-thirds—despite reductions in per capita income of 20% or more over the past decade.

• In the Arab States the number of people with access to safe water more than doubled between 1980 and 1995—despite severe economic setbacks.

These advances are no cause for complacency. Many of the gains will remain fragile unless bolstered by strong pro-poor growth and policies to translate that growth into human development and poverty reduction. Countries with poor growth, such as Zimbabwe, have seen some of their gains reversed.

Poverty reduction in industrial countries

Rising unemployment, falling wages and cuts in social services are driving many people into poverty in industrial countries—and threatening the futures of millions more. Many of the poorest are kept at the bottom by social exclusion. The post–cold war reductions in military expenditure should have been seen as a major opportu-

---

Many of the gains will remain fragile unless bolstered by strong pro-poor growth

nity for social investment. Instead, the priority seems to be saving money and reducing services. The very idea of the welfare state has been called into question and is under threat.

The 25 years after the Second World War showed what can be achieved by developing new policies to reduce unemployment and poverty. The same sustained commitment and policy innovation are needed today. The major challenges include providing employment for all, ensuring viable systems of social security, pensions and health services for all, and enabling men and women to share their home and workplace obligations better.

The recent resurgence of poverty in industrial countries is a reminder that fighting poverty must be a continuous process—requiring countries to adapt their safety nets and mechanisms for preventing poverty to changing economic realities.

4. Globalization offers great opportunities—but only if it is managed more carefully and with more concern for global equity.

Proceeding at breakneck speed but without map or compass, globalization has helped reduce poverty in some of the largest and strongest economies—China, India and some of the Asian tigers. But it has also produced losers among and within countries. As trade and foreign investment have expanded, the developing world has seen a widening gap between winners and losers. Meanwhile, many industrial countries have watched unemployment soar to levels not recorded since the 1930s, and income inequality reach levels not recorded since the last century.

The greatest benefits of globalization have been garnered by a fortunate few. A rising tide of wealth is supposed to lift all boats, but some are more seaworthy than others. The yachts and ocean liners are rising in response to new opportunities, but many rafts and rowboats are taking on water—and some are sinking.

The ratio of global trade to GDP has been rising over the past decade, but it has been falling for 44 developing countries, with more than a billion people. The least developed countries, with 10% of the world's people, have only 0.3% of world trade—half their share of two decades ago.

The list goes on:
• More than half of all developing countries have been bypassed by foreign direct investment, two-thirds of which has gone to only eight developing countries.
• Real commodity prices in the 1990s were 45% lower than those in the 1980s—and 10% lower than the lowest level during the Great Depression, reached in 1932.
• The terms of trade for the least developed countries have declined a cumulative 50% over the past 25 years.
• Average tariffs on industrial country imports from the least developed countries are 30% higher than the global average.
• Developing countries lose about $60 billion a year from agricultural subsidies and barriers to textile exports in industrial nations.

The bottom line for poverty and incomes: The share of the poorest 20% of the world's people in global income now stands at a miserable 1.1%, down from 1.4% in 1991 and 2.3% in 1960. It continues to shrink. And the ratio of the income of the top 20% to that of the poorest 20% rose from 30 to 1 in 1960, to 61 to 1 in 1991—and to a startling new high of 78 to 1 in 1994.

To open opportunities, not close them—to create employment and avoid a "rush to the bottom"—requires better management of globalization, nationally and internationally. Better policies, fairer rules and fairer terms for poor and weak countries to enter markets, especially those for agricultural exports, are all part of this.

All countries and all major international economic and financial agencies need to engage more seriously in efforts to formulate better policies towards globalization, not just stand cheering on the sidelines. Poor countries, increasingly marginalized from the world economy, need special support to help them reap the benefits of integration.

The great unanswered question is whether the winds of globalization will be viewed as a great opportunity or a great

Countries must invest liberally in human development so that they are ready to face the challenge of globalization

threat, as a fresh breeze or a violent hurricane, by some of the poorer nations.

The answer lies in our policy actions. At the national level, countries must invest liberally in human development so that they are ready to face the challenge of globalization and compete in open markets. Indeed, poor countries can leapfrog several decades of development if they combine their low wages with basic education, technical skills and export-led growth, taking advantage of the rapidly opening global markets. This is the policy message of the East Asian tigers.

At the same time, poor countries need much stronger support from the international community—through concessional assistance, debt relief, trade preferences, technical cooperation and national capacity-building—if they are to make their way in the fiercely competitive global markets. What is true for national markets is true for global markets: an enabling environment must be created for the poor if they are to take full advantage of the new opportunities.

5. In all these areas the state must provide an enabling environment for broad-based political support and alliances for pro-poor policies and markets.

The state cannot relinquish its responsibilities in providing basic education and health care for all, reforming institutions to improve access to productive assets, shifting macroeconomic policy towards the goal of full employment and mobilizing resources to eradicate poverty and, through taxation, to control inequality. In every area of policy the state must advance the interests of poor people and promote pro-poor markets.

It is not the resources or the economic solutions that are lacking—it is the political momentum to tackle poverty head-on. An environment must be created in which state policies, as well as market forces, civil activism and community mobilization, contribute to the fullest possible extent to the eradication of poverty.

For this to happen, the following conditions are essential:

- Poor people must be politically empowered to organize themselves for collective action and to influence the circumstances and decisions affecting their lives. For their interests to be advanced, they must be visible on the political map.
- Community groups, professional associations, trade unions, private companies, the media, political parties and government institutions need to join in broad-based partnerships for poverty eradication. Such alliances can be built on common interests and brokered compromises.
- Democratic space needs to be maintained by the state to foster peaceful expression of people's demands and to resist pressures from the economically powerful.

A strategy for poverty eradication must therefore focus not only on what needs to be done, but on how to ensure that action is actually taken. Enabling policies for poverty eradication include such fundamental reforms as promoting broader political participation, ensuring accountability and transparency of government, preventing the criminalization of politics, promoting free flows of information and ensuring a strong role for community groups and NGOs in policy-making and legislative decision-making. The legitimacy and strength of the state depend in part on its capacity to mobilize and be mobilized in the fight against poverty.

6. Special international support is needed for special situations—to reduce the poorest countries' debt faster, to increase their share of aid and to open agricultural markets for their exports.

Without special support, international pledges of solidarity, human rights and worldwide poverty eradication ring hollow.

The least developed countries, most of them in Sub-Saharan Africa, face the biggest challenges in eradicating poverty in the next two or three decades. These are the countries in greatest economic difficulty—and most often in conflict. And these are the countries in which human poverty is growing fastest.

Yet Sub-Saharan Africa has many examples of success—and with sustained support the progress could be accelerated.

The state must advance the interests of poor people and promote pro-poor markets

Five vital lines of action:

Conflict prevention and resolution, peace-building and reconstruction. A broader, more sustained approach is needed, directed to the whole continuum of peace-building, prevention of further conflict and reconstruction in ways that help build new momentum in which all groups in a country have a stake.

Reducing poverty and inequality would help avert many conflicts. And a pro-poor development strategy needs to be at the core of postconflict reconstruction. Restoring health services and moving towards education for all can help restore normalcy and serve as a focus for peace-building. The construction of housing and public buildings can provide employment. But controls on arms sales are needed, along with greater transparency in arms trade.

Debt relief for human development and poverty eradication. Debt is a millstone around the necks of Sub-Saharan and other least developed countries. The debt of the 41 highly indebted poor countries now totals $215 billion, up from $183 billion in 1990 and $55 billion in 1980. Though the recent multilateral initiative to provide debt relief to these countries is welcome, the relief will be selective—and often take three to six years to have effect.

Desperately needed: more action, not more proposals. The benefits of debt relief could be channelled to support education, health care, credit and pro-poor rural development.

More aid, better directed. Despite rapidly growing poverty in most of the poorest and least developed countries, aid has been declining. A new impetus is needed, in the form of strong support for poverty reduction. That support needs to be translated into three actions:
• More aid for the Sub-Saharan and other least developed countries.
• A shift in the use of aid away from expatriate technical assistance personnel and towards long-term support for national capacity.
• A greater concentration of aid on countries demonstrating serious commitment to poverty reduction and human development.

Special support is also needed for slowing the spread of HIV/AIDS. Thailand and Uganda have had some success in this. But there has been little progress in most other developing countries, partly because the disease has yet to be acknowledged as not just a medical problem but also a development problem. Tackling it means dealing with ingrained cultural values and prejudices—particularly those relating to gender—and adopting a multisectoral approach targeted at communities in need.

The opening of global markets, especially for Africa's agricultural exports. Blunting Africa's opportunities for rapid advance is its lack of access to agricultural markets in the industrial countries. Fairer access for Africa's exports, especially its agricultural products, is thus a test of the international commitment to poverty reduction in the region.

Strengthening the United Nations' role and leadership. Rather than downsizing their vision for the United Nations, all governments need to expand their view of its role.

A grand alliance to eradicate poverty should be a powerful integrating force for all the development efforts of the UN system—a focus for advocacy, action and support. Already poverty reduction is the overriding priority for UNDP and among the central priorities for several of the main UN organizations. A system-wide action plan has been prepared, focused on coordinated followup to all the global conferences of the 1990s, with poverty reduction central.

All this could be taken much further, especially at the country level. Despite commitments at global conferences, no more than 30 countries have set clear goals for poverty eradication, and fewer still have serious strategies to achieve the goals.

But more than 100 countries have prepared plans of action to reduce different aspects of poverty, such as by expanding education, improving food security and ensuring reproductive health. These could be brought together in more comprehensive programmes. The UN system could help in this. It could also support efforts to incorporate poverty into mainstream economic policy, development programmes, data collection and monitoring.

The time has come to create a world that is more humane, more stable, more just

Combining growth with a small but steady redistribution towards poverty eradication could ensure all the resources required

Recently, the members of the OECD Development Assistance Committee declared their support for halving income poverty by 2015 and for achieving education and health for all. Poverty eradication could become a focus of international support for many countries, bringing together all concerned UN organizations under the leadership of the government. The Special Initiative for Africa, for example, could be the focus for such collective support. All such efforts must be participatory, involving the poor themselves.

Eradicating absolute poverty in the first decades of the 21st century is feasible, affordable and a moral imperative.

Eradicating poverty everywhere is more than a moral imperative and a commitment to human solidarity. It is a practical possibility. The time has come to eradicate the worst aspects of human poverty within a decade or two—to create a world that is more humane, more stable, more just.

At the World Summit for Social Development in Copenhagen, governments committed themselves to eradicating poverty. As follow-up action, they agreed to set national goals and prepare strategies geared to reducing overall poverty substantially, reducing inequalities, and eradicating extreme poverty in the shortest time possible—by target dates to be set by each country.

These commitments, and the success many countries have had in reducing poverty rapidly, make inaction immoral. But accelerated action will be spurred only if all countries develop a new vision of the possibility of poverty eradication and a stronger sense of how they will gain from it—through greater security, greater stability and greater prosperity.

The costs of eradicating poverty are less than people imagine—about 1% of global income and no more than 2–3% of national income in all but the poorest countries. Further cuts in military spending, with the savings channelled to poverty reduction and pro-poor growth, would go far towards providing the resources required. The challenge of mobilizing resources is thus mostly a challenge of restructuring priorities—and of steadily mainstreaming these priorities into a new programme of pro-poor growth. Combining growth with a small but steady redistribution towards poverty eradication could ensure all the resources required within this generation.

To restate: The unprecedented progress in reducing poverty in the 20th century sets the stage for eradicating absolute poverty in the early 21st century—a moral imperative, an attainable goal. No longer inevitable, poverty should be relegated to history—along with slavery, colonialism and nuclear warfare.

Absolute and relative poverty

Absolute poverty refers to some absolute standard of minimum requirement, while relative poverty refers to falling behind most others in the community. With respect to income, a person is absolutely poor if her income is less than the defined income poverty line, while she is relatively poor if she belongs to a bottom income group (such as the poorest 10%).

Functionings and capability

The functionings of a person refer to the valuable things the person can do or be (such as being well nourished, living long and taking part in the life of a community). The capability of a person stands for the different combinations of functionings the person can achieve; it reflects the freedom to achieve functionings.

Ultra-poverty

Ultra-poverty is said to occur when a household cannot meet 80% of the FAO-WHO minimum calorie requirements, even when using 80% of its income to buy food.

Incidence of poverty

The incidence of poverty, expressed as a headcount ratio, is simply an estimate of the percentage of people below the poverty line. It does not indicate anything about the depth or severity of poverty and thus does not capture any worsening of the conditions of those already in poverty.

Depth of poverty

The depth of poverty can be measured as the average distance below the poverty line, expressed as a proportion of that line. This average is formed over the entire population, poor and non-poor. Because this measure—also called the poverty gap—shows the average distance of the poor from the poverty line, it is able to capture a worsening of their conditions.

Severity of poverty

The severity of poverty can be measured as a weighted average of the squared distance below the poverty line, expressed as a proportion of that line. The weights are given by each individual gap. Again, the average is formed over the entire population. Since the weights increase with poverty, this measure is sensitive to inequality among the poor.

Transient and chronic poverty

Transient poverty refers to short-term, temporary or seasonal poverty, and chronic poverty to long-term or structural poverty.

Vulnerability

Vulnerability has two faces: external exposure to shocks, stress and risk; and internal defencelessness, a lack of means to cope without suffering damaging loss.

Poverty lines

• POVERTY LINES FOR INTERNATIONAL COMPARISON. A poverty line set at $1 (1985 PPP$) a day per person is used by the World Bank for international comparison. This poverty line is based on consumption.

A poverty line of $2 (PPP$) a day is suggested for Latin America and the Caribbean. For Eastern Europe and the CIS countries, a poverty line of $4 (1990 PPP$) has been used. For comparison among industrial countries, a poverty line corresponding to the US poverty line of $14.40 (1985 PPP$) a day per person has been used.

• NATIONAL POVERTY LINES. Developing countries that have set national poverty lines have generally used the food poverty method. These lines indicate the insufficiency of economic resources to meet basic minimum needs in food. There are three approaches to measuring food poverty.

Cost-of-basic-needs method. This approach sets the poverty line at the cost of a basic diet for the main age, gender and activity groups, plus a few essential non-food items. A survey then establishes the proportion of people living in households with consumption (or sometimes income) below this line. The basic diet may consist of the least expensive foods needed to meet basic nutritional requirements, the typical adult diet in the lowest consumption quintile or the investigator's notion of a minimal but decent diet. The choice of both the food and the non-food components included is necessarily arbitrary.

Food energy method. This method focuses on the consumption expenditure at which a person's typical food energy intake is just sufficient to meet a predetermined food energy requirement. Dietary energy intake, as the dependent variable, is regressed against household consumption per adult equivalent. The poverty line is then set at the level of total consumption per person at which the statistical expectation of dietary energy intake exactly meets average dietary energy requirements. The problem with this method is the *caviar caveat*: groups that choose a costly bundle of foods are rewarded with a higher poverty line than that for more frugal eaters.

Food share method. This method derives the cost of a consumption plan to acquire just sufficient nutrients. If the cost of basic nutrients is a third of total consumption, the poverty line is fixed at three times that cost.

All three approaches are sensitive to the price level used to determine the cost of the bundle. And all three concentrate mainly on calories or dietary energy, because protein deficiency due to inadequate economic resources is perceived to be rare in most societies.

In industrial countries too national poverty lines are used to measure relative poverty. The European Commission has suggested a poverty line for these countries of half the median adjusted disposable personal income.

The concept of human development

The process of widening people's choices and the level of well-being they achieve are at the core of the notion of human development. Such choices are neither finite nor static. But regardless of the level of development, the three essential choices for people are to lead a long and healthy life, to acquire knowledge and to have access to the resources needed for a decent standard of living. Human development does not end there, however. Other choices, highly valued by many people, range from political, economic and social freedom to opportunities for being creative and productive and enjoying self-respect and guaranteed human rights.

Income clearly is only one option that people would like to have, though an important one. But it is not the sum total of their lives. Income is also a means, with human development the end.

Human development index

The human development index measures the average achievements in a country in three basic dimensions of human development—longevity, knowledge and a decent standard of living. A composite index, the HDI thus contains three variables: life expectancy, educational attainment (adult literacy and combined primary, secondary and tertiary enrolment) and real GDP per capita (in PPP$).

Human poverty index

The human poverty index measures deprivation in basic human development in the same dimensions as the HDI. The variables used are the percentage of people expected to die before age 40, the percentage of adults who are illiterate, and overall economic provisioning in terms of the percentage of people without access to health services and safe water and the percentage of underweight children under five.

Gender-related development index

The gender-related development index measures achievements in the same dimensions and variables as the HDI does, but takes account of inequality in achievement between women and men. The greater the gender disparity in basic human development, the lower a country's GDI compared with its HDI. The GDI is simply the HDI discounted, or adjusted downwards, for gender inequality.

Gender empowerment measure

The gender empowerment measure indicates whether women are able to actively participate in economic and political life. It focuses on participation, measuring gender inequality in key areas of economic and political participation and decision-making. It thus differs from the GDI, an indicator of gender inequality in basic capabilities.

CHAPTER 1

 Poverty in the human development perspective: concept and measurement

It is in the deprivation of the lives that people can lead that poverty manifests itself. Poverty can involve not only the lack of the necessities of material well-being, but the denial of opportunities for living a tolerable life. Life can be prematurely shortened. It can be made difficult, painful or hazardous. It can be deprived of knowledge and communication. And it can be robbed of dignity, confidence and self-respect—as well as the respect of others. All are aspects of poverty that limit and blight the lives of many millions in the world today.

Defining poverty in the human development perspective

Since its launch in 1990 the *Human Development Report* has defined human development as the process of enlarging people's choices. The most critical ones are to lead a long and healthy life, to be educated and to enjoy a decent standard of living. Additional choices include political freedom, other guaranteed human rights and various ingredients of self-respect—including what Adam Smith called the ability to mix with others without being "ashamed to appear in public". These are among the essential choices, the absence of which can block many other opportunities. Human development is thus a process of widening people's choices as well as raising the level of well-being achieved.

If human development is about enlarging choices, poverty means that opportunities and choices most basic to human development are denied—to lead a long, healthy, creative life and to enjoy a decent standard of living, freedom, dignity, self-respect and the respect of others.

The contrast between human development and human poverty reflects two different ways of evaluating development. One way, the "conglomerative perspective", focuses on the advances made by all groups in each community, from the rich to the poor. This contrasts with an alternative viewpoint, the "deprivational perspective", in which development is judged by the way the poor and the deprived fare in each community. Lack of progress in reducing the disadvantages of the deprived cannot be "washed away" by large advances—no matter how large—made by the better-off people.

Interest in the process of development concerns both perspectives. At a very basic level, the lives and successes of everyone should count, and it would be a mistake to make our understanding of the process of development completely insensitive to the gains and losses of those who happen to fare better than others. It would go against the right of each citizen to be counted, and also clash with the comprehensive concerns of universalist ethics. Yet a part—a big part—of the general interest in the progress of a nation concentrates specifically on the state of the disadvantaged.

Successive *Human Development Report*s have been concerned with both ways of looking at progress. This Report explores in particular the deprivations in human development, including a measure of human development from a deprivational perspective.

Poverty has many dimensions

Concerns with identifying people affected by poverty and the desire to measure it have at times obscured the fact that poverty is too complex to be reduced to a single dimension

Poverty means that opportunities and choices most basic to human development are denied

of human life. It has become common for countries to establish an income-based or consumption-based poverty line. Although income focuses on an important dimension of poverty, it gives only a partial picture of the many ways human lives can be blighted. Someone can enjoy good health and live quite long but be illiterate and thus cut off from learning, from communication and from interactions with others. Another person may be literate and quite well educated but prone to premature death because of epidemiological characteristics or physical disposition. Yet a third may be excluded from participating in the important decision-making processes affecting her life. The deprivation of none of them can be fully captured by the level of their income.

Also, people perceive deprivation in different ways—and each person and community defines the deprivation and disadvantages that affect their lives.

Poverty of lives and opportunities—or human poverty—is multidimensional in character and diverse rather than uniform in content.

How does human poverty relate to other approaches?

Over the years the concept of poverty has been defined in different ways (box 1.1).

Poverty in the human development approach draws on each of these perspectives, but draws particularly on the capability perspective. In the capability concept the poverty of a life lies not merely in the impoverished state in which the person actually lives, but also in the lack of real opportunity—due to social constraints as well as personal circumstances—to lead valuable and valued lives.

In the capability concept the focus is on the functionings that a person can or cannot achieve, given the opportunities she has. Functionings refer to the various valuable things a person can do or be, such as living long, being healthy, being well nourished, mixing well with others in the community and so on.

The capability approach concentrates on functioning information, supplemented by considering, where possible, the options a person had but did not choose to use. For example, a rich and healthy person who becomes ill nourished through fasting can be distinguished from a person who is forced into malnutrition through a lack of means or as a result of suffering from a parasitic disease. In practice such discrimination is difficult when dealing with aggregate statistics (as opposed to detailed micro studies of individuals), and the practical uses of the capability concept in poverty analysis have been mainly with simple functioning data. The *Human Development Report* too presents information that is essentially about living conditions and functionings.

In choosing particular aspects of living for special investigation in a poverty study, there is need for public discussion. There is an inescapable element of judgement in any such selection. In constructing any index of poverty (such as the human poverty index presented in this Report), the selections and the weights have to be explicitly stated and clarified so that public scrutiny can occur. It is very important that the standards to be used are not determined on a top-down basis, but are open to—if possible, emerge from—a participatory, democratic process. One of the purposes of the *Human Development Report* has been precisely to facilitate such a process, and this applies to poverty analysis as well.

BOX 1.1

Three perspectives on poverty

• *Income perspective.* A person is poor if, and only if, her income level is below the defined poverty line. Many countries have adopted income poverty lines to monitor progress in reducing poverty incidence. Often the cut-off poverty line is defined in terms of having enough income for a specified amount of food.

• *Basic needs perspective.* Poverty is deprivation of material requirements for minimally acceptable fulfilment of human needs, including food. This concept of deprivation goes well beyond the lack of private income: it includes the need for basic health and education and essential services that have to be provided by the community to prevent people from falling into poverty. It also recognizes the need for employment and participation.

• *Capability perspective.* Poverty represents the absence of some basic capabilities to function—a person lacking the opportunity to achieve some minimally acceptable levels of these functionings. The functionings relevant to this analysis can vary from such physical ones as being well nourished, being adequately clothed and sheltered and avoiding preventable morbidity, to more complex social achievements such as partaking in the life of the community. The capability approach reconciles the notions of absolute and relative poverty, since relative deprivation in incomes and commodities can lead to an absolute deprivation in minimum capabilities.

The "sustainable livelihood approach" to the study of poverty has particularly emphasized the need for local participation. In this approach each community can define criteria of well-being and the key elements of deprivation as they appear in the local context. This process brings out the concerns and worries of vulnerable people that are persistently neglected in national statistics and in many studies of poverty (box 1.2).

In the 1970s the concept of *social exclusion* came into the literature to analyse the condition of those who are not necessarily income-poor—though many are that too—but who are kept out of the mainstream of society even if not income-poor. The inadequacy of traditional definitions of poverty, based on incomes and consumption, was widely acknowledged to explain these new concerns.

Measurement of poverty and the human poverty index

Can the concept of human poverty be targeted and monitored? Can an overall measure of poverty be developed that can inform as well as be used for policy? Can an internationally comparable measure be defined?

This Report introduces a human poverty index (HPI) in an attempt to bring together in a composite index the different features of deprivation in the quality of life to arrive at an aggregate judgement on the extent of poverty in a community. *Human Development Report 1996* attempted this through a particular version of the "capability poverty measure". The HPI pursues the same approach, focusing on a broader and more representative set of variables, in a consistent relationship to the human development index (HDI).

Like many other concepts, human poverty is larger than any particular measure, including the HPI. As a concept, human poverty includes many aspects that cannot be measured—or are not being measured. It is difficult to reflect them in a composite measure of human poverty. Critical dimensions of human poverty excluded from the HPI for these reasons

are lack of political freedom, inability to participate in decision-making, lack of personal security, inability to participate in the life of a community and threats to sustainability and intergenerational equity.

Poverty depends on the context

The nature of the main deprivations varies with the social and economic conditions of the community in question. The choice of indicators in the HPI cannot but be sensitive to the social context of a country. For example, an index that concentrates on illiteracy and premature mortality may be able to discriminate between Pakistan and Sri Lanka more easily than it can between, say, France and Germany.

Issues of poverty in the developing countries involve hunger, illiteracy, epidemics and the lack of health services or safe water—which may not be so central in the more developed countries, where hunger is rare, literacy is close to universal, most epidemics are well controlled, health services are typically widespread and safe water is easy to tap. Not surprisingly, studies of poverty in the more affluent countries concentrate on such variables as social exclusion. These can be forceful deprivations and very hard to eliminate in all countries. But they take on relatively greater prominence in the affluent ones. There is

Human poverty includes many aspects that cannot be measured— or are not being measured

BOX 1.2

Criteria of ill-being

The following criteria, drawn from various participatory studies, were used by local people in Asia and Sub-Saharan Africa for defining poverty and ill-being:
• Being disabled (for example, blind, crippled, mentally impaired, chronically sick).
• Lacking land, livestock, farm equipment, a grinding mill.
• Being unable to decently bury their dead.
• Being unable to send their children to school.
• Having more mouths to feed, fewer hands to help.
• Lacking able-bodied family members who can feed their families in a crisis.
• Having bad housing.
• Suffering the effects of destructive behaviours (for example, alcoholism).
• Being "poor in people", lacking social support.
• Having to put children in employment.
• Being single parents.
• Having to accept demeaning or low-status work.
• Having food security for only a few months each year.
• Being dependent on common property resources.

Source: Chambers 1997.

no real possibility of constructing an index of human poverty that would be equally relevant in the different types of countries.

Given the pervasiveness of poverty in poor countries, the HPI developed is aimed at that context and the variables chosen reflect that (box 1.3). The nature of poverty in rich countries deserves a specialized study—and a more specialized index—focusing on those deprivations particularly relevant for those countries.

The three indicators of the human poverty index

The HPI presented in this Report concentrates on the deprivation in three essential elements of human life already reflected in the HDI—longevity, knowledge and decent a living standard.

The first deprivation relates to survival—the vulnerability to death at a relatively early age—and is represented in the HPI by the percentage of people expected to die before age 40.

The second dimension relates to knowledge—being excluded from the world of reading and communication—and is measured by the percentage of adults who are illiterate.

The third aspect relates to a decent standard of living, in particular, overall economic provisioning. This is represented by a composite of three variables—the percentage of people with access to health services and to safe water, and the percentage of malnourished children under five.

A few observations must be made about this last variable and about why income does not figure in the HPI. The logic underlying the construction of the economic provisioning variable is that the GNP included in the HDI is actually an amalgam of private and public facilities, since public services are paid out of aggregate national income.

Private income could not be an adequate indicator of an individual's economic facilities, which also include crucial public services (such as health care arrangements and a safe water supply). But why is private income not chosen to supplement the information on public facilities?

One of the problems in assessing the prevalence of income poverty is that the use of the same poverty line in different countries can be very misleading because of the variation in "necessary" commodities. Depending on the prevailing patterns of consumption—clothing, accommodation and such tools of communication and interaction as radios and telephones—many provisions are taken to be essential for social participation in one community without being treated as such in another. As a result, the minimum income needed to escape social estrangement can be quite different between communities.

Given the social pressure, these felt "needs" may compete—for relatively poor people in rich countries—even with the provision of resources for food, nutrition and health care. This can explain the prevalence of some hunger and malnutrition, especially among children, even in the United States, where incomes are high but inequalities generate a heavy burden of "necessity" in the direction of socially obligated consumption, often to the detriment of health and nutritional spending. So, the assessment of poverty on the basis of a low minimum cut-off income used for poor countries fails to show any poverty in generally affluent societies, even when the relatively poor in those societies may lack social participation and may even suffer from hunger and malnutrition.

An alternative is to use different poverty lines in different countries. But it is not easy to decide what the appropriate variations would be and how the respective poverty lines could be estimated. The official national lines cannot serve this purpose, since they reflect other influences, especially political ones, and cannot be used for international comparisons. The general need for a variable cut-off line of poverty is easier to appreciate than it is to find adequate values for variable poverty lines in different communities.

A more practical possibility is to be less ambitious and focus on material deprivation in hunger and malnutrition, not on income. A very high proportion of personal income goes to food and nourishment, especially for poor people in poor countries.

For this we can use information on food intake, which relates to personal incomes. Alternatively, there are estimates of malnutrition, but these are influenced by a number of variables, such as metabolic rate, climatic conditions, activity patterns and epidemiology. Since our concern is with the lives that people can lead, there is a case for going straight to the prevalence of malnutrition, and this is what is done in the HPI, concentrating specifically on the malnutrition of children, which is relatively easier to measure and for which usable data are more uniformly available.

For public provisions, access to health services and to safe water were chosen. Combining these two access variables with the prevalence of malnutrition gives a fairly broad picture of economic provisioning—private and public—to supplement the information on survival and literacy.

These are the basic informational ingredients of the HPI. It must be emphasized that there is some inescapable arbitrariness in any such choice. The choice was made on the basis of balancing considerations of relevance on the one hand, and the availability and quality of data on the other. There are inevitable compromises made, and it would be idle to pretend that even the variables that have been included have high-quality data for every country. There has been an attempt, in these selections, to strike a balance between the demands of relevance and the need for tolerably usable data, and these choices would certainly remain open to criticism and public scrutiny.

Weighting and aggregation

The procedures for constructing the HPI, including weighting and aggregation, are presented in detail in technical note 1.

The process of aggregation can be sensitive to the overlaps in the three dimensions of the HPI. For example, consider a case in which in each of the three categories of deprivation, 30% of people fail to meet the minimum requirement. This can be so because the same 30% fail in all three fields. But it can also be that a different 30% fail in each category. Or we may have some combination of the two extremes. In the first extreme case only 30% are affected by poverty, but they are deprived on all three fronts. In contrast, in the second extreme case as many as 90% of the population are deprived altogether, but each group has inadequacy in merely one field. Even though information on overlaps (or covariance) is not easy to obtain (since data regarding the different variables come from different sources), these distinctions can be important in describing poverty. They can also be crucial for causal analysis, since deprivation of one kind often feeds others.

However, when it comes to constructing an index, it is not easy to decide whether 30% of people with inadequacies of all three

---

BOX 1.3

The HPI—useful for policy-makers?

The human poverty index can be used in at least three ways.

1. *As a tool for advocacy.* If poverty is to be eradicated, public opinion and support needs to be mobilized to the cause. The HPI can help summarize the extent of poverty along several dimensions, the distance to go, the progress made. Income poverty also needs to be measured—but income alone is too narrow a measure.

2. *As a planning tool for identifying areas of concentrated poverty within a country.* The HDI has been used in many countries to rank districts or counties as a guide to identifying those most severely disadvantaged in terms of human development. Several countries, such as the Philippines, have used such analyses as a planning tool. The HPI can be used in a similar way, to identify those most seriously affected by human poverty. Though ranking by any one index alone would be possible—say, by illiteracy rate, lack of access to health services or the percentage in income poverty—the HPI makes possible a ranking in relation to a combination of basic deprivations, not one alone.

3. *As a research tool.* The HDI has been used especially when a researcher wants a composite measure of development. For such uses, other indicators have sometimes been added to the HDI. The HPI could be similarly used and enriched—especially if other measures of poverty and human deprivation were added, such as unemployment.

Although greeted with controversy when first launched in 1990, the HDI has found an increasing following as a simple measure of human development. The HDI provides an alternative to GNP, for assessing a country's standing in basic human development or its progress in human development over time. It does not displace economic measures but can serve as a simple composite complement to other measures like GNP.

The HPI can similarly serve as a useful complement to income measures of poverty. It will serve as a strong reminder that eradicating poverty will always require more than increasing the incomes of the poorest.

Further work is merited to explore how the HPI and the HDI could be enriched and made more robust in situations where a wider range of data on different aspects of poverty and human development are available.

What the HPI does not show. The HPI provides a measure of the incidence of human poverty in a country (or among some other group), say 25%. This means that judged by the HPI, an "average" of some 25% of the country's population is affected by the various forms of human poverty or deficiency included in the measure. But unlike with a headcount measure, it is not possible to associate the incidence of human poverty with a specific group of people or number of people.

---

types represents larger social poverty than 90% of people having one deficiency each. It is a matter of the importance to be given to depth vis-à-vis breadth. For the purpose of the HPI, the two cases have been treated as equivalent, so that in some sense depth and breadth have been equally considered.

There is a further issue to be addressed in deriving an aggregate index, namely that of substitutability between the three components of the HPI. This is done through an explicit procedure of using an additional weight (α). The procedure is fully described and examined in technical note 1. When α is taken to be 1, perfect substitutability is presumed, and the aggregate is obtained by simply averaging the three deprivations. The opposite case of no substitutability corresponds to α being taken to be infinity. In that case the largest of the percentage shortfalls rules the roost. For example, if 30% fail in field one, 50% in field two and 45% in field three, then the overall extent of poverty, in this case, is simply 50%.

Perfect substitutability is too extreme an assumption, and goes against the sensible requirement that as the deprivation in some field becomes relatively more acute, the weight placed on removing deprivation in that field should increase. Nor is the other extreme, zero substitutability, very easy to support, since it implies that any increase in deprivation in any category other than the one with the highest rate of deprivation must leave the aggregate poverty measure completely unchanged. Both extremes are avoided by choosing an intermediate value of α.

The human development index and the human poverty index

While human development focuses on progress in a community as a whole, human poverty focuses on the situation and progress of the most deprived people in the community.

The distinction between the two is analogous to the distinction between GNP and the income-based poverty index. In the income-based perspective, poverty incidence is needed to monitor progress in eliminating poverty. In the same way, the HPI is needed

to judge the extent of human poverty in a country and to monitor its progress.

The growth rate of GNP per person gives an account of progress seen in the conglomerative perspective—everyone's income counts in the GNP total. In contrast, the reduction of an income-based poverty index—such as the decline in the proportion of people below the poverty-line income—uses the deprivational perspective, concentrating only on the incomes of the poor. In this income-based perspective, it would make little sense to argue that since GNP is already based on income information, any income-based poverty measure must be a substitute for GNP. Nor would it be sensible to suggest that the availability of GNP as an indicator makes it redundant to seek a measure of income poverty. GNP and the income poverty measures use the income information in different perspectives—with GNP taking a conglomerative view and the income poverty measures focusing specifically on people poor in income.

Perspective	Income	Human life
Conglomerative	GNP per capita	HDI
Deprivational	Headcount index	HPI

The relationship between the HDI and the HPI has to be seen in a similar way. Both have to use the rich categories of information associated with human development—characteristics of human lives and quality of living that go far beyond what income information can provide. But while the HDI uses these characteristics in the conglomerative perspective, the HPI must use them in the deprivational perspective. The availability of GNP measures does not obviate the need for an income-based poverty indicator, nor does the HDI measure eliminate the need for an HPI.

Values and rankings of the human poverty index

Estimates of the HPI have been prepared for 78 developing countries having adequate data (table 1.1). The procedure for computing the index and the full results are presented in technical note 2. The HPI value indicates the proportion of the population affected by the three key deprivations in their lives—showing how widespread human poverty is.

At the top of the rankings are Trinidad and Tobago, Cuba, Chile, Singapore, Costa Rica—these countries have reduced human poverty to an HPI value of less than 10%. In other words, these countries have reduced human poverty to the point at which it affects less than 10% of the population.

At the bottom are the seven countries whose HPI exceeds 50%—Niger, Sierra Leone, Burkina Faso, Ethiopia, Mali, Cambodia and Mozambique. And in almost half the 78 countries covered, the HPI exceeds 34%, implying that about a third of their people suffer human poverty.

How does the HPI compare with income-based measures of poverty?
• Some countries have done better in reducing income poverty than human poverty. In Côte d'Ivoire and Egypt less than

TABLE 1.1
HPI ranking for developing countries

Country	Human poverty index (HPI) value (%)	HPI rank	HPI rank minus HDI rank	HPI rank minus $1-a-day poverty rank	Country	Human poverty index (HPI) value (%)	HPI rank	HPI rank minus HDI rank	HPI rank minus $1-a-day poverty rank
Trinidad and Tobago	4.1	1	−4	..	Cameroon	31.4	41	−4	..
Cuba	5.1	2	−18	..	Papua New Guinea	32.0	42	2	..
Chile	5.4	3	1	−13	Ghana	32.6	43	−1	..
Singapore	6.6	4	3	..	Egypt	34.8	44	14	15
Costa Rica	6.6	5	2	−15	Zambia	35.1	45	−8	−14
Colombia	10.7	6	−3	−6	Guatemala	35.5	46	12	−9
Mexico	10.9	7	−1	−9	India	36.7	47	−2	..
Jordan	10.9	8	−11	1	Rwanda	37.9	48	−29	−2
Panama	11.2	9	2	−13	Togo	39.3	49	−7	..
Uruguay	11.7	10	6	..	Tanzania, U. Rep. of	39.7	50	−8	14
Thailand	11.7	11	1	6	Lao People's Dem. Rep.	40.1	51	4	..
Jamaica	12.1	12	−6	1	Zaire	41.2	52	0	..
Mauritius	12.5	13	2	..	Uganda	41.3	53	−13	−3
United Arab Emirates	14.9	14	8	..	Nigeria	41.6	54	3	9
Ecuador	15.2	15	1	−15	Morocco	41.7	55	19	30
Mongolia	15.7	16	−12	..	Central African Rep.	41.7	56	−4	..
Zimbabwe	17.3	17	−24	−18	Sudan	42.2	57	−8	..
China	17.5	18	−11	−12	Guinea-Bissau	43.6	58	−11	−8
Philippines	17.7	19	−7	−9	Namibia	45.1	59	24	..
Dominican Rep.	18.3	20	−1	−5	Malawi	45.8	60	−8	..
Libyan Arab Jamahiriya	18.8	21	9	..	Haiti	46.2	61	−3	..
Sri Lanka	20.7	22	−1	8	Bhutan	46.3	62	−1	..
Indonesia	20.8	23	−4	3	Côte d'Ivoire	46.3	63	8	18
Syrian Arab Rep.	21.7	24	9	..	Pakistan	46.8	64	14	24
Honduras	22.0	25	−8	−15	Mauritania	47.1	65	6	11
Bolivia	22.5	26	−6	9	Yemen	47.6	66	9	..
Iran, Islamic Rep. of	22.6	27	14	..	Bangladesh	48.3	67	13	..
Peru	22.8	28	6	−14	Senegal	48.7	68	1	0
Botswana	22.9	29	4	−8	Burundi	49.0	69	−3	..
Paraguay	23.2	30	6	..	Madagascar	49.5	70	9	−1
Tunisia	24.4	31	15	15	Guinea	50.0	71	0	19
Kenya	26.1	32	−14	−13	Mozambique	50.1	72	2	..
Viet Nam	26.2	33	−4	..	Cambodia	52.5	73	11	..
Nicaragua	27.2	34	−5	−7	Mali	54.7	74	0	..
Lesotho	27.5	35	−13	−12	Ethiopia	56.2	75	2	14
El Salvador	28.0	36	5	..	Burkina Faso	58.3	76	1	..
Algeria	28.6	37	20	21	Sierra Leone	59.2	77	−1	..
Congo	29.1	38	−4	..	Niger	66.0	78	2	3
Iraq	30.7	39	1	..					
Myanmar	31.2	40	−3	..					

Note: HDI and $1-a-day poverty ranks have been recalculated for the universe of 78 countries. A negative number indicates that the country performs better on the HPI than on the other measure, a positive the opposite.
Source: Human Development Report Office and World Bank 1996b.

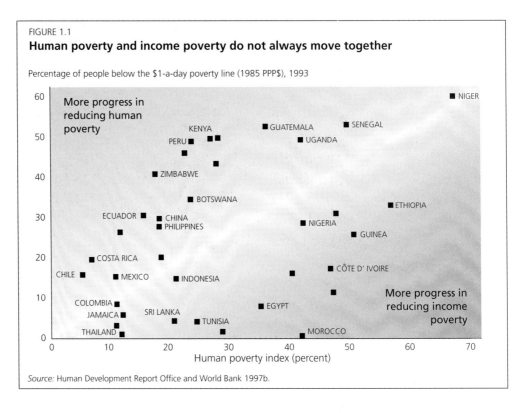

FIGURE 1.1

Human poverty and income poverty do not always move together

Percentage of people below the $1-a-day poverty line (1985 PPP$), 1993

Source: Human Development Report Office and World Bank 1997b.

20% of the people are income-poor, but 35% or more are affected by human poverty. These countries could pay more attention to reducing basic deprivations in choices and opportunities, especially by extending access to basic education and health services.

• Other countries have done better in reducing human poverty than income poverty—China, Costa Rica, Kenya, Peru, the Philippines, Zimbabwe. These countries have invested heavily in reducing deprivations in basic human capabilities.

Progress in reducing poverty in income and progress in reducing poverty in human choices and opportunities do not always move together. Regression analysis indicates a weak relationship between the headcount index of income poverty and HPI (figure 1.1). So, in monitoring progress, the focus should not be on income poverty alone, but on indicators of human poverty as well.

Comparing the HPI with the HDI reveals stark contrasts in some countries. These differences can alert policy-makers to the need to make human development better distributed, more pro-poor (figure 1.2). The HDI measures the overall progress of a country in human development. It can mask unequal distribution of that progress and the widespread human poverty that remains. Countries such as Namibia, Morocco, Pakistan, Egypt, Guatemala and Cambodia rank higher in the HDI than in the HPI—signalling the need for greater attention to human development for the most deprived.

Other countries rank much higher in the HPI than in the HDI—such as Zimbabwe, Cuba, China, Zambia and Viet Nam. In these countries overall progress in

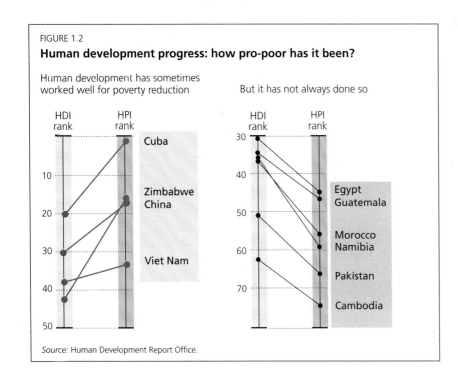

FIGURE 1.2

Human development progress: how pro-poor has it been?

Human development has sometimes worked well for poverty reduction

But it has not always done so

Source: Human Development Report Office.

TABLE 1.2
Trends in HPI for selected developing countries, 1970–90

Country	HPI value (%)		Change in HPI value (%)
	1970	1990	1970–90
Thailand	34	12	66
Mexico	30	11	63
Chile	13	5	59
Costa Rica	15	7	56
Trinidad and Tobago	9	4	54
Sri Lanka	35	21	41
Panama	17	11	36
Mauritius	19	13	35
Peru	28	23	19

Source: Human Development Report Office.

human development was pro-poor, effectively helping the most deprived lift themselves out of human poverty.

The countries at the bottom of the HPI rankings also rank near the bottom in the HDI. In these countries the overall progress in human development has been too low to raise the majority of their people from poverty.

Regional and global human poverty

HPI estimates for regions show that:
• Human poverty affects a quarter of the developing world's population, while income poverty affects a third.
• Human poverty is most widespread in Sub-Saharan Africa and in South Asia, affecting about 40% of the people.
• Progress in reducing human poverty and income poverty do not always go together. The contrasts are most stark in the Arab States, where income poverty was reduced to 4% by 1993 but human poverty was still 32%, and in Latin America and the Caribbean, where human poverty has been reduced to 15% but income poverty is still 24% (figure 1.3).

Trends in human poverty

The trends in human poverty in developing countries with available data show that although all were able to reduce the incidence of human poverty during the past two decades, the extent and pattern of reduction differed (table 1.2).

While Mexico and Thailand were able to reduce the incidence of human poverty by two-thirds, Peru, starting from a similar base, reduced it by less than a fifth. A similar comparison can be made for Costa Rica and Panama.

The disaggregated human poverty index

Estimating separate HPIs for groups or regions reveals disparities and contrasts within countries, and pinpoints concentrations of poverty (figure 1.4).

Brazil—Sharp contrasts exist between the North-East region, with an HPI of 46%, and the South and South-East, with HPIs of only 17% and 14%. These disparities have grown over the past two decades, as the incidence of human poverty declined by two-thirds in the South, but only a third in the North-East.

China—Disaggregated HPIs for Chinese provinces show stark contrasts. Human poverty is far more pervasive in the remote interior provinces of the western region (with an HPI of 44%) than in the coastal region (with an HPI of 18%).

India—Kerala is well ahead, having reduced human poverty to 15%, a clear reflection of the state's policy commitment to equity and human development. In Rajasthan and Bihar human poverty is pervasive—at more than 50%.

FIGURE 1.3
HPI and income poverty incidence

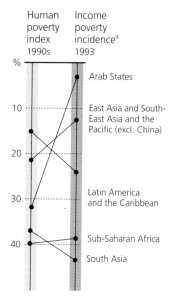

a. Percentage of people below the $1-a-day poverty line (1985 PPP$).
Source: Human Development Report Office.

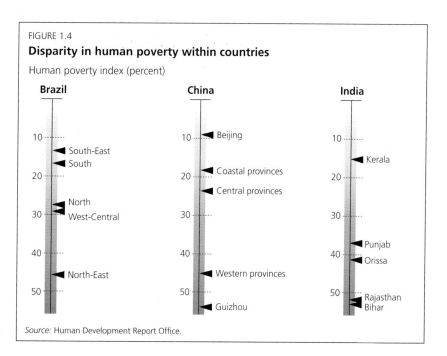

FIGURE 1.4
Disparity in human poverty within countries

Human poverty index (percent)

Source: Human Development Report Office.

CHAPTER 2

Progress and setbacks

Far from continuous, the progress has been marked by ascents and descents

Poverty has degraded human lives for centuries. But one of the great achievements of the 20th century is its dramatic reduction. Income poverty has fallen faster in the past 50 years than in the previous 50 decades. And by the end of the 20th century the number of people deprived in other aspects of life will be reduced to some 1–2 billion, from 2–3 billion three decades ago.

For the developing world in recent decades, the gains have been unprecedented. It has covered as much distance in the past 30 years as the industrial world did in a century. More than three-fourths of the population now can expect to survive to age 40. Adult illiteracy has been reduced by nearly half. Infant mortality has been cut by nearly three-fifths. And even though the South has an average per capita income that is a mere 6% of the North's, it now has a life expectancy and daily calorie supply that are more than four-fifths—and adult literacy that is two-thirds—of the North's.

This progress must be put in perspective, however.

First, far from continuous, the progress has been marked by ascents and descents (box 2.1). Nor has the progress been equally distributed—with some regions too often lagging behind others. Thus even in the 1990s, nearly 32% of people in Sub-Saharan Africa are not expected to survive to age 40, compared with 9% in East Asia. The adult illiteracy rate in South Asia, at nearly 50%, is four times that in South-East Asia and the Pacific. And the per capita GNP of $9,425 in East Asia (excluding China) is more than 18 times the per capita GNP of less than $550 in South Asia and Sub-Saharan Africa.

Second, much human deprivation still remains in the developing world. Nearly a third of the people—1.3 billion—live on less than $1 a day (1985 PPP$). More than 800 million people do not get enough to eat. And more than half a billion are chronically malnourished.

The chronicle of suffering goes on. More than 840 million adults are still illiterate. About 800 million people lack access to health services, and more than 1.2 billion access to safe water. At least a quarter of the human race does not live under relatively pluralistic and democratic regimes.

And on: There are still more than 40 million refugees and internally displaced people, and more than half a billion poor people live in ecologically fragile regions.

And on: Children and women suffer the most. Nearly 160 million children under age five are malnourished, and more than 110 million children are out of school. At 538 million, women constitute nearly two-thirds of the adult illiterates in developing countries. The maternal mortality rate is nearly 500 women per 100,000 live births.

Third, there are still North-South gaps in many areas. The under-five mortality rate of 95 per 1,000 live births in the South is five times that in the North, at 18. The maternal mortality rate of 471 per 100,000 live births in the South is 15 times that in the North, at 31. And per capita energy consumption in the South is only about an eighth of that in the North.

Fourth, deprivation is not limited to developing countries—the industrial countries also suffer. More than 100 million of their people still live below the income poverty line—at 50% of the individual median adjusted disposable income. More than 5 million people are homeless, and more than 37 million are jobless. More than a third of adults do not complete upper-secondary education. More than 130,000 rapes are reported every year, and these are only a fraction of the total.

Fifth, the uneven progress has given rise to disparities among regions, not only globally but also within countries—between poor and rich, women and men and rural and urban, and between ethnic groups. In 1994 the ratio of the income of the richest 20% of the world to that of the poorest 20% was 78 to 1, up from 30 to 1 in 1960. Because of departures from the natural sex ratio in a number of countries, nearly 100 million women are "missing" in the developing world. And in developing countries 72% of urban people, but only 20% of rural people, have access to sanitation.

Finally, the face of poverty is changing. Even though most poor people still live in rural Asia, particularly South Asia, the profile of poverty is rapidly shifting. In the next century a poor person is less likely to be a smallholder in rural Asia, more likely to be an unskilled, low-wage worker in urban Africa and Latin America.

So, coexisting with the impressive achievements in reducing human poverty is a considerable backlog, particularly in developing countries (figures 2.1 and 2.2 and tables 2.1 and 2.2). Human beings have advanced on several fronts—but retreated on several others. The trends in human poverty thus present a mixed picture of unprecedented human progress and unspeakable human misery—of hope and fear.

The analysis of human poverty trends in this chapter focuses on basic capabilities, participation, human security and environment, pointing to unevenness in progress over time and among regions. The chapter also examines economic well-being and income. Annex tables show progress by countries and regions in the different dimensions of human poverty.

Human poverty—progress and deprivation

Deprivation in basic capabilities encompasses deprivation in years of life, health, housing, knowledge, participation, personal security and environment. When these different kinds of deprivation interact, they severely constrain human choices. The performance of countries in improving the basic capabilities of their people can vary widely. But as Oman's experience shows, if a country puts concerted effort into overcoming deprivation in basic capabilities, it can with great

Two great ascents from human poverty

There have been two great "ascents" from human poverty in recent history: the first in industrial countries during the late 19th and the early 20th centuries, and the second in developing countries, Eastern Europe and the former Soviet Union in the aftermath of the Second World War. They had similar elements, but the second had a larger scale and a faster timetable.

The first ascent

Early in the industrial revolution poverty increased as farmers and peasants crowded the slums of industrial Europe, providing cheap labour for the "dark satanic mills". But a later stage of the industrial revolution offered relief from grinding poverty, with the emergence of social movements, cooperatives and unionism. Some of the most significant developments occurred during 1850–1925, in Great Britain and elsewhere, with progress in primary education, public health, sanitation and housing. In Sweden between 1850 and 1870, the number of primary school students more than doubled, from 270,000 to 556,000. And between 1861 and 1891–1900 Sweden's infant mortality rate declined from 139 to 102 per 1,000 live births.

The period also saw the beginnings of the modern welfare state. The seeds can be found in Germany, where Bismarck, reacting to the increasing popularity of socialist ideas, announced an innovative social insurance programme for work-related accidents, sickness and old age in 1881. Before the First World War Germany, Denmark and Great Britain were among the leaders in social insurance; the United States didn't adopt its Social Security Act until 1935. In the period following the Second World War the welfare state emerged. By the 1960s public and private action had achieved universal access to education, health services and pensions, and the first stage of the war on poverty was over.

The second ascent

The years following the Second World War saw the reduction of poverty in Eastern Europe, the former Soviet Union and most developing countries. The 1950s and 1960s were the "golden era" of postwar development. Newly freed from colonialism, many developing countries were ready to take advantage of advances in agriculture and health that increased food supplies and reduced mortality. Economic conditions were promising, and most governments favoured strategies to fight human poverty.

Many developing countries benefited from assistance for antipoverty strategies offered to attract them into one or the other of the competing blocs of the cold war. Progress in human poverty was often accompanied by increasing social and political progress, such as freedom from feudalism, bonded labour and social exclusion on the basis of caste and creed and expanding rights for women.

Eastern Europe and the former Soviet Union also made advances during the 1950s and 1960s. Infant mortality was reduced by half, from 81 to 41 per 1,000 live births. Life expectancy increased from 58 to 66 years for men, and from 63 to 74 years for women. And income poverty was declining. In Hungary between the early 1950s and 1972, the proportion of people living below the poverty line fell from 60% to 14%.

Source: de Vydler 1995, Lipton 1997, Kamerman and Kahn 1996 and Ruminska-Zimny 1997.

FIGURE 2.1a

Trends in human and income poverty

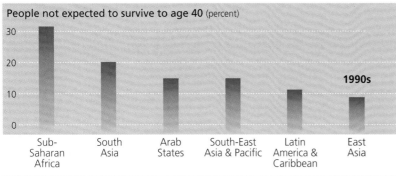

People not expected to survive to age 40 (percent)

1990s

Sub-Saharan Africa | South Asia | Arab States | South-East Asia & Pacific | Latin America & Caribbean | East Asia

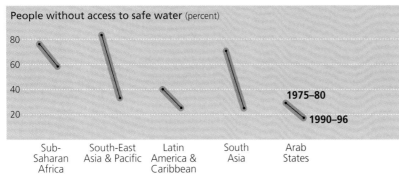

People without access to safe water (percent)

1975–80

1990–96

Sub-Saharan Africa | South-East Asia & Pacific | Latin America & Caribbean | South Asia | Arab States

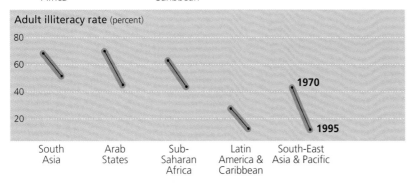

Adult illiteracy rate (percent)

1970

1995

South Asia | Arab States | Sub-Saharan Africa | Latin America & Caribbean | South-East Asia & Pacific

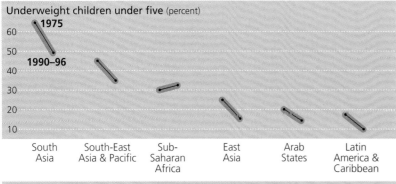

Underweight children under five (percent)

1975

1990–96

South Asia | South-East Asia & Pacific | Sub-Saharan Africa | East Asia | Arab States | Latin America & Caribbean

Population below the income poverty line (percent)

1987   1993

South Asia | Sub-Saharan Africa | East Asia & South-East Asia & Pacific | Latin America & Caribbean | East Asia & South-East Asia & Pacific (excl. China) | Arab States

Source: Human Development Report Office.

FIGURE 2.1b

Fastest and slowest progress
People without access to safe water

1990–96

1975=100

129 Malawi
114 Zambia
101 Tanzania
91 Papua New Guinea
89 Nicaragua

29 Chile
22 Thailand, Costa Rica
19 Saudi Arabia

5 Tunisia

People who are illiterate

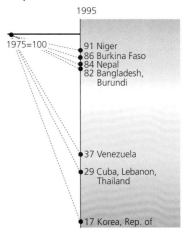

1995

1975=100

91 Niger
86 Burkina Faso
84 Nepal
82 Bangladesh, Burundi

37 Venezuela
29 Cuba, Lebanon, Thailand

17 Korea, Rep. of

Underweight children under five

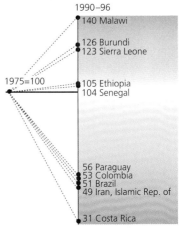

1990–96

140 Malawi

126 Burundi
123 Sierra Leone

1975=100

105 Ethiopia
104 Senegal

56 Paraguay
53 Colombia
51 Brazil
49 Iran, Islamic Rep. of

31 Costa Rica

FIGURE 2.2a
The backlog in poverty

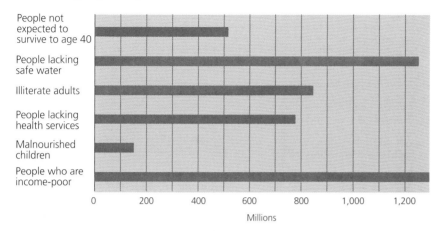

FIGURE 2.2b
507 million people not expected to survive to age 40

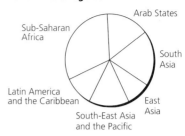

1.2 billion people without access to safe water

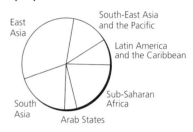

TABLE 2.1
Trends in income poverty in developing countries
(poverty line at $1 a day per person, 1985 PPP$)

Region or country group	People below the poverty line (%)		Share of all poor people (%)		Number of poor people (millions)
	1987	1993	1987	1993	1993
Arab States	5	4	1	1	11
East Asia and South-East Asia and the Pacific	30	26	38	34	446
East Asia and South-East Asia and the Pacific (excl. China)	23	14	10	7	94
Latin America and the Caribbean[a]	22	24	7	9	110
South Asia	45	43	39	39	515
Sub-Saharan Africa	38	39	15	17	219
Developing countries	34	32	100	100	1,301

a. Poverty line of $2 a day.
Source: Human Development Report Office.

842 million illiterate adults

158 million malnourished children under five

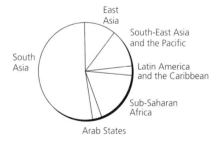

TABLE 2.2
Human poverty in developing countries
(millions)

Region or country group	Illiterate adults 1995	People lacking access to health services 1990–95	People lacking access to safe water 1990–96	Mal-nourished children under 5 1990–96	Maternal mortality rate (per 100,000 live births) 1990	People not expected to survive to age 40[a] 1990s
All developing countries	842	766[b]	1,213	158[b]	471	507
Least developed countries	143	241	218	34	1,030	123
Arab States	59	29	54	5	380	26
East Asia	167	144	398	17	95	81
Latin America and the Caribbean	42	55	109	5	190	36
South Asia	407	264	230	82	554	184
South-East Asia and the Pacific	38	69	162	20	447	52
Sub-Saharan Africa	122	205	249	28	971	124

a. Among population aged 0–39. b. Excludes Cyprus and Turkey.
Source: Human Development Report Office.

1.3 billion people living below the income poverty line

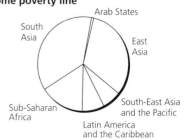

rapidity make a big difference in the lives of its people (box 2.2).

Years of life

One major indicator of human poverty is a short life. Dying before age 40 represents a severe deprivation. In developing countries nearly a fifth of the people are not expected to survive to this age, four times the proportion in industrial countries. But in East Asia fewer than 10% of the people are expected to die before reaching age 40, compared with nearly 33% in Sub-Saharan Africa.

Deprivation in years of life is also reflected in child mortality. In 1960–94 the infant mortality rate in developing countries was cut by nearly three-fifths—from 150 per 1,000 live births to 64 (figure 2.3). But in Sub-Saharan Africa the rate is still nearly 100 per 1,000 live births. South Asia's under-five mortality rate—at 112 per 1,000 live births— is nearly three times that in East Asia and nearly six times that in industrial countries.

Maternal mortality—a major contributor to high mortality in developing countries—reflects serious neglect of women in society but can be easily avoided with little additional investment in maternal health care. The maternal mortality rate in the developing world is 471 per 100,000 live births, more than 15 times the rate in industrial countries (figure 2.4). Sub-Saharan Africa's maternal mortality rate of 971 per 100,000 live births is more than 10 times that in East Asia.

Progress in deprivation in years of life is reflected in longer life expectancy. In developing countries life expectancy at birth increased by 16 years during 1960–94, from 46 years to 62 (figure 2.5). Latin America's life expectancy, at 69, is only five years shorter than that in industrial countries, while Sub-Saharan Africa's of 50 years is 12 years lower than the developing country average.

Health

Around 17 million people in developing countries die each year from such curable infectious and parasitic diseases as diarrhoea, measles, malaria and tuberculosis. Of the world's 23 million people living with HIV/AIDS, more than 90% are in developing countries. Sub-Saharan Africa has nearly two-thirds of all those infected, almost 14 million people. South Asia and South-East Asia and the Pacific have nearly 5.2 million, with numbers growing more rapidly than in any other region.

Deprivation in health starts with lack of access to health care and other services (figure 2.6). There have been considerable improvements in health care in the past three decades, and about 80% of the people in developing countries now have access to health services—though nearly 50% of the people in Sub-Saharan Africa do not. The developing countries have one doctor for every 6,000 people, the industrial countries one for every 350. Among developing regions the ratio ranges from one doctor per 18,000 people in Sub-Saharan Africa to roughly one per 1,000 people in Latin America and the Caribbean.

Between 1975–80 and 1990–96 the share of people in developing countries

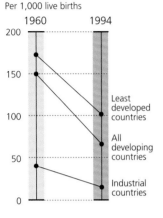

FIGURE 2.3
Trends in infant mortality
Per 1,000 live births

Source: Human Development Report Office.

BOX 2.2
Oman—an impressive record of accelerated human progress

Beginning in 1970, Oman undertook a comprehensive programme of human development, achieving some of the most rapid advances ever recorded. Life expectancy has increased by 30 years, from 40 years in 1970 to 70 years in 1994. Infant mortality was reduced from more than 200 per 1,000 live births in 1960 to less than 30 in 1994.

Improvements in education have been even more impressive. In 1970 there were only three schools—all primary—providing an education for 900 pupils—all boys. By 1994 there were 454,000 students in 920 schools, and 49% were girls.

Most health problems associated with poverty and lack of schooling have been controlled or eradicated. Trachoma leading to blindness, once affecting more than half of schoolchildren, has virtually disappeared. Maternal deaths declined to 27 per 100,000 live births in 1994.

Advances in health and education have been accompanied by rapid advances in other areas of human devel-

opment. Nearly three-quarters of houses now have running water and flushing toilets, and 9 of 10 have electric light and electricity or gas to cook with. Pensions are provided for the disabled, the elderly, widowed or divorced women and orphans. Oman has the highest number of televisions per capita in the developing world, with 730 per 1,000 people.

Oil revenues, of course, made possible such rapid progress and such a high standard of living. But without the commitment to human development, Oman might have been wealthy but unhealthy.

Oman has been a global pace-setter in human development. But there is still scope to enhance human development by translating income growth into the lives of the people. The female literacy rate is two-thirds the male rate, and the fertility rate, at 6.9, is one of the highest in the world. Oman has established an ambitious strategy to take its people to the year 2020 and ensure a better quality of life for all of them.

Source: Hill and Chen 1996 and Oman Ministry of Development and UNICEF 1995.

with access to safe water increased by more than half, from 41% to 69%. In East Asia 94% of the people have access to safe water, in Sub-Saharan Africa 42%.

Per capita food production in developing countries has increased by 22% since 1980, held back by a 3% decline in Sub-Saharan Africa. The share of underweight children under five in developing countries declined from 41% to 22% between 1975 and 1990–96. In the Arab States about 15% of the children under five are underweight, and in South Asia 50% are—though Thailand, through well-conceived and well-implemented policies, has made a big dent in malnutrition (box 2.3). More than half the pregnant women in developing countries suffer from anaemia, though the share ranges from 25% in East Asia to 78% in South Asia, where trained health personnel attend only a third of births.

The health backlog in the developing world is enormous. Nearly 800 million people lack access to health services, 264 million in South Asia and 29 million in the Arab States. And nearly 1.2 billion people lack access to safe water, nearly 400 million in East Asia and 54 million in the Arab States.

Industrial countries have health problems too. More than 300 people per 1,000 are likely to die from heart disease after 65, and more than 200 from cancer. Nearly 2 million people are infected with HIV. More than 40% of adult males smoke, the cause of many life-threatening diseases. Nor is there always support for the ill—in the United States more than 47 million people have no health insurance.

Health is even worse in Eastern Europe and the CIS countries, where both the adult and the infant mortality rates have risen in a number of countries. In addition, 2 million deaths since 1989 can be attributed to sharp increases in cardiovascular disease and violence. Malnutrition is also on the rise. In Ukraine the average daily intake of calories plummeted from more than 3,500 in 1989 to 2,800 in 1994. Children have been hit hardest. New cases of diphtheria among Russian children increased 29-fold—from 500 in 1989 to 15,000 in 1993. And most people are uncertain about their

health care prospects—health facilities are deteriorating and there is little likelihood of updating equipment.

Housing

Housing is fundamental to the formation of individual capabilities and to family and community ties. But more than a billion people in developing countries live without adequate shelter or in unacceptable housing. At least 600 million people live in dwellings that threaten their health and lives.

Adding to the housing problem is the insecurity due to the threat of eviction. Evictions often come with "justifications": urban beautification, claims of illegal occupation of state lands, construction of infrastructure, major international events, and political, military and ethnic reasons. And evictions require force—and often result in violence. Legal loopholes and highly paid lawyers are more accessible to the rich than to poor people, unaware of their rights but conscious that their survival is seriously threatened.

The most extreme housing deprivation is to have no home, and worldwide, an estimated 100 million are homeless. Children are worst affected—in Brazil more than 200,000 children spend their lives on the streets.

Homelessness is growing in industrial countries. In New York nearly a quarter of a million people, more than 3% of the city's population, have stayed in a shelter at some point in the past five years. London has about 400,000 registered homeless. In France the estimates range from 200,000 to 600,000. In Moscow 60,000 children are thought to live on the streets—in Romania, about 3,000.

Poor housing is often connected with poor sanitation that exposes people to infection. About 40% of the people in developing countries have access to proper sanitation, but the range runs from 32% in South Asia to 68% in Latin America and the Caribbean. The backlog: significant, with more than 2.5 billion people in developing countries having no access to proper sanitation.

FIGURE 2.4

Maternal mortality rate, 1990

Per 100,000 live births

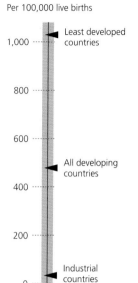

Source: Human Development Report Office.

FIGURE 2.5

Trends in life expectancy

Life expectancy (years)

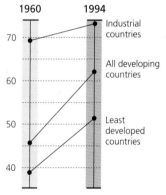

Source: Human Development Report Office.

FIGURE 2.6

People without access to health services

Percentage of the population, 1990–95

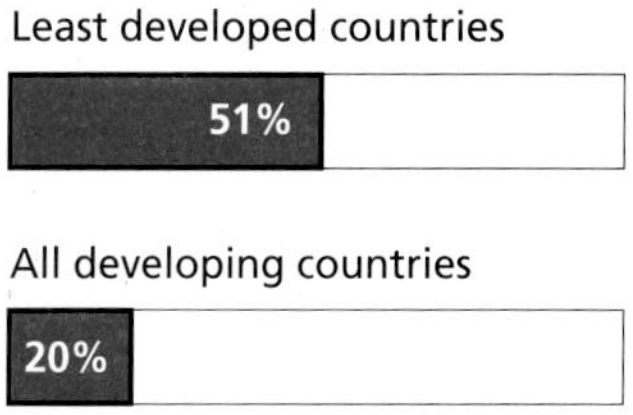

Least developed countries

51%

All developing countries

20%

Source: Human Development Report Office.

Knowledge

FIGURE 2.7

Adult illiteracy rate

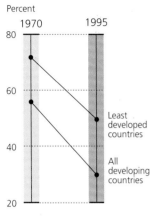

Percent

Source: Human Development Report Office.

Between 1970 and 1995 the adult illiteracy rate in developing countries declined by nearly half—from 57% to 30% (figure 2.7). The fastest decline has been in the Arab States, which reduced adult illiteracy from 70% in 1970 to 43% in 1995. South Asia recorded the slowest decline—from 68% to 50% between 1970 and 1995.

There is still a significant backlog. The developing world has more than 840 million illiterate adults, 538 million of them women. The female illiteracy rate is still nearly 40% in developing countries (figure 2.8). Nearly half the developing world's illiterate adults (407 million) are in South Asia—only 38 million in South-East Asia and the Pacific.

In developing countries some 110 million children are out of school at the primary level and 275 million at the secondary level. There are significant regional variations. At the primary level, nearly half the children out of school (50 million) are in South Asia; 10 million are in the Arab States.

Although industrial countries have near-universal education and close to 100% literacy, more than 15% of secondary-school-age children are not enrolled in school (table 2.5). The industrial world's postsecondary natural and applied science enrolment—at 30% of total enrolment—is less than the 47% in East Asia. In Bulgaria and Russia between 1990 and 1995, the combined primary and secondary enrolment ratios declined by 4–6%. In six Eastern European countries more than 20% of secondary-school-age children are not enrolled in school (table 2.3).

Developing countries have about 200 radios per 1,000 people, a fifth of the ratio in industrial countries, and 140 televisions per 1,000 people, a little more than a fourth of that in industrial countries. The regional range: 25 televisions per 1,000 people in Sub-Saharan Africa, 200 in Latin America and the Caribbean. The industrial countries' 350 main telephone lines per 1,000 people is more than four times the ratio in developing countries.

Participation

About two-thirds of the world's people live under relatively pluralistic, democratic regimes. Since 1980 nearly 45 general elections have been held in East Asia, and nearly 40 parliamentary elections in South Asia. In Sub-Saharan Africa more than half the states are now undertaking democratic reforms and renewing civil society—with nearly 30 multiparty presidential elections since 1990 (more than 20 the first in the country) and legalized opposition parties in more than 30 countries. In Latin America and the Caribbean nearly 150 general elections were held during 1974–94. Several Arab states have strengthened their multi-

---

BOX 2.3

How Thailand eradicated serious malnutrition in a decade

During the nine years from 1982 to 1991 Thailand dramatically reduced severe and moderate malnutrition, almost eradicating it. In 1982 more than half of preschool children were malnourished, 15% moderately or severely. By 1991 malnutrition had been reduced by two-thirds, with severe and moderate malnutrition virtually eradicated. More than 80% of preschoolers were nutritionally normal.

What accounts for the dramatic success? A programme of accelerated action that focused on nutrition, with four critical elements:
• Protein-energy malnutrition was identified as the most important nutritional problem, and for the first time the National Economic and Social Development Plan included a separate national plan for food and nutrition. The plan set goals to eradicate all severe protein-energy malnutrition in preschool children and to reduce moderate protein-energy malnutrition by 50% and mild by 25%.
• Comprehensive nutritional surveillance was instituted through growth monitoring. All preschool children were weighed and checked every three months at community weighing posts.
• A programme of nutrition education and communication encouraged breastfeeding, timely introduction of supplementary foods and proper hygiene and

spread correct information about food beliefs and taboos.
• Household and community food security was strengthened by promoting home gardening, fruit trees, fish ponds and prevention of epidemic diseases in poultry. School lunch programmes were established in 5,000 schools in poor areas, and food fortification was introduced to iodize salt.

All this was in the context of a poverty alleviation plan for some 7.5 million poor people in the north, northeast and south of Thailand.

What does the dramatic progress in Thailand show?
• The need to establish broad-ranging, integrated food and nutrition programmes as part of poverty reduction efforts.
• The need for some form of local organization in which village-level workers or volunteers encourage and support the families of children who are lagging.
• The potential for very rapid progress, especially after periods of economic growth that may have neglected human development.

Thus, through a comprehensive approach, Thailand has been able to virtually eradicate severe and moderate malnutrition. And today, Thailand ranks eleventh among 78 developing countries in the human poverty index, with an HPI of 12%.

Source: Winichagoon and others 1992.

party systems, and since 1990 there have been 22 general elections in the region. And Eastern Europe and the CIS countries have undergone a significant democratization since 1990. All these reforms have opened opportunities for people to take part in the processes that shape their lives.

People are also taking a bigger part in civil society. NGOs in developing countries are increasing in number and taking on bigger roles in voicing people's aspirations and working as pressure groups.

Trade unions have always been strong institutions of civil society. But except in such Scandinavian countries as Denmark, Finland and Sweden, where union membership has risen significantly in the past two decades, union membership has been falling in industrial countries (the Netherlands, Portugal, the United States). In developing countries a smaller part of the workforce tends to be unionized because fewer workers are in the formal sector.

Political space has always been monopolized by men. Although women are half the electorate, they hold only 13% of parliamentary seats and 7% of national cabinet posts. Women are better represented in local government, with their local representation surpassing their national in 46 countries studied. India, in a significant move, reserved a third of its local council seats for women in 1994, allowing at least 800,000 women to enter the local political pipeline to national leadership.

Women's participation in various aspects of economic and community life has increased. The female economic activity rate is now nearly 70% of the male rate in developing countries, ranging from 86% in East Asia to 50% in Latin America and the Caribbean. Women are also increasingly taking part in appraisals of poverty, which have been important in understanding the wellbeing of poor people. In Guinea, for example, although household surveys have not found that the incidence of income poverty is higher among women than among men, participatory poverty appraisals show widespread agreement that women are more vulnerable and of lower status.

Often constraining women's social and political participation is high fertility. But over the past 25 years fertility in developing countries has fallen by 40%.

Personal security

One of the less quantifiable aspects of deprivation, but one felt strongly in most poor communities, is a lack of personal security. Crime and violence are on the rise almost everywhere, and most of the victims are poor.

In the 1970s and 1980s reported crimes worldwide increased by 5% a year—2.5 times the growth in population. In the United States there are 2 million victims of violent crime every year. In many developing countries killings of minors have increased by more than 40% in the 1990s. In Bulgaria reported crimes more than quadrupled from an annual average of 50,000 during the 1980s to 223,000 in 1994. And in the Czech Republic and Hungary crime rates have tripled since 1989.

Internal conflicts also frequently threaten personal security. At the end of 1995 there were nearly 16 million refugees who had fled to other countries, 26 million people who were internally displaced and 4 million people who were "refugee-like"— more than 80% of them women and children. These people have lost their homes, their livelihoods, their security—and are constantly vulnerable. Another constant threat to security—some 110 million landmines lie in wait for victims in at least 68 countries.

Among the worst threats of violence are those against women. It is estimated that a third of married women in developing countries are battered by their husbands during their lifetime. In India the most conservative estimate puts dowry deaths at 5,000 in 1992. And nearly 130,000 rapes are reported annually in the industrial countries, a shocking figure but an understatement of the reality.

Children, who should be most protected in any society, are subject to many abuses. In the United States every year nearly 3 million children are reported to be victims of abuse and neglect. About 75 million children aged 10–14 labour in devel-

Political space has always been monopolized by men

FIGURE 2.8
Female illiteracy rate

Percentage of women who are illiterate, 1995

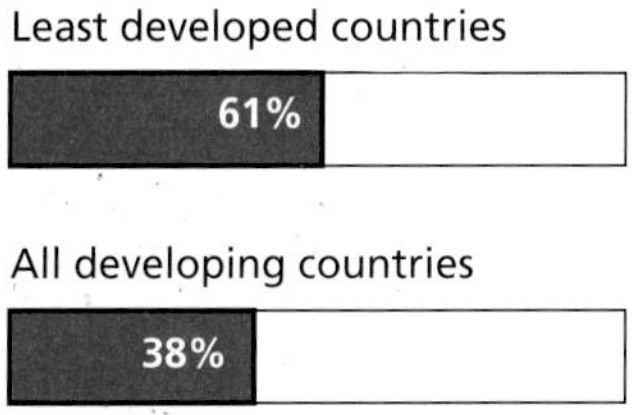

Least developed countries

61%	

All developing countries

38%	

Source: Human Development Report Office.

oping countries—45 million of them in Asia, 24 million in Africa—often working in slavery, prostitution and hazardous conditions. Each year an estimated 1 million children, mostly girls in Asia, are forced into prostitution.

Environment

Continued environmental deterioration is a source of continued impoverishment. Poor people depend on natural resources for their livelihoods—especially on common property resources. And they are more likely than the better off to live in vulnerable areas. Today nearly half a billion poor people in developing countries live in ecologically fragile regions. Thus poor people suffer most from deterioration in the environment—because of the threat to their livelihoods, but also because of aggravated health risks from pollution.

Environmental threats around the world stem from degradation of local ecosystems and of the global system. The

water supply per capita in developing countries today is only a third of what it was in 1970. More than 55% of the people in the Arab States suffer from serious water scarcity—with less than 1,000 cubic metres of water available per capita each year. In the developing world some 8–10 million acres of forest land are lost every year.

In Sub-Saharan Africa 65 million hectares of productive land have become desert in the past 50 years. Salinization damages 25% of the irrigated land in Central Asia and 20% in Pakistan.

Air pollution is also serious. About 700 million people, mainly women and children in poor rural areas, inhale indoor smoke from burning biomass fuel. In the industrial world air pollution is devastating Europe's forests, causing economic losses of $35 billion a year. And it costs farmers more than $4 billion a year in Germany, more than $2 billion a year in Poland. Also linked to environmental degradation are natural disasters, striking an average of nearly 120 million people each year since 1970.

Solid wastes, if poorly managed, can contaminate water, soil and air. A city dweller in industrial countries produces 2–10 times as much garbage as a city dweller in the developing world. But in developing countries a third to a half of urban solid wastes go uncollected, with serious health implications.

Some environmental degradation—polluted air, greenhouse gases—migrates across borders, affecting poorer countries and people. One possible effect: Bangladesh produces only 0.3% of global greenhouse emissions but could see its land area shrink 17% with a one-metre rise in sea level from global warming.

Income poverty

Amenable to econometric analysis and statistical exercises, the measurement of income poverty has dominated the literature. Those measuring income poverty have focused more on its incidence than on its depth and severity. The incidence of income poverty is usually measured by a headcount index, which represents the percentage of people below the chosen poverty line.

Continuing environmental deterioration is a source of continuing impoverishment

---

BOX 2.4

Income poverty in Sub-Saharan Africa

Income poverty runs deep in Sub-Saharan Africa and is a serious threat to economic and social stability. People in this region, along with South Asia, are among the poorest in the world. In 1992 about 45% of Sub-Saharan Africa's population was income-poor according to national poverty lines. In Gambia and Zambia nearly two-thirds of the people were income-poor; in Cameroon, Guinea-Bissau and Uganda, more than half; and in Côte d'Ivoire, Kenya and Nigeria, more than a third. The poverty gap in Sub-Saharan Africa, at 15%, is nearly twice that in East Asia and South-East Asia and the Pacific (excluding China), at 8%.

The growth of income in Sub-Saharan Africa has been dismal in recent decades. Between 1970 and 1992 per capita GDP (PPP$) grew by only $73, compared with growth of $420 in South Asia and $900 in East Asia, regions with incomes comparable to those of Sub-Saharan Africa in 1970.

Between 1981 and 1989 the region saw a cumulative decline of 21% in real GNP per capita. This decline extended both to countries undertaking structural adjustment and to non-adjusting countries, exacerbating the conditions of the poor. Of the 35 countries in the region for which data are available, per capita GNP fell in 27. The most severe declines were in Gabon (58%), Nigeria (nearly 50%), Côte d'Ivoire (42%), Mozambique and Niger (more than 30%), Zaire (more than 25%) and Congo and Zambia (more than 20%).

Countries with adjustment programmes were more successful in improving macroeconomic balances towards the end of the 1980s, after making greater income sacrifices early in the decade. Nonetheless, 11 adjusting countries had falling per capita incomes in 1985–90, as did the region as a whole.

Thus income poverty was high and increasing in many countries of Sub-Saharan Africa in the 1980s. And the situation remains alarming in the 1990s.

Source: Stewart 1995a and World Bank 1996d.

Often, an international poverty line is chosen to compare the incidence of poverty across borders. The World Bank uses a poverty line of $1 (1985 PPP$) a day per person to compare poverty in most of the developing world. (For an explanation of the $1-a-day poverty line see the glossary of poverty and human development.) For Latin America and the Caribbean a poverty line of $2 (1985 PPP$) a day per person is suggested. For countries in Eastern Europe and the CIS $4 (1990 PPP$) a day per person has been used. The figure suggested for industrial countries is $14.40 (1985 PPP$), which corresponds to the income poverty line in the United States. Some countries have also constructed national poverty lines, most based on food poverty (see the glossary). In industrial countries national poverty lines are sometimes set at 50% of the median disposable income of individuals. Setting national poverty lines at different levels can produce quite varied results, a constraint that any discussion of income poverty trends should recognize (see the last two columns of annex table A2.1).

Developing countries

In developing countries the proportion of people in income poverty by the $1-a-day measure declined from 34% to 32% in 1987–93, but the number of income-poor people increased from 1.2 billion to 1.3 billion (see table 2.1). The share of poor people declined rather slowly in East and South Asia, and in Sub-Saharan Africa and Latin America and the Caribbean it even increased (box 2.4). In 1993 South Asia was home to two-fifths of the world's poor people (515 million), and East Asia and South-East Asia and the Pacific to a third (446 million).

For examining historical trends, the only possibility is to use national income poverty lines. The "big five" in Asia—with three-fifths of the developing world's people and two-fifths of the income-poor—have made impressive progress in reducing income poverty according to national poverty lines (figure 2.9). (See pages 49–52 for a discussion of poverty trends and strategies in two of these countries, China and India—the

world's two most populous countries and home to many poor people.)

Other Asian economies have also seen major reductions in poverty. Big gains were made in the 1970s and 1980s by Hong Kong, the Republic of Korea, Singapore and Taiwan (province of China)—and more recently by Malaysia, the Philippines, Thailand and Viet Nam.

In Latin America and the Caribbean the incidence of poverty according to national poverty lines fell significantly in the 1950s, and even faster in the 1960s and 1970s (figure 2.10). But the 1980s were disastrous—with income poverty in the

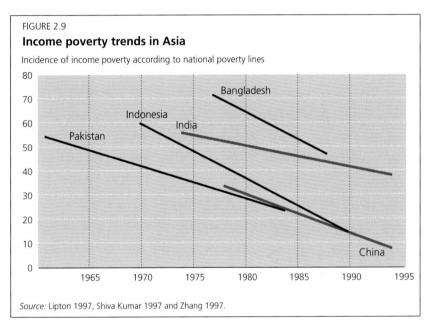

FIGURE 2.9
Income poverty trends in Asia
Incidence of income poverty according to national poverty lines

Source: Lipton 1997, Shiva Kumar 1997 and Zhang 1997.

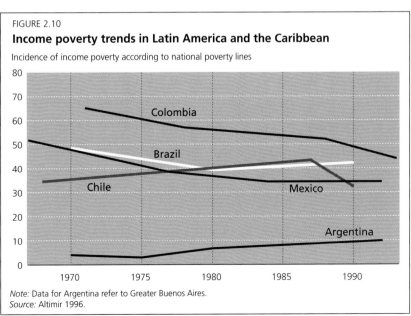

FIGURE 2.10
Income poverty trends in Latin America and the Caribbean
Incidence of income poverty according to national poverty lines

Note: Data for Argentina refer to Greater Buenos Aires.
Source: Altimir 1996.

region reverting to levels higher than those in the 1970s. Only in the early 1990s did poverty again begin to decline in a few Latin American and Caribbean countries (Chile, Colombia).

For Sub-Saharan Africa the most recent estimates show that 266 million of its 590 million people are income-poor by national poverty lines—a much higher proportion than in any other region except South Asia. The depth of poverty—that is, how far incomes fall below the poverty line—is greater in Sub-Saharan Africa than anywhere else in the world.

In the Arab States in the 1980s the incidence of poverty by national poverty lines was about 25%, implying that about 66 million people were income-poor during that decade.

Eastern Europe and the CIS countries

During the postwar decades Eastern Europe and the former Soviet Union reduced income poverty substantially, as rapid industrialization opened new choices and opportunities and education and health care expanded rapidly.

But this progress stagnated, even reversed, in the 1970s and 1980s. Based on national poverty lines, income poverty increased among Polish urban workers from 6% to 25% between 1978 and 1987, and among Yugoslav workers from 9% to 20%. At the same time, social services and health standards deteriorated.

A much steeper and broader decline accompanied the move to market economies in the late 1980s. If $4 (1990 PPP$) a day is taken as the poverty line, the average incidence of income poverty for the region increased sevenfold between 1988 and 1994—from 4% to 32% (figure 2.11). The number of poor people in the region increased from 14 million to more than 119 million.

In 1993–94, with almost 60 million poor people, Russia alone accounted for nearly half the income-poor in Eastern Europe and the CIS.

Income poverty among the elderly and children has increased dramatically (table 2.4 and figure 2.11). Among older people it

increased sixfold in Bulgaria in 1989–94, from 4% to 28%, and among children in Romania threefold, from 9% to 36%.

Industrial countries

The immediate postwar decades saw a substantial reduction in income poverty in the industrial countries. The United States reduced its incidence from 80% in 1939 to 16% in 1969, and Japan from 10% in 1960 to 7% in the early 1970s. By the early 1970s income poverty in all the major OECD countries had fallen to 10–20%.

But by the 1980s and the early 1990s this progress was in jeopardy. The incidence of income poverty increased substantially in the United Kingdom and marginally in Belgium, Finland, Germany, the Netherlands, Norway and the United States—but fell in Canada, Denmark, France and Spain and remained stable in Sweden (figure 2.12).

By the early 1990s more than 100 million people in industrial economies were income-poor, judged by a poverty line of 50% of the median adjusted disposable income for individuals. But if the criterion is the US poverty line of $14.40 (1985 PPP$) a day, the number of income-poor in industrial countries becomes 80 million. Whatever the yardstick, poverty is a huge problem (table 2.6).

Income poverty among the elderly and children is staggering. In Australia, the United Kingdom and the United States more than 20% of the aged are income-poor. And one in every four children in the United States is income-poor—one in six in Australia, Canada and the United Kingdom. Income poverty is alarmingly high in one-parent families and families headed by elderly women.

How do redistributive policies affect income poverty? In Belgium the government's transfer payments help reduce poverty by 81%, from 28% to 6%. In the United States the reduction is only 29%—from 27% to 19%. Transfer payments can have an even stronger impact on the poverty of the elderly and children. In Sweden, for example, transfers reduce poverty among children by 84%—from 18% to 3%.

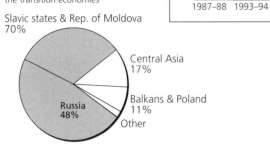

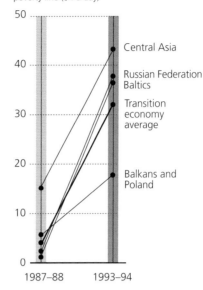

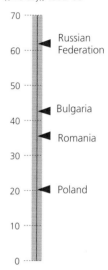

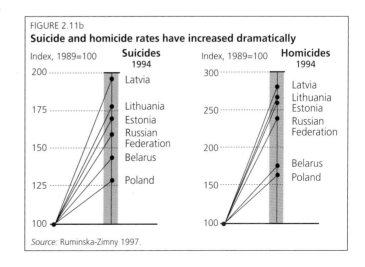

FIGURE 2.11a

Increasing poverty in transition economies

The incidence of income poverty has increased sevenfold since 1988, pushing an additional 105 million people below the poverty line.

People living below the income poverty line ($4 a day)

119.2 million

13.6 million

1987–88   1993–94

Distribution of poor people in the transition economies

Slavic states & Rep. of Moldova 70%

Russia 48%

Central Asia 17%

Balkans & Poland 11%

Other

Source: Milanovic 1996.

The prevalence of income poverty has increased at a similar rate in all groups except the Balkan states and Poland.

Percentage of the population living below the income poverty line ($4 a day)

Central Asia

Russian Federation Baltics

Transition economy average

Balkans and Poland

1987–88   1993–94

Children experience the highest rates of income poverty.

Percentage of children living below the income poverty line ($4 a day), 1992–95

Russian Federation

Bulgaria

Romania

Poland

TABLE 2.3

Human poverty in selected countries of Eastern Europe and the CIS

Country	Population not expected to survive to age 40 (%) 1990[a]	Secondary-school-age children not enrolled in school (%) 1993–95	Unemployment rate (%) 1995
Bulgaria	6.2[b]	40	11.1[c]
Croatia	4.5[b]	34	17.6[c]
Czech Rep.	3.7[b]	12	2.9
Georgia	5.6[b]	29	3.4[c]
Hungary	8.2[b]	27	10.4
Latvia	8.1[b]	22	6.6
Lithuania	6.5[b]	20	7.3[c]
Poland	5.0[b]	17	14.9
Romania	7.1[b]	27	8.9[c]

a. Data refer to 1990 or a year around 1990. b. Calculated by Kenneth Hill. c. Official unemployment rate; registered unemployment only.
Source: Kenneth Hill, UNESCO 1997 and UNECE 1996.

TABLE 2.4

Income poverty among children and the aged, 1989–93

(percentage below the poverty line)

Country	Children 1989	Children 1993	Aged 1989	Aged 1993
Russian Federation	40[a]	62[b]	23[a]	34[b]
Bulgaria	2[c]	43[d]	4[c]	28[d]
Romania	9	36	12	19
Estonia	27[a]	34[d]	38[a]	38[d]
Poland	8	20[a]	5	3[a]
Slovakia	0	9	0	1
Hungary	2	7	1	1
Czech Rep.	0	1[a]	0	1[a]

Note: Poverty line is set at 60% of a low income, which is considered to be 35–45% of the average 1989 wage.
a. 1992. b. 1995. c. 1990. d. 1994.
Source: UNICEF 1995a.

FIGURE 2.11b

Suicide and homicide rates have increased dramatically

Index, 1989=100   **Suicides** 1994

200

Latvia

175

Lithuania
Estonia
Russian Federation

150

Belarus

125

Poland

100

Index, 1989=100   **Homicides** 1994

300

Latvia
Lithuania
Estonia

250

Russian Federation

200

Belarus
Poland

150

100

Source: Ruminska-Zimny 1997.

FIGURE 2.12a
Progress and setbacks in income poverty

Index of poverty rate

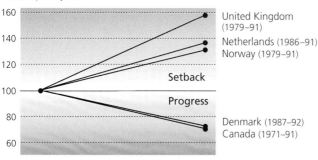

Note: In the figures on this page poverty is measured at 50% of the median adjusted disposable personal income for individuals.
Source: Smeeding 1996.

FIGURE 2.12b
Children and the aged are more likely to be income-poor

Percentage living below the income poverty line, 1989–92

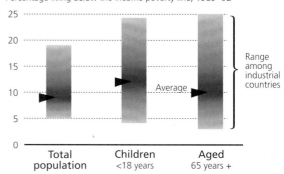

Source: Smeeding 1996.

TABLE 2.5
Human poverty in selected industrial countries

Country	Population not expected to survive to age 40 (%) 1990[a]	Secondary-school-age children not enrolled in school (%) 1993–95	Unemployment rate (%) 1995
Australia	3.5	18	8.5
Belgium	3.5	12	9.5
Canada	3.1	9	9.5
Finland	3.1	4	17.1
France	4.0	10	11.6
Germany	3.0	14	8.2
Ireland	2.9	16	12.9
Japan	2.2	4	3.1
Netherlands	2.5	14	6.5
New Zealand	4.3	5	6.3
Norway	2.7	8	4.9
Spain	3.0	10	22.7
Sweden	2.7	7	9.2
United Kingdom	2.6	16	8.7
USA	4.0	11	5.5

a. Data refer to 1990 or a year around 1990.
Source: Hill 1997, UNESCO 1997 and OECD 1996b.

TABLE 2.6
Income poverty in selected industrial countries

Country	Year	Population below the poverty line (%)
Ireland	1987	37
Spain	1990	21
Netherlands	1991	14
USA	1994	14
United Kingdom	1991	13
France	1984	12
Belgium	1992	12
Germany	1989	12
Australia	1989	8
Denmark	1992	8
Canada	1991	6
Sweden	1992	5
Japan	1992	4
Luxembourg	1985	4
Finland	1991	4
Norway	1991	3

Note: Poverty is measured at $14.40 (1985 PPP$) a day per person, which corresponds to the US poverty line.
Source: Smeeding 1996.

TABLE 2.7
Distribution of income poverty

Country	Share of population in income poverty[a] (%) 1989–94	Children in one-parent income-poor households (%) 1989–92
United States	19	59
United Kingdom	15	49
Australia	13	61
Japan	12	..
Canada	12	58
Spain	10	37
Netherlands	7	34
OECD average	9	..

a. Poverty is measured at 60% of the median adjusted disposable personal income for individuals, the standard used by OECD and the European Union.
Source: Smeeding 1996.

FIGURE 2.12c
Among the aged, income poverty incidence is higher for women

Children in one-parent homes are more likely to grow up in income poverty

Percentage living below the income poverty line, 1989–92

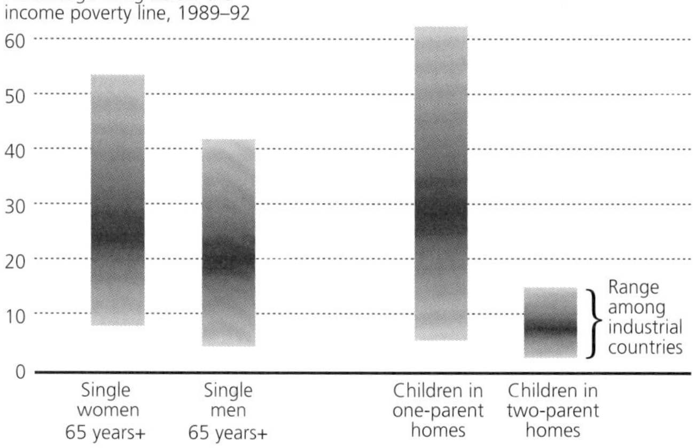

Source: Smeeding 1996.

In recent decades social exclusion in industrial countries has been linked with exclusion from the mainstream labour market, showing up in long-term unemployment, youth unemployment and part-time employment.

Income poverty's links to deprivation

High income poverty is associated with high human poverty, and low income poverty with low human poverty. But the two forms of poverty can move in different directions. High income poverty can coexist with low human poverty (Peru and Zimbabwe), and low income poverty can coexist with high human poverty (Côte d'Ivoire and Egypt). The contrasts between the HPI and the headcount index of income poverty discussed in chapter 1 show these relationships. Analysis of different indicators of human poverty reveals more about the dynamics of income and human poverty.

The relationship between income poverty and human poverty can change. During 1970–90 Malaysia and the Republic of Korea reduced income poverty and some aspects of human poverty by more than half (figure 2.13). Colombia and Costa Rica also cut human poverty by half, but not income

poverty. So income poverty and human poverty generally go hand in hand, but not automatically or always.

Pakistan and Mauritania, for example, have the same illiteracy rate (around 64%), but the income poverty rate at $1 a day is 12% in Pakistan and 31% in Mauritania. Similarly, illiteracy is less than 12% in Peru and Thailand, but Peru's income poverty is 49%, Thailand's 0.1%.

Income poverty's ties with child malnutrition are also weak—no surprise. Child malnutrition depends not so much on the income or food available as on the health care available to children and women. Income poverty explains only about 10% of the variation in child malnutrition.

Income poverty has been reduced under a wide range of political regimes—from China and Viet Nam on the one hand to Costa Rica, Jamaica and Sri Lanka on the other. But the Vietnamese experience shows that both human and income poverty can be reduced through a combination of rigorous analysis of the problem and formulation and implementation of proper policies (box 2.5).

The lack of continuity and the unevenness of progress in human and income poverty over time have resulted in not only a backlog, but also striking disparities.

Income poverty and human poverty can move in different directions

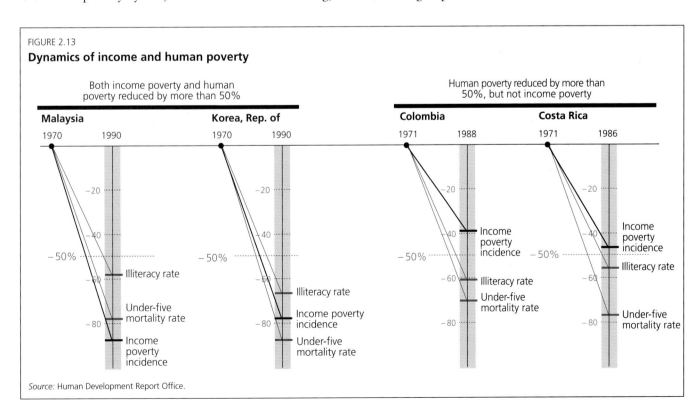

FIGURE 2.13

Dynamics of income and human poverty

Source: Human Development Report Office.

The many disparities

And inequalities: between poor and rich, women and men, rural and urban, developed and underdeveloped regions and different ethnic groups. Seldom are these inequalities isolated—instead, they are interrelated and overlapping. Inequalities and poverty do not always move in the same direction. In some cases they increase or decrease together—in others they move in opposite directions.

BOX 2.5

Doi Moi—eliminating human and income poverty in Viet Nam

Viet Nam has approached poverty at two levels, seeking first to understand the phenomenon and then to formulate strategies to overcome it. The centre-piece of the government's socio-economic development strategy since 1986 has been *Doi Moi,* the reform process aimed at transforming the Vietnamese economy from a centrally planned system to one that is market-based and dynamic.

While Viet Nam has reduced income poverty by an estimated 35% since launching *Doi Moi,* the incidence remains high, ranging from less than 20% according to a national poverty line to around 50% based on an internationally comparable income poverty line. Income poverty is concentrated among ethnic minorities, who live mostly in the northern uplands and central highlands.

Even with a per capita income of $200, Viet Nam has made much progress in reducing human poverty. It has achieved a life expectancy of 66 years, an adult literacy rate of 93% and access to health service for 90% of its population. And between 1990 and 1995 it reduced under-five mortality from 55 per 1,000 live births to 46. As measured by the HPI, human poverty in Viet Nam is now 26%.

Much of the remaining poverty in Viet Nam appears to be linked to five broad underlying causes:
• Isolation—geographic, linguistic and social.
• Excessive risks—such as typhoons, floods and illness.
• Lack of access to productive

resources, particularly land and credit.
• Unsustainable financial and environmental conditions.
• Inadequate participation of the people in planning and implementing development programmes.

A major aim of *Doi Moi* has been to create an enabling environment based on growth, stability and equity to ensure that poor people can better help themselves and that poverty reduction is sustainable. This broad-based strategy has been quite successful, in part because, besides creating an enabling environment for poor people, it has emphasized a supportive environment for the non-poor and some social assistance for those who may not rise on the tide of development.

In rural areas Viet Nam has taken significant steps in land reform. Between 1992 and 1995 the number of borrowers from the Viet Nam Bank of Agriculture increased almost sevenfold—from 900,000 to 7 million. And construction of rural infrastructure through local initiatives has been initiated to reduce isolation and the risks of poverty.

An important future challenge is to further develop the enabling environment of growth, stability and equity while working to ensure that poor people can participate in that environment—by strengthening the economy, incentives, institutions, organizations, families and human resources.

The government aims to eliminate chronic hunger by 1999, to eradicate income poverty by 2010 and, ultimately, to catch up with its more prosperous neighbours in East Asia.

Source: UNDP and UNICEF 1996.

Income disparity

In every region the per capita income of the richest 20% is naturally much higher than that of the poorest 20%—but by differing degrees. In the developing world it is 8 times as high, in industrial countries 7 times as high. And in South Asia it is 5 times as high, in Latin America and the Caribbean 19 times as high. The biggest range: the per capita income of the richest 20% in industrial countries ($32,198 in PPP$) is 11 times that in South Asia ($2,833 in PPP$) (annex table A2.1).

Regional figures may conceal large variations among countries. In Eastern Europe and the CIS countries the per capita income of the highest quintile is 7 times that of the lowest quintile—in Russia 14 times. In industrial countries the per capita income of the highest quintile is 7 times that of the lowest—in Japan only 4 times. Although no figure was available for Sub-Saharan Africa as a whole, income disparity is significant in some countries of the region. In Lesotho the per capita income of the richest 20% is 22 times that of the poorest 20%. For South Africa the figure is 19 times, and for Kenya 18 times.

At a global level, between 1989 and 1996 the number of billionaires increased from 157 to 447. Today the net wealth of the 10 richest billionaires is $133 billion, more than 1.5 times the total national income of all the least developed countries. The wealth of the single richest Mexican in 1995 was $6.6 billion, equal to the combined income of the 17 million poorest Mexicans. These, of course, are comparisons of wealth and income. But a comparison of wealth alone, if possible, would be even starker, since the wealth of the poorest people is generally much less than their income.

Income disparity is often linked with disparity in access to social services and productive resources and in the pattern of public expenditure. In urban Kenya the net primary enrolment ratio in the 1980s was 45% for the poorest 10% and 72% for the richest 10%. In rural Bangladesh in 1992 large landowners constituted only 7% of rural households but received 37% of the institutional credit. In Nigeria only 12% of public health spending in 1992 went to the poorest 20%, while 33% went to the richest 20%.

Gender disparity

The disparity between women and men in income poverty and in different dimensions of human poverty can be illustrated by repeating some of the more striking facts. In developing countries there are still 60% more women than men among illiterate adults, female enrolment even at the primary level is 13% lower than male enrolment, and female wages are only three-fourths of male wages. In industrial countries unemployment is higher among women than men, and women constitute three-fourths of the unpaid family workers.

Gender disparity can be seen in proper perspective through the lens of the gender-related development index (GDI) and the gender empowerment measure (GEM). The GDI attempts to capture achievement in the same set of basic capabilities included in the human development index (HDI)—life expectancy, educational attainment and income—but adjusts the HDI for gender inequality. The GEM measures gender inequality in key areas of economic and political participation and decision-making. It thus differs from the GDI, an indicator of gender inequality in basic capabilities. (The methods for constructing the GDI and the GEM are described in technical note 2 and the full results are in indicator tables 2 and 3.)

Results of the gender-related development index

For this Report the GDI was calculated for 146 countries (table 2.8). Ten countries (Armenia, Azerbaijan, Benin, Botswana, Latvia, Lebanon, Kazakstan, Kyrgyzstan, Mongolia, South Africa) have shifted in rank by 10 or more places compared with last year's GDI. The rank changes of these countries, all either in Eastern Europe and the CIS or in Sub-Saharan Africa, are due mainly to revisions of the data for life

expectancy and real GDP per capita (PPP$).

Canada tops the GDI rankings. The second- and third-ranking countries are in the Nordic belt—Norway and Sweden. Several developing countries and areas do well in the GDI rankings: Barbados (17), the Bahamas (18), Singapore (27), Hong Kong (28), Uruguay (31), Trinidad and Tobago (32), Cyprus (33), the Republic of Korea (35), Costa Rica (36) and Thailand (39). These countries have succeeded in enhancing the basic human capabilities of both women and men.

The bottom five places are occupied by Sierra Leone, Niger, Burkina Faso, Mali and Ethiopia, in ascending order. Women in these countries face a double deprivation: overall achievements in human development are low in these societies, and women's achievements are lower than men's.

Several conclusions can be drawn from the GDI rankings.

First, no society treats its women as well as its men. This is evident from the fact that the GDI value for every country is lower than its HDI value. As many as 39 countries have a GDI value of less than 0.500, showing that women in these countries suffer the double deprivation of low overall achievement in human development and lower achievement than men. And only 41 countries have a GDI value of more than 0.800, underscoring the point that substantial progress in gender equality has been made in only a few societies.

Second, gender inequality is strongly associated with human poverty. The four countries ranking lowest in the GDI—Sierra Leone, Niger, Burkina Faso and Mali—also rank lowest in the human poverty index (HPI). Similarly, of the four developing countries ranking highest in the HPI, three—Costa Rica, Singapore and Trinidad and Tobago—also rank among the highest in the GDI.

Third, gender inequality is not always associated with income poverty. For example, Ecuador (73) and Peru (76) do relatively well in the GDI rankings, but their income poverty is quite high, with 49% of people in Peru below the $1-a-day income

Gender inequality is strongly associated with human poverty

poverty line, and 31% in Ecuador. By contrast, both Côte d'Ivoire (18%) and Tanzania (16%) have a low incidence of income poverty by the $1-a-day poverty line, but quite low GDI ranks—with Côte d'Ivoire at 126 and Tanzania at 123.

Fourth, the countries showing a marked improvement in their GDI ranks relative to their HDI ranks are fairly diverse. They include such industrial countries as Norway and Sweden, most of Eastern Europe and the CIS countries and such developing countries as the Bahamas, Barbados and Viet Nam. This shows that gender equality can be achieved at different income levels and stages of development. It also shows that it can be achieved across a range of cultures and political ideologies.

TABLE 2.8
Gender disparity—GDI and HDI ranks

GDI rank		HDI rank	HDI rank minus GDI rank	GDI rank		HDI rank	HDI rank minus GDI rank	GDI rank		HDI rank	HDI rank minus GDI rank
1	Canada	1	0	51	Kuwait	48	−3	101	Viet Nam	105	4
2	Norway	3	1	52	Estonia	60	8	102	Gabon	104	2
3	Sweden	10	7	53	Fiji	43	−10	103	Honduras	101	−2
4	Iceland	5	1	54	Mauritius	53	−1	104	Cape Verde	106	2
5	USA	4	−1	55	Lithuania	64	9	105	Morocco	103	−2
6	France	2	−4	56	Bahrain	40	−16	106	Nicaragua	108	2
7	Finland	8	1	57	Croatia	65	8	107	Guatemala	102	−5
8	New Zealand	9	1	58	Turkey	63	5	108	Papua New Guinea	109	1
9	Australia	14	5	59	Romania	67	8	109	Zimbabwe	110	1
10	Denmark	18	8	60	Brazil	58	−2	110	Myanmar	111	1
11	Netherlands	6	−5	61	United Arab Emirates	41	−20	111	Ghana	112	1
12	Japan	7	−5	62	Macedonia, FYR	68	6	112	Kenya	114	2
13	United Kingdom	15	2	63	Jamaica	71	8	113	Lesotho	117	4
14	Belgium	13	−1	64	Qatar	49	−15	114	Lao People's Dem. Rep.	116	2
15	Austria	12	−3	65	Turkmenistan	72	7	115	Cameroon	113	−2
16	Germany	19	3	66	Lebanon	56	−10	116	Equatorial Guinea	115	−1
17	Barbados	25	8	67	Latvia	76	9	117	Iraq	107	−10
18	Bahamas	28	10	68	Cuba	73	5	118	India	118	0
19	Spain	11	−8	69	Kazakstan	79	10	119	Comoros	120	1
20	Switzerland	16	−4	70	Sri Lanka	77	7	120	Pakistan	119	−1
21	Greece	20	−1	71	South Africa	76	5	121	Nigeria	121	0
22	Israel	23	1	72	Ukraine	81	9	122	Zambia	122	0
23	Italy	21	−2	73	Ecuador	61	−12	123	Tanzania, U. Rep. of	127	4
24	Slovenia	34	10	74	Tunisia	69	−5	124	Benin	125	1
25	Czech Rep.	37	12	75	Dominican Rep.	74	−1	125	Togo	126	1
26	Slovakia	39	13	76	Peru	75	−1	126	Côte d'Ivoire	124	−2
27	Singapore	26	−1	77	Libyan Arab Jamahiriya	55	−22	127	Mauritania	126	−1
28	Hong Kong	22	−6	78	Uzbekistan	85	7	128	Bangladesh	123	−5
29	Ireland	17	−12	79	Botswana	82	3	129	Central African Rep.	129	0
30	Portugal	30	0	80	Mongolia	86	6	130	Haiti	131	1
31	Uruguay	36	5	81	Philippines	83	2	131	Nepal	130	−1
32	Trinidad and Tobago	38	6	82	Paraguay	80	−2	132	Uganda	133	1
33	Cyprus	24	−9	83	Armenia	88	5	133	Malawi	135	2
34	Hungary	45	11	84	Syrian Arab Rep.	68	−16	134	Senegal	134	0
35	Korea, Rep. of	31	−4	85	Albania	87	2	135	Sudan	132	−3
36	Costa Rica	32	−4	86	Indonesia	84	−2	136	Guinea-Bissau	136	0
37	Poland	50	13	87	Georgia	90	3	137	Chad	137	0
38	Luxembourg	27	−11	88	Kyrgyzstan	92	4	138	Gambia	138	0
39	Thailand	51	12	89	Azerbaijan	91	2	139	Mozambique	139	0
40	Colombia	47	7	90	China	93	3	140	Guinea	140	0
41	Panama	42	1	91	Guyana	89	−2	141	Burundi	141	0
42	Belarus	54	12	92	Algeria	70	−22	142	Ethiopia	142	0
43	Venezuela	44	1	93	Moldova, Rep. of	95	2	143	Mali	143	0
44	Chile	29	−15	94	Maldives	96	2	144	Burkina Faso	144	0
45	Malaysia	52	7	95	Saudi Arabia	62	−33	145	Niger	145	0
46	Russian Federation	57	11	96	Tajikistan	100	4	146	Sierra Leone	146	0
47	Argentina	35	−12	97	El Salvador	97	0				
48	Malta	33	−15	98	Swaziland	99	1				
49	Bulgaria	59	10	99	Bolivia	98	−1				
50	Mexico	46	−4	100	Egypt	94	−6				

Note: HDI ranks have been recalculated for the universe of 146 countries. A positive difference between a country's HDI and GDI ranks indicates that it performs relatively better on gender equality than on average achievements alone.
Source: Human Development Report Office.

Results of the gender empowerment measure

The GEM was estimated for 94 countries (table 2.9). Four of the top five in the GEM rankings are Nordic countries—Norway (1), Sweden (2), Denmark (3) and Finland (4). These countries are not only good at strengthening the basic capabilities of women, they have also opened many opportunities for them to participate in economic and political fields.

Some developing countries outperform much richer industrial countries in gender equality in political, economic and professional activities. Barbados is ahead of Belgium and Italy, Trinidad and Tobago outranks Portugal, and the Bahamas leads the United Kingdom. France lags behind Suriname, Colombia and Botswana, and Japan behind China, Guatemala and Mexico. The GEM value of Greece, at 0.391, is only 65% that of Barbados, at 0.602.

Some developing countries outperform much richer industrial countries in gender equality

TABLE 2.9
Gender disparity—GEM, GDI and HDI ranks

GEM rank		GDI rank	HDI rank	GEM rank		GDI rank	HDI rank
1	Norway	2	3	51	Honduras	66	69
2	Sweden	3	9	52	Thailand	34	42
3	Denmark	9	17	53	Peru	53	55
4	Finland	6	7	54	Uruguay	26	31
5	New Zealand	7	8	55	Venezuela	37	36
6	Canada	1	1	56	Greece	20	19
7	USA	4	4	57	Chile	38	27
8	Austria	14	11	58	Brazil	46	47
9	Germany	15	18	59	Indonesia	57	61
10	Netherlands	10	5	60	Cyprus	28	22
11	Australia	8	13	61	Swaziland	63	68
12	Switzerland	19	15	62	Bolivia	64	67
13	Luxembourg	33	25	63	Haiti	82	88
14	Barbados	16	23	64	Paraguay	56	58
15	Belgium	13	12	65	Cameroon	73	77
16	Italy	22	20	66	Kuwait	42	40
17	Trinidad and Tobago	27	32	67	Maldives	61	65
18	Portugal	25	28	68	Fiji	43	35
19	Bahamas	17	26	69	Burkina Faso	87	93
20	United Kingdom	12	14	70	Sri Lanka	49	57
21	Spain	18	10	71	Zambia	77	83
22	South Africa	50	56	72	Morocco	68	71
23	Cuba	48	53	73	Korea, Rep. of	30	29
24	Ireland	24	16	74	Algeria	60	52
25	Hungary	29	37	75	Egypt	65	64
26	Costa Rica	31	30	76	Bangladesh	80	84
27	Bulgaria	40	48	77	Sierra Leone	88	94
28	China	58	63	78	Tunisia	51	51
29	Guatemala	69	70	79	Equatorial Guinea	74	78
30	Israel	21	21	80	Malawi	83	90
31	Mexico	41	38	81	Iran, Islamic Rep. of	..	49
32	Belize	..	45	82	Turkey	45	50
33	Guyana	59	62	83	Mali	86	92
34	Japan	11	6	84	United Arab Emirates	47	33
35	Philippines	55	60	85	Papua New Guinea	70	74
36	Panama	36	34	86	India	75	80
37	Suriname	..	46	87	Sudan	84	89
38	Colombia	35	39	88	Congo	..	76
39	Botswana	54	59	89	Zaire	..	82
40	France	5	2	90	Central African Rep.	81	87
41	Lesotho	72	79	91	Solomon Islands	..	72
42	Poland	32	41	92	Pakistan	76	81
43	Mozambique	85	91	93	Togo	78	85
44	El Salvador	62	66	94	Mauritania	79	86
45	Zimbabwe	71	75				
46	Dominican Rep.	52	54				
47	Singapore	23	24				
48	Malaysia	39	43				
49	Mauritius	44	44				
50	Cape Verde	67	73				

Note: GDI and HDI ranks have been recalculated for the universe of 94 countries.
Source: Human Development Report Office.

The three countries with the worst GEM ranks—Mauritania (94), Togo (93) and Pakistan (92)—also have very high HPI values: 47% for Mauritania and Pakistan, and 39% for Togo. But among countries with higher GEM rankings—such as Trinidad and Tobago (17), Cuba (23) and Costa Rica (26)—are some of those with the lowest HPI values. For Trinidad and Tobago the HPI is 4%, for Cuba 5% and for Costa Rica 7%. Thus in these six countries there is a strong association between the extent of human poverty and opportunities for women.

By contrast, the link between income poverty and opportunities for women is not always positive. For example, Guatemala (29) and Guyana (33) place quite high in the GEM rankings, but the incidence of income poverty by the $1-a-day poverty line is extremely high in both countries—in Guatemala 53%, and in Guyana 46%. Morocco (72) and Tunisia (78) place quite low in the GEM rankings, but have income poverty of only 1% and 3% by the $1-a-day yardstick. Thus even in income-poor societies, women may enjoy opportunities to participate in economic and political activities.

The GEM results show that no country has a GEM equal to or exceeding 0.800. Only 14 countries have a GEM of more than 0.600. And 21 countries have a GEM of less than 0.300. The low values make it clear that many countries have much further to travel in extending broad economic and political opportunities to women.

Rural-urban disparity

The rural-urban disparity in human and income poverty is pronounced. In developing countries 43% of rural men are illiterate, more than twice the share in urban areas. For women the shares are 66% and 38%. This rural-urban disparity in literacy reflects the rural-urban disparity in access to social services (figure 2.14).

When the HDI for Turkey was disaggregated by rural and urban areas, the HDI for urban males was found to be 15% higher than that for rural males. And the HDI for urban females was estimated to be 13% higher than that for rural females.

There also are rural-urban disparities in income poverty. In 1990, 36% of urban people in South Asia were living in income poverty, compared with 47% of rural people. In Latin America and the Caribbean the incidence of rural poverty, at 58%, is 1.8 times the incidence of urban poverty, at 33%.

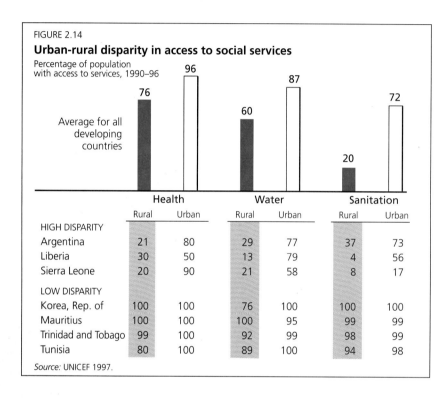

FIGURE 2.14

Urban-rural disparity in access to social services

Percentage of population with access to services, 1990–96

	Health		Water		Sanitation	
	Rural	Urban	Rural	Urban	Rural	Urban
HIGH DISPARITY						
Argentina	21	80	29	77	37	73
Liberia	30	50	13	79	4	56
Sierra Leone	20	90	21	58	8	17
LOW DISPARITY						
Korea, Rep. of	100	100	76	100	100	100
Mauritius	100	100	100	95	99	99
Trinidad and Tobago	99	100	92	99	98	99
Tunisia	80	100	89	100	94	98

Source: UNICEF 1997.

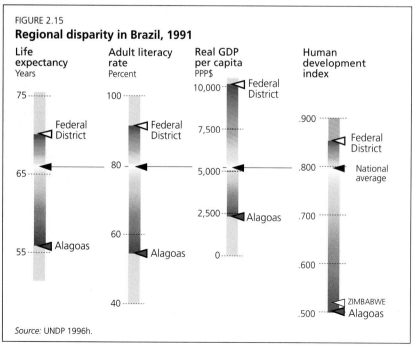

FIGURE 2.15

Regional disparity in Brazil, 1991

Source: UNDP 1996h.

Regional disparity within countries

Uneven progress in reducing human and income poverty has resulted in different forms of regional disparity within countries. In India life expectancy in the State of Kerala is 72 years, but in Madhya Pradesh it is only 54 years. In Brazil in 1991, the adult literacy rate in the Federal District was 91%, while in Alagoas Province it was only 55%. Similar disparities exist in other areas of human development and in the HDI (figure 2.15).

Regional variation in income poverty can also be significant. In the Philippines income poverty in the National Capital Region in 1991 was only 15%, compared with 56% in the province of Bicol. In Indonesia the incidence of income poverty was less than 10% in Jakarta, Yogyakarta and Bali, but more than 40% in East Nussa Tengara, Iran Jaya, West Kalimantan and East Timor. Such disparities are also observed in human development (figure 2.16).

Ethnic disparity

Uneven progress in reducing human poverty is reflected too in disparities among different ethnic groups in a country. For example, in Viet Nam income poverty is more pronounced among ethnic minorities living mainly in the northern uplands and central highlands. People in these groups earn only 60% as much as the Kinh, or Vietnamese. In South Africa only 3% of whites—but 18% of blacks—are not expected to survive to age 40. And while about 8% of whites lack an education, 16% of blacks do.

Ethnic disparity in human poverty is also significant in industrial countries. In Canada 35% of Inuit men are unemployed, compared with 10% of other Canadian men. And in the United States 31% of Hispanics aged 25–65 have not completed ninth grade, but only 6% of whites have not.

In many parts of the world disparities in income and human poverty disproportionately affect the indigenous people (box 2.6).

What the 1997 HDI reveals

Since 1990 the *Human Development Report* has presented the human development index to capture as many aspects of human development as possible in one simple,

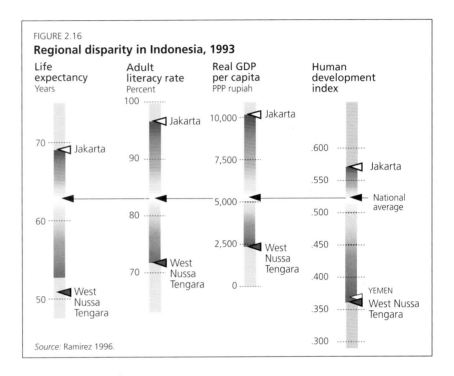

FIGURE 2.16
Regional disparity in Indonesia, 1993

Source: Ramirez 1996.

---

composite index and to produce a ranking of human development achievements.

The concept of human development is much deeper and richer than what can be captured in any composite index or even by a detailed set of statistical indicators. Yet it is useful to simplify a complex reality—and that is what the HDI sets out to do. It is a composite index of achievements in basic human capabilities in three fundamental dimensions—a long and healthy life, knowledge and a decent standard of living. Three variables have been chosen to represent these three dimensions—life expectancy, educational attainment and income.

The HDI value for each country indicates how far the country has to go to attain certain defined goals: an average life span of 85 years, access to education for all and a decent standard of living. The HDI reduces all three basic indicators to a common measuring rod by measuring achievement in each as the relative distance from the desirable goal. The maximum and minimum values for each variable are reduced to a scale between 0 and 1, with each country at some point on this scale. (The method for constructing the HDI is explained in detail in technical note 2.)

The HDI shows the distance a country has to travel to reach the maximum possible value of 1 and also allows intercountry comparisons. The difference between the maximum possible value of the HDI and the HDI value achieved by a country shows the country's shortfall in HDI. A challenge for every country is to find ways to reduce this shortfall. As explained in chapter 1, the HDI measures the overall progress of a country in human development, while the HPI identifies the deprivation in human development.

The ranking of countries by their HDI values leads to the following observations, the highlights of this year's exercise:

• Of the 175 countries for which the HDI was calculated, 64 are in the high human development category, 66 in the medium category and 45 in the low category. Thus, of the world's 5.6 billion people, 1.3 billion (23%) are in the high human development category, 2.6 billion (45%) in the medium

In the HDI rankings, Hong Kong, Cyprus and Barbados lead among developing countries

TABLE 2.10
HDI ranking for industrial countries, 1994

Country	HDI value	HDI rank	Real GDP per capita (PPP$) 1994	Real GDP per capita (PPP$) rank minus HDI rank[a]
Canada	0.960	1	21,459	7
France	0.946	2	20,510	13
Norway	0.943	3	21,346	6
USA	0.942	4	26,397	−1
Iceland	0.942	5	20,566	9
Netherlands	0.940	6	19,238	13
Japan	0.940	7	21,581	0
Finland	0.940	8	17,417	15
New Zealand	0.937	9	16,851	15
Sweden	0.936	10	18,540	11
Spain	0.934	11	14,324	19
Austria	0.932	12	20,667	1
Belgium	0.932	13	20,985	−1
Australia	0.931	14	19,285	4
United Kingdom	0.931	15	18,620	5
Switzerland	0.930	16	24,967	−12
Ireland	0.929	17	16,061	8
Denmark	0.927	18	21,341	−8
Germany	0.924	19	19,675	−3
Greece	0.923	20	11,265	15
Italy	0.921	21	19,363	−4
Israel	0.913	23	16,023	3
Luxembourg	0.899	27	34,155	−26
Portugal	0.890	31	12,326	3
Malta	0.887	34	13,009	−1
Slovenia	0.886	35	10,404	3
Czech Rep.	0.882	39	9,201	3
Slovakia	0.873	42	6,389	12
Hungary	0.857	48	6,437	5
Poland	0.834	58	5,002	14
Belarus	0.806	62	4,713	13
Russian Federation	0.792	67	4,828	7
Bulgaria	0.780	69	4,533	9
Estonia	0.776	71	4,294	8
Lithuania	0.762	76	4,011	8
Croatia	0.760	77	3,960	10
Romania	0.748	79	4,037	3
Macedonia, FYR	0.748	80	3,965	5
Turkmenistan	0.723	85	3,469	12
Latvia	0.711	92	3,332	6
Kazakstan	0.709	93	3,284	6
Ukraine	0.689	95	2,718	14
Uzbekistan	0.662	100	2,438	14
Albania	0.655	102	2,788	4
Armenia	0.651	103	1,737	24
Georgia	0.637	105	1,585	31
Azerbaijan	0.636	106	1,670	25
Kyrgyzstan	0.635	107	1,930	18
Moldova, Rep. of	0.612	110	1,576	28
Tajikistan	0.580	115	1,117	35

a. A positive figure indicates that the HDI rank is better than the real GDP per capita (PPP$) rank, a negative the opposite.
Source: Human Development Report Office.

TABLE 2.11
HDI ranking for developing countries, 1994

Country	HDI value	HDI rank	Real GDP per capita (PPP$) 1994	Real GDP per capita (PPP$) rank minus HDI rank[a]	Country	HDI value	HDI rank	Real GDP per capita (PPP$) 1994	Real GDP per capita (PPP$) rank minus HDI rank[a]
Hong Kong	0.914	22	22,310	−17	Bolivia	0.589	113	2,598	−1
Cyprus	0.907	24	13,071	8	Swaziland	0.582	114	2,821	−10
Barbados	0.907	25	11,051	11	Honduras	0.575	116	2,050	7
Singapore	0.900	26	20,987	−15	Guatemala	0.572	117	3,208	−16
Bahamas	0.894	28	15,875	0	Namibia	0.570	118	4,027	−35
Antigua and Barbuda	0.892	29	8,977	16	Morocco	0.566	119	3,681	−26
Chile	0.891	30	9,129	13	Gabon	0.562	120	3,641	−25
Korea, Rep. of	0.890	32	10,656	5	Viet Nam	0.557	121	1,208	26
Costa Rica	0.889	33	5,919	27	Solomon Islands	0.556	122	2,118	0
Argentina	0.884	36	8,937	10	Cape Verde	0.547	123	1,862	3
Uruguay	0.883	37	6,752	15	Vanuatu	0.547	124	2,276	−7
Brunei Darussalam	0.882	38	30,447	−36	São Tomé and Principe	0.534	125	1,704	3
Trinidad and Tobago	0.880	40	9,124	4	Iraq	0.531	126	3,159	−24
Dominica	0.873	41	6,118	16	Nicaragua	0.530	127	1,580	10
Bahrain	0.870	43	15,321	−14	Papua New Guinea	0.525	128	2,821	−24
United Arab Emirates	0.866	44	16,000	−17	Zimbabwe	0.513	129	2,196	−10
Panama	0.864	45	6,104	14	Congo	0.500	130	2,410	−14
Fiji	0.863	46	5,763	16	Myanmar	0.475	131	1,051	25
Venezuela	0.861	47	8,120	1	Ghana	0.468	132	1,960	−8
Saint Kitts and Nevis	0.853	49	9,436	−9	Cameroon	0.468	133	2,120	−12
Mexico	0.853	50	7,384	0	Kenya	0.463	134	1,404	5
Colombia	0.848	51	6,107	7	Equatorial Guinea	0.462	135	1,673	−5
Seychelles	0.845	52	7,891	−3	Lao People's Dem. Rep.	0.459	136	2,484	−23
Kuwait	0.844	53	21,875	−47	Lesotho	0.457	137	1,109	14
Grenada	0.843	54	5,137	17	India	0.446	138	1,348	5
Qatar	0.840	55	18,403	−33	Pakistan	0.445	139	2,154	−19
Saint Lucia	0.838	56	6,182	−1	Comoros	0.412	140	1,366	1
Saint Vincent	0.836	57	5,650	6	Nigeria	0.393	141	1,351	1
Thailand	0.833	59	7,104	−8	Zaire	0.381	142	429	31
Malaysia	0.832	60	8,865	−13	Zambia	0.369	143	962	15
Mauritius	0.831	61	13,172	−30	Bangladesh	0.368	144	1,331	0
Belize	0.806	63	5,590	1	Côte d'Ivoire	0.368	145	1,668	−13
Libyan Arab Jamahiriya	0.801	64	6,125	−8	Benin	0.368	146	1,696	−17
Lebanon	0.794	65	4,863	8	Togo	0.365	147	1,109	4
Suriname	0.792	66	4,711	10	Yemen	0.361	148	805	14
Brazil	0.783	68	5,362	0	Tanzania, U. Rep. of	0.357	149	656	21
Iran, Islamic Rep. of	0.780	70	5,766	−9	Mauritania	0.355	150	1,593	−15
Ecuador	0.775	72	4,626	5	Central African Rep.	0.355	151	1,130	−2
Saudi Arabia	0.774	73	9,338	−32	Madagascar	0.350	152	694	16
Turkey	0.772	74	5,193	−4	Cambodia	0.348	153	1,084	1
Korea, Dem. People's Rep. of	0.765	75	3,965	10	Nepal	0.347	154	1,137	−6
Syrian Arab Rep.	0.755	78	5,397	−12	Bhutan	0.338	155	1,289	−10
Tunisia	0.748	81	5,319	−12	Haiti	0.338	156	896	5
Algeria	0.737	82	5,442	−17	Angola	0.335	157	1,600	−24
Jamaica	0.736	83	3,816	7	Sudan	0.333	158	1,084	−4
Jordan	0.730	84	4,187	−3	Uganda	0.328	159	1,370	−19
Cuba	0.723	86	3,000	17	Senegal	0.326	160	1,596	−26
Dominican Rep.	0.718	87	3,933	1	Malawi	0.320	161	694	7
Oman	0.718	88	10,078	−49	Djibouti	0.319	162	1,270	−16
Peru	0.717	89	3,645	5	Guinea-Bissau	0.291	163	793	1
South Africa	0.716	90	4,291	−10	Chad	0.288	164	700	2
Sri Lanka	0.711	91	3,277	9	Gambia	0.281	165	939	−5
Paraguay	0.706	94	3,531	2	Mozambique	0.281	166	986	−9
Samoa (Western)	0.684	96	2,726	12	Guinea	0.271	167	1,103	−14
Botswana	0.673	97	5,367	−30	Eritrea	0.269	168	960	−9
Philippines	0.672	98	2,681	12	Burundi	0.247	169	698	−2
Indonesia	0.668	99	3,740	−7	Ethiopia	0.244	170	427	4
Mongolia	0.661	101	3,766	−10	Mali	0.229	171	543	1
Guyana	0.649	104	2,729	3	Burkina Faso	0.221	172	796	−9
China	0.626	108	2,604	3	Niger	0.206	173	787	−8
Egypt	0.614	109	3,846	−20	Rwanda	0.187	174	352	1
Maldives	0.611	111	2,200	7	Sierra Leone	0.176	175	643	−4
El Salvador	0.592	112	2,417	3					

a. A positive figure indicates that the HDI rank is better than the real GDP per capita (PPP$) rank, a negative the opposite.
Source: Human Development Report Office.

category and 1.8 billion (32%) in the low category.

• The HDI values and rankings for some countries have changed since last year, reflecting recent revisions of data by UN and other international organizations, particularly for life expectancy and real GDP per capita (PPP$).

• Canada, France and Norway lead the HDI rankings. Among developing countries, Hong Kong, Cyprus and Barbados lead.

The HDI ranking of countries differs significantly from their ranking by real GDP per capita (tables 2.10 and 2.11). Ten countries have an HDI rank at least 20 places higher than their GDP rank. Among them are Costa Rica and Viet Nam, which have effectively translated the benefits of economic growth into improvements in the lives of their people. For 17 countries the GDP rank is higher than the HDI rank, implying considerable scope for distributing the benefits of economic growth more equitably. Thus countries can have similar incomes but different human development achievements—or similar HDIs but very different incomes (figure 2.17 and table 2.12).

One important finding of this year's HDI exercise is that the HDI values of 30 countries fell between 1993 and 1994 (table 2.13). Two important observations: First, the decline mostly reflects a significant fall in life expectancy or real GDP per capita (PPP$) or both. Second, the 30 countries are either in Sub-Saharan Africa or in Eastern Europe and the CIS or are countries in conflict. In many Sub-Saharan African countries, such as Botswana and Rwanda, the shorter life expectancy reflects the toll of HIV/AIDS. The shortened life expectancy, particularly among men, in Eastern Europe and the CIS countries (for example, Armenia and Russia) reflects the

FIGURE 2.17

Similar income, different human development, 1994

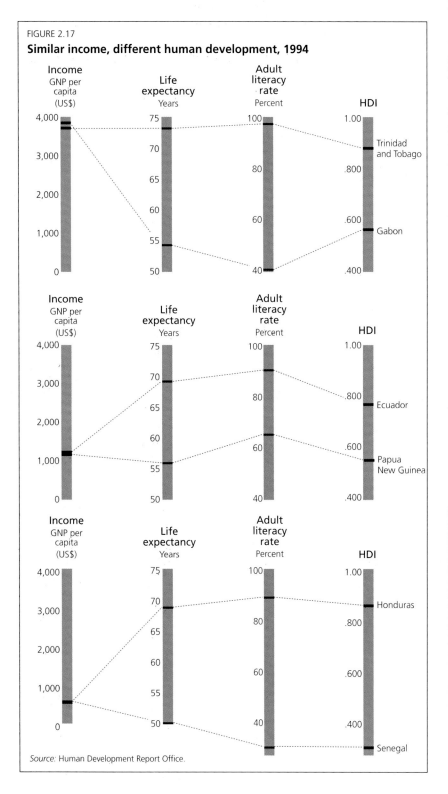

Source: Human Development Report Office.

TABLE 2.12

Similar HDI, different income, 1994

Country	HDI value	GNP per capita (US$)
New Zealand	0.937	13,350
Sweden	0.936	25,530
Barbados	0.907	6,560
Singapore	0.900	22,500
Brazil	0.783	2,970
Bulgaria	0.780	1,250
South Africa	0.716	3,040
Sri Lanka	0.711	640
São Tomé and Principe	0.534	1,150
Vanuatu	0.547	250
Lao People's Dem. Rep.	0.459	320
Lesotho	0.457	720
Gambia	0.281	330
Mozambique	0.281	90

Source: Human Development Report Office.

changing reality in those countries. Because of economic stagnation and decline, real GDP per capita (PPP$) has fallen in recent years in both Sub-Saharan Africa (for example, Gambia and Guinea) and Eastern Europe and the CIS (Moldova and Tajikistan). And countries in conflict (for example, Rwanda and Sudan) have lost on both fronts.

The changing face of poverty

The trend analysis of human and income poverty prompts some questions about the overall situation.

• *How big is the poverty problem?* In developing countries as a group, human poverty affects more than a quarter of the population.

• *Where is poverty most pervasive?* Sub-Saharan Africa and South Asia have the highest incidence of both income poverty (by the $1-a-day poverty line) and human

poverty—at about 40%. The incidence of human poverty in Sub-Saharan Africa is 42%, and that of income poverty 39%. In South Asia human poverty is 38%, and income poverty 43%. But the cause for greatest concern for Sub-Saharan Africa is that poverty is increasing—both in proportion and in absolute numbers—and the increase is occurring in both human poverty and income poverty.

• *Where are the poor?* South Asia is home to two-fifths (515 million of 1.3 billion) of the income-poor of developing countries and almost half of those in human poverty. East Asia, South Asia and South-East Asia and the Pacific combined account for 960 million of the 1.3 billion income-poor in developing countries, and more than two-thirds of the people in human poverty.

• *Where are the stark contrasts between human and income poverty?* Latin America and the Caribbean has reduced the incidence of human poverty to about 15%, but

TABLE 2.13
Countries whose HDI value has decreased since last year

HDI rank	Country	HDI value 1993	HDI value 1994	1994 HDI value minus 1993 HDI value	1996 HDI rank minus 1997 HDI rank[a]	Change in life expectancy at birth (%)	Change in adult literacy rate (%)	Change in combined first-, second- and third-level gross enrolment ratio (%)	Change in real GDP per capita (PPP$) (%)
174	Rwanda	0.332	0.187	−0.145	−18	−52.1	2.1	−5.4	−52.4
92	Latvia	0.820	0.711	−0.110	−34	−1.6	0.0	−7.1	−33.5
126	Iraq	0.599	0.531	−0.068	−14	−13.8	2.0	−3.8	−7.4
97	Botswana	0.741	0.673	−0.068	−23	−19.8	1.0	−0.4	2.8
110	Moldova, Rep. of	0.663	0.612	−0.051	−9	0.1	2.6	−12.3	−33.5
143	Zambia	0.411	0.369	−0.043	−4	−12.4	0.5	−1.4	−13.3
175	Sierra Leone	0.219	0.176	−0.042	−1	−14.3	2.4	−0.7	−25.2
127	Nicaragua	0.568	0.530	−0.038	−7	0.3	0.5	1.6	−30.7
115	Tajikistan	0.616	0.580	−0.036	−7	−5.1	0.0	−0.4	−19.1
167	Guinea	0.306	0.271	−0.036	−5	0.9	2.7	1.7	−38.7
169	Burundi	0.282	0.247	−0.035	0	−13.6	2.7	−0.3	4.2
93	Kazakstan	0.740	0.709	−0.031	−18	−3.2	0.0	11.8	−11.5
95	Ukraine	0.719	0.689	−0.030	−12	−1.4	4.0	−0.4	−16.4
103	Armenia	0.680	0.651	−0.030	−7	−2.7	0.0	0.3	−14.9
106	Azerbaijan	0.665	0.636	−0.029	−7	0.4	0.0	0.6	−23.7
107	Kyrgyzstan	0.663	0.635	−0.028	−5	−2.1	0.0	4.9	−16.8
158	Sudan	0.359	0.333	−0.026	−9	−4.1	2.3	−0.6	−19.7
156	Haiti	0.359	0.338	−0.022	−8	−4.2	1.6	−2.4	−14.7
129	Zimbabwe	0.534	0.513	−0.021	−2	−8.1	0.8	−2.2	4.6
147	Togo	0.385	0.365	−0.020	−4	−8.3	2.4	−1.6	8.7
130	Congo	0.517	0.500	−0.017	−2	0.1	2.5	0.0	−12.4
100	Uzbekistan	0.679	0.662	−0.017	−3	−2.8	0.0	0.4	−2.9
96	Samoa (Western)	0.700	0.684	−0.016	−5	0.5	0.0	0.4	−9.1
124	Vanuatu	0.562	0.547	−0.015	−2	0.8	−1.5	−0.6	−9.0
133	Cameroon	0.481	0.468	−0.014	−3	−2.1	2.1	−4.4	−4.5
68	Brazil	0.796	0.783	−0.013	−9	−0.2	0.4	0.6	−2.5
67	Russian Federation	0.804	0.792	−0.012	−9	−2.6	0.0	−1.1	1.4
165	Gambia	0.292	0.281	−0.011	−1	0.9	1.6	0.6	−21.1
84	Jordan	0.741	0.730	−0.011	−11	0.6	0.8	0.0	−4.4
134	Kenya	0.473	0.463	−0.010	−3	−3.5	1.7	−1.4	0.3

a. A positive figure indicates that the 1994 rank is better than the 1993 rank, a negative the opposite.
Source: Human Development Report Office.

its income poverty is about 24%. In fact, apart from Sub-Saharan Africa, it is the only region where the incidence of income poverty has increased.

The Arab States have been able to reduce income poverty to 4%, but their human poverty is about 34%, not far from South Asia's 38%.

A comparison of the profile of people in income poverty in the 1970s with that in the 1990s shows that income poverty is still concentrated in rural areas of Asia, particularly in South Asia. But the face of income poverty is rapidly changing (box 2.7). Today

a poor person is more likely to be African, to be a child, a woman or an elderly person in an urban area, to be landless, to live in an environmentally fragile area and to be a refugee or a displaced person.

Progress in reducing human and income poverty is marked by discontinuity and unevenness. The resulting disparity and the remaining backlog create and re-create human poverty, a continuing and perpetuating process that the poor constantly struggle to overcome. Chapter 3 looks at this process in a rapidly changing world.

BOX 2.7

The changing face of income poverty

In 1993 more than 500 million of the developing world's 1.3 billion income-poor people—those subsisting on less than $1 a day—lived in South Asia, a majority of them in rural areas. But the face of poverty is constantly changing. Compared with 1970, an income-poor person today is:

Less likely to be	*More likely to be*	*And likely to be poor as a result of*
Asian	African or Latin American	• Economic stagnation and slow employment growth • Increasing disparity • Lack of pro-poor growth • Increased marginalization from global trade and financial flows • Higher fertility and the spread of HIV/AIDS • Accelerated degradation of natural resources • Increased displacement from home and country
An adult male	A child, a woman or elderly (in some countries)	• Increased cuts in social welfare • Greater disintegration of the family • Higher unemployment, particularly chronic unemployment and involuntary part-time work • High costs of social and economic transition • Increased time burdens
A small farmer	An unskilled, low-wage worker	• Continuing globalization and trade liberalization • Increased liberalization of labour markets
Rural	Urban	• Rapid demographic change and migration to urban areas • Growth of the low-productivity informal sector • Worsening access to productive resources • Inadequate development of urban housing and physical infrastructure
Settled	A refugee or internally displaced	• Increasing wars and conflicts • Deepening economic and environmental crises

Source: Lipton and Maxwell 1992 and Human Development Report Office.

China

In the past 45 years or so China has made impressive reductions in human poverty. Between 1949 and 1995 it reduced infant mortality from 200 per 1,000 live births to 42, and increased life expectancy at birth from 35 years to 69. Today almost all children go to school, and adult illiteracy, 80% in the 1950s, has fallen to 19%.

For decades after the mid-1950s, life in rural China continued to be harsh. In 1959–62 more than 30 million people, most of them peasants, died in the Great Famine. And even in the 1970s hungry peasants swamped cities to beg for food. In 1978 the government, concerned about rural poverty, carried out a special investigation that concluded that 260 million people lived below the poverty line—a third of the rural population.

From 1978 onwards, the government took measures to attack rural poverty:

• *Land reform.* Most collective land was distributed to households. This provided peasants with greater incentives to increase output, and productivity in household agriculture rose to a level about 40% higher than that in collectives.

• *Market orientation.* Reforms also improved incentives by allowing people to sell more food on the open market. The government would purchase less: it cut quotas on grain procurement and reduced the number of products that it controlled through planning. It also loosened restrictions on private trade between regions.

• *Price reform.* The government raised agricultural prices. In the early stages of reform it increased the average procurement price for major crops by 22%, and retail prices for pork, eggs, fish and other items by 33%. These increases are estimated to account for 20% of the improvement in rural per capita incomes in 1978–84.

All these measures contributed to a dramatic increase in output. In the 26 years before 1978 agricul-

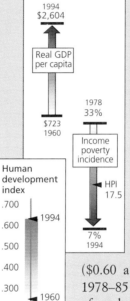

tural output had been growing by 3% a year. But in 1978–84 it grew by more than 7% a year. Agricultural growth led to big increases in rural incomes, which more than doubled between 1978 and 1984.

Rural development was not restricted to agriculture. The government also encouraged township and village enterprises—reducing or abolishing their taxes and giving them more autonomy in production and marketing. As a result, between 1978 and 1992 their share of gross national industrial production increased from 12% to 39%. This created millions of new jobs. Between 1978 and 1992 employment in these enterprises increased from 28 million to 124 million—or from 7% of total employment to 21%.

The expansion of rural agricultural and industrial output had a dramatic effect on income poverty. Based on the national poverty line ($0.60 a day), the incidence of poverty in 1978–85 fell from 33% to 9%, and the number of rural poor from 260 million to 97 million.

In the second half of the 1980s, however, the progress in reducing income poverty went into reverse. By 1989 the number of income-poor people in rural areas increased to 103 million. Educational achievements also faltered: between 1982 and 1987 adult illiteracy rose from 24% to 27%. Moreover, surveys in 1988 and 1989 revealed a wide gender gap; in rural areas women earned around 20% less than men. In private enterprises in urban areas they earned only 56% of men's wages.

Why the setback? It resulted partly from a shift in development strategy. After the mid-1980s the emphasis moved away from agriculture and towards industrial and export sectors. The government redirected public investment and fiscal incentives to the coastal regions—allowing them, for example, to retain more local tax and foreign exchange revenues and giving them greater freedom to use bank loans for local investment.

Although this coastal development strategy, coupled with globalization, helped to reduce income poverty in the coastal areas, the poor interior provinces, especially the isolated mountainous areas with poor infrastructure, were left behind. Not surprisingly, interregional disparities began to widen. In 1990 the HPI value for the interior regions, at 44%, was more than twice that in the coastal regions, at 18%.

At the same time, there was a weakening in public services after the central government transferred part of the responsibility for education and public health to local governments. These were not priorities for local governments.

The central government also reduced its commitment to alleviating rural income poverty. In the 1980s government spending on rural relief and poverty alleviation fell both in real terms and as a proportion of all government expenditure. By 1990 total spending on urban food subsidies was five times as much as the combined expenditure on health, education, relief and other services in poorer rural areas.

At the beginning of the 1990s the government became increasingly concerned about the increases in poverty and started to take measures to reverse the trend. Its approach was formalized in 1994 with the 8-7 Poverty Reduction Programme, which aims to eliminate absolute poverty by the year 2000. (The 8 stands for the 80 million people living in income poverty, the 7 for the programme's seven-year period.)

This programme is strengthening the institutional structure for poverty reduction. The State Council funded several antipoverty units, including the Poor Area Development Office, the China Development Foundation for Poor Areas and the Cadre Training Centre. All these agencies would report to a strengthened Leading Group for the Economic Development of Poor Areas, responsible for coordinating antipoverty programmes at the ministerial level. Similar decentralized institutions were established at the provincial and county levels.

There was also a strong financial commitment: the total annual funds from the central government to alleviate income poverty amounted to 15.3 billion yuan ($1.8 billion). The spending of these funds would also be monitored more carefully, to avoid luxury projects. Previously, there had been some diversion of central government funds. According to a 1994 survey, only 70% of poverty alleviation funds and 60% of development funds were reaching the 592 poor counties for which they were intended.

The central government increased investment and loans in poor areas and gave the areas financial and monetary preferences. It arranged partnerships between the more developed provinces and municipalities and the poorer ones. Beijing helps Inner Mongolia, for example, and Tianjin helps Yunnan. The mayor of Shenzhen has allocated 200 million yuan ($24 million) to development projects in Guizhou, and 17 million yuan ($2 million) for social welfare and infrastructure.

The renewed commitment to poverty reduction was already showing results by 1992. Poverty reduction resumed, though not at the same pace as before. Between 1991 and mid-1995 the number of rural people living in income poverty fell from 94 million to 65 million.

The central government has also stepped up investment in reducing human poverty, increasing expenditure on basic education and health care from 18% to 22% of total government expenditures between 1992 and 1994. But much remains to be done.

• *Water.* Up to a third of the rural population has an inadequate supply of drinking water—130 million people use untreated surface water contaminated by domestic, industrial or agro-chemical wastes, and 43 million people live in water-scarce areas.

• *Sanitation.* Today 97% of the rural population (and 73% of the total population) do not have access to adequate sanitation.

• *Health.* Services in poor rural areas are still inferior to those in cities. Around 60% of births in poor rural areas are unattended, and maternal mortality is 202 per 100,000 live births in many counties—more than twice the national average.

• *Education.* In 1991–92 more than 2 million children were not enrolled in school, of whom 70% were girls. And in many rural areas women are 70% of the illiterate population.

• *Minorities.* Minority groups generally live in areas where the soil is too poor for even subsistence crop production, so they are net buyers of food and have been hit hard by higher prices. The incidence of poverty in these groups is much higher than in the general population.

Although China has gone through different phases—with both advances and setbacks—progress in recent decades has been remarkable. But there is a long way to go before China eliminates income poverty—and even further before it eradicates human poverty.

Source: Zhang 1997.

India

In the 1930s Jawaharlal Nehru described India under British rule as "a servile state with its splendid strength caged up, hardly daring to breathe freely, governed by strangers from afar, her people poor beyond compare, short lived and incapable of resisting disease and epidemic". On being sworn in as India's first prime minister in 1947, Nehru called for "the ending of poverty and ignorance and disease and inequality of opportunity". Mahatma Gandhi too steadfastly argued that India would become truly independent only when its poorest were free of human suffering and poverty.

Since then, India has had 50 years of plans and programmes to promote development and eradicate poverty. What has been achieved? Certainly, there has been progress in agriculture, industry and, more recently, income poverty reduction. But the record is mixed—and India remains a country of stark contrasts and disparities.

• *Food and nutrition.* Between 1951 and 1995 food grain production increased fourfold and famines were virtually eliminated. Yet 53% of children under age four—60 million—remain undernourished.

• *Education.* In 1961–91 literacy more than doubled, yet half the population is still illiterate. And for females aged seven and above, the proportion is 61%. More than 45% of children do not reach grade five.

• *Health.* In 1961–92 life expectancy almost doubled to 61 years, and by 1995 infant mortality had been more than halved to 74 per 1,000 live births. Even so, each year there are 2.2 million infant deaths, most of them avoidable.

• *Safe water.* More than 90% of the population has access to safe drinking water. But declining water tables, quality problems and contamination threaten the advances.

• *Gender.* Because of systematic deprivation, women have always fared worse than men. Though the gap has been narrowing in recent years, India is still one of a handful of countries with fewer women than men—927 females for every 1,000 males.

• *Income poverty.* The share of people in income poverty has fluctuated wildly in the past but the trend is downwards. In 1977–81 rural poverty declined from almost 50% to around 36%, and urban poverty from 40% to 33%. By 1994 rural poverty in India was 39%, and urban poverty 30%.

Many people would credit the reductions in human poverty (and even more so those in income poverty) to economic growth. Yes, growth has been substantial. In 1950–94 the index of industrial production increased 13-fold, and per capita net national product more than doubled. But the trends in income poverty over this period are far from uniform.

• *1951 to mid-1970s: fluctuation.* In 1951 the proportion of the rural population living below the income poverty line was 47%. It rose to 64% in 1954–55, fell to 45% in 1960–61, then rose again, to 51%, in 1977–78.

• *Mid-1970s to end of the 1980s: significant, steady improvement.* Between 1977–78 and 1985–86 rural income poverty fell from 51% to 39%; by 1989–90 it had fallen to 34%. Income poverty also fell in urban areas, from 40% to 33% between 1977–78 and 1989–90.

• *After 1991: progress and setbacks.* During the period following economic reform there was first a rise, then a fall in income poverty. In 1989–90 the incidence of income poverty in rural areas was 34%; in 1992, 43%; and in 1993–94, 39%. In urban areas in these years it was 33%, 34% and 30%. But these national aggregates mask wide variation among states. Four states managed to reduce income poverty by more than 50%—Andhra Pradesh, Haryana, Kerala and Punjab. Other states were less successful, and today 50% of India's rural income-poor live in three states: Bihar, Madhya Pradesh and Uttar Pradesh.

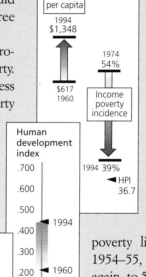

How much of the reduction in poverty can be ascribed to economic growth? Growth was slower in 1950–75, averaging 3.6% a year. Over the next 10 years, when income poverty fell the most, growth rose to 4% a year, and in 1986–91 it averaged 6% a year. But equating growth with poverty reduction is too simplistic. In the second half of the 1980s, for example, despite rapid economic growth, income poverty fell little. Statistical analyses suggest that economic growth explains at best around 50% of the reduction in income poverty.

Whether growth translates into human poverty reduction depends on social and political factors. Kerala, for example, ensured big reductions in income poverty, despite slow economic growth, through political activism and rapid, equitable expansion of opportunities.

Nationwide, India did not see a consistent drop in poverty in the first period because of a greater emphasis on total output than on distribution. In rural areas, where three-quarters of the poor people live, the green revolution increased agricultural production, but inadequate efforts were made to distribute the benefits equitably. Land and tenancy reforms were introduced, but seldom implemented. Similarly, in urban areas the focus was on heavy industry and public enterprises rather than on the microenterprises that employ most of the poor people.

Imbalances were also evident in human poverty. A large share of the (limited) education budget was spent on higher education—at the expense of basic education. Health services were concentrated in urban areas, where they could best serve the middle classes. Nor was there much participation. Village and local institutions were replaced by bureaucracies that administered centrally developed programmes. All this added to inequality. And those most affected were the scheduled castes and scheduled tribes, which have higher rates of illiteracy and child mortality.

The better performance in the second period is largely a result of pro-poor policies and programmes. As part of a strategy to alleviate poverty, the government introduced new programmes for employment and asset generation and required banks to direct 40% of lending to priority sectors. Rural non-agricultural employment increased sharply, as did real agricultural wages.

But the most important part of the pro-poor effort was a massive increase in public spending. In 1976–90 real per capita development spending grew by 6% a year—twice the 3% annual growth in GDP. Comparisons among states show the significance of public spending: income poverty levels are closely correlated with public spending levels.

But state comparisons also show that reducing human poverty demands much more than income growth. Many aspects of deprivation—from poor health to discrimination to domestic violence—have little to do with income. Haryana's per capita income is among the highest and fastest growing in India. Yet its infant mortality rate, at 68 per 1,000 live births, is four times Kerala's. Women in Haryana suffer systematic deprivation, reflected in one of the lowest female to male ratios in the country— 865 to 1,000. If all of India had Kerala's birth and child death rates, there would be 1.5 million fewer infant deaths in the country every year, and a dramatic reduction in population growth. The disaggregated HPI for India shows similar variations: while Kerala has reduced its HPI to 15%, for Bihar and Rajasthan the HPI is more than 50%.

As for the future, the Ninth Five-Year Plan (1997–2002) calls for eradicating income poverty by the year 2005. The planning commission interprets this goal as reducing income poverty to around 5% over the next 10 years.

Is this realistic? There are reasons for optimism. First, the official policies for eradicating poverty focus on human development priorities—including basic health, basic education, safe drinking water and special attention for socially disadvantaged groups. Second, since the post-1991 reforms, economic conditions have been more favourable. Third, democratic participation is opening up—not just through local government but also through people's organizations and through women's groups, often organized around credit or income-generating activities.

But there is also cause for concern. The focus on reducing fiscal deficits is forcing major cuts in public spending, and the emphasis on state minimalism is leading to abdication of state responsibilities in key areas affecting the lives of poor people. This can be seen, for example, in the failure to provide free and compulsory elementary education—a commitment under the Constitution of India—to abolish child labour, to provide adequately for the social and economic security of marginalized communities, to assure poor people of employment opportunities, to improve living conditions in slums, to prevent pollution and to not only correct but also to forestall market failures. India needs sustained public action if it is to eliminate the worst forms of human poverty and promote an equitable expansion of social, economic and political opportunities.

Source: Shiva Kumar 1997.

PROFILE OF HUMAN POVERTY

HDI rank	SURVIVAL People not expected to survive to age 40 (as % of total population) 1990[a]	SURVIVAL Population without access to health services (%) 1990–95	SURVIVAL Population without access to safe water (%) 1990–96	EDUCATION Adult illiteracy rate (%) 1995	EDUCATION Children not reaching grade 5 (%) 1990–95	PERSONAL SECURITY Refugees by country of asylum (thousands) 1995	PERSONAL SECURITY People killed and affected by disasters (annual average; thousands) 1969–93	SUSTAIN-ABILITY Forest and woodland (% change) 1980–93	INCOME Real GDP per capita (PPP$) Poorest 20% 1980–94	INCOME Real GDP per capita (PPP$) Richest 20% 1980–94	INCOME Population in poverty (%) $1 a day (PPP$) 1989–94	INCOME Population in poverty (%) National poverty line 1989–94
High human development	5.0	..	..	..	8	2,272T	2,088T	15.6	5,042	35,189	..	..
1 Canada	3.1	..	..	..	3	144.2	19.8	45.1	5,971	42,110	6[b]	..
2 France	4.0	..	..	..	4	170.2	33.5	2.2	5,359	40,098	12[b,c]	..
3 Norway	2.7	..	..	..	0	22.5	..	0	6,315	37,379	3[b]	..
4 USA	4.0	..	..	..	..	645.5	30.5	-2.9	5,800	51,705	14[b]	..
5 Iceland	2.6	..	..	..	..	(..)	0.2	..	..	..	..	..
6 Netherlands	2.5	..	..	..	..	72.0	0.5	20.3	7,109	31,992	14[b]	..
7 Japan	2.2	..	3	..	0	0	141.3	-0.4	8,987	38,738	5[b]	..
8 Finland	3.1	..	..	..	0	13.3	..	-0.6	5,141	30,682	4[b]	..
9 New Zealand	4.3	..	3	..	6	1.2	2.0	4.1	4,264	37,369	..	..
10 Sweden	2.7	..	..	..	2	43.2	..	0.3	7,160	33,026	5[b]	..
11 Spain	3.0	..	..	..	4	7.1	32.4	3.5	5,669	24,998	21[b]	..
12 Austria	3.7	..	..	..	3	37.5	..	-1.3	..	..	..	..
13 Belgium	3.5	..	..	..	..	31.7	0.1	0	7,718	35,172	12[b]	..
14 Australia	3.5	..	..	..	1	35.6	2.9	36.9	4,077	39,098	8[b]	..
15 United Kingdom	2.6	..	..	..	..	20.4	0.3	16.0	3,963	38,164	13[b]	..
16 Switzerland	3.4	..	..	..	0	57.3	0.1	19.0	5,907	50,666	..	..
17 Ireland	2.9	..	..	..	0	0.4	0.2	0	..	..	37[b,c]	..
18 Denmark	3.4	..	..	..	0	35.6	..	-9.7	5,454	38,986	8[b]	..
19 Germany	3.0	..	..	..	0	569.0	4.7	4.1	6,594	37,963	12[b]	..
20 Greece	3.8	..	..	..	0	4.5	29.1	0	..	..	..	..
21 Italy	3.0	..	..	..	0	80.0	75.5	6.5	6,174	37,228	2[b]	..
22 Hong Kong	2.4	..	0	7.8	..	1.5	1.6	4.8	5,821	50,666	..	..
23 Israel	2.8	..	..	..	0	..	..	8.6	4,539	29,957	..	..
24 Cyprus	3.1	..	..	..	0	0.1	0.1	0	..	..	..	..
25 Barbados	4.2	..	..	2.6	..	..	..	0	..	..	..	..
26 Singapore	3.2	..	0[c]	8.9	0	0	..	0	4,934	47,311	..	..
27 Luxembourg	3.8	..	..	..	..	0.3	..	..	..	..	4[b,c]	..
28 Bahamas	5.5	..	..	1.8	..	..	..	0	..	..	..	..
29 Antigua and Barbuda	..	..	..	..	..	..	3.0	..	..	..	..	12
30 Chile	4.6	3[c]	..	4.8	5	0.3	168.4	0	1,558	27,145	15	..
31 Portugal	4.7	..	..	..	..	1.4	1.6	15.8	..	..	..	..
32 Korea, Rep. of	4.8	0	7	2.0	0	..	80.9	-1.6	..	..	..	..
33 Costa Rica	4.1	..	4	5.2	12	24.2	10.1	-14.2	1,136	14,399	19	11
34 Malta	4.0	..	..	..	0	0.3	..	..	..	..	..	..
35 Slovenia	..	..	..	..	0	22.3	..	0.6	..	..	1[d]	..
36 Argentina	6.3	29[c]	29	3.8	..	12.0	510.7	0	..	..	..	26
37 Uruguay	5.4	18[c]	25[c]	2.7	6	0.1	0.9	0	..	..	..	..
38 Brunei Darussalam	4.6	..	..	11.8	0	..	..	0	..	..	..	..
39 Czech Rep.	3.7	..	..	..	2	2.7	..	0	4,426	15,764	1[d]	..
40 Trinidad and Tobago	5.4	0	3	2.1	5	..	2.0	2.2	..	..	..	21
41 Dominica	..	..	..	..	7	..	..	0	..	..	..	33
42 Slovakia	4.1	..	..	..	3	1.9	..	..	3,344	8,823	1[d]	..
43 Bahrain	6.5	..	..	14.8	1	..	..	..	..	..	..	..
44 United Arab Emirates	3.6	1	5	20.8	1	0.4	..	0	..	..	..	..
45 Panama	6.2	30	7	9.2	18	0.9	7.0	-21.8	589	17,611	26	..
46 Fiji	6.6	..	..	8.4	13	..	51.1	0	..	..	..	..
47 Venezuela	6.1	..	21	8.9	22	11.2	5.2	-9.3	1,505	24,411	12	31
48 Hungary	8.2	..	..	..	2	11.4	..	9.6	2,878	11,088	2[d]	25
49 Saint Kitts and Nevis	..	..	..	..	..	..	..	0	..	..	..	15
50 Mexico	8.3	7	17	10.4	16	39.6	87.6	1.8	1,437	19,383	15	34
51 Colombia	6.3	19	15	8.7	41	5.5	242.6	-6.2	1,042	16,154	7	19
52 Seychelles	..	..	..	..	1	..	..	0	..	..	..	..
53 Kuwait	3.8	0[c]	..	21.4	1	30.0	..	0	..	..	..	..
54 Grenada	..	..	..	..	..	..	..	0	..	..	..	20
55 Qatar	7.4	..	..	20.6	2	..	..	..	..	..	..	..
56 Saint Lucia	..	..	..	..	5	..	..	0	..	..	..	25
57 Saint Vincent	..	..	..	..	..	..	1.7	0	..	..	..	17
58 Poland	5.0	..	..	..	0	0.6	0.9	1.2	2,186	8,605	13[d]	24
59 Thailand	8.9	10[c]	11	6.2	12	101.4	480.7	-18.4	1,778	16,732	(.)	13
60 Malaysia	7.2	..	22	16.5	2	0.2	14.9	5.5	1,923	22,447	6	16
61 Mauritius	6.2	0[c]	1	17.1	0	..	39.5	-24.1	..	..	..	11
62 Belarus	5.9	..	..	..	1	(..)	1.6	-7.7	2,355	6,981	23[d]	37
63 Belize	4.9	..	..	..	32	8.7	3.7	0	..	..	..	35
64 Libyan Arab Jamahiriya	16.2	5	3	23.8	..	3.3	..	40.0	..	..	..	..

PROFILE OF HUMAN POVERTY

HDI rank	People not expected to survive to age 40 (as % of total population) 1990[a]	Population without access to health services (%) 1990–95	Population without access to safe water (%) 1990–96	Adult illiteracy rate (%) 1995	Children not reaching grade 5 (%) 1990–95	Refugees by country of asylum (thousands) 1995	People killed and affected by disasters (annual average; thousands) 1969–93	Forest and woodland (% change) 1980–93	Real GDP per capita (PPP$) Poorest 20% 1980–94	Real GDP per capita (PPP$) Richest 20% 1980–94	$1 a day (PPP$) 1989–94	National poverty line 1989–94
Medium human development	11.2	13	31	19.4	13	5,544T	32,568T	–1.1	870	7,178	..	..
65 Lebanon	8.4	5	6	7.6	..	348.3	2.1	–5.9	..	..	..	..
66 Suriname	7.8	..	..	7.0	..	(..)	0.2	0.7	..	..	..	..
67 Russian Federation	9.6	..	..	..	3	42.3	2.0	3.1	881	12,804	38 d	31
68 Brazil	14.0	..	27	16.7	30	2.0	1,878.7	–5.9	578	18,563	29	17
69 Bulgaria	6.2	..	..	..	7	0.1	..	0.8	1,793	8,489	33 d	..
70 Iran, Islamic Rep. of	11.7	12	10	31.4	10	2,024.5	72.9	0	..	..	..	..
71 Estonia	7.3	..	..	..	0	..	..	21.8	1,191	8,357	40 d	..
72 Ecuador	9.9	..	32	9.9	33 c	14.5	62.2	0.7	1,188	11,572	30	35
73 Saudi Arabia	8.8	3 c	5 c	37.2	6	13.3	0.1	50.0	..	..	..	..
74 Turkey	13.1	..	20	17.7	11	9.9	33.4	0	..	..	..	..
75 Korea, Dem. People's Rep. of	7.0	..	..	..	..	..	..	0	..	..	..	..
76 Lithuania	6.5	..	..	..	6	..	..	2.0	1,260	6,547	46 d	..
77 Croatia	4.5	..	..	..	2	188.6	..	3.8	..	..	..	..
78 Syrian Arab Rep.	10.3	10	15	29.2	8	374.3	5.4	39.5	..	..	..	..
79 Romania	7.1	..	..	..	7	0.2	58.3	1.7	1,714	6,485	22 d	..
80 Macedonia, FYR	6.6	..	..	..	5	9.0	..	..	..	..	..	..
81 Tunisia	10.5	..	2	33.3	8	0.1	18.5	25.2	1,460	11,459	4	14
82 Algeria	10.6	2	22	38.4	8	206.8	34.5	–8.8	1,922	12,839	2 c	..
83 Jamaica	4.3	10 c	14	15.0	4	2.0	54.2	–5.1	922	7,553	5	32
84 Jordan	9.2	3 c	2	13.4	2	1,288.9	0.8	11.1	1,292	10,972	3	15
85 Turkmenistan	13.6	0	26	..	..	3.0	..	–14.9	1,048	6,694	48 d	..
86 Cuba	6.2	0	11	4.3	5	1.8	62.2	4.4	..	..	..	..
87 Dominican Rep.	10.2	22	35	17.9	42	1.0	101.9	–5.5	775	10,277	20	21
88 Oman	8.8	4	18	..	4	..	0.2	..	..	..	..	..
89 Peru	13.4	56	28	11.3	..	0.7	514.3	–0.1	813	8,366	49	32
90 South Africa	17.0	..	1	18.2	24	91.8	262.6	0	516	9,897	24	..
91 Sri Lanka	7.9	..	43	9.8	8	0	579.3	19.3	1,348	5,954	4	22
92 Latvia	8.1	..	..	..	5	..	..	3.4	2,405	9,193	23 d	..
93 Kazakstan	9.3	..	..	..	..	(..)	1.2	–9.4	1,391	7,494	50 d	..
94 Paraguay	9.2	37 c	58	7.9	29	0.1	17.7	–36.3	..	..	..	22
95 Ukraine	6.3	..	..	..	3	5.2	16.3	47.6	1,544	5,753	41 d	32
96 Samoa (Western)	11.2	..	..	..	..	..	..	0	..	..	..	..
97 Botswana	15.9	..	7 c	30.2	16	0.3	170.9	0	..	..	35 c	..
98 Philippines	12.8	29	14	5.4	33	0.1	2,050.6	9.2	842	6,190	28 c	41
99 Indonesia	14.8	7	38	16.2	8	0	316.3	–5.0	1,422	6,654	15	8
100 Uzbekistan	9.9	..	38	..	0	0.9	2.0	–45.8	..	..	29 d	..
101 Mongolia	16.0	5 c	20	17.1	..	..	4.0	–9.4	..	..	..	36
102 Albania	6.1	..	..	..	8	(..)	140.0	3.4	..	..	..	..
103 Armenia	6.9	..	..	..	..	218.0	52.0	..	..	..	..	..
104 Guyana	15.8	..	..	1.9	..	..	10.9	0.8	..	..	..	43
105 Georgia	5.6	..	..	..	..	0.1	4.3	–8.8	..	..	..	30
106 Azerbaijan	7.3	..	..	..	7	233.7	..	–15.9	..	..	..	..
107 Kyrgyzstan	9.9	..	..	..	..	13.2	6.0	–13.6	..	..	76 d	40
108 China	9.1	12	33	18.5	12	288.3	23,655.0	..	722	5,114	29	11
109 Egypt	16.6	1	21	48.6	2	7.7	3.3	0	1,653	7,809	8	..
110 Moldova, Rep. of	10.0	..	45	..	..	..	..	100.5	818	4,918	65 d	..
111 Maldives	18.0	..	..	6.8	7	..	0.5	0	..	..	..	..
112 El Salvador	11.7	60	31	28.5	42	0.2	65.0	–25.7	..	..	..	38
113 Bolivia	19.6	33	34	16.9	40	0.7	162.2	0	703	6,049	7	..
114 Swaziland	23.9	..	..	23.3	22	0.5	62.1	16.5	..	..	..	..
115 Tajikistan	11.4	..	..	..	..	0.4	3.2	–0.6	..	..	..	53
116 Honduras	10.8	31	13	27.3	..	0.1	49.2	..	399	6,027	47	53
117 Guatemala	14.5	43	36	44.4	..	1.5	157.8	27.8	357	10,710	53	58
118 Namibia	21.1	41	43	..	18	1.4	10.0	–2.3	..	..	..	..
119 Morocco	12.3	30 c	45	56.3	20	0.4	17.3	15.2	1,079	7,570	1	13
120 Gabon	29.0	..	32 c	36.8	50 c	0.8	0.4	–0.6	..	..	..	..
121 Viet Nam	12.1	10	57	6.3	..	(..)	1,579.0	–19.3	406	2,288	..	51
122 Solomon Islands	7.7	..	..	..	19	..	8.9	–4.3	..	..	..	..
123 Cape Verde	14.6	..	..	28.4	..	..	0.3	0	..	..	..	44
124 Vanuatu	14.0	..	..	..	..	..	7.1	0	..	..	..	..

PROFILE OF HUMAN POVERTY

HDI rank		SURVIVAL — People not expected to survive to age 40 (as % of total population) 1990[a]	Population without access to health services (%) 1990–95	Population without access to safe water (%) 1990–96	EDUCATION — Adult illiteracy rate (%) 1995	Children not reaching grade 5 (%) 1990–95	PERSONAL SECURITY — Refugees by country of asylum (thousands) 1995	People killed and affected by disasters (annual average; thousands) 1969–93	SUSTAINABILITY — Forest and woodland (% change) 1980–93	INCOME — Real GDP per capita (PPP$) Poorest 20% 1980–94	Real GDP per capita (PPP$) Richest 20% 1980–94	Population in poverty (%) $1 a day (PPP$) 1989–94	Population in poverty (%) National poverty line 1989–94
125	São Tomé and Principe	..	..	..	..	..	..	7.5	..	..	..	..	46
126	Iraq	15.4	7 c	22	42.0	28 c	123.3	..	0	..	..	..	..
127	Nicaragua	13.6	17 c	47	34.3	51	0.6	59.4	−29.0	479	6,293	44	50
128	Papua New Guinea	28.6	4 c	72	27.8	29	9.5	7.7	0	..	..	..	..
129	Zimbabwe	18.4	15	23	14.9	24	0.3	184.2	−7.4	420	6,542	41	26
130	Congo	22.1	17 c	66	25.1	47	15.0	..	−1.2	..	..	..	..
	Low human development	25.3	30	29	49.0	38	6,601T	84,956T	−4.3	530	2,870	..	..
131	Myanmar	25.6	40	40	16.9	..	..	238.5	1.1	..	..	..	..
132	Ghana	24.9	40 c	35	35.5	20	89.2	501.1	−9.9	790	4,220	..	31
133	Cameroon	25.4	20	50	36.6	34	45.9	40.7	0	..	..	..	..
134	Kenya	22.3	23	47	21.9	23	239.5	141.8	0	238	4,347	50	37
135	Equatorial Guinea	36.5	..	..	21.5	..	..	..	0.4	..	..	..	..
136	Lao People's Dem. Rep.	32.7	33 c	48	43.4	47	..	191.7	−9.0	700	2,931	..	46
137	Lesotho	23.9	20 c	44	28.7	40	(..)	34.0	..	137	2,945	50 c	26
138	India	19.4	15	19	48.0	38	274.1	63,271.2	1.5	527	2,641	53	..
139	Pakistan	22.6	45 c	26	62.2	52	867.6	982.8	22.1	907	4,288	12	34
140	Comoros	26.3	..	..	42.7	22	..	15.4	14.3	..	..	..	..
141	Nigeria	33.8	49	49	42.9	8	8.1	124.5	−24.2	308	3,796	29	21
142	Zaire	30.0	74 c	58	22.7	36	1,326.5	33.0	−2.2	..	..	..	..
143	Zambia	35.1	..	73	21.8	..	130.6	103.2	−2.9	216	2,797	85	86
144	Bangladesh	26.4	55	3	61.9	53 c	51.1	10,927.5	−13.3	606	2,445	29	48
145	Côte d'Ivoire	23.1	..	25	59.9	27	297.9	0.4	−28.3	551	3,572	18 c	..
146	Benin	29.5	82 c	50	63.0	45	23.5	136.4	−14.4	..	..	..	33
147	Togo	28.4	..	37	48.3	50	11.0	24.1	−11.8	..	..	..	17
148	Yemen	25.6	62	39	..	..	40.3	121.1	−50.7	..	..	..	..
149	Tanzania, U. Rep. of	30.6	58	62	32.2	17	829.7	140.7	−20.5	217	1,430	16	50
150	Mauritania	31.7	37	34 c	62.3	28	40.4	253.1	−2.7	290	3,743	31 c	57 c
151	Central African Rep.	35.4	48	62	40.0	35 c	33.8	0.6	0	..	..	..	..
152	Madagascar	32.1	62	71	..	72	(..)	254.8	0	203	1,750	72	59
153	Cambodia	31.9	47 c	64	..	50	0	41.6	−11.9	..	..	..	..
154	Nepal	19.9	..	37	72.5	48	124.8	252.1	3.6	455	1,975	53 c	..
155	Bhutan	33.2	35 c	42	57.8	18	..	..	20.3	..	..	..	..
156	Haiti	27.1	40	72	55.0	53	..	159.8	0	..	..	..	..
157	Angola	38.9	..	68	..	66	10.9	279.8	−3.5	..	..	..	..
158	Sudan	25.2	30	40	53.9	6	558.2	986.9	−7.5	..	..	..	..
159	Uganda	39.0	51	62	38.2	45	229.3	57.4	−9.2	309	2,189	50	55
160	Senegal	25.3	10	48	66.9	12 c	68.6	291.1	−5.5	299	5,010	54	..
161	Malawi	38.3	65	63	43.6	63	1.0	459.7	−1.1	..	..	..	..
162	Djibouti	35.6	..	..	53.8	6	25.7	27.7	0	..	..	..	..
163	Guinea-Bissau	43.2	60	41	45.1	80 c	15.3	0.4	0	90	2,533	87	49
164	Chad	34.0	70	76	51.9	54	0.1	283.3	0	..	..	..	..
165	Gambia	40.6	7	52	61.4	13	7.2	29.4	0	..	..	..	64
166	Mozambique	43.8	61 c	37	59.9	65	0.1	1,179.7	−9.4	..	..	..	..
167	Guinea	41.3	20	45	64.1	20	633.0	1.0	−4.7	270	4,518	26	..
168	Eritrea	34.1	..	..	..	21	1.1	0.3	0	..	..	..	..
169	Burundi	33.8	20	41	64.7	26	142.7	0.3	0	..	..	..	..
170	Ethiopia	35.7	54	75	64.5	42	393.5	2,402.3	−11.1	..	..	34 c	..
171	Mali	28.4	60	55	69.0	15	15.6	209.3	−4.9	..	..	..	..
172	Burkina Faso	36.1	10	22	80.8	39	29.5	279.1	0	..	..	..	..
173	Niger	43.2	1	46	86.4	18	22.6	313.4	−3.9	296	1,742	61	..
174	Rwanda	42.1	20	..	39.5	40	7.8	164.2	−5.8	359	1,447	46 c	53
175	Sierra Leone	52.1	62	66	68.6	..	4.7	0.5	−3.5	..	..	..	75

PROFILE OF HUMAN POVERTY

	SURVIVAL			EDUCATION		PERSONAL SECURITY		SUSTAIN-ABILITY	INCOME			
	People not expected to survive to age 40 (as % of total population) 1990ª	Population without access to health services (%) 1990–95	Population without access to safe water (%) 1990–96	Adult illiteracy rate (%) 1995	Children not reaching grade 5 (%) 1990–95	Refugees by country of asylum (thousands) 1995	People killed and affected by disasters (annual average; thousands) 1969–93	Forest and woodland (% change) 1980–93	Real GDP per capita (PPP$) Poorest 20% 1980–94	Richest 20% 1980–94	Population in poverty (%) $1 a day (PPP$) 1993	National poverty line 1989–94
All developing countries	18.0	20	29	29.6	25	11,670T	118,950T	–4.1	768	6,194	32	..
Industrial countries	5.2	..	..	..	2	2,747T	663T	12.5	4,810	32,198	..	..
World	16.4	..	..	..	23	14,417T	119,613T	3.2	1,787	12,747	..	..
Arab States	15.5	13	24	43.2	9	3,021T	1,218T	–3.6	..	..	4	..
East Asia	8.9	12	32	17.8	12	290T	23,742T	..	748	5,342	26 ᵉ	..
East Asia (excl. China)	6.0	..	..	3.2	..	..	87T	–5.3	..	..	14 ᵉ	..
Latin America & the Caribbean	10.8	..	25	13.4	27	128T	4,398T	–4.6	932	17,391	24	..
Latin America & the Caribbean (excl. Mexico & Brazil)	9.8	30	27	12.2	30	86T	2,432T	–3.7	..	..	..	..
South Asia	19.9	22	18	49.6	39	3,342T	76,086T	2.6	586	2,833	43	..
South Asia (excl. India)	21.0	42	17	54.1	42	3,068T	12,815T	5.3	778	3,459	..	..
South-East Asia & the Pacific	15.1	15	35	12.3	16	..	4,988T	–4.0	1,253	8,269	14	..
Sub-Saharan Africa	31.9	47	49	42.2	29	4,889T	8,485T	–4.5	..	..	39	..
Least developed countries	31.6	51	43	50.4	43	4,710T	19,619T	–4.4	..	..	..	..
North America	3.9	..	..	..	..	790T	50T	22.8	5,817	50,769	..	..
Eastern Europe & the CIS	8.2	..	..	..	3	754T	288T	2.9	1,509	9,959	..	..
Western and Southern Europe	3.3	..	..	..	2	1,146T	178T	1.5	6,156	36,088	..	..
OECD	5.2	..	..	..	6	2,057T	496T	20.1	5,764	39,274	..	..
European Union	3.2	..	..	..	2	1,087T	178T	1.9	5,780	36,137	..	..
Nordic countries	2.9	..	..	..	8	115T	0T	–0.2	6,179	34,666	..	..

a. Data refer to 1990 or a year around 1990.
b. Income poverty line is $14.40 (1985 PPP$) a day per person.
c. Data refer to a year or period other than that specified in the column heading.
d. Income poverty line is $4 (1990 PPP$) a day per person.
e. Includes South-East Asia and the Pacific.
Source: Column 1: see technical note table 2.1; *columns 2 and 3:* calculated on the basis of data from UNICEF 1997; *column 4:* calculated on the basis of data from UNESCO 1996a; *column 5:* calculated on the basis of data from UNESCO 1996d and UNICEF 1997; *column 6:* UNHCR 1996a; *column 7:* International Federation of Red Cross and Red Crescent Societies 1995; *column 8:* WRI 1996b; *columns 9 and 10:* UNDP 1996d; *columns 11 and 12:* $1-a-day data are from World Bank 1997b, $4-a-day data are from Milanovic 1996, $14.40-a-day data are from Smeeding 1996 and national poverty line data are from World Bank 1996e and Lipton 1996g.

HUMAN POVERTY OF WOMEN AND CHILDREN

	SURVIVAL					EDUCATION			POLITICAL PARTICIPATION			INCOME
HDI rank	Maternal mortality rate (per 100,000 live births) 1990	Children dying before age 1 (thousands) 1995	Under-weight children under age five (%) 1990–96	Adult Illiteracy Female rate (%) 1995	Adult Illiteracy Female rate as % of male rate 1995	Female primary enrolment ratio (as % of male) 1995	Female secondary enrolment ratio (as % of male) 1993–95	Children not in primary school (%) 1993–95	Child economic activity rate (% age 10–14) 1995	Parliamentary seats held by women (as % of total)[a] 1996	Female unpaid family workers (as % of total) 1990	Female economic activity rate (as % of male) 1995
High human development	56	279T	..	..	..	..	103	6	..	13	68	69
1 Canada	6	5	..	..	..	..	101	4	..	19	80	80
2 France	15	10	..	..	..	..	105	1	..	6	82	76
3 Norway	6	1	..	..	..	..	100	1	..	39	67	82
4 USA	12	61	..	..	..	..	100	4	..	11	76	80
5 Iceland	..	..	..	..	..	..	..	..	..	25	..	83
6 Netherlands	12	2	..	..	..	..	104 [b]	7	..	28	91	65
7 Japan	18	11	..	..	..	..	101	0	..	8	82	66
8 Finland	11	1	..	..	..	..	101	1	..	34	38	86
9 New Zealand	25	1	..	..	..	..	104	1	..	29	66	77
10 Sweden	7	1	..	..	..	..	100	1	..	40	67	90
11 Spain	7	6	..	..	..	..	105 [b]	0 [b]	..	20	62	54
12 Austria	10	1	..	..	..	..	101	0	..	25	75	65
13 Belgium	10	2	..	..	..	..	103	2	..	15	85	65
14 Australia	9	3	..	..	..	..	105	1	..	21	59	74
15 United Kingdom	9	10	..	..	..	..	105 [b]	0	..	8	..	73
16 Switzerland	6	1	..	..	..	..	94 [b]	0	..	20	..	65
17 Ireland	10	1	..	..	..	..	105	0	..	14	37	49
18 Denmark	9	1	..	..	..	..	102 [b]	2	..	33	97	84
19 Germany	22	9	..	..	..	..	101	3	..	26	..	69
20 Greece	10	2	..	..	..	..	99	9	..	6	76	55
21 Italy	12	8	..	..	..	..	..	..	0.4	10	63	57
22 Hong Kong	7	1	..	12	298	..	106	9	..	..	77	62
23 Israel	7	2	..	..	..	..	..	..	..	8	72	65
24 Cyprus	..	0	..	..	..	..	102	3	..	5	83	62
25 Barbados	..	..	..	3	165	95	92 [b]	22 [b]	..	18	67	80
26 Singapore	10	1	..	14	331	99	..	1 [b]	..	3	77	63
27 Luxembourg	..	..	..	..	..	..	102 [b]	19 [b]	..	20	84	56
28 Bahamas	..	0	..	2	138	99	101 [b]	5	..	11	72	84
29 Antigua and Barbuda	..	..	..	..	..	100	..	..	..	11	..	..
30 Chile	65	8	1	5	110	99	110	13	..	7	42	46
31 Portugal	15	2	..	..	..	..	..	0	1.8	13	60	71
32 Korea, Rep. of	130	14	..	3	458	101	100	7	..	3	87	68
33 Costa Rica	60	2	2	5	96	102	109 [b]	8	5.4	16	34	43
34 Malta	..	..	..	..	..	..	99	0	..	6	..	35
35 Slovenia	13	0	..	..	..	..	..	0	..	8	62	81
36 Argentina	100	33	..	4	101	89	113 [b]	5 [b]	4.5	20	..	43
37 Uruguay	85	2	7	2	75	100	..	5	1.9	7	40	65
38 Brunei Darussalam	..	0	..	17	225	99	111	9	..	..	55	56
39 Czech Rep.	15	2	..	..	..	..	102	15	..	..	76	86
40 Trinidad and Tobago	90	1	7	3	247	100	119 [b]	11 [b]	..	19	54	56
41 Dominica	..	..	..	..	..	82	..	..	..	9	50	..
42 Slovakia	..	2	..	..	..	..	..	..	..	15	66	87
43 Bahrain	..	0	..	21	188	100	104	0	..	..	8	31
44 United Arab Emirates	26	1	..	20	96	99	112	17	..	0	9	27
45 Panama	55	3	7	10	113	98	110 [b]	9 [b]	3.6	10	15	52
46 Fiji	..	1	..	11	174	100	..	1 [b]	..	6	20	39
47 Venezuela	120	25	6	10	118	84	150 [b]	12 [b]	0.9	6	34	50
48 Hungary	30	3	..	..	..	..	107	7	0.2	11	82	74
49 Saint Kitts and Nevis	..	..	..	..	..	..	..	..	..	13	..	..
50 Mexico	110	153	14	13	154	100	..	0	6.7	14	11	45
51 Colombia	100	46	8	9	98	68	113	15	6.6	10	74	59
52 Seychelles	..	..	..	..	..	..	..	..	..	27	60	..
53 Kuwait	29	1	6	25	141	100	100	39	..	0	4	50
54 Grenada	..	..	..	..	..	100	..	..	..	..	4	..
55 Qatar	..	0	..	20	97	78	103	20	..	..	4	29
56 Saint Lucia	..	..	..	..	..	100	..	..	..	14	..	..
57 Saint Vincent	..	..	..	..	..	100	..	..	..	10	42	..
58 Poland	19	13	..	..	..	..	109	3	..	13	76	81
59 Thailand	200	62	26	8	212	70	..	..	16.2	7	64	87
60 Malaysia	80	13	23	22	200	83	..	..	3.2	10	64	59
61 Mauritius	120	1	16	21	164	..	..	5	2.9	8	48	46
62 Belarus	37	3	..	..	..	..	..	14	..	..	..	84
63 Belize	..	0	..	..	..	99	138 [b]	1	3.7	11	..	30
64 Libyan Arab Jamahiriya	220	28	5	37	307	97	75 [b]	3 [b]	0.3	..	..	28

HUMAN POVERTY OF WOMEN AND CHILDREN

	SURVIVAL					EDUCATION				POLITICAL PARTICIPATION		INCOME
HDI rank	Maternal mortality rate (per 100,000 live births) 1990	Children dying before age 1 (thousands) 1995	Under-weight children under age five (%) 1990–96	Illiteracy Female rate (%) 1995	Illiteracy Female rate as % of male rate 1995	Female primary enrolment ratio (as % of male) 1995	Female secondary enrolment (as % of male) 1993–95	Children not in primary school (%) 1993–95	Child economic activity rate (% age 10–14) 1995	Parliamentary seats held by women (as % of total)[a] 1996	Female unpaid family workers (as % of total) 1990	Female economic activity rate (as % of male) 1995
Medium human development	193	2,294T	18	27	166	93	..	4	10.5	15	..	75
65 Lebanon	300	5	..	10	183	94	..	..	..	2	..	37
66 Suriname	..	1	..	9	185	96	..	..	..	16	42	46
67 Russian Federation	75	62	..	..	..	..	..	7	..	8	..	83
68 Brazil	220	293	7	17	101	102	123[b]	10	16.1	7	46	53
69 Bulgaria	27	3	..	..	..	..	102	10	..	13	..	89
70 Iran, Islamic Rep. of	120	200	16	41	182	93	..	3[b]	4.7	4	43	33
71 Estonia	41	0	..	..	..	..	108[b]	76	..	13	..	85
72 Ecuador	150	29	17	12	148	91	..	..	5.4	..	27	36
73 Saudi Arabia	130	33	..	50	175	89	83	38	..	..	..	19
74 Turkey	180	132	10	28	333	..	70	6	11.9	3	69	57
75 Korea, Dem. People's Rep. of	70	22	..	..	..	..	..	..	..	20	69	78
76 Lithuania	36	1	..	..	..	..	..	..	..	18	..	83
77 Croatia	..	1	..	..	..	..	108	18	..	7	74	72
78 Syrian Arab Rep.	180	33	12	44	308	91	90	9	5.8	10	5	36
79 Romania	130	12	..	..	..	..	103	8	0.2	6	67	78
80 Macedonia, FYR	..	209	..	..	..	..	102	15	..	3	..	..
81 Tunisia	170	18	9	45	213	96	85[b]	3	..	7	49	45
82 Algeria	160	84	13	51	195	92	90	5	1.6	7	6	33
83 Jamaica	120	1	10	11	57	96	111[b]	0[b]	..	12	..	86
84 Jordan	150	13	9	21	312	101	106[b]	11[b]	0.6	3	4	28
85 Turkmenistan	55	14	..	..	..	..	..	..	..	18	..	81
86 Cuba	95	3	..	5	123	101	115	4	..	23	5	61
87 Dominican Rep.	110	15	10	18	99	105	144	19	16.0	10	43	42
88 Oman	190	5	12	..	..	96	95	29	0.4	..	..	19
89 Peru	280	62	11	17	312	91	..	13	2.5	11	..	41
90 South Africa	230	127	9	18	101	..	121	4	..	24	..	59
91 Sri Lanka	140	11	38	13	194	100	..	..	2.4	5	56	54
92 Latvia	40	1	..	..	..	..	101	16	..	9	..	85
93 Kazakstan	80	22	..	..	..	..	..	..	..	11	91	82
94 Paraguay	160	13	4	9	144	101	106	11	7.9	6	..	41
95 Ukraine	50	19	..	..	..	..	..	..	..	4	..	81
96 Samoa (Western)	..	1	..	..	..	81	..	..	..	4	8	..
97 Botswana	250	6	15	40	206	..	114	4	16.9	9	35	81
98 Philippines	280	152	30	6	113	98	102[b]	0	8.0	12	53	60
99 Indonesia	650	500	35	22	212	93	87	3	9.6	13	66	65
100 Uzbekistan	55	58	..	..	..	..	..	..	..	6	..	84
101 Mongolia	65	8	12	23	200	107	138	25	1.7	8	..	88
102 Albania	65	5	..	..	..	..	..	4	0.9	12	..	72
103 Armenia	50	3	..	..	..	..	..	..	..	6	..	87
104 Guyana	..	2	..	3	185	100	..	..	..	20	..	48
105 Georgia	33	4	..	..	..	..	99	18	..	7	..	79
106 Azerbaijan	22	11	..	..	..	..	..	..	..	12	..	75
107 Kyrgyzstan	110	10	..	..	..	..	..	0	..	5	..	84
108 China	95	1,722	16	27	269	98	..	1	11.6	21	..	87
109 Egypt	170	206	9	61	168	99	86	11	11.2	2	62	41
110 Moldova, Rep. of	60	3	..	..	..	..	..	..	..	5	..	86
111 Maldives	..	1	..	7	104	..	..	..	5.9	6	29	77
112 El Salvador	300	14	11	30	114	66	116	21	15.2	11	58	50
113 Bolivia	650	36	16	24	253	96	84	9	14.3	6	79	59
114 Swaziland	..	5	..	24	111	..	118	5	13.9	8	59	55
115 Tajikistan	130	2	..	..	..	..	..	..	..	3	..	76
116 Honduras	220	16	18	27	100	101	..	10	8.5	8	..	43
117 Guatemala	200	35	27	51	137	50	..	42[b]	16.3	13	21	36
118 Namibia	370	7	26	..	..	..	138[b]	8	22.0	..	69	68
119 Morocco	610	81	9	69	159	75	64[b]	28	..	1	31	..
120 Gabon	500	7	..	47	178	..	..	..	17.9	6	..	78
121 Viet Nam	160	157	45	9	251	80	..	..	9.1	19	..	94
122 Solomon Islands	..	1	..	..	..	..	..	..	29.2	2	..	93
123 Cape Verde	..	1	..	36	195	99	100	0	14.3	11	54	57
124 Vanuatu	..	0	..	..	..	..	79[b]	26[b]	..	..	..	..

	SURVIVAL					EDUCATION				POLITICAL PARTICIPATION		INCOME

HDI rank	Maternal mortality rate (per 100,000 live births) 1990	Children dying before age 1 (thousands) 1995	Under-weight children under age five (%) 1990–96	Illiteracy Female rate (%) 1995	Illiteracy Female rate as % of male rate 1995	Female primary enrolment ratio (as % of male) 1995	Female secondary enrolment (as % of male) 1993–95	Children not in primary school (%) 1993–95	Child economic activity rate (% age 10–14) 1995	Parliamentary seats held by women (as % of total)[a] 1996	Female unpaid family workers (as % of total) 1990	Female economic activity rate (as % of male) 1995
125 São Tomé and Principe	..	..	..	..	..	..	..	..	..	7	54	..
126 Iraq	310	169	12	55	188	89	68 b	21	3.0	..	50	23
127 Nicaragua	160	14	12	33	94	104	114	14	14.1	11	..	54
128 Papua New Guinea	930	18	35	37	196	87	..	..	19.2	0	..	76
129 Zimbabwe	570	60	16	20	209	..	..	0 b	29.4	15	..	79
130 Congo	890	20	24	33	194	..	..	..	26.2	2	65	73
Low human development	753	5,037T	45	62	156	74	..	..	22.3	7	43	58
131 Myanmar	580	212	43	22	198	87	..	..	24.5	..	..	76
132 Ghana	740	105	27	46	193	..	..	..	13.2	..	63	101
133 Cameroon	550	65	14	48	192	..	..	24	25.2	12	70	59
134 Kenya	650	137	23	30	219	..	..	9 b	41.3	3	..	86
135 Equatorial Guinea	..	4	..	32	306	96	..	..	..	9	74	..
136 Lao People's Dem. Rep.	650	40	44	56	182	87	71	32	27.1	9	..	86
137 Lesotho	610	11	21	38	199	118	183	35	21.9	11	39	56
138 India	570	3,671	53	62	181	78	..	..	14.4	7	..	50
139 Pakistan	340	819	38	76	151	68	..	..	17.7	3	33	38
140 Comoros	..	4	..	50	138	66	..	47	39.3	0	..	76
141 Nigeria	1,000	790	36	53	161	78	..	..	25.8	..	46	55
142 Zaire	870	386	34	32	241	90	62	39	29.6	5	..	76
143 Zambia	940	75	28	29	200	97	74	25	16.3	10	54	79
144 Bangladesh	850	537	67	74	146	88	54 b	38 b	30.1	9	6	76
145 Côte d'Ivoire	810	91	24	70	140	..	..	48	20.5	8	62	51
146 Benin	990	41	..	74	145	60	..	48 b	27.6	7	40	89
147 Togo	640	31	24	63	191	72	38 b	22	28.6	1	54	65
148 Yemen	1,400	123	39	..	..	49	..	..	20.1	1	69	39
149 Tanzania, U. Rep. of	770	21	29	43	210	..	..	52	39.5	17	88	95
150 Mauritania	930	17	23	74	146	51	..	44	24.0	1	38	77
151 Central Africa Rep.	700	25	27	48	151	56	..	42	31.1	4	55	83
152 Madagascar	490	108	34	..	..	113	..	..	35.8	4	..	81
153 Cambodia	900	78	40	..	..	44	..	..	24.7	6	..	104
154 Nepal	1,500	145	49	86	146	58	..	..	45.2	5	55	68
155 Bhutan	1,600	16	38	72	164	25	..	..	55.3	2	..	66
156 Haiti	1,000	43	28	58	111	39	..	74 b	25.4	3	37	73
157 Angola	1,500	133	..	..	..	..	..	..	27.1	10	..	84
158 Sudan	660	144	34	65	155	85 ·	..	..	29.4	5	..	40
159 Uganda	1,200	235	23	50	190	91	..	..	45.3	18	74	90
160 Senegal	1,200	46	20	77	135	..	..	46	31.4	12	..	74
161 Malawi	560	142	30	58	208	102	100	0	35.2	6	58	94
162 Djibouti	..	5	..	67	169	78	..	68	..	0	22	..
163 Guinea-Bissau	910	12	23	58	180	82	25 b	44 b	37.9	10	4	65
164 Chad	1,500	65	..	65	172	54	..	..	38.3	17	..	78
165 Gambia	1,100	12	..	75	159	72	54	45	37.2	..	64	79
166 Mozambique	1,500	171	27	77	181	77	63	61	33.8	25	82	92
167 Guinea	1,600	90	26	78	156	49	38 b	63 b	34.1	7	60	91
168 Eritrea	1,400	27	41	..	..	89	88	69	39.6	21	..	89
169 Burundi	1,300	63	37	78	153	69	67 b	48 b	49.1	..	60	91
170 Ethiopia	1,400	625	48	75	137	29	..	..	42.3	..	67	70
171 Mali	1,200	163	31	77	127	68	50 b	75	54.5	2	53	84
172 Burkina Faso	930	98	30	91	129	67	56	71	51.1	9	66	86
173 Niger	1,200	113	36	93	118	36	38 b	77 b	45.2	..	24	77
174 Rwanda	1,300	71	29	48	160	106	78 b	24 b	41.7	17	70	93
175 Sierra Leone	1,800	75	29	82	150	100	..	..	15.5	6	74	54

HUMAN POVERTY OF WOMEN AND CHILDREN

	SURVIVAL			EDUCATION						POLITICAL PARTICIPATION	INCOME	
	Maternal mortality rate (per 100,000 live births) 1990	Children dying before age 1 (thousands) 1995	Under-weight children under age five (%) 1990–96	Illiteracy Female rate (%) 1995	Illiteracy Female rate as % of male rate 1995	Female primary enrolment ratio (as % of male) 1995	Female secondary enrolment (as % of male) 1993–95	Children not in primary school (%) 1993–95	Child economic activity rate (% age 10–14) 1995	Parliamentary seats held by women (as % of total)[a] 1996	Female unpaid family workers (as % of total) 1990	Female economic activity rate (as % of male) 1995
All developing countries	471	7,404T	31	38	159	88	..	9	16.0	12	48	67
Industrial countries	31	206T	..	..	..	..	..	5	..	4	75	75
World	416	7,610T	..	..	..	..	..	8	15.8	13	57	68
Arab States	380	475T	16	56	176	91	92	15	10.4	4	40	37
East Asia	95	883T	16	26	249	102	..	1	11.5	20	80	86
East Asia (excl. China)	99	22T	..	5	235	..	..	8	..	9	80	71
Latin America & the Caribbean	190	424T	11	15	119	93	..	13	10.9	10	38	50
Latin America & the Caribbean (excl. Mexico & Brazil)	204	202T	12	14	119	92	..	15	8.4	12	47	49
South Asia	554	2,700T	50	63	157	77	..	..	16.2	7	29	51
South Asia (excl. India)	520	865T	43	65	154	77	..	..	20.4	6	29	54
South-East Asia & the Pacific	447	618T	36	16	198	86	..	..	11.3	12	63	73
Sub-Saharan Africa	971	2,259T	31	51	158	79	..	37	32.7	12	57	74
Least developed countries	1,030	2,177T	42	61	155	75	..	45	32.6	9	43	76
North America	12	33T	..	..	..	..	101	4	..	12	76	80
Eastern Europe & the CIS	63	137T	..	..	..	..	..	8	..	8	..	82
Western and Southern Europe	14	23T	..	..	..	..	102	3	..	18	71	66
OECD	34	213T	..	..	..	..	102	4	..	13	68	69
European Union	13	27T	..	..	..	..	103	3	..	16	71	67
Nordic countries	8	2T	..	..	..	..	101	1	..	37	67	86

a. Data are as of January 1997.
b. Data refer to latest available years.
Source: Columns 1 and 3: UNICEF 1997; *column 2:* UN 1996b; *columns 4 and 5:* UNESCO 1996b; *column 6:* UNESCO 1996c; *columns 7 and 8:* UNESCO 1995b and 1997; *columns 9 and 12:* ILO 1996b; *column 10:* IPU 1997; *column 11:* UN 1995d.

CHAPTER 3

 # Resisting new forces of poverty in a changing world

A dynamic process, poverty is a constant struggle. Individuals, households and communities have to cope with the deprivations limiting their lives—seizing any opportunity for escape. But as they struggle, the world around them changes, presenting both new opportunities and new threats.

Some people lift themselves from poverty. Others stay poor. And still others become newly poor. Poverty is thus constantly being created and re-created. It disappears in some places but reappears elsewhere, at other times.

How do individuals, households and communities resist, escape and recover from poverty? What new conditions jeopardize past gains and threaten to produce more poverty? This chapter explores how poor people are fighting poverty in the rapidly changing world at the end of the 20th century.

Vulnerability, assets and coping strategies

Poor people cope with a wide range of adversities—cholera epidemics, rising prices, failed rains—against which they are defenceless, and this vulnerability to deepening poverty defines their lives. The poorest stay in poverty throughout the year, over the years, for a lifetime and pass poverty to the next generations—the chronically poor (box 3.1). The defining challenge of poverty eradication is to strengthen people's ability to cope with these adversities—to build resistance and resilience, to seize opportunities for escape.

Most individuals, households and communities develop complex and innovative strategies to survive poverty and adversity, tapping assets that help them cope. A family

that loses a job may rent out a room to make up for the lost income. A woman facing crop failure might mortgage her wedding jewelry. Coping with the illness of a parent, children as young as 10 might go out to work.

People's assets reduce vulnerability and build resilience against poverty. The more

---

BOX 3.1

Socially disadvantaged means chronically poor

Chronic poverty—sustained over many years and sometimes carried from one generation to the next—has a more serious effect on people than transient poverty.

Studies of poverty that follow the progress of the same people over time show that long-term poverty is more likely for certain social groups—such as immigrants in Germany and African Americans in the United States (box table 3.1.1). Of all the reasons for falling into poverty, the most common are linked to employment or marital status.

Evidence from a village in a drought-prone region in India between 1975 and 1993 showed that while 40% of households stayed in poverty for six or more years, about 10% suffered poverty for only one or two years (box table 3.1.2).

Another approach is to estimate the differences in *exit time* from income poverty (with a given rate of GNP growth) according to the depth of poverty. Data in three Indian states show that scheduled castes and tribes suffer deeper poverty and that their exit time would be much longer.

BOX TABLE 3.1.1
The ins and outs of poverty for families with children in the 1980s

	Average poverty rate (%)[a]	Those who escaped (%)[a]	Poor for three years or more (%)[b]
Germany			
Nationals	7	27	1
Foreigners	18	20	4
United States			
White	15	17	10
African			
American	49	8	42

a. The proportion of those in poverty whose income rose to 60% of the median at some later date. b. The proportion of the population that has an income less than 50% of the median each year of a three-year period.
Source: Duncan and others 1995.

BOX TABLE 3.1.2
Exit times from income poverty for rural households in India

	Household expenditures (as % of national poverty line) 1960–90	Exit time (years)
Bihar		
Scheduled caste	64	30
Scheduled tribe	66	23
Other	94	10
Orissa		
Scheduled caste	76	10
Scheduled tribe	64	17
Other	94	2
West Bengal		
Scheduled caste	75	12
Scheduled tribe	70	14
Other	88	5

Source: Shiva Kumar 1996.

assets they have, the less their vulnerability and the greater their ability to cope with poverty, to resist it and to escape it. But any erosion of these assets increases their vulnerability and insecurity.

Building people's assets, empowering them to fight poverty, should be the centrepiece of poverty eradication. The state has a responsibility to address structural inequalities in the distribution of assets, especially land, credit, housing and social services. But public policy and development efforts too often ignore:

- The potential to build on people's assets.
- The threat of those assets being eroded.
- The need to supply missing assets critical for survival and for equal participation in society.

In economic terms an *asset* usually refers to capital, whether physical or financial, from which people may derive a future stream of income. But the assets used to resist poverty encompass a broader range of

tangible and non-tangible resources—classified broadly as economic, social, environmental and personal. Time might be considered one of these assets (box 3.2).

Economic assets

Economic assets include land, livestock, housing, labour and financial capital, which provide a basis for generating income and production. Except for labour, these assets are often missing or scarcely accessible for poor people.

Land is critical for rural people—and for the three-quarters of the world's income-poor who depend on agriculture for their livelihood. About a quarter of the rural poor in developing countries are landless or do not have adequate security of tenure or title. And even those who have land often have holdings too small or unproductive to provide a secure livelihood.

Housing—and a secure right to it—are as critical an asset for the urban household as land is for the farmer. The home is commonly where the microentrepreneur starts a business. But housing rights are rarely protected, and the threat of eviction is a reality for many urban dwellers.

Capital, derived from credit and savings, is another key asset that allows poor people to seize market opportunities—such as investing in a small business or using farm inputs. Credit and savings also help families through crises—drought, recession, illness—without having to resort to measures such as selling off other assets or taking children out of school. Only 2–5% of the 500 million poorest households in the world have access to institutional credit.

Social and political assets

People's ability to draw on relationships with other people, especially on the basis of trust and reciprocity, is an asset—social capital.

In times of stress the first resort for help is usually family or other members of the community. Faced with an illness, women in poor neighbourhoods may share cooking and child care. And people borrow from one another—to meet immediate needs for

The assets to resist poverty encompass a broad range of resources, tangible and non-tangible

---

BOX 3.2

Is time an asset?

Lack of time is an important factor in the vulnerability of poor people and in their access to opportunities.

There are only 24 hours in a day, but does everyone need the same number of hours for survival? Does everyone have the same amount of disposable time—and the same ability to determine how to use time?

No. Much depends on whether a person is a woman or a man and on the size of the household and the conditions in which the person lives.

Women especially suffer from a shortage of time because of the triple load they carry: child-bearing and -rearing, family and household management and production or income-earning activities. Time-use studies find that in almost every country women spend more hours than men in work—paid and unpaid. *Human Development Report 1995* showed that of the total time spent in work, women on average account for 53% and men for 47%. As demands on women's time increase, they share their work with their daughters and with other children, but very

rarely are household responsibilities transferred to men.

Some circumstances—such as having a water supply close to home and transport to the workplace—increase the time available. Others—such as deforestation and pollution—reduce the time available and increase the vulnerability of women.

The importance of time for poor people has policy implications. For example, in setting a poverty line based on the income required for survival, policymakers need to recognize that survival income will vary depending on how much time is spent caring for children and the sick and how much is available for income-earning work.

Policies that impose a financial burden on families, such as a reduction in health care benefits, may also impose a time burden—with further repercussions for the ability to escape poverty. And policies that reduce the time burden of poor people, such as by improving the water supply, can remove a critical constraint on their ability to escape poverty.

food, water, electricity or health care. Sometimes combining family units to create larger households can also strengthen resilience against poverty.

Such relationships of trust and reciprocity are also the basis of community organizations, which might negotiate with government agencies for better services, such as schools, dispensaries or water. Groups can also form to take collective political action, often building alliances beyond the community (chapter 5).

Social assets can be eroded by stresses in social relations, however, especially from violence, alcoholism and other destructive behaviour—and a lack of time to invest in social relations.

Encouraging and nurturing social and political assets are an important part of providing an enabling environment for helping the poor resist poverty.

Environmental and infrastructure assets

People rely on both natural resources and infrastructure to secure health and livelihoods.

Roads and transport provide access to markets and jobs and reduce isolation. Social infrastructure enhances health and knowledge. Water and electricity can be tapped in setting up microenterprises. So cuts in public spending on infrastructure dig deeply into the assets of people.

Access to these assets is very unevenly distributed, and poorer communities often lack basic social services that are more plentifully available in richer communities. On average in developing countries, the proportion of people without access to safe water is only 13% in urban areas but 40% in rural areas. And female illiteracy is 38% in urban areas, compared with 66% in rural areas. But even in urban areas households with less income pay more for services. Water is piped into the rich suburbs but trucked into the slums—where the poor pay more, sometimes in cash, almost always on time.

In times of stress, people draw even more on the natural environment, as a reserve and as an important part of their coping strategy. In times of crop failure, farmers who normally cultivate maize or rice might gather fruit or other food from the forest. The depletion and pollution of natural reserves erode an important asset. Those affected might become ecological refugees, moving to other rural areas or to cities.

Personal strengths

The greatest personal asset is good health—not just physical well-being but also the toughness to cope with adversity.

Personal strengths also include skills and talents. So people's resilience against poverty can be strengthened by education and training that open a wider range of opportunities. But people without formal education have many skills—traditional knowledge and other physical and intellectual skills—that can be tapped to fight poverty.

Upward and downward spirals

All these assets, though listed separately, are linked and often mutually reinforcing. Mobilizing social assets can improve the management of environmental assets. People working together can help maintain such common property as ponds, woodlots, pastures and drinking water supplies—and ensure their sustainability. Social assets can also reinforce economic assets. The community solidarity that leads to collective political action to negotiate for better schools can bolster economic assets by increasing the chances of employment.

But the loss of any one of these assets can lead to the loss of many others, inducing a downward spiral. Lost income puts stress on human relationships and can lead to the loss of social and political assets—and to conflict and violence. In poor urban communities in Hungary, Mexico, the Philippines and Zambia, women linked rising domestic violence directly to declining male earnings, often combined with alcohol abuse.

Economic pressure can also pit parents against children, often because of greater reliance on children's labour. Children may

Social and political assets are important for helping the poor resist poverty

rebel against the added responsibilities—parents may lack time and energy to supervise their children. And children may not study or help in the home, or they might take up drinking, petty crime and other destructive behaviour.

Escalating crime and violence and growing drug and alcohol abuse threaten personal safety. Women especially become reluctant to go out at night, and become isolated as a result. All this reduces people's ability to participate in community activities, eroding their social assets and increasing their vulnerability.

Economic crises push households beyond the point at which they can sustain reciprocity—so community credit systems break down. There may also be less co-operation generally—women who have to spend more time at work have less time for community activities.

Downward spirals of poverty frequently mean environmental degradation, and environmental shocks can heighten poverty. Droughts that lead to crop failure, for example, cause poor people to scavenge more intensively for wood or edible plants or wildlife. They also cause herders to keep their livestock close to water holes. All this can cause greater deforestation and soil erosion.

Environmental crises can then erode social assets, as people facing diminishing resources are forced to compete with one another. In the Niger delta and surrounding drylands, many groups survive on livestock, farming and fishing. But successive droughts have broken down reciprocal relationships.

The result of these downward spirals: poverty deepens, and people become less able to pull themselves out of poverty as families sell their land and animals or curtail their children's education. The loss of assets transforms transient poverty into chronic poverty that can extend to the next generation.

A strategy for poverty eradication must take into account all these interlocking factors, including the different ways that women and men mobilize assets to escape poverty (box 3.3). Building on and reinforcing the assets of poor people helps them fight poverty themselves.

Grass-roots development programmes that have done this have been among the most effective. One has encouraged a Ugandan community stricken by HIV/AIDS to develop a community adoption programme for orphans, helped by a UN volunteer. Another has encouraged forest management through community negotiations with logging companies, helped by a bilateral aid programme.

And institutional and policy reforms are needed to give better access and secure rights to all the critical assets that are unevenly distributed. These include land, housing, credit, physical infrastructure, education, health and other social services (box 3.4).

BOX 3.3

What does the feminization of poverty mean?

Women are poorer than men because more households headed by women fall below the income poverty line than households headed by men. True? Yes and no.

Surveys of household consumption and expenditure in many countries of North and South America, Europe and the CIS show the incidence of income poverty to be high among female-headed households. But elsewhere there is no difference between male- and female-headed households—in Indonesia, Morocco, Viet Nam and Zimbabwe, for example.

Women and men experience poverty in different ways. And the feminization of poverty may be a question less of whether more women than men are poor than of the severity of poverty and the greater hardship women face in lifting themselves and their children out of the trap. The wide range of biases in society—unequal opportunities in education, employment and asset ownership among them—mean that women have fewer opportunities. Poverty accentuates gender gaps, and when adversity strikes, it is women who often are the most vulnerable.

In Zimbabwe gender equality was achieved in primary school enrolment by 1990. But when user fees were introduced as part of a structural adjustment programme, gender bias began to re-emerge in rural areas.

In Pakistan the gender gap in education is pronounced, with 77% illiteracy among women in 1995 but 51% among men—and with primary school enrolment among girls at 68% of that for boys. Women have fewer employment opportunities than men in rural areas: they rarely find work outside agriculture, so their lack of access to land is particularly crippling.

China has made enormous progress in gender equality, but it is still the girls who are more deprived in poor families. More than 80% of the children who dropped out of school in 1990 were girls, mostly in rural and remote mountainous areas and among minority groups. There are twice as many illiterate women as men.

In Mexico poverty is mainly rural, especially among large families. Many poor women start work in childhood as domestic servants, and with working days of up to 12 hours they cannot attend school. They tend to marry young and have children while still adolescents. In the shifts in the economic environment during the structural adjustment of the 1980s, women's wages fell from 80% of men's in 1980 to 57% in 1992.

In Russia, despite high levels of education, women are concentrated in low-wage occupations, and they were the first to be let go during the transition.

Source: Moghadam 1996.

New global pressures, creating and re-creating poverty

The dramatic changes that mark the last decades of the 20th century present many opportunities. But they also pose threats that could undermine much of the success in reducing poverty. The HDI, rising since first reported in 1990, has for the first time fallen for as many as 30 countries.

The world is rapidly changing, with the globalization and liberalization of the world economy, with the rise of new conflicts, with the spread of HIV/AIDS, with the steady deterioration of environmental resources, with demographic changes, with the failures of economic growth in Sub-Saharan Africa, Latin America and the Caribbean and the Arab States and with the transition to free market economic systems and democratic government. All this change puts added stress on the lives of people. And the people who already suffer deprivation in many aspects of their lives suffer most.

These are among the factors driving the poverty trends described in chapter 2—and shifting the poverty profile around the world (see box 2.7). Of the 30 countries with declining HDIs, 10 are in Eastern Europe and the CIS, 12 are in Sub-Saharan Africa, and the rest are spread among other regions. The main reasons for these declines: falling GDP in Sub-Saharan Africa, Latin America and the Caribbean and the transition economies and falling life expectancy due to armed conflict and HIV/AIDS.

Conflicts and displaced persons

The casualties of conflict still represent only a small proportion of the world's poor people. But 9 of the 30 countries whose HDI values declined are among those with a deadly, population-displacing conflict.

The end of the cold war settled several long-standing disputes. But there has been a steady rise in the number of conflicts within national borders. Of the 30 armed struggles in 1995, none was a war between states. Instead, they were civil wars, guerrilla wars, separatist movements and ethnic violence over territory or government. In the past five years at least 1 million people have died from conflicts.

Wars strike poor households and communities because they strike civilian populations at large. Past battles were often between standing armies, but wars today affect primarily civilians. During the First World War few casualties were civilians—in Cambodia and Rwanda more than 90% were.

Many of the casualties are women and children. Around 2 million children died as a result of armed conflict in the past decade—partly because of the proliferation of light weapons and the indiscriminate use of land-mines. In 68 countries 110 million land-mines lie undetonated.

The poor are also exposed because modern wars are fought mainly in poorer countries—all of today's conflicts are in developing countries or in Eastern Europe and the CIS. Even when people flee the fighting, they take refuge in neighbouring, equally poor countries.

In 1995 there were 46 million displaced people—one in every 120 people in the

---

BOX 3.4

Gender, poverty and property rights in South Asia

In most of South Asia the majority of poor women depend on agriculture for their livelihood—even more than men, who have broader opportunities. In rural India in 1993–94, 86% of women workers were in agriculture, compared with 74% of men.

But few women own or control land—and this handicaps them in warding off poverty for themselves and their families. Lack of access to land is especially critical for the 20% or so of rural households in Bangladesh and India that are headed by women as a result of widowhood, desertion or male migration.

Many factors obstruct women's access to land. Legal: inheritance laws for agricultural land favour men in many communities. Social: son preferences, patrilocal marriages and in some regions female-seclusion practices restrict women's ability to claim and manage land. And administrative: under land reform and settlement schemes land is typically distributed to male heads of household.

Land titles secure production opportunities for women, increase their bargaining power with employers and provide mortgageable or saleable assets for times of crisis. In most regions landless households tend to be more prone to poverty than those with even small plots.

Property rights for women would reduce the risk of poverty for themselves and for their families. Many studies show an antifemale bias in resource allocation within households.

Unequal access to land and property rights is widespread not just in South Asia but in all regions. In Zimbabwe the 1980 constitution did not guarantee women legal rights of joint ownership. And the land reform scheme considered only widowed women with dependents eligible, excluding women on their own—single, deserted, divorced. Land reform elsewhere, such as in China and Cuba, also left most women out.

Source: Agarwal 1996 and Folbre 1996.

FIGURE 3.1

Projected reversals in human development due to HIV/AIDS

▷ Without HIV/AIDS ▶ Accounting for HIV/AIDS

Projected life expectancy in 2010

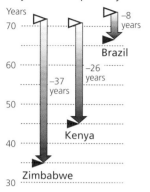

Projected child mortality in 2010

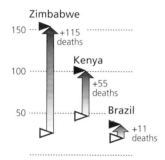

Source: Stanecki and Way 1996.

world—who had been forced to flee from home. Of them, 26 million were displaced in their own country, 16 million were refugees in other countries, and 4 million were considered "refugee-like". Of the total, 40 million were in developing countries, 6 million in industrial or transition countries. At the end of 1994, 23 countries with low human development had 50,000 refugees or more. Consider Sudan, with 4 million internally displaced people and 730,000 refugees from other countries.

The number of refugees alone has increased dramatically—from 2.5 million in 1960 to 16 million in 1995. The numbers for Asia and Eastern Europe and the CIS countries peaked in 1992–93, but the numbers continue to rise in Sub-Saharan Africa.

Conflicts in poor countries block or handicap poverty eradication efforts. Quite apart from the direct impact of widespread destruction, conflicts divert important resources from development.

In addition to those affected by warfare, many poor people fall victim to the supposedly "peaceful" alternative—economic sanctions. Although sanctions are aimed primarily at those in power in renegade regimes, the politically connected and wealthy are able to avoid much of the impact—leaving poor people to suffer most.

In Haiti during sanctions drinking water supplies were cut by half. Garbage collection ceased, and sewage treatment plants were not maintained. One study found that the price of staple foods increased fivefold and that the proportion of malnourished children increased from 5% to 23%.

In Iraq under sanctions life expectancy fell from 65 years in 1990 to 57 years in 1994. Today an estimated 30% of the population lives in human poverty.

Economic sanctions are a blunt instrument. They need to be re-evaluated as a policy choice. Sanctions can be far better targeted to the political elite by freezing bank accounts, denying travel visas and air connections, imposing arms embargoes and taking other actions that lessen the damage inflicted on the general population.

Before sanctions are imposed, their likely effect on people, especially the poor and most vulnerable groups in society, should be assessed. Ways must be found to allow imports of drugs and medical supplies and to process applications for exemptions for imports for humanitarian activities.

Poverty cannot be eliminated without progress in conflict prevention—and without addressing the special needs of the casualties. One of the main problems for poor households and communities caught up in conflict is the inadequacy of today's system of global governance—it simply was not designed for dealing with internal conflicts. Stronger and more effective international instruments and mechanisms are needed to address:

• The internally displaced who are outside the scope of the Geneva Convention.

• Rapid conflict resolution.

• Reconstruction programmes after conflict, especially demilitarization and mine removal.

• Control of arms sales, especially of arms that maim or kill civilians.

Finally, without human development, peace will continue to be threatened by poverty (box 3.5). Poverty and conflict feed each other. Economic stagnation and competition over livelihoods, resources and

---

BOX 3.5

Eradicating poverty—essential for consolidating peace

Despite much progress on the political front, Palestinians have yet to collect the elusive peace dividend. Indeed, per capita income has dropped as much as 25% since 1992. Closure of the Occupied Territories means that Palestinians cannot take jobs in the Israeli economy, and merchandise traffic in and out of the territories has been cut substantially—60% for Gaza and 40% for the West Bank. Two-thirds of the population live below the locally defined income poverty line.

With the institutions of the Palestinian Authority in place by mid-1996, tackling poverty took on renewed urgency. Poverty eradication was viewed as essential both for its development benefits and for continuation of the peace process.

With the support of the international community, the Palestinians have accomplished two urgent tasks. They launched an emergency programme to mitigate the effects of unemployment (and poverty) caused by the closure of the territories. And they set up the basic institutions of open, participatory governance.

A broader and longer-term human development strategy also is being formulated, aimed at building capacity for governance in the Palestinian Authority and at employment generation, private sector growth, gender-sensitive policymaking, rural development and the provision of health, education and housing services. These policies aim to instil hope for the future and confidence in the long-term benefits of peace.

Source: UNDP 1997.

opportunities contribute to social conflicts of all kinds—between farmers and pastoralists, between ethnic groups, between people of different religions. These conflicts feed or give rise to confrontations, civil wars, even genocide.

HIV/AIDS

The HIV/AIDS pandemic is creating a new wave of impoverishment—and reversing earlier gains. Among the 30 countries with declines in HDI values, several suffered these setbacks in part because of HIV/AIDS—Botswana, Burundi, Cameroon, Congo, Kenya, Rwanda, Togo and Zimbabwe. Botswana and Zimbabwe made huge strides during the 1970s and 1980s but have lost 5–10 years in life expectancy, bringing them back to the 1960s.

Projections to 2010 put life expectancy in Botswana at 33 years (it would have been 61 without AIDS) and in Burkina Faso at 35 years (rather than 61). Child mortality is likely to increase to 148 per 1,000 live births in Botswana (not decline to 38). In 18 of the 22 mostly Sub-Saharan African countries studied, HIV/AIDS would reduce life expectancy by at least 10 years, and in 14 it would push child mortality up by at least 50 deaths per 1,000 live births (figure 3.1). These are consequences not only of HIV/AIDS-related deaths, but also of the impact of the pandemic on development. Other diseases blight the lives of many more. Every year, malaria affects at least 500 million and kills 2 million and diarrhoea kills nearly 3 million children. But HIV/AIDS has had the most devastating impact in the decade since it hit. If unchecked, it will reverse poverty gains quickly and dramatically.

The impact of HIV/AIDS on poverty shows the two-way relationship between poverty and illness. The common perception of AIDS in the 1980s was as a disease of promiscuity and drugs in the industrial countries—there is no doubt now that AIDS is closely linked to poverty. Poverty offers a fertile breeding ground for the epidemic's spread, and infection sets off a cascade of economic and social disintegration and impoverishment.

Of the 23 million people with HIV/AIDS, 94% are in the developing world, with most in Sub-Saharan Africa (14 million) and South and South-East Asia (5.2 million) (figure 3.2). The incidence of HIV infection in poorer countries (750 per 100,000 people) is more than 10 times that in industrial countries. And the spread is faster—especially in South and South-East Asia and in Eastern Europe. Of the 3.1 million new infections among adults in 1996, 1.3 million were in Sub-Saharan Africa and 1.5 million in South and South-East Asia. The spread of HIV/AIDS has slowed in North America and Western Europe, and there is some evidence of falling rates of infection in two of the high-incidence developing countries, Thailand and Uganda.

High-income earners and elites are not spared infection. But often, as in Brazil, Thailand and Uganda, the victims are predominantly the very poorest—particularly exposed since they often lack education, information and access to social and health services. They are also most exposed to the social dislocation from rapid urbanization, civil unrest and armed conflict.

The pandemic in Latin America and the Caribbean is concentrated among the urban poor in the shanty towns of Mexico City, São Paulo and Rio de Janeiro. In the United States the rate of increase between 1989 and 1994 was 14% for white men but 61% for Hispanics and 79% for African Americans. Particularly hard hit in the United States are African American women: they make up two-thirds of all HIV-infected women, and more African American children are infected than children of all other races combined.

Women in poor communities are especially vulnerable. In most cultures they have little power to refuse sex, and if they insist on using a condom they may risk physical or economic retaliation. In societies tolerant of men's extramarital sex, women are exposed to the promiscuity of their partners.

When HIV/AIDS strikes, the effect can be catastrophic for the family. Besides the loss of income, the expense of caring for the stricken rapidly eats up the family's financial

FIGURE 3.2

HIV infection by region, 1996

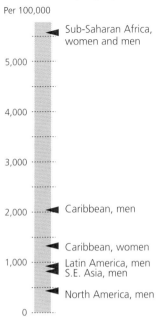

Per 100,000

Sub-Saharan Africa, women and men
Caribbean, men
Caribbean, women
Latin America, men
S.E. Asia, men
North America, men

Regional shares of people living with HIV/AIDS

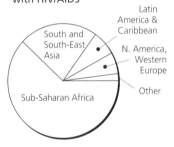

Latin America & Caribbean
South and South-East Asia
N. America, Western Europe
Sub-Saharan Africa
Other

Source: UNAIDS 1996b.

reserves. One study in rural Thailand showed that more than half of a household's income could be spent on caring for the sick. Families may have to sell such economic assets as land or cattle, deepening their poverty, or go into debt borrowing at high interest rates. They may also prejudice any escape from poverty by taking their children out of school. One of the most tragic consequences: the rising number of orphans. One study of 15 countries in Sub-Saharan Africa projects a doubling in the number of orphans by 2005—to 4.2 million.

The projected increase in child mortality is not only a result of high rates of mother to child infection at birth. The reduced capacity of a household to secure a livelihood when its productive members are sick or have died also affects the health and mortality of children. And the epidemic puts a tremendous burden on already overstretched health services, reducing the quality of care.

Stemming the spread of HIV/AIDS requires changing behaviour and strengthening the assets of people and communities to cope as well as possible. Concerted national efforts aimed at changing behaviour are beginning to show results. The involvement in policy and programmes of people living with HIV/AIDS and of the communities most affected is proving essential for effective response to the epidemic. In Thailand, which has had one of the most comprehensive campaigns to change high-risk behaviour, infection among military conscripts dropped from 3.6% to 2.5% between 1993 and 1995. Uganda has also led in prevention strategies, reducing the rate of infection among some pregnant women from 21% in the early 1990s to 15% in the mid-1990s (box 3.6).

Yet the epidemic continues to spread. In many countries it has yet to be acknowledged as a developmental problem. And tackling it means dealing with ingrained cultural values and prejudices—particularly those about women—and adopting a multisectoral strategy. The legal, ethical and human rights issues are complex. Few countries have really taken them on—with most failing even to offer voluntary and confidential HIV testing.

Most of the international effort so far has been scientific research, producing knowledge and drugs to prolong survival. But treatments at $25,000 per person a year are unimaginable for the poor. There has been little progress in bringing prevention and relief to the millions of poor individuals, households and communities most affected.

Environmental degradation on marginal lands

Almost half the world's poorest people—more than 500 million by the most conservative estimate—live on marginal lands in the Sahel and in the upper watersheds of the Andes and Himalayas. Under current policies and conditions, that number will rise to 800 million by 2020. The livelihoods of all these people are directly and acutely affected by natural resource degradation.

Marginal lands include drylands, swamps, saline lands and steep slopes (but sometimes the definition is broadened to cover all degraded or fragile areas or all areas lacking favourable natural resources and socio-economic conditions). By defini-

---

BOX 3.6

Successes in the response to HIV—Thailand and Uganda

Two of the countries most affected by HIV/AIDS—Thailand and Uganda—have also demonstrated some of the best ways to tackle the problem. Both quickly recognized that the issues are not just medical but developmental—and that the response needed to be broad and multisectoral. Surveys show that this approach is bringing results. More people are avoiding high-risk behaviour, and rates of infection are coming down for some groups. The experience in both countries demonstrates the importance of:

• *Providing political leadership*—The problem was accepted as a special responsibility of the prime minister in Thailand and of the president in Uganda. There were also appropriate budgets. Thailand spent $47 million per year—$0.80 per capita, well above India's $0.01 per capita. In addition, the subject was debated freely and openly.

• *Empowering communities*—The campaign actively involved communities and NGOs. They helped shape national policies and strategies, not just fill in gaps in government services.

• *Mobilizing employers*—A national dialogue involving government, NGOs and employers led to a consensus on the need to protect a healthy and productive workforce. Rather than discriminating against workers living with HIV, employers agreed to help deal with the economic and social consequences of the epidemic.

• *Addressing socio-economic issues*—The programmes addressed key issues affecting vulnerability, including urbanization, migration, poverty and gender disparity—as well as cross-border factors. They also focused on human rights, such as the right to confidential testing and access to basic treatment. And they addressed the special needs of children—particularly orphans.

Source: Lavollay 1996.

---

tion, the ecosystems of these areas are fragile. Soils are susceptible to erosion. Rainfall is highly unstable. The areas are often isolated, unreached by well-developed socio-economic infrastructure. And the recent environmental stresses of deforestation, prolonged droughts, erosion and dwindling surface and ground water all increase the risks for the poor and vulnerable.

These areas are by no means "marginal" for the world population. Drylands alone are home to some 1.5 billion people, 35% of the developing world's population—about 37% of the people in Asia (1.1 billion), 34% in Sub-Saharan Africa (180 million), 59% in the Arab States (140 million) and 26% in Latin America and the Caribbean (120 million).

In China almost all of the 65 million officially recognized income-poor live in remote and mountainous rural areas. In many of these villages at least half the boys and nearly all the girls do not attend school. Overall, the highest incidence of poverty occurs in arid zones. A recent study of 10 Sahelian countries showed human poverty worsening from wetter to drier zones; the HPI is only 26% in humid zones but soars to 61% in arid zones (figure 3.3).

The links between environmental degradation and poverty—in all its dimensions—are thus strong and complex. Progress in eradicating poverty needs actions to reverse two trends.

First, the growing claims on common property resources are making the poor even less secure, and population pressure is adding to the demands. Such resources—not just water, fuel and grazing areas but also nuts, berries and medicinal herbs—are particularly important in the most arid zones, providing livelihoods for many of the very poorest in a community. A study in seven states in India showed that the poorest families derived 15–25% of their income from these resources.

With traditional social structures weakened by social change, traditional rights are not always upheld and protected. Conflicts between farmers and herders are proliferating in Africa, Asia and elsewhere. Market forces also put pressure on common property resources, and policies protect neither

the environment nor the poor. In Brazil a tax exemption for agricultural land made it attractive for rich groups to buy and cut forests, adding to the impoverishment of those depending on the forests.

Second, low levels of agricultural productivity combine with population growth and marginal lands to create a downward spiral, particularly in Sub-Saharan Africa. There, population growth has outstripped growth in agricultural production, which averaged about 2% a year in 1965–80, then 1.8% in the 1980s. Food imports rose by 185% between 1974 and 1990, food aid by 295%.

Growing populations have led to such environmentally damaging adaptations as overgrazing, shortened fallow periods and the extension of cultivation onto rangelands and slopes. People fleeing drought, armed conflict and economic downturns in cities also add to the pressure. And environmental degradation creates incentives to have larger families.

What is needed to reverse these trends? One key is much higher priority for technological progress in agricultural systems that can intensify production and lessen stresses on the environment. In the Machakos District in Kenya, the population has been growing fast, but poverty has nevertheless declined and pressure on the environment has eased. Intensive action and investment in development overall—especially to improve productivity and the sustainability of the environment—are the reason. Paradoxically, the increases in population—and thus in the labour force—permitted the adoption of labour-intensive conservation measures. Elsewhere in Kenya and in Burkina Faso, Burundi and Nigeria, people also have found environmentally sustainable solutions.

Such experiences show that marginal areas need not be marginal for development. They can support large populations, and investing in these areas is not an economic loss.

Poverty in marginal ecological zones needs greater policy attention. Investment in sustainable technology should rise to the top of the international and national research agendas, which have so far favoured production in resource-rich areas.

More than 500 million of the world's poorest people live on marginal lands

FIGURE 3.3

Poverty increases as rainfall decreases

HPI for 10 countries in the West African Sahel (percent)

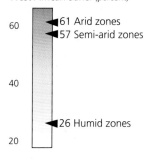

61 Arid zones
57 Semi-arid zones

26 Humid zones

Source: WRI 1996a.

It is time to shift attention from resource-rich to resource-poor people's livelihoods, from rice and wheat to millet and sorghum, from irrigated systems to low-rainfall, integrated-livelihood systems (box 3.7)

The second green revolution—technology for sustainable development on marginal lands

The technological force behind the reduction of rural poverty has been the development of high-yielding varieties now widely used in developing countries—on 74% of areas growing rice, 70% wheat and 57% maize. The varieties are especially widespread in China, India, South-East Asia and the Pacific and many parts of Latin America and the Caribbean where advances have been made in reducing rural poverty.

But the same technological breakthroughs have not occurred for crops like sorghum, millet and cassava—the staple crops grown by poor farmers, consumed by poor people and grown on less productive marginal lands. Investments are needed to develop the technology for the poor farmer's green revolution.

Yields for these crops have grown only slowly in contrast to the dramatic rise for wheat, rice and maize (box figure 3.7). This is part of the story of lagging agricultural production and rural poverty in Africa, where increases in production and yields have been slowing and falling behind population growth.

The second green revolution—for poor farmers on marginal lands—should not be a copy of the first. It should aim at environmental sustainability, low-cost inputs and higher returns for small-scale holdings—and at minimizing risk for poor farmers. It should focus less on crops and more on systems, on finding ways to diversify production and use the range of natural resources available. It should focus on tree crops, agroforestry and mixed livestock, pasture and crops. The revolution must learn from indigenous systems developed over centuries that have enabled people to survive in the most hostile and fragile environments. It must also consolidate the community's capacity for collective action and bolster social capital.

BOX FIGURE 3.7

Poor people's food crops have benefited little from advances in technology

Yields in 1990–94 indexed to 1970–74
1970–74=100

Source: CGIAR 1996.

A serious obstacle to poverty reduction is the inadequate effort made so far to develop technologies for marginal lands—only a quarter of international agricultural research resources have been devoted to marginal lands. Researchers are attracted to more profitable activities, especially biotechnology for industrial countries. Higher priority is also required at the national level. All countries that had technological breakthroughs had well-functioning national research systems that emphasized major food staples. Sri Lanka in 1966–83 successfully directed research to small farmers and lagging zones. In Africa the parlous state of agricultural research is a serious obstacle to poverty-reducing growth.

Source: Broca and Ohram 1991 and Lipton 1996a.

Changing demographic structures

One of the most dramatic changes of the 20th century in developing countries, the demographic transition—from high birth and death rates to low birth and death rates—brings rapid increases in population size and density. It also changes the age structure of the population and of families. And in the process it can either help or handicap the escape from poverty.

Early in the transition—with many more children than adults and rapid population growth—the demographic structure handicaps poverty reduction. It weakens the potential for savings. It reduces the resources for improving health and education. And it puts pressure on natural resources. It also weakens women's health, equality and autonomy—because women end up with reduced options for education and income-earning work.

The situation reverses later in the transition, when the age structure is less heavily weighted towards the very young. Adults with fewer or older children can save more, pay more taxes and have more time for productive activities—and improve their health and skills.

A large and dense population can also contribute to poverty reduction. Some areas in Sub-Saharan Africa suffer from low population densities that make it very expensive per capita to provide infrastructure and services. A larger and more concentrated population can increase demand and generate trade. More important, it stimulates creativity and innovation—and speeds improvements in access to basic services.

Countries in the later stages of the transition have succeeded most in bringing down mass poverty—the greatest number of them in East Asia and South-East Asia and the Pacific, and in South Asia and Latin America and the Caribbean. Fertility rates remain high in Sub-Saharan Africa, the Arab States and South Asia (figure 3.4). Differences between rich and poor groups are similar across countries. Brazil's average annual population growth rate was 2.6% during 1955–95—though 1.6% for the half initially richer and 3.2% for the half initially poorer.

Why do poor parents see large families as advantageous or even necessary for survival? The need for children to support parents in old age and the security that comes from having many children when many die in childhood are well known. Less well understood is the need for more children in households that face demands on time just for survival.

Children in the poorest families are often out of school and working from a very young age, as young as five. They do the work that their mothers lack the time to perform. In rural areas where environmental degradation adds to the time needed to fetch water and fuel, a solution for already overworked women is to have more children. In dry seasons women spend up to five hours a day on these tasks in Africa and India. Women are already time-poor, and having more children, especially girls, can ease the load.

Under these circumstances, having many children builds assets and reduces vulnerability. Thus it is a rational coping strategy in the face of acute time shortage. It secures survival even if it means reducing opportunities for education and savings—two key means for households to work their way out of poverty. High fertility is thus a brake on escape from poverty in the long term and a coping strategy for building assets for the poor family in the short term.

Accelerating the demographic transition will help speed poverty reduction, especially in much of Sub-Saharan Africa, South Asia and the Arab States, where fertility rates among younger women continue to be high.

Accelerating the transition means creating conditions that encourage parents to have fewer children. Better health conditions mean more children survive. Expanding employment opportunities encourage parents to invest in the education of each child.

Even more important is to relieve the constraints on women's time and promote a greater role for them in household decision-making—and to educate girls, the single most important factor associated with lower fertility.

Failures of economic growth

Economic growth can be a powerful means to eradicate poverty. It can raise the productivity and incomes of poor people, expanding opportunities and choices in a variety of ways. Sustained national GDP growth, combined with rising wages and productivity, was an important part of the historic ascent from poverty, in the industrial countries—and in the past 30 years in such countries as China, Indonesia and Malaysia, which have dramatically reduced poverty in income and other critical dimensions.

But these successes contrast with present realities. In too many countries growth has failed to reduce poverty, either because growth has been too slow or stagnant or because its quality and structure have been insufficiently pro-poor.

And there is controversy about the importance of economic growth to poverty reduction. Growth optimists point out that poverty usually declines more quickly in faster-growing countries and that most of the poor gain almost everywhere during periods of rapid growth. Growth pessimists point to the damage that adjustments that facilitate growth can cause, particularly to the disruptions that harm the poor—including shifts in employment patterns, changing prices and environmental pollution.

In fact, both optimists and pessimists have a case. Economic growth does contribute to poverty reduction, but there are still losers from the adjustments that growth requires. And economic growth explains only about half of poverty reduction. The rest depends on good policy to harness the growth for poverty reduction.

Having no economic growth is almost entirely bad for poor people. Without economic growth, it is almost never possible to reduce income poverty, and even advances against other aspects of human poverty, such as illiteracy or child mortality, cannot be sustained without economic growth (box 3.8).

The war between growth optimists and pessimists is both phony and counterproductive. It detracts attention from the much more important issues for poverty reduction:

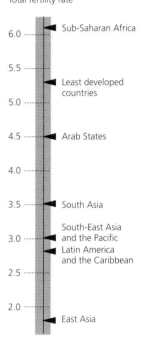

FIGURE 3.4
Fertility rate by region, 1994

Total fertility rate

6.0 — Sub-Saharan Africa

5.5

5.0 — Least developed countries

4.5 — Arab States

4.0

3.5 — South Asia

3.0 — South-East Asia and the Pacific
— Latin America and the Caribbean

2.5

2.0 — East Asia

Source: UN 1996b.

The phony war between growth optimists and growth pessimists

Isn't economic growth, as many ask, bad for poor people? Growth pessimists emphasize how particular groups have become poor because of changes accompanying growth—shifts in employment patterns, environmental pollution, social dislocation and cultural destruction. Growth optimists emphasize how economic growth has boosted the incomes of poor families.

Both are right.

Growth typically helps poor families increase their incomes. Careful review of evidence on income distribution and poverty available for the first time in many countries shows that in most places and times, faster growth is associated with proportionate gains in income for all income groups, including the poorest. Correspondingly, during periods of economic decline, everyone loses. Moreover, as *Human Development Report 1996* showed, economic growth does not have to increase income inequalities.

But there is wide variation in how well growth reduces poverty—and some exceptions. A recent review of 95 time periods around the world shows that the income of the poor generally improved during periods of growth. But in some cases it worsened. And in two cases the income of the poor improved during periods of economic decline (box table 3.8.1).

Another analysis, looking at 59 nationwide household surveys, shows wide variation in the incidence of income poverty for countries with similar levels of income (box table 3.8.2). International variation in average private consumption is associated with 50% of the variation in the incidence of poverty. With average income of $114–$130 a month, the predicted incidence of poverty would be 6–7%. But six countries with this level of income

had an incidence of poverty ranging from 2% to 26%.

Even if growth helps the vast majority of poor people, some become worse off. Growth inevitably induces changes and adjustments that harm the poor—reductions in government employment, social services and expenditures. In some countries even efficient market-led growth—such as technical progress or trade expansion—reduces demand for unskilled workers. In South Asia people with little education but specific skills in craft production are sidelined by technical progress. In these dislocations it is often the less educated, adaptable and mobile who lose—but also those who have less political and social clout, especially women.

Even less automatic are the links between economic growth and reduction in other aspects of human poverty—such as illiteracy, a short life span, ill health, lack of personal security.

Distribution, government policies and public provision hugely affect the translation of a given level of consumption—and probably its growth—into poverty reduction.

BOX TABLE 3.8.2
Growth explains only part of poverty reduction
Countries with average private consumption of $114–$130 a month

Country	Population below the $1-a-day poverty line (%) 1989–93
Panama	26
South Africa	24
Mexico	15
Bolivia	7
Turkmenistan	5
Lithuania	2

Source: Lipton 1996d and UNDP 1997.

BOX TABLE 3.8.1
Economic growth normally helps people escape from consumption poverty but neither worsens nor helps equality

Indicator	Periods of growth (88) Improved	Periods of growth (88) Worsened	Periods of decline (7) Improved	Periods of decline (7) Worsened
Inequality	45	43	2	5
Income of the poor	77	11	2	5

Source: Deininger and Squire 1996.

• How to accelerate growth.
• How to forge a pattern of growth that promotes poverty reduction—pro-poor growth.

The need to accelerate growth

A serious obstacle to reducing mass absolute poverty in recent decades has been economic stagnation and decline. While Asia achieved poverty reduction with high growth, in other regions both growth and poverty reduction have been slow or negative. In 97 of 166 countries, per capita incomes in 1994 were lower than the peaks before 1990—in 37 of them before 1970.

How much does growth need to be raised to make substantial inroads into income poverty? A recent study estimates that a 20% drop in the proportion of people living on less than $1 a day requires about a 10% increase in mean income. This implies that per capita GDP growth of 3% a year would be needed to halve the incidence of poverty in a decade.

The 3% rate is far higher than the growth rates in countries with mass poverty, except in East Asia, where per capita growth was 12.4% in 1990–94, and South-East Asia and the Pacific, where it was 5.1%. Per capita growth was negative in Sub-Saharan Africa (–2.4%) and the Arab States (–4.5%) and very low in Latin America and the Caribbean (1.3%).

After the "lost decade" of the 1980s, the 1990s are thought to be a decade of recovery. But the recovery has been slow, reaching too few countries. Thirty countries had a growth rate averaging 3% per capita or more over 1990–94. And projections to 1997 show the number falling to 24 countries, 14 of them in Asia (table 3.1).

To halve poverty in even 20 years would still require a dramatic acceleration in economic growth beyond current rates. In Sub-Saharan Africa, for example, annual per capita growth would have to be 1.4%, compared with the –2.4% in 1990–94.

Promoting pro-poor growth

Economic growth, though essential for poverty reduction, is not enough. Growth must be pro-poor, expanding the opportunities and life choices of poor people. Economic growth contributes most to poverty reduction when it expands the employment, productivity and wages of poor people—and when public resources are spent to promote human development. *Human Development Report 1996* showed how a virtuous cycle of economic growth and human development takes over when the pattern of growth is labour-using and employment-generating—and when there are rapid improvements in human skills and health. In fact, reducing poverty can be good for growth (box 3.9).

Another important condition is initial equality. Income poverty is reduced more quickly where equality is greater. Recent studies have estimated that annual per capita GDP growth of 10% would reduce the incidence of income poverty by 30% in relatively egalitarian societies, with a Gini coefficient of 0.25, and by only 10% in less equal societies, with a Gini coefficient of 0.50.

Growth does not help poverty reduction when big chunks of GDP go out of the country in public spending that neither advances human development nor benefits the poor—such as to pay international debt or purchase weapons.

How effectively economic growth is channelled to improving the incomes of the poorest can be seen by comparing the growth of average per capita income with the growth of the incomes of the poorest 20%. In Brazil in 1971–89, real GNP per capita grew by 3.1% annually, but the income of the poorest 20% grew by only 0.8%. In 1968–88 in the United Kingdom, GNP per capita grew by 2.2%—the income of the poorest 20% by only 0.3%. Sweden also had 2.2% growth in that period, but the income of the poorest 20% grew by 6.3% (figure 3.5). No wonder income poverty in the United Kingdom rose from 9% to 15% during the 1980s.

Comparisons of per capita GDP with the incidence of poverty—as measured both by the headcount index of income poverty and by the HPI—also show how well countries have translated economic growth into poverty eradication. At similar GDP per capita levels, Honduras has almost three times the proportion of people in income poverty (below the $1-a-day PPP cut-off line) as Indonesia, Ecuador four times as much as Colombia, and South Africa five times as much as Malaysia.

Some countries have used GDP growth much more effectively than others to reduce human poverty. In Namibia human poverty affects four times the proportion of people (45%) as in Jordan (11%), though GDP per capita in the two countries is

Growth does not help poverty reduction when big chunks of GDP go out of the country

TABLE 3.1
Countries with per capita GDP growth of 3% or more

Region	Number of countries 1990–94	Number of countries 1995–97	Regional per capita growth (%) 1990–94
East Asia	3	3	12.4
South-East Asia and the Pacific	8	7	5.1
South Asia	4	4	2.1
Latin America and the Caribbean	7	2	1.3
Sub-Saharan Africa	5	5	–2.4
Arab States	2	2	–4.5
Developing countries	30	24	4.5
Eastern Europe and the CIS	0	5	–9.1

Source: Human Development Report Office.

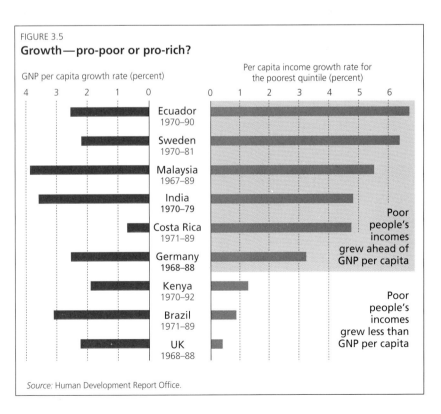

FIGURE 3.5
Growth—pro-poor or pro-rich?

Source: Human Development Report Office.

about the same. Similar contrasts abound. Cambodia and Sierra Leone have human poverty twice as widespread as that in Viet Nam, though all three countries have per capita incomes that are among the lowest in the world (figure 3.6).

Similarly, among countries with incomes of around $2,500–$3,000, Bolivia, China and the Philippines reduced human poverty to less than 20%, while in the Lao People's Democratic Republic and Papua New Guinea the HPI is more than 30%.

These comparisons need to be viewed in historical perspective. The HPI need not be read as a reflection of poor government commitment today. Namibia's high HPI, indicating more widespread poverty than in countries with similar levels of human development, reflects the legacies of its pre-independence past.

Another way of seeing how growth affects poverty is to consider the growth elasticity of poverty reduction. The higher the elasticity, the better—the more each percentage point of growth will reduce poverty. Countries in Sub-Saharan Africa and Latin America and the Caribbean have some of the lowest elasticities—0.2 in Zambia, 0.8 in Senegal and elsewhere, 0.7

in Guatemala and Honduras and 0.9 in Brazil and Panama. At the other end of the scale is East Asia, where the elasticities tend to be well above 2—for Indonesia 2.8, for Malaysia 3.4 and for rural China 3.0. Poverty reduction in East Asia benefited from fast growth and from pro-poor growth. Of 11 countries in Asia with data, 9 had elasticities of 2 or higher. Of 15 countries in Sub-Saharan Africa, only one had an elasticity above 1. Among countries of Latin America and the Caribbean the record is mixed, with elasticities ranging from less than 1 to 5.

Economic growth has brought big gains in poverty reduction in Indonesia, the Republic of Korea and Malaysia since the 1970s. Their growth strategies expanded economic opportunities for poor people, with relatively equitable distribution of financial and physical capital, including land. And the resources generated by economic growth were heavily channelled into human development, especially into improving health, education and skills.

In China policy shifts in 1978 favouring small-scale agriculture drove the acceleration of both growth and poverty reduction. But in the late 1980s policies shifted to favour industry, and poverty reduction began to lag and inequality to increase. To redress this situation China introduced an aggressive antipoverty programme, again emphasizing rural development (see pages 49–50).

The key elements of a pro-poor growth strategy naturally depend on the situation in a country. But everywhere, an essential precondition is to make poverty eradication a priority objective of the national development strategy. Malaysia demonstrates the success that can be achieved by integrating poverty as a major consideration in sectoral and national development strategies—and by setting targets for reducing the number of people living below a nationally defined poverty line (box 3.10). Other important priorities for most developing countries include:
• Raising the productivity of small-scale agriculture.
• Promoting microenterprises and the informal sector.
• Emphasizing labour-intensive industrialization to expand opportunities.

FIGURE 3.6

Similar incomes, different progress in reducing human poverty

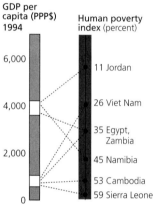

Source: Lipton 1996d.

• Accelerating the expansion of human capabilities.

• Establishing a pro-poor economic policy framework.

Raising the productivity of small-scale agriculture. The majority of poor people—about three-quarters in most developing countries—depend on agriculture for their livelihoods, either as smallholders or as labourers. Growth in smallholder agricultural productivity was a major factor in poverty reduction in China in 1978–85, in Indonesia and Malaysia in 1970–80 and in Japan, the Republic of Korea and Taiwan (province of China) in the 1950s and 1960s.

Improving the productivity of small-scale agriculture does more than benefit the farmers. It also creates employment on the farm and off—and reduces food prices. The poor benefit most because around 70% of their consumption is food, mostly staples—and regular supplies and stable prices create food security.

Growth that has neglected agriculture has done little for the poor. In Brazil the rapid growth of the 1950s and early 1960s emphasized capital-intensive industrialization, bringing few benefits to the poor. During the same period in India, states with fast industrial growth saw little change in either rural or urban poverty—those with fast services growth did better, and those with fast agricultural growth did best of all.

Some critical policy conditions for this small-farmer strategy: technological progress, good price policies and access to land.

The green revolution helped millions of small farmers and urban food buyers escape poverty. But these breakthroughs were for wheat, rice and maize grown in fairly good farming conditions. Much less progress has been made for "poor farmer crops", such as millet, sorghum and cassava, and "poor farmer conditions", where rainfall is low and uncertain, the soil salty or poorly drained (see box 3.7).

Prices are too often biased against agriculture. The most common problem is an overvalued exchange rate, which reduces the cost of capital imports and biases agriculture towards capital-intensive technologies that use little labour. Another problem for agriculture is export taxes. The solution

is not to subsidize agriculture, since the subsidies would be pocketed by richer farmers. Better to free markets and remove their biases against the poor.

Malaysia mainstreams poverty reduction

In 1970 about 60% of the Malaysian population was reckoned to be living below the income poverty line. This fell to 21% by 1985 and to 14% in 1993, and the target is 7% for 2000. Malaysia has mainstreamed poverty reduction as an explicit objective of its national development strategy.

The initial stimulus for this strategy came from tragic but fortunately short-lived ethnic riots in 1969 combined with election results that dramatically reduced the strength of the ruling coalition. These events made clear the inadequacy of the laissez faire, trickle-down development strategy that had been followed since independence and that had widened income differences even while achieving 6% growth in the 1960s.

In 1971 the government introduced a new economic policy combining clear goals for growth with equity, active government participation in the economy and "consistent pragmatism" in macroeconomic policy. Although viewed at the time with apprehension by some pro-market economists (including the Harvard advisory team), the new strategy both accelerated economic growth and reduced inequality. Growth reached an average rate of 6.7% in 1971–90, while the Gini coefficient fell from 0.513 to 0.445. The income share of the poorest 40% of the population rose from 11.5% to 13.8%. Key parts of the strategy:

Industrialization and export diversification. Between 1970 and 1994 the share of manufactures in exports grew from 12% to 77%, and industrial production rose from 14% to 32% of total production while agriculture fell from 29% to 15%.

Rural development. Special efforts were made to increase rural productivity through innovative programmes, including resettlement of the landless, rehabilitation and consolidation of land, downstream processing of farm goods and industrial and vocational training for rural manpower and

youths to enable and encourage them to become employed in non-farm occupations.

Employment-led urban development. The urban strategy focused on expanding opportunities for self-employment in the informal sector. It also supported labour-intensive public works to alleviate high youth unemployment. And it provided tax exemptions for foreign and domestic companies employing more than 50 workers. Employment more than doubled, and the unemployment rate fell from 8% in 1970 to less than 3% in 1994.

Partnership between the private sector and the state. The 1980s brought some policy shifts assigning the private sector the role of engine of growth. Malaysia patterned its policy on the Japanese model, building and sustaining a close working relationship between the public and private sectors to attract foreign direct investment.

In 1988 attention turned to the needs of the poorest of the poor, with the Development Programme for the Hard-Core Poor. The hard-core poor include many Malaysians in rural areas, the Orang Asli in peninsular Malaysia and some of the indigenous people in Sabah and Sarawak.

The programme focuses on increasing employability and incomes, improving housing, ensuring food supplements for children, and providing educational assistance and interest-free loans to purchase shares in a unit trust. Hard-core poverty (less than half the official poverty line) fell to 7% in 1983 and to 3% in 1993 and is set to be virtually eradicated by 2000.

Vision 2020, a long-term perspective adopted in 1990, sees Malaysia becoming a caring society, economically just, dynamic and robust. The eradication of poverty is thus underlined with an important and explicit focus on values (religious, spiritual, moral, ethical and democratic) in the Malaysian concept of development.

Source: Malaysia Economic Planning Unit 1994.

It may also be necessary to manage food stocks and prices in favour of the poor, particularly when harvests are bad. India responded to the drought of 1987–88 with relief works offering employment and food. But it failed to respond similarly in 1992–93, and food prices rose significantly—hurting the urban poor and the rural poor who were net buyers of food.

One of the keys to well-distributed growth is well-distributed land. Asian economies have shown this, though they have achieved equitable distribution in different ways. Indonesia started with relatively equal land distribution, though it has also relocated people from crowded Java to relieve population pressure. Malaysia too has settled hundreds of thousands of poor farmers on new plantations—at great cost. Japan, the Republic of Korea and Taiwan (province of China) all based their development on more formal programmes of land reform. And China first created large communes and later, in 1978–84, converted the commune land to family farms.

For India land reform has been less of a priority—perhaps because most of the rural poor have access to some land. Nevertheless, distribution is very unequal, and only a couple of states have made progress in redistributing land.

Promoting microenterprises and the informal sector. If not on agriculture, most poor people in developing countries depend for their incomes on the informal sector—typically microenterprises in services, manufacturing and trading, in both rural and urban areas. People all over the world have shown their creativity and energy in exploiting market opportunities in the informal sector. But rarely do governments create an environment favourable to microenterprises. Rarely do they provide access to financial credit and savings mechanisms. Rarely, security of housing rights. And rarely, improved infrastructure, especially for water, energy and roads. All are ingredients critical to successful microenterprise.

Microenterprises are the incubators for industrialization. East Asian economies reduced poverty through agricultural intensification first, then through labour-intensive industrial development.

These countries followed Japan in having poverty reduction follow employment-creating growth. Even in this highly industrialized country, by far the majority of the workers outside agriculture—80% in the 1950s and 50% today—are either self-employed or work in small and medium-size industries employing fewer than 100 people. Deliberate government policies to improve the productivity of these small firms had a big part in the pro-poor economic growth of the 1970s. A critical factor is equitable access to low-cost institutional credit (box 3.11).

Emphasizing labour-intensive industrialization. How much economic growth expands the employment opportunities of people depends on its pattern and structure. As *Human Development Report 1996* showed, economic growth can expand opportunities rapidly but can also be "jobless". Focusing growth strategies on labour-intensive activities—textiles, clothing, electronics—and intensifying small-scale agriculture were important to the success of East Asian economies in achieving high growth, full employment and rising wages.

Elsewhere, industrialization has brought fewer benefits for the poor. Brazil, India and Mexico have industrialized without substantially reducing poverty—mainly because

---

BOX 3.11

Beyond microcredit to credit reform and a pro-poor financial sector

Providing credit through specialized microcredit institutions targeting poor families is one way to achieve more equitable access to financial services.

A well-known example of such institutions is the Grameen Bank in Bangladesh, now providing credit to more than 2 million people, mostly women, with a default rate of only 2–3%.

Japan established specialized credit schemes and institutions in the 1950s and 1960s, such as the People's Finance Corporation, the Small Business Finance Corporation and the credit guarantee scheme. Since the mid-1970s a financial market organized by private banks has gradually developed for small and medium-size enterprises. They now account for about 70% of the lending of city banks in Japan.

A second way is to facilitate savings. The introduction of the postal savings system in Japan, and then in the Republic of Korea, Malaysia and Singapore, gave many poor people the access to finance and services they needed to seize market opportunities.

A third way is to free up financial markets. Excessive regulation can result in an antipoor bias by increasing transaction costs and reinforcing the tendency towards a few large loans rather than many small loans.

A fourth solution is to link commercial financial markets and microfinance institutions.

Source: Genda 1997 and von Pischke 1996.

they distorted prices, interest rates and exchange rates to favour capital-intensive investment. Reinforcing this tendency were labour laws and policies favouring workers fortunate enough to have jobs in the formal sector. These workers have enjoyed considerable job security and above-market wage rates. Unwilling to extend these expensive privileges to others, employers have avoided taking on more staff, investing instead in labour-saving technology.

Accelerating the expansion of human capabilities. Not only ends for reducing human poverty, rapid improvements in human capabilities and economic growth can be mutually reinforcing. When a good share of the resources generated by economic growth are channeled to human development, and when the pattern of economic growth generates demand for increasing skills, a virtuous spiral of growth and human development, of reduction in income poverty and human poverty, results. As *Human Development Report 1996* showed, Indonesia, the Republic of Korea and Malaysia all followed this model. Countries that invested less in human development, such as Egypt and Pakistan, are left with a large backlog of human poverty.

Establishing a pro-poor economic policy framework. Rather than tack antipoverty measures on as a palliative afterthought, countries need to make poverty eradication an explicit objective of economic policy. All countries share a desire to maintain a stable macroeconomic environment—low inflation, low deficits in national budgets and the balance of payments—and to ensure an economic structure that keeps them competitive in the world economy. And most countries have been facing the need to adjust—by changing their patterns of public spending, investment and output—to achieve these objectives in a changing global environment.

Is structural adjustment with growth and poverty reduction possible? In the 1980s many developing countries tackled macroeconomic imbalances. A handful of countries did manage to adjust, improve macroeconomic balances, become more competitive in world markets and also achieve growth and poverty reduction—

including Chile, Colombia, Indonesia and to some extent Ghana. But many more did not manage to recover and grow for a protracted period—and are still struggling to restore steady economic growth.

Stabilization policies can contribute to the contraction of economic activity and can work against growth. In countries where the public sector is dominant, reducing public expenditures has a ripple effect. Many small contractors and suppliers for anything from road construction to paper go into debt as business dries up and as the government fails to pay. (The internal debt in many African countries is also significant.)

Freeing markets should expand the opportunities for entrepreneurs—but for many, especially the poorest, the market does not ensure equal access to the opportunities that the new policies should bring—or to the infrastructure needed to take advantage of the opportunities. In both Sub-Saharan Africa and the transition economies the responses to market incentives have been uneven.

New forms of adjustment are needed that promote both growth and poverty reduction. Adjustment through reallocation and growth rather than adjustment through contraction is one option to explore. This means maintaining investments in human, physical and natural resources but reallocating them to activities that respond to market opportunities.

The positive experiences of the past two decades show the potential for maintaining expansionary rather than recessionary policies, and the important role of high expenditures for human priority concerns—primary education and health, low-cost water supply and sanitation. Market-oriented reform in China, Indonesia and Viet Nam show that adjustment, poverty reduction and growth can go together (box 3.12).

Unemployment, welfare restructuring and social exclusion in industrial countries

Although poverty is considered eradicated or reduced to a minimum in industrial countries, they have been experiencing "new poverty" in recent years. The slow-

New forms of adjustment are needed that promote both growth and poverty reduction

Pro-poor structural adjustment

Poor people living in countries under-taking stabilization and structural adjustment since the 1980s have had widely contrasting experiences. Some countries—such as Colombia, Costa Rica, Indonesia, the Republic of Korea and Malaysia—managed to achieve not only stabilization but also growth combined with improvements in income and social indicators for the poor. But in such countries as Brazil, Tanzania and Zambia the number of poor people grew, inequalities between rich and poor groups were exacerbated, and poor people suffered a decline in access to critical social services—schools, water supplies and health centres. The policy lessons:

Adjustment with growth through expansionary macroeconomic policies. Likely to involve a more gradual process of reducing fiscal imbalances, this approach emphasizes promoting exports rather than cutting imports, and switching or restructuring investments. Ghana and Indonesia are positive examples of this approach, Mexico and Sierra Leone negative ones. External finance helps, including aid flows, private flows and debt concessions.

Pro-poor structural changes. Many countries that reduced poverty while adjusting promoted structural changes to increase the access of poor people to the opportunities of growth and development. Colombia, Costa Rica, Indonesia, Malaysia and Paraguay increased equality. But Chile, Côte d'Ivoire, Uruguay and

rural Thailand reduced income poverty but not inequality.

Pro-poor meso policies to protect expenditures on social services and physical infrastructure. Social services for the poor can improve rather than deteriorate during adjustment if budgets are balanced by raising revenue rather than cutting spending and allocations focus on priorities. In Ghana improved tax collection more than doubled revenues—from 5% of GDP in 1983 to 12% by 1990. Social spending could then be increased, and real per capita expenditure on education rose by 51% and that on health by 66%.

Avoid user charges except for the better off. User charges often deny access to basic services for the poor. While Colombia, Costa Rica, Indonesia and Malaysia did not resort to user charges, others did—and found that the poor suffered and revenue rose little. In Zimbabwe attendance at rural clinics fell by a quarter.

Emergency support policies. During economic decline and stabilization, emergency support can enable people to secure minimum living standards, prevent malnutrition and keep children in school, avoiding a downward spiral into chronic poverty. Successful policies include employment schemes such as AGETIP in Senegal, pensions for the incapacitated and the aged, nutrition interventions such as the targeted food subsidy scheme in Chile and drought relief as in Zimbabwe.

Source: Stewart 1995a.

down in economic growth in the 1980s is often blamed for this new poverty. But how economic growth affects poverty depends on the pattern of growth as much in these countries as it does in China or Mali. Mainstreaming poverty eradication as a priority goal of national economic policies is as relevant in industrial as in developing countries.

Many of the forces of globalization—the information revolution, the new pattern and scale of trade, financial deregulation—are transforming industrial economies, to the detriment of many of the poor. These forces are reshaping the labour market, de-emphasizing unskilled, rigid and production-line employment and boosting growth in jobs that put a premium on education, skills, mobility and flexibility.

A key priority for pro-poor economic policy is to secure employment for all people. Unemployment is at a postwar high in many countries—in early 1997 even Germany had 12% unemployment—and growing in most OECD countries. In 1995 it ranged from 3% in Japan to 23% in Spain, affecting 36 million people. Most affected are women, ethnic minorities and the youth. Many young people have never held a job.

Unemployment contributes to social exclusion. Jobs and incomes are not just an economic necessity—they are a way of participating in community life. As the significance of family and community has faded, work has become the primary space for interacting with others and for establishing an identity.

A related problem is the growing poverty of many in work. With the labour market fragmented, jobs for the relatively unskilled have been available only at falling real wages. Real wages have been cut by making jobs part time, temporary, insecure—or just low paid. At the bottom of the labour market, low-paid jobs have grown—offering a wage income so far below the median that people with such jobs qualify for supplements. In all countries women are particularly affected (figure 3.7).

Among OECD countries the issues and responses vary in intensity and character. In the United States unemployment remains relatively low, and the problem is more one of low wages and the "working poor". Social welfare programmes have been under attack, hitting children and the elderly particularly hard. Today a quarter of US children are in households below the poverty line. Indeed, in most industrial countries children are poor in disproportionate numbers. About half or more of the children in single-parent households are below the poverty line in Australia, Canada, the United Kingdom and the United States—but only 5% in Finland and 8% in Sweden.

Most of the policy responses to poverty in the industrial countries have focused on upgrading labour, through better education or retraining, or offering employers subsidies to take on the long-term unemployed. Little is being done to increase the demand for labour through pro-poor growth policies.

Budgets in all countries are under immense pressure. Partly this is the price of failure: most countries are burdened by the high costs of unemployment payments. But it is also deliberate policy: governments, particularly those in the European Union aiming to meet the Maastricht criteria, have concentrated on keeping inflation low, reducing public debt and stabilizing exchange rates. The race to fulfil the criteria for a single currency has meant separate and damaging deflationary policy in each EU country. These policies all contribute to further impoverishment and are matters of public choice.

What needs to be done? Welfare provisions need to be rethought. But poverty reduction also needs to be mainstreamed into economic policies, as in poor countries. Four actions should be considered:

1. Reaffirm the commitment to full employment. Inflation is now everywhere—partly because of increased competition and globalization. In Europe the Maastricht Treaty should add to its convergence conditions full employment and growth. Low inflation, by itself, does not generate growth or full employment.

2. Renew the commitment to a redistributive strategy to eliminate poverty in the rich countries. The pressures of globalization make this even more imperative. To compete globally, the rich countries need a healthier, better-educated, more productive citizenry. Part of the strategy to reduce poverty should be a restructuring of taxation, to raise thresholds and free the low paid from income tax liability while raising the basic rate for the better paid, who have been receiving a disproportionately large share of recent income gains. A fairer tax system would command greater public support.

3. Change the structure of taxes and benefits to encourage the unemployed to take a job. This requires making some benefits depend not on the status of being unemployed but on some other need-based criterion. Earned-income tax credits or other tax concessions for the working poor are a start. But the problem often lies with other benefits—rent subsidies, food stamps and the like, which depend on being unemployed or economically inactive.

4. Upgrade the entitlements of the elderly, the single mother with small children, the long-term unemployed, the chronically sick—to take them out of poverty. In the post–cold war era there can be a much greater reduction in defence and arms spending than has so far been achieved—permitting reallocations to eradicate poverty.

Integrating antipoverty measures in the policies of the transition economies

The dramatic fall in GDP in the transition economies of Eastern Europe and the CIS brought an equally dramatic rise in income poverty—from 4% in 1988 to 32% in 1994, from 14 million people to 119 million. The impact of economic decline has been much more widespread, disruptive and costly in people's lives than was expected. In these countries the search for pro-poor growth strategies is as relevant as in Brazil, Mozambique or the United Kingdom.

Just as pro-poor structural adjustment policies are needed, so are pro-poor transition policies. The main policies exacerbating poverty have been cuts in public spending on social services, reductions in welfare provision and removal of consumer subsidies.

The increasing poverty has affected all social classes. One important factor is unemployment, now in double digits in all countries. But falling wages are an even more important cause of poor incomes—in Russia 66% of people below the poverty line have jobs (figure 3.8). And even those low wages may be far in arrears. In Russia in 1993 and 1994, only 40% of workers were paid in full and on time.

Shrinking public budgets have hurt children, a result of cutbacks in family benefits, including maternity benefits, child care and preschool education. In Russia since 1992, the proportion of children under six who are below the poverty line has increased

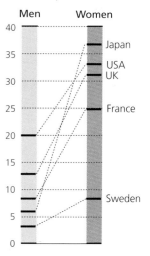

FIGURE 3.7

Women are more likely to work in low-paid employment

Percentage of workers who are low paid, 1993–95

Source: OECD 1996d.

from 40% to 62%, the incidence of chronic malnutrition from 9% to 14%. Even primary school enrolment is falling—by 3% in Estonia since 1989, 4% in Bulgaria and 12% in Georgia. In Russia life expectancy for men has fallen by 5 years to 58 years—the same as that in Bolivia and Lesotho, and lower than that in India.

But the transition has been especially costly for women. In employment priority is given to men, still seen as the primary bread winners. And the decline in family income and public services means that women have to take on the added burden of doing more work unpaid, leaving less time for their own needs and development. This change has been particularly difficult for single mothers, whose numbers are on the rise with more divorces, more deaths of middle-aged men and more births to unmarried mothers. In Poland in 1992, 67% of single mothers lived below the subsistence minimum.

Life has become more stressful as people are forced to adopt ever more desperate survival strategies. Kyrgyz women who previously gave food to neighbours and relatives in need now find it stressful to sell that food to survive. Such feelings are intensified by cultural values that see poverty as the result of personal failure—even in today's changed circumstances.

The transition to market economies was expected to cause disruption but not such disaster. The focus so far has been overwhelmingly on radical reform to stimulate economic growth, with little effort to construct new systems of welfare provision. The dismantled social welfare policies have not been replaced by the social safety nets needed in market economies.

Economic growth is beginning to revive in a few—but not all—transition economies. But economic growth alone will not solve their problems. The policies for transition need to be recentred on human development goals, and antipoverty measures that enable people to build up their assets must be incorporated from the outset.

A new strategy is required that strengthens the role of the state in the division of responsibilities among the state, the market and civil society. The state must take the lead in addressing labour market aspects of poverty—creating jobs through retraining and public works, supporting small business, increasing labour mobility and changing housing policies. It also must focus more on social policies—reversing the erosion in access to basic social services, health and education and providing an effective safety net for those left behind. The state should address distributive aspects of the transition—the growing disparities among regions and between winners and losers, poor and non-poor.

The welfare system has to be adjusted to market rules, with targeted improvements. But the key issue is downsizing the universal system of social benefits and redistributing entitlements. So far, governments have proceeded on a piecemeal basis and under pressure from the losers—sectors and social groups. There has been little discussion of the concept of such changes or of the model to follow. Maintaining a basic level of universal benefits should be an important part of efforts to prevent the erosion of gains already achieved in human development in the region.

Socialism failed to eradicate poverty. And despite ideological claims to the contrary, it did not create the conditions for sustainable human development. The command economy restricted people's political and economic freedom. And inefficiency prevented the economy from generating enough resources to meet people's needs. But the fall of socialism eliminated the positive pressure to provide a safety net for those left behind. Now the poor need to organize politically to ensure that their interests are reflected in the new economic policy framework.

Towards an agenda for poverty eradication

With poverty constantly being created and re-created, its eradication requires vigilance. The priorities for developing countries:
• Restoring and accelerating economic growth, especially in Sub-Saharan Africa, the low-income countries in Latin America and the Caribbean and among the Arab States that are experiencing stagnation or decline, and the transition economies of Eastern Europe and the CIS.

FIGURE 3.8

Wages have declined drastically in transition economies

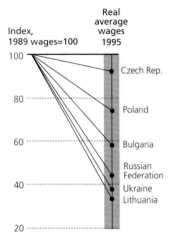

Source: Milanovic 1996.

- Promoting pro-poor growth to improve incomes and productivity in smallholder agriculture, especially in resource-poor areas, and in microenterprises in urban and rural areas.

- Reversing environmental degradation, especially on the marginal lands where more than 500 million poor people live.

- Stemming the spread of HIV/AIDS among poor people through multisectoral, people-centred programmes.

- Accelerating the demographic transition in countries where fertility rates are still high, especially in Sub-Saharan Africa, South Asia and the Arab States.

- Developing instruments to improve the processes for peace-building, conflict resolution and conflict prevention—as well as to help displaced persons.

Strengthening the abilities of the poor to fight poverty—and build their assets—should underpin the strategy for poverty eradication. Besides the efforts of the poor themselves, this will require policy and institutional changes to:

- Ensure access of the poor to the critical economic assets of land, credit and housing.

- Ensure access of the poor to health services and education opportunities that can build their capabilities.

- Create a policy environment that promotes pro-poor growth.

Such a strategy requires a favourable global environment as well as political commitments and power shifts in every country—subjects explored in the next two chapters.

CHAPTER 4

Globalization—poor nations, poor people

Poor countries and poor people too often find their interests neglected

A dominant economic theme of the 1990s, globalization encapsulates both a description and a prescription. The description is the widening and deepening of international flows of trade, finance and information in a single, integrated global market (box 4.1). The prescription is to liberalize national and global markets in the belief that free flows of trade, finance and information will produce the best outcome for growth and human welfare. All is presented with an air of inevitability and overwhelming conviction. Not since the heyday of free trade in the 19th century has economic theory elicited such widespread certainty.

The principles of free global markets are nevertheless applied selectively. If this were not so, the global market for unskilled labour would be as free as the market for industrial country exports or capital. Global negotiations are moving rapidly towards a free world market in foreign investment and services. But intervention in agriculture and textiles, an obstacle to developing countries, remains high. Lacking power, poor countries and poor people too often find their interests neglected and undermined.

Globalization has its winners and its losers. With the expansion of trade and foreign investment, developing countries have seen the gaps among themselves widen. Meanwhile, in many industrial countries unemployment has soared to levels not seen since the 1930s, and income inequality to levels not recorded since the last century.

A rising tide of wealth is supposed to lift all boats. But some are more seaworthy than others. The yachts and ocean liners are indeed rising in response to new opportunities, but the rafts and rowboats are taking on water—and some are sinking fast.

Inequality is not inherent in globalization. Because liberalization exposes domestic producers to volatile global markets and to capital flows that are large relative to the economy, it increases risks—but it also increases potential rewards. For poverty eradication the challenge is to identify policies that enable poor people to participate in markets on more equitable terms, nationally and globally.

Globalization has many aspects. This chapter focuses on its economic impact on poor nations and poor people.

Globalization and poor countries

For the world the benefits of liberalization should exceed the costs. During 1995–2001 the results of the Uruguay Round of the GATT (General Agreement on Tariffs and Trade) are expected to increase global income by an estimated $212–$510 billion—gains from greater efficiency and higher rates of return on capital, as well as from the expansion of trade.

The overall gains obscure a more complex balance sheet of winners and losers. Projected losses are heavily outweighed by the gains, but those losses will be concentrated in a group of countries that can least afford them—and for some the costs will be significant. The least developed countries stand to lose up to $600 million a year, and Sub-Saharan Africa $1.2 billion.

This scenario has disturbing implications for poverty and human welfare. Foreign exchange losses will translate into pressure on incomes, a diminishing ability to sustain imports and increased dependence on aid at a time when aid itself is under severe pressure. Revenue from trade will be lost, undermining the capacity of governments to develop the economic and social infrastructure on which sustained reduction in human poverty depends.

Many poorer countries have seen little of the expansion in world trade. Although developing countries' share of world population grew during 1970–91, their share of world trade scarcely changed. But among them, Asian countries saw their share of trade grow from 4.6% to 12.5%, while other

---

BOX 4.1

The shrinking world

Contacts between the world's people are widening and deepening as natural and artificial barriers fall. Huge declines in transport and communication costs have reduced natural barriers. Shipping is much cheaper: between 1920 and 1990 maritime transport costs fell by more than two-thirds. Between 1960 and 1990 operating costs per mile for the world's airlines fell by 60%.

Communication is also much easier and cheaper. Between 1940 and 1970 the cost of an international telephone call fell by more than 80%, and between 1970 and 1990 by 90%. In the 1980s telecommunication traffic was expanding by 20% a year. The Internet, the take-off point for the information superhighway, is now used by 50 million people, with the number of subscribers tapping into it doubling every year.

Toppling trade barriers
Artificial barriers have been eased with the reduction in trade barriers (tariffs, quotas and so on) and exchange controls. In 1947 the average tariff on manufactured imports was 47%; by 1980 it was only 6%, and with full implementation of the Uruguay Round, it should fall to 3%.

Other artificial barriers were removed with the resolution of political conflicts that have divided the world for decades, such as the cold war and the apartheid system in South Africa.

Spurred by the fall of barriers, global trade grew 12-fold in the postwar period. Now more than $4 trillion a year, it is expected to grow 6% annually for the next 10 years.

The rising tide of finance
The expansion of capital flows has been even more dramatic. Flows of foreign direct investment in 1995 reached $315 billion, nearly a sixfold increase over the level for 1981–85. Over the same period world trade increased by little more than half.

Less visible, but infinitely more powerful, are the world's financial markets. Between the mid-1970s and 1996 the daily turnover in the world's foreign exchange markets increased from around $1 billion to $1.2 trillion. Most private capital flows went to industrial countries, but a growing share is going to developing countries. Between 1987 and 1994 the flows to developing countries rose from $25 billion to $172 billion, and in 1995 they received a third of the global foreign direct investment flows.

These changes are significant, but need to be placed in historical context. Much of this has happened before. For 17 industrial countries for which there are data, exports as a share of GDP in 1913 were 12.9%, not much below the 1993 level of 14.5%. And capital transfers as a share of industrial country GDP are still smaller than in the 1890s. Earlier eras of globalization also saw far greater movement of people around the world. Today immigration is more restricted.

The modern era of globalization is distinguished less by the scale of the flows than by their character. In trade, for example, a much smaller share by value consists of commodities (partly a reflection of lower prices relative to manufactures) and a larger share is services and intracompany trade. Finance too is different: net flows may be similar, but gross flows are larger—and the flows come from a wider variety of sources. And multinational corporations are leaders in mobilizing capital and generating technology.

Global technology . . .
Some of the changes in international trade and finance reflect advances in technology. The lightning speed of transactions means that countries and companies now must respond rapidly if they are not to be left behind.

Technological change is also affecting the nature of investment. Previously, high-technology production had been limited to rich countries with high wages. Today technology is more easily tranferred to developing countries, where sophisticated production can be combined with relatively low wages.

The increasing ease with which technology can accompany capital across borders threatens to break the links between high productivity, high technology and high wages. For example, Mexico's worker productivity rose from a fifth to a third of the US level between 1989 and 1993, in part as a consequence of increased foreign investment and sophisticated technology geared towards production for the US market. But the average wage gap has narrowed far more slowly, with the Mexican wage still only a sixth of the US wage. The availability of higher levels of technology all over the world is putting pressure on the wages and employment of low-skilled workers.

. . . and a global culture
Normally, globalization refers to the international flow of trade and capital. But the international spread of cultures has been at least as important as the spread of economic processes. Today a global culture is emerging. Through many media—from music to movies to books—international ideas and values are being mixed with, and superimposed on, national identities. The spread of ideas through television and video has seen revolutionary developments. There now are more than 1.2 billion TV sets around the world. The United States exports more than 120,000 hours of television programming a year to Europe alone, and the global trade in programming is growing by more than 15% a year.

Popular culture exerts more powerful pressure than ever before. From Manila to Managua, Beirut to Beijing, in the East, West, North and South, styles in dress (jeans, hair-dos, t-shirts), sports, music, eating habits and social and cultural attitudes have become global trends. Even crimes—whether relating to drugs, abuse of women, embezzlement or corruption—transcend frontiers and have become similar everywhere. In so many ways, the world has shrunk.

Source: Berry, Horton and Mazumdar 1997, *The Economist* 1996, Watkins 1995, World Commission on Culture and Development 1995, UNRISD 1995a, Watkins 1997 and World Bank 1995a and 1996b.

regions' shares declined. The least developed countries, with 10% of the world's people, have 0.3% of world trade—half their share two decades ago.

The imbalance is also evident in the ratio of trade to GDP (figure 4.1). For the world this ratio has been rising over the past decade, but for 44 developing countries with more than a billion people, it has been falling.

Many countries have also been bypassed by finance, with most foreign direct investment (FDI) going to the industrial "triad" of North America, Europe and Japan. Together with the eight Chinese coastal provinces and Beijing, these economies receive more than 90% of global FDI. The rest of the world, with more than 70% of the population, gets less than 10%, and for a third of developing countries the ratio of FDI to GDP has fallen over the past decade. Since investment flows are often tied up with transfers of technology, this means that huge regions of the world are being left out of technological advance.

Why are these flows so skewed? For several reasons—some the result of national policy failures, others the result of external forces.

Bad policy

Poor macroeconomic policy, particularly large fiscal deficits, creates instability that discourages investors. And when deficits are financed by external borrowing, this can overvalue the currency, again deterring foreign investors and exporters.

Governments also impede trade and investment more directly. Tariffs that overprotect local producers for long periods also keep out imports of capital and intermediate goods that could be used to increase productivity. And if producers are not exposed to international competition, they have less incentive to adopt the international standards of quality control and process efficiency vital for export competitiveness. Protection also discourages investment by multinationals, through the bureaucratic delays associated with it: complex systems of manufacturing demand the integration of output from different coun-

tries, and this requires prompt, reliable schedules. Governments can also impede incoming investment with policies that lack transparency or consistency, depriving investors of predictable and productive environments.

Neglecting investments in people also makes it difficult to expand exports and attract investors. Lacking basic skills, people cannot adapt to changing market conditions or shift to more sophisticated exports. And neglecting infrastructure, particularly transport and communications, reduces access to global opportunities. In Tanzania, as in many African countries, small-scale farmers have been constrained in responding to the higher prices resulting from liberalization by the lack of roads linking them to markets.

Bad terms

But not all the blame for limited benefits from globalization can be laid at the door of governments. Even when globalization reaches poor countries, it often arrives on very unfavourable terms. Since the early 1970s the least developed countries have suffered a cumulative decline of 50% in their terms of trade (figure 4.2). For developing countries as a group the cumulative terms-of-trade losses amounted to $290 billion between 1980 and 1991. Much of this catastrophic fall was due to the decline in real commodity prices—in 1990 they were 45% lower than in 1980 and 10% lower than the lowest prices during the Great Depression, in 1932. But poor prices were not confined to commodities. Developing countries' terms of trade for manufactured goods also fell—by 35% during 1970–91.

Poor countries also suffer unfavourable terms in finance. With inferior credit ratings and the expectation of national currency depreciations, they paid interest rates that were in effect four times as high as those charged rich countries during the 1980s. In part as a result of these high interest rates, debt remains a millstone for many poor countries: Sub-Saharan African governments transfer to Northern creditors four times what they spend on the health of their people.

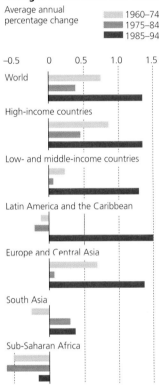

FIGURE 4.1

Changes in real trade-GDP ratios

Average annual percentage change

1960–74
1975–84
1985–94

–0.5   0   0.5   1.0   1.5

World

High-income countries

Low- and middle-income countries

Latin America and the Caribbean

Europe and Central Asia

South Asia

Sub-Saharan Africa

Source: World Bank 1996b.

Beyond the human cost, debt creates economic obstacles. For the poorest countries debt repayments typically soak up about a fifth of export earnings, seriously depleting their limited stock of foreign exchange and undermining their ability to engage in international trade on more equitable terms.

A positive development was the introduction in 1996 of the Highly Indebted Poor Countries Initiative, which aims at reducing the debt stock and sets a ceiling on debt service payments. Welcome as it is, it requires compliance with at least two International Monetary Fund (IMF) stabilization programmes, which may postpone debt relief for some of the poorest countries for up to six years—at considerable human and economic cost.

Besides unfavourable terms in trade and finance, the poor countries also suffer unfavourable terms in the flow of people. Even countries founded on immigration, such as Australia, Canada and the United States, are becoming much choosier about whom they will let in. They give preference to those who are highly skilled—a flow that continues to cause a brain drain from developing countries. And while increasingly restrictive in admitting refugees, they welcome those who arrive with large amounts of capital.

Bad rules

Poor countries often lose out because the rules of the game are biased against them— particularly those relating to international trade. The Uruguay Round hardly changed the picture. Developing countries, with three-quarters of the world's people, will get only a quarter to a third of the income gains generated—hardly an equitable distribution—and most of that will go to a few powerful exporters in Asia and Latin America.

The Uruguay Round left intact most of the protection for industry and agriculture in industrial countries, while ignoring issues of vital concern to poor countries—notably the problem of debt and the management of primary commodity markets.

• *Tariffs*—Goods from the industrial countries enjoyed much greater tariff reductions in the Uruguay Round than those from developing countries—45% compared with 20–25%. While developing countries as a group now face tariffs 10% higher than the global average, the least developed countries face tariffs 30% higher—because tariffs remain high on the goods with greatest potential for the poorest countries, such as textiles, leather and agricultural commodities.

Another problem is tariff escalation— the practice of setting higher tariffs on processed goods than on raw materials. This locks developing countries into volatile primary commodity markets, where real prices are declining, and obstructs an obvious way for them to add value to their exports. For some commodities of special significance to developing countries—such as leather, oilseeds, textile fibres and beverages—tariffs will continue to be 8–26% higher on the final product than on the underlying raw materials.

• *Non-tariff barriers*—As successive GATT agreements reduced tariff barriers, industrial countries increasingly switched to non-tariff barriers—quotas, antidumping measures and "voluntary" export restraints. Before the Uruguay Round non-tariff barriers affected 18% of developing country exports, but this share should now fall to 5.5%. That said, the scope for evading the spirit, if not the letter, of the Uruguay Round agreements remains considerable.

Antidumping measures are aimed at exporters that sell below cost to drive competitors in the importing country out of business and then exploit their larger market shares, charging higher prices. Antidumping actions, and their accompanying penalties, are one of the most popular forms of protection. They more than doubled in number between 1989 and 1994, affecting a large share of exports to industrial countries. Antidumping cases brought by the European Union during the 1980s covered imports roughly equal in value to all its agricultural imports. The United States and the European Union have applied antidumping measures against a wide range of developing country exports—everything from steel to colour televisions to toys.

FIGURE 4.2

Declining terms of trade
Average annual rate of change

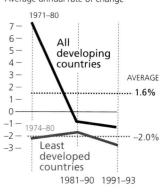

Source: Berry, Horton and Mazumdar 1997.

Rules about what justifies antidumping actions are vague. An OECD study found that in more than 90% of US and EU antidumping actions, the goods being imported posed little or no threat to national industries. The Uruguay Round has made the rules more uniform, but they retain some highly arbitrary criteria.

BOX 4.2

Level playing field?

Contrary to the post–Uruguay Round image of the world agricultural market as a level playing field, the major exporters, notably the European Union and the United States, have continued to subsidize production and exports. In 1995 the industrial countries spent $182 billion on subsidies. As poor countries open their economies, they expose many poor agricultural producers to overwhelming and unfair competition from subsidized imports.

The problem is acutely illustrated by the Philippines. Under the 1994 agriculture agreement of the Uruguay Round, the Philippines is liberalizing imports of a wide range of agricultural commodities. For maize, among those most immediately affected, tariffs on imports will be halved over the next eight years and minimum import quantities expanded. So, depending on world price trends, maize imported from the United States could be available at prices 30% below current market prices by the end of the decade. Domestic farm-gate prices will decline to the import price.

What does this mean for producers in the Philippines? Maize is the second most important crop produced in the country after rice, involving around 1.2 million households. The main maize-producing area is the island of Mindanao, where many of the poorest households derive more than three-quarters of their income from maize sales. More than half the population lives below the poverty line, and a third of the children under five suffer from malnutrition. Any decline in household income could have disastrous effects.

According to Oxfam, the liberalization of maize imports could mean the loss of up to half a million livelihoods on Mindanao. Claims that, in the long run,

trade liberalization will increase average incomes need to be set against these human costs. Viewed from Mindanao, Keynes's observation that "in the long run we are all dead" carries rather more resonance.

Such facts suggest that whatever sway the concept of a level playing field in world agriculture may exercise over the imagination of free traders, it is conspicuous by its absence in the real world. The full extent of the unequal competition into which producers in the Philippines are being forced is graphically illustrated by another fact. According to the OECD, the per capita transfer to US farmers amounted to $29,000 in 1995. In the main maize-producing areas of Mindanao and the Cagayan Valley, average per capita incomes amount to less than $300. So each US farmer receives in subsidies roughly 100 times the income of a maize farmer in the Philippines.

In the real world, as distinct from the imaginary one inhabited by free traders, survival in agricultural markets depends less on comparative advantage than on comparative access to subsidies. Liberalizing local food markets in the face of such unequal competition is not a prescription for improving efficiency, but a recipe for the destruction of livelihoods on a massive scale.

Implementation of the Uruguay Round agriculture agreement over the next five years will not materially change this picture. No effective disciplines on export subsidization were agreed to in the Uruguay Round, allowing the United States and the European Union to continue past practices, though under slightly different rules. Agriculture remains the only area of international trade in which export dumping is accepted as a legitimate trade practice.

Source: Watkins 1997 and Oxfam International 1996c.

• *Textiles*—Textiles and clothing are relatively simple industries, and countries embarking on industrialization usually begin with them. They account for 24% of exports for Sub-Saharan Africa, 14% for Asia and 8% for Latin America and the Caribbean. For Bangladesh and Sri Lanka they account for half of all export earnings.

Countries exporting textiles and clothing are limited to specific quotas, above which high tariffs are applied. This systematic management of world trade in textiles and clothing started in 1961 with the Multi-Fibre Arrangement (MFA) and continued with its four successors.

Estimates of the foreign exchange losses that developing countries suffer as a result of MFA quotas on these exports range from $4 billion to $15 billion a year. The Uruguay Round agreement on textiles and clothing will phase out the MFA quotas and reduce tariffs over a 10-year period, but only to an average tariff of 12%—three times the average levied on industrial country imports.

The removal of quotas will benefit the more efficient, low-wage producers in China, Indonesia and Thailand. By contrast, Bangladesh, Nepal and Sri Lanka will lose. According to one estimate, Bangladesh could lose up to a fifth of its exports—one of its main weapons against poverty. Of the million or more workers in garment factories in Bangladesh, around 90% are women—poorly paid, but often providing the family's main source of income. They have little prospect of work elsewhere.

• *Agriculture*—Agricultural commodities have always had a special status in world trade, and industrial countries have resolutely subsidized agricultural exports. The United States and the European Union, which dominate world markets, give heavy subsidies to their farmers—equal to roughly half the value of agricultural output in these economies.

This subsidization in rich countries hits developing countries hard. First, it keeps world prices low, so they can get little for their commodities. Second, it excludes them from food markets in the rich countries. Third, it exposes their domestic food producers to dumping in the form of cheap food imports, which reduces incentives for food production and thus undermines self-reliance and livelihoods (box 4.2).

Cheap food imports have positive short-term income benefits for food-deficit poor countries. They also help poor households, which spend much of their income on food. But many of the 88 countries categorized by FAO as low-income food-deficit countries are not in a position to sustain food imports. And purchasing food imports may not be the most productive use of one of their scarcest resources, their foreign exchange. Collectively, the 88 low-income food-deficit countries spend half their foreign exchange on food imports. Yet in many of these countries smallholder farmers are more than capable of feeding the population.

One estimate suggests that if industrial countries were to reduce agricultural subsidies and protection by just 30%, developing countries would earn an extra $45 billion a year. The Uruguay Round agreement on agriculture requires only a 21% reduction in the volume of subsidized exports—and allows income support to farmers.

• *Intellectual property rights*—The Uruguay Round extended the life and enforced the protection of patents and other intellectual property rights—increasing the cost of technology transfers to developing countries. Early on, industrial countries exploited a fairly free flow of ideas and technology. In the 19th century the United States adapted and developed European technologies with little regard for patent rights. And after the Second World War Japan did much the same with US technology. Now those same countries are enforcing policies that will impose steep licensing charges on developing countries for using foreign technology. In a knowledge-intensive global economy access to technology on reasonable terms determines whether countries can take advantage of the opportunities that globalization offers.

Globalization is thus proceeding apace, but largely for the benefit of the more dynamic and powerful countries in the North and the South. The loss to developing countries from unequal access to trade, labour and finance was estimated by *Human Development Report 1992* at $500 billion a year, 10 times what they receive annually in foreign assistance. Arguments that the benefits will necessarily trickle down to the poorest countries seem far-fetched.

Globalization and poor people

Even less certain than globalization's benefits for poor countries are its benefits for poor people within countries.

In developing countries

Pointing to China and India, together home to more than half a billion of the world's income-poor, many would argue that globalization has reduced poverty. In China globalization and poverty reduction seem to have gone hand in hand, and government policies strengthened the link (see pages 49–50 in chapter 2). The country is now the largest recipient of FDI in the developing world, and in the past 15 years has increased its exports more than tenfold. And it has reduced the share of its people in income poverty from a third to a tenth, while also making major improvements in health and education.

In India since the start of a gradual liberalization in 1991, FDI flows have doubled every year, and exports are up by more than 50%. Poverty has been reduced not just in income but also in health and education (see pages 51–52 in chapter 2).

Similar stories could be told for Bangladesh, Indonesia and Viet Nam—all liberalized their trade and investment regimes, and all have to some extent reduced poverty.

National policies have been crucial in establishing mutually reinforcing relationships for globalization-induced growth to improve human development and reduce poverty, in turn equipping countries to take advantage of global markets.

The Uruguay Round should push up world agricultural prices and benefit agriculture in general. Where landownership is not concentrated and production is labour intensive, as in some parts of Asia and much of Sub-Saharan Africa, the poorest producers should gain from better prices. But

Globalization is proceeding largely for the benefit of the dynamic and powerful countries

where land is monopolized by a small elite and used for highly mechanized production of cash crops for export, as in Latin America, ownership could concentrate still further and intensify rural poverty (box 4.3).

BOX 4.3

Winners and losers in Mexico

Since the mid-1980s Mexico has been a world pace-setter in pursuing policies conducive to globalization. It has deregulated financial markets, exposed agriculture and manufacturing to increased competition through the reduction of trade barriers and privatized public assets on a large scale—including most of the commercial banking system. By the early 1990s almost 90% of imports fell into liberalized categories. All this marked a profound departure from the highly regulated economy that Mexico had been until 1980. Indeed, in many respects, the shift has been as revolutionary as that in the formerly communist countries.

Liberalization and deregulation have led to widely divergent sets of opportunities and threats for different regions and socio-economic groups. For owners of capital, the privatization of state industries and the 1992 land reform allowing investors to purchase smallholder land have created new sources of wealth. In the midst of one of the worst economic crises the country has ever faced, the number of billionaires increased from 10 to 15. In 1996 their combined wealth was equal to 9% of Mexico's GDP. Large-scale commercial farms and private industries geared towards the North American market have also benefited. New jobs are being created in the northern states, which span the *maquiladora* zone and the commercial farming areas along the Pacific coast and in the irrigated valley of El Bajo. But these are not the states in which the social dislocation and loss of livelihoods are occurring on the largest scale.

The share of the population living in absolute poverty increased from 19% in 1984 to 24% in 1989. In urban areas the number of people living in absolute poverty then fell slightly until 1992. But in rural areas, where more than 80% of those in absolute poverty live, the number of poor people increased throughout the period, rising from 6.7 million to 8.8

million. While evidence for the period since 1992 is sparse, poverty levels have probably worsened since the 1994 financial collapse. More than one million Mexicans lost their jobs in the wake of the crisis.

Analysis suggests that Mexico will gain in net income terms as a result of specialization facilitated by the North American Free Trade Agreement. But behind this overall projection are the losers—mostly producers of maize, the country's staple food. Maize accounts for around half of Mexico's agricultural land area—and maize production plays a key part in rural livelihoods.

Most smallholders are net-deficit households, selling maize after the harvest and then performing wage labour to buy it after household supplies run out. The vast majority of Mexico's maize farmers operate on poor land with limited access to credit, inputs and equipment. In rain-fed areas yields average around a fifth of those in the US Midwest, with which Mexico's maize farmers will have to compete as trade restrictions are withdrawn.

According to one study, between 700,000 and 800,000 livelihoods will be lost as maize prices fall as a result of competition from cheaper imports. This will affect 15% of the economically active population in agriculture, with profound implications for rural poverty and regional inequality. More than 30% of the rural population lives below the income poverty line, and the poorest rural areas have significantly less access to water, electricity and housing. With real wages in rural labour markets declining and unemployment rising, off-farm employment is unlikely to compensate for income losses from maize. As a result, households will be forced into increasingly desperate survival strategies, including migrating to commercial farm areas, to urban centres and to the United States.

Source: Watkins 1997.

In the urban areas poor people will suffer if food prices rise, but they will gain from employment in new export industries. Those likely to benefit most are young women hired by multinationals. New employment opportunities increase their incomes and often their power in households. And they encourage poor households to educate daughters as well as sons—reducing gender gaps in the next generation.

Globalization has profound implications for states. Everywhere the imperative to liberalize has demanded a shrinking of state involvement in national life, producing a wave of privatizations of public enterprises and, generally, job cuts. And everywhere the opening of financial markets has limited governments' ability to run deficits—requiring them to slash health spending and food subsidies that benefit poor people.

It is difficult to establish the effects of globalization on poverty. Basic trade theory argues that poor people gain from trade liberalization. Developing countries have a comparative advantage in abundant, low-cost, unskilled labour. If they concentrate on goods whose production is simple and labour intensive, greater integration into global markets should increase their exports and output, raising the demand for unskilled labour and raising the incomes of the poor relative to those of the non-poor.

Moreover, countries move up the trade ladder, exporting more sophisticated products, leaving space on the ladder below for later-industrializing countries. All this helps reduce poverty. The countries on the higher rungs benefit most, but even those on the lower rungs should see poverty fall. And free trade should also help poor consumers—without trade protection, local prices should fall to world prices.

There should also be benefits for employment from a liberal financial regime. Removing restrictions on capital flows should attract more FDI, creating more jobs for the poor by integrating them into international systems of production.

But things don't always turn out this way. Liberalization has in some cases been accompanied by greater inequality, with a falling share of income for the poorest 20%, as in several Latin American countries—Argentina, Chile, the Dominican Republic, Ecuador, Mexico and Uruguay. In 16 of 18 countries in Eastern Europe and the CIS income distribution has worsened and poverty has increased during liberalization. And China, with all its growth, has seen poverty reduction in the central and western regions lag behind that in the export-intensive coastal regions.

Why should liberalization, which in theory should narrow income gaps, leave the poor worse off? One explanation is that manufacturing tends to be dominated by large companies in the formal sector, where wages in any case are usually higher than in the small-scale or informal sector. If there are weak links from the formal to the small-scale or informal sector, globalization merely accentuates the disadvantage of informal sector workers. Another explanation is that liberalization makes it easier to bring in capital goods, increasing productivity but raising the demand for skilled rather than unskilled labour.

Globalization can also shift patterns of consumption. Luxury cars and soft drinks can rapidly become a part of daily life, heightening relative deprivation. The pattern can increase absolute poverty by undermining the production of goods on which poor people rely. A flood of imported wheat can shift consumption away from sorghum or cassava, making them scarcer in local markets.

Sweeping liberalization can also expose the poor to sudden shocks. Some bounce back as the economy improves; others are left trapped in poverty.

In industrial countries

In industrial countries the era of globalization has been characterized by an increase in overall income but also a rise in unemployment and inequality. In 1995, 34 million people were out of work in the OECD countries—7.5% of the workforce—and since 1979 unemployment in the European Union has more than doubled, to 11%.

What's to blame? Some say competition from cheap labour in the developing world.

But the role of developing country trade is probably exaggerated. Analysis shows that it explains at most 10% of the rise in wage inequality and manufacturing unemployment in industrial countries. Even if the net effect of developing country trade reduced the demand for low-skill labour in manufacturing by 10%, the effect would be small, since manufacturing typically accounts for less than a fifth of the demand for low-skill labour. Fiscal retrenchment and labour-saving technological change have had a much greater impact on unemployment and inequality.

The scale of developing country exports in industrial country markets is also often exaggerated. For OECD countries imports from developing countries account for only 3% of the market for manufactured goods. And the industrial countries still have a positive trade balance in manufactures with the developing countries—equal to more than 1% of GDP on average.

Moreover, the two countries most affected by developing country manufacturing, the United States and Canada, do not have the highest unemployment. Among OECD countries Canada has enjoyed the largest increase in manufacturing employment. So, the arguments blaming unemployment on imports need careful examination.

National policy in an era of globalization

How to open more opportunities for the poorest countries? How to ensure that the benefits of global integration are more equally shared? The immediate responsibility lies with national governments, perhaps powerless to steer world markets, but able to minimize the damage and maximize the opportunities. Policies for reducing poverty and empowering the poor can become part of a strategy for empowering nations in a globalizing world. Following are some key policy options for such a strategy.

1. *Manage trade and capital flows more carefully.* National governments can exercise more discretion when adopting policies of liberalization. A selective approach to the global market would follow the example of

Empowering the poor can be part of a strategy for empowering nations

most East Asian economies—with some time-bound, performance-related protection for potentially viable industries, some industrial intervention and some management of foreign direct investment (box 4.4).

2. Invest in poor people. Globalization adds extra urgency to this. The diffusion of new technology increases the payoff to higher levels of human capital and to more flexible sets of skills. Those without the necessary education will be left even further behind.

3. Foster small enterprises. One of the most important ways for globalization to reduce poverty is through the incubators of microenterprises and small and medium-size firms—they are more labour-intensive than large firms and will provide the bulk of new jobs for the poor for some time. Subcontractors to larger enterprises and bridges between the informal and formal sectors, these firms increase competitiveness by reducing fixed costs and providing flexibility.

Such links have been forged effectively in Japan and in some of its Asian neighbours. But these links are much less common in Africa and Latin America—the legacy of protection that gave large firms few incentives to link up with smaller companies.

Small enterprises that can export should be supported in making this leap. Otherwise, production will continue to be dominated by larger and less labour-intensive firms. And small enterprises vulnerable to imports may merit temporary protection.

4. Manage new technology. Labour-saving technologies that are developed elsewhere and require advanced skills may be inappropriate in developing countries.

Though vital, technological change will always be a double-edged sword—and its relationship with poverty reduction is complicated and poorly understood. The benefits of investment in technology can be maximized if it is accompanied by strong policies to create human capital and foster small enterprises.

5. Reduce poverty and provide safety nets. Globalization redistributes opportunities and benefits in a way that can lead to rising inequality. Policies to reduce poverty and moderate income inequality can counter the disruption from globalization. Safety nets are needed to catch those hurt by the disruption and to help them move in a new direction.

6. Improve governance. Globalization usually weakens the state's influence—but in many ways it demands a stronger state, to help people reap its benefits and mitigate its costs. Better governance is vital not just to ensure the rule of law and protect against international organized crime, but also to maintain and expand social and economic infrastructure.

BOX 4.4

Global prospects, analytical suspects

Many governments increasingly see their role as not to regulate markets but to facilitate their relentless expansion. Among other things, this involves removing barriers to trade and exploiting the country's comparative advantage—which for many developing countries is cheap labour.

This strategy is based on a conviction that export growth will lead to overall economic growth—a belief supported by an array of empirical studies showing that exports and economic growth tend to go together. But do exports lead to growth, or is it the other way round? Nobody is really sure.

Regardless of the answer, there are two reasons for caution. The first danger is dropping trade barriers too soon, before local industry is sufficiently robust to withstand foreign competition. A surge in imports can harm small and medium-size manufacturing—on which many of the poor depend for employment. The record of East Asia shows that the normal prelude and complement to the creation of a successful export manufacturing sector is a period of protection for infant industries. Their comparative advantages were more often created than discovered.

The second danger is that, if developing countries collectively increase the supply of certain exports, they will drive global prices down. The benefits will go to the consumers of poor countries' exports, many of whom are better off than the producers.

Like trade, capital flows to poor countries also raise questions about whether there should be restrictions—beyond such obvious ones as those on foreign direct investment in environmentally damaging industries. Against much evidence of the potential benefits from capital inflows, there are some concerns. A new concept, the "tequila effect", was created when billions of dollars flowed out of Mexico in December 1994—precipitating not just a national financial crisis but also a global one. In Latin America the two countries with the most successful recent growth performance—Chile and Colombia—both apply controls on capital. The capital account needs to be managed carefully to avoid currency overvaluation and exchange rate fluctuations—both of which harm small and medium-size exporters.

There are also concerns about the relationship of foreign and local capital. More efficient foreign producers may crowd out local entrepreneurs from more profitable activities and repatriate the proceeds rather than reinvest them locally. They may also monopolize the scarce supply of skilled labour, hurting national companies.

If, in addition, national governments go out of their way to attract foreign direct investment by offering to relax labour or health standards, that will hurt the poor and set off a "race to the bottom" that will lower standards worldwide.

Source: Berry, Horton and Mazumdar 1997.

Group solutions and concerted action

Many policies that governments wish to adopt are possible only in concert with others, such as through regional trading groups. These groups can increase trade, facilitate financial flows and enhance transport links. By forming such groups, poor countries could thus combine increased competition with economies of scale and a better division of labour—while retaining some protection from competition from more advanced countries. Such groups traditionally have a high failure rate, but some have recently found new energy— CARICOM (for the Caribbean) and ASEAN (for South-East Asia).

Even outside regional groups, developing countries, especially the poorer ones, will carry greater weight if they coordinate their actions and bargain as groups. Some such groups could exercise producer power over supplies, as OPEC countries did. Concerted action by commodity exporters could help stabilize commodity prices at levels that do not consign people to poverty. Exporter groups could establish buffer stocks, production quotas and stockpiles—financed by a tax on importers and exporters. A link could be established between such supply management and diversification of exports, with some of the gain in export revenue being used to finance diversification.

Developing countries sharing similar external indebtedness could coordinate negotiations of international solutions to the debt problem. Ironically, the more powerful creditors have insisted on a case-by-case approach, undercutting collective negotiation by debtors.

Bargaining that capitalizes on national power endowments could be a useful supplement to multilateralism for developing countries. To a large extent this was the strategy of Japan, Europe and the United States in the Uruguay Round. The main difficulty for the poor countries: they have less power than the rich.

International policy options

Are states becoming irrelevant? At one level they are being resisted by ethnic and other groups pressing for greater autonomy and self-determination. At another they are being bypassed by multinational corporations that care little about local jurisdictions. They seem to have become too big for the small things, and too small for the big.

The big things pose enormous challenges for international governance— challenges related to the growing interdependence of countries and people as well as to the persistent impoverishment of much of the world. While the world has shrunk, the mechanisms for managing the system in a stable, sustainable way for the benefit of all have lagged behind. The accelerating process of globalization is expanding global opportunities without distributing them equitably. The playing fields of globalization more often than not slope against the interests of people and countries.

Pro-active national efforts are essential for translating globalization into poverty reduction. International efforts must share the responsibility for providing the much-needed public good of equity and social cohesion through cooperation in its widest sense. Globalization increases both the benefits from providing this international public good and the penalties from neglecting it.

Today's global integration is wiping away national borders and weakening national policies. A system of global policies is needed to make markets work for people, not people for markets.

To seize the opportunities of globalization, the poorest developing countries need:

1. A more supportive macroeconomic policy environment for poverty eradication. The world clearly needs much more effective macroeconomic policy management at the global level—with more stable sources of international liquidity, better surveillance, faster crisis response mechanisms and a larger multinational lender of last resort. Existing organizations serve these purposes inadequately. Indeed, by stressing the importance of controlling inflation and focusing on the need for reform in deficit countries, they often place the burden squarely on the shoulders of the poor—with a deflationary impact on the world economy.

States have become too big for the small things, and too small for the big

TABLE 4.1
State and corporate power, 1994
(US$ billions)

Country or corporation	Total GDP or corporate sales
Indonesia	174.6
General Motors	168.8
Turkey	149.8
Denmark	146.1
Ford	137.1
South Africa	123.3
Toyota	111.1
Exxon	110.0
Royal Dutch/Shell	109.8
Norway	109.6
Poland	92.8
Portugal	91.6
IBM	72.0
Malaysia	68.5
Venezuela	59.0
Pakistan	57.1
Unilever	49.7
Nestlé	47.8
Sony	47.6
Egypt	43.9
Nigeria	30.4
Top five corporations	871.4
Least developed countries	76.5
South Asia	451.3
Sub-Saharan Africa	246.8

Source: Fortune Magazine 1996, World Bank 1995d and UNRISD 1995.

2. A fairer institutional environment for global trade. There is an urgent need to treat the products of developing countries on a par with those of industrial countries—and to accelerate the liberalization of markets of interest to poor countries, such as textiles, and institute a comprehensive ban on dumping agricultural exports.

In addition, concrete and substantive actions are required for the least developed countries, including:

• Eliminating tariff escalation for semi-processed tropical agricultural products and natural resources.

• Deepening tariff cuts and eliminating duties under preferential schemes.

• Exempting textile imports from small exporters from restrictions, regardless of whether the exporters are members of the World Trade Organization (WTO).

• Banning product-specific restrictions against exports from the least developed countries.

These options are considered in the Comprehensive and Integrated WTO Plan of Action for the Least Developed Countries. But no detailed recommendations have been adopted or implemented.

3. A partnership with multinational corporations to promote growth for poverty reduction. At the international level there is nothing equivalent to national legislation ensuring fair taxation, environmental management and labour rights and protecting against monopolies. Remarkable, considering that some multinational corporations command more wealth and economic power than most states do. Indeed, of the world's 100 largest economies, 50 are megacorporations. The 350 largest corporations now account for 40% of global trade, and their turnover exceeds the GDP of many countries (table 4.1).

What's needed? An incentive system that, while avoiding excessive regulation, encourages multinational corporations to contribute to poverty reduction and be publicly accountable and socially responsible. Both industrial and developing countries have interests here. Those of the industrial include preventing tax evasion.

4. Action to stop the race to the bottom. In a world of cutthroat competition, countries underbid each other in labour costs, labour standards and environmental protection—to produce as cheaply as possible for the international market. Many countries unilaterally try to restrain these races to the bottom. And some may come under external pressure if they tolerate dangerous working conditions and child labour, with human rights issues a basis for unilateral trade sanctions. A more efficient and equitable approach would be to strengthen institutions such as the International Labour Organisation—to support respect for labour rights—and to develop similar institutions for international environmental protection.

International coordination is also needed to avoid races to attract international investors by offering overly generous tax incentives that erode the tax base.

5. Selective support for global technology priorities. Global research and development has been biased towards the needs of rich countries—and now this bias is being accentuated with the shift from publicly financed research towards research by companies keen to appropriate the benefits. Resources are shifting away from research with public-good characteristics, such as that which led to the green revolution, and towards research focusing on more appropriable goods, such as biotechnology. Similarly, research by pharmaceutical companies is dealing more with the ailments of rich countries than with those of the developing world.

Today competitiveness in trade and in attracting capital is more knowledge-intensive than ever before. Through information superhighways, new technology is eliminating some problems of access to knowledge. But the poor are left with little access to these superhighways, lacking both the vehicles—personal computers, telephones, televisions—and the education and skills to drive them. Many countries need assistance in managing the information revolution to avoid marginalization and exploitation.

6. Action on global debt. The highly indebted poor countries need debt relief now—not at some indeterminate point in the future. Providing effective relief to the

20 worst-affected countries would cost between \$5.5 billion and \$7.7 billion—less than the cost of one Stealth bomber and roughly equivalent to the cost of building the Euro-Disney theme park in France. The meagre financial costs contrast with the appalling human costs of inaction. The Group of Seven and the Bretton Woods institutions should aim to end the debt crisis for the poorest countries by 2000. Such relief would require special measures to convert debt reduction into poverty reduction—reorienting national priorities towards human development objectives. Relieved of their annual debt repayments, the severely indebted countries could use the funds for investments that in Africa alone would save the lives of about 21 million children by 2000 and provide 90 million girls and women with access to basic education.

7. *Better access to finance for poor countries.* If poor countries are to participate in globalization on more advantageous terms, they need better access to finance. Private capital is bypassing areas of desperate need, especially Africa. And public finance delivered through bilateral and multilateral assistance is not filling the gap.

Bilateral aid has fallen to 0.28% of industrial country GDP on average—the lowest since aid targets were set. This trend must be reversed, and the quality of aid must be improved, with a stronger focus on poverty eradication. Considerable resources could be mobilized by restructuring aid budgets. Adopting the 20:20 initiative, which calls for earmarking 20% of aid flows and 20% of developing country budgets for basic social services, could contribute enormously to human development and the eventual eradication of poverty.

• • •

In many respects the world is sailing through the current era of globalization with neither compass nor map. Too little is known about the links between globalization and poverty, an area that demands

much more intensive study. But regardless of the future direction of globalization, we know enough about the basic measures that need to be taken to attack poverty. The speed of globalization makes them all the more urgent.

UNfair criticism?

The United Nations has been part of the process of globalization from the beginning. Through agreements negotiated at the United Nations, and with the technical support of UN staff and experts, it makes possible such essential elements of globalization as international mail delivery, the allocation of frequencies for international communications, the standardization of international trade laws and investment codes, customs formalities, global environmental initiatives, rules governing the disposal of industrial waste, the fight against global pandemics, the preservation of the common cultural heritage, the collection and analysis of statistics at a global level, even international air travel. The United Nations encourages globalization—but also seeks to ensure that the process is fair and efficient, that all countries and all people—especially the poorest—can benefit.

For the past five decades the United Nations has been at the forefront of international efforts to reduce poverty—defining needs, outlining policies, sharing experience and taking and supporting action. WHO helped mobilize worldwide action for the eradication of smallpox. FAO created early warning and monitoring networks for food security. UNESCO aided national literacy and education campaigns. ILO supported the World Employment Programme and pioneering work in employment, and its funding programmes have made possible many practical efforts in poverty reduction. UNICEF effectively promoted universal immunization in the 1980s and mobilized global efforts to address the needs of children and women. UNFPA contributed to family planning and to balanced population growth. UNDP helped countries build their own capacity for

poverty eradication through sustainable human development.

Many of the advances in health, education, nutrition, population, environmental sustainability and other aspects of poverty reduction had their original inspiration in a UN resolution or in a programme or country project supported by a UN body. At the World Summit for Social Development in Copenhagen, heads of state and government convened not to discuss arms control or to broker peace agreements, but to recommit the international community to the goals of poverty eradication.

The United Nations has made many contributions to the great ideas on development. Six Nobel Prize laureates in economics have worked for the United Nations. Many global policy initiatives began within the United Nations and then were implemented elsewhere, including the International Development Association at the World Bank, the Compensatory Finance Facility at the IMF and the Generalized System of Preferences at UNCTAD. And in the past decade such publications as UNICEF's *Adjustment with a Human Face* and UNDP's *Human Development Report*s have influenced the international and national debates on development.

Serving a global community of 185 states and some 6 billion people, the UN has \$4.6 billion a year to spend on economic and social development—less than the annual budget of New York's State University. This is the equivalent of 80 cents per human being, compared with the \$134 a person spent annually on arms and the military. Is the United Nations too expensive for a globalizing world?

Source: Childers 1995, Commission on Global Governance 1995, Kennedy and Russett 1995 and UNDPI 1996.

CHAPTER 5

The politics of poverty eradication

*What is lacking
is political
momentum
to tackle poverty
head on*

Politics, not just economics, determines what we do—or don't do—to address human poverty. And what is lacking is not the resources or the economic solutions—but the political momentum to tackle poverty head on.

Much is known about what is needed to eradicate poverty—job-led growth, access to credit, redistribution of land, investment in basic social services, promotion of the informal sector and sound macroeconomic policies. But too little attention has gone to finding ways to ensure that such actions are taken. How can an environment be created that ensures that state policies, market forces, civil activism and community mobilization contribute to the eradication of poverty? What political reform is needed to ensure pro-poor policies and pro-poor markets?

A political strategy for poverty eradication has three essential elements:

Political empowerment of poor people. People must organize for collective action to influence the circumstances and decisions affecting their lives. To advance their interests, their voices must be heard in the corridors of power.

Partnerships for change. All agents in society—trade unions, the media, community groups, private companies, political parties, academic institutions, professional associations—need to come together in a partnership to address human poverty in all its dimensions. And that partnership must be based on common interests and brokered compromises. Society must be open enough to tolerate a complex web of interests and coalitions and to ensure stability and progress towards human development.

An enabling and responsible state. The state needs to foster peaceful expression of people's priorities and to ensure democratic space for brokering the interests of society's many groups. Thus it needs to promote participation and encourage private-public partnerships. It also needs to be transparent and accountable—and to resist pressure from the economically powerful.

A formidable challenge

Building peaceful political momentum for poverty eradication is a formidable challenge. Poverty often serves the vested interests of the economically powerful, who may benefit from exploiting the pool of low-paid labour (box 5.1).

The realities of economic, social and political disparities and injustices are so overwhelming that few believe that things can change. And some think that only violence and confrontation can produce real change in favour of the poor. Poverty is brutal. It can provoke violent reactions. Those who profit from the status quo have often defended their position with violence. And when disappointment and frustration have risen to a crisis point, the poor have sometimes turned to armed struggle.

Progress in human development and in eradicating human poverty has often been won through uprisings and rebellions against states that have advanced the interests of the economically powerful while tolerating rigid class divisions, unbearable economic conditions and human suffering and poverty.

History is marked by uprisings and rebellions sparked by poverty. English peasants revolted against an impoverishing poll tax in 1381. German peasants rose up against their feudal overlords in opposition to serfdom in 1524.

Among developing countries, India has a long tradition of peasants' movements. As far back as the 17th and 18th centuries, when India was ruled by the British East India Company, peasants rose up against their British landlords.

In Bangladesh as recently as the 1950s, there was another large-scale peasants' movement, a response to unjust share-cropping practices. Although sharecroppers were responsible for providing all the inputs, including labour, they received only a third of the yield, with two-thirds going to the landlords. The Three-Division Movement that arose in opposition to this exploitation demanded a 50:50 split. Violence erupted, and the authorities responded with force. But ultimately the peasants' demands prevailed, and the principle of equal distribution of sharecroppers' production was enacted into law.

Full-scale revolutions have their roots in people's reactions to poverty and economic injustice. Spontaneous uprisings instigated the French Revolution in 1789, the revolutionary movements throughout Europe in 1848 and the Bolshevik Revolution in 1917. The wars of independence in Africa and Asia in the 19th and 20th centuries were not only an expression of nationalism—they were also a struggle against economic and social injustice. The civil rights movement in the United States in the 1960s too was a struggle for economic and social emancipation—at times resulting in violence despite the pacifist philosophy of its leader, Martin Luther King Jr.

Sometimes it was the violence itself that sabotaged the achievements of these struggles. Many revolutions replaced one evil with another through harsh recriminations, self-serving leadership, misguided utopianism or betrayals.

Naturally, not all progress in eradicating poverty was achieved through confrontation. Some strides in reducing poverty, especially since 1960, have been gradual and peaceful, as with the formation of welfare states in industrial countries and the reduction of infant mortality, the increase in life expectancy and other achievements in developing countries.

This chapter looks at the need for peaceful—but fundamental—reform through collective action and democracy. The challenge facing today's leaders, activists and citizens is to learn from history and work towards non-violent change, understanding the risks of confrontation and the backlashes it can produce. Avoiding violence and chaos is in all people's interest, and the imperative of avoiding disorder must be the motivation to share power more equitably.

The need for collective action

Achievements in eradicating human poverty depend first and foremost on people's ability to articulate their demands and mobilize for collective action. Isolated and dispersed, poor people have no power and no influence over political decisions that affect their lives. But organized, they have the power to ensure that their interests are advanced. As a group they can influence state policies and push for the allocation of adequate resources to human development priorities, for markets that are more people-friendly and for economic growth that is pro-poor. It is the pressure from people to defend their rights and to remove obstacles and enhance their life opportunities that will eradicate human poverty.

Putting local initiatives and community action at the centre of poverty eradication strategies is the only way, though a difficult one, to ensure that those strategies are truly

---

BOX 5.1

Vested interests in perpetuating poverty

Poor people are often seen as an economic burden on society. Yet poverty often serves the vested interests of the economically powerful, who may depend on the poverty-stricken to ensure that their societies run smoothly. A mobile pool of low-paid and unorganized workers is useful for doing the "dirty, dangerous and difficult" work that others refuse to do. In industrial countries many jobs considered menial are taken by immigrants, legal and illegal. With no legal protection or opportunity for collective action, workers are often exploited, receiving wages far below the minimum.

Source: Øyen 1997.

The poor can also be politically convenient. In some countries they serve as scapegoats for the ills of society, as immigrant workers do in Europe and North America. But they can also serve as a useful pool of voters for politicians who claim to serve their interests—even if they never consult them.

In the end, poverty reduction must involve some redistribution of resources—economic, social or political—and that will sometimes be vigorously opposed. Any strategy to eradicate poverty must therefore take into account the fact that many people have a vested interest in the perpetuation of poverty.

people-centred. This has profound implications. Poor people must no longer be seen as beneficiaries of government largesse, but instead as legitimate claimants of entitlements. That is why years of action by community groups and others have focused increasingly on rights—to employment, to health, to reproductive freedom, to participation. This approach recognizes the inherent dignity of all members of the human family—a dignity that states have a duty to protect.

People's mobilization for collective action to eradicate poverty may take many forms.

Community mobilization

Poor people must mobilize themselves and build solidarity to improve their life opportunities. Individual empowerment is the starting point of community action. As the women's movement has so successfully demonstrated, the personal is political (box 5.2).

At the core of collective action against poverty is self-help. Under normal circumstances most communities already have systems of mutual support. As chapter 3 shows, one of the main assets people have to defend themselves against poverty is the network of family and community to which they can turn to cope with sudden crises.

At times, however, these networks are stretched beyond breaking point. Historical processes such as wars or colonization have sometimes weakened the social capital of communities. This has happened, for example, in large areas of Indochina—Cambodia, the Lao People's Democratic Republic and Viet Nam—as a result of the Viet Nam War and its aftermath.

Much the same could be said of the impact of colonialism in Africa. The belittling of African culture and identity and imposition of Western values sabotaged social cohesion and solidarity in many communities. Strengthening cultural traditions can be an important part of building the capacity for taking collective action.

There are striking examples of communities coming together to fight poverty. In Senegal villagers have set up development associations for village improvement, water management, road construction, cooperative marketing, mosque building and a range of other activities.

The emergence of "local corporatism" in recent years in China is another example of small-scale economic solidarity. Township and village enterprises are spreading fast in rural areas of Guangdong, Hebei and Jiangsu Provinces. Part of the profits are put into community funds to help support adult education and finance informal insurance schemes for protection in case of illness.

In many other countries cooperative associations based on traditional forms of solidarity manage small irrigation systems, ensuring that the poorest households get the water they need. In the Philippines these self-managed schemes are called *zanjeros,* in Thailand *muang-fai* and in Bali *subaks.*

Community organizations, whatever the terms used to describe them, are multiplying the world over. Kenya has 23,000 registered women's groups, and the Philippines about 12,000 people's organizations. In India the state of Tamil Nadu

---

BOX 5.2

Alagamma gains control of her life

Empowerment is about change in favour of those who previously exercised little control over their lives. This has two sides. The first is control over resources (financial, physical and human). The second is control over ideology (beliefs, values and attitudes).

Alagamma is an illiterate Indian woman of scheduled caste. She used to earn a pittance from Ganesan, a quarrying contractor, by breaking granite blocks into smaller stones. Her entire family was bonded to Ganesan because her father once borrowed money from him secured on their quarter acre of land.

Then the government gave quarrying rights to groups of women workers like Alagamma, breaking the hold of contractors and the Indian mafia.

Alagamma and her father took Rs 1,000 ($40) to the shop where Ganesan was sitting. They told him that they had come to repay the money they had borrowed eight years ago and reclaim their quarter acre. Ganesan was not inclined to take the money and told them to come back in two or three years. But Alagamma and her father were adamant: they told Ganesan they would plough their land the next day. And they did.

Empowerment starts with changes in consciousness and in self-perception. This can be the most explosively creative, energy-releasing transformation, one from which there is no looking back. Empowerment taps powerful reservoirs of hope and enthusiasm among people used to viewing themselves negatively.

Governments, NGOs and other institutions do not empower people; people empower themselves. But through policies and actions governments can either create a supportive environment or put up barriers to empowerment.

Source: G. Sen 1997.

alone has more than 25,000 community organizations. Counting non-registered groups would push the figures even higher.

Non-governmental organizations

A vibrant civil society working towards the eradication of poverty also depends on the mobilization of people in more formal organizations. Strong communities of NGOs are particularly active in some countries—such as Bangladesh, Brazil, India, Indonesia, Kenya, the Philippines, Thailand and Zimbabwe—playing a vital role in poverty eradication and in advocating people-friendly development strategies. In Thailand, for example, government-NGO consultations and partnerships are frequent and dynamic in many important policy areas—from environmental protection to housing rights for slum dwellers to HIV/AIDS prevention. NGOs must have the space and freedom to play this essential role.

NGOs can be an important force for poverty eradication—pressing for land reform, for example, or protecting slum dwellers from property developers (box 5.3). They can also represent people's views and priorities in contacts with governments.

In addition, NGOs can reinforce and complement government activities—tending to be more flexible, more responsive and more effective than official agencies in reaching some communities. This role should not be seen as "filling gaps" because it does not relieve governments of their responsibilities, a result that might be repugnant to some proponents of NGOs. But there are many productive partnerships achieving things that governments alone could not. In India, for example, government resources combined with NGO energy and creativity reaped spectacular results in the Total Literacy Campaign.

Trade unions

Throughout the 20th century and before, trade unions have played a vital part in promoting better living and working conditions. In the industrial countries years of trade union activism were part of the struggle for higher wages, better benefits, shorter working hours and stronger safety precautions in the workplace. But trade unions have also had a much broader social and political impact. In many countries trade unions were influential in the development of welfare states and people-friendly markets (box 5.4).

But their power has been waning, and membership is down almost everywhere. In the United States union membership declined from 23% of the labor force in 1970 to 16% in 1990. In France it has fallen from 22% to 10%, and in Spain from 26% to 10%. Only in the Nordic countries has union membership increased since 1970.

In developing countries the shares tend to be smaller, because there are fewer workers in the formal sector. In Sub-Saharan Africa only 1–2% of workers are

---

BOX 5.3

Empowering the urban poor in Mumbai, India

In developing countries NGOs play an indispensable role in helping to reduce and eliminate poverty. Their activities vary widely, but their aims are the same.

Yuva—Youth for Unity and Voluntary Action—is one of many NGOs working in Mumbai (Bombay) for the rights of the urban poor. It organizes youth and women for social action in housing, health, education and the judicial system and offers counseling. Yuva is also active in policy advocacy—and made its voice heard at the Habitat II conference in Istanbul in 1996.

One of its main activities is providing support to pavement dwellers, who are under constant threat of being evicted and of having their makeshift homes bulldozed by the municipal authorities. Often when people are evicted, the authorities offer to relocate them to the outskirts of the city, far from their work and from their children's schools. Most soon trickle back to their old locations, and the cycle starts again.

These people can find themselves powerless in the vice between politicians and large urban developers—a situation that also offers considerable scope for petty corruption by local officials.

Yuva educates people about their rights—with respect to housing, employment and schooling for their children. Recognizing that, as elsewhere, most responsibility for household survival falls on women, Yuva also supports such activities as women's savings funds.

One of the pavement dwellers, Lalitabai, explains their concerns: "We have lived here for many years, most of us for more than 15 years. We have ration cards, and our names are on the voting lists. We have a right to this ground. We are saying that we will not move from here until we have been given land and a house. And not housing miles away in the jungle outside Mumbai. No, what use would that be to us? We need housing here so we can continue to work in our jobs."

The success of organizations such as Yuva will always depend on the determination and courage of the poor people with whom they work. These qualities are clearly demonstrated by another pavement dweller, Shantabai, who says: "If we were not alert, they would simply come and take away our belongings. But we will fight them. We know this is a just fight. They claim they are enforcing the law, but we have been told and we know that these laws are wrong. It is right to resist them."

Source: G. Sen 1997.

unionized—and they tend to be the ones with better-paying, stable jobs. In Latin America and the Caribbean the share is about 20%.

As developing countries industrialize, unions become more important. In the Republic of Korea they have been the impetus for democratization. But in Asia generally, they are under pressure from governments and from multinational corporations, which often make their absence a condition of investment.

Trade unions have had trouble adapting to the changing times. They have lost influence as the workforce has shifted away from the ranks of production-line workers and towards the more dispersed workers in the services sector. The rapid increase in unemployment has further weakened the economic clout of trade unions. Many critics of trade unions now accuse them of contributing to unemployment and poverty by pushing the price of labour too high. If trade unions are to remain relevant, they clearly need to reinvent themselves—to represent a new generation of workers in a context of reduced demand for labour and to build broader alliances.

People's movements

Another essential form of collective action is the self-mobilization of people into large movements. Although these movements are often equated with unrest and violence, it is often the resistance to them by repressive regimes and corporate interests that causes the violence—not the movements themselves. To be effective, people's movements must emerge spontaneously from grass-roots initiatives, not be controlled or manipulated from above. This is not to downplay the importance of leadership in harnessing the energies of people towards common goals.

The most spectacular example of a people's movement: the enormously strong women's movement. Global in reach, empowering half the world's people, the women's movement has driven the progress towards gender equality. The recognition of equality as a human right, the near-universal right to vote and the increasing equality in educational enrolment in most countries—these are just some of the revolutionary achievements of this century-old movement.

Another notable example: the struggle against British rule in India, led by Mahatma Gandhi. His policies of *ahimsa* (non-violence) and *satyagraha* (passive resistance) have been the inspiration for many popular movements since—notably the civil rights movement in the United States. Gandhi's legacy includes the aspiration to eradicate the unjust social and economic aspects of the caste system.

Some movements—such as the anti-apartheid movement in South Africa and the movement for democracy in the Philippines that brought Corazon Aquino

---

BOX 5.4

Trade unions led poverty reduction in Germany

Trade unions work solely for the benefit of their members. True? Not always. Many have had a much broader social and political impact—such as those in Germany.

Since the late 19th century the work week in German industry has been virtually halved. The union movement has also succeeded in ensuring the steady extension of financial safeguards against the kind of economic downturns that led to rampant poverty and misery in the 1870s and 1930s.

Many things now taken for granted are social rights that were fought for and won with much struggle by the trade unions: freedom of association, the right to strike and to bargain collectively, industrial health and safety standards, industrial law, universal suffrage, co-determination and worker participation in the workplace and the company and representation on public bodies responsible for everything from social insurance to radio.

Trade unions proved to be the biggest organized force working not only for social reform but also for democracy. Alongside other associations and political parties and often against strong opposition, they struggled for a more people-friendly market and a "social state", basic political rights and democratization. Trade unions became "schools" and guarantors of democracy. With the creation of the Federal Republic, they strongly supported the strengthening of democratic traditions and the creation of a "social market economy".

In the postwar era the German economy has been a powerful exporter. Social progress did not inhibit international competitiveness—contrary to what some critics of the social welfare state and strong unions still contend.

Although in Germany labour does not have the same influence over national politics as it does in Austria or Sweden, workers councils and co-determination at local levels have been decisive in guaranteeing social progress, even in times of slow growth. Both unions and management are prohibited from taking actions that could endanger the welfare of the company. The outcome is referred to as "socially oriented business policy".

The German labour union movement stands in stark contrast to the antagonistic labour relations in the United Kingdom and the United States. The underlying difference is that the German model is based on negotiation and compromise, the Anglo-American model on exclusion and polarization.

Source: Schneider 1991 and Block 1995.

to power—have profoundly affected national human development.

Smaller movements focused on specific issues or reacting to a specific threat are also important collective action. Many local groups have mobilized against development projects or private company activities that threaten the natural environment and the livelihoods that depend on it. Others have focused on more general environmental concerns—for example, the Green Belt movement in Kenya (box 5.5). And still others have focused on health and nutrition issues—such as the Hunger Campaign in Brazil (box 5.6).

The need for partnerships

The success of political mobilization against poverty hinges on winning broad and diverse support. Poor people alone, however well organized, cannot force the policy shifts for poverty eradication. All groups in society must be involved—not just those representing the poor. Alliances, partnerships and compromises are the only viable vehicles for peaceful, sustained reform.

What does it take to mobilize those alliances and partnerships? A clear, shared vision of the future that provides an unshakable focus for action. And not just for the poor. Visionary ideals can rally groups normally seen as elite—politicians, academics and other leading members of society—to form alliances with the poor.

When enough people rally to a cause, many ideals can become realistic. Consider the abolition of slavery in the 19th century. And consider many of the welfare reforms of the 20th century, which would have seemed unthinkable a few decades before. Idealists should thus continue to think the unthinkable, but with clear commitment, presenting their proposals with the same detail and elaboration typically devoted to a meticulous defence of the status quo.

Reformers need to work out the best strategy for negotiating their way through the power structure. Each strategy must of course take local circumstances into account, but experience shows the value of

some general approaches, such as finding common interests and exploiting differences among elite groups.

*Finding and creating areas
of common interest*

No child should die of hunger. On this the whole community can probably agree. The community may also agree that all citizens, regardless of their ability to pay, should have basic health and education services. Common interests may also reinforce these common concerns. Reducing levels of infectious disease by spraying or immunization makes everyone safer. Similarly, a more literate population benefits all of society through the associated productivity gains.

Common interests also abound between employers and employees. Enlightened employers want their workers to be well fed and energetic, and so are likely to support low food prices. But they also want workers to be literate and skilled,

and so will support investment in education and training.

Alliances may also be possible between groups that seem to have little in common. In Norway urban and rural poor found a common interest in promoting rural development that discouraged migration to the towns and kept industrial labour in short supply (box 5.7).

Common interests can also emerge between beneficiaries and providers of social services. Nurses, social workers, extension workers, paramedical personnel, primary school teachers—all stand to benefit from an expansion of services. And since they are often better organized and more vocal than the poor, they can be powerful allies.

In Kenya and Sri Lanka in the 1980s, for example, resources devoted to primary education increased partly as a result of pressure from powerful teachers unions. And in Peru in the 1980s, primary education expanded largely because of efforts by political parties to win the votes of teachers.

Just last year in Zimbabwe, nurses went on strike to demand not only higher wages but also more public investment in health care. The government assumed that this was mere pleading on behalf of a certain group of employees. In fact, despite the disruption to health services, the strike enjoyed widespread popular support.

Exploiting differences among elites

Most ruling elites are coalitions of different groups, and the poor can sometimes take advantage of this.

In 19th-century Britain factory workers allied themselves first with the industrialists—to support the repeal of the Corn Laws, which kept the price of food high. But they also allied themselves with the landowners against the industrialists when it came to supporting laws that protected the workforce. Both landowners and industrialists protested that they would be ruined—but both agriculture and industry flourished for a quarter of a century. As has been shown many times, promoting the interests of the poor does not run counter to the long-term interests of the rich.

BOX 5.7

A rural-urban alliance for poverty reduction in Norway

Almost everybody in society benefits from the reduction and eradication of poverty, and disparate groups can be brought together to work towards that goal once a common interest has been identified. Let's take a simple example.

In Norway poverty was virtually eliminated in the first half of the 20th century—largely thanks to an alliance between rural smallholders and urban industrial workers.

In 1900 Norway was a poor country. Although natural resources, especially fish, were plentiful and the country was sparsely populated, rural people (70% of the population) lived in hunger and poverty.

Like many developing countries today, Norway could have remained a rich country with poor people. Why didn't it? Three reasons:
• *Education.* Early investment in education ensured that by 1900 illiteracy was virtually zero.
• *Secure land tenure.* Land was of little commercial value, so even poor people had secure tenure and thus access to natural resources.
• *Democratic institutions.* By 1913 universal adult suffrage meant that the rural poor were strongly represented in parliament.

Source: Brox 1996.

This last point is particularly important. Unlike in many other European countries, in Norway democracy came first and industrialization second. A modern economy developed under a government representing the people, resulting in more equitable and people-centred policies to alleviate poverty.

Also distinguishing the Norwegian experience is the solid alliance that emerged between rural smallholders and urban workers. Both groups had a strong interest in accelerating rural development. For the rural poor this was a matter of direct self-interest. For urban workers it meant preventing large-scale migration to the cities, which would lead to a labour surplus and weaken the trade unions.

The strength of the rural poor lay in their voting numbers, while that of urban workers lay in their ability to disrupt production. Their coalition was so successful in ensuring heavy investment in rural areas that as late as 1960 half the population still lived there.

Only recently has this equilibrium been disturbed, with unemployment rising in both rural and urban areas.

Another example is the expansion of food stamps in the United States in the 1960s. In this case the interests of poor people coincided with those of people in the food-producing rural districts, whose representatives in Congress allied themselves with welfare-minded liberals.

The need for an activist state

Individuals and groups can do a great deal on their own to combat poverty. But much will depend on the environment created by government action. The state has a central role—not just through its activities but through its influence on many other elements of society. And the call for people's mobilization must not be a justification for the state to abdicate its responsibilities.

In the era of structural adjustment many states have slashed expenditures on social services, often with the argument that the gap can be filled by community self-help. At times the pressure on spending has motivated the introduction of user fees for health services—in countries where there is no capacity for effective means-testing and where people cannot afford even the lowest fees. This is a perversion of the ideals of self-help.

A poverty eradication strategy requires not a retreating, weak state but an active, strong one, and that strength should be used to enable the poor rather than disable them.

The disabling state

Some states use much of their power for actions that run counter to the interests of poor people. Politicians use government resources to strengthen their hold on power. Public officials demand bribes before they allow access to government benefits (box 5.8). And well-connected citizens use political influence to gain preferential access to public resources. The result: not just inefficient and inequitable allocation of resources, but also less freedom and more human deprivation.

In the worst cases politicians have used their offices ruthlessly to amass personal wealth and power and benefit those on whose support they depend—with no regard for efficiency or the public interest. The most extreme examples include Trujillo in the Dominican Republic, Somoza in Nicaragua, Amin in Uganda, Marcos in the Philippines and the Duvaliers in Haiti.

But it is not necessary to point to a handful of dictatorships to find ways in which governments are dominated by vested interests. Health and education services are fre-

---

BOX 5.8

Poverty and corruption

Like blackmail, corruption makes you pay to end the nuisance it creates: it puts sand in the gears of the administrative machinery and charges you for its removal.

Corruption in government increases poverty in many ways. Most directly, it diverts resources to the rich people, who can afford to pay bribes, and away from the poor people, who cannot. But it also skews decisions in favour of capital-intensive enterprise (where the pickings are greater) and away from labour-intensive activities more likely to benefit the poor.

Corruption also weakens governments and lessens their ability to fight poverty. It reduces tax revenues and thus the resources available for public services. And if administrations are assumed to be corrupt, honest people tend to avoid public service, so the quality of personnel suffers. More generally, corruption eats away at the fabric of public life—leading to increased lawlessness and undermining social and political stability.

To focus attention on this issue, a recently established NGO, Transparency International, publishes an annual Corruption Perception Index based on a survey of international businesspeople's perception of corruption in the countries in which they operate. In 1996, according to this index, the most corrupt country was judged to be Nigeria, followed by Pakistan, Kenya, Bangladesh and China; the least corrupt was New Zealand.

Many countries are now making greater efforts to root out corruption. They are introducing systems to improve transparency and accountability in public administration, including regular independent auditing and incentives and protection for whistle-blowers.

In Botswana the parliament passed the Corruption and Economic Crime Act in August 1994. This act establishes a directorate, reporting to the president, with a mandate to prevent, investigate and report on corruption. The act also provides a comprehensive legal framework for the government's anticorruption drive, which is already showing results.

Other countries are addressing what is often considered the root cause of corruption—inadequate government salaries. Uganda has tripled the salaries of teachers in the hope that this will reduce the widespread practice of selling grades and test results. And Philippine tax authorities have reduced corruption through employee bonuses and merit-based promotions.

Corruption also requires an international response, and corporations from industrial countries must bear some of the responsibility. They often consider paying bribes a reasonable way to do business—and it is frequently tax-deductible. The US government has made corruption by US citizens of officials in other countries a criminal offence, something that other countries are now also considering.

Discussions about corruption have intensified at the United Nations, and in 1996 the Economic and Social Council adopted the United Nations Declaration against Corruption and Bribery in International Commercial Transactions. In addition, the Crime Prevention and Criminal Justice Branch of the UN Secretariat continues to provide guidelines and recommendations to governments on rooting out corruption.

Source: Transparency International 1996 and Frisch 1996.

---

quently biased towards the wealthy in urban areas. Food policy too is often skewed towards the well off: prices are kept low so that urban officials and the military get subsidized supplies—at the expense of poor farmers and landless labourers.

The structure and operations of the economy may be pro-rich and antipoor, biased towards serving vested interests. Government policy can lead to underpriced capital, overpriced labour and an overvalued exchange rate—encouraging techniques that are capital and import intensive. And governments may support monopolies and cartels rather than labour-intensive microenterprises in the informal sector or small-scale agriculture. In Malawi until recently, smallholder farmers were forbidden to grow some of the more profitable cash crops, protecting the interests of a powerful consortium of estate owners.

Market competition offers an important way in which people, especially poor people, can escape economic domination by exploitative government, big landlords and big retailers. But for markets to help in this way there must be real competition, not monopolies. Worst of all are markets corrupted by biased government influence—when the market enters the government and the government sells off monopoly power to the highest bidder.

Various forces can encourage real competition, even where governments are weak or self-seeking. First, there are the profit-seeking ambitions of producers and retailers, who can be relied on to argue their own case. Second, there are influences and interests from abroad—foreign competitors eager to enter the market and donor governments and others wanting opportunities for their own exporters and investors. Third, there are the international agencies, supporting the doctrine of free trade and free competition. The result is rarely a textbook example of perfect competition, but poor people can often benefit from this diffusion of market power—and can certainly fare better than they would under a monopoly or under total government domination of the economy.

Probably the most shocking example of states' use of power contrary to the interests of poor people is the squandering of limited budgetary resources in the continued obsession with military might. Global defence spending amounted to roughly $800 billion in 1995 (in 1995 prices). South Asia spent $15 billion in 1995, more than what it would cost annually to achieve basic health and nutrition for all worldwide. Sub-Saharan Africa spent $8 billion, about the same as the estimated annual cost of achieving universal access to safe water and sanitation in all developing countries. And East Asia spent $51 billion, nine times the annual amount needed to ensure basic education for all worldwide.

If a government is more concerned about its military establishment than its people, the imbalance shows up in the ratio of military to social spending. Some countries have corrected this imbalance; others have not (table 5.1).

States can also add to impoverishment by squandering resources on prestige projects. Abortive projects have become a graveyard of white elephants in many poor countries. Factories have been built that have failed to reach full production capacity and need big state subsidies to keep going. Railways have been built that are now impassable because of lack of maintenance. Large sums have been spent on presidential palaces and other showpieces. And other infrastructure projects that are built might have some benefit, but not for poor people. A political decision to build a new international airport—one that will replace an old but fully functional airport—might run into strong opposition from local organizations demanding that the millions of dollars be invested instead in human development.

The enabling state

Fortunately, this bleak view of the state is only a partial one. The interaction among people, markets and states is generally more subtle. Many states can and do act in the common interest or in the interest of poor people—taking measures to, say, protect children, redistribute wealth or reduce poverty.

South Africa stands out as an example of a country with a political commitment to

Government that acts in the interest of poor people is easier to achieve in democratic systems

poverty eradication and a strategy based on public-private partnerships and a people-driven process of development. The political momentum of the struggle against apartheid is now driving the struggle against human poverty (box 5.9).

Government that acts in the interest of poor people is easier to achieve in democratic systems where the poor represent a significant electoral bloc. In Malaysia the government has promoted the interests of the Malays, who, although the majority of the population, are generally poorer than other groups. In Zimbabwe after independence, the government took many measures to benefit the poor majority, including a big shift in education priorities—between 1980 and 1984 it doubled the expenditure per primary student. And in Malawi after the 1994 shift to democracy, the government introduced free primary education, which increased net enrolment from 53% to 76%.

But free elections are not sufficient to motivate states to become more enabling and responsible. Studies on the link between development and type of government have established no clear correlation between electoral democracy and successful eradication of poverty. One important reason is low voter turnout. It is especially low in some industrial countries, implying that many poor people do not use their vote to influence policies (table 5.2).

TABLE 5.1
Big military spenders

Country	Military expenditure as % of GDP 1995	Military expenditure as % of combined education and health expenditure 1991
Korea, Dem. People's Rep. of	25.2	..
Oman	15.1	283
Iraq	14.8	271
Croatia	12.6	..
Kuwait	11.8	88
Saudi Arabia	10.6	151
Israel	9.2	106
Russian Federation	7.4	132
Tajikistan	6.9	..
Pakistan	6.5	125
Myanmar	6.2	222
Brunei Darussalam	6.0	125
China	5.7	114

Source: IISS 1993 and 1996.

BOX 5.9

South Africa—the struggle continues

"My government's commitment to creating a people-centred society of liberty binds us to the pursuit of the goals of freedom from want, freedom from hunger, freedom from deprivation, freedom from ignorance, freedom from suppression and freedom from fear. These freedoms are fundamental to the guarantee of human dignity." In these words at the opening of the first democratically elected parliament in South Africa, President Nelson Mandela captured the hopes, aspirations and needs of the population, particularly of the black majority.

For many the situation has not yet changed much—the landless; the homeless; the black African majority, more than 40% of whom live in absolute poverty; women and children, who are the majority of those living in deprivation, especially in rural areas; and the growing numbers of those who are unemployed, underemployed or living on less than $1 a day.

South Africa must operate in an increasingly competitive global environment with a limited pool of skills and an economic system that needs major restructuring to promote growth. The level of inequality is among the highest in the world, and crime and violence of all sorts, particularly against women and children, are on the rise. Government spending must be redirected towards those in greatest need. But cuts in social expenditures make sustainable development based on progressive redistribution difficult to achieve.

South Africa is in search of ways to eradicate poverty through a people-driven process—one that has people and government working in a new partnership to identify common priorities. This partnership would work towards processes for restoring and redistributing land; a legal framework to ensure more equitable access to loans, housing, education, health care and paid work; and the effective promotion of racial and gender equity.

A participatory study, conducted in more than 150 communities nationwide, surveyed people's perceptions of the problems affecting them and of the most effective ways to transform their situation. People expressed a desire to be informed and to participate in new ways of governance. An essential need voiced by the people is for channels of communication that are accessible, appropriate and timely. "We cannot draw up collective plans and strategies with government if the bureaucracy is antipeople and the language inaccessible," said one person.

Another need is for solutions to the violence—institutional, political, criminal and domestic—that people face in their daily lives. As another person said: "We are at war in our townships, we live in fear for our lives every day, and nothing is being done to safeguard us or our children. How much more must we take before something is done? We will no longer wait for others to do anything for us, because whether we live or die does not matter to those who have the resources. We will empower ourselves through mass action and education to solve our problems ourselves."

The new constitution has created an environment in which partnerships, coalitions and alliances can be forged, based on past common struggles against apartheid. This will unleash a process driven by people at the grass roots that could mobilize both human and material resources to address widening and deepening poverty.

The political success that has been achieved provides the space for critical action, based on a shared history of struggle. A range of people's organizations are emerging, born out of political resistance and unique strategies of local mobilization. These organizations can work with the new government to plan joint strategies to energize reconstruction and development. And they can push for government support of a people-driven, sustainable process of development—a process that generates work, ensures sustainable livelihoods, builds a sense of pride and reclaims the community as a dynamic force for social transformation.

Source: Taylor 1996 and 1997.

During the cold war era the threat of communism was an important force in motivating non-communist regimes—whether or not they were democratic—to improve the conditions of poor people. Just as Bismarck introduced social policies to stem the tide of socialism in Germany, the governments of such countries as Indonesia, the Republic of Korea, Malaysia and Thailand advanced the interests of the poor to avoid social unrest and political upheaval. With this motivating force removed, it has now become even more critical to find ways to build political commitment to poverty eradication. The fall of communism has left only one prevailing economic ideology in the political marketplace. Does the lack of competition mean that the concerns of poor people are forgotten?

Most states are neither wholly harmful nor wholly beneficial. They are not monoliths, but collections of institutions and structures. This complexity offers the potential for checks and balances that can restrain corrupt officials and predatory government. It also offers openings for reform and alliances within state structures.

States committed to building the political momentum and policy environment for the eradication of poverty can take steps in several important areas. More important, even states that are not fully committed can be encouraged to take such steps, through lobbying, democratic pressure and international influence. These actions put poor people on the political map and support a society-wide mobilization and partnership for pro-poor action.

• *Promote political participation by all.* The government must enable people's active participation at many levels of debate, dialogue and decision-making. This requires tolerant government institutions and free discussions of policy, development and change. Such an open atmosphere is greatly assisted by freedom of speech, democratic institutions, free elections and respect for human rights. And ensuring the full partic-

---

BOX 5.10

The power of participation

The great value of participatory rural appraisals (which are not exclusively rural) is in the way they empower communities and build their capacity for self-help, solidarity and collective action. Such appraisals can be best described as a family of approaches, methods and behaviours that enable people to express and analyse the realities of their lives and conditions, plan what action to take and monitor and evaluate results. They provide ways to give poor people a voice, enabling them to express and analyse their problems and priorities. Used well, they can generate important (and often surprising) insights that can contribute to policies better fitted to serving the needs of poor people. More fundamentally, they can challenge the perceptions of those in authority and begin to change attitudes and agendas.

The methods used enable people to share information, and stimulate discussion and analysis. Many appraisals use visual tools. Maps show where people live and where water, forests, farmland, schools and health facilities are located. Flow diagrams help to analyse problems and find solutions. Seasonal calendars aid in planning agricultural activities, and matrices in comparing the merits of different crop varieties.

Participatory rural appraisals have also proved to be of direct value to policy-makers. By obtaining information from communities, the appraisals can build a detailed picture of the complexity and diversity of local people's realities—and do it far better than such conventional survey techniques as questionnaires. They provide an opportunity to meet people face to face and a means of gaining quick and accurate assessments of the implications and impact of policies.

In Jamaica an appraisal showed that the stigma of living in an area with a reputation for violence makes it difficult to find a job. In Zambia an appraisal identified the wide gap between policy and practice on exemptions from health care charges for the destitute, showing that the poorest often lose out. In Honduras and Panama appraisals showed that the areas where indigenous people's land rights were threatened also had the greatest biological diversity in the country, strengthening the people's claim to the land and the right to manage and conserve its resources. In Scotland an appraisal identified villagers' interest in purchasing and managing forests to generate jobs.

Participatory rural appraisals have evolved and spread with astonishing speed since the early 1990s. Originating mainly among NGOs in East Africa and South Asia, they have since been adopted by government departments, training institutes, aid agencies and universities around the globe. They are now used in at least 100 countries.

Source: IDS 1996b and Attwood 1996.

TABLE 5.2
Political participation in industrial countries

Country	Eligible voters voting (%) 1991–94
Lowest turnout	
USA	39
Switzerland	46
Russian Federation	50
Poland	53
Finland	68
France	69
Highest turnout	
Malta	96
Belgium	93
Latvia	90
Iceland	88
Slovenia	86
Denmark	84

Source: UNECE 1995b.

ipation of women and minorities is likely to require affirmative action.

• *Encourage public-private partnerships.* Ideally, the relationship between governments and NGOs should be one of partnership, resulting, as in many countries, in a constructive division of labour in which the standard service delivery by provincial and district authorities is complemented by the more flexible, responsive activities of NGOs. To support such partnership, governments should create an adequate space for NGOs and engage them in policy dialogue. Partnerships with private sector firms also hold promise.

• *Facilitate bottom-up planning.* Governments have to offer adequate means for communities to feed in views, information and policy recommendations through every tier of administration. A useful tool for participatory planning and one that is proving highly appropriate is participatory rural appraisal (box 5.10).

• *Ensure accountability and transparency.* All organizations, public and private, should be accountable not just to their shareholders or members but to society as a whole. This also means that NGOs should be held accountable not just to their donors but also to the communities they serve.

• *Prevent the criminalization of politics.* State action for human development and poverty eradication requires a clear separation of economic and political power. In the complex web of power relations and self-serving economic interests, weak governments cannot find a counterweight to economically powerful groups and individuals, leaving corruption a major obstacle to poverty eradication. Legal mechanisms, institutional arrangements and political commitments are needed to fight corruption at every level.

• *Protect the freedom of the press.* A free press is essential for providing people with the information they need to make rational choices about political action. It helps establish the right political incentives for policy-makers.

• *Promote judicial activism.* NGOs, community groups and people's movements are using legal action to achieve their goals. Many countries already have a legal framework recognizing economic, social and political rights, with constitutions that commit the government to human development—laws often underused. In other countries activism is needed to amend laws, do away with biases and anachronisms and contribute to a pro-poor legal framework for just settlements.

• *Promote civic education.* People need to understand how their own political system work—or could work. Governments should make greater efforts to ensure that people are aware of their history, their constitution and their rights. If they lack the resources for this work, they should encourage NGOs to do it.

The need for democratic space

Ending human poverty requires an activist state to create the political conditions for fundamental reform. Above all, this requires a democratic space in which people can articulate demands, act collectively and fight for a more equitable distribution of power. Only then will adequate resources be invested in human development priorities, and access to productive assets become more equitable. Only then will macroeconomic management be more pro-poor, and markets provide ample opportunities for the poor to improve their standard of living.

Since 1986 the proportion of governments that are democratically elected has risen from 40% to 60%. Although an important start, a democratically elected government is not enough, however. The challenge now is to ensure that democratic practices and principles permeate every level and dimension of society. When it comes to eradicating poverty, political reform is not an option—it is an imperative.

Ending human poverty requires a democratic space in which people can articulate demands, act collectively and fight for a more equitable distribution of power

CHAPTER 6

Eradicating human poverty worldwide —an agenda for the 21st century

The success of many countries in rapidly reducing many aspects of poverty makes inaction immoral

Eradicating poverty everywhere is more than a moral imperative and a commitment to human solidarity. It is a practical possibility—and in the long run an economic imperative for global prosperity. And because poverty is no longer inevitable, it should no longer be tolerated. The time has come to eradicate the worst aspects of human poverty in a decade or two—to create a world that is more humane, more stable, more just.

Reaching this goal early in the 21st century is more feasible than most people realize. True, there are the obstacles of vested interests and opposition. But scepticism and disbelief are just as disabling.

Freedom from poverty has long been an international commitment and a human right. The 1948 Universal Declaration of Human Rights stated the principle: "Everyone has the right to a standard of living adequate for the health and well-being of himself and his family, including food, clothing, housing and medical care and necessary social services" (box 6.1).

During the 1990s this commitment has been made more specific—and linked to time-bound targets—in the declarations and plans of action adopted in major global conferences on children (1990), environment and sustainable development (1992), human rights (1993), population and development (1994), social development (1995), women (1995), human settlements (1996) and food security (1996).

At the World Summit for Social Development in Copenhagen—the largest summit ever, with 117 heads of state present and 185 governments represented—countries for the first time made clear commitments to eradicate poverty, not merely alleviate it: "We commit ourselves to the goal of eradicating poverty in the world, through decisive national actions and international cooperation, as an ethical, social, political and economic imperative of humankind." They also committed themselves to follow-up action and implementation in partnership with all actors of civil society:

- To set national goals.
- To prepare strategies geared to reducing overall poverty substantially in the shortest time possible.
- To reduce inequalities.

BOX 6.1

Human poverty is a denial of human rights

Human poverty constitutes a denial of fundamental human rights. To promote social progress and raise the standard of living within the wider concept of freedom, international human rights law—as enshrined in the UN Charter, the Universal Declaration of Human Rights and other treaties and declarations—recognizes economic and social rights, with the aim of attacking poverty and its consequences. Among these rights are an adequate standard of living, food, housing, education, health, work, social security and a share in the benefits of social progress.

International law recognizes that many countries do not have the resources to achieve some of these rights immediately; nevertheless, states are obliged to take steps, to the extent that their resources allow, to progressively realize economic, social and cultural rights. International law also obliges the international community to assist poorer countries in addressing their resource problems, and commitments have been made at UN conferences to increase development assistance, focusing on human development priorities and the eradication of poverty.

All countries except Somalia and the United States have ratified the Convention on the Rights of the Child. Well over two-thirds of all countries have ratified other conventions related to poverty and human rights.

BOX TABLE 6.1
Ratification status of major human rights conventions, 1 March 1997

Convention	Countries that have ratified or acceded	Countries that have not ratified or acceded
Economic, social and cultural rights, 1966	135	57
Civil and political rights, 1966	136	56
Elimination of discrimination against women, 1979	153	39
Rights of the child, 1989	190	2

Source: United Nations Centre for Human Rights 1997.

- To eradicate absolute poverty by a target date to be specified in each country in its national context (box 6.2).

These commitments and the success of many countries in rapidly reducing many aspects of poverty make inaction immoral. But accelerated action will be spurred only if all countries, including the industrial, develop a new vision of the possibility of eradicating poverty and a stronger sense of how they will gain from it—through greater security, greater stability and greater prosperity.

The potential benefits of reducing poverty are often doubted—but once they appear, they are taken for granted. In country after country, incorporating the deprived into the market and the power structure has brought broader benefits. The same has happened when poor countries have been brought into the global economy, ending the marginalization of people and economies and achieving greater balance.

The scale of the challenge

What will it take to eradicate severe and absolute poverty the world over?

The numbers in human poverty are huge, whether counting those in conflict, children out of school, households without secure sources of food or access to safe water and sanitation, or the 1.3 billion people estimated to be struggling to survive on less than the equivalent of $1 a day. Notwithstanding the scale, the long-run

trends have been positive (figure 6.1). The numbers escaping from poverty have dramatically increased in the past few decades. The challenge ahead is to regain momentum, and when the rate of advance is insufficient, to accelerate it—and when there have been setbacks, to reverse them.

In a few countries, including at least one or two in most regions, poverty is rapidly decreasing, and many of the goals for the year 2000 or even beyond have already been achieved (table 6.1). These countries are the fortunate exceptions.

For most countries a major acceleration is still required if severe and absolute poverty is to be eradicated in a decade or two. Advances in life expectancy, child mortality and basic health and education, including the enrolment of girls, are continuing, but not fast enough.

The weakness of pro-poor policies and the slowness of growth are most serious for about 100 developing and transition countries. But the failures of pro-poor growth are most serious in Sub-Saharan and other least developed countries.

For the better-off countries, including most of the industrial countries, the challenge is not to achieve faster growth but to find new ways to reduce poverty and hold the line against new poverty and unemployment with the more or less steady growth already being achieved.

Moderating inequality is the first step in ending poverty. Since 1960 global inequality has increased beyond anything ever

FIGURE 6.1

If trends of the past continue…
1980–95 trends for all developing countries projected into the future

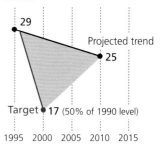

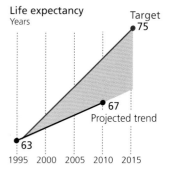

Source: Human Development Report Office.

TABLE 6.1
A few countries have already reached some of the goals for 2000 and beyond

Goal	Sub-Saharan Africa	Arab States	South Asia	East Asia	South-East Asia and the Pacific	Latin America and the Caribbean	Eastern Europe and CIS	Total
Life expectancy above 70 years	1	6	1	3	6	23	13	53
Under-five mortality rate below 70 per 1,000 live births	4	13	2	4	10	31	23	87
Net primary enrolment ratio of 100%	0	2	1	0	0	1	..	4
Girls' primary enrolment equal to or greater than boys'	5	3	1	2	1	16	..	28
Countries in region	44	18	8	5	15	33	25	148

Note: The life expectancy goal is for 2005 (ICPD 1994), the under-five mortality goal for 2000 (WSSD 1995), the enrolment goal for 2000 (UNESCO 1996c) and the girls' primary enrolment goal for 2005 (WSSD 1995).
Source: For life expectancy, UN 1996b; for under-five mortality rate, UNICEF 1997; and for net enrolment, UNESCO 1996b.

BOX 6.2

Progress and challenges in key areas of poverty eradication

Clear agreements to reduce poverty were made in all the global conferences of the 1990s—but a giant step forward was taken in 1995 with the new political commitment to eradicate poverty. Some of the specific goals:

• By 2000, reach a life expectancy at birth of not less than 60 years in every country, by 2005, a life expectancy greater than 70 years and by 2015, life expectancy greater than 75 years.

• By 2000, reduce under-five child mortality by a third from the 1990 level or to 70 per 1,000 live births, whichever is less, and by 2015, to less than 45 per 1,000 live births.

• By 2000, reduce maternal mortality by half from the 1990 level, and by 2015, by another half.

• By 2000, reduce severe and moderate malnutrition among children under age five by half from the 1990 level, giving special attention to the gender gap in nutrition.

• By 2000, achieve universal access to high-quality and affordable primary health care, removing all programme-related barriers to use of family planning by 2005. Eliminate polio, guinea worm disease, iodine deficiency disorders and vitamin A deficiency.

• By 2000, achieve universal access to basic education and the completion of primary education by at least 80% of primary-school-age children, and by 2015, universal primary education in all countries.

• By 2000, reduce adult illiteracy by at least half from its 1990 level; by 2005, close the gender gap in primary and secondary school education; and by 2020, reduce female illiteracy by at least half from its 1990 level.

More—and better—schooling

School enrolment at all levels has expanded by leaps and bounds in developing countries in the past 40 years. But many children receive little or no education or drop out at an early stage.

The World Conference on Education for All in 1990 resulted in agreement on a stepped-up programme to increase the coverage and quality of primary schooling and to expand adult education. The target: basic education and literacy for all by early in the 21st century.

By 1995 more than 100 countries had developed plans and strategies to achieve education for all, and about half had increased budgetary resources to support the plan. Total primary enrolment has risen by about 50 million since 1990, with the number of school-age children out of school falling from 130 million to 110 million.

Three priorities:

• Most countries need to raise the quality of primary schooling, with more resources needed for books and other learning materials and for improving the quality and pay of primary school teachers.

• Gender inequalities must be rapidly ended and policies adopted to offset the pressures hindering the enrolment and performance of girls.

• The international community needs to give stronger support to the poorest and least developed countries truly committed to the goal of education for all.

Reproductive health and family planning

Firmly anchored in a human rights framework, the programme of action of the International Conference on Population and Development in 1994 made the empowerment of women, gender equality and equity and reproductive rights and reproductive health, including family planning, the focus for follow-up action.

• Several countries have reoriented their policies and family planning programmes to adopt the broader reproductive health approach advocated. Prominent among them are India, Indonesia, Kenya, Lesotho, the Marshall Islands, Mexico, Mongolia, Peru and Zambia.

• Institutions to safeguard women's rights and to promote women's empowerment have been established in many countries, including the Directorate for Gender Equity in Colombia, the Women's Rights Commission in Peru and the Ministry for Women's Affairs and Women's Rights in Haiti.

• Increasing the role and responsibility of men in family planning, parenting and reproductive health is being emphasized in the Dominican Republic, Mauritius, Myanmar, Papua New Guinea and the Philippines.

• India has replaced its target approach to family planning with an approach integrating family planning with other aspects of reproductive health, emphasizing quality of care and meeting the needs of women and men.

To sustain the momentum generated at the 1994 conference, the international community must strengthen collaboration and cooperation in:

• Integrating population issues into sustainable development strategies.

• Vigorously advocating the empowerment of women and reproductive rights and reproductive health for all.

• Giving special attention to the reproductive health information and service needs of youth and adolescents and other vulnerable and marginalized groups.

• Preventing and controlling HIV/AIDS.

• Developing new partnerships with NGOs, the private sector and civil society.

• Mobilizing resources for expanded and accelerated programme implementation.

Advances in access to water

Improving access to water has been one of the fastest areas of advance since 1980, with rapid improvements in all regions and even in countries in economic decline.

Access to safe water and adequate sanitation for all is a basic need, important not only for health but for household cleanliness and for saving time and back-breaking treks to water-holes, especially for women. It is the basic input for change in the quality of life.

Since 1980 the share of people with access to water has more than doubled in rural areas and increased somewhat in urban areas, despite big increases in population.

Source: ICPD 1994, WSSD 1995, FWCW 1995, WSC 1990, UNFPA 1996a, 1996b, 1996c and 1997, UNESCO 1996c, Colclough and Lewin 1993, WHO and UNICEF 1997, Mason and others 1997 and RESULTS Educational Fund 1997.

In most countries advances have accelerated but progress is still too slow. The key problem has been lack of political commitment and lack of priority for the sector in national planning. While some attention was given to towns and cities, rural areas remained neglected, and operations and maintenance were virtually ignored. Sanitation was most neglected, and in 1995 coverage was about 63% in urban areas and 18% in rural.

Projections show that access to safe water for all can be achieved in urban areas with only a modest increase in coverage. In rural areas a major acceleration in the provision of water supplies is needed in all regions (except South-East Asia and the Pacific) to achieve safe water for all by 2010.

Nutrition's worrying slowdown

In developing countries about 160 million preschool children (half the total) are underweight, a number that has remained fairly steady. Of these, about 85 million are in South Asia alone—but the number in Sub-Saharan Africa has risen from about 20 million to almost 30 million in the past 10 years. The prevalence of malnutrition has been falling worldwide, but only by just about enough to offset population growth.

The goal of halving the prevalence of malnutrition in the 1990s was adopted by the World Summit for Children in 1990 and reaffirmed by the International Conference on Nutrition in 1992. Some countries managed an average reduction in prevalence of about two percentage points a year (say, from 40% to 20% in 10 years), Thailand for long enough to reach the goal, Indonesia and Sri Lanka for shorter periods.

Unless the rate of improvement is accelerated, the prospect of overcoming malnutrition will recede. At recent rates, it would take 200 years to eradicate malnutrition in South Asia, and in Sub-Saharan Africa an improving trend has yet to be established.

Many countries with widespread malnutrition now have policies to speed up improvements. Additional resources are needed to meet nutritional goals—but with the crucial step taken of deciding what to do, finding the resources should be less of a problem. Around $2–$10 a child per year—roughly $1 billion a year—could bring significant progress. But in some countries with large populations and high prevalence, such as Ethiopia and India, appropriate strategies are not yet in place.

Targeting gender inequality

The eradication of poverty requires equal opportunities and the full and equal participation of women and men as agents and beneficiaries of people-centred sustainable development.

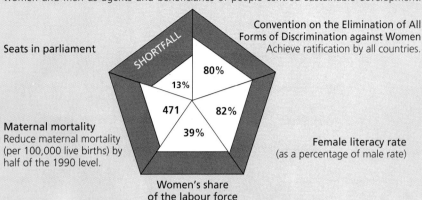

Seats in parliament

SHORTFALL

80%

13%

471

82%

39%

Convention on the Elimination of All Forms of Discrimination against Women
Achieve ratification by all countries.

Female literacy rate
(as a percentage of male rate)

Women's share of the labour force

Maternal mortality
Reduce maternal mortality (per 100,000 live births) by half of the 1990 level.

The platform of action adopted at the Fourth World Conference on Women at Beijing reaffirmed the objective of achieving equal rights, responsibilities, opportunities and participation for men and women in political, civil, economic, social and cultural life, with the full enjoyment by women and the girl-child of all human rights and fundamental freedoms.

Microcredit for poor people

Only 0.2% of global commercial lending reaches the poorest billion, 20% of the world's people. And microcredit programs now reach only about 8 million very poor people in developing countries.

The Microcredit Summit in 1997 set the target of reaching the 100 million poorest families, especially the women in those families, with credit for self-employment and other financial and business services by 2005. This requires an estimated $21.6 billion. A little more than half may need to come through grants and concessional loans, the rest from commercial credit markets, institutional earnings and the savings of the public, including the savings of the poor. Experience shows that financial institutions targeting the poor are sustainable after five to seven years.

Reaching the summit's objectives requires a complex strategy. Support from international agencies and donors is required, especially in the initial years. The challenge is to create new structures or new and more flexible instruments to link microcredit programmes with sources of funds, including the private sector.

Needed: pro-poor growth

All countries need to set clear targets for reducing the incidence of income poverty—but so far only a handful have done so, such as China, Malaysia, Viet Nam and Zimbabwe. And surprisingly, most countries do not have a poverty line for income. Without cut-off lines and targets,

efforts to monitor reductions in income poverty lack focus and direction.

Economic growth is necessary for reducing income poverty. But economic growth has failed badly over the past two decades in about 100 countries—in some 70 developing countries since 1980 or so and in some 30 countries in Eastern Europe and the CIS, mostly since the late 1980s.

Economic growth in general fell desperately short of the 3% per capita target needed to double incomes in a generation and to halve the incidence of poverty in a decade. There has been modest improvement in some countries in the 1990s, with 30 achieving per capita growth of 3% or more during 1990–94 (15 in Asia, 7 in Latin America and the Caribbean, 5 in Sub-Saharan Africa and 2 Arab states). But outside Asia, 59 countries recorded declines in per capita income during 1990–94 and another 22 grew less than 1% a year.

There have been welcome signs of some increases in growth in 1995, and a few more increases are forecast for 1996 and 1997. But almost all these increases are insufficient for more than a handful of countries to reach growth of 3% a year per capita. Indeed, outside Asia, only nine countries are forecast to achieve 3% growth in 1995–97, and this progress is offset by projections of slowing growth for at least six others from earlier rates above 3%.

Reducing income poverty also requires expanding employment opportunities for the poorest—so growth needs to be the kind that creates jobs and increases the productivity and income of the poor.

experienced. By 1991 the share of the richest 20% in the global economy had grown to 85%, while the share of the poorest 20% had fallen from 2.3% to 1.4%. By 1994 the share of the richest had soared to 86%, and the share of the poorest had shrunk to 1.1%. So, over the past 35 years the ratio of the incomes of the richest 20% to those of the poorest 20% has increased from 30 to 1 in 1960 to 61 to 1 in 1991 and to 78 to 1 in 1994.

Since the publication of last year's *Human Development Report*, the recorded number of billionaires in the world has increased from 358 to 447, with the value of their combined assets now exceeding the combined incomes of the poorest 50% of the world's people, up from 45% the year before.

These are obscenities of excess in a world where 160 million children are malnourished, 840 million people live without secure sources of food and 1.2 billion lack access to safe drinking water. These inequalities demand action.

Six essential actions

Earlier chapters have set out the actions required to eradicate poverty in the 21st century. In summary, we must:

1. Empower individuals, households and communities to gain greater control over their life and resources by:
• Ensuring their access to assets as a protection against vulnerability. Access to credit and other financial services is vital, as is security of tenure, especially for housing and land.
• Ensuring food security for households and all their members.
• Ensuring education and health for all, along with access to reproductive health care, family planning and safe water and sanitation. This goal needs to be achieved within a decade or two, not postponed for another generation.
• Building social safety nets to prevent people from falling into destitution and to rescue them from disaster.

2. Strengthen gender equality to empower women and to release their vast underused energy and creativity. Poverty

eradication without gender equality is impossible and a contradiction in terms. Among key priorities are equal access to education and health, to job opportunities and to land and credit and actions to end domestic violence.

3. Accelerate pro-poor growth in the 100 or so developing and transition countries whose economies are growing only slowly, stagnating or declining. A minimum target should be 3% annual per capita growth.

Pro-poor growth is not just growth. It is growth that:
• Restores full employment and opportunity expansion as a high priority of economic policy.
• Creates an enabling environment for small-scale agriculture, microenterprises and the informal sector.
• Restructures public expenditure and taxation to support poverty reduction and social security.
• Reverses environmental degradation and secures sustainable livelihoods, especially on the marginal lands on which about half the world's poorest people depend for their livelihoods.

In short, pro-poor growth means mainstreaming poverty reduction into national policy-making—easy to say, tough to achieve.

4. mprove the management of globalization, nationally and internationally—to open opportunities, not close them. Needed are better policies, fairer rules and fairer terms for poor and weak countries to enter markets, especially those for agricultural and textile exports. The aim must be to create employment and avoid a "rush to the bottom". But mainstreaming poverty reduction in international action is difficult—even when explicitly required in international agreements.

5. Ensure an active state, committed to eradicating poverty and providing an enabling environment for broad political participation and partnerships for pro-poor growth.

A strategy for poverty eradication must focus not only on what needs to be done, but on how to ensure that action is taken. This requires such fundamental reforms as promoting political participation by all, ensuring accountability and transparency in government, preventing the criminalization of politics, promoting a free flow of information and freedom of the press and ensuring a strong role for community groups and NGOs in policy-making and legislative decision-making. The legitimacy and strength of the state are based on its capacity to mobilize and be mobilized in the fight against poverty.

6. *Take special actions for special situations*—to support progress in the poorest and weakest countries and to prevent reversals:

• Conflict prevention and resolution, and peace-building efforts in war-torn countries combining political initiatives with support for economic and social reconstruction. Even in crisis, human development is possible.

• More effective support for Sub-Saharan African and other least developed countries, combining faster action on debt relief, higher priority in aid allocations and a sharper focus in aid on poverty reduction and on achieving education and health for all by 2015.

Country-by-country action must always be the starting point. But to be effective and sustained, national action must be reinforced and supported by regional and global action, especially in the poorest and least developed countries.

National policy-making

Different countries follow—and should follow—widely different paths for making policy and plans to reduce poverty. Several elements are usually essential:

• *Clear national objectives* for poverty reduction and eradication, set through a participatory process, with a core set of measurable and time-bound targets.

• *National assessments* of the main causes of poverty together with a strategy document setting out the policies and actions needed to eradicate poverty. Experience shows the value of developing programmes of action focused on priority groups and priority sectors. Some 100 countries have prepared plans of action for basic education, nutrition and reproductive health—often in

support of goals and commitments agreed to at the global conferences of the 1990s. Even more countries—150—have prepared national plans of action to accelerate implementation of the goals for children agreed to at the World Summit for Children in 1990 (box 6.3).

• *Mainstreaming poverty reduction* within national economic policy. Too often poverty reduction gets sidelined by the economic priorities of structural adjustment. Countries that have reduced poverty while adjusting have shown that poverty reduction should be part of the goals and the process of structural adjustment. This has now been accepted as a principle of international policy on adjustment, though it is not yet always practiced.

• *Mobilizing broad support,* drawing on the strengths and capabilities of a broad net-

---

BOX 6.3

Are global goals ever achieved? Yes

Goals set at UN conferences are often met with scepticism. But the achievements following the World Summit for Children in 1990 show that a different response may be warranted.

This first-ever summit on human issues set 7 major (and 20 supporting) goals, most to be achieved by the year 2000. Mid-decade goals were added later—for Sub-Saharan Africa, South Asia, East Asia, the Arab States and Latin America and the Caribbean.

Most progress has been made in immunization, polio, diarrhoeal diseases, iodine deficiency, guinea worm disease, access to safe drinking water and promotion of breast-feeding.

• One hundred twenty-nine developing countries have reached the 1990 goal of 80% immunization coverage—and by 1995, 59 developing countries had already reached the target for the year 2000 of more than 90%.

• With polio now eliminated in 110 countries, its eradication by 2000 looks "promising".

• Low-cost oral rehydration (against the effects of diarrhoeal disease) is now widely practiced, saving the lives of 1 million or so children a year.

• Iodine deficiency, the biggest preventable cause of mental deficiency, is on the retreat. Around 1.5 billion more

people had access to iodized salt in 1995 than in 1990. Some 12 million more are being saved from the impact of severe iodine deficiency each year.

• The number of children in primary school has risen by 50 million—and the number of school-age children not in school has fallen from 130 million to 110 million.

• Child mortality has declined in all regions. Worldwide, some 7 million more lives are being saved each year than in 1980.

In addition, the summit has helped to raise general awareness of children's needs and increase the commitment to meeting them. One hundred ninety countries have now ratified the Convention on the Rights of the Child. More than 50 have started reporting regularly on implementation.

Low-cost and cost-effective actions were a big part of the success, making it possible to achieve the goals by restructuring budgets rather than by making big increases in spending.

Monitoring was also vital. By 1995 almost 100 countries had undertaken household sample surveys, most covering 6,000–8,000 households, providing up-to-date information to assess progress. These are widely used at the country level to mobilize and maintain support.

Source: UNICEF 1996c.

---

work of actors—in government, academia, the media, the private sector, voluntary and non-governmental organizations and the social services and other professions.

• *Budgetary commitments* to allocating the resources needed to keep the strategy on track. A priority is to enhance the effectiveness of spending aimed at reducing poverty—both to improve its impact and as the best argument for increasing such spending.

• *Monitoring* to assess progress, guide corrections when the strategy goes off track and maintain public awareness and support.

Also key to success is mobilizing and sustaining public support, often easiest in local initiatives. The past decade or two have seen many successful local initiatives in all parts of the world—by mayors for urban renewal and poverty reduction, by religious groups worldwide in support of immunization, by literacy teachers for minority groups, by women's groups for fairer opportunities. Such local initiatives offer a base for building broader—even national—initiatives. A critical step is to transform commitment into national consensus, mobilizing a movement involving many groups—parliament, non-governmental organizations, religious organizations, professional associations, the private sector.

Costs?

The costs of eradicating poverty are less than people imagine: about 1% of global income—and no more than 2–3% of national income in all but the poorest countries (box 6.4). Moreover, there undoubtedly is room in most countries to restructure spending and reduce waste—even after the cutbacks and retrenchments of recent years. And there may be scope for drawing on private sources, including contributions from those using government services.

With creative organization and genuine participation, poor people have demonstrated an enormous capacity to contribute to activities and schemes in which they have a stake and the assurance of some control.

But the greatest potential comes from the additional resources that would be available from successful pro-poor growth. Channelling a fraction of these resources each year into poverty reduction and further investment in pro-poor growth could establish an accelerated pattern of self-sustaining, pro-poor growth. "Redistribution with growth", as such a strategy has been called, was followed in the 1960s and 1970s by many of the now-successful Asian countries, which in the initial phases were often helped by strong external support.

International action

Ways need to be found to bring these fundamental issues into the mainstream of international economic policy-making and action. Poverty reduction is still too often

---

BOX 6.4

The price tag for poverty eradication

Many assert that poverty eradication is not affordable. In a world economy of $25 trillion, this argument is patently false.

The additional cost of achieving basic social services for all in developing countries is estimated at about $40 billion a year over the 10 years to 2005.

Less than 0.2% of world income, this sum is about 1% of developing country income—or half the GNP share that the United States transferred each year to Europe during 1948–52 as part of the Marshall Plan for postwar reconstruction.

Most of the resources can come from restructuring existing budgets. For universal access to basic social services, about $30 billion could come from national budgets and perhaps $10 billion from aid. The 20:20 guideline endorsed in Copenhagen and first proposed in the *Human Development Report* would achieve this.

The investment needed to accelerate growth and empower everyone to escape poverty is impossible to calculate as a global sum. But to get some sense of its magnitude, it is possible to roughly estimate the cost of closing the gap between the annual income of poor people and the minimum income at which they would no longer be in extreme poverty. This figure is also small—amounting to about another $40 billion a year.

So, to provide universal access to basic social services and transfers to alleviate income poverty would—with efficient targeting—cost roughly $80 billion. That is less than 0.5% of global income and less than the combined net worth of the seven richest men in the world.

But poverty can be sustainably eradicated only through pro-poor growth, not through transfers. And most countries have more than enough to generate the resources needed to eradicate income poverty and to provide basic social services for all.

Lack of political commitment, not financial resources, is the real obstacle to poverty eradication. Eradicating absolute poverty is eminently affordable.

BOX TABLE 6.4

The cost of achieving universal access to basic social services
(US$ billions)

Need	Annual cost
Basic education for all	6
Basic health and nutrition	13
Reproductive health and family planning	12
Low-cost water supply and sanitation	9
Total for basic social services	40

Source: UNDP, UNFPA and UNICEF 1994.

seen as a matter for developing countries—not a global concern in which every country has a stake.

What has dominated the global economic agenda? So far, trade, property rights, finance, financial stability and governance. What's off the radar:
- Poverty eradication.
- Unemployment and the need for a long-term employment strategy.
- Marginalization of the poorest and least developed countries, and the need to achieve a long-run balance in the global economy.
- The need for environmental sustainability in the global economy.

These gaps in the global agenda point to five imperatives for international action:
- New initiatives for conflict prevention and resolution, and for peace-building in war-torn countries leading to reconstruction and poverty-reducing development. For such initiatives to be sustainable, and in some cases even possible, stronger controls on arms sales and greater reductions in military spending are needed.
- Supportive international action in priority areas of health (HIV/AIDS), nutrition, basic education, environmental protection and agricultural technology (research on technical packages for Africa). Such action is vital to provide the global infrastructure for long-term poverty reduction.
- More effective debt relief—larger in scale, faster in operation. Many proposals have been introduced over the past decade, but the levels and rates of implementation are pathetic in relation to the problems that debt poses for the severely indebted low-income countries. Only with debt reduction can poverty be reduced in many of these countries.
- Better focusing of aid on the least developed countries in Sub-Saharan Africa and elsewhere, especially those pursuing serious programmes to reduce poverty. A larger share of aid needs to go to the poorest countries and to their poverty reduction programmes. Allocations for expatriate technical assistance are excessive and should be reduced. Implementation of the 20:20 guidelines would mobilize more support for action in basic social services (box 6.5).

- Reduction of military expenditures, with the peace dividend channelled to poverty reduction and pro-poor growth. Half the world's governments still spend more to guard against military attack than to defeat the enemies of good health. Despite declines in the past five years, nuclear stockpiles still have a destructive potential 700 times that of all the explosive power used in the 20th century's three major wars. And world military spending amounts to 1.75 times that in 1960, at $797 billion in 1995 (more than $1.5 million a minute). There is much scope for regional action. In 1994 African ministers called for more public spending on human development and an urgent one-third reduction in military spending.

BOX 6.5

The 20:20 vision

The 20:20 Initiative, first proposed in *Human Development Report 1992,* was endorsed by the World Summit for Social Development in 1995. It lays down guidelines to mobilize the resources required to achieve access to basic social services for all. The idea is that governments should allocate about 20% of their budgets—and donors 20% of their aid budgets—to basic social services, sufficient for universal coverage.

In April 1996, at the invitation of Norway and the Netherlands, representatives of 40 governments gathered in Oslo—along with NGOs, UN agencies and the Bretton Woods institutions—to discuss implementation of the 20:20 Initiative. Options were explored for establishing agreements between governments and donors to enhance the funding of basic social services.

The resulting Oslo Consensus encouraged support and agreed on a common definition of basic social services to include "basic education, primary health care, including reproductive health and population programmes, nutrition programmes and safe drinking water and sanitation, as well as the institutional capacity for delivering those services."

What has happened since? Partial data suggest that 13% of national budgets and 10% of donor funding are being allocated to basic services. But there is evidence of a gradual increase in recent years. Within the framework of the OECD Development Assistance Committee, donor governments are discussing ways to improve the monitoring of bilateral assistance for basic services.

In Oslo some developing countries expressed interest in pursuing 20:20 development agreements with donors. UNICEF is helping them examine budgetary spending and the scope for restructuring public spending in favour of basic social services. UNDP is helping governments to integrate their social services into broader poverty reduction efforts.

The Oslo Consensus called for Consultative Group and Round Table conferences to review allocations to basic social services in the light of the 20:20 guidelines. Ethiopia has placed reform and funding for education high on the agenda for its next Consultative Group Meeting. All these developments are signs that developing countries and donors are devoting increased attention—and funding—to securing basic social services for all.

Source: UNDP 1994 and Mehrotra and Thet 1996.

Donor commitments to support poverty reduction

In 1996 donor countries laid out their plans for helping to reduce poverty in developing countries through a global partnership. In their vision for the 21st century they committed themselves to helping developing countries to:

• Cut by half the proportion of people living in income poverty by 2015.

• Ensure universal primary education by 2015.

• Advance towards gender equality and the empowerment of women by eliminating gender disparity in primary and secondary education by 2005.

• Reduce by two-thirds mortality among infants and children under five and reduce by three-fourths maternal mortality—all by 2015.

• Provide reproductive health services to all individuals of appropriate age no later than 2015 through the primary health care system.

• Prepare plans for ending environmental degradation.

These aims are intended to support national programs, not supplant them.

Source: OECD 1996e.

Rio plus five—taking stock of missed opportunities

The commitments made at the United Nations Conference on Environment and Development (UNCED) in 1992, encapsulated in Agenda 21, give equal weight to poverty and environment, recognizing the intrinsic relationship between the two in the context of sustainable development. But the political appeal of environmental issues in the North has allowed environmentalists to steal the show during the followup to the conference. Agenda 21 recognizes that a specific antipoverty strategy is one of the basic conditions for ensuring sustainable development. But this kind of focus on poverty has been missing from the global mechanisms established to support and monitor implementation of Agenda 21.

The UN Commission on Sustainable Development, charged with monitoring followup to UNCED and Agenda 21, has not made poverty a theme of its discussions. And the Global Environment Facility, the financing mechanism for meeting the global environmental goals of Agenda 21, is not geared to take account of the poverty-environment relationship. Meanwhile, the UN Commission on Social Development, charged with monitoring followup to the World Summit for Social Development, where poverty was the central concern, does not view poverty reduction in the context of its relationship to environmental protection and sustainable use of resources.

This "fault line" must be recognized and repaired. What is needed are global policies and mechanisms, bilateral and multilateral financing criteria and domestic policies and expenditure patterns that lead to the creation of assets for poor people, especially those who derive their livelihoods from natural resources. All these need to ensure that resources are invested in:

• Improving environmental health.

• Sustaining natural resources and ecosystems to ensure food, shelter, living space and livelihoods for poor people.

• Maximizing the potential of environmental protection activities to create sustainable employment and income.

• Supporting local communities in their role as custodians of their environment and natural resources.

• Ensuring rights of tenure, land use and access to physical resources and credit for poor people.

• Accelerating technological innovations needed to increase productivity and sustain livelihoods in marginal environments.

All these actions would build up the asset base of poor people and communities and help eliminate persistent poverty.

In the five years since UNCED the need to contribute to poverty reduction while attempting to apply Agenda 21 has been ignored. The world has an opportunity to redress this neglect this year as the United Nations reviews the progress made on Agenda 21 and corrects its course.

Regional action

In the past decade regional organizations have increasingly become forces for poverty reduction.

• SAARC (South Asian Association for Regional Cooperation) took initiatives on its formation in the mid-1980s to improve child health and survival. More recently, the SAARC programme for poverty reduction has been a source of innovation in social mobilization. The Dhaka Declaration of the SAARC Heads of State of 1992 endorses the goal of poverty eradication by 2002.

• SADC (Southern African Development Community) started with a political focus—to establish a common front against apartheid. But with the end of apartheid SADC has demonstrated its potential for subregional action for more human concerns—such as drought relief and improving conditions for children.

• The European Union has devoted much attention to social policy and to efforts to tackle social exclusion, including grants to reduce poverty and unemployment in marginal regions of Europe.

Two regional actions have great potential for helping to eradicate poverty: regional pacts to reduce military spending and reallocate it to poverty reduction and human security, and peer review of poverty plans and experience. Peer review could help in sharing experience and mobilizing more action without the one-sidedness of conditionality. It was the system the Marshall Plan used so successfully 50 years ago for postwar European reconstruction.

Poverty eradication and the United Nations

Poverty eradication is already a major focus for the United Nations, and followup to the World Summit for Social Development and the other global conferences has been made a focus for systemwide coordination. But more could undoubtedly be done, especially at the country level, to make poverty eradication a much stronger integrating framework for many of the development activities of the UN system.

Already support for poverty eradication is the highest priority of UNDP, and poverty reduction is among the central priorities of the main funding organizations of the United Nations—IFAD with its focus on rural poverty, UNFPA with its focus on women, reproductive health and family planning, UNIFEM with its emphasis on women's empowerment, UNICEF with its focus on children and the girl-child, UNHCR with its support for refugees, and the World Food Programme, which provides large-scale support in both emergency and non-emergency situations.

These organizations and the specialized agencies (FAO, UNESCO, ILO and WHO) and others (such as UNCTAD, UNCHS and UNEP) in the UN system have clear roles in follow-up action to the global conferences. But all could become part of a stronger global effort for poverty eradication through clear support for country-by-country action. A critical issue is how to establish more effective and creative partnerships with the World Bank, the regional development banks, the International Monetary Fund and the World Trade Organization.

National and international civil society should be a major player in all such efforts. Non-governmental organizations have long been leaders in support of poverty reduction, often extremely effective in pioneering approaches that empower poor people at low cost.

A big development of recent years is the greater recognition of the benefits of partnership—of working more closely together and recognizing the valuable contributions of others in what might otherwise be neglected areas. Partnership does not have to mean uncritical support for everything each group is doing, even when there is a shared focus on poverty reduction. Honest disagreement on such issues as the impact of adjustment on the poor or fees for health services has led to important reappraisals and changes in policy and approach. Indeed, these changes appear to be focusing international policy and support more on the needs and capabilities of poor people.

A grand alliance to eradicate poverty is a powerful integrating theme of the devel-opment efforts of the UN system—a focus for advocacy, action, support and regular reporting. UNDP is committed to playing a full and supportive part in this, including in its role as the UN resident coordinator in many countries. Poverty eradication is becoming a central focus of country assessments in which concerned UN organizations will join, under the leadership of the government. Better collection, publication and analysis of data showing whether and how countries are reducing poverty will be important for maintaining momentum (box 6.8). Partnerships between the UN system and the donor and NGO communities must be strengthened around nationally defined goals for poverty eradication.

The costs of inaction

Implementing this agenda will not be easy. But the costs of accelerated action must be measured against the costs of delay and inaction—against political conflict and instability, continuing disease and environ-

No longer inevitable, poverty should be relegated to history

BOX 6.8

Monitoring progress in eradicating poverty

All countries need to establish or expand a system for regularly monitoring basic indicators of poverty and human deprivation and advances in human development. Such monitoring can serve several purposes:
- Establishing public accountability for progress in poverty reduction.
- Guiding progress and identifying the need for mid-course corrections.
- Mobilizing public support and action, especially by NGOs.

The monitoring of poverty and human development has taken big strides over the past decade or two. There now are 150 sample surveys of nutritional status, covering nearly 100 countries. In 1975 there were four. And about 90 countries have mounted sample surveys—150 in all, each covering around 8,000 households—to assess progress in reaching the goals of the 1990s.

The World Bank has supported poverty assessments in some 50 countries, many using participatory rural appraisals.

Initiatives are under way to improve the monitoring of access to safe water and sanitation, basic education, reproductive health care and family planning.

National human development reports have been produced in some 70 countries, and more are under preparation with support from UNDP. These provide frank assessments of progress and setbacks, and analyses of policies affecting human development.

One interesting development: non-governmental organizations and networks are mounting their own monitoring of followup to the World Summit for Social Development and other global conferences. They also provide an annual report, *Social Watch,* to measure country and global performance (ITM 1997).

Monitoring requires not only the collection of relevant data, but the capacity to quickly process, analyse and publish them. Publicizing the results through the media typically generates popular interest and greater political commitment.

mental degradation in large parts of the world, affronts to humanity and human sensibilities. In today's world of instant communication and growing global awareness, the pains of poverty cannot be hidden amidst the excesses of wealth and the inequalities.

What are the costs of eradicating poverty? As already asserted, only about 1% of global income—and no more than 2–3% of national income in all but the poorest countries. Further cuts in military spending, with the savings channelled to poverty reduction and pro-poor growth, would go far towards providing the resources required.

The unprecedented progress in reducing poverty in the 20th century sets the stage for eradicating absolute poverty in the early 21st century—a moral imperative, an attainable goal. No longer inevitable, poverty should be relegated to history—along with slavery, colonialism and nuclear warfare.

Technical note 1. Properties of the human poverty index

This technical note states, establishes and discusses some important properties of the human poverty index. Intended as an aid to understanding the index, these properties are derived with respect to a more general definition of the human poverty index $P(\alpha)$ than that actually used in this Report. This allows the possibility that the weights on the three poverty subindices may differ, so that $P(\alpha)$ is a weighted mean of order α of P_1, P_2 and P_3.

Thus, letting $w_i > 0$ be the weight on $P_i (\geq 0)$, for $i = 1, 2, 3$, we define the generalized mean $P(\alpha)$ as

(1)
$$P(\alpha) = \left(\frac{w_1 P_1^\alpha + w_2 P_2^\alpha + w_3 P_3^\alpha}{w_1 + w_2 + w_3} \right)^{1/\alpha}.$$

The weighted mean reduces to the ordinary mean of order α when $w_i = 1$ for every i. With $w_1 = w_2 = w_3 = 1$, we have simply

(2)
$$P(\alpha) = \left[\left(\frac{1}{3} \right) P_1^\alpha + \left(\frac{1}{3} \right) P_2^\alpha + \left(\frac{1}{3} \right) P_3^\alpha \right]^{1/\alpha}.$$

The mean of order 1 ($\alpha = 1$) is the simple weighted or unweighted arithmetic mean of P_1, P_2 and P_3. Thus

$$P(1) = \frac{w_1 P_1 + w_2 P_2 + w_3 P_3}{w_1 + w_2 + w_3}$$
$$= \frac{1}{3} \left(P_1 + P_2 + P_3 \right) \qquad \text{when } w_i = 1 \text{ for every } i.$$

Can the human poverty index $P(\alpha)$ be interpreted as a headcount or incidence of poverty? While P_1, P_2 and P_3 are the headcount or incidence of poverty in each of three separate dimensions, $P(\alpha)$ cannot be generally thought of as the headcount ratio with respect to a poverty line (hyperplane) drawn in the product space of the three variables. Instead, $P(\alpha)$ is an average, albeit of order α, of the three subindices P_1, P_2 and P_3. If the incidence of poverty happened to be the *same* in every dimension, then $P(\alpha)$ would clearly be equal to this common number, since

$$\left[\frac{w_1 P(\alpha)^\alpha + w_2 P(\alpha)^\alpha + w_3 P(\alpha)^\alpha}{w_1 + w_2 + w_3} \right]^{1/\alpha} = P(\alpha) = \left(\frac{w_1 P_1^\alpha + w_2 P_2^\alpha + w_3 P_3^\alpha}{w_1 + w_2 + w_3} \right)^{1/\alpha}.$$

This observation allows us to interpret $P(\alpha)$ as the degree of overall poverty that is equivalent to having a headcount ratio of $P(\alpha)\%$ in every dimension.

The first property of $P(\alpha)$ that we establish is central to understanding it as a mean of P_1, P_2 and P_3. This property is that $P(\alpha)$ always lies between the smallest and largest values of P_i, for $i = 1, 2, 3$.

PROPOSITION 1.

$$\min \left\{ P_1, P_2, P_3 \right\} \leq P(\alpha) \leq \max \left\{ P_1, P_2, P_3 \right\}.$$

PROOF. By definition of $P(\alpha)$, we have

(3) $\quad P(\alpha)^\alpha = \dfrac{w_1}{w_1 + w_2 + w_3} P_1^\alpha + \dfrac{w_2}{w_1 + w_2 + w_3} P_2^\alpha + \dfrac{w_3}{w_1 + w_2 + w_3} P_3^\alpha.$

But for each $i = 1, 2, 3$,

$$\min \left\{ P_1, P_2, P_3 \right\} \leq P_i \leq \max \left\{ P_1, P_2, P_3 \right\}.$$

Therefore, since $\alpha > 0$,

$$\left[\min \left\{ P_1, P_2, P_3 \right\} \right]^\alpha \leq P_i^\alpha \leq \left[\max \left\{ P_1, P_2, P_3 \right\} \right]^\alpha.$$

Using the right-hand-side inequality for each P_i^α in equation 3 gives

$$P(\alpha)^\alpha \leq \frac{w_1 + w_2 + w_3}{w_1 + w_2 + w_3} \left[\max \left\{ P_1, P_2, P_3 \right\} \right]^\alpha$$
$$= \left[\max \left\{ P_1, P_2, P_3 \right\} \right]^\alpha.$$

Similarly,

$$P(\alpha)^\alpha \geq \left[\min \left\{ P_1, P_2, P_3 \right\} \right]^\alpha.$$

Hence

$$\left[\min \left\{ P_1, P_2, P_3 \right\} \right]^\alpha \leq P(\alpha)^\alpha \leq \left[\max \left\{ P_1, P_2, P_3 \right\} \right]^\alpha.$$

Since $\alpha > 0$, it follows that

$$\min \left\{ P_1, P_2, P_3 \right\} \leq P(\alpha) \leq \max \left\{ P_1, P_2, P_3 \right\}. \quad \square$$

The generalized mean $P(\alpha)$ is constructed for values of $\alpha \geq 1$. As shown, its limiting value when $\alpha = 1$ is simply the arithmetic mean of P_1, P_2 and P_3. In proposition 7 we show that the larger α is, the larger $P(\alpha)$ will be. For expositional reasons, it is convenient to demonstrate at this stage that as α tends to infinity, the limiting value of $P(\alpha)$ is max $\{P_1, P_2, P_3\}$.

PROPOSITION 2. As $\alpha \to \infty$,

$$P(\alpha) \to \max \left\{ P_1, P_2, P_3 \right\}.$$

PROOF. Let P_k be the largest—or in the case of ties, one of the largest—P_i, for $i = 1, 2, 3$. Thus

$$P_k = \max \left\{ P_1, P_2, P_3 \right\}.$$

Then from proposition 1, for any $\alpha > 0$, we have

(4)
$$P(\alpha) \leq P_k = \max \left\{ P_1, P_2, P_3 \right\}.$$

Now

$$P(\alpha)^\alpha = \frac{w_1}{w_1 + w_2 + w_3} P_1^\alpha + \frac{w_2}{w_1 + w_2 + w_3} P_2^\alpha + \frac{w_3}{w_1 + w_2 + w_3} P_3^\alpha$$
$$\geq \frac{w_k}{w_1 + w_2 + w_3} P_k^\alpha \qquad \text{since } P_k \text{ is one of } P_1, P_2 \text{ or } P_3.$$

Technical note 1 is from the *Human Development Report 1997* background paper by Sudhir Anand and Amartya K. Sen, "Concepts of Human Development and Poverty: A Multidimensional Perspective."

Therefore, since $\alpha > 0$,

$$P(\alpha) \geq \left(\frac{w_k}{w_1 + w_2 + w_3} \right)^{1/\alpha} P_k.$$

Letting $\alpha \to \infty$, $\left(\dfrac{w_k}{w_1 + w_2 + w_3} \right)^{1/\alpha} \to 1$,

so that $\quad \lim\limits_{\alpha \to \infty} P(\alpha) \geq P_k.$

But from equation 4 we also have

$$\lim_{\alpha \to \infty} P(\alpha) \leq P_k.$$

Hence

$$\lim_{\alpha \to \infty} P(\alpha) = P_k = \max\left\{ P_1, P_2, P_3 \right\}. \quad \square$$

The next property of $P(\alpha)$ that we demonstrate is that the index is homogeneous of degree 1 in the subindices P_1, P_2 and P_3. In other words, if the incidence of poverty in each dimension is halved (multiplied by $\lambda > 0$), the value of the aggregate index $P(\alpha)$ will be halved (changed to λ multiplied by $P(\alpha)$).

PROPOSITION 3. $P(\alpha)$ is homogeneous of degree 1 in (P_1, P_2, P_3).

PROOF. Let $\lambda > 0$ be a scalar number, and let $P(\alpha)$ be the value of the human poverty index corresponding to (P_1, P_2, P_3).

Then

$$P(\alpha) = \left(\frac{w_1 P_1^\alpha + w_2 P_2^\alpha + w_3 P_3^\alpha}{w_1 + w_2 + w_3} \right)^{1/\alpha}.$$

The value of the human poverty index corresponding to $(\lambda P_1, \lambda P_2, \lambda P_3)$ is then given by

$$\left[\frac{w_1 (\lambda P_1)^\alpha + w_2 (\lambda P_2)^\alpha + w_3 (\lambda P_3)^\alpha}{w_1 + w_2 + w_3} \right]^{1/\alpha} = \left[\frac{\lambda^\alpha (w_1 P_1^\alpha + w_2 P_2^\alpha + w_3 P_3^\alpha)}{w_1 + w_2 + w_3} \right]^{1/\alpha}$$
$$= \lambda P(\alpha). \quad \square$$

The next property of $P(\alpha)$ that we derive is that $P(\alpha)$ is monotonic increasing in each P_i, for $i = 1, 2, 3$.

PROPOSITION 4. For each $i = 1, 2, 3$,

$$\frac{\partial P(\alpha)}{\partial P_i} > 0.$$

PROOF. From the definition of the generalized mean $P(\alpha)$ we have

$$(w_1 + w_2 + w_3)\, P(\alpha)^\alpha = w_1 P_1^\alpha + w_2 P_2^\alpha + w_3 P_3^\alpha.$$

Differentiating partially with respect to P_i,

$$(w_1 + w_2 + w_3)\, \alpha P(\alpha)^{\alpha-1} \frac{\partial P(\alpha)}{\partial P_i} = w_i \alpha P_i^{\alpha-1}.$$

Therefore

$$(5) \qquad \frac{\partial P(\alpha)}{\partial P_i} = \frac{w_i}{w_1 + w_2 + w_3} \left[\frac{P_i}{P(\alpha)} \right]^{\alpha-1}$$
$$> 0 \quad \text{because } w_i > 0. \quad \square$$

In the unit weights case ($w_i = 1$, for $i = 1, 2, 3$) this reduces to

$$\frac{\partial P(\alpha)}{\partial P_i} = \frac{1}{3} \left[\frac{P_i}{P(\alpha)} \right]^{\alpha-1}.$$

Moreover, for $\alpha = 1$, so that $P(1)$ is simply the weighted or unweighted arithmetic mean of P_i, we have

$$\frac{\partial P(1)}{\partial P_i} = \frac{w_i}{w_1 + w_2 + w_3}$$

or

$$\frac{\partial P(1)}{\partial P_i} = \frac{1}{3}.$$

For an aggregate poverty index $P(\alpha)$ composed of distinct poverty subindices P_1, P_2 and P_3, it seems clearly desirable that $P(\alpha)$ should be increasing in each P_i. Also desirable is that $P(\alpha)$ should increase at an increasing rate in P_i—in other words, that $P(\alpha)$ should be convex with respect to P_i. This is equivalent to saying that $P(\alpha)$ decreases with reductions in P_i, and at a diminishing rate. The next proposition establishes that our aggregator function $P(\alpha)$, for $\alpha > 1$, does satisfy this property.

PROPOSITION 5. For each $i = 1, 2, 3$,

$$\frac{\partial^2 P(\alpha)}{\partial P_i^2} > 0.$$

PROOF.

$$\frac{\partial^2 P(\alpha)}{\partial P_i^2} = \frac{\partial}{\partial P_i} \left[\frac{\partial P(\alpha)}{\partial P_i} \right]$$
$$= \frac{w_i}{w_1 + w_2 + w_3} \frac{\partial}{\partial P_i} \left\{ \left[\frac{P_i}{P(\alpha)} \right]^{\alpha-1} \right\}$$

from equation 5.

Now

$$\frac{\partial}{\partial P_i} \left[\frac{P_i}{P(\alpha)} \right]^{\alpha-1} = (\alpha - 1) \left[\frac{P_i}{P(\alpha)} \right]^{\alpha-2} \frac{\partial}{\partial P_i} \left[\frac{P_i}{P(\alpha)} \right]$$
$$= (\alpha - 1) \left[\frac{P_i}{P(\alpha)} \right]^{\alpha-2} \left[P(\alpha) - P_i \frac{\partial P(\alpha)}{\partial P_i} \right] \bigg/ P(\alpha)^2$$
$$= (\alpha - 1) \frac{P_i^{\alpha-2}}{P(\alpha)^\alpha} \left[P(\alpha) - \frac{P_i w_i P_i^{\alpha-1}}{(w_1 + w_2 + w_3)\, P(\alpha)^{\alpha-1}} \right]$$

substituting for $\dfrac{\partial P(\alpha)}{\partial P_i}$ from equation 5

$$= \frac{(\alpha - 1) P_i^{\alpha-2}}{P(\alpha)^\alpha} \left[\frac{(w_1 + w_2 + w_3) P(\alpha)^\alpha - w_i P_i^\alpha}{(w_1 + w_2 + w_3) P(\alpha)^{\alpha-1}} \right].$$

Hence

$$\frac{\partial^2 P(\alpha)}{\partial P_i^2} = \frac{w_i P_i^{\alpha-2}(\alpha-1)}{(w_1 + w_2 + w_3)^2 P(\alpha)^{2\alpha-1}} \left[(w_1 + w_2 + w_3)P(\alpha)^\alpha - w_i P_i^\alpha \right]$$
$$> 0$$

because $\alpha > 1$ and

$$(w_1 + w_2 + w_3)P(\alpha)^\alpha - w_i P_i^\alpha = \sum_{j \neq i} w_j P_j^\alpha > 0. \quad \square$$

The next property we consider is the effect on the aggregate index $P(\alpha)$ of increasing the weight w_i on a particular poverty subindex P_i. We expect that increasing the weight on the largest subindex, max $\{P_1, P_2, P_3\}$, will increase $P(\alpha)$, while increasing the weight on the smallest subindex, min $\{P_1, P_2, P_3\}$, will reduce $P(\alpha)$. But what would be the effect of increasing the weight on a middle P_i? The answer depends on the relationship between P_i and $P(\alpha)$.

PROPOSITION 6. For any i,

$$\frac{\partial P(\alpha)}{\partial w_i} \gtreqless 0 \text{ as } P_i \gtreqless P(\alpha).$$

PROOF. From the definition of $P(\alpha)$ we have

$$(w_1 + w_2 + w_3)P(\alpha)^\alpha = w_1 P_1^\alpha + w_2 P_2^\alpha + w_3 P_3^\alpha.$$

Differentiating both sides partially with respect to w_i,

$$(w_1 + w_2 + w_3)\alpha P(\alpha)^{\alpha-1} \frac{\partial P(\alpha)}{\partial w_i} + P(\alpha)^\alpha = P_i^\alpha.$$

Therefore

$$(w_1 + w_2 + w_3)\alpha P(\alpha)^{\alpha-1} \frac{\partial P(\alpha)}{\partial w_i} = P_i^\alpha - P(\alpha)^\alpha.$$

Hence, since $\alpha > 0$,

$$\frac{\partial P(\alpha)}{\partial w_i} \gtreqless 0 \text{ as } P_i^\alpha \gtreqless P(\alpha)^\alpha,$$

that is,

$$\text{as } P_i \gtreqless P(\alpha). \quad \square$$

For $\alpha = 1$ we have

$$\frac{\partial P(1)}{\partial w_i} = \frac{1}{w_1 + w_2 + w_3} \left[P_i - P(1) \right]$$
$$\gtreqless 0 \text{ as } P_i \gtreqless P(1).$$

The next property we consider is the effect on $P(\alpha)$ of raising the parameter value α for given values of the subindices P_i, for $i = 1, 2, 3$. It shows that the value of the aggregate index will be higher when a higher-order mean is formed of P_1, P_2, P_3. In particular, a mean of order $\alpha > 1$ will result in a $P(\alpha)$ that is greater than $P(1)$, the simple arithmetic mean of P_1, P_2, P_3.

PROPOSITION 7. For given P_1, P_2 and P_3 that are not equal, if $\alpha > \gamma > 0$, then $P(\alpha) > P(\gamma)$.

PROOF. Let $\alpha > \gamma > 0$. By definition of $P(\alpha)$ and $P(\gamma)$, we have

$$P(\alpha)^\alpha = \frac{w_1}{w_1 + w_2 + w_3}P_1^\alpha + \frac{w_2}{w_1 + w_2 + w_3}P_2^\alpha + \frac{w_3}{w_1 + w_2 + w_3}P_3^\alpha$$

and

$$P(\gamma)^\gamma = \frac{w_1}{w_1 + w_2 + w_3}P_1^\gamma + \frac{w_2}{w_1 + w_2 + w_3}P_2^\gamma + \frac{w_3}{w_1 + w_2 + w_3}P_3^\gamma.$$

Raising both sides of the second equation to the power (α/γ) (> 1 because $\alpha > \gamma > 0$),

$$\left[P(\gamma)^\gamma \right]^{\alpha/\gamma} = \left(\frac{w_1}{w_1 + w_2 + w_3}P_1^\gamma + \frac{w_2}{w_1 + w_2 + w_3}P_2^\gamma + \frac{w_3}{w_1 + w_2 + w_3}P_3^\gamma \right)^{\alpha/\gamma}.$$

Now $f(x) = x^{\alpha/\gamma}$ is a strictly convex function, since

$$f'(x) = (\alpha/\gamma) x^{(\alpha/\gamma)-1}$$

and

$$f''(x) = (\alpha/\gamma)\left[(\alpha/\gamma) - 1 \right]x^{(\alpha/\gamma)-2}$$
$$> 0 \quad \text{because } (\alpha/\gamma) > 1.$$

Hence, by Jensen's inequality applied to strictly convex functions $f(\cdot)$, since P_1, P_2 and P_3 are not equal, we have the strict inequality

$$f\left(\frac{w_1}{w_1 + w_2 + w_3}P_1^\gamma + \frac{w_2}{w_1 + w_2 + w_3}P_2^\gamma + \frac{w_3}{w_1 + w_2 + w_3}P_3^\gamma \right)$$
$$< \frac{w_1}{w_1 + w_2 + w_3}f(P_1^\gamma) + \frac{w_2}{w_1 + w_2 + w_3}f(P_2^\gamma) + \frac{w_3}{w_1 + w_2 + w_3}f(P_3^\gamma).$$

Using the strictly convex function $f(x) = x^{\alpha/\gamma}$ gives

$$\left[P(\gamma)^\gamma \right]^{\alpha/\gamma} < \frac{w_1}{w_1 + w_2 + w_3}P_1^\alpha + \frac{w_2}{w_1 + w_2 + w_3}P_2^\alpha + \frac{w_3}{w_1 + w_2 + w_3}P_3^\alpha,$$

that is,

$$P(\gamma)^\alpha < P(\alpha)^\alpha.$$

Since $\alpha > 0$, it follows that

$$P(\gamma) < P(\alpha). \quad \square$$

Letting $\gamma = 1$ and $\alpha > 1$, we have the corollary that

$$P(\alpha) > P(1) = \frac{w_1 P_1 + w_2 P_2 + w_3 P_3}{w_1 + w_2 + w_3},$$

the simple weighted arithmetic mean of P_1, P_2 and P_3.

We next investigate the "decomposability" of the human poverty index among groups within a country. Suppose the population of a country is divided into m mutually exclusive and exhaustive groups. The groups may be defined in terms of stratum (urban, rural), region (by state, province or district) or gender (male, female). Let n_j be the size of population group j, for $j = 1, 2, \ldots, m$, and let n be the size of the total population of the country. Then

$$n = \sum_{j=1}^{m} n_j.$$

Let P_{1j}, P_{2j} and P_{3j} be the values of the three poverty subindices P_1, P_2 and P_3 for group j, where $j = 1, 2, \ldots, m$. Finally, let $P_j(\alpha)$ denote the mean of order α of P_{1j}, P_{2j} and P_{3j} for group j. By definition, we have

$$P_j(\alpha) = \left(\frac{w_1 P_{1j}^{\alpha} + w_2 P_{2j}^{\alpha} + w_3 P_{3j}^{\alpha}}{w_1 + w_2 + w_3} \right)^{1/\alpha}, \text{ for } j = 1, 2, \ldots, m.$$

What is the relationship between $P(\alpha)$ and the $P_j(\alpha)$ for $j = 1, 2, \ldots, m$? Strict decomposability of the index $P(\alpha)$ would require that $P(\alpha)$ be a population-weighted average of the $P_j(\alpha)$, the population weights being n_j /n. But strict decomposability does not generally obtain.

The relationship between the values of a given subindex for different groups (for example, P_{1j}, for $j = 1, 2, \ldots, m$) and the overall value of the subindex (for example, P_1) is straightforward enough. As the indices are simple headcounts of poverty, we have

$$\sum_{j=1}^{m} \frac{n_j}{n} P_{1j} = P_1,$$

$$\sum_{j=1}^{m} \frac{n_j}{n} P_{2j} = P_2,$$

$$\text{and} \sum_{j=1}^{m} \frac{n_j}{n} P_{3j} = P_3.$$

But when the α-averages of P_{1j}, P_{2j} and P_{3j} are formed for each j to give $P_j(\alpha)$, the population-weighted average of the $P_j(\alpha)$s exceeds $P(\alpha)$.

PROPOSITION 8. For $\alpha \geq 1$,

$$\sum_{j=1}^{m} \frac{n_j}{n} P_j(\alpha) \geq P(\alpha).$$

PROOF. For each $j = 1, 2, \ldots, m$, we have

$$\frac{n_j}{n} P_j(\alpha) = \left[\frac{w_1 \left(\frac{n_j}{n} P_{1j} \right)^{\alpha} + w_2 \left(\frac{n_j}{n} P_{2j} \right)^{\alpha} + w_3 \left(\frac{n_j}{n} P_{3j} \right)^{\alpha}}{w_1 + w_2 + w_3} \right]^{1/\alpha}.$$

Applying Minkowski's inequality (Hardy, Littlewood and Pólya 1952, p. 30) to $(n_j/n)P_{1j}$, $(n_j/n)P_{2j}$, $(n_j/n)P_{3j}$ for $j = 1, 2, \ldots, m$ yields

$$\sum_{j=1}^{m} \left[\frac{w_1 \left(\frac{n_j}{n} P_{1j} \right)^{\alpha} + w_2 \left(\frac{n_j}{n} P_{2j} \right)^{\alpha} + w_3 \left(\frac{n_j}{n} P_{3j} \right)^{\alpha}}{w_1 + w_2 + w_3} \right]^{1/\alpha}$$

$$\geq \left[\frac{w_1 \left(\sum_{j=1}^{m} \frac{n_j}{n} P_{1j} \right)^{\alpha} + w_2 \left(\sum_{j=1}^{m} \frac{n_j}{n} P_{2j} \right)^{\alpha} + w_3 \left(\sum_{j=1}^{m} \frac{n_j}{n} P_{3j} \right)^{\alpha}}{w_1 + w_2 + w_3} \right]^{1/\alpha}.$$

Hence

$$\sum_{j=1}^{m} \frac{n_j}{n} P_j(\alpha) \geq \left(\frac{w_1 P_1^{\alpha} + w_2 P_2^{\alpha} + w_3 P_3^{\alpha}}{w_1 + w_2 + w_3} \right)^{1/\alpha}.$$

Therefore

$$\sum_{j=1}^{m} \frac{n_j}{n} P_j(\alpha) \geq P(\alpha). \quad \square$$

The weak inequality in proposition 8 will be a strict inequality unless either $\alpha = 1$ or (P_{1j}, P_{2j}, P_{3j}) and (P_{1k}, P_{2k}, P_{3k}) are proportional for all j and k.

A simple example with non-proportionality of the group poverty subindices shows why decomposability (equality in proposition 8) does not obtain for $\alpha > 1$. Suppose the population is divided into two mutually exclusive and exhaustive groups $j = 1, 2$ of equal size ($n_1/n = n_2/n = \frac{1}{2}$), with values of poverty subindices as follows:

$$(P_{11}, P_{21}, P_{31}) = (0.25, 0.5, 0.75),$$
$$\text{and } (P_{12}, P_{22}, P_{32}) = (0.75, 0.5, 0.25).$$

Hence

$$(P_1, P_2, P_3) = (0.5, 0.5, 0.5),$$

and obviously $P(\alpha) = 0.5$.

Now for group 1

$$P_1(\alpha) = [(\tfrac{1}{3})(0.25)^{\alpha} + (\tfrac{1}{3})(0.5)^{\alpha} + (\tfrac{1}{3})(0.75)^{\alpha}]^{1/\alpha}$$
$$> 0.5, \quad \text{by proposition 7 since } \alpha > 1,$$

and for group 2

$$P_2(\alpha) = [(\tfrac{1}{3})(0.75)^{\alpha} + (\tfrac{1}{3})(0.5)^{\alpha} + (\tfrac{1}{3})(0.25)^{\alpha}]^{1/\alpha}$$
$$> 0.5, \quad \text{by proposition 7 since } \alpha > 1.$$

Therefore

$$(\tfrac{1}{2})P_1(\alpha) + (\tfrac{1}{2})P_2(\alpha) > (\tfrac{1}{2})(0.5) + (\tfrac{1}{2})(0.5)$$
$$= 0.5$$
$$= P(\alpha).$$

Taking the group arithmetic means of each poverty subindex tends to reduce or leave unchanged the relative disparity among the three poverty subindices. As a result of this feature the α-average of the arithmetic means of group subindices is smaller than the arithmetic mean of α-averages of group subindices.

Finally, for a given value of $\alpha (\geq 1)$, we discuss the degree of substitutability between the poverty subindices P_1, P_2 and P_3 in the aggregate measure $P(\alpha)$. The elasticity of substitution between, say, P_1 and P_2 along an iso-$P(\alpha)$ curve (holding P_3 constant) is defined as the percentage change in (P_1/P_2) for a unit percentage change in the slope of the tangent along this curve (projected onto P_1-P_2 space at the given value of P_3). For the index $P(\alpha)$ the elasticity of substitution is constant along each level set of $P(\alpha)$ and the same for different level sets. By proposition 3, $P(\alpha)$ is homogeneous of degree 1 in (P_1, P_2, P_3), and therefore its level sets are homothetic.

PROPOSITION 9. The elasticity of substitution σ between any two subindices of $P(\alpha)$, that is, between any two of P_1, P_2 and P_3, is constant and equal to $1/(\alpha-1)$.

PROOF. Consider the elasticity of substitution between P_1 and P_2, holding P_3 constant. The slope of the tangent along an iso-$P(\alpha)$ curve in P_1-P_2 space is given by

$$x = \frac{\partial P(\alpha)}{\partial P_1} \bigg/ \frac{\partial P(\alpha)}{\partial P_2}.$$

By definition, the elasticity of substitution σ between P_1 and P_2 is

$$\frac{\partial \log(P_1/P_2)}{\partial \log x}.$$

From equation 5 in proposition 4 we have

$$\frac{\partial P(\alpha)}{\partial P_1} \bigg/ \frac{\partial P(\alpha)}{\partial P_2} = \frac{w_1}{w_2}\left(\frac{P_1}{P_2}\right)^{\alpha-1} = x.$$

Therefore

$$\frac{P_1}{P_2} = \left(\frac{w_2}{w_1}\right)^{1/(\alpha-1)} x^{1/(\alpha-1)}$$

and

$$\log\left(\frac{P_1}{P_2}\right) = \frac{1}{\alpha-1}\log\left(\frac{w_2}{w_1}\right) + \frac{1}{\alpha-1}\log x.$$

Hence the elasticity of substitution

$$\sigma = \frac{\partial \log(P_1/P_2)}{\partial \log x} = \frac{1}{\alpha-1}. \quad \square$$

Thus, if $\alpha = 1$, there is infinite, or perfect, substitutability between P_1 and P_2. And as $\alpha \to \infty$, there is no substitutability between P_1 and P_2. As α increases from 1, the elasticity of substitution decreases monotonically from ∞ to 0.

If we choose $\alpha = 1$ (the case of perfect substitutability), the aggregate index $P(\alpha)$ is the simple arithmetic mean of the three subindices P_1, P_2, P_3. As α tends to infinity, the substitutability becomes zero, and the aggregate index tends to the maximum of the three subindices, max $\{P_1, P_2, P_3\}$. In general, the elasticity of substitution between any two of the subindices, holding the other constant, is $\sigma = 1/(\alpha - 1)$.

With $\alpha = 1$ and infinite substitutability, the impact on $P(\alpha)$ from a unit increase (or decrease) of any subindex is the same, irrespective of the level of deprivation in the different dimensions. This contradicts the usual assumption that as the extent of deprivation in any dimension increases (given the others), the weight on further additions to deprivation in that dimension should also increase. For this we need $\alpha > 1$. The value of α also influences, correspondingly, the relative weight to be placed on deprivation in the different dimensions. Consider, for example, $P_1 = 60\%$ and $P_2 = 30\%$ (with, say, $P_3 = 45\%$). In this case, for any α the relative impact of a unit increase in P_1 compared with a unit increase in P_2, which is given in general by $(P_1/P_2)^{\alpha-1}$, equals $2^{\alpha-1}$. With $\alpha = 1$, the relative impact is given by 1. As was remarked earlier, as α tends to infinity, P_1 becomes the only determinant of $P(\alpha)$, so that its impact is infinitely larger than that of a unit increase in P_2, which has, in this case, no impact at all.

The relative impact increases as α is raised from 1. With $\alpha = 3$, the relative impact is 4, giving the dimension of doubly greater deprivation (P_1) much greater weight. The relative impact rises very fast with the raising of α, as is clear from the formula. For $\alpha = 5$, the relative impact of a unit increase in P_1 is as much as 16 times that of a unit increase in P_2.

For calculating the human poverty index, $\alpha = 3$ has been chosen. This gives an elasticity of substitution of $1/2$ and places greater weight on those dimensions in which deprivation is larger. It does not, however, have the extremism of zero substitutability (given by α tending to infinity), nor the very high values of relative impact that are generated as α is raised (increasing the relative impact, in the case discussed above, from 4 to 16 as α goes from 3 to 5). There is an inescapable arbitrariness in the choice of α. The right way to deal with this issue is to explain clearly what is being assumed, as has been attempted here, so that public criticism of this assumption is possible.

As a matter of intellectual continuity, it should be mentioned that the value of $\alpha = 3$ corresponds exactly to the weighting used to calculate the gender-related development index (GDI).

Technical note 2. Computing the indices

The human development index

The HDI is based on three indicators: longevity, as measured by life expectancy at birth; educational attainment, as measured by a combination of adult literacy (two-thirds weight) and combined primary, secondary and tertiary enrolment ratios (one-third weight); and standard of living, as measured by real GDP per capita (PPP$).

For the construction of the index, fixed minimum and maximum values have been established for each of these indicators:
- Life expectancy at birth: 25 years and 85 years
- Adult literacy: 0% and 100%
- Combined gross enrolment ratio: 0% and 100%
- Real GDP per capita (PPP$): $100 and $40,000 (PPP$).

For any component of the HDI, individual indices can be computed according to the general formula:

$$\text{Index} = \frac{\text{Actual } x_i \text{ value} - \text{minimum } x_i \text{ value}}{\text{Maximum } x_i \text{ value} - \text{minimum } x_i \text{ value}} \; .$$

If, for example, the life expectancy at birth in a country is 65 years, then the index of life expectancy for this country would be

$$\frac{65 - 25}{85 - 25} = \frac{40}{60} = 0.667.$$

The construction of the income index is a little more complex. The world average income of $5,835 (PPP$) in 1994 is taken as the threshold level (y^*), and any income above this level is discounted using the following formulation based on Atkinson's formula for the utility of income:

$$
\begin{aligned}
W(y) &= y^* \text{ for } 0 < y < y^* \\
&= y^* + 2[(y - y^*)^{1/2}] \text{ for } y^* \leq y \leq 2y^* \\
&= y^* + 2(y^{*1/2}) + 3[(y - 2y^*)^{1/3}] \text{ for } 2y^* \leq y \leq 3y^* \\
y &= y^* + 2(y^{*1/2}) + 3[(y - 2y^*)^{1/3}] + n\{[1 - (n-1)y^*]\}^{1/n} \\
&\qquad\qquad\qquad\qquad \text{for } (n-1)y^* \leq y \leq ny^*.
\end{aligned}
$$

To calculate the discounted value of the maximum income of $40,000 (PPP$), the following form of Atkinson's formula is used:

$$
\begin{aligned}
W(y) &= y^* + 2(y^{*1/2}) + 3(y^{*1/3}) + 4(y^{*1/4}) + 5(y^{*1/5}) \\
&+ 6(y^{*1/6}) + 7(y^{*1/7}) + 8[(40,000 - 7y^*)^{1/8}] \; .
\end{aligned}
$$

This is because $40,000 (PPP$) is between $7y^*$ and $8y^*$. With the above formulation, the discounted value of the maximum income of $40,000 (PPP$) is $6,154 (PPP$).

The construction of the HDI is illustrated with two examples—Greece and Gabon, an industrial and a developing country.

Country	Life expectancy (years)	Adult literacy rate (%)	Combined enrolment ratio (%)	Real GDP per capita (PPP$)
Greece	77.8	96.7	82	11,265
Gabon	54.1	62.6	60	3,641

Life expectancy index

$$\text{Greece} = \frac{77.8 - 25}{85 - 25} = \frac{52.8}{60} = 0.880$$

$$\text{Gabon} = \frac{54.1 - 25}{85 - 25} = \frac{29.1}{60} = 0.485$$

Adult literacy index

$$\text{Greece} = \frac{96.7 - 0}{100 - 0} = \frac{96.7}{100} = 0.967$$

$$\text{Gabon} = \frac{62.6 - 0}{100 - 0} = \frac{62.6}{100} = 0.626$$

Combined primary, secondary and tertiary enrolment ratio index

$$\text{Greece} = \frac{82 - 0}{100 - 0} = 0.820$$

$$\text{Gabon} = \frac{60 - 0}{100 - 0} = 0.600$$

Educational attainment index

$$\text{Greece} = [2(0.967) + 1(0.820)] \div 3 = 0.918$$

$$\text{Gabon} = [2(0.625) + 1(0.600)] \div 3 = 0.617$$

Adjusted real GDP per capita (PPP$) index

Greece's real GDP per capita at $11,265 (PPP$) is above the threshold level, but less than twice the threshold. Thus the adjusted real GDP per capita for Greece would be $5,982 (PPP$) because $5,982 = [5,835 + 2(11,265 - 5,835)^{1/2}]$.

Gabon's real GDP per capita at $3,641 (PPP$) is less than the threshold level, so it needs no adjustment.

Thus the adjusted real GDP per capita (PPP$) indices for Greece and Gabon would be:

$$\text{Greece} = \frac{5,982 - 100}{6,154 - 100} = \frac{5,882}{6,054} = 0.972$$

$$\text{Gabon} = \frac{3,641 - 100}{6,154 - 100} = \frac{3,541}{6,054} = 0.584$$

Human development index

The HDI is a simple average of the life expectancy index, educational attainment index and adjusted real GDP per capita (PPP$) index, and so is derived by dividing the sum of these three indices by 3.

Country	Life expectancy index	Educational attainment index	Adjusted real GDP per capita (PPP$) index	HDI
Greece	0.880	0.918	0.972	0.923
Gabon	0.485	0.617	0.584	0.562

The gender-related development index and the gender empowerment measure

For comparisons among countries, the GDI and the GEM are limited to data widely available in international data sets. For this year's Report we have endeavoured to use the most recent, reliable and internally consistent data. Collecting more extensive and more reliable gender-disaggregated data is a challenge that the international community should squarely face. We continue to publish results on the GDI and the GEM—based on the best available estimates—in the expectation that it will help increase the demand for such data.

The gender-related development index

The GDI uses the same variables as the HDI. The difference is that the GDI adjusts the average achievement of each country in life expectancy, educational attainment and income in accordance with the disparity in achievement between women and men. (For a detailed explanation of the GDI methodology see technical note 1 in *Human Development Report 1995*). For this gender-sensitive adjustment we use a weighting formula that expresses a moderate aversion to inequality, setting the weighting parameter, $\in$, equal to 2. This is the harmonic mean of the male and female values.

The GDI also adjusts the maximum and minimum values for life expectancy, to account for the fact that women tend to live longer than men. For women the maximum value is 87.5 years and the minimum value 27.5 years; for men the corresponding values are 82.5 and 22.5 years.

Calculating the index for income is fairly complex. Female and male shares of earned income are derived from data on the ratio of the average female wage to the average male wage and the female and male percentage shares of the economically active population aged 15 and above. Where data on the wage ratio are not available, we use a value of 75%, the weighted mean of the wage ratio for all countries with wage data. Before income is indexed, the average adjusted real GDP per capita of each country is discounted on the basis of the disparity in the female and male shares of earned income in proportion to the female and male population shares.

The indices for life expectancy, educational attainment and income are added together with equal weight to derive the final GDI value.

Illustration of the GDI methodology

We choose Norway to illustrate the steps for calculating the gender-related development index. The parameter of inequality aversion, $\in$, equals 2. (Any discrepancies in results are due to rounding.)

Percentage share of total population
Females   51
Males   49
Life expectancy at birth (years)
Females   80.4
Males   74.6
Adult literacy rate (percent)
Females   99
Males   99
Combined primary, secondary and tertiary gross enrolment ratio (percent)
Females   93
Males   92

STEP ONE
Computing the equally distributed life expectancy index

Life expectancy index
Females $(80.4 - 27.5)/60 = 0.882$
Males $(74.6 - 22.5)/60 = 0.868$

The equally distributed life expectancy index
{[(female population share × (female life expectancy index)$^{-1}$] + [male population share × (male life expectancy index)$^{-1}$]}$^{-1}$
$[0.51(0.882)^{-1} + 0.49(0.868)^{-1}]^{-1} = 0.875$

STEP TWO
Computing the equally distributed educational attainment index

Adult literacy index
Females $(99 - 0)/100 = 0.990$
Males $(99 - 0)/100 = 0.990$
Combined gross enrolment index
Females $(93 - 0)/100 = 0.930$
Males $(92 - 0)/100 = 0.920$
Educational attainment index
2/3(adult literacy index) + 1/3(combined gross enrolment index)
Females $2/3(0.990) + 1/3(0.930) = 0.970$
Males $2/3(0.990) + 1/3(0.920) = 0.967$

The equally distributed educational attainment index
{[female population share × (educational attainment index)$^{-1}$] + [male population share × (educational attainment index)$^{-1}$]}$^{-1}$
$[0.51(0.970)^{-1} + 0.49(0.967)^{-1}]^{-1} = 0.968$

STEP THREE
Computing the equally distributed income index

Percentage share of the economically active population
Females   45.5
Males   54.5

Ratio of female non-agricultural wage to male non-agricultural wage: 0.870

Adjusted real GDP per capita: PPP$6,073 (see the section above on the HDI)

A. Computing proportional income shares

Average wage (W) = (female share of economically active population × female wage) + (male economically active population × 1)
$(0.455 \times 0.870) + (0.545 \times 1) = 0.941$

Female wage to average wage (W)
$0.870/0.941 = 0.925$
Male wage to average wage (W)
$1/0.941 = 1.063$

Share of earned income
Note: [(female wage/average wage) × female share of economically active population] + [(male wage/average wage) × male share of economically active population] = 1
Females
Female wage/female economically active population
$0.9247 \times 0.4553 = 0.4210$
Males
Male wage/male economically active population
$1.063 \times 0.545 = 0.579$

Female and male proportional income shares
Females
Female share of earned income/female population share
$0.421/0.505 = 0.834$
Males
Male share of earned income/male population share
$0.579/0.495 = 1.169$

B. Computing the equally distributed income index

The weighting parameter ($\in$ = 2) is applied.
{[female population share × (female proportional income share)$^{-1}$] + [male population share × (male proportional income share)$^{-1}$]}$^{-1}$

$[0.505\ (0.834)^{-1} + 0.495\ (1.169)^{-1}]^{-1} = 0.972$
$0.972 \times 6{,}073 = 5{,}903$
$(5{,}903 - 100)/(6{,}154 - 100) = 0.959$

STEP FOUR
Computing the gender-related development index (GDI)

$1/3(0.875 + 0.968 + 0.959) = 0.934$

The gender empowerment measure

The GEM uses variables constructed explicitly to measure the relative empowerment of women and men in political and economic spheres of activity.

The first two variables are chosen to reflect economic participation and decision-making power: women's and men's percentage shares of administrative and managerial positions and their percentage shares of professional and technical jobs. These are broad, loosely defined occupational categories. Because the relevant population for each is different, we calculate a seperate index for each and then add the two together. The third variable, women's and men's percentage shares of parliamentary seats, is chosen to reflect political participation and decision-making power.

For all three variables we use the methodology of population-weighted ($1 - \in$) averaging to derive an "equally distributed equivalent percentage" (EDEP) for both sexes taken together. Each variable is indexed by dividing the EDEP by 50%.

An income variable is used to reflect power over economic resources. It is calculated in the same manner as for the GDI except that unadjusted rather than adjusted real GDP per capita is used. The maximum value for income is thus PPP$40,000 and the minimum PPP$100.

The three indices—for economic participation and decision-making, political participation and decision-making, and power over economic resources—are added together to derive the final GEM value.

Illustration of the GEM methodology

We choose Cameroon to illustrate the steps in calculating the GEM. The parameter of inequality aversion, $\in$, equals 2. (Any discrepancies in results are due to rounding.)

STEP ONE
Computing indices for parliamentary representation and administrative and managerial, and professional and technical, positions

Percentage share of parliamentary representation
Females   12.1
Males   87.8
Percentage share of administrative and managerial positions
Females   10.1
Males   89.9
Percentage share of professional and technical positions
Females   24.4
Males   75.6
Percentage share of population
Females   50.38
Males   49.62

Computing the EDEP for parliamentary representation
$[0.4962(87.8)^{-1} + 0.5038(12.1)^{-1}] = 21.3$

Computing the EDEP for administrative and managerial positions
$[0.4962(89.9)^{-1} + 0.5038(10.1)^{-1}] = 18.05$

Computing the EDEP for professional and technical positions
$[0.4962(75.6)^{-1} + 0.5038(24.4)^{-1}] = 36.75$

Indexing parliamentary representation
$21.30/50 = 0.426$

Indexing administrative and managerial positions
$18.05/50 = 0.361$

Indexing professional and technical positions
$36.75/50 = 0.735$

Combining the indices for administrative and managerial, and professional and technical, positions
$(0.361 + 0.735)/2 = 0.548$

STEP TWO
Computing the index for share of earned income

Percentage share of economically active population
Females   37.4
Males   62.6

Ratio of female non-agricultural wage to male non-agricultural wage: 75%

Unadjusted real GDP per capita: PPP$2,120

Ratio of female wage to average wage (W) and of male wage to average wage (W):
$W = 0.374(0.75) + 0.626(1) = 0.9065$
Female wage to average wage: $0.75/0.9065 = 0.8274$
Male wage to average wage: $1/0.9065 = 1.1031$

Share of earned income
Note: [(female wage/average wage) × female share of economically active population] + [(male wage/average wage) × male share of economically active population] = 1
Females $0.8274 \times 0.374 = 0.3094$
Males $1.1031 \times 0.626 = 0.6095$

Female and male proportional income shares
Females $0.3094/0.5038 = 0.6141$
Males $0.6905/0.4962 = 1.3916$

Computing the equally distributed income index
$[0.4962(1.3916)^{-1} + 0.5038(0.6141)^{-1}]^{-1} = 0.8496$
$0.8496 \times 2{,}120 = 1{,}801$
$(1{,}801 - 100)/(40{,}000 - 100) = 0.0426$

STEP THREE
Computing the GEM
$[1/3(0.0426 + 0.0548 + 0.426)] = 0.3389$

The human poverty index

The HPI concentrates on deprivation in three essential elements of human life already reflected in the HDI—longevity, knowledge and a decent standard of living. The first deprivation relates to survival—the vulnerability to death at a relatively early age. The second relates to knowledge—being excluded from the world of reading and communication. The third relates to a decent living standard in terms of overall economic provisioning.

In constructing the HPI, the deprivation in longevity is represented by the percentage of people not expected to survive to age 40 (P_1), and the deprivation in knowledge by the percentage of adults who are illiterate (P_2). The deprivation in a decent living standard in terms of overall economic provisioning is represented by a composite (P_3) of three variables—the percentage of people without access to safe water (P_{31}), the percentage of people without access to health services (P_{32}) and the percentage of moderately and severely underweight children under five (P_{33}).

The composite variable P is constructed by taking a simple average of the three variables P_{31}, P_{32} and P_{33}. Thus

$$P_3 = \frac{P_{31} + P_{32} + P_{33}}{3} .$$

Following the analysis in chapter 1 and technical note 1, the formula of HPI is given by

$$\text{HPI} = [(P_1^3 + P_2^3 + P_3^3) - 3]^{1/3}.$$

As an example, we compute the HPI for Egypt.

Calculating P_3

Country	P_1 (%)	P_2 (%)	P_{31} (%)	P_{32} (%)	P_{33} (%)
Egypt	16.6	49.5	21.0	1.0	9.0

$$P_3 = \frac{21 + 1 + 9}{3} = \frac{31}{3} = 10.33$$

STEP TWO
Constructing the HPI

$$
\begin{aligned}
\text{HPI} &= [1/3(16.6^3 + 49.5^3 + 10.33^3)]^{1/3} \\
&= [1/3(4{,}574.30 + 121{,}287.38 + 1{,}102.30)]^{1/3} \\
&= [1/3(126{,}963.98)^{1/3} \\
&= (42{,}321.33)^{1/3} \\
&= 34.8
\end{aligned}
$$

Human poverty index

HPI rank		Survival deprivation People not expected to survive to age 40 (%) 1990[a] (P_1)	Deprivation in education and knowledge Adult illiteracy rate (%) 1994 (P_2)	Deprivation in economic provisioning (P_3)				Human poverty index (HPI) value (%)
				Population without access to safe water (%) 1990–96 (P_{31})	Population without access to health services (%) 1990–95 (P_{32})	Underweight children under age five (%) 1990–96 (P_{33})	Overall (P_3)	
1	Trinidad and Tobago	5.4[b]	2.1	3	0	7[c]	3	4.1
2	Cuba	6.2[d,e]	4.6	11	0	1[f]	4	5.1
3	Chile	4.6[d,e]	5.0	15[c]	3[c]	1	6	5.4
4	Singapore	3.2[d,e]	9.0	0[c]	0[c]	14[c]	5	6.6
5	Costa Rica	4.1[b]	5.3	4	20[c]	2	9	6.6
6	Colombia	6.3[b]	8.9	15	19	8	14	10.7
7	Mexico	8.3[b]	10.8	17	7	14[c]	13	10.9
8	Jordan	9.2[b]	14.5	2	3[c]	9	5	10.9
9	Panama	6.2[d,e]	9.5	7	30	7	15	11.2
10	Uruguay	5.4[d,e]	2.9	25[c]	18[c]	7[c]	17	11.7
11	Thailand	8.9[b]	6.5	11	10[c]	26[c]	16	11.7
12	Jamaica	4.3[b]	15.6	14	10[c]	10	11	12.1
13	Mauritius	6.2[d,e]	17.6	1	0[c]	16	6	12.5
14	United Arab Emirates	3.6[b]	21.4	5	1	6[g]	4	14.9
15	Ecuador	9.9[b]	10.4	32	12[c]	17[c]	20	15.2
16	Mongolia	16.0[h,i]	17.8	20	5[c]	12	12	15.7
17	Zimbabwe	18.4[d,j]	15.3	23	15	16	18	17.3
18	China	9.1[d,k]	19.1	33	12	16	20	17.5
19	Philippines	12.8[d,l]	5.6	14	29	30	24	17.7
20	Dominican Rep.	10.2[b]	18.5	35	22	10	22	18.3
21	Libyan Arab Jamahiriya	16.2[b]	25.0	3	5	5	4	18.8
22	Sri Lanka	7.9[d,e]	9.9	43	7[c]	38	29	20.7
23	Indonesia	14.8[d,j]	16.8	38	7	35	27	20.8
24	Syrian Arab Rep.	10.3[b]	30.2	15	10	12	12	21.7
25	Honduras	10.8[b]	28.0	13	31	18	21	22.0
26	Bolivia	19.6[d,j]	17.5	34	33	16	28	22.5
27	Iran, Islamic Rep. of	11.7[b]	31.4[m]	10	12	16	13	22.6
28	Peru	13.4[d,j]	11.7	28	56	11	32	22.8
29	Botswana	15.9[b]	31.3	7[c]	11[c]	15[c]	11	22.9
30	Paraguay	9.2[b]	8.1	58	37[c]	4	33	23.2
31	Tunisia	10.5[b]	34.8	2	10[c]	9	7	24.4
32	Kenya	22.3[b]	23.0	47	23	23	31	26.1
33	Viet Nam	12.1[b]	7.0	57	10	45	37	26.2
34	Nicaragua	13.6[b]	34.7	47	17[c]	12	25	27.2
35	Lesotho	23.9[b]	29.5	44	20[c]	21	28	27.5
36	El Salvador	11.7[b]	29.1	31	60	11	34	28.0
37	Algeria	10.6[b]	40.6	22	2	13	12	28.6
38	Congo	22.1[b]	26.1	66	17[c]	24[c]	36	29.1
39	Iraq	15.4[b]	43.2	22	7[c]	12	14	30.7
40	Myanmar	25.6[b]	17.3	40	40	43	41	31.2
41	Cameroon	25.4[b]	37.9	50	20	14	28	31.4
42	Papua New Guinea	28.6[b]	28.8	72	4[c]	35[c]	37	32.0
43	Ghana	24.9[b]	36.6	35	40[c]	27	34	32.6
44	Egypt	16.6[de]	49.5	21	1	9	10	34.8
45	Zambia	35.1[b]	23.4	73	25[c]	28	42	35.1
46	Guatemala	14.5[d,e]	44.3	36	43	27	35	35.5
47	India	19.4[d,k]	48.8	19	15	53	29	36.7
48	Rwanda	42.1[b]	40.8	34[c]	20	29	28	37.9
49	Togo	28.4[b]	49.6	37	39[c]	24[c]	33	39.3
50	Tanzania, U. Rep. of	30.6[b]	33.2	62	58	29	50	39.7
51	Lao People's Dem. Rep.	32.7[h,i]	44.2	48	33[c]	44	42	40.1
52	Zaire	30.0[b]	23.6	58	74[c]	34	55	41.2
53	Uganda	39.0[d,n]	38.9	62	51	23[c]	45	41.3
54	Nigeria	33.8[b]	44.4	49	49	36	45	41.6
55	Morocco	12.3[d,j]	57.9	45	30[c]	9	28	41.7

Human poverty index (continued)

HPI rank	Survival deprivation People not expected to survive to age 40 (%) 1990[a] (P_1)	Deprivation in education and knowledge Adult illiteracy rate (%) 1994 (P_2)	Deprivation in economic provisioning (P_3)				Human poverty index (HPI) value (%)
			Population without access to safe water (%) 1990–96 (P_{31})	Population without access to health services (%) 1990–95 (P_{32})	Underweight children under age five (%) 1990–96 (P_{33})	Overall (P_3)	
56 Central African Rep.	35.4[d,j]	42.8	62	48	27	46	41.7
57 Sudan	25.2[b]	55.2	40	30	34	35	42.2
58 Guinea-Bissau	43.2[h,i]	46.1	41	60	23[c]	41	43.6
59 Namibia	21.1[d,j]	60.0[o]	43	41	26	37	45.1
60 Malawi	38.3[d,j]	44.2	63	65	30	53	45.8
61 Haiti	27.1[b]	55.9	72	40	28	47	46.2
62 Bhutan	33.2[h,i]	58.9	42	35[c]	38[c]	38	46.3
63 Côte d'Ivoire	23.1[d,n]	60.6	25	70[c]	24	40	46.3
64 Pakistan	22.6[b]	62.9	26	45[c]	38	36	46.8
65 Mauritania	31.7[h,i]	63.1	34[c]	37	23	31	47.1
66 Yemen	25.6[b]	58.9[o]	39	62	39	47	47.6
67 Bangladesh	26.4[b]	62.7	3	55	67	42	48.3
68 Senegal	25.3[d,p]	67.9	48	10	20	26	48.7
69 Burundi	33.8[b]	65.4	41	20	37	33	49.0
70 Madagascar	32.1[d,j]	54.2[q]	71	62	34	56	49.5
71 Guinea	41.3[h,i]	65.2	45	20	26	30	50.0
72 Mozambique	43.8[b]	60.5	37	61[c]	27	42	50.1
73 Cambodia	31.9[h,i]	65.0[r]	64	47[c]	40	50	52.5
74 Mali	28.4[d,n]	70.7	55	60	31[c]	49	54.7
75 Ethiopia	35.7[b]	65.5	75	54	48	59	56.2
76 Burkina Faso	36.1[b]	81.3	22	10	30	21	58.3
77 Sierra Leone	52.1[b]	69.7	66	62	29	52	59.2
78 Niger	43.2[d]	86.9	46	68[r]	36	50	66.0

a. Data refer to 1990 or a year around 1990. b. Obtained by combining two sets of mortality risk estimates: UNICEF estimates of the probability of dying by age 5 and UN Population Division estimates of the probability of dying between the ages of 5 and 40 ($_{35}q_5$). Estimates were interpolated using the Coale-Demeny "West" family of model life tables. For all countries life expectancy at birth in 1990 is estimated as the arithmetic average of estimates for that period in UN 1996b, as explained in Hill 1997. c. Data refer to a year or period other than that specified in the column heading, differ from the standard definition or refer to only part of a country. d. UNICEF estimates of the probability of dying by age 5 plus independent estimates (Hill 1997) of the probability of dying between the ages of 5 and 40. e. Based on registration of deaths around 1990. f. Wasting (moderate or severe). g. UNICEF field office source. h. UN Population Division, based on life expectancy at birth. i. UN Population Division, obtained by finding estimated life expectancy at birth in 1990 (obtained by linear interpolation between the 1985–90 and 1990–95 estimates) and then finding the implied $_{40}q_0$ and $_{60}q_0$ values in the Coale-Demeny "West" model life tables. Keyfitz and Flieger national life tables were used to calculate the ratio of life expectancy at birth to $_{40}q_0$ and $_{60}q_0$ around 1970 and around 1985; for each country the ratios for 1990 were then estimated by linear extrapolation. These ratios were plotted against time and found to change in similar ways over time across countries, giving a series of parallel lines. The estimated ratio and estimated life expectancy at birth were then used to obtain estimated risks of dying by age 40 and age 60, as explained in Hill 1997. j. Based on Demographic and Health Survey direct sisterhood estimates of probability of dying between the ages of 5 and 50, extended from 50 to 60 using a Coale-Demeny "West" model life table fitted to $_{45}q_5$, as explained in Hill 1997. k. World Bank 1993. l. Based on registered deaths after adjusting for estimated completeness. m. UNESCO 1995. Data are for 1995. n. Based on Demographic and Health Survey direct sisterhood estimates of probability of dying between the ages of 15 and 50, extended to cover ages 5 to 14 and 50 to 60 using a Coale-Demeny "West" model life table fitted to $_{35}q_{15}$. o. UNDP 1996d. p. Pison and others 1995. q. Human Development Report Office estimate based on national sources. r. UNICEF 1996b.
Source: *Column 1:* Hill 1997; *column 2:* calculated on the basis of data from UNESCO 1996b; *columns 3 and 4:* calculated on the basis of data from UNICEF 1997; *column 5:* UNICEF 1997.

References

Background papers for Human Development Report 1997

Altimir, Oscar. 1996. "Poverty Trends in Selected Latin American Countries."

Anand, Sudhir, and Amartya K. Sen. 1997. "Concepts of Human Development and Poverty: A Multidimensional Perspective."

Berry, Albert, Susan Horton and Dipak Mazumdar. 1997. "Globalization, Adjustment, Inequality and Poverty."

Desai, Meghnad. 1997. "Poverty and Social Exclusion in Advanced/OECD Countries."

Genda, Yuji. 1997. "Poverty in Japan."

Kamerman, Sheila, and Alfred Kahn. 1996. "The Problem of Poverty in the Advanced Industrialized Countries and the Policy and Program Response."

Lavollay, Michel. 1996. "HIV/AIDS: An Allegory of Human Deprivation."

Lipton, Michael. 1996a. "Agricultural Research, the Poor and the Environment."

———. 1996b. "Defining and Measuring Poverty: Conceptual Issues."

———. 1996c. "Growth and Poverty Reduction: Which Way Round?"

———. 1996d. "How Economic Growth Affects Poverty."

———. 1996e. "Interactions between Poverty and Population Change, and Some Linkages to Environmental Depletion."

———. 1996f. "Poverty and Its Links to Human Underdevelopment: Some Stylized Facts."

———. 1996g. "Poverty-Basic and Annex Tables: Notes on Method."

———. 1997. "The Evolution of Private Consumption Poverty in the Developing World, 1960–1997."

Mason, John, Tom Scialfa, Kavita Sethuraman, Naisu Zhu and Jamie Van Leeuwen. 1997. "World Nutrition Trends and Situation."

Mathonnat, Jacky. 1996. "Etudes sur les Depenses Publiques d'Education et de Sante dans les Pays en Developpement."

Matsunaga, Yasuyuki. 1997a. "Conflict and Deprivation: The Dynamics of Political Violence in the Post–Cold War Period."

———. 1997b. "Poverty and Displaced Populations: Policy Implications of Involuntary Displacement."

Moghadam, Valentine. 1996. "The Feminization of Poverty? Notes on a Concept and Trends."

Parikh, Jyoti. 1996. "Poverty-Environment-Development Nexus."

Ruggeri Laderchi, Caterina. 1996. "Poverty: Some Issues, Concepts and Definitions."

Ruminska-Zimny, Ewa. 1997. "Human Poverty in Transition Economies."

Sen, Gita. 1997. "Empowerment as an Approach to Poverty."

Shiva Kumar, A.K. 1997. "Poverty and Human Development: The Indian Experience."

Smeeding, Timothy. 1996. "Financial Poverty in Developed Countries: The Evidence from the LIS."

Streeten, Paul. 1996. "The Political Economy of Fighting Poverty."

von Pischke, J.D. 1996. "Poverty, Human Development and Financial Services."

Watanabe, Eimi. 1996. "Country Poverty Strategies: A Survey."

Watkins, Kevin. 1997. "Globalisation and Liberalisation: The Implication for Poverty, Distribution and Inequality."

WRI (World Resources Institute). 1996. "Background Data for Human Development Report 1997."

Zhang, Amei. 1997. "Poverty Alleviation in China: Commitment, Policies and Expenditures."

Special contributions

Agarwal, Bina. 1996. "Gender, Poverty and Property Rights in South Asia."

Attwood, Heidi. 1996. "PRA: What Is It and Why Should We Use It? and Illustrations of Poor People's Perceptions of Poverty and Well-Being as Disclosed through PRA Expenditures."

Brox, Ottar. 1996. "Out of Poverty: The Case of Norway."

Correa, Sonia. 1997. "Brazil: The Citizen Action against Hunger and Misery." Brazilian Institute for Economic and Social Analysis.

Darbellay, Elaine. 1996. "Poverty in Nigeria."

———. 1997a. "Poverty in Ghana."

———. 1997b. "Poverty in Kenya."

———. 1997c. "Poverty in the Russian Federation."

Hill, Kenneth. 1997. "Derivation of Risks of Dying by Ages 40 and 60 and Calculations of Survival Rates: A Note."

Ishikawa, Tsuneo. 1996. "Poverty and Inequality in Japan: An Estimate."

Maathai, Wangari. 1997. "The Green Belt Movement."

Øyen, Else. 1997. "The Utility of Poverty."

Ramirez, Alejandro. 1996. "Consumption Poverty, Capabilities Poverty and Human Development in Indonesia."

Roche, Douglas. 1996. "After the World Court Opinion."

Shiva Kumar, A.K. 1996. "Exit Time from Poverty."

Taylor, Vivienne. 1997. "South Africa: Transcending the Legacy of Apartheid and Poverty."

UNV (United Nations Volunteers). 1997. "Case Studies of Success in Volunteers for Poverty Eradication."

Bibliographic note

Chapter 1 draws on the following: Anand and Sen 1997 and Lipton 1996b.

Chapter 2 draws on the following: Altimir 1996, Anand and Sen 1997, Darbellay 1996, 1997a, 1997b and 1997c, *Fortune Magazine* 1996, HABITAT 1996, Kamerman and Kahn 1996, Lipton 1996b, 1996f and 1996g, Mason and others 1997, Matsunaga 1997a and 1997b, Milanovic 1996, Psacharopoulos and Patrinos 1994, Ramirez 1996, Ruggeri Laderchi 1996, Ruminska-Zimny 1997, A. Sen 1990, B. Sen 1992, Shaffer 1996, Shiva Kumar 1996 and 1997, Smeeding 1996, Swaminathan 1995, UNAIDS 1996, UNDP 1996h, UNDP and UNICEF 1996, UNESCWA 1996, UNHCR 1996, UNRISD 1995, World Bank 1996d, Worldwatch Institute 1996, WRI 1994 and 1996b and Zhang 1997.

Chapter 3 draws on the following: Agarwal 1994, Bardhan 1996, Broca and Ohram 1991, Bruno, Ravallion and Squire 1996, CESR 1997, Chambers 1997, Cleaver and Schreiber 1994, Datt and Ravallion forthcoming, Davies 1993 and 1996, Deininger and Squire 1996, Desai 1997, Folbre 1996, Genda 1997, Hazell and Garrett 1996, Human Development Center 1997, Jazairy, Alamgir and Panuccio 1992, Kamerman and Kahn 1996, Kumar 1997, Lavollay 1996, Lipton 1995, 1996a, 1996b, 1996d and 1996e, Lipton and Maxwell 1992, Lipton and Osmani 1996, Lipton and Ravallion 1995, Mann and Tarantola 1996, Matsunaga 1997a and 1997b, Moghadam 1996, Moser 1996, Ravallion forthcoming, Ravallion and Chen 1996, Ruminska-Zimny 1997, G. Sen 1997, UNAIDS 1996, UNDP 1995c, 1996b and 1996d, US Department of Health and Human Services 1996, von Pischke 1996, World Bank 1992 and 1995b, WRI 1996b and Zhang 1997.

Chapter 4 draws on the following: Berry, Horton and Mazumdar 1997, Boyer and Drache 1996, Childers 1995, Commission on Global Governance 1995, *The Economist* 1996, *Fortune Magazine* 1996, Kennedy and Russett 1995, Oxfam International 1996a and 1996b, Stewart 1995b, UNCTAD 1996a, UNDPI 1996, UNRISD 1995, Watkins 1995 and 1997 and World Bank 1995a and 1996b.

Chapter 5 draws on the following: Athreya and Chunkath 1996, Ba 1990, Berger 1976, Block 1995, Crawford 1995, Freedom House 1995, Frisch 1996, Ghai and Vivian 1992, Government of Malawi and UNICEF 1996, Haq 1995, Human Development Center 1997, IDS 1996b, IISS 1996, Kapadia 1996, Kohli 1994, Kothari 1993, Lal and Myint 1996, Lewis 1996, Riddell 1992, Rodrik 1996, Saggar and Pan 1994, Schneider 1991, G. Sen 1995, Streeten 1993, Taylor 1996, Transparency International 1996, UNDP 1996b and 1996c and UNECE 1996.

Chapter 6 draws on the following: Chenery and others 1974, Colclough and Lewin 1993, Dreze and Sen 1995, Eatwell 1996, Erikson 1996, ITM 1996, OECD 1996e, Øyen, Miller and Samad 1996, UNDP 1995b, UNESCO 1996 and UNICEF 1995b and 1996.

References

Agarwal, Bina. 1994. *A Field of One's Own: Gender and Land Rights in South Asia.* New York: Cambridge University Press.

Anand, Sudhir. 1977. "Aspects of Poverty in Malaysia." *Review of Income and Wealth* 23(1): 1–16.

———. 1983. *Inequality and Poverty in Malaysia: Measurement and Decomposition.* New York: Oxford University Press.

———. 1993. "Inequality between and within Nations." Harvard University, Center for Population and Development Studies, Cambridge, Mass.

Anand, Sudhir, and Amartya K. Sen. 1993. "Human Development Index: Methodology and Measurement." Human Development Report Office Occasional Paper 12. UNDP, New York.

———. 1995. "Gender Inequality in Human Development: Theories and Measurement." Human Development Report Office Occasional Paper 19. UNDP, New York.

ARF (Addiction Research Foundation). 1994. "Statistical Information, International Profile 1994." Ontario, Canada.

Arrow, Kenneth J. 1965. "Aspects of the Theory of Risk-Bearing." Yrjö Jahnsson Lectures. Helsinki: Yrjö Jahnssonin Säätiö.

Association of Iroquois and Allied Indians. 1996. "Fact Sheet on Health and Social Conditions in First Nations Communities."

Athreya, V.B., and S.R. Chunkath. 1996. *Literacy and Empowerment.* New Delhi: Sage Publications.

Atkinson, Anthony B. 1970. "On the Measurement of Inequality." *Journal of Economic Theory* 2(3): 244–63.

———. 1973. "How Progressive Should Income Tax Be?" In M. Parkin, ed., *Essays on Modern Economics.* London: Longman. Reprinted in E.S. Phelps, ed., *Economic Justice.* Harmondsworth, England: Penguin.

———. 1987. "On the Measurement of Poverty." *Econometrica* 55(4): 749–64.

Atkinson, Anthony B., and François Bourguignon. 1982. "The Comparison of Multi-Dimensional Distributions of Economic Status." *Review of Economic Studies* 49: 183–201.

Ba, Hassan. 1990. "Village Associations on the Riverbanks of Senegal: The New Development Actors." *Voices from Africa* 2(January): 83–104. UNCTAD/NGLS, Geneva.

Bardhan, Pranab. 1996. "Method in Madness? A Political-Economy Analysis of Ethnic Conflicts in Less Developed Countries." Economics Department Working Paper. University of California at Berkeley.

Basu, Kaushik. 1987. "Achievements, Capabilities, and the Concept of Well-Being." *Social Choice and Welfare* 4: 69–76.

Berger, Peter L. 1976. *Pyramids of Sacrifice: Political Ethics and Social Change.* New York: Anchor Books.

Blackorby, Charles, and David Donaldson. 1978. "Measures of Relative Equality and Their Meaning in Terms of Social Welfare." *Journal of Economic Theory* 18.

———. 1984. "Ethically Significant Ordinal Indexes of Relative Inequality." In R.L. Basmann and G.F. Rhodes, eds., *Advances in Econometrics* 3. London: JAI Press.

Block, Thorsten. 1995. "Human Development and Economic Growth in Germany." Background paper for *Human Development Report 1996*. UNDP, New York.

Boyer, Robert, and Daniel Drache, eds. 1996. *States against Markets: The Limits of Globalization.* London and New York: Routledge.

Broca, Sumiter, and Peter Ohram. 1991. "Study on the Location of the Poor." Paper prepared for the Technical Advisory Committee to the Consultative Group for International Agricultural Research. International Food Policy Research Institute, Washington, DC.

Bruno, Michael, Martin Ravallion and Lyn Squire. 1996. "Equity and Growth in Developing Countries: Old and New Perspectives on the Policy Issue." Policy Research Working Paper 1563. World Bank, Washington, DC.

CESR (Center for Economic and Social Rights). 1996. "UN-Sanctioned Suffering: A Human Rights Assessment of United Nations Sanctions on Iraq."

———. 1997. "A Human Rights Assessment of Sanctions: The Case of Iraq."

CGIAR (Consultative Group for International Agricultural Research). 1996. "1971–96: Twenty-Five Years of Food and Agricultural Improvement in Developing Countries." Washington, DC.

Chambers, Robert. 1997. *Whose Reality Counts? Putting the First Last.* London: Intermediate Technology Publications.

Chenery, Hollis, Montek S. Ahluwalia, C.I.G. Bell, John H. Duloy and Richard Jolly. 1974. *Redistribution with Growth.* London: Oxford University Press.

Childers, Erskine. 1995. "The UN at 50: Midlife Crisis." *World Press Review* 42(June): 8–22.

Cleaver, Kevin, and Gotz A. Schreiber. 1994. *Reversing the Spiral: The Population, Agriculture, and Environment Nexus in Sub-Saharan Africa.* Washington, DC: World Bank.

Colclough, Christopher, and Keith Lewin. 1993. *Educating All the Children.* Oxford: Oxford University Press.

Commission on Global Governance. 1995. *Our Global Neighbourhood.* New York: Oxford University Press.

Cornia, Giovanni Andrea. 1996. "Labour Market Shocks, Psychosocial Stress and the Transition Mortality Crisis." Research in Progress 4. Helsinki: WIDER (World Institute for Development Economics Research).

Datt, Gaurav, and Martin Ravallion. Forthcoming. "Why Have Some Indian States Done Better than Others at Reducing Rural Poverty?" *Economica.*

Davies, Susanna. 1993. "Versatile Livelihoods: Strategic Adaptation to Food Insecurity in the Mahalian Sahel." University of Sussex, Institute of Development Studies.

———. 1996. *Adaptable Livelihoods: Coping with Food Security in the Mahalian Sahel.* New York: St. Martin's Press.

Deininger, Klaus, and Lyn Squire. 1996. "A New Data Set Measuring Income Inequality." *The World Bank Economic Review* 10(3): 565–91.

Desai, Meghnad J. 1991. "Human Development: Concepts and Measurement." *European Economic Review* 35: 350–57.

de Vydler, Stefan. 1995. "Country Study on Sweden." Background paper for *Human Development Report 1996.* UNDP, New York.

Diamond, Peter A., and Michael Rothschild, eds. 1989. *Uncertainty in Economics: Readings and Exercises.* Rev. ed. New York: Academic Press.

———. 1989. *Hunger and Public Action.* Oxford: Clarendon Press.

Dreze, Jean, and Amartya K. Sen. 1995. *India: Economic Development and Social Opportunity.* Delhi: Oxford University Press.

Duncan, Greg. J., Björn Gustafsson, Richard Hauser, Günther Schmaus, Stephen Jenkins, Hans Messinger, Ruud Muffels, Brian Nolan, Jean-Claude Ray and Wolfgang Vosges. 1995. "Poverty and Social Assistance Dynamics in the United States, Canada and Europe." In Katherine McFate, Roger Lawson and William Julius Wilson, eds., *Poverty, Inequality and the Future of Social Policy: Western States in the New World Order.* New York: Russell Sage Foundation.

Eatwell, John. 1996. "International Financial Liberalization: The Impact on World Development." ODS Discussion Paper 12. UNDP, New York.

The Economist. 1996. "Why the Net Should Grow Up." 19 October, p. 17.

Erikson, John. 1996. "The International Response to Conflict and Genocide: Lessons from the Rwanda Experience: Synthesis Report." Steering Committee of the Joint Evaluation of Emergency Assistance to Rwanda, Copenhagen.

Eurostat and UN (United Nations). 1995. *Women and Men in Europe and North America.* Geneva.

FAO (Food and Agriculture Organization of the United Nations). 1994. *1994 Country Tables: Basic Data on the Agricultural Sector.* Economic and Social Policy Department. Rome.

———. 1996. *The Sixth World Food Survey.* Rome.

Folbre, Nancy. 1996. "Engendering Economics: New Perspectives on Women, Work, and Demographic Change." In Michael Bruno and Boris Pleskovic, eds., *Annual World Bank Conference on Development Economics 1995.* Washington, DC: World Bank.

Fortune Magazine. 1996. "Fortune 500." 29 April, p. F-1.

Foster, James E. 1984. "On Economic Poverty: A Survey of Aggregate Measures." *Advances in Econometrics* 3: 215–51.

———. 1985. "Inequality Measurement." In H.P. Young, ed., *Fair Allocation.* Providence, RI: American Mathematical Society.

Foster, James E., Joel Greer and Erik Thorbecke. 1984. "A Class of Decomposable Poverty Measures." *Econometrica* 52(3): 761–65.

Freedom House. 1995. "Freedom in the World." New York.

Frisch, Dieter. 1996. "The Effects of Corruption on Development." *Courier* 158(July–August): 68–70.

FWCW (Fourth World Conference on Women). 1995. "Report of the Fourth World Conference on Women." Beijing, 4–15 September.

Ghai, Dharam, and Jessica M. Vivian, eds. 1992. *Grassroots Environmental Action: People's Participation in Sustainable Development.* London: Routledge.

Government of Malawi and UNICEF (United Nations Children's Fund). 1996. "Malawi: Programme Plan of Operation for Youth and Education, 1997–2001." Lilongwe.

HABITAT (United Nations Centre for Human Settlements). 1996. *An Urbanized World: Global Report on Human Settlements.* Nairobi.

Hammond, Peter J. 1975. "A Note on Extreme Inequality Aversion." *Journal of Economic Theory* 11: 465–67.

Haq, Mahbub ul. 1995. *Reflections on Human Development.* Oxford: Oxford University Press.

Hardy, G.H., J.E. Littlewood and G. Polya. 1952. *Inequalities.* 2nd ed. Cambridge: Cambridge University Press.

Hazell, Peter, and James L. Garrett. 1996. "Reducing Poverty and Protecting the Environment: The Overlooked Potential of Less-Favored Lands." *2020 Vision Brief* 39 (October).

Hill, Alan G., and Lincoln Chen. 1996. *Oman's Leap to Good Health.* New York: WHO-UNICEF.

Human Development Center. 1997. *Human Development in South Asia 1997.* Karachi: Oxford University Press.

ICPD (International Conference on Population and Development). 1994. "Recommendation for the Further Implementation of the World Population Plan of Action." Cairo, 3–4 September.

IDS (Institute for Development Studies). 1989. "Vulnerability: How the Poor Cope." *IDS Bulletin* 20(2). Sussex.

———. 1996a. "Poverty, Policy and Aid." *IDS Bulletin* 27 (2). Sussex.

———. 1996b. "The Power of Participation: PRA and Policy." *Policy Briefing Issue* 7(August). Sussex.

IILS (International Institute for Labour Studies) and UNDP (United Nations Development Programme). 1995. *Social Exclusion and Anti-Poverty Strategies.* Geneva: IILS.

IISS (International Institute for Strategic Studies). 1993. *The Military Balance 1993–94.* London: Brasseys.

———. 1996. *The Military Balance 1996–97.* Oxford: Oxford University Press.

ILO (International Labour Office). 1994. *Yearbook of Labour Statistics 1994.* Geneva.

———. 1995a. *World Labour Report 1995.* Geneva.

———. 1995b. *Yearbook of Labour Statistics 1995.* Geneva.

———. 1996a. "Child Labour: What Is to Be Done?" Paper prepared for the Informal Tripartite Meeting at the Ministerial Level. Geneva, 12 June.

———. 1996b. *Estimates and Projections of the Economically Active Population, 1950–2010.* 4th ed. Diskette. Geneva.

IMF (International Monetary Fund). Various editions. *Government Finance Statistics Yearbook.* Washington, DC.

International Federation of Red Cross and Red Crescent Societies. 1995. *World Disasters Report 1995.* Geneva.

IPU (Inter-Parliamentary Union). 1997. *Democracy Still in the Making.* Geneva.

ITM (Instituto del Tercer Mundo). 1996. *Social Watch 2000: The Starting Point.* Montevideo.

ITU (International Telecommunication Union). 1996. *World Telecommunication Indicators.* Diskette. Geneva.

Jazairy, Idriss, Mohiuddin Alamgir and Theresa Panuccio. 1992. *The State of World Rural Poverty: An Inquiry into Its Causes and Consequences.* Published for IFAD (International Fund for Agricultural Development) by New York University Press.

Johansen, Frida. 1993. *Poverty Reduction in East Asia: The Silent Revolution.* World Bank Discussion Paper 223. Washington, DC.

Kapadia, K. 1996. "Housing Rights of the Urban Poor: Battle for Mumbai's Streets." *Economic and Political Weekly* 31(24).

Kennedy, Paul, and Bruce Russett. 1995. "Reforming the United Nations." *Foreign Affairs* (September/October).

Kohli, Atul. 1994. "Democracy in the Developing World: Trends and Prospects." Background paper for *Human Development Report 1994.* UNDP, New York.

Kolm, Serge C. 1969. "The Optimal Production of Social Justice." In J. Margolis and H. Guitton, eds., *Public Economics.* London: Macmillan.

Kothari, Smitu. 1993. "Social Movements and the Redefinition of Democracy." Background paper for *Human Development Report 1994.* UNDP, New York.

Lal, Deepak, and H. Myint. 1996. *The Political Economy of Poverty, Equity and Growth.* Oxford: Clarendon Press.

Lewis, Paul. 1996. "A World Fed up with Bribes." *New York Times,* 28 November.

Lipton, Michael. 1995. "Successes in Anti-Poverty." Issues in Development Discussion Paper 8. International Labour Office, Geneva.

Lipton, Michael, and Simon Maxwell. 1992. "The New Poverty Agenda: An Overview." Institute of Development Studies Discussion Paper 306. University of Sussex.

Lipton, Michael, and Siddiqur Osmani with Arian de Haan. 1996. "The Quality of Life in Emerging Asia." University of Sussex.

Lipton, Michael, and Martin Ravallion. 1995. "Poverty and Policy." In Jere Behrman and T.N. Srinivasan, eds., *Handbook of Development Economics.* Vol. 3. Amsterdam: North Holland.

Malaysia Economic Planning Unit. 1994. "Poverty Eradication, Expansion of Productive Employment and Social Integration in Malaysia, 1971–94." Prime Minister's Department, Kuala Lumpur.

Mann, Jonathan, and Daniel J.M. Tarantola, eds. 1996. *AIDS in the World II: Global Dimensions, Social Roots and Responses.* New York: Oxford University Press for the Global AIDS Policy Coalition.

Martinetti, Enrica Chiappero. 1994. "A New Approach to Evaluation of Well-Being and Poverty by Fuzzy Set Theory." *Giornale deggli Economisti e Annali di Economia* (July–September): 367–88.

Mehrotra, Santosh, and Aung Tun Thet. 1996. "Public Expenditure on Basic Social Services: The Scope for Budget Restructuring in Selected Asian and African Economies." UNICEF Staff Working Paper 14. New York.

Milanovic, Branco. 1996. "Income, Inequality and Poverty during the Transition." Research Paper Series 11. World Bank, Washington, DC.

Moser, Caroline O.N. 1996. *Confronting Crisis: A Comparative Study of Household Responses to Poverty and Vulnerability in Four Poor Urban Communities.* Environmentally Sustainable Development Studies and Monographs 8. Washington, DC: World Bank.

Moser, Caroline O.N., and Jeremy Holland. 1997. *Urban Poverty and Violence in Jamaica.* Latin American and Caribbean Studies. Washington, DC: World Bank.

Nussbaum, Martha C. 1988. "Nature, Function, and Capability: Aristotle on Political Distribution." *Oxford Studies in Ancient Philosophy* (supplementary issue).

OECD (Organisation for Economic Co-operation and Development). 1994a. *Development Co-operation: Development Assistance Committee Report 1994.* Paris.

———. 1994b. *Employment Outlook.* Paris.

———. 1995a. *Employment Outlook.* Paris.

———. 1995b. *Environmental Data: Compendium 1995.* Paris.

———. 1996a. *Development Co-operation: Development Assistance Committee Report 1996.* Paris.

———. 1996b. *Economic Outlook.* 60th issue. Paris.

———. 1996c. *Education at a Glance 1996.* Paris.

———. 1996d. *Employment Outlook.* Paris.

———. 1996e. *Shaping the 21st Century: The Contribution of Development Cooperation.* Paris: OECD.

Oman Ministry of Development and UNICEF (United Nations Children's Fund). 1995. "Situation Analysis of Children and Women in the Sultanate of Oman." Muscat.

Orshansky, Molly. 1965. "Counting the Poor: Another Look at the Poverty Profile." *Social Security Bulletin* 28: 3–29.

Osmani, Siddiq R. 1982. *Economic Inequality and Group Welfare.* Oxford: Clarendon Press.

Oxfam International. 1996a. "Debt Relief and Poverty Reduction: New Hope for Uganda." Oxfam International Position Paper. Oxford.

———. 1996b. "Multilateral Debt: The Human Costs." Oxfam International Position Paper. Oxford.

———. 1996c. "Trade Liberalization as a Threat to Livelihoods: The Corn Sector in the Philippines." Oxford.

Øyen, Else, S.M. Miller and Syed Abdus Samad. 1996. *Poverty: A Global Review Handbook on International Poverty Research.* Oslo: Scandinavian University Press.

Pisson, Gilles, and others, eds. 1995. *Population Dynamics of Senegal.* Washington, DC: National Academy Press.

Pratt, John W. 1964. "Risk Aversion in the Small and in the Large." *Econometrica* 32: 122–36.

Psacharopoulos, George, and Harry A. Patrinos, eds. 1994. *Indigenous People and Poverty in Latin America: An Empirical Analysis.* Regional and Sectoral Studies Series. Washington, DC: World Bank.

Psacharopoulos, George, and Zafiris Tzannatos, eds. 1992. *Case Studies on Women's Employment and Pay in Latin America.* Washington, DC: World Bank.

Ravallion, Martin. 1994. *Poverty Comparisons.* Chur, Switzerland: Harwood Academic Publishers.

———. Forthcoming. "Can High-Inequality Developing Countries Escape Absolute Poverty?" *Economic Letters.*

Ravallion, Martin, and Shaohua Chen. 1996. "What Can New Survey Data Tell Us about Recent Changes in Distribution and Poverty?" Policy Research Working Paper 1694. World Bank, Washington, DC.

RESULTS Educational Fund. 1997. "The Micro Credit Summit Declaration and Plan of Action." Washington, DC, 2–4 February.

Riddell, Roger. 1992. "Grassroots Participation and the Role of NGOs." Background paper for *Human Development Report 1993.* UNDP, New York.

Rodrik, Dani. 1996. "Understanding Economic Policy Reform." *Journal of Economic Literature* 34(March): 9–41.

Rogers, Gerry, Charles Gore and Jose B. Figueiredo. 1995. *Social Exclusion: Rhetoric, Reality, Responses.* Geneva: ILO and UNDP.

Rothschild, Michael, and Joseph E. Stiglitz. 1970. "Increasing Risk: I. A Definition." *Journal of Economic Theory* 2(3): 225–43.

Saggar, I., and I. Pan. 1994. "SCs and STs in Eastern India: Inequality and Poverty Estimates." *Economic and Political Weekly,* 5 March.

Schneider, Michael. 1991. *A Brief History of the German Trade Unions.* Bonn: Verlag J.H.W. Dietz Nachf.

Sen, Amartya K. 1973. *On Economic Inequality.* Oxford: Clarendon Press.

———. 1976. "Poverty: An Ordinal Approach to Measurement." *Econometrica* 46: 219–31.

———. 1979. "Issues in the Measurement of Poverty." *Scandinavian Journal of Economics* 81(2): 285–307.

———. 1983. "Poor, Relatively Speaking." *Oxford Economic Papers* 35.

———. 1990. "More than 100 Million Women Are Missing." *New York Review of Books* 37(20): 61–66.

———. 1992. *Inequality Reexamined.* Oxford: Clarendon Press; and Cambridge, Mass.: Harvard University Press.

———. 1993. "Life Expectancy and Inequality: Some Conceptual Issues." In P.K. Bardhan, M. Datta-Chaudhuri and T.N. Krishnan, eds., *Development and Change.* Bombay: Oxford University Press.

———. 1997. *On Economic Inequality. With a New Annex by James E. Foster and Amartya K. Sen.* Oxford: Clarendon Press.

Sen, Binayak. 1992. "Institutional Credit in Bangladesh." Background paper for *Human Development Report 1993.* UNDP, New York.

Shaffer, Paul. 1996. "Poverty and Gender in the Republic of Guinea." Canadian International Development Agency, Ottawa.

SIPRI (Stockholm International Peace Research Institute). 1996. *SIPRI Yearbook 1996.* New York: Oxford University Press.

Stanecki, Karen A., and Peter O. Way. 1996. "The Demographic Impacts of HIV/AIDS: Perspectives from the World Population Profile, 1996." US Bureau of the Census, Population Division, International Programs Center, Washington, DC.

Stern, Nicholas H. 1977. "Welfare Weights and the Elasticity of the Marginal Valuation of Income." In M. Artis and R. Nobay, eds., *Current Economic Problems.* Oxford: Basil Blackwell.

Stewart, Frances. 1995a. *Adjustment and Poverty: Options and Choices.* London: Routledge.

———. 1995b. "Biases in Global Markets: Can the Forces of Inequality and Marginalisation Be Modified?" In Mahbub ul Haq, Richard Jolly, Paul Streeten and Khadija Haq, eds., *The UN and the Bretton Woods Institutions.* London: Macmillan.

Streeten, Paul. 1993. "Markets and States: Against Minimalism." *World Development* 21(8): 1281–98.

Streeten, Paul, with Shahid J. Burki, Mahbub ul Haq, Norman Hicks and Frances Stewart. 1981. *First Things First: Meeting Basic Human Needs in the Developing Countries.* New York: Oxford University Press.

Summers, Robert, and Alan Heston. 1991. "Penn World Tables (Mark 5): An Expanded Set of International Comparisons, 1950–1988." *Quarterly Journal of Economics* 106: 327–68.

Swaminathan, Madhura. 1995. "Aspects of Urban Poverty in Bombay." *Environment and Urbanization* 7(1): 133–43.

Taylor, Vivienne. 1996. "Social Mobilization, Reconstruction and Development: Lessons from the Mass Democratic Movement." Cape Town: UWC Press for the Southern African Development Education and Policy Research Unit.

Transparency International. 1996. *Sharpening the Response against Global Corruption: Transparency International Global Report 1996.* Berlin.

UN (United Nations). 1993a. "Statistical Chart on World Families." Statistical Division and the Secretariat for the International Year of the Family. New York.

———. 1993b. *Statistical Yearbook 1990/91.* 38th issue. Statistical Division. New York. ST/ESA/STAT/ SER.S/14.E/F/93.XVII.1.

———. 1994a. *Statistical Yearbook 1992.* 39th issue. Statistical Division. New York. ST/ESA/STAT/ SER.S/15.E/F/94.XVII.1.

———. 1994b. *Women's Indicators and Statistics Database.* Version 3. CD-ROM. Statistical Division. New York.

———. 1995a. "Ninth United Nations Congress on the Prevention of Crime and the Treatment of Offenders." Background paper by the Secretariat on International Action against Corruption. New York.

———. 1995b. *Statistical Yearbook 1993.* 40th issue. Statistical Division. New York.

———. 1995c. "World Urbanization Prospects: The 1994 Revision." Database. Population Division. New York.

———. 1995d. *The World's Women 1970–95: Trends and Statistics.* New York.

———. 1996a. *Energy Statistics Yearbook 1994.* New York.

———. 1996b. "World Population Prospects 1950–2050." Database. 1996 revision. Population Division. New York.

———. 1996c. "The Realization of Economic, Social and Cultural Rights; Final Report on Human Rights and Extreme Poverty." Submitted by the Special Rapporteur, Leandro Despouy, Economic and Social Council, Commission on Human Rights, 28 June, New York.

———. 1997. "World Population Monitoring—Issues of International Migration and Development: Selected Aspects." Population Division. New York. Draft.

UNAIDS (Joint United Nations Programme on HIV/AIDS). 1996a. *The Current Global Situation of AIDS.* Geneva.

———. 1996b. *HIV/AIDS: The Global Epidemic, Fact Sheet.* Geneva.

———. 1997. Correspondence received on AIDS cases reported to WHO by country/territory through 20 November 1996. Geneva.

UNCSDHA (United Nations Centre for Social Development and Humanitarian Affairs). 1995. "Results of the Fourth United Nations Survey of Crime Trends and Operations of the Criminal Justice System (1986–90)—Interim Report by the Secretariat." Vienna.

UNCTAD (United Nations Conference on Trade and Development). 1996a. *Globalization and Liberalization: Effects of International Economic Relations on Poverty.* New York and Geneva.

———. 1996b. *World Investment Report 1996: Investment, Trade and International Policy Arrangements.* New York and Geneva.

UNDP (United Nations Development Programme). 1994. *Human Development Report 1994.* New York: Oxford University Press.

———. 1995a. *Human Development Report 1995.* New York: Oxford University Press.

———. 1995b. *Poverty Eradication: A Policy Framework for Country Strategies.* New York.

———. 1995c. "Wheeling and Dealing: HIV and Development on the Shan State Borders of Myanmar." Study paper 3. HIV and Development Programme. New York.

———. 1996a. "Democratic Governance and the Social Condition in the Anglophone Caribbean." New York.

———. 1996b. *Development and the HIV Epidemic: A Forward-Looking Evaluation of the Approach of the UNDP HIV and Development Programme.* New York.

———. 1996c. "Governance for Sustainable Development." UNDP Policy Document. New York.

———. 1996d. *Human Development Report 1996.* New York: Oxford University Press.

———. 1996e. *Human Development under Transition: Summaries of National Human Development Reports 1996, Europe and CIS.* RBEC (Regional Bureau for Europe and the Commonwealth of Independent States). New York.

———. 1996f. *Human Settlements under Transition: The Case of Eastern Europe and the CIS.* RBEC (Regional Bureau for Europe and the Commonwealth of Independent States). New York.

———. 1996g. "Preventing and Eradicating Poverty." Report on the experts' meeting on poverty alleviation and sustainable livelihoods in the Arab States. Damascus, 28–29 February.

———. 1996h. "Relatório Sobre o Desenvolvimento Humano Brasil." Brasilia.

———. 1997. "Programme of Assistance to the Palestinian People: Report of the Administrator." New York.

———. Forthcoming. "Human Security for the New Millennium: Elements for a Poverty Eradication Strategy in the Arab States." New York.

UNDP (United Nations Development Programme), UNFPA (United Nations Population Fund) and UNICEF (United Nations Children's Fund). 1994. *The 20:20 Initiative.* New York: UNDP.

UNDP (United Nations Development Programme) and UNICEF (United Nations Children's Fund). 1996. "Catching Up: Capacity Development for Poverty Elimination in Viet Nam." Hanoi.

UNDPI (United Nations Department of Public Information). 1996. "Setting the Record Straight: Some Facts about the United Nations." New York.

UNECE (United Nations Economic Commission for Europe). 1995a. *Statistics of Traffic Accidents in Europe and North America.* New York and Geneva.

———. 1995b. *Trends in Europe and North America: The Statistical Yearbook of the Economic Commission for Europe.* New York and Geneva: United Nations.

———. 1996. Database. Geneva.

———. 1997. Correspondence on GNP per capita. Received January.

UNESCO (United Nations Educational, Scientific and Cultural Organization). 1993. *World Education Report 1993.* Paris.

———. 1995a. *Statistical Yearbook 1995.* Paris.

———. 1995b. *World Education Report 1995.* Paris.

———. 1996a. Correspondence on adult literacy. Received November. Division of Statistics. Paris.

———. 1996b. Correspondence on adult literacy and combined primary, secondary and tertiary enrolment. Received December. Division of Statistics. Paris.

———. 1996c. "Education for All: Achieving the Goal." Mid-Decade Meeting of the International Consultative Forum on Education for All. Amman, 16–19 June.

———. 1996d. *Statistical Yearbook 1996*. Paris.

———. 1997. Correspondence on education enrolments and expenditures. Received January. Paris.

UNESCWA (United Nations Economic and Social Commission for Western Africa). 1996. *Poverty in Western Africa: A Social Perspective*. Eradicating Poverty Studies Series 1. E/ESCWA/SD/1996/8. New York.

UNFPA (United Nations Population Fund). 1996a. *Expert Consultation on Reproductive Health and Family Planning: Directions for UNFPA Assistance*. Technical Report 31. New York.

———. 1996b. *Implementation of the Programme of Action of the International Conference on Population and Development*. A/51/350. New York.

———. 1996c. *Monitoring of Population Programmes: Report of the Secretary-General*. E/CN.9/1996/3. New York.

———. 1997. *The State of World Population 1997—The Right to Choose: Reproductive Rights and Reproductive Health*. New York.

UNHCR (United Nations High Commissioner for Refugees). 1996a. *Populations of Concern to UNHCR: A Statistical Overview*. Geneva.

———. 1996b. *UNHCR by the Numbers*. Geneva.

UNICEF (United Nations Children's Fund). 1995a. *Poverty, Children and Policy: Responses for a Brighter Future*. Economies in Transition: Regional Monitoring Report 3. Florence.

———. 1995b. *Progress of Nations*. New York.

———. 1996a. *Progress of Nations*. New York.

———. 1996b. *The State of the World's Children 1996*. New York: Oxford University Press.

———. 1996c. *World Summit for Children Followup: Mid-Decade Review 1996*. Secretary-General's Report. New York.

———. 1997. *The State of the World's Children 1997*. New York: Oxford University Press.

United Nations Centre for Human Rights. 1997. "Human Rights: International Instruments—Chart of Ratifications as of 31 December 1996." ST/HR/4/Rev.13. Geneva.

UNRISD (United Nations Research Institute for Social Development). 1995. *States of Disarray: The Social Effects of Globalisation*. Geneva.

US Department of Health and Human Services. 1996. "Update: Mortality Attributable to HIV Infection among Persons Aged 25–44 Years—United States 1994." *Morbidity and Mortality Weekly Report* 45(6): 121–25.

Watkins, Kevin, ed. 1995. *Oxfam Poverty Report*. Oxford: Oxfam.

WHO (World Health Organization). 1993. *World Health Statistics Annual 1993*. Geneva.

———. 1994. *World Health Statistics Annual 1994*. Geneva.

———. 1996a. *Tabac Alerte*. Special issue. Geneva.

———. 1996b. *World Health Report 1996*. Geneva.

WHO (World Health Organization) and UNICEF (United Nations Children's Fund). 1997. "Special Tabulations on Access to Water Supply and Sanitation for 1980 and 1995." Monitoring unit. New York.

Winichagoon, P., and others, eds. 1992. "Integrating Food and Nutrition into Development: Thailand's Experience and Future Visions." Mahidol University, Institute of Nutrition, Thailand.

World Bank. 1990. *World Development Report 1990*. New York: Oxford University Press.

———. 1992. *World Development Report 1992*. New York: Oxford University Press.

———. 1993. *World Development Report 1993*. New York: Oxford University Press.

———. 1995a. *Global Economic Prospects and the Developing Countries 1995*. Washington, DC.

———. 1995b. *The Social Impact of Adjustment Operations: An Overview*. Report 14776. Washington, DC.

———. 1995c. *Social Indicators of Development*. Baltimore: Johns Hopkins University Press.

———. 1995d. *World Data 1995*. CD-ROM. Washington, DC.

———. 1995e. *World Development Report 1995*. New York: Oxford University Press.

———. 1996a. Correspondence on GDP. Received May. Washington, DC.

———. 1996b. *Global Economic Prospects and the Developing Countries 1996*. Washington, DC.

———. 1996c. *Poverty Reduction and the World Bank: Progress and Challenges in the 1990s*. Washington, DC.

———. 1996d. "Taking Action to Reduce Poverty in Sub-Saharan Africa: An Overview." Washington, DC.

———. 1996e. *Trends in Developing Economies 1996*. Washington, DC.

———. 1996f. *World Bank Atlas 1996*. Washington, DC.

———. 1996g. *World Debt Tables 1995–96*. Washington, DC.

———. 1996h. *World Development Report 1996*. New York: Oxford University Press.

———. 1997a. Correspondence on unpublished World Bank data on GNP per capita estimates using the GDP/GNP ratio for 1994. Received January. Washington, DC.

———. 1997b. *World Development Indicators 1997*. Washington, DC.

World Commission on Culture and Development. 1995. *Our Creative Diversity*. Paris: UNESCO.

Worldwatch Institute. 1996. *Worldwatch* 9(4).

Worldwide Government Directories. 1995. *Worldwide Government Directory with International Organizations*. Bethesda, Md.

WRI (World Resources Institute). 1994. *World Resources 1994–95*. New York: Oxford University Press.

———. 1996a. Correspondence on the Gini coefficient. Received December. Washington, DC.

———. 1996b. *World Resources 1996–97*. New York: Oxford University Press.

WSC (World Summit for Children). 1990. "World Declaration on the Survival, Protection and Development of Children, and Plan of Action for Implementing the Declaration in the 1990s." New York, 29–30 September.

WSSD (World Summit for Social Development). 1995. "Report of the World Summit for Social Development." Copenhagen, 6–12 March.

HUMAN
DEVELOPMENT
INDICATORS

Indicators

TABLE 1   Human development index   146 — All countries

TABLE 2   Gender-related development index   149 — All countries

TABLE 3   Gender empowerment measure   152 — All countries

TABLE 4   Regional comparisons of human development values   155 — All countries

TABLE 5   Trends in human development and per capita income   158 — All countries

TABLE 6   Trends in human development and economic growth   161 — All countries

TABLE 7   Profile of human development   164 — Developing countries
- Life expectancy at birth
- Population with access to health services
- Population with access to safe water
- Population with access to sanitation
- Daily calorie supply per capita
- Adult literacy rate
- Combined first- and second-level gross enrolment ratio
- Daily newspapers
- Televisions
- Real GDP per capita
- GNP per capita

TABLE 8   Trends in human development   166 — Developing countries
- Life expectancy at birth
- Infant mortality rate
- Population with access to safe water
- Underweight children under age five
- Adult literacy rate
- Gross enrolment ratio for all levels
- Real GDP per capita

TABLE 9   South-North gaps   168 — Developing countries
- Life expectancy at birth
- Adult literacy
- Daily calorie supply per capita
- Access to safe water
- Under-five mortality

TABLE 10   Women and capabilities   170 — Developing countries
- Female net primary enrolment ratio
- Female net secondary enrolment ratio
- Female tertiary students
- Female life expectancy at birth
- Total fertility

TABLE 11   Women and political and economic participation   172 — Developing countries
- Administrators and managers
- Professional and technical workers
- Clerical and sales workers
- Service workers
- Women in government

TABLE 12   Child survival and development   174 — Developing countries
- Pregnant women aged 15–49 with anaemia
- Births attended by trained health personnel
- Low-birth-weight infants
- Maternal mortality rate
- Infant mortality rate
- Under-five mortality rate
- Mothers breast-feeding at six months
- Oral rehydration therapy use rate
- Underweight children under age five

TABLE 13   Health profile   176 Developing countries

- One-year-olds fully immunized against tuberculosis
- One-year-olds fully immunized against measles
- AIDS cases
- Tuberculosis cases
- Malaria cases
- Cigarette consumption per adult
- Population per doctor
- Population per nurse
- People with disabilities
- Public expenditure on health as % of GNP
- Public expenditure on health as % of GDP

TABLE 14   Food security   178 Developing countries

- Food production per capita index
- Agricultural production as % of GDP
- Food consumption as % of total household consumption
- Daily calorie supply per capita
- Per capita food supply from fish and seafood
- Food imports as % of merchandise imports
- Cereal imports
- Food aid in cereals

TABLE 15   Education imbalances   180 Developing countries

- Compulsory education
- Secondary technical enrolment
- Tertiary natural and applied science enrolment
- Tertiary students abroad
- R & D scientists and technicians
- Public expenditure on education as % of GNP
- Public expenditure on education as % of total government expenditure
- Public expenditure on primary and secondary education
- Public expenditure on higher education

TABLE 16   Employment   182 Developing countries

- Labour force as % of total population
- Women's share of adult labour force
- Percentage of labour force in agriculture
- Percentage of labour force in industry
- Percentage of labour force in services
- Real earnings per employee annual growth rate

TABLE 17   Communication profile   184 Developing countries

- Radios
- Televisions
- Book titles published
- Printing and writing paper consumed
- Post offices
- Main telephone lines
- International telephone calls
- Fax machines
- Mobile cellular telephone subscribers
- Internet users
- Personal computers

TABLE 18   Social investment   186 Developing countries

- Social security benefits expenditure
- Percentage of central government expenditure on social security and welfare
- Percentage of central government expenditure on housing and community amenities
- Percentage of central government expenditure on health
- Percentage of central government expenditure on education

TABLE 19   Military expenditure and resource use imbalances   188 Developing countries

- Defence expenditure
- Defence expenditure as % of GDP
- Defence expenditure per capita
- Military expenditure as % of combined education and health expenditure
- Imports of conventional weapons
- Total armed forces

TABLE 20   Resource flows   190 Developing countries

- Total external debt
- Total external debt as % of GNP
- Debt service ratio
- Total net official development assistance received, 1995
- Net foreign direct investment
- Export-import ratio
- Terms of trade
- Current account balance before official transfers

TABLE 21   Growing urbanization   192 Developing countries

- Urban population as % of total
- Urban population annual growth rate
- Population in cities of more than 750,000 as % of total population
- Population in cities of more than 750,000 as % of urban population
- Largest city
- Largest city population
- Largest city growth rate

TABLE 31   Education profile   208   Industrial countries
- Full-time students per 100 people
- Secondary full-time net enrolment ratio
- Upper-secondary technical enrolment
- Tertiary net enrolment ratio
- Tertiary natural and applied science enrolment

- Public expenditure on higher education
- Public expenditure per tertiary student
- Public expenditure on education
- Total expenditure on education

TABLE 32   Employment   209   Industrial countries
- Labour force as % of total population
- Women's share of adult labour force
- Percentage of labour force in agriculture
- Percentage of labour force in industry
- Percentage of labour force in services

- Future labour force replacement ratio
- Real earnings per employee annual growth rate
- Labour force unionized
- Weekly hours of work
- Expenditure on labour market programmes

TABLE 33   Unemployment   210   Industrial countries
- Unemployed people
- Total unemployment rate
- Male unemployment rate
- Female unemployment rate
- Youth unemployment rate
- Incidence of long-term unemployment, more than 6 months

- Incidence of long-term unemployment, more than 12 months
- Discouraged workers
- Involuntary part-time workers
- Unemployment benefits expenditure

TABLE 34   Communication profile   211   Industrial countries
- Radios
- Televisions
- Book titles published
- Printing and writing paper consumed
- Main telephone lines

- International telephone calls
- Fax machines
- Mobile cellular telephone subscribers
- Internet users
- Personal computers

TABLE 35   Social investment   212   Industrial countries
- Social security benefits expenditure
- Percentage of central government expenditure on social security and welfare
- Percentage of central government expenditure on housing and community amenities

- Percentage of central government expenditure on health
- Percentage of central government expenditure on education

TABLE 36   Social stress and social change   213   Industrial countries
- Prisoners
- Young adult prisoners
- Intentional homicides by men
- Drug crimes
- Reported adult rapes
- Injuries and deaths from road accidents

- Suicides
- Divorces
- Single-female-parent homes
- Live births per 1,000 women aged 15–19
- One-person-households headed by women aged 65 and above

TABLE 37   Aid flows   214   Industrial countries
- Net official development assistance (ODA) disbursed
- ODA as % of GNP, average for 1984/85
- ODA as % of GNP, 1995
- ODA as % of central government budget
- ODA per capita of donor country

- Multilateral ODA as % of GNP
- Government subsidies to NGOs
- Aid by NGOs as % of GNP
- Aid to least developed countries

TABLE 38   Military expenditure and resource use imbalances   215   Industrial countries
- Defence expenditure
- Defence expenditure as % of GDP
- Defence expenditure per capita
- Military expenditure as % of combined education and health expenditure

- ODA disbursed as % of defence expenditure
- Exports of conventional weapons
- Total armed forces

102 Albania	19 Germany	88 Oman
82 Algeria	132 Ghana	139 Pakistan
157 Angola	20 Greece	45 Panama
29 Antigua and Barbuda	54 Grenada	128 Papua New Guinea
36 Argentina	117 Guatemala	94 Paraguay
103 Armenia	167 Guinea	89 Peru
14 Australia	163 Guinea-Bissau	98 Philippines
12 Austria	104 Guyana	58 Poland
106 Azerbaijan	156 Haiti	31 Portugal
28 Bahamas	116 Honduras	55 Qatar
43 Bahrain	22 Hong Kong	79 Romania
144 Bangladesh	48 Hungary	67 Russian Federation
25 Barbados	5 Iceland	174 Rwanda
62 Belarus	138 India	49 Saint Kitts and Nevis
13 Belgium	99 Indonesia	56 Saint Lucia
63 Belize	70 Iran, Islamic Rep. of	57 Saint Vincent
146 Benin	126 Iraq	96 Samoa (Western)
155 Bhutan	17 Ireland	125 São Tomé and Principe
113 Bolivia	23 Israel	73 Saudi Arabia
97 Botswana	21 Italy	160 Senegal
68 Brazil	83 Jamaica	52 Seychelles
38 Brunei Darussalam	7 Japan	175 Sierra Leone
69 Bulgaria	84 Jordan	26 Singapore
172 Burkina Faso	93 Kazakstan	42 Slovakia
169 Burundi	134 Kenya	35 Slovenia
153 Cambodia	75 Korea, Dem. People's Rep. of	122 Solomon Islands
133 Cameroon	32 Korea, Rep. of	90 South Africa
1 Canada	53 Kuwait	11 Spain
123 Cape Verde	107 Kyrgyzstan	91 Sri Lanka
151 Central African Rep.	136 Lao People's Dem. Rep.	158 Sudan
164 Chad	92 Latvia	66 Suriname
30 Chile	65 Lebanon	114 Swaziland
108 China	137 Lesotho	10 Sweden
51 Colombia	64 Libyan Arab Jamahiriya	16 Switzerland
140 Comoros	76 Lithuania	78 Syrian Arab Rep.
130 Congo	27 Luxembourg	115 Tajikistan
33 Costa Rica	80 Macedonia, FYR	149 Tanzania, U. Rep. of
145 Côte d'Ivoire	152 Madagascar	59 Thailand
77 Croatia	161 Malawi	147 Togo
86 Cuba	60 Malaysia	40 Trinidad and Tobago
24 Cyprus	111 Maldives	81 Tunisia
39 Czech Rep.	171 Mali	74 Turkey
18 Denmark	34 Malta	85 Turkmenistan
162 Djibouti	150 Mauritania	159 Uganda
41 Dominica	61 Mauritius	95 Ukraine
87 Dominican Rep.	50 Mexico	44 United Arab Emirates
72 Ecuador	110 Moldova, Rep. of	15 United Kingdom
109 Egypt	101 Mongolia	37 Uruguay
112 El Salvador	119 Morocco	4 USA
135 Equatorial Guinea	166 Mozambique	100 Uzbekistan
168 Eritrea	131 Myanmar	124 Vanuatu
71 Estonia	118 Namibia	47 Venezuela
170 Ethiopia	154 Nepal	121 Viet Nam
46 Fiji	6 Netherlands	148 Yemen
8 Finland	9 New Zealand	142 Zaire
2 France	127 Nicaragua	143 Zambia
120 Gabon	173 Niger	129 Zimbabwe
165 Gambia	141 Nigeria	
105 Georgia	3 Norway	

The *Human Development Report* has presented data on broad aspects of human development since its inception in 1990. This has required a far-ranging array of statistics that reflect people's well-being and the opportunities that they actually enjoy.

As a standard practice, this year's Report, like earlier ones, relies on national estimates reported by the United Nations and its agencies and by other internationally recognized organizations, and thus on the standardization and consistency of data produced by these offices. The few exceptions in which data from other sources have been used are noted in the relevant tables.

Data standards and methodology

Even when standardized international sources are used, a number of problems remain for any user of statistical data.

First, despite the considerable efforts of international organizations to collect, process and disseminate social and economic statistics and to standardize definitions and data collection methods, limitations remain in the coverage, consistency and comparability of data across time and countries. Second, dramatic shifts and breaks in statistical series can occur when statistical administrations and research bodies seek to update or improve their estimates using new sources of data, such as censuses and surveys.

Such concerns arise in preparing the human development index (HDI). For example, for the 1996 revision of the United Nations database "World Population Prospects 1950–2050" (UN 1996b), released on 15 November 1996, the United Nations Population Division derived estimates and projections from population censuses—supplemented with information from national survey data—using specialized demographic techniques. It made significant adjustments to the 1994 revision to incorporate the demographic impact of HIV/AIDS and to accommodate the extensive migratory movements within Europe and elsewhere and the rapid growth in the number of refugees in Africa and

elsewhere (UN 1996b).[1] And it incorporated newly available data reflecting significant changes in the demographic profiles of countries in Eastern Europe and the Commonwealth of Independent States (CIS).

Changes in the population estimates have an effect on other indicators—such as enrolment ratios for different levels of schooling published by UNESCO. These are defined as the ratio of the number of children enrolled in a schooling level to the number of children in the relevant age group. The age group indicator depends on the estimates of age- and sex-specific populations published by the United Nations Population Division. Data on enrolment are affected by the methodology and timing used by the administrative registries, population censuses and education surveys at the national level. In addition, independent of the variations in population estimates and enrolment data, UNESCO may periodically revise the methodology used for its projections and estimations of literacy and enrolment. Consequently, the reader must take into account the potential for fluctuation in both literacy and enrolment rates when making comparisons across time and countries.

Estimates of income used in the HDI are GDP converted to international dollars by using purchasing power parities (PPP) established by the World Bank, based on the results of surveys by the International Comparison Programme (ICP).

Revision and updating of the PPP-based income estimates lead to fluctuations across time and country series. The real GDP per capita (PPP$) estimates used in *Human Development Report 1997* integrate the results from the 1993 ICP, which cover the OECD member countries and Eastern Europe and the CIS, and the most recent version of the Penn World Tables (Mark 5.6).

Another problem is uneven data availability across country groups. Some issues, such as literacy, are well documented in the developing countries but less so in the industrial countries, or vice versa. In such cases the Report presents the limited data available, primarily from official national reporting systems and compiled by the United Nations, with the caveat that these data may not be readily used for international comparisons.

The transition in the Eastern European and CIS countries has led to a break in most of their statistical series, so the data available for recent years present problems of reliability, consistency and comparability at the international level and are often subject to revision.

The quality of data also suffers in countries in which there is war or civil strife. Where the availability and quality of estimates have become extremely limited, reporting of the data in the *Human Development Report* has been interrupted. But other countries where data have become available have been included for the first time this year, such as Eritrea and FYR Macedonia.

Another major problem is the extremely limited availability of data on such important human development issues as crime, violence, employment, the environment, child labour, gender equality, income distribution, maternal mortality, informal sector activities and non-market unpaid work.

Country classification

The main criterion for classifying countries is the HDI. Countries are classified into three groups: high human development, with HDI values of 0.800 and above; medium human development, with HDI values of 0.500 to 0.799; and low human development, with HDI values below 0.500. For analytic purposes, aggregate measures for the medium and low human development countries are also computed after excluding China and India from their respective groups because the magnitudes of their populations, GDP and other measures overwhelm those of the smaller countries.

The regional classification of countries corresponds to the Regional Bureaux of

UNDP and the income classification to the definitions in the World Bank's *World Development Report 1996*, except as noted otherwise.

Indicator tables

In the indicator tables countries and areas are ranked in descending order by their HDI value. Where estimates have been calculated using established international statistical series, the estimates are footnoted and the sources given in the notes at the end of each table. These notes also give the data sources for each column. The first source listed is the main international source for the indicator. The indicator tables no longer include estimates derived from sources other than the documented sources, except for table 1 (human development index). Short citations of sources are given, corresponding to the full references in the complete list of data sources used in preparing the indicator tables. This list appears after the indicator tables.

Not all countries have been included in the indicator tables, owing to the lack of comparable data.

Unless otherwise stated, the summary measures for the human development, income and regional groups of countries are weighted by population subgroups or other requisite indicators. Summary measures are not presented in cases where there were no data for the majority of countries in a group or appropriate weighting procedures were unavailable. Where appropriate, the summary aggregate is presented as the total for the region, rather than as a weighted average. Unless otherwise indicated, multiyear averages of growth rates are expressed as compound annual rates of change. Year-to-year growth rates are expressed as annual percentage changes.

In the absence of the phrase "annual", "annual rate" or "growth rate", a hyphen between two years indicates that the data were collected during one of the years shown. A slash between two years indicates an average for the years shown, such as 1993/94. The following signs have been used:

.. Data not available

(.) Less than half the unit shown

(..)Less than one-tenth the unit shown

– Not applicable

T Total

Improving human development statistics

A major goal of the Report is to encourage national governments, international bodies and policy-makers to participate in improving statistical indicators of human development.

The *Human Development Report* will continue to refine statistical data and to press countries and the global community to support the production and analysis of better human and social data.

Note

1. The 1996 revision incorporates the demographic impact of HIV/AIDS in the population estimates and projections for the 28 developing countries where HIV seroprevalence had reached 2% in 1994 or where the absolute number of infected adults was large: Benin, Botswana, Brazil, Burkina Faso, Burundi, Cameroon, Central African Republic, Chad, Congo, Côte d'Ivoire, Eritrea, Guinea-Bissau, Haiti, India, Kenya, Lesotho, Malawi, Mozambique, Namibia, Rwanda, Sierra Leone, Tanzania, Thailand, Togo, Uganda, Zaire, Zambia and Zimbabwe.

1 Human development index

HDI rank	Life expectancy at birth (years) 1994	Adult literacy rate (%) 1994	Combined first-, second- and third-level gross enrolment ratio (%) 1994	Real GDP per capita (PPP$) 1994	Adjusted real GDP per capita (PPP$) 1994	Life expectancy index	Education index	GDP index	Human development index (HDI) value 1994	Real GDP per capita (PPP$) rank minus HDI rank[a]
High human development	74.6	97.0	80	17,052	6,040	0.83	0.91	0.98	0.907	–
1 Canada	79.0	99.0	100[b]	21,459	6,073	0.90	0.99	0.99	0.960	7
2 France	78.7	99.0	89	20,510	6,071	0.89	0.96	0.99	0.946	13
3 Norway	77.5	99.0	92	21,346	6,073	0.88	0.97	0.99	0.943	6
4 USA	76.2	99.0	96	26,397	6,101	0.85	0.98	0.99	0.942	-1
5 Iceland	79.1	99.0	83	20,566	6,071	0.90	0.94	0.99	0.942	9
6 Netherlands	77.3	99.0	91	19,238	6,067	0.87	0.96	0.99	0.940	13
7 Japan	79.8	99.0	78	21,581	6,074	0.91	0.92	0.99	0.940	0
8 Finland	76.3	99.0	97	17,417	6,041	0.85	0.98	0.98	0.940	15
9 New Zealand	76.4	99.0	94	16,851	6,039	0.86	0.97	0.98	0.937	15
10 Sweden	78.3	99.0	82	18,540	6,064	0.89	0.93	0.99	0.936	11
11 Spain	77.6	97.1[c]	90	14,324	6,029	0.88	0.95	0.98	0.934	19
12 Austria	76.6	99.0	87	20,667	6,072	0.86	0.95	0.99	0.932	1
13 Belgium	76.8	99.0	86	20,985	6,072	0.86	0.95	0.99	0.932	-1
14 Australia	78.1	99.0	79	19,285	6,068	0.89	0.92	0.99	0.931	4
15 United Kingdom	76.7	99.0	86	18,620	6,065	0.86	0.95	0.99	0.931	5
16 Switzerland	78.1	99.0	76	24,967	6,098	0.88	0.91	0.99	0.930	-12
17 Ireland	76.3	99.0	88	16,061	6,037	0.85	0.95	0.98	0.929	8
18 Denmark	75.2	99.0	89	21,341	6,073	0.84	0.96	0.99	0.927	-8
19 Germany	76.3	99.0	81	19,675[d]	6,069	0.86	0.93	0.99	0.924	-3
20 Greece	77.8	96.7[c]	82	11,265	5,982	0.88	0.92	0.97	0.923	15
21 Italy	77.8	98.1[c]	73	19,363	6,068	0.88	0.90	0.99	0.921	-4
22 Hong Kong	79.0	92.3	72	22,310	6,075	0.90	0.86	0.99	0.914	-17
23 Israel	77.5	95.0	75	16,023	6,037	0.87	0.88	0.98	0.913	3
24 Cyprus	77.1	94.0	75	13,071[e,f]	6,021	0.87	0.88	0.98	0.907	8
25 Barbados	75.9	97.3	76	11,051	5,979	0.85	0.90	0.97	0.907	11
26 Singapore	77.1	91.0	72	20,987	6,072	0.87	0.85	0.99	0.900	-15
27 Luxembourg	75.9	99.0	58	34,155	6,130	0.85	0.85	1.00	0.899	-26
28 Bahamas	72.9	98.1	75	15,875	6,036	0.80	0.90	0.98	0.894	0
29 Antigua and Barbuda	74.0	96.0	76	8,977[e]	5,947	0.82	0.89	0.97	0.892	16
30 Chile	75.1	95.0	72	9,129	5,950	0.83	0.87	0.97	0.891	13
31 Portugal	74.6	89.6[c]	81	12,326	6,014	0.83	0.87	0.98	0.890	3
32 Korea, Rep. of	71.5	97.9	82	10,656	5,974	0.77	0.93	0.97	0.890	5
33 Costa Rica	76.6	94.7	68	5,919	5,853	0.86	0.86	0.95	0.889	27
34 Malta	76.4	86.0[g]	76	13,009[e,f]	6,021	0.86	0.83	0.98	0.887	-1
35 Slovenia	73.1	96.0	74	10,404[e]	5,970	0.80	0.89	0.97	0.886	3
36 Argentina	72.4	96.0	77	8,937	5,946	0.79	0.90	0.97	0.884	10
37 Uruguay	72.6	97.1	75	6,752	5,895	0.79	0.90	0.96	0.883	15
38 Brunei Darussalam	74.9	87.9	70	30,447[e,f]	6,125	0.83	0.82	1.00	0.882	-36
39 Czech Rep.	72.2	99.0	70	9,201	5,951	0.79	0.89	0.97	0.882	3
40 Trinidad and Tobago	72.9	97.9	67	9,124	5,949	0.80	0.88	0.97	0.880	4
41 Dominica	72.0	94.0	77	6,118[e]	5,868	0.78	0.88	0.95	0.873	16
42 Slovakia	70.8	99.0	72	6,389	5,882	0.76	0.90	0.96	0.873	12
43 Bahrain	72.0	84.4	85	15,321	6,036	0.78	0.85	0.98	0.870	-14
44 United Arab Emirates	74.2	78.6	82	16,000[h]	6,036	0.82	0.80	0.98	0.866	-17
45 Panama	73.2	90.5	70	6,104	5,868	0.80	0.84	0.95	0.864	14
46 Fiji	71.8	91.3	79	5,763	5,763	0.78	0.87	0.94	0.863	16
47 Venezuela	72.1	91.0	68	8,120	5,930	0.79	0.83	0.96	0.861	1
48 Hungary	68.8	99.0	67	6,437	5,884	0.73	0.88	0.96	0.857	5
49 Saint Kitts and Nevis	69.0[g]	90.0[g]	78	9,436	5,955	0.73	0.86	0.97	0.853	-9
50 Mexico	72.0	89.2	66	7,384	5,913	0.78	0.81	0.96	0.853	0
51 Colombia	70.1	91.1	70	6,107	5,868	0.75	0.84	0.95	0.848	7
52 Seychelles	72.0[g]	88.0[g]	61	7,891[e]	5,925	0.78	0.79	0.96	0.845	-3
53 Kuwait	75.2	77.8	57	21,875	6,074	0.84	0.71	0.99	0.844	-47
54 Grenada	72.0[g]	98.0[g]	78	5,137[e]	5,137	0.78	0.91	0.83	0.843	17
55 Qatar	70.9	78.9	73	18,403	6,063	0.76	0.77	0.99	0.840	-33
56 Saint Lucia	71.0[g]	82.0[g]	74	6,182[e]	5,872	0.77	0.79	0.95	0.838	-1
57 Saint Vincent	72.0[g]	82.0[g]	78	5,650[e]	5,650	0.78	0.81	0.92	0.836	6
58 Poland	71.2	99.0	79	5,002	5,002	0.77	0.92	0.81	0.834	14
59 Thailand	69.5	93.5	53	7,104	5,906	0.74	0.80	0.96	0.833	-8
60 Malaysia	71.2	83.0	62	8,865	5,945	0.77	0.76	0.97	0.832	-13
61 Mauritius	70.7	82.4	61	13,172	6,022	0.76	0.75	0.98	0.831	-30
62 Belarus	69.2	97.9	80	4,713	4,713	0.74	0.92	0.76	0.806	13
63 Belize	74.0	70.0[g]	68	5,590	5,590	0.82	0.69	0.91	0.806	1
64 Libyan Arab Jamahiriya	63.8	75.0	91	6,125[e]	5,869	0.65	0.80	0.95	0.801	-8

HDI rank		Life expectancy at birth (years) 1994	Adult literacy rate (%) 1994	Combined first-, second- and third-level gross enrolment ratio (%) 1994	Real GDP per capita (PPP$) 1994	Adjusted real GDP per capita (PPP$) 1994	Life expectancy index	Education index	GDP index	Human development index (HDI) value 1994	Real GDP per capita (PPP$) rank minus HDI rank[a]
	Medium human development	67.1	82.6	64	3,352	3,352	0.70	0.76	0.54	0.667	–
65	Lebanon	69.0	92.0	75	4,863 [e,f]	4,863	0.73	0.86	0.79	0.794	8
66	Suriname	70.7	92.7	71	4,711	4,711	0.76	0.85	0.76	0.792	10
67	Russian Federation	65.7	98.7	78	4,828	4,828	0.68	0.92	0.78	0.792	7
68	Brazil	66.4	82.7	72	5,362	5,362	0.69	0.79	0.87	0.783	0
69	Bulgaria	71.1	93.0	66	4,533	4,533	0.77	0.84	0.73	0.780	9
70	Iran, Islamic Rep. of	68.2	68.6 [c]	68	5,766	5,766	0.72	0.68	0.94	0.780	-9
71	Estonia	69.2	99.0	72	4,294	4,294	0.74	0.90	0.69	0.776	8
72	Ecuador	69.3	89.6	72	4,626	4,626	0.74	0.84	0.75	0.775	5
73	Saudi Arabia	70.3	61.8	56	9,338	5,953	0.76	0.60	0.97	0.774	-32
74	Turkey	68.2	81.6	63	5,193	5,193	0.72	0.75	0.84	0.772	-4
75	Korea, Dem. People's Rep. of	71.4	95.0	75	3,965 [e,f]	3,965	0.77	0.88	0.64	0.765	10
76	Lithuania	70.1	98.4 [g]	70	4,011	4,011	0.75	0.89	0.65	0.762	8
77	Croatia	71.3	97.0	67	3,960 [d]	3,960	0.77	0.87	0.64	0.760	10
78	Syrian Arab Rep.	67.8	69.8	64	5,397	5,397	0.71	0.68	0.87	0.755	-12
79	Romania	69.5	96.9 [g]	62	4,037	4,037	0.74	0.85	0.65	0.748	3
80	Macedonia, FYR	71.7	94.0	60	3,965 [f]	3,965	0.78	0.83	0.64	0.748	5
81	Tunisia	68.4	65.2	67	5,319	5,319	0.72	0.66	0.86	0.748	-12
82	Algeria	67.8	59.4	66	5,442	5,442	0.71	0.62	0.88	0.737	-17
83	Jamaica	73.9	84.4	65	3,816	3,816	0.82	0.78	0.61	0.736	7
84	Jordan	68.5	85.5	66	4,187	4,187	0.73	0.79	0.68	0.730	-3
85	Turkmenistan	64.7	97.7 [g]	90	3,469 [e]	3,469	0.66	0.95	0.56	0.723	12
86	Cuba	75.6	95.4	63	3,000 [e]	3,000	0.84	0.85	0.48	0.723	17
87	Dominican Rep.	70.0	81.5	68	3,933	3,933	0.75	0.77	0.63	0.718	1
88	Oman	70.0	35.0	60	10,078	5,965	0.75	0.43	0.97	0.718	-49
89	Peru	67.4	88.3	81	3,645	3,645	0.71	0.86	0.59	0.717	5
90	South Africa	63.7	81.4	81	4,291	4,291	0.64	0.81	0.69	0.716	-10
91	Sri Lanka	72.2	90.1	66	3,277	3,277	0.79	0.82	0.52	0.711	9
92	Latvia	67.9	99.0	67	3,332	3,332	0.71	0.88	0.53	0.711	6
93	Kazakstan	67.5	97.5	73	3,284	3,284	0.71	0.89	0.53	0.709	6
94	Paraguay	68.8	91.9	62	3,531	3,531	0.73	0.82	0.57	0.706	2
95	Ukraine	68.4	98.8 [c]	76	2,718	2,718	0.72	0.91	0.43	0.689	14
96	Samoa (Western)	68.1	98.0 [g]	74	2,726 [e]	2,726	0.72	0.90	0.43	0.684	12
97	Botswana	52.3	68.7	71	5,367	5,367	0.45	0.69	0.87	0.673	-30
98	Philippines	67.0	94.4	78	2,681	2,681	0.70	0.89	0.43	0.672	12
99	Indonesia	63.5	83.2	62	3,740	3,740	0.64	0.76	0.60	0.668	-7
100	Uzbekistan	67.5	97.2 [g]	73	2,438	2,438	0.71	0.89	0.39	0.662	14
101	Mongolia	64.4	82.2	52	3,766	3,766	0.66	0.72	0.61	0.661	-10
102	Albania	70.5	85.0	59	2,788 [e,f]	2,788	0.76	0.76	0.44	0.655	4
103	Armenia	70.8	98.8	78	1,737	1,737	0.76	0.92	0.27	0.651	24
104	Guyana	63.2	97.9	67	2,729	2,729	0.64	0.88	0.43	0.649	3
105	Georgia	73.1	94.9	69	1,585	1,585	0.80	0.86	0.25	0.637	31
106	Azerbaijan	71.0	96.3	72	1,670	1,670	0.77	0.88	0.26	0.636	25
107	Kyrgyzstan	67.8	97.0 [g]	73	1,930	1,930	0.71	0.89	0.30	0.635	18
108	China	68.9	80.9	58	2,604	2,604	0.73	0.73	0.41	0.626	3
109	Egypt	64.3	50.5	69	3,846	3,846	0.66	0.57	0.62	0.614	-20
110	Moldova, Rep. of	67.7	98.9 [c]	67	1,576 [d]	1,576	0.71	0.88	0.24	0.612	28
111	Maldives	62.8	93.0	71	2,200	2,200	0.63	0.86	0.35	0.611	7
112	El Salvador	69.3	70.9	55	2,417	2,417	0.74	0.66	0.38	0.592	3
113	Bolivia	60.1	82.5	66	2,598	2,598	0.59	0.77	0.41	0.589	-1
114	Swaziland	58.3	75.2	72	2,821	2,821	0.55	0.74	0.45	0.582	-10
115	Tajikistan	66.8	96.7 [g]	69	1,117	1,117	0.70	0.87	0.17	0.580	35
116	Honduras	68.4	72.0	60	2,050	2,050	0.72	0.68	0.32	0.575	7
117	Guatemala	65.6	55.7	46	3,208	3,208	0.68	0.52	0.51	0.572	-16
118	Namibia	55.9	40.0	84	4,027	4,027	0.52	0.55	0.65	0.570	-35
119	Morocco	65.3	42.1	46	3,681	3,681	0.67	0.43	0.59	0.566	-26
120	Gabon	54.1	62.6	60	3,641 [e]	3,641	0.49	0.62	0.58	0.562	-25
121	Viet Nam	66.0	93.0	55	1,208 [e,f]	1,208	0.68	0.80	0.18	0.557	26
122	Solomon Islands	70.8	62.0	47	2,118	2,118	0.76	0.57	0.33	0.556	0
123	Cape Verde	65.3	69.9	64	1,862	1,862	0.67	0.68	0.29	0.547	3
124	Vanuatu	65.9	64.0 [g]	52	2,276	2,276	0.68	0.60	0.36	0.547	-7
125	São Tomé and Principe	67.0 [i]	67.0 [i]	57	1,704 [e,f]	1,704	0.70	0.64	0.26	0.534	3
126	Iraq	57.0	56.8	53	3,159 [e,f]	3,159	0.53	0.56	0.51	0.531	-24
127	Nicaragua	67.3	65.3	62	1,580 [e]	1,580	0.70	0.64	0.24	0.530	10
128	Papua New Guinea	56.4	71.2	38	2,821	2,821	0.52	0.60	0.45	0.525	-24
129	Zimbabwe	49.0	84.7	68	2,196	2,196	0.40	0.79	0.35	0.513	-10
130	Congo	51.3	73.9	56	2,410	2,410	0.44	0.68	0.38	0.500	-14

HDI rank	Life expectancy at birth (years) 1994	Adult literacy rate (%) 1994	Combined first-, second- and third-level gross enrolment ratio (%) 1994	Real GDP per capita (PPP$) 1994	Adjusted real GDP per capita (PPP$) 1994	Life expectancy index	Education index	GDP index	Human development index (HDI) value 1994	Real GDP per capita (PPP$) rank minus HDI rank[a]
Low human development	56.1	49.9	47	1,308	1,308	0.52	0.49	0.20	0.403	–
131 Myanmar	58.4	82.7	48	1,051	1,051	0.56	0.71	0.16	0.475	25
132 Ghana	56.6	63.4	44	1,960	1,960	0.53	0.57	0.31	0.468	-8
133 Cameroon	55.1	62.1	46	2,120	2,120	0.50	0.57	0.33	0.468	-12
134 Kenya	53.6	77.0	55	1,404	1,404	0.48	0.70	0.22	0.463	5
135 Equatorial Guinea	48.6	77.8	64	1,673 e,f	1,673	0.39	0.73	0.26	0.462	-5
136 Lao People's Dem. Rep.	51.7	55.8	50	2,484 e	2,484	0.45	0.54	0.39	0.459	-23
137 Lesotho	57.9	70.5	56	1,109	1,109	0.55	0.66	0.17	0.457	14
138 India	61.3	51.2	56	1,348	1,348	0.60	0.53	0.21	0.446	5
139 Pakistan	62.3	37.1	38	2,154	2,154	0.62	0.37	0.34	0.445	-19
140 Comoros	56.1	56.7	39	1,366	1,366	0.52	0.51	0.21	0.412	1
141 Nigeria	51.0	55.6	50	1,351	1,351	0.43	0.54	0.21	0.393	1
142 Zaire	52.2	76.4	38	429 e	429	0.45	0.64	0.05	0.381	31
143 Zambia	42.6	76.6	48	962	962	0.29	0.67	0.14	0.369	15
144 Bangladesh	56.4	37.3	39	1,331	1,331	0.52	0.38	0.20	0.368	0
145 Côte d'Ivoire	52.1	39.4	39	1,668	1,668	0.45	0.39	0.26	0.368	-13
146 Benin	54.2	35.5	35	1,696	1,696	0.49	0.35	0.26	0.368	-17
147 Togo	50.6	50.4	50	1,109	1,109	0.43	0.50	0.17	0.365	4
148 Yemen	56.2	41.1	52	805 e,f	805	0.52	0.45	0.12	0.361	14
149 Tanzania, U. Rep. of	50.3	66.8	34	656	656	0.42	0.56	0.09	0.357	21
150 Mauritania	52.1	36.9	36	1,593	1,593	0.45	0.37	0.25	0.355	-15
151 Central African Rep.	48.3	57.2	37	1,130	1,130	0.39	0.50	0.17	0.355	-2
152 Madagascar	57.2	45.8 i	33	694	694	0.54	0.42	0.10	0.350	16
153 Cambodia	52.4	35.0 g	58	1,084 e,f	1,084	0.46	0.43	0.16	0.348	1
154 Nepal	55.3	27.0	55	1,137	1,137	0.51	0.36	0.17	0.347	-6
155 Bhutan	51.5	41.1	31	1,289	1,289	0.44	0.38	0.20	0.338	-10
156 Haiti	54.4	44.1	29	896	896	0.49	0.39	0.13	0.338	5
157 Angola	47.2	42.5	31	1,600	1,600	0.37	0.39	0.25	0.335	-24
158 Sudan	51.0	44.8	31	1,084 e,f	1,084	0.43	0.40	0.16	0.333	-4
159 Uganda	40.2	61.1	34	1,370	1,370	0.25	0.52	0.21	0.328	-19
160 Senegal	49.9	32.1	31	1,596	1,596	0.41	0.32	0.25	0.326	-26
161 Malawi	41.1	55.8	67	694	694	0.27	0.60	0.10	0.320	7
162 Djibouti	48.8	45.0	20	1,270 e,f	1,270	0.40	0.37	0.19	0.319	-16
163 Guinea-Bissau	43.2	53.9	29	793	793	0.30	0.46	0.11	0.291	1
164 Chad	47.0	47.0	25	700	700	0.37	0.40	0.10	0.288	2
165 Gambia	45.6	37.2	34	939 e	939	0.34	0.36	0.14	0.281	-5
166 Mozambique	46.0	39.5	25	986	986	0.35	0.35	0.15	0.281	-9
167 Guinea	45.1	34.8	24	1,103 e	1,103	0.34	0.31	0.17	0.271	-14
168 Eritrea	50.1	25.0	24	960 e,f	960	0.42	0.25	0.14	0.269	-9
169 Burundi	43.5	34.6	31	698	698	0.31	0.33	0.10	0.247	-2
170 Ethiopia	48.2	34.5	18	427	427	0.39	0.29	0.05	0.244	4
171 Mali	46.6	29.3	17	543	543	0.36	0.25	0.07	0.229	1
172 Burkina Faso	46.4	18.7	20	796	796	0.36	0.19	0.11	0.221	-9
173 Niger	47.1	13.1	15	787	787	0.37	0.14	0.11	0.206	-8
174 Rwanda	22.6 k	59.2	37	352	352	0.00	0.52	0.04	0.187	1
175 Sierra Leone	33.6	30.3	28	643	643	0.14	0.30	0.09	0.176	-4
All developing countries	61.8	69.7	56	2,904	2,904	0.61	0.65	0.46	0.576	–
Least developed countries	50.4	48.1	36	965	965	0.42	0.44	0.14	0.336	–
Sub-Saharan Africa	50.0	55.9	42	1,377	1,377	0.42	0.51	0.21	0.380	–
Industrial countries	74.1	98.5	83	15,986	6,037	0.82	0.93	0.98	0.911	–
World	63.2	77.1	60	5,798	5,798	0.64	0.71	0.94	0.764	–

Note: Figures in italics are Human Development Report Office estimates. Countries with the same HDI value are ranked on the basis of the fourth decimal place, not shown here.
a. A positive figure indicates that the HDI rank is better than the real GDP per capita rank (PPP$), a negative the opposite.
b. Capped at 100.
c. UNESCO 1995b. Data refer to 1995.
d. UNECE estimate based on data from the 1993 European Comparison Programme.
e. Preliminary update of the Penn World Tables using an expanded set of international comparisons, as described in Summers and Heston 1991.
f. Extrapolations are provisional.
g. UNICEF 1997.
h. Estimate based on World Bank calculations using GDP-GNP ratio from UNDP 1996d.
i. World Bank 1995c.
j. Human Development Report Office estimate based on national sources.
k. 1985-90 data from UN 1996b.
Source: Column 1: calculated on the basis of data from UN 1996b; *column 2:* UNESCO 1996b; *column 3:* UNESCO 1996a; *column 4:* unless otherwise noted, calculated on the basis of estimates from World Bank 1997a.

HDI rank	Gender-related development index (GDI) rank	Life expectancy at birth (years) 1994		Adult literacy rate (%) 1994		Combined primary, secondary and tertiary gross enrolment ratio (%) 1994		Earned income share (%) 1994[a]		GDI value 1994	HDI rank minus GDI rank[b]
		Female	Male	Female	Male	Female	Male	Female	Male		
High human development	–	77.7	71.4	96.6	97.4	80.0	78.9	34.7	65.4	0.874	–
1 Canada	1	81.7	76.3	99.0	99.0	100.0[c]	100.0[c]	37.8[d]	62.2[d]	0.939	0
2 France	6	83.0	74.3	99.0	99.0	91.0	87.0	39.0	61.0	0.926	-4
3 Norway	2	80.4	74.6	99.0	99.0	93.0	92.0	42.1	57.9	0.934	1
4 USA	5	79.5	72.8	99.0	99.0	98.0	93.0	40.7	59.3	0.928	-1
5 Iceland	4	80.8	77.4	99.0	99.0	81.0	82.0	42.0	58.0	0.932	1
6 Netherlands	11	80.2	74.3	99.0	99.0	88.0	93.0	33.5	66.5	0.901	-5
7 Japan	12	82.8	76.6	99.0	99.0	77.0	79.0	33.9[d]	66.1[d]	0.901	-5
8 Finland	7	79.9	72.4	99.0	99.0	100.0[c]	92.0	41.5	58.5	0.925	1
9 New Zealand	8	79.2	73.6	99.0	99.0	96.0	91.0	38.8	61.2	0.918	1
10 Sweden	3	80.9	75.8	99.0	99.0	84.0	81.0	45.1	54.9	0.932	7
11 Spain	19	81.3	73.9	97.1	97.1	94.0	87.0	29.4[d]	70.6[d]	0.874	-8
12 Austria	15	79.6	73.2	99.0	99.0	85.0	88.0	33.7[d]	66.3[d]	0.890	-3
13 Belgium	14	80.2	73.3	99.0	99.0	86.0	86.0	33.4	66.6	0.891	-1
14 Australia	9	81.0	75.2	99.0	99.0	80.0	77.0	39.8	60.2	0.917	5
15 United Kingdom	13	79.3	74.1	99.0	99.0	86.0	85.0	35.0	65.0	0.896	2
16 Switzerland	20	81.5	74.6	99.0	99.0	73.0	78.0	30.2	69.8	0.874	-4
17 Ireland	29	79.0	73.6	99.0	99.0	89.0	87.0	25.8	74.2	0.851	-12
18 Denmark	10	77.8	72.6	99.0	99.0	90.0	87.0	41.7	58.3	0.916	8
19 Germany	16	79.3	72.8	99.0	99.0	7^.0	83.0	34.8	65.2	0.886	3
20 Greece	21	80.4	75.2	96.7	96.7	80.0	83.0	31.2	68.8	0.873	-1
21 Italy	23	80.9	74.6	98.1	98.1	74.0	72.0	31.0[d]	69.0[d]	0.867	-2
22 Hong Kong	28	81.8	76.0	89.1	96.0	73.0	72.0	27.1	72.9	0.852	-6
23 Israel	22	79.1	75.7	95.0	95.0	76.0	74.0	32.9[d]	67.1[d]	0.872	1
24 Cyprus	33	79.2	74.9	94.0	94.0	75.0	75.0	27.1	72.9	0.837	-9
25 Barbados	17	78.2	73.2	96.6	97.9	76.0	74.0	39.5[d]	60.5[d]	0.885	8
26 Singapore	27	79.3	74.9	87.2	95.6	71.0	73.0	30.7	69.3	0.853	-1
27 Luxembourg	38	79.1	72.5	99.0	99.0	59.0	57.0	25.3	74.7	0.813	-11
28 Bahamas	18	76.5	70.1	97.7	98.4	77.0	73.0	39.5[d]	60.5[d]	0.880	10
29 Antigua and Barbuda	..	..	..	..	..	..	..	..	..	..	..
30 Chile	44	77.9	72.1	95.0	95.4	71.0	72.0	21.9[e]	78.1[e]	0.785	-15
31 Portugal	30	78.3	71.0	89.6	89.6	84.0	77.0	34.1	65.9	0.850	0
32 Korea, Rep. of	35	75.2	67.7	96.8	99.0	78.0	86.0	27.7	72.3	0.826	-4
33 Costa Rica	36	78.9	74.3	95.0	94.6	67.0	69.0	27.2	72.8	0.825	-4
34 Malta	48	78.6	74.1	86.0	86.0	75.0	79.0	20.9[d]	79.1[d]	0.773	-15
35 Slovenia	24	77.5	68.4	96.0	96.0	76.0	72.0	39.3[d]	60.7[d]	0.866	10
36 Argentina	47	76.0	68.9	96.0	96.0	79.0	76.0	22.0[e]	78.0[e]	0.777	-12
37 Uruguay	31	75.9	69.4	97.3	96.7	80.0	70.0	33.4[e]	66.6[e]	0.842	5
38 Brunei Darussalam	..	..	..	..	..	..	..	..	..	..	..
39 Czech Rep.	25	75.2	69.2	99.0	99.0	70.0	69.0	38.1	61.9	0.859	12
40 Trinidad and Tobago	32	75.4	70.8	97.2	98.6	67.0	67.0	29.7[d]	70.3[d]	0.841	6
41 Dominica	..	..	..	..	..	..	..	..	..	..	..
42 Slovakia	26	75.5	66.3	99.0	99.0	73.0	71.0	40.7[d]	59.3[d]	0.859	13
43 Bahrain	56	74.5	70.1	77.6	87.7	87.0	83.0	14.7[d]	85.3[d]	0.742	-16
44 United Arab Emirates	61	75.7	73.3	77.9	78.0	85.0	80.0	10.0[d]	90.0[d]	0.727	-20
45 Panama	41	75.3	71.3	89.7	91.2	71.0	69.0	27.5[d]	72.5[d]	0.802	1
46 Fiji	53	74.1	69.9	89.2	93.7	78.0	80.0	21.4[d]	78.6[d]	0.763	-10
47 Venezuela	43	75.1	69.3	90.3	91.6	69.0	66.0	26.8[d]	73.2[d]	0.792	1
48 Hungary	34	73.8	64.2	99.0	99.0	68.0	66.0	39.5	60.5	0.837	11
49 Saint Kitts and Nevis	..	..	..	..	..	..	..	..	..	..	..
50 Mexico	50	75.0	69.1	86.7	91.5	65.0	67.0	25.1[d]	74.9[d]	0.770	-4
51 Colombia	40	72.8	67.4	91.3	91.1	72.0	67.0	33.3[e]	66.7[e]	0.811	7
52 Seychelles	..	..	..	..	..	..	..	..	..	..	..
53 Kuwait	51	77.5	73.5	72.6	80.4	57.0	56.0	24.5[d]	75.5[d]	0.769	-3
54 Grenada	..	..	..	..	..	..	..	..	..	..	..
55 Qatar	64	74.6	69.1	78.3	78.2	74.0	71.0	9.7[d]	90.3[d]	0.713	-15
56 Saint Lucia	..	..	..	..	..	..	..	..	..	..	..
57 Saint Vincent	..	..	..	..	..	..	..	..	..	..	..
58 Poland	37	75.8	66.6	99.0	99.0	80.0	79.0	38.9[d]	61.1[d]	0.818	13
59 Thailand	39	72.2	66.8	90.7	95.6	53.0	53.0	37.2	62.8	0.812	12
60 Malaysia	45	73.5	69.0	77.5	88.2	63.0	61.0	30.2[d]	69.8[d]	0.782	7
61 Mauritius	54	74.2	67.4	78.4	86.8	62.0	61.0	25.4[d]	74.6[d]	0.752	-1
62 Belarus	42	74.6	63.8	97.9	97.9	81.0	79.0	41.6[d]	58.4[d]	0.792	12
63 Belize	..	..	..	..	..	..	..	..	..	..	..
64 Libyan Arab Jamahiriya	77	65.8	62.3	57.2	88.9	90.0	91.0	16.0[d]	84.0[d]	0.655	-22

HDI rank	Gender-related development index (GDI) rank	Life expectancy at birth (years) 1994		Adult literacy rate (%) 1994		Combined primary, secondary and tertiary gross enrolment ratio (%) 1994		Earned income share (%) 1994[a]		GDI value 1994	HDI rank minus GDI rank[b]
		Female	Male	Female	Male	Female	Male	Female	Male		
Medium human development	–	69.5	64.7	76.1	88.9	60.8	65.2	35.7	64.4	0.643	–
65 Lebanon	66	70.9	67.1	89.5	94.3	76.0	74.0	22.5 [d]	77.5 [d]	0.708	-10
66 Suriname	..	..	..	..	..	..	..	..	..	..	..
67 Russian Federation	46	72.2	59.2	*98.7*	*98.7*	82.0	75.0	41.3 [d]	58.7 [d]	0.778	11
68 Brazil	60	70.5	62.5	82.5	82.8	72.0	72.0	28.7 [e]	71.3 [e]	0.728	-2
69 Bulgaria	49	74.9	67.7	*93.0*	*93.0*	69.0	64.0	41.0 [d]	59.0 [d]	0.772	10
70 Iran, Islamic Rep. of	..	..	..	..	..	..	..	..	..	..	..
71 Estonia	52	75.0	63.3	*99.0*	*99.0*	74.0	69.0	42.0 [d]	58.0 [d]	0.764	8
72 Ecuador	73	72.0	66.8	87.8	91.8	71.0	73.0	18.4 [e]	81.6 [e]	0.675	-12
73 Saudi Arabia	95	72.1	69.0	47.6	70.6	53.0	59.0	9.7 [d]	90.3 [d]	0.581	-33
74 Turkey	58	70.6	65.9	71.1	91.7	55.0	70.0	33.2	66.8	0.737	5
75 Korea, Dem. People's Rep. of	..	..	..	..	..	..	..	..	..	..	..
76 Lithuania	55	75.9	64.2	*98.4*	*98.4*	72.0	68.0	40.8 [d]	59.2 [d]	0.750	9
77 Croatia	57	75.8	67.1	*97.0*	*97.0*	68.0	67.0	36.5 [d]	63.5 [d]	0.741	8
78 Syrian Arab Rep.	84	69.9	65.8	53.0	84.8	59.0	68.0	20.6 [d]	79.4 [d]	0.646	-18
79 Romania	59	73.3	65.9	*96.9*	*96.9*	62.0	62.0	37.5 [d]	62.5 [d]	0.733	8
80 Macedonia, FYR	62	73.9	69.4	*94.0*	*94.0*	61.0	60.0	33.9 [d]	66.1 [d]	0.726	6
81 Tunisia	74	69.4	67.4	50.4	77.9	64.0	71.0	24.5 [d]	75.5 [d]	0.668	-5
82 Algeria	92	69.0	66.6	43.5	71.8	61.0	70.0	19.1 [d]	80.9 [d]	0.614	-22
83 Jamaica	63	76.1	71.7	88.4	79.6	67.0	64.0	39.2 [d]	60.8 [d]	0.726	8
84 Jordan	..	..	..	..	..	..	..	..	..	..	..
85 Turkmenistan	65	68.1	61.3	*97.7*	*97.7*	90.0	90.0	38.2 [d]	61.8 [d]	0.712	7
86 Cuba	68	77.5	73.7	94.8	95.9	65.0	61.0	31.1 [d]	68.9 [d]	0.699	5
87 Dominican Rep.	75	72.1	68.0	81.2	81.2	69.0	67.0	23.1 [d]	76.9 [d]	0.658	-1
88 Oman	..	..	..	..	..	..	..	..	..	..	..
89 Peru	76	69.9	65.1	82.2	94.5	77.0	84.0	22.9 [d]	77.1 [d]	0.656	-1
90 South Africa	71	66.8	60.8	81.2	81.4	82.0	80.0	30.8 [d]	69.2 [d]	0.681	5
91 Sri Lanka	70	74.6	70.0	86.9	93.2	68.0	65.0	34.5	65.5	0.694	7
92 Latvia	67	74.2	61.5	*99.0*	*99.0*	69.0	66.0	42.6 [d]	57.4 [d]	0.702	11
93 Kazakstan	69	72.3	62.6	*97.5*	*97.5*	75.0	71.0	39.2 [d]	60.8 [d]	0.698	10
94 Paraguay	82	71.1	66.6	90.2	93.2	62.0	62.0	22.7 [d]	77.3	0.649	-2
95 Ukraine	72	73.8	62.9	*98.8*	*98.8*	78.0	75.0	41.4 [d]	58.6 [d]	0.681	9
96 Samoa (Western)	..	..	..	..	..	..	..	..	..	..	..
97 Botswana	79	53.7	50.5	58.0	79.3	72.0	70.0	38.9 [d]	61.1 [d]	0.652	3
98 Philippines	81	68.9	65.2	93.9	94.8	80.0	75.0	30.7 [d]	69.3 [d]	0.650	2
99 Indonesia	86	65.3	61.8	77.1	89.4	59.0	65.0	32.9 [d]	67.1 [d]	0.642	-2
100 Uzbekistan	78	70.7	64.2	*97.2*	*97.2*	71.0	75.0	39.0 [d]	61.0 [d]	0.655	7
101 Mongolia	80	65.8	63.0	75.8	87.9	59.0	45.0	39.2 [d]	60.8 [d]	0.650	6
102 Albania	85	73.7	67.7	*85.0*	*85.0*	60.0	59.0	34.0 [d]	66.0 [d]	0.643	2
103 Armenia	83	74.5	67.1	*98.8*	*98.8*	83.0	74.0	40.3 [d]	59.7 [d]	0.647	5
104 Guyana	91	66.7	60.0	97.4	98.5	67.0	66.0	26.4 [d]	73.6 [d]	0.615	-2
105 Georgia	87	77.2	68.8	*94.9*	*94.9*	69.0	68.0	39.3 [d]	60.7 [d]	0.630	3
106 Azerbaijan	89	74.9	66.8	*96.3*	*96.3*	71.0	74.0	36.8 [d]	63.2 [d]	0.628	2
107 Kyrgyzstan	88	72.1	63.3	*97.0*	*97.0*	74.0	71.0	39.5 [d]	60.5 [d]	0.628	4
108 China	90	71.1	66.9	70.9	89.6	55.0	61.0	38.1 [d]	61.9 [d]	0.617	3
109 Egypt	100	65.6	63.1	36.7	62.6	63.0	75.0	24.9	75.1	0.555	6
110 Moldova, Rep. of	93	71.8	63.3	*98.9*	*98.9*	68.0	66.0	41.4 [d]	58.6 [d]	0.608	2
111 Maldives	94	61.5	64.2	92.9	93.1	70.0	70.0	35.4 [d]	64.6 [d]	0.600	2
112 El Salvador	97	72.9	65.6	68.7	72.8	55.0	55.0	27.6 [d]	72.4 [d]	0.563	0
113 Bolivia	99	61.7	58.5	75.2	90.4	61.0	72.0	27.0 [e]	73.0 [e]	0.557	-1
114 Swaziland	98	60.5	56.0	73.3	76.4	70.0	74.0	34.9	65.1	0.563	1
115 Tajikistan	96	70.0	63.7	*96.7*	*96.7*	67.0	70.0	36.4 [d]	63.6 [d]	0.575	4
116 Honduras	103	70.8	66.1	71.6	71.7	61.0	59.0	23.8 [d]	76.2 [d]	0.544	-2
117 Guatemala	107	68.2	63.2	48.3	62.2	42.0	50.0	20.6 [d]	79.4 [d]	0.510	-5
118 Namibia	..	..	..	..	..	..	..	..	..	..	..
119 Morocco	105	66.9	63.6	27.7	54.5	39.0	52.0	28.4 [d]	71.6 [d]	0.515	-2
120 Gabon	102	55.8	52.5	51.8	74.1	60.0	60.0	37.3 [d]	62.7 [d]	0.546	2
121 Viet Nam	101	68.1	63.6	89.9	95.7	52.0	57.0	42.3 [d]	57.7 [d]	0.552	4
122 Solomon Islands	..	..	..	..	..	..	..	..	..	..	..
123 Cape Verde	104	66.1	64.1	59.8	79.4	62.0	65.0	32.4 [d]	67.6 [d]	0.523	2
124 Vanuatu	..	..	..	..	..	..	..	..	..	..	..
125 São Tomé and Principe	..	..	..	..	..	..	..	..	..	..	..
126 Iraq	117	58.0	55.8	42.2	69.5	46.0	59.0	13.9 [d]	86.1 [d]	0.433	-10
127 Nicaragua	106	69.7	64.9	66.0	64.3	63.0	61.0	29.5 [d]	70.5 [d]	0.515	2
128 Papua New Guinea	108	57.3	55.8	60.7	79.8	34.0	41.0	34.8 [d]	65.2 [d]	0.508	1
129 Zimbabwe	109	50.1	48.1	79.0	90.2	64.0	72.0	37.4 [d]	62.6 [d]	0.503	1
130 Congo	..	..	..	..	..	..	..	..	..	..	..

HDI rank	Gender-related development index (GDI) rank	Life expectancy at birth (years) 1994		Adult literacy rate (%) 1994		Combined primary, secondary and tertiary gross enrolment ratio (%) 1994		Earned income share (%) 1994[a]		GDI value 1994	HDI rank minus GDI rank[b]
		Female	Male	Female	Male	Female	Male	Female	Male		
Low human development	–	57.3	55.9	35.8	61.8	40.2	54.4	27.9	72.3	0.391	–
131 Myanmar	110	60.0	56.8	76.8	88.6	47.0	48.0	36.6 [d]	63.4 [d]	0.469	1
132 Ghana	111	58.5	54.8	51.0	75.2	38.0	50.0	43.5 [d]	56.5 [d]	0.459	1
133 Cameroon	115	56.5	53.7	49.5	74.0	42.0	51.0	30.9 [d]	69.1 [d]	0.444	-2
134 Kenya	112	54.8	52.3	67.8	85.2	54.0	56.0	42.0	58.0	0.458	2
135 Equatorial Guinea	116	50.2	47.0	67.3	88.9	59.0	70.0	29.0 [d]	71.0 [d]	0.441	-1
136 Lao People's Dem. Rep.	114	53.3	50.3	42.7	68.6	42.0	58.0	39.9 [d]	60.1 [d]	0.444	2
137 Lesotho	113	59.4	56.8	60.9	80.3	60.0	51.0	30.3 [e]	69.7 [e]	0.446	4
138 India	118	61.4	61.1	36.1	64.5	47.0	63.0	25.7 [d]	74.3 [d]	0.419	0
139 Pakistan	120	63.3	61.3	23.3	49.0	25.0	50.0	20.8 [d]	79.2 [d]	0.392	-1
140 Comoros	119	56.6	55.6	49.4	63.4	35.0	42.0	35.6 [d]	64.4 [d]	0.402	1
141 Nigeria	121	52.6	49.5	43.8	66.1	44.0	55.0	29.5 [d]	70.5 [d]	0.372	0
142 Zaire	..	..	..	..	..	..	..	..	..	..	..
143 Zambia	122	43.3	41.7	69.3	84.4	44.0	51.0	38.8	61.2	0.362	0
144 Bangladesh	128	56.5	56.3	24.3	48.4	34.0	45.0	23.1	76.9	0.339	-5
145 Côte d'Ivoire	126	53.5	50.9	27.5	49.4	32.0	47.0	27.0 [d]	73.0 [d]	0.341	-2
146 Benin	124	56.8	51.7	23.0	46.6	23.0	48.0	40.5 [d]	59.5 [d]	0.349	1
147 Togo	125	52.2	49.1	34.4	65.6	37.0	62.0	33.3 [d]	66.7 [d]	0.342	1
148 Yemen	..	56.7	55.7	..	..	..	..	..	..	..	..
149 Tanzania, U. Rep. of	123	51.7	48.9	54.3	78.8	33.0	35.0	47.3	52.7	0.352	4
150 Mauritania	127	53.7	50.5	25.6	48.4	31.0	42.0	37.2 [d]	62.8 [d]	0.341	1
151 Central African Rep.	129	50.9	45.9	43.9	66.7	27.0	47.0	39.1	60.9	0.338	0
152 Madagascar	..	..	..	..	..	..	..	..	..	..	..
153 Cambodia	..	..	..	..	..	..	..	..	..	..	..
154 Nepal	131	54.9	55.8	12.8	39.7	42.0	68.0	33.0 [d]	67.0 [d]	0.321	-1
155 Bhutan	..	53.2	49.8	..	..	..	..	..	..	..	..
156 Haiti	130	56.1	52.8	40.4	46.9	28.0	30.0	36.2 [d]	63.8 [d]	0.332	1
157 Angola	..	..	..	..	..	..	..	..	..	..	..
158 Sudan	135	52.4	49.6	31.3	56.4	28.0	35.0	22.7 [d]	77.3 [d]	0.306	-3
159 Uganda	132	41.1	39.3	48.7	73.2	30.0	39.0	40.7 [d]	59.3 [d]	0.318	1
160 Senegal	134	50.9	48.9	21.2	42.1	25.0	37.0	35.7 [d]	64.3 [d]	0.309	0
161 Malawi	133	41.5	40.6	40.4	71.7	63.0	71.0	42.0 [d]	58.0 [d]	0.310	2
162 Djibouti	..	..	..	..	..	..	..	..	..	..	..
163 Guinea-Bissau	136	44.8	41.7	40.7	67.1	21.0	38.0	33.6 [d]	66.4 [d]	0.276	0
164 Chad	137	48.7	45.4	32.7	60.7	15.0	35.0	37.3 [e]	62.7 [e]	0.270	0
165 Gambia	138	47.2	44.0	22.7	50.9	27.0	41.0	37.8 [d]	62.2 [d]	0.263	0
166 Mozambique	139	47.5	44.5	22.1	55.8	21.0	30.0	41.3 [d]	58.7 [d]	0.262	0
167 Guinea	140	45.6	44.6	20.3	48.4	15.0	33.0	40.3 [d]	59.7 [d]	0.250	0
168 Eritrea	..	51.6	48.6	..	..	..	..	..	..	..	..
169 Burundi	141	45.0	41.9	21.0	48.2	27.0	35.0	41.7 [d]	58.3 [d]	0.233	0
170 Ethiopia	142	49.8	46.7	24.1	44.5	14.0	21.0	34.1 [d]	65.9 [d]	0.233	0
171 Mali	143	48.3	45.0	20.2	36.7	13.0	21.0	39.4 [d]	60.6 [d]	0.218	0
172 Burkina Faso	144	47.5	45.4	8.6	28.8	15.0	25.0	39.7 [d]	60.3 [d]	0.206	0
173 Niger	145	48.7	45.5	5.6	20.5	11.0	19.0	37.2 [d]	62.8 [d]	0.193	0
174 Rwanda	..	..	..	..	..	..	..	..	..	..	..
175 Sierra Leone	146	35.2	32.1	16.7	43.7	22.0	34.0	29.7 [d]	70.3 [d]	0.155	0
All developing countries	–	63.5	60.6	60.3	78.4	51.6	60.3	31.7	68.4	0.555	–
Least developed countries	–	51.2	49.1	34.7	56.6	30.7	40.0	33.1	67.2	0.323	–
Sub-Saharan Africa	–	51.5	48.5	44.4	64.3	38.4	46.6	35.5	64.6	0.374	–
Industrial countries	–	77.8	70.2	98.5	98.5	83.9	81.5	37.7	62.4	0.856	–
World	–	65.4	61.8	70.8	83.5	57.1	63.9	33.3	66.9	0.637	–

Note: Figures in italics are Human Development Report Office estimates.
a. Data refer to 1994 or latest available year.
b. The HDI ranks used in this column are those recalculated for the universe of 146 countries. See table 2.8 in chapter 2. A positive figure indicates that the GDI rank is better than the HDI rank, a negative the opposite.
c. Capped at 100.
d. No wage data available. An estimate of 75%, the mean for all countries with wage data available, was used for the ratio of the female non-agricultural wage to the male non-agricultural wage.
e. Wage data based on Psacharopoulos and Tzannatos 1992.
Source: Columns 2 and 3: Human Development Report Office calculations based on data from UN 1996b; *columns 4 and 5:* Human Development Report Office calculations based on estimates from UNESCO 1996b; *columns 6 and 7:* UNESCO 1996b; *columns 8 and 9:* calculations based on estimates from the following: for real GDP per capita (PPP$), World Bank 1997a; for share of economically active population, ILO 1995b and 1996b; and for female wages as a percentage of male wages, ILO 1995b, UN 1994b and Psacharopoulos and Tzannatos 1992.

HDI rank	Gender empowerment measure (GEM) rank	Seats held in parliament (% women)[a]	Administrators and managers (% women)[b]	Professional and technical workers (% women)[b]	Earned income share (% to women)[b,c]	GEM value
High human development	–	12.6	25.3	47.2	40	0.549
1 Canada	6	19.3	42.2	56.1	38 [d]	0.700
2 France	40	6.1	9.4	41.4	39	0.452
3 Norway	1	39.4	30.9	57.5	42	0.795
4 USA	7	11.2	42.0	52.7	41	0.671
5 Iceland	..	..	..	..	..	..
6 Netherlands	10	28.4	15.0	44.2	34	0.660
7 Japan	34	7.7	8.5	41.8	34 [d]	0.465
8 Finland	4	33.5	26.4	62.3	41	0.719
9 New Zealand	5	29.2	32.3	47.8	39	0.718
10 Sweden	2	40.4	38.9	64.4	45	0.784
11 Spain	21	19.8	12.0	48.1	29 [d]	0.542
12 Austria	8	25.1	19.2	48.6	34 [d]	0.667
13 Belgium	15	15.4	18.8	50.5	33	0.591
14 Australia	11	20.5	43.3	25.0	40	0.659
15 United Kingdom	20	7.8	33.0	43.7	35	0.543
16 Switzerland	12	20.3	27.8	23.8	30	0.642
17 Ireland	24	13.7	17.3	48.0	26	0.521
18 Denmark	3	33.0	20.0	62.8	42	0.728
19 Germany	9	25.5	19.2	43.0	35	0.661
20 Greece	56	6.3	12.1	44.2	31	0.391
21 Italy	16	10.0	37.6	46.3	31 [d]	0.573
22 Hong Kong	..	..	..	..	..	..
23 Israel	30	7.5	18.7	54.1	33 [d]	0.475
24 Cyprus	60	5.4	10.2	40.8	27	0.375
25 Barbados	14	18.4	37.0	52.1	40 [d]	0.602
26 Singapore	47	2.5	34.3	16.1	31	0.423
27 Luxembourg	13	20.0	8.6	37.7	25	0.631
28 Bahamas	19	10.8	26.3	56.9	39 [d]	0.544
29 Antigua and Barbuda	..	..	..	..	..	..
30 Chile	57	7.2	17.4	34.0	22 [e]	0.384
31 Portugal	18	13.0	36.6	52.4	34	0.556
32 Korea, Rep. of	73	3.0	4.2	45.0	28	0.302
33 Costa Rica	26	15.8	21.1	44.9	27	0.494
34 Malta	..	..	..	..	..	..
35 Slovenia	..	..	..	..	..	..
36 Argentina	..	..	..	..	..	..
37 Uruguay	54	6.9	25.3	62.6	33 [e]	0.414
38 Brunei Darussalam	..	..	..	..	..	..
39 Czech Rep.	..	..	..	..	..	..
40 Trinidad and Tobago	17	19.4	23.3	53.3	30 [d]	0.571
41 Dominica	..	..	..	..	..	..
42 Slovakia	..	..	..	..	..	..
43 Bahrain	..	..	..	..	..	..
44 United Arab Emirates	84	0	1.6	25.1	10 [d]	0.237
45 Panama	36	9.7	27.6	49.2	28 [d]	0.459
46 Fiji	68	5.8	9.6	44.7	21 [d]	0.329
47 Venezuela	55	6.3	17.6	55.2	27 [d]	0.394
48 Hungary	25	11.4	58.2	49.0	40	0.510
49 Saint Kitts and Nevis	..	..	..	..	..	..
50 Mexico	31	13.9	20.0	43.6	25 [d]	0.473
51 Colombia	38	9.8	27.2	41.8	33 [e]	0.455
52 Seychelles	..	..	..	..	..	..
53 Kuwait	66	0	5.2	36.8	25 [d]	0.333
54 Grenada	..	..	..	..	..	..
55 Qatar	..	..	..	..	..	..
56 Saint Lucia	..	..	..	..	..	..
57 Saint Vincent	..	..	..	..	..	..
58 Poland	42	13.0	15.6	60.4	39 [d]	0.433
59 Thailand	52	6.6	21.8	52.4	37	0.417
60 Malaysia	48	10.3	11.9	44.5	30 [d]	0.422
61 Mauritius	49	7.6	14.3	41.4	25 [d]	0.419
62 Belarus	..	..	..	..	..	..
63 Belize	32	10.8	36.6	38.8	18 [d]	0.470
64 Libyan Arab Jamahiriya	..	..	..	..	..	..

HDI rank	Gender empowerment measure (GEM) rank	Seats held in parliament (% women)[a]	Administrators and managers (% women)[b]	Professional and technical workers (% women)[b]	Earned income share (% to women)[b,c]	GEM value
Medium human development	–	16.4	12.7	44.3	30	0.436
65 Lebanon	..		..	..	..	..
66 Suriname	37	15.7	21.5	69.9	26 [d]	0.457
67 Russian Federation	..	..	..	..	..	..
68 Brazil	58	6.7	17.3	57.2	29 [e]	0.377
69 Bulgaria	27	13.3	28.9	57.0	41 [d]	0.487
70 Iran, Islamic Rep. of	81	4.0	3.5	32.6	19 [d]	0.251
71 Estonia	..	..	..	..	..	..
72 Ecuador	..	..	..	..	..	..
73 Saudi Arabia	..	..	..	..	..	..
74 Turkey	82	2.4	6.6	29.3	33	0.250
75 Korea, Dem. People's Rep. of	..	..	..	..	..	..
76 Lithuania	..	..	..	..	..	..
77 Croatia	..	..	..	..	..	..
78 Syrian Arab Rep.	..	..	..	..	..	..
79 Romania	..	..	..	..	..	..
80 Macedonia, FYR	..	..	..	..	..	..
81 Tunisia	78	6.7	7.3	17.6	25 [d]	0.260
82 Algeria	74	6.6	5.9	27.6	19 [d]	0.282
83 Jamaica	..	..	..	..	..	..
84 Jordan	..	..	..	..	..	..
85 Turkmenistan	..	..	..	..	..	..
86 Cuba	23	22.8	18.5	47.8	31 [d]	0.523
87 Dominican Rep.	46	10.0	21.2	49.5	23 [d]	0.424
88 Oman	..	..	..	..	..	..
89 Peru	53	10.8	20.0	41.1	23 [d]	0.416
90 South Africa	22	23.7	17.4	46.7	31 [d]	0.531
91 Sri Lanka	70	5.3	16.9	24.5	34	0.307
92 Latvia	..	..	..	..	..	..
93 Kazakstan	..	..	..	..	..	..
94 Paraguay	64	5.6	14.5	50.9	23	0.341
95 Ukraine	..	..	..	..	..	..
96 Samoa (Western)	..	..	..	..	..	..
97 Botswana	39	8.5	36.1	61.4	39 [d]	0.455
98 Philippines	35	11.5	33.7	62.7	31 [d]	0.459
99 Indonesia	59	12.6	6.6	40.8	33 [d]	0.375
100 Uzbekistan	..	..	..	..	..	..
101 Mongolia	..	..	..	..	..	..
102 Albania	..	..	..	..	..	..
103 Armenia	..	..	..	..	..	..
104 Guyana	33	20.0	12.8	47.5	26 [d]	0.469
105 Georgia	..	..	..	..	..	..
106 Azerbaijan	..	..	..	..	..	..
107 Kyrgyzstan	..	..	..	..	..	..
108 China	28	21.0	11.6	45.1	38 [d]	0.481
109 Egypt	75	2.0	16.0	28.7	25	0.278
110 Moldova, Rep. of	..	..	..	..	..	..
111 Maldives	67	6.3	14.0	34.6	35 [d]	0.330
112 El Salvador	44	10.7	25.3	44.5	28 [d]	0.429
113 Bolivia	62	6.4	16.8	41.9	27 [e]	0.350
114 Swaziland	61	8.4	14.5	54.3	35	0.366
115 Tajikistan	..	..	..	..	..	..
116 Honduras	51	7.8	30.6	49.8	24 [d]	0.417
117 Guatemala	29	12.5	32.4	45.2	21 [d]	0.476
118 Namibia	..	..	..	..	..	..
119 Morocco	72	0.6	25.6	31.3	28 [d]	0.303
120 Gabon	..	..	..	..	..	..
121 Viet Nam	..	..	..	..	..	..
122 Solomon Islands	91	2.1	2.6	27.4	40 [d]	0.197
123 Cape Verde	50	11.1	23.3	48.4	32 [d]	0.418
124 Vanuatu	..	..	..	..	..	..
125 São Tomé and Principe	..	..	..	..	..	..
126 Iraq	..	..	..	..	..	..
127 Nicaragua	..	..	..	..	..	..
128 Papua New Guinea	85	..	11.6	29.5	35 [d]	0.232
129 Zimbabwe	45	14.7	15.4	40.0	37 [d]	0.429
130 Congo	88	2.2	6.1	28.5	36 [d]	0.217

HDI rank	Gender empowerment measure (GEM) rank	Seats held in parliament (% women)[a]	Administrators and managers (% women)[b]	Professional and technical workers (% women)[b]	Earned income share (% to women)[b,c]	GEM value
Low human development	–	7.2	3.5	21.1	30	0.233
131 Myanmar	..	..	..	..	..	..
132 Ghana	..	..	..	..	..	..
133 Cameroon	65	12.2	10.1	24.4	31 [d]	0.339
134 Kenya	..	..	..	..	..	..
135 Equatorial Guinea	79	8.8	1.6	26.8	29 [d]	0.256
136 Lao People's Dem. Rep.	..	..	..	..	..	..
137 Lesotho	41	11.2	33.4	56.6	30 [e]	0.450
138 India	86	7.3	2.3	20.5	26 [d]	0.228
139 Pakistan	92	3.4	3.4	20.1	21 [d]	0.189
140 Comoros	..	..	..	..	..	..
141 Nigeria	..	..	..	..	..	..
142 Zaire	89	5.0	9.0	16.6	37 [d]	0.211
143 Zambia	71	9.7	6.1	31.9	39	0.303
144 Bangladesh	76	9.1	5.1	23.1	23	0.273
145 Côte d'Ivoire	..	..	..	..	..	..
146 Benin	..	..	..	..	..	..
147 Togo	93	1.2	7.9	21.2	33 [d]	0.182
148 Yemen	..	..	..	..	..	..
149 Tanzania, U. Rep. of	..	..	..	..	..	..
150 Mauritania	94	0.7	7.7	20.7	37 [d]	0.177
151 Central African Rep.	90	3.5	9.0	18.9	39	0.205
152 Madagascar	..	..	..	..	..	..
153 Cambodia	..	..	..	..	..	..
154 Nepal	..	..	..	..	..	..
155 Bhutan	..	..	..	..	..	..
156 Haiti	63	2.7	32.6	39.3	36 [d]	0.345
157 Angola	..	..	..	..	..	..
158 Sudan	87	5.3	2.4	28.8	23 [d]	0.225
159 Uganda	..	..	..	..	..	..
160 Senegal	..	..	..	..	..	..
161 Malawi	80	5.6	4.8	34.7	42 [d]	0.255
162 Djibouti	..	..	..	..	..	..
163 Guinea-Bissau	..	..	..	..	..	..
164 Chad	..	..	..	..	..	..
165 Gambia	..	..	..	..	..	..
166 Mozambique	43	25.2	11.3	20.4	41 [d]	0.430
167 Guinea	..	..	..	..	..	..
168 Eritrea	..	..	..	..	..	..
169 Burundi	..	..	..	..	..	..
170 Ethiopia	..	..	..	..	..	..
171 Mali	83	2.3	19.7	19.0	39 [d]	0.239
172 Burkina Faso	69	8.8	13.5	25.8	40 [d]	0.318
173 Niger	..	..	..	..	..	..
174 Rwanda	..	..	..	..	..	..
175 Sierra Leone	77	6.3	8.0	32.0	30 [d]	0.273
All developing countries	–	12.7	10.0	36.7	30	0.367
Least developed countries	–	..	..	..	..	..
Sub-Saharan Africa	–	..	..	..	..	..
Industrial countries	–	13.6	27.4	47.8	40	0.586
World	–	12.9	14.1	39.3	30	0.418

a. Data are as of 1 January 1997. A value of 0 was converted to 0.001 for purposes of calculation.
b. Data refer to latest available year.
c. The manufacturing wage was used for the Central African Republic, Finland, Greece, Ireland, Norway and Sweden.
d. No wage data available. An estimate of 75%, the mean for all countries with wage data available, was used for the ratio of the female non-agricultural wage to the male non-agricultural wage.
e. Wage data based on Psacharopoulos and Tzannatos 1992.
Source: Column 2: IPU 1997; *columns 3 and 4:* ILO 1994 and 1995a and UN 1994b; *column 5:* Human Development Report Office calculations based on estimates from the following: for real GDP per capita (PPP$), World Bank 1997a; for share of economically active population, ILO 1995b and 1996b; and for female wages as a percentage of male wages, ILO 1995b, UN 1994b and Psacharopoulos and Tzannatos 1992.

HDI rank	Human development index (HDI) value 1994	Gender-related development index (GDI) value 1994	Gender empowerment measure (GEM) value 1994	HDI value as % of highest in region 1994	GDI value as % of highest in region 1994	GEM value as % of highest in region 1994
Sub-Saharan Africa	0.845 [a]	0.752 [a]	0.531 [a]	–	–	–
52 Seychelles	**0.845** [a]	..	0.419	100	..	..
61 Mauritius	0.831	**0.752** [a]	0.419	98	100	79
90 South Africa	0.716	0.681	**0.531** [a]	85	91	100
97 Botswana	0.673	0.652	0.455	80	87	86
114 Swaziland	0.582	0.563	0.366	69	75	69
118 Namibia	0.570	..	..	67	..	..
120 Gabon	0.562	0.546	..	67	73	..
123 Cape Verde	0.547	0.523	0.418	65	70	79
125 São Tomé and Principe	0.534	..	..	63	..	..
129 Zimbabwe	0.513	0.503	0.429	61	67	81
130 Congo	0.500	..	0.217	59	..	41
132 Ghana	0.468	0.459	..	55	61	..
133 Cameroon	0.468	0.444	0.339	55	59	64
134 Kenya	0.463	0.458	..	55	61	..
135 Equatorial Guinea	0.462	0.441	0.256	55	59	48
137 Lesotho	0.457	0.446	0.450	54	59	85
140 Comoros	0.412	0.402	..	49	54	..
141 Nigeria	0.393	0.372	..	46	49	..
142 Zaire	0.381	..	0.211	45	..	40
143 Zambia	0.369	0.362	0.303	44	48	57
145 Côte d'Ivoire	0.368	0.341	..	44	45	..
146 Benin	0.368	0.349	..	44	46	..
147 Togo	0.365	0.342	0.182	43	45	34
149 Tanzania, U. Rep. of	0.357	0.352	..	42	47	..
150 Mauritania	0.355	0.341	0.177	42	45	33
151 Central African Rep.	0.355	0.338	0.205	42	45	39
152 Madagascar	0.350	..	..	41	..	..
157 Angola	0.335	..	..	40	..	..
159 Uganda	0.328	0.318	..	39	42	..
160 Senegal	0.326	0.309	..	39	41	..
161 Malawi	0.320	0.310	0.255	38	41	48
163 Guinea-Bissau	0.291	0.276	..	34	37	..
164 Chad	0.288	0.270	..	34	36	..
165 Gambia	0.281	0.263	..	33	35	..
166 Mozambique	0.281	0.262	0.430	33	35	81
167 Guinea	0.271	0.250	..	32	33	..
168 Eritrea	0.269	..	..	32	..	..
169 Burundi	0.247	0.233	..	29	31	..
170 Ethiopia	0.244	0.233	..	29	31	..
171 Mali	0.229	0.218	0.239	27	29	45
172 Burkina Faso	0.221	0.206	0.318	26	27	60
173 Niger	0.206	0.193	..	24	26	..
174 Rwanda	0.187	..	..	22	..	..
175 Sierra Leone	0.176	0.155	0.273	21	21	51
East Asia	0.914 [a]	0.852 [a]	0.481 [a]	–	–	–
22 Hong Kong	**0.914** [a]	**0.852** [a]	..	100	100	..
32 Korea, Rep. of	0.890	0.826	0.302	97	97	63
75 Korea, Dem. People's Rep. of	0.765	..	..	84	..	..
101 Mongolia	0.661	0.650	..	72	76	..
108 China	0.626	0.617	**0.481** [a]	68	72	100
South Asia	0.780 [a]	0.694 [a]	0.330 [a]	–	–	–
70 Iran, Islamic Rep. of	**0.780** [a]	..	0.251	100	..	76
91 Sri Lanka	0.711	**0.694** [a]	0.307	91	100	93
111 Maldives	0.611	0.600	**0.330** [a]	78	86	100
138 India	0.446	0.419	0.228	57	60	69
139 Pakistan	0.445	0.392	0.189	57	56	57
144 Bangladesh	0.368	0.339	0.273	47	49	83
154 Nepal	0.347	0.321	..	44	46	..
155 Bhutan	0.338	..	..	43	..	..
South-East Asia and the Pacific	0.900 [a]	0.853 [a]	0.459 [a]	–	–	–
26 Singapore	**0.900** [a]	**0.853** [a]	0.423	100	100	92
38 Brunei Darussalam	0.882	..	..	98	..	..
46 Fiji	0.863	0.763	0.329	96	90	72
59 Thailand	0.833	0.812	0.417	93	95	91
60 Malaysia	0.832	0.782	0.422	92	92	92

HDI rank		Human development index (HDI) value 1994	Gender-related development index (GDI) value 1994	Gender empowerment measure (GEM) value 1994	HDI value as % of highest in region 1994	GDI value as % of highest in region 1994	GEM value as % of highest in region 1994
96	Samoa	0.684	..		76		
98	Philippines	0.672	0.650	**0.459** [a]	75	76	100
99	Indonesia	0.668	0.642	0.375	74	75	82
121	Viet Nam	0.557	0.552	..	62	65	
122	Solomon Islands	0.556	..	0.197	62		43
124	Vanuatu	0.547	..	..	61		
128	Papua New Guinea	0.525	0.508	0.232	58	60	50
131	Myanmar	0.475	0.469	..	53	55	
136	Lao People's Dem. Rep.	0.459	0.444	..	51	52	
153	Cambodia	0.348	..	..	39		
Arab States		**0.870** [a]	**0.769** [a]	**0.333** [a]	–	–	–
43	Bahrain	**0.870** [a]	0.742	..	100	97	
44	United Arab Emirates	0.866	0.727	0.237	100	95	71
53	Kuwait	0.844	**0.769** [a]	**0.333** [a]	97	100	100
55	Qatar	0.840	0.713	..	97	93	
64	Libyan Arab Jamahiriya	0.801	0.655	..	92	85	
65	Lebanon	0.794	0.708	..	91	92	
73	Saudi Arabia	0.774	0.581	..	89	76	
78	Syrian Arab Rep.	0.755	0.646	..	87	84	
81	Tunisia	0.748	0.668	0.260	86	87	78
82	Algeria	0.737	0.614	0.282	85	80	85
84	Jordan	0.730	..	..	84		
88	Oman	0.718	..	..	83		
109	Egypt	0.614	0.555	0.278	71	72	83
119	Morocco	0.566	0.515	0.303	65	67	91
126	Iraq	0.531	0.433	..	61	56	
148	Yemen	0.361	..	..	42		
158	Sudan	0.333	0.306	0.225	38	40	68
162	Djibouti	0.319	..	..	37		
Latin America and the Caribbean		**0.907** [a]	**0.885** [a]	**0.602** [a]	–	–	–
25	Barbados	**0.907** [a]	**0.885** [a]	**0.602** [a]	100	100	100
28	Bahamas	0.894	0.880	0.544	99	99	90
29	Antigua and Barbuda	0.892	..	..	98		
30	Chile	0.891	0.785	0.384	98	89	64
33	Costa Rica	0.889	0.825	0.494	98	93	82
36	Argentina	0.884	0.777	..	97	88	
37	Uruguay	0.883	0.842	0.414	97	95	69
40	Trinidad and Tobago	0.880	0.841	0.571	97	95	95
41	Dominica	0.873	..	..	96		
45	Panama	0.864	0.802	0.459	95	91	76
47	Venezuela	0.861	0.792	0.394	95	89	66
49	Saint Kitts and Nevis	0.853	..	..	94		
50	Mexico	0.853	0.770	0.473	94	87	79
51	Colombia	0.848	0.811	0.455	94	92	76
54	Grenada	0.843	..	..	93		
56	Saint Lucia	0.838	..	..	92		
57	Saint Vincent	0.836	..	..	92		
63	Belize	0.806	..	0.470	89		78
66	Suriname	0.792	..	0.457	87		76
68	Brazil	0.783	0.728	0.377	86	82	63
72	Ecuador	0.775	0.675	..	85	76	
83	Jamaica	0.736	0.726	..	81	82	
86	Cuba	0.723	0.699	0.523	80	79	87
87	Dominican Rep.	0.718	0.658	0.424	79	74	70
89	Peru	0.717	0.656	0.416	79	74	69
94	Paraguay	0.706	0.649	0.341	78	73	57
104	Guyana	0.649	0.615	0.469	72	69	78
112	El Salvador	0.592	0.563	0.429	65	64	71
113	Bolivia	0.589	0.557	0.350	65	63	58
116	Honduras	0.575	0.544	0.417	63	62	69
117	Guatemala	0.572	0.510	0.476	63	58	79
127	Nicaragua	0.530	0.515	..	58	58	
156	Haiti	0.338	0.332	0.345	37	37	57

HDI rank	Human development index (HDI) value 1994	Gender-related development index (GDI) value 1994	Gender empowerment measure (GEM) value 1994	HDI value as % of highest in region 1994	GDI value as % of highest in region 1994	GEM value as % of highest in region 1994
Other developing countries						
24 Cyprus	0.907	0.837	0.375	99 [b]	95 [b]	62 [b]
74 Turkey	0.772	0.737	0.250	84 [b]	83 [b]	42 [b]
All developing countries	0.914 [a]	0.885 [a]	0.602 [a]	–	–	–
Eastern Europe and CIS	0.886 [a]	0.866 [a]	0.510 [a]	–	–	–
35 Slovenia	**0.886** [a]	**0.866** [a]	..	100	100	..
39 Czech Rep.	0.882	0.859	..	100	99	..
42 Slovakia	0.873	0.859	..	99	99	..
48 Hungary	0.857	0.837	**0.510** [a]	97	97	100
58 Poland	0.834	0.818	0.433	94	94	85
62 Belarus	0.806	0.792	..	91	92	..
67 Russian Federation	0.792	0.778	..	89	90	..
69 Bulgaria	0.780	0.772	0.487	88	89	95
71 Estonia	0.776	0.764	..	88	88	..
76 Lithuania	0.762	0.750	..	86	87	..
77 Croatia	0.760	0.741	..	86	86	..
79 Romania	0.748	0.733	..	84	85	..
80 Macedonia, FYR	0.748	0.726	..	84	84	..
85 Turkmenistan	0.723	0.712	..	82	82	..
92 Latvia	0.711	0.702	..	80	81	..
93 Kazakstan	0.709	0.698	..	80	81	..
95 Ukraine	0.689	0.681	..	78	79	..
100 Uzbekistan	0.662	0.655	..	75	76	..
102 Albania	0.655	0.643	..	74	74	..
103 Armenia	0.651	0.647	..	73	75	..
105 Georgia	0.637	0.630	..	72	73	..
106 Azerbaijan	0.636	0.628	..	72	73	..
107 Kyrgyzstan	0.635	0.628	..	72	73	..
110 Moldova, Rep. of	0.612	0.608	..	69	70	..
115 Tajikistan	0.580	0.575	..	65	66	..
OECD	0.960 [a]	0.939 [a]	0.795 [a]	–	–	–
1 Canada	**0.960** [a]	**0.939** [a]	0.700	100	100	88
2 France	0.946	0.926	0.452	99	99	57
3 Norway	0.943	0.934	**0.795** [a]	98	100	100
4 USA	0.942	0.928	0.671	98	99	84
5 Iceland	0.942	0.932	..	98	99	..
6 Netherlands	0.940	0.901	0.660	98	96	83
7 Japan	0.940	0.901	0.465	98	96	58
8 Finland	0.940	0.925	0.719	98	99	90
9 New Zealand	0.937	0.918	0.718	98	98	90
10 Sweden	0.936	0.932	0.784	97	99	99
11 Spain	0.934	0.874	0.542	97	93	68
12 Austria	0.932	0.890	0.667	97	95	84
13 Belgium	0.932	0.891	0.591	97	95	74
14 Australia	0.931	0.917	0.659	97	98	83
15 United Kingdom	0.931	0.896	0.543	97	95	68
16 Switzerland	0.930	0.874	0.642	97	93	81
17 Ireland	0.929	0.851	0.521	97	91	66
18 Denmark	0.927	0.916	0.728	97	98	92
19 Germany	0.924	0.886	0.661	96	94	83
20 Greece	0.923	0.873	0.391	96	93	49
21 Italy	0.921	0.867	0.573	96	92	72
27 Luxembourg	0.899	0.813	0.631	94	87	79
31 Portugal	0.890	0.850	0.556	93	91	70
29 Czech Republic	0.882	0.859	..	92	92	..
48 Hungary	0.857	0.837	0.510	89	89	64
50 Mexico	0.853	0.770	0.473	89	82	60
58 Poland	0.834	0.818	0.433	87	87	54
74 Turkey	0.772	0.737	0.250	80	79	31
Other industrial countries						
23 Israel	0.913	0.872	0.475	95 [c]	93 [c]	60 [c]
34 Malta	0.887	0.773	..	92 [c]	82 [c]	..
Industrial countries	0.960 [a]	0.939 [a]	0.795 [a]	–	–	–
World	0.960 [a]	0.939 [a]	0.795 [a]	–	–	–

a. Indicates highest value achieved in the region or country group.
b. As a percentage of the highest value for developing countries.
c. As a percentage of the highest value for industrial countries.
Source: Human Development Report Office.

5 Trends in human development and per capita income

	Human development index (HDI) value					GDP per capita (1987 US$)				
HDI rank	1960	1970	1980	1992	1994	1960	1970	1980	1990	1994
High human development	..	..	..	..	0.901	5,984	8,679	10,398	12,447	12,744
1 Canada	0.865	0.887	0.911	0.932	0.960	7,261	10,097	13,520	15,894	15,940
2 France	0.853	0.871	0.895	0.927	0.946	7,219	11,166	14,564	17,490	17,768
3 Norway	0.865	0.878	0.901	0.928	0.943	7,895	10,886	16,307	20,064	22,378
4 USA	0.865	0.881	0.905	0.925	0.942	10,707	13,794	16,389	19,461	20,500
5 Iceland	0.853	0.863	0.890	0.914	0.942	6,624	7,419	18,214	21,450	20,927
6 Netherlands	0.855	0.867	0.888	0.923	0.940	7,943	11,464	14,072	16,273	16,861
7 Japan	0.686	0.875	0.906	0.929	0.940	4,706	11,579	16,070	22,733	23,791
8 Finland	0.811	0.855	0.880	0.911	0.940	7,351	11,221	15,068	19,582	17,579
9 New Zealand	0.852	0.861	0.877	0.907	0.937	7,444	8,827	9,934	11,067	11,866
10 Sweden	0.867	0.881	0.899	0.928	0.936	9,873	14,451	16,884	20,021	18,927
11 Spain	0.636	0.820	0.851	0.888	0.934	2,828	5,207	6,630	8,522	8,881
12 Austria	0.797	0.857	0.880	0.917	0.932	6,727	10,045	14,167	17,136	17,690
13 Belgium	0.826	0.851	0.873	0.916	0.932	6,363	9,752	13,163	15,705	16,181
14 Australia	0.850	0.862	0.890	0.926	0.931	6,989	9,651	11,453	13,235	14,245
15 United Kingdom	0.857	0.873	0.892	0.919	0.931	6,795	8,463	10,161	12,933	13,132
16 Switzerland	0.853	0.872	0.897	0.931	0.930	15,779	21,689	24,037	27,323	26,936
17 Ireland	0.710	0.829	0.862	0.892	0.929	3,904	5,648	7,791	10,871	12,697
18 Denmark	0.857	0.879	0.888	0.912	0.927	9,835	14,081	16,889	20,538	21,966
19 Germany	0.841	0.856	0.881	0.918	0.924	6,869	9,913	12,865	15,853	..
20 Greece	0.573	0.723	0.839	0.874	0.923	1,570	3,100	4,453	4,828	5,055
21 Italy	0.755	0.831	0.857	0.891	0.921	5,296	8,606	11,827	14,567	15,058
22 Hong Kong	0.561	0.737	0.830	0.875	0.914	1,631	3,128	5,939	9,896	11,611
23 Israel	0.719	0.827	0.862	0.900	0.913	3,537	5,847	7,798	9,250	10,064
24 Cyprus	0.579	0.733	0.844	0.873	0.907	..	..	4,046	6,639	7,542
25 Barbados	0.678	0.824	0.856	0.894	0.907	2,290	4,282	5,490	6,002	5,843
26 Singapore	0.519	0.682	0.780	0.836	0.900	1,510	2,761	5,581	9,877	12,548
27 Luxembourg	0.826	0.843	0.869	0.908	0.899	9,704	12,702	15,320	20,796	21,221
28 Bahamas	..	..	..	..	0.894	6,770	9,624	10,265	11,240	10,290
29 Antigua and Barbuda	..	..	..	..	0.892	..	..	2,982	5,255	5,699
30 Chile	0.584	0.682	0.753	0.848	0.891	1,162	1,397	1,580	1,914	2,378
31 Portugal	0.460	0.588	0.736	0.838	0.890	1,402	2,535	3,730	4,932	5,077
32 Korea, Rep. of	0.398	0.523	0.666	0.859	0.890	520	967	1,953	4,132	5,210
33 Costa Rica	0.550	0.647	0.746	0.848	0.889	1,053	1,351	1,767	1,692	..
34 Malta	0.517	0.615	0.802	0.843	0.887	989	1,652	4,171	5,596	..
35 Slovenia	..	..	..	..	0.886	..	..	..	..	..
36 Argentina	0.667	0.748	0.790	0.853	0.884	2,701	3,460	3,914	3,099	3,947
37 Uruguay	0.737	0.762	0.830	0.859	0.883	1,937	2,022	2,590	2,425	2,795
38 Brunei Darussalam	..	..	..	..	0.882	..	..	17,052	11,193	10,040
39 Czech Rep.	..	..	..	..	0.882	..	..	..	3,701	3,013
40 Trinidad and Tobago	0.737	0.789	0.816	0.855	0.880	2,442	3,183	5,218	3,759	3,711
41 Dominica	..	..	..	..	0.873	1,192	1,307	1,129	2,018	2,161
42 Slovakia	..	..	..	..	0.873	..	..	..	3,198	2,512
43 Bahrain	..	..	..	..	0.870	..	..	9,661	7,432	7,644
44 United Arab Emirates	0.515	0.601	0.719	0.771	0.866	..	..	30,712	18,603	..
45 Panama	0.485	0.592	0.687	0.816	0.864	1,068	1,710	2,255	1,967	2,369
46 Fiji	..	..	..	..	0.863	1,116	1,404	1,864	1,952	..
47 Venezuela	0.600	0.728	0.784	0.820	0.861	2,815	3,261	3,022	2,537	2,651
48 Hungary	0.625	0.705	0.838	0.863	0.857	742	1,350	2,059	2,456	2,282
49 Saint Kitts and Nevis	..	..	..	..	0.853	..	..	1,782	3,085	3,577
50 Mexico	0.517	0.642	0.758	0.804	0.853	938	1,360	1,936	1,814	1,891
51 Colombia	0.469	0.554	0.656	0.813	0.848	639	796	1,094	1,224	1,326
52 Seychelles	..	..	..	..	0.845	1,803	2,044	3,536	4,400	4,974
53 Kuwait	..	..	..	..	0.844	..	35,871	18,434	..	..
54 Grenada	..	..	..	..	0.843	..	..	..	1,969	..
55 Qatar	..	..	..	..	0.840	..	..	..	..	..
56 Saint Lucia	..	..	..	..	0.838	..	..	..	2,722	2,665
57 Saint Vincent	..	..	..	..	0.836	743	797	939	1,620	1,793
58 Poland	..	..	..	..	0.834	..	..	1,749	1,683	1,803
59 Thailand	0.373	0.465	0.551	0.798	0.833	300	487	718	1,299	1,703
60 Malaysia	0.330	0.471	0.687	0.794	0.832	708	995	1,678	2,335	2,905
61 Mauritius	0.486	0.524	0.626	0.778	0.831	815	864	1,241	2,064	2,399
62 Belarus	..	..	..	..	0.806	515	980	1,774	2,628	1,792
63 Belize	..	..	..	..	0.806	750	939	1,592	1,950	2,123
64 Libyan Arab Jamahiriya	..	..	..	..	0.801	3,275	17,025	13,219	..	..

HDI rank	Human development index (HDI) value					GDP per capita (1987 US$)				
	1960	1970	1980	1992	1994	1960	1970	1980	1990	1994
Medium human development	..	..	..	..	0.667	307	442	737	794	860
65 Lebanon	..	..	..	..	0.794	97	131	241	274	328
66 Suriname	..	..	..	..	0.792	..	659	794	1,979	2,035
67 Russian Federation	..	..	..	..	..	..	..	..	..	..
68 Brazil	0.394	0.507	0.673	0.756	0.783	823	1,145	2,049	1,947	1,993
69 Bulgaria	..	..	..	..	0.780	..	..	2,344	3,080	2,554
70 Iran, Islamic Rep. of	0.306	0.406	0.497	0.672	0.780	..	..	2,970	2,523	2,933
71 Estonia	..	..	..	..	0.776	1,498	2,580	3,936	3,719	2,454
72 Ecuador	0.422	0.485	0.613	0.718	0.775	..	668	1,226	1,170	1,241
73 Saudi Arabia	0.448	0.511	0.629	0.742	0.774	..	6,625	9,978	5,351	5,246
74 Turkey	0.333	0.441	0.549	0.739	0.772	753	999	1,293	1,738	1,754
75 Korea, Dem. People's Rep. of	..	..	..	..	0.765	..	..	..	..	..
76 Lithuania	..	..	..	..	0.762	727	1,494	2,158	2,697	1,033
77 Croatia	..	..	..	..	0.760	..	..	..	..	..
78 Syrian Arab Rep.	0.318	0.419	0.658	0.727	0.755	..	635	1,168	1,020	..
79 Romania	..	..	..	..	0.748	..	..	..	..	..
80 Macedonia, FYR	..	..	..	..	0.748	..	..	..	..	..
81 Tunisia	0.258	0.340	0.499	0.690	0.748	..	716	1,172	1,315	1,428
82 Algeria	0.264	0.323	0.476	0.553	0.737	1,988	2,097	2,675	2,654	2,348
83 Jamaica	0.529	0.662	0.654	0.749	0.736	1,154	1,555	1,289	1,461	1,586
84 Jordan	0.296	0.405	0.553	0.628	0.730	..	..	..	1,507	1,629
85 Turkmenistan	..	..	..	..	0.723	858	1,105	1,218	1,316	..
86 Cuba	..	..	..	..	0.723	..	..	..	..	..
87 Dominican Rep.	0.385	0.455	0.541	0.638	0.718	386	494	744	773	839
88 Oman	..	..	..	..	0.718	750	3,367	3,587	5,253	5,683
89 Peru	0.420	0.528	0.590	0.642	0.717	964	1,214	1,316	987	988
90 South Africa	0.464	0.591	0.629	0.650	0.716	1,808	2,396	2,561	2,286	2,141
91 Sri Lanka	0.475	0.506	0.552	0.665	0.711	204	252	332	440	522
92 Latvia	..	..	..	..	0.711	1,020	1,774	2,695	3,546	1,767
93 Kazakstan	..	..	..	..	0.709	793	1,255	1,761	1,720	918
94 Paraguay	0.474	0.511	0.602	0.679	0.706	525	604	1,047	1,004	1,012
95 Ukraine	..	..	..	..	0.689	655	1,127	1,627	2,092	1,125
96 Samoa (Western)	..	..	..	..	0.684	..	..	..	..	..
97 Botswana	0.207	0.284	0.414	0.670	0.673	238	303	897	1,675	1,784
98 Philippines	0.419	0.489	0.557	0.621	0.672	418	496	680	636	615
99 Indonesia	0.223	0.306	0.418	0.586	0.668	190	221	354	517	676
100 Uzbekistan	..	..	..	..	0.662	357	532	734	822	612
101 Mongolia	..	..	..	..	0.661	..	..	1,360	1,721	1,267
102 Albania	..	..	..	..	0.655	..	..	696	639	526
103 Armenia	..	..	..	..	0.651	2,043	3,428	5,774	1,653	551
104 Guyana	..	..	..	..	0.649	475	540	587	395	519
105 Georgia	..	..	..	..	0.637	715	1,183	1,980	1,774	454
106 Azerbaijan	..	..	..	..	0.636	52	65	1,066	1,026	410
107 Kyrgyzstan	..	..	..	..	0.635	435	655	814	1,075	497
108 China	0.248	0.372	0.475	0.644	0.626	75	89	134	269	435
109 Egypt	0.210	0.269	0.360	0.551	0.614	237	316	551	734	722
110 Moldova, Rep. of	..	..	..	..	0.612	..	..	..	..	..
111 Maldives	..	..	..	..	0.611	..	..	..	543	665
112 El Salvador	0.339	0.422	0.454	0.543	0.592	769	950	1,033	909	952
113 Bolivia	0.308	0.369	0.442	0.530	0.589	610	754	876	731	780
114 Swaziland	..	..	..	..	0.582	310	610	732	822	768
115 Tajikistan	..	..	..	..	0.580	384	577	723	685	281
116 Honduras	0.280	0.350	0.435	0.524	0.575	691	804	999	927	896
117 Guatemala	0.311	0.392	0.477	0.564	0.572	616	795	1,045	858	897
118 Namibia	..	..	..	..	0.570	..	..	1,792	1,479	1,575
119 Morocco	0.198	0.282	0.383	0.549	0.566	484	575	782	909	942
120 Gabon	0.259	0.378	0.468	0.525	0.562	2,307	3,600	4,697	4,447	3,639
121 Viet Nam	..	..	..	..	0.557	..	..	..	606	760
122 Solomon Islands	..	..	..	..	0.556	..	404	434	585	623
123 Cape Verde	..	..	..	..	0.547	..	298	415	605	654
124 Vanuatu	..	..	..	..	0.547	..	..	807	904	821
125 São Tomé and Principe	..	..	..	..	0.534	..	517	712	496	486
126 Iraq	0.348	0.452	0.581	0.614	0.531	3,420	4,437	6,600	1,621	..
127 Nicaragua	0.344	0.462	0.534	0.583	0.530	1,295	1,809	1,376	920	..
128 Papua New Guinea	0.208	0.325	0.348	0.408	0.525	570	877	881	802	1,124
129 Zimbabwe	0.284	0.326	0.386	0.474	0.513	460	613	597	646	629
130 Congo	0.241	0.307	0.368	0.461	0.500	511	601	901	1,090	933

HDI rank	Human development index (HDI) value					GDP per capita (1987 US$)				
	1960	1970	1980	1992	1994	1960	1970	1980	1990	1993
Low human development	..	..	..	..	0.403	227	261	285	344	364
131 Myanmar	0.243	0.318	0.356	0.406	0.475	195	204	260	238	268
132 Ghana	0.233	0.283	0.323	0.382	0.468	497	517	434	386	412
133 Cameroon	0.191	0.253	0.332	0.447	0.468	601	582	962	898	661
134 Kenya	0.192	0.254	0.340	0.434	0.463	218	246	372	395	372
135 Equatorial Guinea	..	..	..	..	0.462	..	..	..	357	420
136 Lao People's Dem. Rep.	..	..	..	..	0.459	..	..	..	310	349
137 Lesotho	0.245	0.307	0.404	0.476	0.457	616	745	674	..	..
138 India	0.206	0.254	0.296	0.382	0.446	206	241	262	377	407
139 Pakistan	0.183	0.244	0.287	0.393	0.445	135	206	251	349	373
140 Comoros	..	..	..	..	0.412	..	..	459	462	437
141 Nigeria	0.184	0.230	0.297	0.348	0.393	329	348	421	358	349
142 Zaire	0.179	0.235	0.286	0.341	0.381	288	309	241	197	..
143 Zambia	0.258	0.315	0.342	0.352	0.369	412	440	375	291	253
144 Bangladesh	0.166	0.199	0.234	0.309	0.368	146	162	142	183	196
145 Côte d'Ivoire	0.168	0.243	0.330	0.370	0.368	500	1,050	1,216	823	708
146 Benin	0.130	0.162	0.197	0.261	0.368	320	356	359	353	362
147 Togo	0.123	0.183	0.255	0.311	0.365	244	400	472	391	317
148 Yemen	0.092	0.138	0.253	0.323	0.361	..	..	..	..	..
149 Tanzania, U. Rep. of	0.162	0.211	0.282	0.306	0.357	123	160	165	171	153
150 Mauritania	..	..	..	..	0.355	359	581	523	472	494
151 Central African Rep.	0.160	0.196	0.226	0.249	0.355	426	445	412	379	348
152 Madagascar	0.237	0.291	0.344	0.396	0.350	340	357	311	244	205
153 Cambodia	..	..	..	..	0.348	..	..	..	131	124
154 Nepal	0.128	0.162	0.209	0.289	0.347	148	155	147	181	203
155 Bhutan	..	..	..	..	0.338	..	..	..	..	..
156 Haiti	0.174	0.218	0.295	0.354	0.338	386	333	428	339	226
157 Angola	0.139	0.195	0.212	0.271	0.335	..	..	..	..	..
158 Sudan	0.160	0.188	0.229	0.276	0.333	814	729	784	670	765
159 Uganda	0.185	0.213	0.215	0.272	0.328	..	..	..	462	511
160 Senegal	0.146	0.176	0.233	0.322	0.326	713	723	663	687	615
161 Malawi	0.144	0.176	0.216	0.260	0.320	102	125	168	140	132
162 Djibouti	..	..	..	..	0.319	..	..	1,232	716	..
163 Guinea-Bissau	0.091	0.125	0.148	0.224	0.291	..	202	146	202	216
164 Chad	0.112	0.135	0.151	0.212	0.288	213	198	128	182	173
165 Gambia	0.068	0.107	0.148	0.215	0.281	189	240	289	296	268
166 Mozambique	0.169	0.248	0.247	0.252	0.281	..	..	129	111	133
167 Guinea	0.083	0.111	0.148	0.191	0.271	..	..	..	403	397
168 Eritrea	..	..	..	..	0.269	..	..	..	..	..
169 Burundi	0.131	0.157	0.219	0.276	0.247	125	161	195	227	191
170 Ethiopia	..	..	..	..	0.244	..	..	..	165	153
171 Mali	0.083	0.102	0.146	0.214	0.229	217	240	288	260	248
172 Burkina Faso	0.086	0.116	0.151	0.203	0.221	173	185	219	245	253
173 Niger	0.090	0.134	0.163	0.209	0.206	556	552	455	308	275
174 Rwanda	0.185	0.215	0.244	0.274	0.187	..	..	..	..	..
175 Sierra Leone	0.095	0.155	0.177	0.209	0.176	119	164	159	147	145
All developing countries	..	..	..	..	0.576	330	461	671	723	823
Least developed countries	..	..	..	..	0.336	247	259	252	242	254
Sub-Saharan Africa	..	..	..	..	0.380	495	598	634	514	507
Industrial countries	..	..	..	..	0.911	6,448	9,546	11,562	14,119	14,473
World	..	..	..	..	0.764	2,049	2,756	3,205	3,470	3,402

Note: HDI values for 1960-92 are not strictly comparable with HDI values for 1994.
Source: Columns 6-10: World Bank 1995d and 1996a.

Trends in human development and economic growth

HDI rank	Reduction in shortfall (1-HDI) in human development index (HDI) value (%)			GDP per capita (1987 US$)						
	1960-70	1970-80	1980-92	1960[a]	Lowest value during 1960-94[a]	Year	Highest value during 1960-94[a]	Year	1994[a]	Average annual rate of change (%) 1960-94[a]
High human development	..	..	..	..	..	..	..	..	..	..
1 Canada	16.0	21.4	23.7	7,261	7,261	1960	16,162	1989	15,940	2.3
2 France	12.5	18.2	30.6	7,219	7,219	1960	17,768	1994	17,768	2.7
3 Norway	9.6	18.6	27.5	7,895	7,895	1960	22,378	1994	22,378	3.1
4 USA	11.5	20.8	20.7	10,707	10,707	1960	20,500	1994	20,500	1.9
5 Iceland	6.9	19.6	22.0	6,624	4,743	1961	21,928	1987	20,927	3.4
6 Netherlands	8.1	15.6	31.5	7,943	7,858	1961	16,861	1994	16,861	2.2
7 Japan	60.4	24.8	24.1	4,706	4,706	1960	23,848	1992	23,791	4.9
8 Finland	23.4	17.3	25.6	7,351	7,351	1960	19,652	1989	17,579	2.6
9 New Zealand	6.1	11.5	24.2	7,444	7,444	1960	11,866	1994	11,866	1.4
10 Sweden	11.0	14.7	28.9	9,873	9,873	1960	20,021	1991	18,927	1.9
11 Spain	50.6	17.4	24.6	2,828	2,828	1960	8,881	1994	8,881	3.4
12 Austria	29.6	15.8	30.9	6,727	6,727	1960	17,725	1992	17,690	2.9
13 Belgium	14.6	14.4	34.0	6,363	6,363	1960	16,253	1992	16,181	2.8
14 Australia	7.9	20.8	32.4	6,989	6,989	1960	14,245	1994	14,245	2.1
15 United Kingdom	11.1	14.7	25.2	6,795	6,795	1960	13,132	1994	13,132	2.0
16 Switzerland	12.7	19.8	32.9	15,779	15,779	1960	27,323	1990	26,936	1.6
17 Ireland	41.2	19.0	21.9	3,904	3,904	1960	12,697	1994	12,697	3.5
18 Denmark	15.0	8.1	21.2	9,835	9,835	1960	21,966	1994	21,966	2.4
19 Germany	9.4	17.7	30.8	6,869	6,869	1960	18,142	1992	17,839[b]	2.9
20 Greece	35.1	41.8	21.9	1,570	1,570	1960	5,055	1994	5,055	3.5
21 Italy	30.8	15.8	23.5	5,296	5,296	1960	15,058	1994	15,058	3.1
22 Hong Kong	40.1	35.2	26.6	1,631	1,631	1960	11,611	1994	11,611	5.9
23 Israel	38.5	20.2	27.6	3,537	3,537	1960	10,064	1994	10,064	3.1
24 Cyprus	36.5	41.7	18.5	2,394[c]	2,394	1975	7,542	1994	7,542	6.2
25 Barbados	45.3	18.3	26.2	2,290	2,290	1960	6,370	1989	5,843	2.8
26 Singapore	34.0	30.8	25.4	1,510	1,510	1960	12,548	1994	12,548	6.4
27 Luxembourg	9.9	16.2	30.0	9,704	9,704	1960	21,299	1992	21,221	2.3
28 Bahamas	..	..	..	6,770	6,443	1975	11,297	1989	10,290	1.2
29 Antigua and Barbuda	..	..	..	2,982[d]	2,982	1980	5,699	1994	5,699	4.7
30 Chile	23.6	22.3	38.5	1,162	1,162	1960	2,378	1994	2,378	2.1
31 Portugal	23.8	35.9	38.6	1,402	1,402	1960	5,102	1992	5,077	3.9
32 Korea, Rep. of	20.9	30.0	57.8	520	520	1960	5,210	1994	5,210	7.0
33 Costa Rica	21.4	28.2	40.1	1,053	1,004	1961	1,863	1993	1,863[b]	1.7
34 Malta	20.3	48.5	20.7	989	950	1962	6,302	1993	6,302[b]	5.8
35 Slovenia	..	..	..	..	..	..	..	..	..	..
36 Argentina	24.5	16.4	30.1	2,701	2,607	1963	3,947	1994	3,947	1.1
37 Uruguay	9.7	28.4	17.1	1,937	1,864	1967	2,795	1994	2,795	1.1
38 Brunei Darussalam	..	..	..	13,320[e]	10,040	1994	19,203	1979	10,040	-1.3
39 Czech Rep.	..	..	..	3,402[f]	2,958	1993	3,746	1989	3,013	-1.2
40 Trinidad and Tobago	19.7	13.1	21.0	2,442	2,442	1960	5,372	1981	3,711	1.2
41 Dominica	..	..	..	1,192	958	1979	2,171	1993	2,161	1.8
42 Slovakia	..	..	..	2,957[f]	2,408	1993	3,298	1989	2,512	-1.6
43 Bahrain	..	..	..	9,661[d]	7,157	1987	9,661	1980	7,644	-1.7
44 United Arab Emirates	17.8	29.6	18.4	33,348[e]	15,019	1988	33,348	1973	18,603[g]	-3.4
45 Panama	20.8	23.4	41.2	1,068	1,068	1960	2,377	1987	2,369	2.4
46 Fiji	..	..	..	1,116	1,075	1966	1,990	1993	1,990[b]	1.8
47 Venezuela	32.0	20.5	16.7	2,815	2,436	1989	3,395	1977	2,651	-0.2
48 Hungary	21.2	45.2	15.3	742	742	1960	2,509	1989	2,282	3.4
49 Saint Kitts and Nevis	..	..	..	1,417[h]	1,417	1977	3,577	1994	3,577	5.6
50 Mexico	25.8	32.5	18.9	938	938	1960	2,056	1981	1,891	2.1
51 Colombia	16.1	22.9	45.6	639	639	1960	1,326	1994	1,326	2.2
52 Seychelles	..	..	..	1,803	1,677	1961	4,974	1994	4,974	3.0
53 Kuwait	..	..	..	51,488[i]	10,301	1992	51,488	1962	10,301[j]	-5.2
54 Grenada	..	..	..	1,408[f]	1,408	1984	2,010	1991	1,988[b]	3.9
55 Qatar	..	..	..	..	..	..	..	..	..	..
56 Saint Lucia	..	..	..	1,904[k]	1,904	1985	2,937	1993	2,665	3.8
57 Saint Vincent	..	..	..	743	671	1967	1,793	1994	1,793	2.6
58 Poland	..	..	..	1,749[d]	1,473	1982	1,803	1994	1,803	0.2
59 Thailand	14.6	16.0	55.1	300	300	1960	1,703	1994	1,703	5.2
60 Malaysia	21.0	40.9	34.1	708	708	1960	2,905	1994	2,905	4.2
61 Mauritius	7.3	21.4	40.7	815	815	1960	2,399	1994	2,399	3.2
62 Belarus	..	..	..	515	515	1960	2,679	1989	1,792	3.7
63 Belize	..	..	..	750	750	1960	2,161	1993	2,123	3.1
64 Libyan Arab Jamahiriya	..	..	..	3,275	3,275	1960	17,025	1970	5,360[l]	1.7

		Reduction in shortfall (1-HDI) in human development index (HDI) value (%)			GDP per capita (1987 US$)						
HDI rank		1960-70	1970-80	1980-92	1960[a]	Lowest value during 1960-94[a]	Year	Highest value during 1960-94[a]	Year	1994[a]	Average annual rate of change (%) 1960-94[a]
Medium human development		..	..	..	..	..	..	..	..	..	..
65	Lebanon	..	..	..	..	..	..	..	..	..	..
66	Suriname	..	..	..	659 [m]	659	1970	2,844	1987	2,035	4.8
67	Russian Federation	..	..	..	..	..	..	..	..	..	..
68	Brazil	18.7	33.7	25.3	823	823	1960	2,097	1987	1,993	2.6
69	Bulgaria	..	..	..	2,344 [d]	2,344	1980	3,511	1988	2,554	0.6
70	Iran, Islamic Rep. of	14.3	15.4	34.8	4,302 [n]	2,375	1989	4,953	1976	2,933	-1.9
71	Estonia	..	..	..	1,498	1,498	1960	4,208	1983	2,454	1.5
72	Ecuador	11.0	24.8	27.2	626 [o]	622	1966	1,241	1994	1,241	2.4
73	Saudi Arabia	11.3	24.1	30.5	3,930 [i]	3,930	1962	9,978	1980	5,246	0.9
74	Turkey	16.2	19.3	42.1	753	745	1961	1,893	1993	1,754	2.5
75	Korea, Dem. People's Rep. of	..	..	..	..	..	..	..	..	..	..
76	Lithuania	..	..	..	727	727	1960	2,808	1989	1,033	1.0
77	Croatia	..	..	..	..	..	..	..	..	..	..
78	Syrian Arab Rep.	14.7	41.1	20.3	641 [p]	554	1966	1,236	1981	1,063 [q]	1.8
79	Romania	..	..	..	1,114 [c]	1,091	1992	1,828	1986	1,274	0.7
80	Macedonia, FYR	..	..	..	..	..	..	..	..	..	..
81	Tunisia	11.0	24.1	38.2	547 [r]	547	1961	1,428	1994	1,428	2.9
82	Algeria	8.0	22.6	14.7	1,988	1,327	1962	2,966	1985	2,348	0.5
83	Jamaica	28.1	-2.3	27.5	1,154	1,133	1962	1,850	1972	1,586	0.9
84	Jordan	15.5	24.8	16.9	2,253 [s]	1,374	1991	2,293	1987	1,629	-2.9
85	Turkmenistan	..	..	..	858	858	1960	1,430	1988	1,130 [j]	0.9
86	Cuba	..	..	..	..	..	..	..	..	..	..
87	Dominican Rep.	11.3	15.8	21.1	386	365	1961	839	1994	839	2.3
88	Oman	..	..	..	750	740	1961	5,768	1993	5,683	6.1
89	Peru	18.7	13.0	12.7	964	953	1992	1,379	1981	988	0.1
90	South Africa	23.8	9.2	5.7	1,808	1,808	1960	2,629	1981	2,141	0.5
91	Sri Lanka	5.8	9.3	25.3	204	204	1960	522	1994	522	2.8
92	Latvia	..	..	..	1,020	1,020	1960	3,604	1989	1,767	1.6
93	Kazakstan	..	..	..	793	793	1960	1,866	1988	918	0.4
94	Paraguay	7.0	18.7	19.3	525	525	1960	1,101	1981	1,012	1.9
95	Ukraine	..	..	..	655	655	1960	2,170	1989	1,125	1.6
96	Samoa (Western)	..	..	..	..	..	..	..	..	..	..
97	Botswana	9.7	18.1	43.7	238	223	1965	1,828	1992	1,784	6.1
98	Philippines	12.0	13.3	14.4	418	418	1960	693	1982	615	1.1
99	Indonesia	10.6	16.1	28.9	190	187	1967	676	1994	676	3.8
100	Uzbekistan	..	..	..	357	357	1960	825	1989	612	1.6
101	Mongolia	..	..	..	1,360 [d]	1,267	1994	1,809	1989	1,267	-0.5
102	Albania	..	..	..	696 [d]	419	1992	727	1982	526	-2.0
103	Armenia	..	..	..	2,043	551	1994	6,366	1983	551	-3.8
104	Guyana	..	..	..	475	395	1990	632	1976	519	0.3
105	Georgia	..	..	..	715	454	1994	2,358	1985	454	-1.3
106	Azerbaijan	..	..	..	52	49	1961	1,288	1987	410	6.2
107	Kyrgyzstan	..	..	..	435	435	1960	1,075	1990	497	0.4
108	China	16.4	16.4	32.2	75	46	1962	435	1994	435	5.3
109	Egypt	7.4	12.4	29.9	237	237	1960	735	1991	722	3.3
110	Moldova, Rep. of	..	..	..	..	..	..	..	..	..	..
111	Maldives	..	..	..	394 [k]	394	1985	665	1994	665	6.0
112	El Salvador	12.6	5.6	16.3	769	769	1960	1,195	1978	952	0.6
113	Bolivia	8.9	11.5	15.8	610	610	1960	927	1978	780	0.7
114	Swaziland	..	..	..	310	310	1960	823	1989	768	2.7
115	Tajikistan	..	..	..	384	281	1994	779	1988	281	-0.9
116	Honduras	9.8	13.0	15.8	691	680	1961	1,028	1979	896	0.8
117	Guatemala	11.7	14.0	16.6	616	616	1960	1,045	1980	897	1.1
118	Namibia	..	..	..	1,792 [d]	1,479	1990	1,792	1980	1,575	-0.9
119	Morocco	10.6	14.1	26.9	484	463	1961	942	1994	942	2.0
120	Gabon	16.1	14.5	10.7	2,307	2,307	1960	8,287	1976	3,639	1.3
121	Viet Nam	..	..	..	526 [f]	526	1984	760	1994	760	3.7
122	Solomon Islands	..	..	..	416 [t]	277	1972	623	1994	623	1.6
123	Cape Verde	..	..	..	298 [m]	248	1974	654	1994	654	3.3
124	Vanuatu	..	..	..	936 [u]	787	1992	953	1984	821	-0.9
125	São Tomé and Principe	..	..	..	517 [m]	485	1974	712	1980	486	-0.3
126	Iraq	15.9	23.5	8.0	3,420	781	1991	8,315	1979	781 [q]	-4.7
127	Nicaragua	18.0	13.4	10.5	1,295	816	1993	2,125	1977	816 [b]	-1.4
128	Papua New Guinea	14.8	3.3	9.2	570	570	1960	1,124	1994	1,124	2.0
129	Zimbabwe	5.8	8.9	14.3	460	460	1960	699	1974	629	0.9
130	Congo	8.7	8.8	14.7	511	511	1960	1,333	1984	933	1.8

	Reduction in shortfall (1-HDI) in human development index (HDI) value (%)			GDP per capita (1987 US$)							
HDI rank	1960-70	1970-80	1980-92	1960[a]	Lowest value during 1960-94[a]	Year	Highest value during 1960-94[a]	Year	1994[a]	Average annual rate of change (%) 1960-94[a]
Low human development	..	..	..	..	..	..	..	..	..	..
131 Myanmar	10.0	5.5	7.8	195	180	1967	295	1985	268	0.9
132 Ghana	6.5	5.7	8.7	497	338	1983	531	1971	412	-0.6
133 Cameroon	7.6	10.6	17.2	601	543	1967	1,243	1986	661	0.3
134 Kenya	7.7	11.5	14.2	218	195	1961	395	1990	372	1.6
135 Equatorial Guinea	..	..	..	352[c]	345	1991	420	1994	420	0.9
136 Lao People's Dem. Rep.				285[f]	270	1988	349	1994	349	2.0
137 Lesotho	8.2	14.1	12.0	97	97	1960	328	1994	328	3.6
138 India	5.9	5.7	12.2	206	206	1960	407	1994	407	2.0
139 Pakistan	7.4	5.7	14.8	135	135	1960	375	1992	373	3.0
140 Comoros	..	..	..	459[d]	437	1994	501	1984	437	-0.4
141 Nigeria	5.7	8.7	7.2	329	256	1967	437	1977	349	0.2
142 Zaire	6.8	6.7	7.7	288	153	1992	332	1974	153[i]	-2.0
143 Zambia	7.7	3.9	1.6	412	253	1994	478	1965	253	-1.4
144 Bangladesh	4.0	4.4	9.7	146	127	1973	196	1994	196	0.9
145 Côte d'Ivoire	9.0	11.5	6.0	500	500	1960	1,452	1978	708	1.0
146 Benin	3.8	4.2	7.9	320	309	1962	391	1985	362	0.4
147 Togo	6.9	8.7	7.5	244	244	1960	472	1980	317	0.8
148 Yemen	5.0	13.4	9.3	..	..	..	..	..	..	..
149 Tanzania, U. Rep. of	5.8	9.0	3.4	123	118	1961	173	1975	153	0.6
150 Mauritania	..	..	..	359	354	1963	581	1970	494	0.9
151 Central African Rep.	4.3	3.7	3.0	426	330	1993	466	1978	348	-0.6
152 Madagascar	7.0	7.5	8.0	340	205	1994	364	1971	205	-1.5
153 Cambodia	..	..	..	123[v]	123	1987	148	1993	124	0.1
154 Nepal	3.9	5.6	10.1	148	146	1973	203	1994	203	0.9
155 Bhutan	..	..	..	..	..	..	..	..	..	..
156 Haiti	5.4	9.8	8.4	386	226	1994	428	1980	226	-1.6
157 Angola	6.5	2.1	7.5	..	..	..	..	..	..	..
158 Sudan	3.4	5.0	6.1	814	643	1973	966	1977	765	-0.2
159 Uganda	3.5	0.2	7.3	452[s]	404	1986	511	1994	511	1.1
160 Senegal	3.5	6.9	11.6	713	615	1994	752	1965	615	-0.4
161 Malawi	3.8	4.9	5.6	102	102	1960	172	1979	132	0.8
162 Djibouti	..	..	..	1,262[u]	710	1991	1,301	1978	674[b]	-4.4
163 Guinea-Bissau	3.7	2.6	9.0	202[m]	146	1980	216	1994	216	0.3
164 Chad	2.6	1.9	7.2	213	127	1981	220	1962	173	-0.6
165 Gambia	4.2	4.6	7.9	189	189	1960	337	1982	268	1.0
166 Mozambique	9.4	-0.1	0.7	129[d]	83	1986	133	1994	133	0.2
167 Guinea	3.0	4.3	5.0	386[c]	386	1975	407	1993	397	0.1
168 Eritrea	..	..	..	..	..	..	..	..	..	..
169 Burundi	3.0	7.3	7.3	125	106	1961	232	1991	191	1.3
170 Ethiopia	..	..	..	187[s]	141	1992	155	1993	153	-1.8
171 Mali	2.0	5.0	7.9	217	212	1962	299	1979	248	0.4
172 Burkina Faso	3.2	4.0	6.1	173	173	1960	254	1991	253	1.1
173 Niger	4.8	3.4	5.5	556	270	1993	623	1963	275	-2.0
174 Rwanda	3.7	3.7	4.0	295	124	1994	357	1983	124	-2.5
175 Sierra Leone	6.6	2.6	3.8	119	119	1960	169	1982	145	0.6
All developing countries	..	..	..	..	..	..	..	..	..	..
Least developed countries	..	..	..	..	..	..	..	..	..	..
Sub-Saharan Africa	..	..	..	..	..	..	..	..	..	..
Industrial countries	..	..	..	..	..	..	..	..	..	..
World	..	..	..	..	..	..	..	..	..	..

a. The earliest year for which data are given is 1960, and the latest year for which data are given is 1994, unless otherwise specified. b. 1993. c. 1975. d. 1980. e. 1973. f. 1984. g. 1990. h. 1977. i. 1962. j. 1992. k. 1985. l. 1989. m. 1970. n. 1974. o. 1965. p. 1963. q. 1991. r. 1961. s. 1983. t. 1967. u. 1979. v. 1987.
Source: Columns 4-8: World Bank 1995d; *column 9:* calculated on the basis of data from World Bank 1997a; *column 10:* calculated on the basis of data from World Bank 1995d and 1996a.

7 Profile of human development

HDI rank	Life expectancy at birth (years) 1994	Population with access to			Daily calorie supply per capita 1992	Adult literacy rate (%) 1994	Combined first- and second-level gross enrolment ratio (%) 1992-94	Daily newspapers (copies per 100 people) 1994	Televisions (per 100 people) 1994	Real GDP per capita (PPP$) 1994	GNP per capita (US$) 1994
		Health services (%) 1990-95	Safe water (%) 1990-96	Sanitation (%) 1990-96							
High human development	71.5	90	85	83	2,894	92.0	86	15	25	8,525	4,963
22 Hong Kong	79.0	..	100	..	3,144	92.3	91	72	36	22,310	21,650
24 Cyprus	77.1	..	..	..	3,782	..	99	11	16	13,071 a,b	10,260
25 Barbados	75.9	..	..	..	3,223	97.3	..	16	26	11,051	6,560
26 Singapore	77.1	..	100 c	..	..	91.0	86	36	38	20,987	22,500
28 Bahamas	72.9	..	..	..	..	98.1	94	13	24	15,875	11,800
29 Antigua and Barbuda	..	..	..	..	..	..	..	..	35	8,977 a	..
30 Chile	75.1	97 c	..	..	2,583	95.0	89	10	25	9,129	3,520
32 Korea, Rep. of	71.5	100	93	100	3,298	97.9	98	40	32	10,656	8,260
33 Costa Rica	76.6	..	96	84	2,889	94.7	81	10	22	5,919	2,400
36 Argentina	72.4	71 c	71	68	2,880	96.0	93	14	32	8,937	8,110
37 Uruguay	72.6	82 c	75 c	61	2,750	97.1	95	24	52	6,752	4,660
38 Brunei Darussalam	74.9	..	..	..	2,745	87.9	89	7	32	30,447 a	14,240
40 Trinidad and Tobago	72.9	100	97	79	2,589	97.9	87	14	31	9,124	3,740
41 Dominica	..	..	..	..	..	..	..	..	7	6,118 a	2,800
43 Bahrain	72.0	..	..	..	..	84.4	100 d	13	42	15,321	7,460
44 United Arab Emirates	74.2	99	95	77	..	78.6	100 d	16	29	16,000 e	..
45 Panama	73.2	70	93	83	2,239	90.5	87	6	17	6,104	2,580
46 Fiji	71.8	..	..	..	3,092	91.3	97	5	7	5,763	2,250
47 Venezuela	72.1	..	79	59	2,622	91.0	85	2	18	8,120	2,760
49 Saint Kitts and Nevis	69.0 f	..	..	..	..	90.0 f	..	..	22	9,436	4,760
50 Mexico	72.0	93	83	72	3,181	89.2	87	11	19	7,384	4,180
51 Colombia	70.1	81	85	85	2,678	91.1	90	6	22	6,107	1,670
52 Seychelles	72.0 f	..	..	..	..	88.0 f	..	4	32	7,891 a	6,680
53 Kuwait	75.2	100 c	..	..	2,535	77.8	66	40	41	21,875	19,420
54 Grenada	72.0 f	..	..	..	2,407	98.0 f	..	..	16	5,137 a	2,630
55 Qatar	70.9	..	..	..	..	78.9	84	15	43	18,403	12,820
56 Saint Lucia	71.0 f	..	..	..	..	82.0 f	..	..	25	6,182 a	3,130
57 Saint Vincent	72.0 f	..	..	..	..	82.0 f	..	..	23	5,650 a	2,140
59 Thailand	69.5	90 c	89	96	2,443	93.5	68	5	25	7,104	2,410
60 Malaysia	71.2	..	78	94	2,884	83.0	78	14	23	8,865	3,480
61 Mauritius	70.7	100 c	99	99	2,696	82.4	80	7	19	13,172	3,150
63 Belize	74.0	..	..	..	2,670	70.0 f	92	..	17	5,590	2,530
64 Libyan Arab Jamahiriya	63.8	95	97	98	3,310	75.0	100 d	1	10	6,125 a	..
Medium human development	67.1	87	69	36	2,730	80.0	86	3	19	3,288	993
Excluding China	65.6	86	73	55	2,731	78.7	85	4	15	4,114	1,638
65 Lebanon	69.0	95	94	63	3,319	92.0	94	17	26	4,863 a,b	..
66 Suriname	70.7	..	..	..	2,548	92.7	..	10	15	4,711	860
68 Brazil	66.4	..	73	44	2,824	82.7	96	5	25	5,362	2,970
70 Iran, Islamic Rep. of	68.2	88	90	81	2,861	68.6 g	84	2	12	5,766	..
72 Ecuador	69.3	..	68	76	2,587	89.6	90	7	13	4,626	1,280
73 Saudi Arabia	70.3	97 c	95 c	86 c	2,751	61.8	66	5	25	9,338	7,050
74 Turkey	68.2	..	80	..	3,429	81.6	80	4	27	5,193	2,500
75 Korea, Dem. People's Rep. of	71.4	..	..	..	2,834	..	..	21	12	3,965 a,b	..
78 Syrian Arab Rep.	67.8	90	85	83	3,175	69.8	77	2	8	5,397	..
81 Tunisia	68.4	..	98	80	3,333	65.2	86	5	9	5,319	1,790
82 Algeria	67.8	98	78	91	2,897	59.4	84	5	7	5,442	1,650
83 Jamaica	73.9	90 c	86	89	2,607	84.4	86	7	30	3,816	1,540
84 Jordan	68.5	97 c	98	77	3,031	85.5	92	5	16	4,187	1,440
86 Cuba	75.6	100	89	92	2,833	95.4	90	12	19	..	..
87 Dominican Rep.	70.0	78	65	78	..	81.5	84	3	9	3,933	1,330
88 Oman	70.0	96	82	78	..	..	74	3	73	10,078	5,140
89 Peru	67.4	44	72	57	1,883	88.3	100 d	9	10	3,645	2,110
90 South Africa	63.7	..	99	53	2,705	81.4	100 d	3	10	4,291	3,040
91 Sri Lanka	72.2	..	57	63	2,275	90.1	87	3	7	3,277	640
94 Paraguay	68.8	63 c	42	41	2,670	91.9	78	4	7	3,531	1,580
96 Samoa (Western)	68.1	..	..	..	..	98.0 f	..	..	..	2,726	1,000
97 Botswana	52.3	..	93 c	55	2,288	68.7	92	2	2	5,367	2,800
98 Philippines	67.0	71	86	77	2,258	94.4	99	7	12	2,681	950
99 Indonesia	63.5	93	62	51	2,755	83.2	80	2	15	3,740	880
101 Mongolia	64.4	95 c	80	74	1,899	82.2	68	9	6	3,766	300
104 Guyana	63.2	..	..	..	2,385	97.9	82	10	4	2,729	530
108 China	68.9	88	67	24	2,729	80.9	88	2	23	2,604	530
109 Egypt	64.3	99	79	32	3,336	50.5	87	6	9	3,846	720
111 Maldives	62.8	..	..	..	2,624	93.0	90	1	4	..	950
112 El Salvador	69.3	40	69	81	2,663	70.9	67	5	23	2,417	1,360
113 Bolivia	60.1	67	66	55	2,100	82.5	77	7	14	2,598	770
114 Swaziland	58.3	..	..	..	2,706	75.2	94	1	7	2,821	1,100
116 Honduras	68.4	69	87	87	2,306	72.0	79	4	8	2,050	600
117 Guatemala	65.6	57	64	59	2,255	55.7	57	2	5	3,208	1,200
118 Namibia	55.9	59	57	34	2,120	..	100 d	10	3	4,027	1,970

HDI rank	Life expectancy at birth (years) 1994	Population with access to			Daily calorie supply per capita 1992	Adult literacy rate (%) 1994	Combined first- and second-level gross enrolment ratio (%) 1992-94	Daily news-papers (copies per 100 people) 1994	Televisions (per 100 people) 1994	Real GDP per capita (PPP$) 1994	GNP per capita (US$) 1994
		Health services (%) 1990-95	Safe water (%) 1990-96	Sanitation (%) 1990-96							
119 Morocco	65.3	70 c	55	41	2,985	42.1	59	1	7	3,681	1,140
120 Gabon	54.1	..	68 c	..	2,511	62.6	..	2	5	3,641 a	3,880
121 Viet Nam	66.0	90	43	22	2,250	93.0	73	1	11	1,208 a,c	200
122 Solomon Islands	70.8	..	..	..	2,222	62.0	64	..	2	2,118	810
123 Cape Verde	65.3	..	..	..	..	69.9	83	..	..	1,862	930
124 Vanuatu	65.9	..	..	..	2,744	64.0 f	66	..	1	2,276	1,150
125 São Tomé and Principe	67.0 h					67.0 h				1,704 a,c	250
126 Iraq	57.0	93 c	78	70	2,122	56.8	69	3	7	3,159 a,c	..
127 Nicaragua	67.3	83 c	53	60	2,296	65.3	79	3	15	1,580 a	340
128 Papua New Guinea	56.4	96 c	28	22	2,615	71.2	50	2	17	2,821	1,240
129 Zimbabwe	49.0	85	77	66	1,989	84.7	86	2	3	2,196	500
130 Congo	51.3	83 c	34	69	2,297	73.9	..	1	1	2,410	620
Low human development	56.1	70	71	35	2,262	50.0	60	..	4	1,306	306
Excluding India	52.5	52	59	42	2,115	48.5	49	1	3	1,261	287
131 Myanmar	58.4	60	60	43	2,598	82.7	65	2	8	1,051	..
132 Ghana	56.6	60	65	55	2,206	63.4	58	2	2	1,960	410
133 Cameroon	55.1	80	50	50	1,981	62.1	58	(.)	8	2,120	680
134 Kenya	53.6	77	53	77	2,075	77.0	72	1	2	1,404	250
135 Equatorial Guinea	48.6	..	..	..	..	77.8	..	(.)	9	1,673 a,c	430
136 Lao People's Dem. Rep.	51.7	67 c	52	28	2,259	55.8	67	(.)	1	2,484 a	320
137 Lesotho	57.9	80 c	56	28	2,201	70.5	72	1	1	1,109	720
138 India	61.3	85	81	29	2,395	51.2	72	..	6	1,348	320
139 Pakistan	62.3	55 c	74	47	2,316	37.1	42	2	2	2,154	430
140 Comoros	56.1	..	..	..	1,897	56.7	50	..	1	1,366	510
141 Nigeria	51.0	51	51	58	2,125	55.6	63	2	4	1,351	280
142 Zaire	52.2	26 c	42	18	2,060	76.4	49	(.)	(.)	429 a	..
143 Zambia	42.6	..	27	64	1,931	76.6	62	1	3	962	350
144 Bangladesh	56.4	45	97	48	2,019	37.3	46	1	1	1,331	220
145 Côte d'Ivoire	52.1	..	75	43	2,491	39.4	48	1	6	1,668	610
146 Benin	54.2	18 c	50	20	2,532	35.5	40	(.)	2	1,696	370
147 Togo	50.6	..	63	23	2,243	50.4	64	(.)	1	1,109 a,c	320
148 Yemen	56.2	38	61	24	2,203	..	70	2	27	805	280
149 Tanzania, U. Rep. of	50.3	42	38	86	2,021	66.8	44	1	(.)	656	140
150 Mauritania	52.1	63	66 c	..	2,685	36.9	44	(.)	4	1,593	480
151 Central African Rep.	48.3	52	38	52	1,691	57.2	42	(.)	1	1,130	370
152 Madagascar	57.2	38	29	3	2,135	45.8 i	42	(.)	2	694	200
153 Cambodia	52.4	53 c	36	14	2,021	35.0 f	75	..	1	1,084 a,c	..
154 Nepal	55.3	..	63	18	1,957	27.0	75	1	(.)	1,137	200
155 Bhutan	51.5	65 c	58	70	..	41.1	..	..	..	1,289	400
156 Haiti	54.4	60	28	24	1,707	44.1	40	1	1	896	230
157 Angola	47.2	..	32	16	1,840	..	45	1	3	..	..
158 Sudan	51.0	70	60	22	2,202	44.8	38	2	8	1,084 a,c	..
159 Uganda	40.2	49	38	64	2,162	61.1	44	(.)	2	1,370	190
160 Senegal	49.9	90	52	58	2,265	32.1	38	1	4	1,596	600
161 Malawi	41.1	35	37	6	1,827	55.8	87	(.)	..	694	170
162 Djibouti	48.8	..	..	..	..	45.0	26	..	5	1,270 a,c	..
163 Guinea-Bissau	43.2	40	59	30	2,556	53.9	38	1	..	793	240
164 Chad	47.0	30	24	21	1,989	47.0	49	(.)	(.)	700	180
165 Gambia	45.6	93	48	37	2,360	37.2	44	(.)	..	939 a	330
166 Mozambique	46.0	39 c	63	54	1,680	39.5	35	1	(.)	986	90
167 Guinea	45.1	80	55	21	2,390	34.8	30	..	1	1,103 a	520
168 Eritrea	50.1	..	..	..	..	25.0	32	..	1	960 a,c	..
169 Burundi	43.5	80	59	51	1,941	34.6	40	(.)	1	698	160
170 Ethiopia	48.2	46	25	19	1,610	34.5	20	(.)	(.)	427	100
171 Mali	46.6	40	45	31	2,279	29.3	20	(.)	1	543	250
172 Burkina Faso	46.4	90	78	18	2,387	18.7	25	(.)	1	796	300
173 Niger	47.1	99	54	15	2,257	13.1	19	(.)	2	787	230
174 Rwanda	22.6 j	80	..	..	1,821	59.2	50	(.)	(.)	352	80
175 Sierra Leone	33.6	38	34	11	1,695	30.3	36	(.)	1	643	160
All developing countries	61.8	80	71	39	2,553	69.7	74	4	14	2,908	1,053
Least developed countries	50.4	49	57	36	2,054	48.4	46	1	2	951	210
Sub-Saharan Africa	50.0	53	51	45	2,096	56.2	53	1	3	1,373	539
Industrial countries	74.1	..	..	..	..	..	98	26	50	15,986	17,221
World	63.2	..	..	..	..	..	78	10	22	5,806	4,797

a. Preliminary update of the Penn World Tables using an expanded set of international comparisons, as described in Summers and Heston 1991. b. Provisional. c. Data refer to a year or period other than that specified in the column heading, differ from the standard definition or refer to only part of the country. d. Capped at 100. e. Calculated using GNP-GDP ratio from UNDP 1996d. f. UNICEF 1997. g. UNESCO 1995b. h. World Bank 1995c. i. Human Development Report Office estimate based on national sources. j. 1985-90 data from UN 1996b.
Source: Column 1: UN 1996b; *columns 2-4:* UNICEF 1997; *column 5:* FAO 1994; *columns 6 and 7:* UNESCO 1996b; *column 8:* UNESCO 1995b; *column 9:* ITU 1996; *column 10:* World Bank 1997a; *column 11:* World Bank 1996g.

8 Trends in human development

HDI rank	Life expectancy at birth (years)		Infant mortality rate (per 1,000 live births)		Population with access to safe water (%)		Underweight children under age five (%)		Adult literacy rate (%)		Gross enrolment ratio for all levels (% age 6-23)		Real GDP per capita (PPP$)	
	1960	1994	1960	1994	1975-80	1990-96	1975	1990-96	1970	1994	1980	1994	1960	1994
High human development	56.5	71.5	90	25	58	87	22	15	80	92	60	68	2,189	8,397
22 Hong Kong	66.2	79.0	43	5	99	100	..	..	..	..	59	72	2,323	22,310
24 Cyprus	68.6	77.1	30	9	..	..	..	..	..	..	..	..	2,039	13,071 [a,b]
25 Barbados	64.2	75.9	74	8	..	..	..	..	..	..	67	76		
26 Singapore	64.5	77.1	36	5	..	..	..	..	..	..	53	72	2,409	20,987
28 Bahamas	63.2	72.9	50	13	..	..	..	..	..	..	70	75	..	..
29 Antigua and Barbuda	..	..	..	..	..	..	..	..	..	..	..	..	..	..
30 Chile	57.1	75.1	114	13	..	..	2	1	89	95	65	72	3,130	9,129
32 Korea, Rep. of	53.9	71.5	85	10	66	93	..	..	88	98	66	82	690	10,656
33 Costa Rica	61.6	76.6	85	13	72	96	10	2	88	95	55	68	2,160	5,919
36 Argentina	64.9	72.4	60	23	..	..	..	..	93	96	65	77	3,381	8,937
37 Uruguay	67.7	72.6	50	19	..	..	6	7	93	97	63	75	4,401	6,752
38 Brunei Darussalam	62.2	74.9	63	9	..	..	..	..	..	..	64	70	..	..
40 Trinidad and Tobago	63.3	72.9	56	15	93	97	14	7	..	..	59	67	4,754	9,124
41 Dominica	..	..	..	..	..	..	..	..	..	..	..	..	..	..
43 Bahrain	55.5	72.0	130	20	..	..	..	..	..	..	58	85	..	..
44 United Arab Emirates	53.0	74.2	145	17	..	..	..	..	..	..	44	82	..	..
45 Panama	60.7	73.2	69	24	77	93	14	7	81	91	66	70	1,533	6,104
46 Fiji	59.0	71.8	71	22	..	..	..	..	..	..	63	79	2,354	5,763
47 Venezuela	59.5	72.1	81	22	79	79	14	6	75	91	58	68	3,899	8,120
49 Saint Kitts and Nevis	..	..	..	..	..	..	..	..	..	..	..	..	..	..
50 Mexico	56.9	72.0	95	32	62	83	19	14	74	89	68	66	2,870	7,384
51 Colombia	56.5	70.1	99	26	64	85	19	8	78	91	53	70	1,874	6,107
52 Seychelles	..	..	..	..	..	..	..	..	..	..	..	..	..	..
53 Kuwait	59.5	75.2	89	17	..	..	..	..	54	78	..	..	..	..
54 Grenada	..	..	..	..	..	..	..	..	..	..	..	..	..	..
55 Qatar	53.0	70.9	145	19	..	..	..	..	..	..	60	73	..	..
56 Saint Lucia	..	..	..	..	..	..	..	..	..	..	..	..	..	..
57 Saint Vincent	..	..	..	..	..	..	..	..	..	..	..	..	..	..
59 Thailand	52.3	69.5	103	29	25	89	36	26	79	94	49	53	985	7,104
60 Malaysia	53.9	71.2	72	12	..	..	31	23	60	83	54	62	1,783	8,865
61 Mauritius	59.2	70.7	70	17	99	99	32	16	..	..	48	61	2,113	13,172
63 Belize	61.4	74.0	74	31	..	..	..	..	..	..	..	..	..	..
64 Libyan Arab Jamahiriya	46.7	63.8	160	64	87	97	..	..	37	75	..	..	..	..
Medium human development	47.6	67.2	143	46	..	..	29	19	..	..	51	62	902	3,288
Excluding China	48.3	65.7	135	49	45	73	33	21	55	79	52	65	1,217	4,275
65 Lebanon	59.6	69.0	68	32	..	..	..	..	69	92	67	75		
66 Suriname	60.1	70.7	70	26	..	..	..	..	..	..	..	..	2,234	4,711
68 Brazil	54.7	66.4	116	45	62	73	18	7	66	83	54	72	1,404	5,362
70 Iran, Islamic Rep. of	49.5	68.2	169	40	51	90	43	16	29	69	46	68	1,985	5,766
72 Ecuador	53.1	69.3	124	47	36	68	20	17	72	90	69	72	1,461	4,626
73 Saudi Arabia	44.4	70.3	170	27	64	95 [c]	..	..	9	62	36	56	..	..
74 Turkey	50.1	68.2	190	44	68	80	15	10	52	82	44	63	1,669	5,193
75 Korea, Dem. People's Rep. of	54.0	71.4	86	23	..	..	..	..	..	..	..	..	..	..
78 Syrian Arab Rep.	49.8	67.8	135	37	..	..	20	12	40	70	60	64	..	..
81 Tunisia	48.3	68.4	159	41	35	98	17	9	31	65	50	67	1,394	5,319
82 Algeria	47.0	67.8	168	51	77	78	23	13	25	59	52	66	1,676	5,442
83 Jamaica	62.7	73.9	63	13	86	86	14	10	97	84	67	65	1,829	3,816
84 Jordan	46.9	68.5	135	33	..	..	18	9	47	86	..	..	1,328	4,187
86 Cuba	63.8	75.6	65	9	..	..	..	..	87	95	72	63	..	..
87 Dominican Rep.	51.8	70.0	125	38	55	65	17	10	67	82	60	68	1,227	3,933
88 Oman	40.1	70.0	214	28	..	..	..	..	..	..	28	60	2,040	10,078
89 Peru	47.7	67.4	142	52	..	..	17	11	71	88	65	81	2,130	3,645
90 South Africa	49.0	63.7	89	51	..	..	..	..	..	..	..	..	2,984	4,291
91 Sri Lanka	62.0	72.2	71	16	19	57	58	38	77	90	58	66	1,389	3,277
94 Paraguay	63.9	68.8	66	42	13	42	9	4	80	92	49	62	1,220	3,531
96 Samoa (Western)	49.8	68.1	134	62	..	..	..	..	..	..	..	..	..	..
97 Botswana	46.5	52.3	116	55	..	..	..	..	41	69	51	71	474	5,367
98 Philippines	52.8	67.0	79	36	..	..	39	30	83	94	61	78	1,183	2,681
99 Indonesia	41.2	63.5	139	53	11	62	51	35	54	83	51	62	490	3,740
101 Mongolia	46.8	64.4	128	57	..	..	..	..	..	..	60	52	..	..
104 Guyana	56.0	63.2	100	62	..	..	..	..	..	..	61	67	1,630	2,729
108 China	47.1	68.9	150	43	..	..	26	16	..	..	50	58	723	2,604
109 Egypt	46.1	64.3	179	63	75	79	17	9	35	51	51	69	557	3,846
111 Maldives	43.6	62.8	160	53	..	..	..	..	..	..	..	..	..	..
112 El Salvador	50.5	69.3	130	41	53	69	22	11	57	71	47	55	1,305	2,417
113 Bolivia	42.7	60.1	167	71	34	66	17	16	57	83	54	66	1,142	2,598
114 Swaziland	40.2	58.3	157	72	..	..	..	..	..	..	59	72	1,182	2,821
116 Honduras	46.3	68.4	145	40	41	87	23	18	53	72	47	6	901	2,050
117 Guatemala	45.6	65.6	125	45	39	64	30	27	44	56	35	46	1,667	3,208
118 Namibia	42.5	55.9	146	63	..	..	..	..	..	..	..	..	..	..

HDI rank	Life expectancy at birth (years)		Infant mortality rate (per 1,000 live births)		Population with access to safe water (%)		Underweight children under age five (%)		Adult literacy rate (%)		Gross enrolment ratio for all levels (% age 6-23)		Real GDP per capita (PPP$)	
	1960	1994	1960	1994	1975-80	1990-96	1975	1990-96	1970	1994	1980	1994	1960	1994
119 Morocco	46.7	65.3	163	58	..	..	19	9	22	42	38	46	854	3,681
120 Gabon	40.8	54.1	171	91	..	..	..	..	33	63	..	..	1,373	3,641 [a]
121 Viet Nam	44.2	66.0	147	41	..	..	55	45	..	..	52	55	..	..
122 Solomon Islands	50.3	70.8	120	25	..	..	..	..	..	..	..	..	..	..
123 Cape Verde	52.0	65.3	110	48	..	..	..	..	..	..	45	64	..	..
124 Vanuatu	46.5	65.9	141	44	..	..	..	..	..	..	..	..	..	..
125 São Tomé and Principe	..	..	..	..	..	..	..	..	..	..	..	..	..	..
126 Iraq	48.5	57.0	139	146	66	78	19	12	34	57	67	53	..	..
127 Nicaragua	47.0	67.3	141	48	46	53	20	12	..	..	53	62	1,756	1,580 [a]
128 Papua New Guinea	40.6	56.4	165	68	20	28	39	35	32	71	28	38	1,136	2,821
129 Zimbabwe	45.3	49.0	109	70	..	..	25	16	55	85	41	68	937	2,196
130 Congo	41.7	51.3	140	90	38	34	43	24	35	74	..	..	1,092	2,410
Low human development	42.1	56.4	167	85	..	..	60	46	32	50	37	47	657	1,337
Excluding India	40.0	52.7	169	94	22	54	44	39	28	49	34	39	716	1,324
131 Myanmar	43.7	58.4	158	86	17	60	41	43	71	83	39	48	341	1,051
132 Ghana	45.0	56.6	132	79	35	65	35	27	31	63	48	44	1,049	1,960
133 Cameroon	39.2	55.1	163	62	..	..	19	14	33	62	48	46	736	2,120
134 Kenya	44.7	53.6	124	70	17	53	25	23	32	77	62	55	635	1,404
135 Equatorial Guinea	36.8	48.6	188	114	..	..	..	..	..	..	57	64	..	..
136 Lao People's Dem. Rep.	40.4	51.7	155	93	..	..	..	..	..	..	44	50	..	..
137 Lesotho	42.9	57.9	149	79	17	56	20	21	..	..	52	56	346	1,109
138 India	44.0	61.3	165	74	..	..	71	53	34	51	40	56	617	1,348
139 Pakistan	43.5	62.3	163	80	25	74	47	38	21	37	19	38	820	2,154
140 Comoros	42.5	56.1	165	88	..	..	..	..	..	..	45	39	..	..
141 Nigeria	39.5	51.0	189	82	..	..	30	36	25	56	50	50	1,133	1,351
142 Zaire	41.3	52.2	153	94	19	42	..	..	42	76	46	38	..	..
143 Zambia	41.5	42.6	135	110	42	27	17	28	52	77	46	48	1,172	962
144 Bangladesh	39.6	56.4	156	85	..	..	84	67	24	37	30	39	621	1,331
145 Côte d'Ivoire	39.2	52.1	165	89	..	..	18	24	18	39	39	39	1,021	1,668
146 Benin	36.9	54.2	179	87	34	50	..	..	16	36	34	35	1,075	1,696
147 Togo	39.3	50.6	182	89	16	63	25	24	17	50	61	50	411	1,109
148 Yemen	35.8	56.2	224	88	..	..	33	39	..	..	..	..	..	..
149 Tanzania, U. Rep. of	40.5	50.3	147	85	39	38	25	29	..	..	44	34	272	656
150 Mauritania	38.5	52.1	177	98	..	..	39	23	..	..	19	36	930	1,593
151 Central African Rep.	38.5	48.3	174	99	..	..	..	..	16	57	33	37	806	1,130
152 Madagascar	40.7	57.2	178	87	..	..	30	34	..	..	60	33	1,013	694
153 Cambodia	42.4	52.4	146	112	..	..	..	..	..	..	..	..	..	..
154 Nepal	38.3	55.3	195	92	8	63	..	..	13	27	28	55	584	1,137
155 Bhutan	37.3	51.5	203	113	..	..	..	..	..	..	..	..	..	..
156 Haiti	42.1	54.4	182	87	12	28	26	28	22	44	..	..	921	896
157 Angola	33.0	47.2	208	120	17	32	..	..	..	..	54	31	..	..
158 Sudan	39.2	51.0	160	86	..	..	..	..	17	45	25	31	..	..
159 Uganda	43.0	40.2	133	121	35	38	28	23	41	61	25	34	371	1,370
160 Senegal	37.2	49.9	172	66	36	52	19	20	12	32	24	31	1,136	1,596
161 Malawi	37.8	41.1	206	147	51	37	19	30	..	..	33	67	423	694
162 Djibouti	36.0	48.8	186	113	..	..	..	..	..	..	19	20	..	..
163 Guinea-Bissau	34.0	43.2	200	138	10	59	..	..	..	..	27	29	..	..
164 Chad	34.8	47.0	195	121	..	..	..	..	11	47	16	25	785	700
165 Gambia	32.3	45.6	213	129	..	..	..	..	..	..	23	34	411	939
166 Mozambique	37.3	46.0	190	116	..	..	..	..	22	40	29	25	1,368	986
167 Guinea	33.5	45.1	203	131	14	55	..	..	14	35	21	24	..	..
168 Eritrea	39.1	50.1	166	103	..	..	..	..	..	..	..	..	..	..
169 Burundi	41.3	43.5	153	122	29	59	27	37	20	35	11	31	473	698
170 Ethiopia	35.9	48.2	187	115	8	25	45	48	..	..	16	18	262	427
171 Mali	34.8	46.6	209	156	..	..	36	31	8	29	..	..	541	543
172 Burkina Faso	36.1	46.4	186	101	25	78	34	30	8	19	8	20	290	796
173 Niger	35.3	47.1	191	121	..	..	50	36	4	13	12	15	604	787
174 Rwanda	42.3	23.1 [c]	150	145	..	..	37	29	32	59	33	37	538	352
175 Sierra Leone	31.5	33.6	219	200	14	34	22	29	13	30	30	28	871	643
All developing countries	46.0	62.1	149	64	41	69	41	32	43	64	46	56	915	2,923
Least developed countries	39.1	50.6	170	103	..	..	..	..	..	..	32	36	561	974
Sub-Saharan Africa	39.9	49.9	166	97	24	42	31	32	27	56	39	39	990	1,460
Industrial countries	68.6	73.8	39	14	..	..	..	..	..	..	..	..	..	..
World	50.2	63.6	129	58	..	..	..	..	..	..	..	..	..	..

a. Preliminary update of the Penn World Tables using an expanded set of international comparisons, as described in Summers and Heston 1991.
b. Provisional.
c. 1985-90 data from UN 1996b.
Source: Columns 1-4: calculated on the basis of estimates from UN 1996b; *columns 5-8:* UNICEF 1997; *columns 9-12:* UNESCO 1996b; *columns 13 and 14:* calculated on the basis of estimates from World Bank 1997a.

	Index: North=100 (see note)									
	Life expectancy at birth		Adult literacy		Daily calorie supply per capita		Access to safe water		Under-five mortality	
HDI rank	1960	1994	1970	1994	1965	1992	1975-80	1990-96	1960	1995
High human development	82	97	81	93	83	91	59	88	36	84
22 Hong Kong	97	100+	..	..	..	..	100	100+	79	100+
24 Cyprus	100	100+	..	..	..	..	..	..	..	..
25 Barbados	94	100+	..	..	..	..	..	..	..	..
26 Singapore	94	100+	..	..	..	..	..	..	100	100+
28 Bahamas	92	99	..	..	..	..	..	..	..	..
29 Antigua and Barbuda	..	..	..	..	..	..	..	..	..	..
30 Chile	83	100+	90	96	87	83	..	..	30	100+
32 Korea, Rep. of	79	97	89	99	77	100	67	94	33	100+
33 Costa Rica	90	100+	89	96	84	93	73	97	36	100+
36 Argentina	95	98	94	97	96	92	..	..	60	67
37 Uruguay	99	98	94	98	85	88	..	..	87	86
38 Brunei Darussalam	91	100+	..	..	..	..	..	..	..	..
40 Trinidad and Tobago	92	99	..	..	83	83	94	98	56	100
41 Dominica	..	..	..	..	..	..	..	..	..	..
43 Bahrain	81	98	..	..	..	..	..	..	..	..
44 United Arab Emirates	77	100+	..	..	..	..	..	..	17	95
45 Panama	88	99	82	91	79	72	78	94	39	90
46 Fiji	86	97	..	..	..	..	..	..	..	..
47 Venezuela	87	98	76	92	76	84	80	80	58	75
49 Saint Kitts and Nevis	..	..	..	..	..	..	..	..	..	..
50 Mexico	83	98	75	90	90	100	63	84	28	56
51 Colombia	82	95	79	92	76	86	65	86	31	50
52 Seychelles	..	..	..	..	..	..	..	..	..	..
53 Kuwait	87	100+	55	79	..	..	..	..	32	100+
54 Grenada	..	..	..	..	..	..	..	..	..	..
55 Qatar	77	96	..	..	..	..	..	..	..	..
56 Saint Lucia	..	..	..	..	..	..	..	..	..	..
57 Saint Vincent	..	..	..	..	..	..	..	..	..	..
59 Thailand	76	94	80	94	77	78	25	90	28	56
60 Malaysia	79	96	61	84	81	93	..	..	39	100+
61 Mauritius	86	96	..	..	83	87	100	100	49	78
63 Belize	90	100	..	..	..	..	..	..	* ..	
64 Libyan Arab Jamahiriya	68	87	37	76	67	100	88	98	15	29
Medium human development	70	91	..	..	71	87	..	..	21	37
Excluding China	70	89	56	80	74	87	..	..	23	36
65 Lebanon	87	93	70	93	80	100	..	..	48	45
66 Suriname	88	96	..	..	..	..	..	..	..	..
68 Brazil	80	90	67	84	81	91	63	74	23	30
70 Iran, Islamic Rep. of	72	92	29	69	70	92	52	91	18	45
72 Ecuador	77	94	73	91	67	83	36	69	23	45
73 Saudi Arabia	65	95	9	62	64	88	65	96	14	53
74 Turkey	73	92	53	82	85	100	69	81	19	36
75 Korea, Dem. People's Rep. of	79	97	..	..	80	91	..	..	34	60
78 Syrian Arab Rep.	73	92	40	71	72	100	..	..	20	50
81 Tunisia	70	93	31	66	76	100	35	99	17	49
82 Algeria	69	92	25	60	58	93	78	79	17	30
83 Jamaica	91	100	98	85	81	84	87	87	54	100+
84 Jordan	68	93	47	86	75	97	..	..	27	72
86 Cuba	93	100+	88	96	82	91	..	..	82	100+
87 Dominican Rep.	75	95	68	82	..	..	56	66	27	41
88 Oman	58	95	..	..	..	..	..	..	14	72
89 Peru	70	91	72	89	79	60	..	..	17	33
90 South Africa	71	86	..	..	86	87	..	..	32	27
91 Sri Lanka	90	98	78	91	81	73	19	58	31	95
94 Paraguay	93	93	81	93	90	86	13	42	45	53
96 Samoa (Western)	73	92	..	..	..	..	..	..	..	..
97 Botswana	68	71	41	69	71	73	..	..	24	35
98 Philippines	77	91	84	95	66	73	..	..	40	34
99 Indonesia	60	86	55	84	65	88	11	63	19	24
101 Mongolia	68	87	..	..	85	61	..	..	22	24
104 Guyana	82	86	..	..	..	..	..	..	..	..
108 China	69	93	..	..	69	88	..	..	20	38
109 Egypt	67	87	35	51	78	100	76	80	16	35
111 Maldives	64	85	..	..	..	..	..	..	..	..
112 El Salvador	74	94	58	72	65	86	54	70	19	45
113 Bolivia	62	81	58	83	62	67	34	67	16	17
114 Swaziland	59	79	..	..	..	..	..	..	..	..
116 Honduras	67	93	54	73	70	74	41	88	20	47
117 Guatemala	66	89	44	56	75	72	39	65	20	27
118 Namibia	62	76	..	..	..	..	..	..	20	23

	Index: North=100 (see note)									
	Life expectancy at birth		Adult literacy		Daily calorie supply per capita		Access to safe water		Under-five mortality	
HDI rank	1960	1994	1970	1994	1965	1992	1975-80	1990-96	1960	1995
119 Morocco	68	88	22	43	74	96	..	..	19	24
120 Gabon	59	73	33	63	65	81	..	..	14	12
121 Viet Nam	64	89	..	..	78	72	..	..	19	40
122 Solomon Islands	73	96	..	..	..	..	..	..	..	..
123 Cape Verde	76	88	..	..	..	..	..	..	..	..
124 Vanuatu	68	89	..	..	..	..	..	..	..	..
125 São Tomé and Principe	..	..	..	..	..	..	..	..	..	..
126 Iraq	71	77	34	57	72	68	67	79	24	25
127 Nicaragua	69	91	..	..	86	74	46	54	20	30
128 Papua New Guinea	59	76	32	72	58	84	20	28	16	19
129 Zimbabwe	66	66	56	86	70	64	..	..	23	24
130 Congo	61	69	35	75	81	74	38	34	19	17
Low human development	61	76	32	51	72	73	..	..	17	14
Excluding India	58	71	28	50	71	68	..	..	16	12
131 Myanmar	64	79	72	84	72	83	17	61	17	12
132 Ghana	66	77	31	64	70	71	35	66	19	14
133 Cameroon	57	75	33	63	81	64	..	..	15	17
134 Kenya	65	73	32	78	79	67	17	54	20	20
135 Equatorial Guinea	54	66	..	..	..	..	..	..	..	..
136 Lao People's Dem. Rep.	59	70	..	..	69	73	..	..	18	13
137 Lesotho	63	78	..	..	72	71	17	57	20	12
138 India	64	83	34	52	72	77	..	..	17	16
139 Pakistan	63	84	21	37	61	74	25	75	18	13
140 Comoros	62	76	..	..	..	..	..	..	..	..
141 Nigeria	58	69	25	56	77	68	..	..	20	9
142 Zaire	60	71	42	77	79	66	19	42	14	10
143 Zambia	61	58	53	77	73	62	42	27	19	9
144 Bangladesh	58	76	24	38	73	65	..	..	17	16
145 Côte d'Ivoire	57	71	18	40	82	80	..	..	14	12
146 Benin	54	73	16	36	71	81	34	51	13	13
147 Togo	57	69	17	51	81	72	16	64	15	14
148 Yemen	52	76	..	..	..	..	..	..	12	16
149 Tanzania, U. Rep. of	59	68	..	..	69	65	39	38	16	11
150 Mauritania	56	71	..	..	71	86	..	..	13	9
151 Central African Rep.	56	66	16	58	73	54	..	..	14	11
152 Madagascar	59	78	..	..	87	69	..	..	11	11
153 Cambodia	62	71	..	..	79	65	..	..	19	10
154 Nepal	56	75	13	27	70	63	8	64	14	16
155 Bhutan	54	70	..	..	..	..	..	..	13	10
156 Haiti	61	74	22	45	71	55	12	28	16	15
157 Angola	48	64	..	..	65	59	17	32	12	6
158 Sudan	57	69	17	45	64	71	..	..	14	16
159 Uganda	63	54	41	62	77	69	35	38	19	10
160 Senegal	54	68	12	32	84	73	36	53	13	16
161 Malawi	55	56	..	..	73	59	52	37	11	8
162 Djibouti	52	66	..	..	..	..	..	..	..	..
163 Guinea-Bissau	50	59	..	..	..	..	10	60	12	8
164 Chad	51	64	11	47	80	64	..	..	13	12
165 Gambia	47	62	..	..	..	..	..	..	11	16
166 Mozambique	54	62	22	40	69	54	..	..	12	7
167 Guinea	49	61	14	35	65	77	14	56	12	8
168 Eritrea	57	68	..	..	..	..	..	..	..	..
169 Burundi	60	59	20	35	83	62	29	60	16	10
170 Ethiopia	52	65	..	..	62	52	8	25	14	9
171 Mali	51	63	8	30	67	73	..	..	10	9
172 Burkina Faso	53	63	8	19	73	77	25	79	13	11
173 Niger	51	64	4	13	69	72	..	..	13	6
174 Rwanda	62	31	32	60	59	58	..	..	21	13
175 Sierra Leone	46	46	13	31	64	54	14	34	11	6
All developing countries	67	84	43	64	72	82	..	..	21	29
Least developed countries	57	68	..	..	71	66	..	..	15	12
Sub-Saharan Africa	58	68	27	56	75	67	100	100	17	12
Industrial countries	100	100	100	100	100	100	100	100	100	100
World	73	86	..	..	..	..	..	..	..	..

Note: North refers to the industrial countries. All figures are expressed in relation to the North average, which is indexed to equal 100. The smaller the figure the bigger the gap, the closer the figure to 100 the smaller the gap, and a figure of 100+ indicates that the country exceeds the North average for that indicator.
Source: Columns 1 and 2: UN 1996b; *columns 3 and 4:* UNESCO 1996b; *columns 5 and 6:* FAO 1994; *columns 7-10:* UNICEF 1997.

10 Women and capabilities

HDI rank	Female net enrolment				Female tertiary students		Female life expectancy at birth		Total fertility	
	Primary		Secondary		Per 100,000 women 1992	Index (1980=100) 1992	Years 1994	Index (1970=100) 1994	Rate 1994	Index (1970=100) 1994
	Ratio 1992	Index (1980=100) 1992	Ratio 1992	Index (1980=100) 1992						
High human development	94	..	..	..	1,749	..	74	117	2.7	52
22 Hong Kong	..	..	..	..	1,320	182	82	110	1.4	39
24 Cyprus	99	99	96	109	859	336	79	109	2.3	87
25 Barbados	88	91	75	88	1,885	114	78	110	2.0	66
26 Singapore	..	..	..	..	..	..	79	112	2.0	66
28 Bahamas	96	..	89	..	..	..	77	110	1.4	43
29 Antigua and Barbuda	..	..	..	..	..	..	..	..	..	..
30 Chile	84	..	55	..	..	..	78	119	2.4	59
32 Korea, Rep. of	100	100	85	131	2,866	338	75	120	1.3	28
33 Costa Rica	88	98	38	88	..	..	79	115	2.9	58
36 Argentina	95	..	62	..	..	..	76	109	2.6	85
37 Uruguay	93	..	..	..	..	..	76	105	2.2	75
38 Brunei Darussalam	86	105	64	119	..	..	78	114	2.7	47
40 Trinidad and Tobago	88	95	67	105	440	99	75	111	1.6	45
41 Dominica	..	..	..	..	..	..	..	..	..	..
43 Bahrain	100	132	87	171	2,011	371	75	117	3.0	46
44 United Arab Emirates	99	132	79	..	1,185	268	76	121	3.5	53
45 Panama	92	103	53	108	..	..	75	113	2.6	48
46 Fiji	100	109	..	..	..	..	74	113	2.8	60
47 Venezuela	90	..	24	150	..	..	75	111	3.0	56
49 Saint Kitts and Nevis	..	..	..	..	..	..	..	..	..	..
50 Mexico	..	..	..	..	1,333	146	75	117	2.7	41
51 Colombia	..	..	..	..	1,578	174	73	116	2.7	49
52 Seychelles	..	..	..	..	..	..	..	..	..	..
53 Kuwait	..	..	..	..	1,569	118	78	114	2.5	36
54 Grenada	..	..	..	..	..	..	..	..	..	..
55 Qatar	78	94	72	139	3,072	183	75	119	3.9	56
56 Saint Lucia	..	..	..	..	..	..	..	..	..	..
57 Saint Vincent	..	..	..	..	..	..	..	..	..	..
59 Thailand	..	..	..	..	2,138	..	72	120	1.0	18
60 Malaysia	..	..	..	..	640	197	74	117	3.4	61
61 Mauritius	94	119	..	..	313	482	74	115	2.7	72
63 Belize	95	..	37	..	..	..	75	112	4.0	63
64 Libyan Arab Jamahiriya	96	..	..	..	1,486	417	66	124	6.4	85
Medium human development	93	..	..	..	538	244	69	120	2.7	46
Excluding China	88	..	..	..	1,145	256	68	124	3.5	58
65 Lebanon	..	..	..	..	2,482	118	71	108	2.8	51
66 Suriname	..	..	..	..	1,127	..	73	112	2.3	42
68 Brazil	..	..	..	..	1,220	107	71	116	1.8	36
70 Iran, Islamic Rep. of	93	..	..	..	764	398	69	127	5.2	78
72 Ecuador	..	..	..	..	..	..	72	121	3.2	51
73 Saudi Arabia	57	154	30	188	1,215	310	72	135	6.4	88
74 Turkey	..	..	..	..	1,111	550	71	121	1.9	36
75 Korea, Dem. People's Rep. of	..	..	..	..	..	..	74	120	2.1	33
78 Syrian Arab Rep.	92	115	39	130	1,419	147	70	122	4.7	61
81 Tunisia	93	129	40	222	869	290	69	128	2.8	43
82 Algeria	89	125	50	208	844	307	69	128	4.1	55
83 Jamaica	100	103	68	100	663	..	76	110	2.6	49
84 Jordan	89	98	37	62	1,906	161	70	126	5.5	70
86 Cuba	98	103	..	..	2,134	140	78	108	1.0	26
87 Dominican Rep.	83	114	29	..	..	..	72	120	2.8	45
88 Oman	71	222	..	..	413	..	72	151	7.2	100
89 Peru	..	..	..	..	..	..	70	127	3.1	49
90 South Africa	93	..	49	..	1,168	..	67	120	4.0	69
91 Sri Lanka	..	..	..	..	402	158	75	114	1.7	38
94 Paraguay	96	112	29	..	832	..	71	105	4.4	74
96 Samoa (Western)	..	..	..	..	..	..	70	119	4.0	55
97 Botswana	100	122	45	265	280	354	54	101	4.8	71
98 Philippines	..	..	..	..	3,140	111	69	118	3.8	67
99 Indonesia	95	115	34	..	751	331	65	134	2.5	47
101 Mongolia	..	..	..	..	..	..	66	122	3.1	43
104 Guyana	..	..	..	..	499	178	67	108	2.3	42
108 China	95	..	..	..	132	236	71	114	1.0	19
109 Egypt	82	..	60	..	1,056	101	66	126	3.5	57
111 Maldives	..	..	..	..	..	..	62	127	6.8	97
112 El Salvador	71	..	..	..	1,281	564	73	123	3.2	50
113 Bolivia	87	118	27	193	..	..	62	128	4.7	73
114 Swaziland	93	..	..	..	311	120	61	126	4.8	73
116 Honduras	91	117	..	..	726	133	71	130	4.8	67
117 Guatemala	..	..	..	..	..	..	68	128	5.3	81
118 Namibia	93	..	35	..	382	..	57	117	5.2	87

HDI rank	Female net enrolment Primary		Female net enrolment Secondary		Female tertiary students		Female life expectancy at birth		Total fertility	
	Ratio 1992	Index (1980=100) 1992	Ratio 1992	Index (1980=100) 1992	Per 100,000 women 1992	Index (1980=100) 1992	Years 1994	Index (1970=100) 1994	Rate 1994	Index (1970=100) 1994
119 Morocco	53	113	24	150	715	262	67	126	3.4	49
120 Gabon	..	..	..	..	225	239	56	122	5.0	119
121 Viet Nam	..	..	..	..	..	..	68	132	3.0	50
122 Solomon Islands	..	..	..	..	..	..	73	118	5.3	78
123 Cape Verde	99	113	..	..	..	..	66	114	3.6	51
124 Vanuatu	..	..	..	..	..	..	68	126	4.6	69
125 São Tomé and Principe	..	..	..	..	..	..	..	..	..	..
126 Iraq	74	79	30	97	..	..	58	104	5.7	79
127 Nicaragua	81	110	28	112	819	80	70	126	4.2	61
128 Papua New Guinea	..	..	..	..	..	..	57	124	5.0	82
129 Zimbabwe	..	..	..	..	320	198	50	96	5.2	70
130 Congo	..	..	..	..	190	151	54	111	6.3	101
Low human development	..	..	..	..	..	..	57	123	4.6	73
Excluding India	..	..	..	..	129	..	54	120	5.7	85
131 Myanmar	..	..	..	..	60	120	60	120	3.3	55
132 Ghana	..	..	..	..	54	92	59	115	5.7	85
133 Cameroon	71	111	..	..	..	..	57	123	5.7	92
134 Kenya	..	..	..	..	102	340	55	106	5.5	67
135 Equatorial Guinea	..	..	..	..	41	..	50	122	5.9	104
136 Lao People's Dem. Rep.	57	..	13	..	60	214	53	127	6.7	109
137 Lesotho	75	96	22	129	209	111	59	118	5.2	90
138 India	..	..	..	..	..	..	61	127	3.0	54
139 Pakistan	..	..	..	..	149	139	63	129	5.5	78
140 Comoros	46	..	..	..	14	..	57	120	6.0	85
141 Nigeria	..	..	..	..	192	..	53	119	6.4	100
142 Zaire	47	78	12	..	..	..	54	115	6.7	108
143 Zambia	..	..	..	..	..	..	43	90	6.0	88
144 Bangladesh	66	138	12	200	132	169	57	131	2.9	42
145 Côte d'Ivoire	..	..	..	..	..	..	54	117	5.8	78
146 Benin	35	..	..	..	60	102	57	128	6.3	90
147 Togo	58	97	..	..	60	113	52	114	6.6	100
148 Yemen	..	..	..	..	147	..	57	138	7.6	100
149 Tanzania, U. Rep. of	..	..	..	..	..	..	52	110	5.9	87
150 Mauritania	..	..	..	..	104	..	54	122	5.4	82
151 Central African Rep.	46	112	..	..	55	458	51	113	5.2	92
152 Madagascar	..	..	..	..	278	..	59	126	6.1	93
153 Cambodia	..	..	..	..	..	..	54	121	4.9	83
154 Nepal	..	..	..	..	270	267	55	132	5.4	89
155 Bhutan	..	..	..	..	..	..	53	131	5.9	100
156 Haiti	26	70	..	..	..	..	56	115	4.7	80
157 Angola	..	..	..	..	..	..	49	127	7.2	111
158 Sudan	..	..	..	..	245	292	52	119	4.9	74
159 Uganda	..	..	..	..	63	315	41	86	7.1	103
160 Senegal	42	140	..	..	117	130	51	126	6.1	87
161 Malawi	48	126	2	..	37	109	42	101	7.2	99
162 Djibouti	26	..	..	..	..	..	50	121	5.8	86
163 Guinea-Bissau	..	..	..	..	..	..	45	119	5.8	109
164 Chad	..	..	..	..	..	..	49	123	5.9	98
165 Gambia	46	139	12	..	..	..	47	126	5.6	86
166 Mozambique	37	112	5	250	16	320	48	110	6.5	100
167 Guinea	..	..	..	..	28	18	46	123	7.0	100
168 Eritrea	24	..	10	..	..	..	52	115	5.8	92
169 Burundi	47	294	4	200	38	173	45	99	6.8	100
170 Ethiopia	..	..	..	..	25	227	50	120	7.0	103
171 Mali	14	..	3	..	19	136	48	123	7.1	100
172 Burkina Faso	24	218	5	250	28	280	48	115	7.2	94
173 Niger	18	..	3	150	18	180	49	122	7.4	94
174 Rwanda	71	125	7	..	19	380	23	49	6.6	81
175 Sierra Leone	..	..	..	..	..	..	35	98	6.5	101
All developing countries	86	..	..	..	559	..	63	121	3.6	60
Least developed countries	..	..	..	..	109	..	52	118	5.6	84
Sub-Saharan Africa	54	..	..	..	222	227	52	114	6.2	93
Industrial countries	96	..	..	..	3,407	134	78	106	1.8	73
World	89	..	..	..	1,377	212	65	119	3.4	61

Source: Columns 1, 3 and 5: UNESCO 1995b; columns 2, 4 and 6: calculated on the basis of data from UNESCO 1995b; columns 7-10: UN 1996b.

11 Women and political and economic participation

HDI rank	Administrators and managers		Professional and technical workers		Clerical and sales workers		Service workers		Women in government		
	Female (%) 1990	Female as % of male 1990	Female (%) 1990	Female as % of male 1990	Female (%) 1990	Female as % of male 1990	Female (%) 1990	Female as % of male 1990	Total[a] (%) 1995	At ministerial level[a] (%) 1995	At sub-ministerial level[a] (%) 1995
High human development	18	23	46	86	47	90	56	136	7	9	7
22 Hong Kong	16	19	42	72	51	104	41	70	..	..	..
24 Cyprus	10	11	41	69	50	100	45	83	5	8	3
25 Barbados	37	59	52	109	65	184	57	132	23	33	24
26 Singapore	34	52	16	19	..	..	41	69	5	0	7
28 Bahamas	26	36	57	132	70	235	62	162	34	20	38
29 Antigua and Barbuda	..	..	..	..	..	..	..	..	30	0	47
30 Chile	17	21	34	52	46	86	73	263	12	16	10
32 Korea, Rep. of	4	4	45	82	44	79	61	156	2	3	1
33 Costa Rica	21	27	45	82	40	68	59	146	21	15	24
36 Argentina	..	..	..	..	..	..	..	..	3	0	4
37 Uruguay	25	34	63	167	46	85	68	210	3	0	5
38 Brunei Darussalam	11	13	35	54	52	109	40	67	2	0	3
40 Trinidad and Tobago	23	30	53	114	59	144	53	112	14	20	10
41 Dominica	36	56	57	130	..	..	69	200	31	8	39
43 Bahrain	..	..	..	..	..	..	..	..	0	0	0
44 United Arab Emirates	2	2	25	34	8	8	25	32	0	0	0
45 Panama	28	38	49	97	58	135	56	126	11	11	11
46 Fiji	10	11	45	81	38	62	48	93	10	9	11
47 Venezuela	18	21	55	123	46	84	58	136	6	4	9
49 Saint Kitts and Nevis	..	..	..	..	..	..	..	..	21	10	28
50 Mexico	20	25	44	77	42	71	45	82	7	14	4
51 Colombia	27	37	42	72	46	84	70	229	25	11	29
52 Seychelles	29	40	58	139	59	143	59	141	21	31	19
53 Kuwait	5	6	37	58	19	23	46	85	6	0	9
54 Grenada	32	46	53	113	64	178	58	140	19	10	24
55 Qatar	1	1	27	37	6	7	27	36	2	0	3
56 Saint Lucia	..	..	..	..	..	..	..	..	5	8	0
57 Saint Vincent	..	..	..	..	..	..	..	..	25	10	50
59 Thailand	22	28	52	110	57	134	56	128	4	4	5
60 Malaysia	12	14	45	80	..	..	..	..	6	8	5
61 Mauritius	14	17	41	71	31	44	41	70	7	4	8
63 Belize	37	58	39	63	..	..	..	..	10	0	14
64 Libyan Arab Jamahiriya	..	..	..	..	..	..	..	..	0	0	0
Medium human development	13	15	44	83	38	66	48	104	5	6	5
Excluding China	14	18	43	84	..	..	41	97	7	5	8
65 Lebanon	..	..	..	..	..	..	..	..	0	0	0
66 Suriname	22	27	70	232	49	96	60	150	14	0	21
68 Brazil	17	21	57	133	..	..	..	..	13	4	15
70 Iran, Islamic Rep. of	4	4	33	48	5	5	7	8	0	0	1
72 Ecuador	32	46	48	92	41	70	64	174	10	7	10
73 Saudi Arabia	..	..	..	..	..	..	..	..	0	0	0
74 Turkey	7	7	29	42	16	20	10	11	5	3	6
75 Korea, Dem. People's Rep. of	..	..	..	..	..	..	..	..	1	1	1
78 Syrian Arab Rep.	..	..	..	..	..	..	..	..	4	7	2
81 Tunisia	7	8	18	21	..	..	..	..	5	3	7
82 Algeria	6	6	28	38	11	13	19	23	2	0	3
83 Jamaica	..	..	60	147	..	..	72	255	13	6	16
84 Jordan	..	..	..	..	..	..	..	..	7	3	0
86 Cuba	19	23	48	91	..	..	..	..	8	4	10
87 Dominican Rep.	21	27	50	98	..	..	..	..	12	3	16
88 Oman	..	..	..	..	..	..	..	..	4	0	4
89 Peru	20	25	41	70	52	109	38	60	10	6	11
90 South Africa	17	21	47	88	..	..	66	196	7	9	6
91 Sri Lanka	17	20	25	33	22	28	38	61	9	13	8
94 Paraguay	15	17	51	104	46	86	72	255	3	0	4
96 Samoa (Western)	12	14	47	88	53	113	54	118	7	7	7
97 Botswana	36	57	61	159	60	151	70	238	11	0	15
98 Philippines	34	51	63	168	63	168	58	138	24	8	26
99 Indonesia	7	7	41	69	44	79	58	135	2	4	1
101 Mongolia	..	..	..	..	..	..	..	..	5	0	9
104 Guyana	13	15	48	90	..	..	..	..	16	11	21
108 China	12	13	45	82	39	65	52	107	4	6	4
109 Egypt	16	19	29	40	29	40	8	9	2	3	2
111 Maldives	14	16	35	53	25	33	12	14	10	5	11
112 El Salvador	25	34	45	80	60	148	72	261	18	6	25
113 Bolivia	17	20	42	72	65	183	73	263	9	0	10
114 Swaziland	15	17	54	119	54	116	45	82	7	0	13
116 Honduras	31	44	50	99	60	147	72	263	17	11	21
117 Guatemala	32	48	45	82	54	118	72	261	18	19	18
118 Namibia	21	26	41	69	..	..	..	..	7	10	6

HDI rank	Administrators and managers		Professional and technical workers		Clerical and sales workers		Service workers		Women in government		
	Female (%) 1990	Female as % of male 1990	Female (%) 1990	Female as % of male 1990	Female (%) 1990	Female as % of male 1990	Female (%) 1990	Female as % of male 1990	Total[a] (%) 1995	At ministerial level[a] (%) 1995	At sub-ministerial level[a] (%) 1995
119 Morocco	26	34	31	46	..	..	..	..	1	0	2
120 Gabon	..	..	..	..	..	..	..	..	6	3	11
121 Viet Nam	..	..	..	..	..	..	..	..	4	7	2
122 Solomon Islands	3	3	27	38	27	37	40	65	0	0	0
123 Cape Verde	23	30	48	94	63	170	57	134	12	13	10
124 Vanuatu	13	15	35	54	..	..	..	..	0	0	0
125 São Tomé and Principe	..	..	..	..	..	..	..	..	4	0	11
126 Iraq	13	15	44	78	7	7	16	19	0	0	0
127 Nicaragua	..	..	..	..	..	..	..	..	11	11	10
128 Papua New Guinea	12	13	30	42	..	..	..	..	2	0	3
129 Zimbabwe	15	18	40	67	34	52	30	42	11	3	19
130 Congo	6	7	29	40	..	..	..	..	4	6	0
Low human development	4	4	22	28	..	..	..	..	6	5	6
Excluding India	7	8	24	32	..	..	..	..	5	6	5
131 Myanmar	..	..	..	..	..	..	..	..	0	0	0
132 Ghana	9	10	36	56	..	..	..	..	11	11	10
133 Cameroon	10	11	24	32	37	59	31	46	5	3	7
134 Kenya	..	..	..	..	..	..	..	..	5	0	6
135 Equatorial Guinea	2	2	27	37	..	..	..	..	3	4	0
136 Lao People's Dem. Rep.	..	..	..	..	..	..	..	..	3	0	4
137 Lesotho	33	50	57	130	59	144	68	209	14	7	16
138 India	2	2	21	26	..	..	..	..	6	4	6
139 Pakistan	3	4	20	25	3	3	14	16	2	4	1
140 Comoros	..	..	22	29	..	..	..	..	3	7	0
141 Nigeria	6	6	26	35	58	140	11	13	4	4	4
142 Zaire	9	10	17	20	..	..	..	..	2	3	0
143 Zambia	6	7	32	47	58	136	22	29	9	7	9
144 Bangladesh	5	5	23	30	4	4	46	87	3	5	3
145 Côte d'Ivoire	..	..	..	..	..	..	..	..	3	8	0
146 Benin	..	..	..	..	..	..	..	..	10	15	5
147 Togo	8	9	21	27	..	..	..	..	3	4	0
148 Yemen	..	..	..	..	..	..	..	..	0	0	0
149 Tanzania, U. Rep. of	..	..	..	..	..	..	..	..	9	16	5
150 Mauritania	8	8	21	26	25	33	45	81	5	4	5
151 Central African Rep.	9	10	19	23	59	146	12	13	5	5	5
152 Madagascar	..	..	..	..	..	..	..	..	0	0	0
153 Cambodia	..	..	..	..	..	..	..	..	5	0	7
154 Nepal	..	..	..	..	..	..	..	..	0	0	0
155 Bhutan	..	..	..	..	..	..	..	..	5	13	0
156 Haiti	33	48	39	65	88	752	65	188	14	17	11
157 Angola	..	..	..	..	..	..	..	..	6	7	6
158 Sudan	2	3	29	40	..	..	..	..	1	0	1
159 Uganda	..	..	..	..	..	..	..	..	10	13	8
160 Senegal	..	..	..	..	..	..	..	..	2	4	0
161 Malawi	5	5	35	53	33	58	28	39	6	5	7
162 Djibouti	2	2	20	25	..	..	..	..	1	0	2
163 Guinea-Bissau	..	..	..	..	..	..	..	..	12	8	16
164 Chad	..	..	..	..	..	..	..	..	3	5	0
165 Gambia	16	18	24	31	..	..	..	..	7	22	2
166 Mozambique	11	13	20	26	..	..	..	..	13	4	15
167 Guinea	..	..	..	..	..	..	..	..	5	15	0
168 Eritrea	..	..	..	..	..	..	..	..	..	..	..
169 Burundi	13	16	30	44	..	..	..	..	4	8	0
170 Ethiopia	11	13	24	31	..	..	..	..	11	12	10
171 Mali	20	25	19	23	57	130	41	71	7	10	0
172 Burkina Faso	14	16	26	35	63	168	22	28	10	11	9
173 Niger	8	9	..	..	..	..	..	..	9	10	9
174 Rwanda	8	9	32	47	32	48	26	35	10	8	13
175 Sierra Leone	8	9	32	47	66	191	15	18	5	4	5
All developing countries	10	12	36	64	..	..	..	..	6	6	6
Least developed countries	9	10	24	33	..	..	..	..	6	8	6
Sub-Saharan Africa	10	12	28	43	..	..	..	..	7	7	7
Industrial countries	27	44	48	95	..	..	..	..	13	12	13
World	14	19	39	71	..	..	..	..	7	7	8

a. Including elected heads of state and governors of central banks. For countries for which the value is zero, no women ministers were reported by the United Nations Division for the Advancement of Women; this information could not be reconfirmed by the Human Development Report Office.
Source: Columns 1-8: UN 1994b; columns 9-11: calculations by the United Nations Division for the Advancement of Women based on data from World Government Directories 1995.

HDI rank	Pregnant women aged 15-49 with anaemia (%) 1975-91	Births attended by trained health personnel (%) 1990-96	Low-birth-weight infants (%) 1990-94	Maternal mortality rate (per 100,000 live births) 1990	Infant mortality rate (per 1,000 live births) 1994	Under-five mortality rate (per 1,000 live births) 1995	Mothers breast-feeding at six months (%) 1980-92	Oral rehydration therapy use rate (%) 1990-96	Under-weight children under age five (%) 1990-96
High human development	..	83	9	119	25	27	..	..	14
22 Hong Kong	..	100	8	7	5	6	..	..	..
24 Cyprus	..	..	..	..	9	10	..	..	..
25 Barbados	29	..	..	..	8	10	17	..	..
26 Singapore	57	100	7	10	5	6	..	..	..
28 Bahamas	12	..	..	..	13	28	..	..	..
29 Antigua and Barbuda	..	..	..	..	..	22	..	..	..
30 Chile	32	98	5	65	13	15	18a	..	1
32 Korea, Rep. of	..	98	9	130	10	9	..	..	..
33 Costa Rica	..	93	6	60	13	16	38	31	2
36 Argentina	..	97	7	100	23	27	36	..	..
37 Uruguay	..	96	8	85	19	21	33	..	7
38 Brunei Darussalam	..	..	..	..	9	10	..	..	..
40 Trinidad and Tobago	..	98	10	90	15	18	49a	..	7
41 Dominica	28	..	..	..	..	21	..	..	..
43 Bahrain	..	..	..	..	20	20	..	..	..
44 United Arab Emirates	..	96	6	26	17	19	..	..	..
45 Panama	..	86	9	55	24	20	53	94	7
46 Fiji	40	..	..	..	22	25	..	..	..
47 Venezuela	52a	69	9	120	22	24	..	..	6
49 Saint Kitts and Nevis	57	..	..	..	..	40	..	3	..
50 Mexico	..	77	8	110	32	32	50a	81	14
51 Colombia	8	85	10	100	26	36	65a	45	8
52 Seychelles	..	..	..	..	..	20	55	..	..
53 Kuwait	..	99	7	29	17	14	..	..	6
54 Grenada	63	..	..	..	..	33	..	..	..
55 Qatar	..	..	..	..	19	23	..	..	..
56 Saint Lucia	22	..	..	..	..	22	..	..	..
57 Saint Vincent	20	..	..	..	..	23	..	..	..
59 Thailand	48	71	13	200	29	32	80	95	26
60 Malaysia	36	94	8	80	12	13	..	..	23
61 Mauritius	..	97	13	120	17	23	55	..	16
63 Belize	65	..	..	..	31	40	..	..	..
64 Libyan Arab Jamahiriya	..	76	..	220	64	63	..	49	5
Medium human development	..	74	11	206	46	52	67	..	18
Excluding China	..	65	12	301	49	57	76	..	20
65 Lebanon	..	45a	10	300	32	40	40	82	..
66 Suriname	..	..	..	..	26	32	..	..	..
68 Brazil	..	81	11	220	45	60	43a	..	7
70 Iran, Islamic Rep. of	..	77	9	120	40	40	..	37	16
72 Ecuador	..	64	13	150	47	40	73a	64	17
73 Saudi Arabia	23	82	7	130	27	34	57	58	..
74 Turkey	..	76	8	180	44	50	91	16	10
75 Korea, Dem. People's Rep. of	..	100	..	70	23	30	..	..	..
78 Syrian Arab Rep.	..	67	11	180	37	36	..	36	12
81 Tunisia	38	69	8	170	41	37	..	..	9
82 Algeria	..	77	9	160	51	61	..	98	13
83 Jamaica	62	82	10	120	13	13	82	..	10
84 Jordan	..	87	7	150	33	25	72a	41	9
86 Cuba	..	90	9	95	9	10	33	..	..
87 Dominican Rep.	..	92	11	110	38	44	45a	..	10
88 Oman	..	87	8	190	28	25	..	85	12
89 Peru	..	52	11	280	52	55	87a	92	11
90 South Africa	..	82	..	230	51	67	..	..	9
91 Sri Lanka	..	94	25	140	16	19	81	34	38
94 Paraguay	..	66	5	160	42	34	69a	33	4
96 Samoa (Western)	..	..	..	..	62	54	..	..	..
97 Botswana	..	78	8	250	55	52	90a	..	15
98 Philippines	48	53	15	280	36	53	..	63	30
99 Indonesia	74	36	14	650	53	75	95a	99	35
101 Mongolia	..	99	6	65	57	74	..	..	12
104 Guyana	58	..	..	..	62	59	..	..	..
108 China	..	84	9	95	43	47	60a	85	16
109 Egypt	75a	46	10	170	63	51	83a	43	9
111 Maldives	..	..	..	..	53	77	..	..	..
112 El Salvador	14	87	11	300	41	40	77a	69	11
113 Bolivia	..	47	12	650	71	105	84	43	16
114 Swaziland	..	..	..	..	72	107	87a	..	..
116 Honduras	..	88	9	220	40	38	28	32	18
117 Guatemala	..	35	14	200	45	67	79a	22	27
118 Namibia	..	68	16	370	63	78	86a	66	26

HDI rank	Pregnant women aged 15-49 with anaemia (%) 1975-91	Births attended by trained health personnel (%) 1990-96	Low-birth-weight infants (%) 1990-94	Maternal mortality rate (per 100,000 live births) 1990	Infant mortality rate (per 1,000 live births) 1994	Under-five mortality rate (per 1,000 live births) 1995	Mothers breast-feeding at six months (%) 1980-92	Oral rehydration therapy use rate (%) 1990-96	Under-weight children under age five (%) 1990-96
119 Morocco	..	40	9	610	58	75	..	29	9
120 Gabon	..	80	..	500	91	148	..	..	..
121 Viet Nam	..	95	17	160	41	45	88	..	45
122 Solomon Islands	30	..	..	..	25	31	..	..	..
123 Cape Verde	48ª	..	..	..	48	73	..	..	..
124 Vanuatu	87	..	..	..	44	58	..	..	..
125 São Tomé and Principe	..	..	..	..	..	81	..	..	..
126 Iraq	..	54	15	310	146	71	45	..	12
127 Nicaragua	..	61	15	160	48	60	25	54	12
128 Papua New Guinea	..	20	23	930	68	95	99	..	35
129 Zimbabwe	..	69	14	570	70	74	92ª	60	16
130 Congo	..	..	16	890	90	108	98ª	41	24
Low human development	79	32	27	753	85	142	84	..	45
Excluding India	..	30	21	895	94	162	93	..	38
131 Myanmar	60	57	16	580	86	150	..	96	43
132 Ghana	..	44	7	740	79	130	92	93	27
133 Cameroon	..	64	13	550	62	106	95	..	14
134 Kenya	40ª	45	16	650	70	90	92ª	76	23
135 Equatorial Guinea	..	..	..	..	114	175	..	..	..
136 Lao People's Dem. Rep.	..	..	18	650	93	134	98	..	44
137 Lesotho	..	40	11	610	79	154	..	42	21
138 India	88	34	33	570	74	115	75ª	31	53
139 Pakistan	..	19	25	340	80	137	88ª	97	38
140 Comoros	..	..	..	..	88	124	..	..	..
141 Nigeria	65ª	31	16	1,000	82	191	99ª	..	36
142 Zaire	..	..	15	870	94	185	99	90	34
143 Zambia	..	51	13	940	110	203	99ª	99	28
144 Bangladesh	58	14	50	850	85	115	97	96	67
145 Côte d'Ivoire	34ª	45	14	810	89	150	81	18	24
146 Benin	46	45	..	990	87	142	89	60	..
147 Togo	47	54	20	640	89	128	87ª	..	24
148 Yemen	..	16	19	1,400	88	110	..	92	39
149 Tanzania, U. Rep. of	..	53	14	770	85	160	90	76	29
150 Mauritania	24	40	11	930	98	195	82	31	23
151 Central African Rep.	..	46	15	700	99	165	..	34	27
152 Madagascar	..	57	17	490	87	164	95	85	34
153 Cambodia	..	47	..	900	112	174	93	..	40
154 Nepal	..	7	..	1,500	92	114	..	27	49
155 Bhutan	30ª	15	..	1,600	113	189	..	85	38
156 Haiti	..	21	15	1,000	87	124	..	31	28
157 Angola	..	15	19	1,500	120	292	..	..	..
158 Sudan	50	69	15	660	86	115	90	..	34
159 Uganda	..	38	..	1,200	121	185	88ª	46	23
160 Senegal	53	46	11	1,200	66	110	91ª	18	20
161 Malawi	..	55	20	560	147	219	..	78	30
162 Djibouti	..	..	..	..	113	158	..	..	..
163 Guinea-Bissau	..	27	20	910	138	227	100	..	23
164 Chad	..	15	..	1,500	121	152	..	..	..
165 Gambia	..	44	..	1,100	129	110	..	..	..
166 Mozambique	58ª	25	20	1,500	116	275	93	83	27
167 Guinea	..	31	21	1,600	131	219	70	38	26
168 Eritrea	..	21	13	1,400	103	195	..	38	41
169 Burundi	..	19	..	1,300	122	176	92ª	..	37
170 Ethiopia	..	14	16	1,400	115	195	..	95	48
171 Mali	50ª	24	17	1,200	156	210	95ª	..	31
172 Burkina Faso	55	42	21	930	101	164	98	100	30
173 Niger	57	15	15	1,200	121	320	..	20	36
174 Rwanda	..	26	17	1,300	145	139	97	47	29
175 Sierra Leone	45	25	11	1,800	200	284	..	..	29
All developing countries	..	54	18	471	64	95	72	67	31
Least developed countries	..	30	23	1,030	103	169	..	82	42
Sub-Saharan Africa	..	38	16	971	97	174	94	73	31
Industrial countries	..	99	6	31	14	18	..	..	..
World	..	58	17	416	58	85	..	..	..

a. Data refer to a year or period other than that specified in the column heading, differ from the standard definition or refer to only part of the country.
Source: Columns 1 and 7: UN 1994b; columns 2-4, 6, 8 and 9: UNICEF 1997; column 5: UN 1996b.

HDI rank	One-year-olds fully immunized against		AIDS cases (per 100,000 people)[a] 1995	Tuberculosis cases (per 100,000 people)[a] 1994	Malaria cases (per 100,000 people)[a] 1992	Cigarette consumption per adult (1970-72=100) 1990-92	Population per doctor 1988-91	Population per nurse 1988-91	People with disabilities (as % of total population) 1985-92	Public expenditure on health	
	Tuberculosis (%) 1992-95	Measles (%) 1995								As % of GNP 1960	As % of GDP 1990
High human development	97	86	7.7	45.3	119.3	98	1,650	1,782	..	1.4	2.1
22 Hong Kong	100	77	0.8	..	..	..	..	..	0.8	..	1.1
24 Cyprus	..	..	0.4	5.1	0.3	..	585	..	2.3	0.6	..
25 Barbados	..	..	36.0	..	..	..	..	..	..	3.0	..
26 Singapore	97	88	2.0	51.3	10.8	64	725	..	0.4	1.0	1.1
28 Bahamas	..	..	141.8	..	..	..	..	..	..	..	..
29 Antigua and Barbuda	..	..	7.6	..	..	..	..	..	..	..	..
30 Chile	96	96	1.9	..	..	79	943	3,846	..	2.0	3.4
32 Korea, Rep. of	93	92	(.)	85.7	..	127	1,205	1,538	..	0.2	2.7
33 Costa Rica	99	94	5.8	9.7	150.4	72	1,136	2,222	..	3.0	..
36 Argentina	96	76	4.7	39.9	2.2	89	329	1,786	..	1.3	2.5
37 Uruguay	99	80	4.0	21.0	..	104	..	..	..	2.6	2.5
38 Brunei Darussalam	..	..	(.)	..	7.3	..	..	..	..	..	..
40 Trinidad and Tobago	..	84	26.0	10.1	0.6	124	1,370	..	1.1	1.7	..
41 Dominica	..	..	7.0	16.9	..	..	..	..	..	..	..
43 Bahrain	..	..	1.4	..	47.4	..	775	..	1.0	..	..
44 United Arab Emirates	98	90	(.)	19.7	173.2	..	1,042	568	..	..	..
45 Panama	100	84	7.7	32.0	18.6	84	562	1,064	1.4	3.0	..
46 Fiji	..	..	(.)	36.3	..	138	..	..	0.9	..	..
47 Venezuela	91	67	2.8	22.8	58.7	93	..	..	3.8	2.6	2.0
49 Saint Kitts and Nevis	..	..	12.2	4.9	..	..	..	..	..	..	..
50 Mexico	98	90	4.6	18.3	17.6	61	621	..	..	1.9	1.6
51 Colombia	99	84	2.5	25.3	367.8	93	1,064	2,632	1.2	0.4	1.8
52 Seychelles	..	..	8.2	..	..	..	..	..	..	..	..
53 Kuwait	..	93	0.3	13.5	78.6	..	..	..	0.4	..	..
54 Grenada	..	..	19.6	3.3	..	..	..	..	..	..	..
55 Qatar	..	..	0.9	..	68.8	..	..	..	0.2	..	..
56 Saint Lucia	..	..	7.0	17.0	..	..	..	..	..	..	..
57 Saint Vincent	..	..	5.4	..	..	..	..	..	..	..	..
59 Thailand	98	90	30.5	82.7	199.4	130	4,762	1,064	0.7	0.4	1.1
60 Malaysia	97	81	0.7	59.4	202.5	116	2,564	..	..	1.1	1.3
61 Mauritius	87	85	0.6	13.5	..	140	1,176	398	2.6	1.5	..
63 Belize	..	..	12.8	28.4	4,127.9	..	..	..	6.6	..	..
64 Libyan Arab Jamahiriya	99	92	(.)	..	2.6	..	962	328	..	1.3	..
Medium human development	91	87	..	49.0	133.2	116	..	..	3.7	0.8	2.3
Excluding China	91	83	3.5	77.0	310.4	112	3,446	2,685	1.8	0.7	2.4
65 Lebanon	..	88	0.3	32.2	0.1	..	413	2,174	..	..	..
66 Suriname	..	..	4.7	12.8	..	161	..	..	..	..	..
68 Brazil	100	88	6.0	55.6	297.1	113	847	3,448	1.8	0.6	2.8
70 Iran, Islamic Rep. of	99	95	(.)	..	96.9	103	..	..	..	0.8	1.5
72 Ecuador	91	62	0.6	86.3	417.6	134	671	1,818	..	0.4	..
73 Saudi Arabia	93	94	0.2	14.2	103.5	175	704	310	..	0.6	3.1
74 Turkey	42	42	(.)	..	78.7	108	1,176	..	1.4	0.8	1.5
75 Korea, Dem. People's Rep. of	99	98	(.)	..	..	91	..	..	..	0.5	..
78 Syrian Arab Rep.	100	98	(.)	37.0	6.9	211	1,220	1,031	1.0	0.4	0.4
81 Tunisia	89	91	0.7	26.9	0.5	127	1,852	407	0.9	1.6	3.3
82 Algeria	93	77	0.1	50.0	0.3	168	1,064	..	..	1.2	5.4
83 Jamaica	100	89	20.6	4.5	0.2	61	7,143	..	..	2.0	..
84 Jordan	..	92	(.)	8.6	5.2	165	649	641	0.5	0.6	1.8
86 Cuba	99	100	1.0	15.4	0.1	85	332	180	1.7	3.0	..
87 Dominican Rep.	74	85	4.9	49.2	12.6	111	935	9,091	..	1.3	2.1
88 Oman	96	98	0.3	14.4	797.4	..	..	..	..	..	..
89 Peru	96	98	3.8	210.1	411.7	85	1,031	..	0.2	1.1	1.9
90 South Africa	95	76	6.8	222.7	..	128	..	..	..	0.5	3.2
91 Sri Lanka	90	88	0.1	35.9	2,045.4	94	7,143	1,754	0.4	2.0	1.8
94 Paraguay	92	75	0.5	39.3	9.3	92	1,587	7,143	..	0.5	1.2
96 Samoa (Western)	..	..	0.6	27.6	..	..	..	..	..	..	..
97 Botswana	81	68	35.9	335.9	1,043.6	..	4,762	469	4.0	1.5	..
98 Philippines	91	86	0.1	271.2	97.9	88	8,333	..	1.1	0.4	1.0
99 Indonesia	86	70	(.)	25.5	72.3	236	7,143	2,857	1.1	0.3	0.7
101 Mongolia	94	85	(.)	71.7	..	..	389	209	..	..	..
104 Guyana	..	..	11.5	32.4	4,040.4	93	..	..	3.9	..	..
108 China	92	93	(.)	30.1	5.7	260	..	..	4.9	1.3	2.1
109 Egypt	95	90	(.)	6.4	..	166	..	..	1.6	0.6	1.0
111 Maldives	..	..	(.)	101.2	11.8	..	..	..	..	..	..
112 El Salvador	100	93	6.6	70.6	70.3	80	1,563	3,333	..	0.9	2.6
113 Bolivia	85	80	0.2	130.3	379.6	108	2,564	7,692	2.6	0.4	2.4
114 Swaziland	..	..	18.0	..	..	..	9,091	595	..	..	..
116 Honduras	99	90	16.1	78.1	810.4	78	1,266	4,545	..	1.0	2.9
117 Guatemala	78	75	1.0	28.8	405.6	52	4,000	7,143	3.8	0.6	2.1
118 Namibia	94	69	119.1	..	..	..	4,545	339	..	..	..

HDI rank	One-year-olds fully immunized against Tuberculosis (%) 1992-95	Measles (%) 1995	AIDS cases (per 100,000 people)[a] 1995	Tuberculosis cases (per 100,000 people)[a] 1994	Malaria cases (per 100,000 people)[a] 1992	Cigarette consumption per adult (1970-72=100) 1990-92	Population per doctor 1988-91	Population per nurse 1988-91	People with disabilities (as % of total population) 1985-92	Public expenditure on health As % of GNP 1960	As % of GDP 1990
119 Morocco	93	88	0.2	116.5	0.8	135	..	..	1.6	1.0	0.9
120 Gabon	73	56	25.3	98.9	..	..	2,500	1,471	..	0.5	..
121 Viet Nam	96	95	0.2	71.5	215.6	..	247	1,149	5.7	..	1.1
122 Solomon Islands	..	..	(.)	90.7	33.6	56	..	..	..	..	..
123 Cape Verde	..	..	5.4	..	..	..	..	..	4.3	..	..
124 Vanuatu	..	..	(.)	92.1	6,289.1	..	..	..	..	..	..
125 São Tomé and Principe	..	..	3.0	..	..	..	..	..	..	..	..
126 Iraq	99	95	(.)	..	253.6	102	1,667	1,370	0.9	1.0	..
127 Nicaragua	100	81	0.2	68.6	1,099.0	106	2,000	3,125	..	0.4	6.7
128 Papua New Guinea	78	63	1.0	126.9	1,588.9	..	..	1,587	..	..	2.8
129 Zimbabwe	95	74	118.6	..	8,026.1	61	7,692	1,639	..	1.2	3.2
130 Congo	94	70	95.6	122.3	..	102	3,571	1,370	..	1.6	..
Low human development	82	65	5.0	101.4	341.5	135	7,745	5,825	1.0	0.6	1.5
Excluding India	72	55	12.1	68.9	..	134	14,212	9,180	0.6	0.7	1.7
131 Myanmar	82	75	1.3	35.2	254.9	167	12,500	..	0.4	0.7	..
132 Ghana	70	46	14.8	52.8	..	61	25,000	3,704	..	1.1	1.7
133 Cameroon	54	46	20.9	57.0	..	274	12,500	1,852	..	1.0	1.0
134 Kenya	92	73	29.1	86.7	..	119	20,000	9,091	..	1.5	2.7
135 Equatorial Guinea	..	..	24.4	91.5	..	..	..	..	..	..	..
136 Lao People's Dem. Rep.	59	68	0.1	24.0	882.3	118	4,545	..	..	0.5	1.0
137 Lesotho	59	74	16.6	219.2	..	..	25,000	2,000	..	1.0	..
138 India	96	78	0.1	122.0	241.6	136	2,439	3,333	0.2	0.5	1.3
139 Pakistan	75	53	(.)	..	69.8	102	2,000	3,448	4.9	0.3	1.8
140 Comoros	..	..	0.3	83.3	..	..	10,000	3,448	..	..	3.3
141 Nigeria	57	40	..	7.8	..	128	5,882	1,639	..	0.3	1.2
142 Zaire	46	39	4.3	..	..	123	14,286	1,351	..	..	0.8
143 Zambia	63	69	45.3	..	..	86	11,111	5,000	1.6	1.0	2.2
144 Bangladesh	94	79	(.)	41.4	107.6	194	12,500	20,000	0.8	..	1.4
145 Côte d'Ivoire	48	57	47.2	..	..	89	11,111	3,226	..	1.5	1.7
146 Benin	91	72	4.0	40.3	..	102	14,286	3,226	..	1.5	2.8
147 Togo	81	65	41.3	28.6	..	88	11,111	3,030	..	1.3	2.5
148 Yemen	87	40	0.1	80.0	274.9	172	4,348	1,818	..	..	1.5
149 Tanzania, U. Rep. of	92	82	95.5	119.3	4,261.7	97	..	..	..	0.5	3.2
150 Mauritania	93	53	1.5	..	..	..	16,667	2,273	..	0.5	..
151 Central African Rep.	73	36	19.6	..	..	..	25,000	11,111	..	1.3	2.6
152 Madagascar	77	60	(.)	74.1	..	170	8,333	3,846	..	1.4	1.3
153 Cambodia	95	75	0.9	155.3	1,015.6	130	..	..	..	0.2	2.2
154 Nepal	61	57	0.1	74.5	78.4	341	16,667	33,333	3.0	0.2	2.2
155 Bhutan	98	85	(.)	66.7	1,617.7	..	11,111	6,667	..	..	..
156 Haiti	68	31	(.)	..	12.2	341	7,143	9,091	..	1.0	3.2
157 Angola	40	32	2.9	68.4	..	100	25,000	..	..	..	..
158 Sudan	88	74	0.9	..	..	88	..	7,143	5.3	1.0	0.5
159 Uganda	98	79	10.3	141.5	..	100	25,000	7,143	..	0.7	1.6
160 Senegal	90	80	4.8	85.3	..	244	16,667	12,500	..	1.5	2.3
161 Malawi	91	70	47.3	..	..	165	50,000	33,333	2.9	0.2	2.9
162 Djibouti	..	..	40.2	566.0	172.1	..	..	..	..	..	..
163 Guinea-Bissau	100	82	7.4	157.3	15,162.2	..	..	..	..	..	..
164 Chad	36	26	9.3	..	..	..	33,333	50,000	..	0.5	4.7
165 Gambia	98	87	5.6	..	..	..	..	..	..	..	..
166 Mozambique	58	40	7.4	167.6	..	124	33,333	5,000	..	..	4.4
167 Guinea	86	69	9.1	45.7	..	..	7,692	..	..	1.0	2.3
168 Eritrea	57	45	20.6	..	..	..	..	..	..	..	..
169 Burundi	77	50	7.7	64.8	..	..	16,667	..	..	0.8	1.7
170 Ethiopia	63	43	7.0	181.8	..	150	33,333	14,286	3.8	0.7	2.3
171 Mali	75	49	4.2	29.4	2,826.8	..	20,000	5,882	2.8	1.0	2.8
172 Burkina Faso	78	55	16.3	..	..	..	33,333	10,000	..	0.6	7.0
173 Niger	32	18	6.8	42.8	..	155	50,000	3,846	..	0.2	3.4
174 Rwanda	86	50	(.)	..	..	..	25,000	8,333	..	0.5	1.9
175 Sierra Leone	60	46	0.6	62.1	..	176	..	..	..	..	1.7
All developing countries	87	76	4.8	69.1	206.4	113	5,833	4,691	2.6	0.9	2.1
Least developed countries	74	59	13.5	84.8	..	133	19,035	13,842	..	..	1.8
Sub-Saharan Africa	69	53	22.2	93.6	..	120	18,514	6,548	..	0.7	2.5
Industrial countries	91	85	5.6	27.2	..	93	..	..	..	..	..
World	87	77	5.0	59.5	..	103	..	..	..	..	..

a. The number of reported cases in adults and children.
Source: Columns 1 and 2: UNICEF 1997; *column 3:* WHO and UNAIDS 1997; *columns 4 and 5:* WHO 1996b; *column 6:* calculated on the basis of estimates from WHO 1996a; *columns 7 and 8:* calculated on the basis of estimates from WHO 1993; *column 9:* UN 1993a; *columns 10 and 11:* World Bank 1993 and UNDP 1994.

HDI rank	Food production per capita index (1979-81=100) 1993	Agricultural production (as % of GDP) 1994	Food consumption (as % of total household consumption) 1980-85	Daily calorie supply per capita 1992	Per capita food supply from fish and seafood Total (kg) 1990-92	Per capita food supply from fish and seafood Change since 1980-82 (%) 1990-92	Food imports (as % of merchandise imports) 1980	Food imports (as % of merchandise imports) 1994	Cereal imports (thousands of metric tons) 1994	Food aid in cereals (thousands of metric tons) 1994-95[a]
High human development	104	8	32	2,894	20	3	12	5	35,810T	..
22 Hong Kong	87	(.)	..	3,144	..	..	12	3	652	..
24 Cyprus	94	..	..	3,782	..	..	..	7	..	..
25 Barbados	64	..	..	3,223	..	..	..	..	..	..
26 Singapore	47	(.)	..	..	..	..	9	3	776	..
28 Bahamas	..	..	..	..	..	..	..	..	..	..
29 Antigua and Barbuda	..	..	..	..	..	..	..	..	..	..
30 Chile	118	..	29	2,583	23	26	15	5	1,277	2
32 Korea, Rep. of	94	7	35	3,298	59	35	10	4	11,936	..
33 Costa Rica	104	15	33	2,889	7	7	9	6	453	2
36 Argentina	94	5	35	2,880	7	10	6	4	28	..
37 Uruguay	113	8	31	2,750	5	0	8	8	277	..
38 Brunei Darussalam	100	..	..	2,745	..	..	..	..	..	..
40 Trinidad and Tobago	85	3	19	2,589	12	-17	11	17	162	..
41 Dominica	..	..	..	..	..	..	..	..	..	..
43 Bahrain	..	..	..	..	..	..	..	7	..	..
44 United Arab Emirates	..	2	..	..	25	19	11	6	759	..
45 Panama	87	11	38	2,239	12	-12	10	8	273	2
46 Fiji	97	..	..	3,092	41	2	..	12	..	..
47 Venezuela	101	5	23	2,622	13	0	15	11	2,015	..
49 Saint Kitts and Nevis	..	..	..	..	..	..	..	..	..	..
50 Mexico	94	8	35 [b,c]	3,181	10	-10	16	9	8,100	44
51 Colombia	114	14	29	2,678	2	-47	12	7	2,353	15
52 Seychelles	..	..	..	..	..	..	..	..	..	..
53 Kuwait	..	(.)	..	2,535	10	-3	15	14	455	..
54 Grenada	78	..	..	2,407	..	..	..	..	..	..
55 Qatar	..	..	..	..	..	..	..	12	..	..
56 Saint Lucia	..	..	..	..	..	..	..	..	..	..
57 Saint Vincent	..	..	..	..	..	..	..	..	..	..
59 Thailand	102	10	30	2,443	25	33	5	2	740	3
60 Malaysia	203	14	23 [b]	2,884	25	-39	12	4	3,509	0
61 Mauritius	99	9	24	2,696	19	16	26	12	255	2
63 Belize	95	..	..	2,670	6	-12	..	13	..	..
64 Libyan Arab Jamahiriya	81	..	..	3,310	2	-73	..	19	1,790	..
Medium human development	133	16	54	2,730	11	68	..	8	80,572T	..
Excluding China	118	14	42	2,731	11	14	13	10	64,241T	1,961T
65 Lebanon	186	..	..	3,319	0	-37	..	14	577	7
66 Suriname	81	..	..	2,548	7	-60	..	13	..	..
68 Brazil	114	13	35	2,824	6	-1	10	9	8,971	33
70 Iran, Islamic Rep. of	126	21	37	2,861	4	161	13	16	5,450	54
72 Ecuador	110	12	30	2,587	10	-6	8	5	486	32
73 Saudi Arabia	340	..	..	2,751	7	-29	14	12	6,182	..
74 Turkey	102	16	40	3,429	6	-20	4	3	878	2
75 Korea, Dem. People's Rep. of	76	..	..	2,834	43	21	..	15	310	..
78 Syrian Arab Rep.	89	..	..	3,175	1	-77	..	10	952	59
81 Tunisia	123	15	37	3,333	10	22	14	7	1,592	22
82 Algeria	119	12	..	2,897	3	10	21	26	7,760	23
83 Jamaica	111	8	36	2,607	16	-14	20	10	335	46
84 Jordan	121	8	35	3,031	2	-24	18	20	1,347	111
86 Cuba	65	..	..	2,833	14	-24	..	21	1,464	3
87 Dominican Rep.	104	15	46	..	8	-1	17	14	895	2
88 Oman	..	3	..	..	..	..	15	13	460	..
89 Peru	..	7	35	1,883	22	4	20	13	2,289	348
90 South Africa	74	5	34	2,705	10	10	3	5	913	..
91 Sri Lanka	81	24	43	2,275	11	-28	20	7	927	342
94 Paraguay	109	24	30	2,670	4	200	..	7	31	1
96 Samoa (Western)	..	..	..	..	..	..	..	..	..	..
97 Botswana	69	5	25	2,288	4	21	..	13	175	7
98 Philippines	88	22	51	2,258	33	-1	8	6	2,219	44
99 Indonesia	145	17	48	2,755	15	22	13	6	5,113	15
101 Mongolia	63	21	..	1,899	1	10	..	23	63	12
104 Guyana	94	..	..	2,385	40	0	..	7	..	..
108 China	145	21	61 [b,c]	2,729	10	107	..	3	16,331	..
109 Egypt	114	20	49	3,336	7	33	32	22	9,200	179
111 Maldives	84	..	..	2,624	..	..	..	..	..	..
112 El Salvador	95	14	33	2,663	2	5	18	11	448	7
113 Bolivia	107	..	33 [b]	2,100	1	-52	19	13	434	175
114 Swaziland	82	..	..	2,706	..	..	..	8	..	..
116 Honduras	89	20	39	2,306	1	-33	10	16	278	73
117 Guatemala	94	25	36	2,255	1	26	8	11	517	144
118 Namibia	72	14	..	2,120	11	7	..	9	112	26

HDI rank	Food production per capita index (1979-81=100) 1993	Agricultural production (as % of GDP) 1994	Food consumption (as % of total household consumption) 1980-85	Daily calorie supply per capita 1992	Per capita food supply from fish and seafood Total (kg) 1990-92	Per capita food supply from fish and seafood Change since 1980-82 (%) 1990-92	Food imports (as % of merchandise imports) 1980	Food imports (as % of merchandise imports) 1994	Cereal imports (thousands of metric tons) 1994	Food aid in cereals (thousands of metric tons) 1994-95[a]
119 Morocco	106	21	38	2,985	7	10	20	11	1,678	13
120 Gabon	78	8	..	2,511	27	-29	19	13	64	..
121 Viet Nam	133	28	..	2,250	14	28	..	5	387	64
122 Solomon Islands	88	..	..	2,222	56	-10	..	14	..	..
123 Cape Verde	..	..	..	..	..	..	..	32	..	..
124 Vanuatu	80	..	..	2,744	..	..	..	..	..	..
125 São Tomé and Principe	..	..	..	–	..	..	..	..	..	..
126 Iraq	87	..	..	2,122	1	-62	..	32	1,099	68
127 Nicaragua	64	33	..	2,296	1	4	15	19	174	33
128 Papua New Guinea	103	28	..	2,615	22	-7	21	14	275	0
129 Zimbabwe	78	15	40	1,989	2	-44	3	3	100	4
130 Congo	79	10	37	2,297	33	16	19	17	86	12
Low human development	113	32	51	2,262	5	19	14	11	12,861 T	4,396 T
Excluding India	102	34	48	2,115	7	5	15	14	12,849 T	4,132 T
131 Myanmar	107	63	..	2,598	15	5	7	15	49	5
132 Ghana	115	46	50 [b]	2,206	25	16	10	9	311	101
133 Cameroon	79	32	24	1,981	10	-26	9	11	226	2
134 Kenya	83	29	38	2,075	7	107	8	15	622	102
135 Equatorial Guinea	..	..	..	..	..	..	..	13	..	..
136 Lao People's Dem. Rep.	..	51	..	2,259	7	-9	..	4	22	10
137 Lesotho	70	14	..	2,201	2	-24	..	12	99	15
138 India	123	30	52	2,395	4	30	9	5	12	264
139 Pakistan	118	25	37	2,316	2	24	13	11	1,916	103
140 Comoros	83	..	..	1,897	..	..	..	37	..	..
141 Nigeria	129	43	48	2,125	5	-67	17	13	1,078	..
142 Zaire	100	..	..	2,060	8	17	..	42	253	83
143 Zambia	99	31	36	1,931	8	-15	5	3	35	11
144 Bangladesh	97	30	59	2,019	7	4	24	14	952	888
145 Côte d'Ivoire	89	41	39	2,491	16	-18	13	16	466	56
146 Benin	119	34	37	2,532	10	-16	26	18	107	15
147 Togo	106	38	..	2,243	12	3	17	10	69	8
148 Yemen	75	..	..	2,203	..	..	28	25	..	91
149 Tanzania, U. Rep. of	76	57	64	2,021	15	27	13	8	195	118
150 Mauritania	81	27	..	2,685	15	34	30	49	206	22
151 Central African Rep.	94	44	..	1,691	5	-11	21	24	52	1
152 Madagascar	86	35	59	2,135	8	29	9	14	140	26
153 Cambodia	141	..	..	2,021	12	76	..	9	58	64
154 Nepal	114	44	57	1,957	1	188	4	11	62	21
155 Bhutan	..	..	..	..	..	..	..	11	..	..
156 Haiti	67	44	..	1,707	4	12	24	77	311	117
157 Angola	72	..	..	1,840	..	..	..	15	475	217
158 Sudan	76	..	60 [b]	2,202	1	-37	..	22	1,022	132
159 Uganda	109	49	..	2,162	14	13	11	4	56	62
160 Senegal	111	17	49	2,265	21	-7	25	29	579	16
161 Malawi	70	31	30	1,827	10	13	8	35	506	204
162 Djibouti	..	..	..	..	..	..	..	27	..	..
163 Guinea-Bissau	110	45	..	2,556	2	-36	20	46	68	2
164 Chad	99	44	..	1,989	5	42	23	6	50	14
165 Gambia	76	28	..	2,360	14	20	23	32	97	2
166 Mozambique	77	33	..	1,680	3	-20	..	16	496	320
167 Guinea	98	24	..	2,390	8	12	..	23	384	29
168 Eritrea	..	..	..	..	..	..	..	..	281	140
169 Burundi	92	53	..	1,941	4	13	13	19	105	48
170 Ethiopia	86	57	49	1,610	0	0	8	20	928	720
171 Mali	91	42	57	2,279	7	-30	19	15	70	17
172 Burkina Faso	132	34	..	2,387	2	36	21	14	110	19
173 Niger	77	39	..	2,257	1	-65	14	22	155	32
174 Rwanda	70	51	29	1,821	0	-25	12	25	97	269
175 Sierra Leone	86	47	56	1,695	13	-40	24	57	141	30
All developing countries	123	15	51	2,553	9	44	13	7	129,243 T	6,427 T
Least developed countries	94	37	..	2,054	7	12	15	16	7,651 T	3,752 T
Sub-Saharan Africa	97	20	45	2,096	8	-8	11	10	10,162 T	2,752 T
Industrial countries	96	3	..	..	29	19	11	6	90,212 T	..
World	118	6	..	..	13	39	11	6	219,455 T	..

a. The time reference for food aid is the crop year, July to June.
b. Data refer to a year or period other than that specified in the column heading.
c. Includes beverages and tobacco.
Source: Columns 1 and 4: FAO 1994; columns 2, 7 and 8: World Bank 1996g; column 3: World Bank 1993; columns 5 and 6: WRI 1996b; columns 9 and 10: World Bank 1997b.

15 Education imbalances

			Secondary technical enrolment (as % of total secondary)	Tertiary natural and applied science enrolment (as % of total tertiary)	Tertiary students abroad (as % of those at home)	R & D scientists and technicians (per 1,000 people)	Public expenditure on				
		Compulsory education (duration in years)					Education (as % of GNP)		Education (as % of total government expenditure)	Primary and secondary education (as % of all levels)	Higher education (as % of all levels)
HDI rank			1988-91	1992	1989-93	1988-95	1980	1993-94	1992-94	1990-94	1990-94
High human development		7	..	31	..	0.5	3.6	4.6	..	..	..
22	Hong Kong	9	10.0	35	50.2	..	..	..	17.0	66	30
24	Cyprus	9	6.6	26	..	0.2	3.5	..	14.2	84	6
25	Barbados	12	..	8	11.2	..	6.5	7.5	18.6	75	19
26	Singapore	0	..	..	25.0	2.2	2.8	3.3	24.2	62	33
28	Bahamas	10	..	..	41.1	..	..	3.9	16.3	..	..
29	Antigua and Barbuda	11	..	..	..	..	3.0	..	..	..	..
30	Chile	8	37.5	41	3.7	0.3	4.6	2.9	13.4	68	20
32	Korea, Rep. of	9	18.6	40	2.7	2.6	3.7	4.5	16.0	80	8
33	Costa Rica	9	22.2	18	1.6	0.5	7.8	4.7	19.2	62	31
36	Argentina	7	..	..	0.4	0.3	2.7	3.8	14.0	72	17
37	Uruguay	6	16.3	22	1.1	0.7	2.3	2.5	13.3	68	25
38	Brunei Darussalam	12	4.6	..	..	0.1	1.2	3.6	..	45	1
40	Trinidad and Tobago	7	0.8	45	38.0	0.2	4.0	4.5	..	73	13
41	Dominica	10	1.1	42	..	..	..	..	..	..	..
43	Bahrain	12	12.7	39	20.3	..	2.9	4.7	..	73	..
44	United Arab Emirates	6	0.8	13	23.8	..	1.3	..	16.3	..	..
45	Panama	6	25.6	21	3.5	..	4.8	5.2	20.9	51	25
46	Fiji	–	9.1	25	21.6	0.1	5.9	5.4	18.6	88	9
47	Venezuela	10	17.6	..	1.1	0.2	4.4	5.1	22.4	26	35
49	Saint Kitts and Nevis	12	..	..	..	..	5.2	..	..	76	12
50	Mexico	6	12.2	34	0.8	0.1	4.7	5.8	..	57	14
51	Colombia	5	21.5	31	0.6	(.)	1.9	3.7	12.9	72	17
52	Seychelles	9	29.0	..	..	0.2	5.8	7.4	..	66	11
53	Kuwait	8	0.3	29	14.0	0.9	2.4	5.6	11.0	57	16
54	Grenada	11	..	..	..	..	..	..	..	..	..
55	Qatar	0	2.7	24	12.0	0.4	2.6	..	..	..	..
56	Saint Lucia	10	..	..	70.7	0.4	..	..	..	74	12
57	Saint Vincent	–	2.8	26	16.4	..	..	6.7	13.8	96	(.)
59	Thailand	6	18.5	19	1.1	0.2	3.4	3.8	18.9	73	17
60	Malaysia	11	2.2	27	28.3	0.1	6.0	5.3	15.5	71	17
61	Mauritius	7	1.4	16	78.9	0.3	5.3	..	..	74	17
63	Belize	10	1.3	..	..	..	..	5.7	15.5	..	..
64	Libyan Arab Jamahiriya	9	17.2	..	2.1	0.2	3.4	..	..	..	..
Medium human development		8	..	38	..	0.3	4.0	2.9	..	..	..
Excluding China		7	..	25	..	0.2	4.3	3.0	..	..	..
65	Lebanon	–	..	..	14.2	..	..	2.0	..	..	..
66	Suriname	11	27.1	6	..	..	6.7	3.6	..	75	8
68	Brazil	8	..	22	0.1	0.2	3.6	1.6	..	56	26
70	Iran, Islamic Rep. of	5	4.6	37	10.5	0.1	7.5	5.9	18.1	64	22
72	Ecuador	6	33.8	21	2.7	0.2	5.6	3.0	..	66	23
73	Saudi Arabia	–	2.8	16	3.4	..	4.1	..	..	80	20
74	Turkey	5	24.5	23	3.2	0.2	2.8	3.3	..	69	21
75	Korea, Dem. People's Rep. of	10	..	..	0.2	..	..	..	..	..	..
78	Syrian Arab Rep.	6	5.9	29	5.1	..	4.6	..	12.5	98	(.)
81	Tunisia	9	3.5	27	12.2	0.4	5.4	6.3	..	77	21
82	Algeria	9	7.0	50	7.1	..	7.8	5.6	17.6	96	(.)
83	Jamaica	6	3.5	22	12.9	(.)	7.0	4.7	..	62	26
84	Jordan	10	23.3	29	17.5	0.1	..	3.8	10.5	90	3
86	Cuba	6	32.2	23	0.4	1.4	7.2	6.6	12.3	57	14
87	Dominican Rep.	8	..	..	0.9	..	2.2	1.9	12.2	64	11
88	Oman	–	2.2	21	21.1	..	2.1	4.5	15.5	93	6
89	Peru	11	..	29	0.7	0.2	3.1	..	..	..	..
90	South Africa	10	..	..	1.0	0.3	..	7.1	22.9	81	15
91	Sri Lanka	11	..	34	10.0	0.2	2.7	3.2	9.4	72	11
94	Paraguay	6	6.9	25	1.4	..	1.5	2.9	..	68	18
96	Samoa (Western)	–	..	..	..	..	..	4.2	10.7	78	..
97	Botswana	–	4.6	28	14.5	..	7.0	8.5	..	80	12
98	Philippines	6	(.)	26	0.3	0.1	1.7	2.4	..	..	..
99	Indonesia	6	12.0	22	1.0	0.2	1.7	1.3	..	47	18
101	Mongolia	8	..	..	6.7	..	..	5.2	..	59	18
104	Guyana	10	3.4	45	14.9	0.1	9.7	5.0	..	..	..
108	China	9	9.1	47	5.7	0.3	2.5	2.6	..	67	17
109	Egypt	5	20.9	18	0.8	0.4	5.7	5.0	11.0	64	37
111	Maldives	–	1.0	..	..	..	..	8.1	13.6	99	..
112	El Salvador	9	..	19	1.2	(.)	3.9	1.6	..	..	..
113	Bolivia	8	..	32	2.0	0.2	4.4	5.4	11.2	51	30
114	Swaziland	7	1.4	43	10.3	..	6.1	6.8	17.5	60	30
116	Honduras	6	30.2	25	2.6	..	3.2	4.0	16.0	65	20
117	Guatemala	6	..	..	1.8	0.1	1.9	1.6	12.8	65	20
118	Namibia	10	1.9	3	..	..	1.5	8.7	..	..	..

HDI rank	Compulsory education (duration in years)	Secondary technical enrolment (as % of total secondary) 1988-91	Tertiary natural and applied science enrolment (as % of total tertiary) 1992	Tertiary students abroad (as % of those at home) 1989-93	R & D scientists and technicians (per 1,000 people) 1988-95	Public expenditure on				
						Education (as % of GNP)		Education (as % of total government expenditure) 1992-94	Primary and secondary education (as % of all levels) 1990-94	Higher education (as % of all levels) 1990-94
						1980	1993-94			
119 Morocco	6	1.5	34	13.9	..	6.1	5.4	22.6	84	16
120 Gabon	10	20.6	..	38.1	0.2	2.7	3.2	..	100	(.)
121 Viet Nam	5	5.6	..	2.7	0.3	..	..	..	..	..
122 Solomon Islands	..	17.3	..	..	..	5.6	4.2	7.9	86	14
123 Cape Verde	6	7.5	..	..	..	..	4.4	19.9	72	3
124 Vanuatu	6	6.9	..	..	..	..	4.8	..	87	3
125 São Tomé and Principe	4	1.4	..	..	..	8.0	..	..	..	..
126 Iraq	6	13.7	..	1.5	..	3.0	..	..	77	21
127 Nicaragua	6	9.1	40	4.5	0.2	3.4	3.8	12.2	78	(.)
128 Papua New Guinea	–	11.6	..	9.4	..	..	..	..	..	..
129 Zimbabwe	8	1.7	25	3.7	..	6.6	8.3	..	79	18
130 Congo	10	6.7	12	32.3	0.3	7.0	8.3	..	..	..
Low human development	7	..	27	..	..	3.3	3.4	..	..	..
Excluding India	6	..	28	..	..	4.0	2.7	..	..	..
131 Myanmar	5	1.2	..	0.4	..	1.7	..	14.4	88	12
132 Ghana	9	2.5	32	38.8	..	3.1	3.1	24.3	64	11
133 Cameroon	–	18.0	28	25.2	..	3.2	3.1	..	87	13
134 Kenya	8	1.6	22	20.3	..	6.8	6.8	..	82	14
135 Equatorial Guinea	8	..	4	..	..	..	1.8	5.6	..	..
136 Lao People's Dem. Rep.	5	2.9	45	24.9	..	..	2.3	..	83	4
137 Lesotho	7	3.6	16	5.5	..	5.1	4.8	..	79	16
138 India	8	1.6	26	1.0	0.1	2.8	3.8	11.5	64	14
139 Pakistan	–	1.6	..	3.9	0.1	2.0	2.7	..	67	18
140 Comoros	9	1.4	29	..	..	..	..	..	74	12
141 Nigeria	6	3.9	36	1.7	(.)	6.4	1.3	7.3	57	25
142 Zaire	6	27.4	..	9.9	..	2.6	..	..	..	..
143 Zambia	7	2.8	25	9.5	..	4.5	2.6	8.7	66	17
144 Bangladesh	5	0.7	25	1.3	..	1.5	2.3	8.7	88	8
145 Côte d'Ivoire	6	9.8	..	15.4	..	7.2	..	..	99	(.)
146 Benin	6	6.1	16	19.1	0.2	..	..	..	..	..
147 Togo	6	6.7	16	22.4	..	5.6	6.1	21.6	60	12
148 Yemen	–	3.6	8	15.9	..	..	..	20.8	..	..
149 Tanzania, U. Rep. of	7	..	..	42.3	..	4.4	5.0	11.4	74	17
150 Mauritania	–	2.6	9	50.2	..	..	..	..	74	22
151 Central African Rep.	6	7.1	9	27.7	0.1	3.8	2.8	..	67	22
152 Madagascar	5	5.0	23	8.8	(.)	4.4	1.9	13.6	82	(.)
153 Cambodia	6	..	..	..	..	..	..	..	..	..
154 Nepal	5	..	14	3.2	(.)	1.8	2.9	13.2	62	28
155 Bhutan	–	..	..	20.0	..	..	..	..	..	..
156 Haiti	6	..	..	22.9	..	1.5	1.4	20.0	72	9
157 Angola	8	5.9	30	38.5	..	..	..	10.7	96	4
158 Sudan	6	4.1	16	13.3	..	4.8	..	..	..	..
159 Uganda	–	2.5	15	6.9	..	1.2	1.9	15.0	..	..
160 Senegal	6	3.3	20	21.0	0.2	..	..	..	69	24
161 Malawi	8	2.4	36	12.8	..	3.4	..	..	66	19
162 Djibouti	6	15.9	..	..	..	..	3.8	11.1	75	14
163 Guinea-Bissau	6	10.3	..	..	..	..	..	..	..	..
164 Chad	8	4.8	..	24.1	..	..	2.2	..	61	8
165 Gambia	–	..	..	..	..	3.3	2.7	12.9	64	9
166 Mozambique	7	6.0	39	34.3	..	4.4	..	..	66	10
167 Guinea	6	9.5	46	19.8	0.2	..	..	..	64	18
168 Eritrea	7	..	..	..	..	..	..	..	65	(.)
169 Burundi	6	12.8	32	17.4	(.)	3.0	3.8	12.2	73	25
170 Ethiopia	6	0.5	43	20.4	..	..	..	13.1	81	11
171 Mali	9	13.4	43	30.1	..	3.8	2.1	13.2	73	23
172 Burkina Faso	6	7.6	20	28.3	..	2.6	3.6	11.1	95	..
173 Niger	8	1.1	21	27.0	..	3.1	3.1	10.8	77	..
174 Rwanda	7	..	21	35.6	(.)	2.7	..	..	82	16
175 Sierra Leone	–	5.3	15	19.0	..	3.8	..	..	53	35
All developing countries	–	..	33	..	0.3	3.8	3.6	..	..	..
Least developed countries	–	..	26	..	..	3.1	2.8	..	..	..
Sub-Saharan Africa	–	..	31	..	..	5.1	5.5	..	..	..
Industrial countries	–	..	30	..	3.3	5.8	5.4	..	..	..
World	–	..	32	..	1.0	5.5	5.1	..	..	..

Source: Column 1: UNESCO 1995b; *column 2:* UNESCO 1993; *column 3:* calculated on the basis of estimates from UNESCO 1995b; *columns 4 and 5:* calculated on the basis of estimates from UNESCO 1995a; *columns 6-10:* calculated on the basis of data from UNESCO 1996d.

16 Employment

HDI rank	Labour force (as % of total population) 1990	Women's share of adult labour force (age 15 and above) 1970	1990	Percentage of labour force in						Real earnings per employee annual growth rate (%) 1970-80	1980-92
				Agriculture 1960	1990	Industry 1960	1990	Services 1960	1990		
High human development	43	31	36	54	31	18	24	28	44	..	..
22 Hong Kong	51	35	37	8	1	52	37	41	62	..	4.8
24 Cyprus	48	33	38	42	14	27	30	31	56	..	..
25 Barbados	50	40	46	26	7	27	23	46	70	..	..
26 Singapore	49	26	38	7	0	23	36	70	64	3.0	5.1
28 Bahamas	49	40	46	20	5	25	15	55	79	..	..
29 Antigua and Barbuda	..	..	..	..	..	..	..	..	..	..	..
30 Chile	38	22	30	30	19	30	25	39	56	8.1	-0.3
32 Korea, Rep. of	46	32	39	61	18	10	35	28	47	10.0	8.4
33 Costa Rica	38	18	28	51	26	18	27	30	47	..	..
36 Argentina	38	25	28	21	12	34	32	45	55	-2.1	-2.2
37 Uruguay	44	26	39	21	14	29	27	50	59	..	-2.3
38 Brunei Darussalam	..	..	..	..	..	..	..	..	..	..	..
40 Trinidad and Tobago	39	30	35	22	11	34	32	44	57	..	..
41 Dominica	..	..	..	..	..	..	..	..	..	..	..
43 Bahrain	44	5	17	14	2	45	30	42	68	..	..
44 United Arab Emirates	51	4	12	29	8	29	27	42	65	..	..
45 Panama	39	25	32	51	26	14	16	35	58	0.2	2.0
46 Fiji	34	12	23	60	46	17	15	23	39	..	..
47 Venezuela	..	..	..	..	..	..	..	..	..	4.9	-5.4
49 Saint Kitts and Nevis	..	..	..	..	..	..	..	..	..	..	..
50 Mexico	37	19	30	55	28	19	24	25	48	..	..
51 Colombia	40	24	36	52	27	19	23	29	50	-0.2	1.0
52 Seychelles	..	..	..	..	..	..	..	..	..	..	..
53 Kuwait	42	8	23	1	1	34	25	64	74	7.0	-1.6
54 Grenada	..	..	..	..	..	..	..	..	..	..	..
55 Qatar	57	4	11	17	3	24	32	59	65	..	..
56 Saint Lucia	..	..	..	..	..	..	..	..	..	..	..
57 Saint Vincent	..	..	..	..	..	..	..	..	..	..	..
59 Thailand	57	48	47	84	64	4	14	12	22	..	..
60 Malaysia	39	31	36	63	27	12	23	25	50	2.0	2.3
61 Mauritius	41	20	30	40	17	26	43	35	40	1.8	0.4
63 Belize	31	20	21	42	34	24	19	34	48	..	..
64 Libyan Arab Jamahiriya	29	16	18	59	11	14	23	26	66	..	..
Medium human development	51	38	42	78	62	9	17	14	22	..	..
Excluding China	40	31	35	66	42	13	20	21	39	..	0.4
65 Lebanon	31	19	27	38	7	23	31	39	62	..	..
66 Suriname	34	22	30	29	21	22	18	49	61	..	..
68 Brazil	44	24	34	55	23	17	23	28	54	5.0	-2.4
70 Iran, Islamic Rep. of	29	19	21	58	32	21	25	21	43	..	-6.8
72 Ecuador	35	19	25	59	33	18	19	23	48	3.3	-0.7
73 Saudi Arabia	34	5	10	71	19	10	20	19	61	..	..
74 Turkey	44	38	33	79	53	10	18	11	29	6.1	3.0
75 Korea, Dem. People's Rep. of	50	46	45	64	38	19	31	17	31	..	..
78 Syrian Arab Rep.	28	23	25	61	33	16	24	23	43	..	..
81 Tunisia	35	24	29	62	28	16	33	23	39	..	..
82 Algeria	28	20	21	71	26	10	31	19	43	-1.3	..
83 Jamaica	49	43	46	42	25	22	23	37	52	-0.2	-1.5
84 Jordan	27	13	18	50	15	24	23	26	61	..	-3.3
86 Cuba	45	20	36	36	18	24	30	41	51	..	..
87 Dominican Rep.	40	22	27	64	25	13	29	24	46	-1.1	..
88 Oman	26	6	12	67	45	12	24	20	32	..	..
89 Peru	35	22	27	52	36	20	18	28	46	..	..
90 South Africa	39	33	37	38	14	27	32	35	55	2.7	0.2
91 Sri Lanka	40	25	34	57	48	13	21	30	31	..	1.4
94 Paraguay	37	26	28	54	39	18	22	27	39	..	..
96 Samoa (Western)	..	..	..	..	..	..	..	..	..	..	..
97 Botswana	44	53	47	93	46	2	20	5	33	..	..
98 Philippines	40	33	37	64	46	14	15	22	39	-3.7	5.2
99 Indonesia	44	30	39	75	55	8	14	18	31	5.2	4.3
101 Mongolia	47	46	46	61	32	19	23	20	45	..	..
104 Guyana	40	21	31	38	22	27	25	35	53	..	..
108 China	59	42	45	83	72	6	15	10	13	..	..
109 Egypt	35	..	..	..	..	..	..	..	..	4.1	-3.6
111 Maldives	41	38	42	70	32	17	31	13	37	..	..
112 El Salvador	36	21	32	62	36	17	21	21	43	2.4	..
113 Bolivia	40	32	37	55	47	24	18	21	36	1.7	-0.8
114 Swaziland	34	34	37	75	39	9	22	16	38	..	..
116 Honduras	34	22	28	72	41	9	20	18	39	..	..
117 Guatemala	35	19	23	66	52	13	17	21	30	-3.2	-1.6
118 Namibia	42	40	41	71	49	13	15	16	36	..	..

HDI rank	Labour force (as % of total population) 1990	Women's share of adult labour force (age 15 and above)		Percentage of labour force in						Real earnings per employee annual growth rate (%)	
				Agriculture		Industry		Services			
	1990	1970	1990	1960	1990	1960	1990	1960	1990	1970-80	1980-92
119 Morocco	38	31	35	73	45	10	25	17	31	..	-2.5
120 Gabon	49	46	44	85	52	6	16	8	33	..	..
121 Viet Nam	51	48	50	82	71	5	14	14	15	..	..
122 Solomon Islands	51	..	..	..	..	..	..	..	..	..	..
123 Cape Verde	37	29	39	57	31	22	30	21	40	..	..
124 Vanuatu	37	21	31	33	12	22	27	44	61	..	..
125 São Tomé and Principe	..	..	..	..	..	..	..	..	..	..	..
126 Iraq	26	16	16	58	16	16	18	25	66	..	..
127 Nicaragua	34	23	35	63	28	15	26	21	46	-2.0	..
128 Papua New Guinea	49	42	41	90	79	4	7	6	14	2.9	..
129 Zimbabwe	46	44	44	81	68	10	8	9	24	1.6	0.1
130 Congo	42	41	43	68	49	10	15	21	37	..	..
Low human development	43	37	35	79	66	9	13	13	21	..	..
Excluding India	44	40	40	83	68	7	10	11	22	..	..
131 Myanmar	51	44	44	81	73	5	10	14	17	..	..
132 Ghana	47	51	51	63	59	14	13	23	28	-14.8	..
133 Cameroon	40	37	37	89	70	4	9	7	21	..	..
134 Kenya	48	45	46	88	80	5	7	8	13	-3.4	-2.1
135 Equatorial Guinea	43	37	35	85	75	4	5	10	20	..	..
136 Lao People's Dem. Rep.	50	45	47	82	78	4	6	14	16	..	..
137 Lesotho	40	39	37	47	40	33	28	19	32	..	..
138 India	43	34	31	75	64	11	16	14	20	0.4	2.5
139 Pakistan	35	22	24	66	52	16	19	19	30	3.4	..
140 Comoros	44	43	43	86	77	6	9	8	13	..	..
141 Nigeria	40	37	35	73	43	10	7	17	50	-0.8	..
142 Zaire	42	45	44	79	68	9	13	11	19	..	..
143 Zambia	42	45	45	85	75	6	8	10	17	-3.2	3.8
144 Bangladesh	49	40	42	88	65	6	16	7	18	-3.0	-0.7
145 Côte d'Ivoire	37	33	32	84	60	4	10	12	30	-0.9	..
146 Benin	46	49	48	85	64	4	8	11	28	..	..
147 Togo	42	39	40	80	66	8	10	12	24	..	..
148 Yemen	30	27	30	82	61	6	17	11	22	..	..
149 Tanzania, U. Rep. of	52	..	..	..	..	..	..	..	..	..	..
150 Mauritania	45	47	44	92	55	2	10	6	34	..	..
151 Central African Rep.	49	49	47	93	80	2	4	5	16	..	..
152 Madagascar	48	45	45	86	78	4	7	10	15	-0.8	..
153 Cambodia	50	49	54	83	74	3	8	14	19	..	..
154 Nepal	47	39	40	95	94	2	0	3	6	..	..
155 Bhutan	51	40	39	95	94	2	1	3	5	..	..
156 Haiti	45	46	43	80	68	6	9	14	23	..	..
157 Angola	47	47	47	81	75	6	8	12	17	..	..
158 Sudan	36	27	27	87	69	3	8	10	22	..	..
159 Uganda	51	48	48	93	85	2	5	5	11	..	..
160 Senegal	45	42	42	84	77	5	8	11	16	..	..
161 Malawi	49	51	50	94	87	3	5	4	8	..	..
162 Djibouti	..	..	..	..	..	..	..	..	..	..	..
163 Guinea-Bissau	48	40	40	91	85	1	2	8	13	..	..
164 Chad	49	42	44	96	83	2	4	3	13	..	..
165 Gambia	50	45	45	94	82	5	8	1	11	..	..
166 Mozambique	53	49	48	88	83	5	8	7	9	..	..
167 Guinea	49	48	47	94	87	1	2	5	11	..	..
168 Eritrea	50	47	47	87	80	4	5	9	15	..	..
169 Burundi	54	50	49	95	92	2	3	3	6	-7.5	..
170 Ethiopia	44	42	41	93	86	2	2	5	12	..	..
171 Mali	50	47	47	94	86	1	2	5	12	..	..
172 Burkina Faso	54	49	47	92	92	3	2	6	6	..	..
173 Niger	49	45	44	94	90	2	4	4	6	..	..
174 Rwanda	52	49	49	95	92	2	3	3	5	..	..
175 Sierra Leone	37	36	36	81	67	9	15	9	17	..	..
All developing countries	47	37	39	77	61	9	16	14	23	..	..
Least developed countries	47	43	43	86	74	5	10	9	17	..	..
Sub-Saharan Africa	45	43	42	81	66	7	9	12	25	..	..
Industrial countries	49	40	44	27	10	35	33	38	57	..	..
World	48	38	40	61	49	17	20	22	31	..	..

Note: Percentage shares of labour force in agriculture, industry and services may not necessarily add to 100 because of rounding.
Source: Columns 1-9: ILO 1996b; columns 10 and 11: World Bank 1995e.

HDI rank	Radios (per 1,000 people) 1994	Televisions (per 100 people) 1994	Book titles published (per 100,000 people) 1992-94	Printing and writing paper consumed (metric tons per 1,000 people) 1994	Post offices (per 100,000 people) 1991	Main telephone lines (per 100 people) 1994	International telephone calls (minutes per person) 1994	Fax machines (per 100 people) 1994	Mobile cellular telephone subscribers (per 100 people) 1992	Internet users (per 10,000 people) 1994	Personal computers (per 100 people) 1994
High human development	419	25	..	19.9	..	14.9	15.8	0.5	1.3	8.8	3.7
22 Hong Kong	677	36	..	153.5	..	54.0	270.5	4.3	8.0	117.3	11.3
24 Cyprus	300	16	142	31.0	..	51.8	145.2	..	3.1	6.6	..
25 Barbados	877	26	..	27.3	..	32.7	98.6	0.6	1.1	..	..
26 Singapore	645	38	..	117.9	24.2	45.5	198.7	..	7.2	102.5	15.3
28 Bahamas	735	24	..	8.0	..	28.3	128.0	..	..	..	..
29 Antigua and Barbuda	427	35	..	..	17.3	30.8	151.6	..	..	..	..
30 Chile	345	25	13	15.9	8.4	11.0	4.5	..	0.7	12.0	2.5
32 Korea, Rep. of	1,017	32	77	37.1	7.7	39.6	8.2	0.8	2.2	22.3	11.3
33 Costa Rica	260	22	29	11.2	..	13.0	16.7	..	0.2	13.3	..
36 Argentina	673	32	26	17.5	..	14.1	5.1	0.1	0.6	2.0	1.4
37 Uruguay	606	52	..	13.7	..	18.4	14.6	0.3	0.2	3.0	..
38 Brunei Darussalam	271	32	16	5.8	4.6	22.1	92.9	0.5	5.5	..	..
40 Trinidad and Tobago	491	31	2	10.6	19.6	15.8	37.3	0.2	0.2	..	..
41 Dominica	600	7	..	12.0	..	23.5	69.5	..	..	..	..
43 Bahrain	556	42	..	11.0	..	24.8	158.3	1.0	3.2	..	..
44 United Arab Emirates	312	29	14	39.3	10.0	27.6	230.8	1.4	4.2	..	..
45 Panama	227	17	..	7.2	..	11.1	13.9	..	..	0.4	..
46 Fiji	607	7	52	11.8	..	7.7	18.5	0.3	0.1	0.4	..
47 Venezuela	443	18	17	12.6	..	10.8	7.3	..	1.5	1.4	1.1
49 Saint Kitts and Nevis	666	22	..	..	18.2	33.2	48.1	..	..	..	..
50 Mexico	256	19	..	11.7	..	9.3	8.4	..	0.6	4.0	2.3
51 Colombia	178	22	..	9.8	..	9.2	3.3	0.2	0.3	1.7	..
52 Seychelles	490	32	..	3.5	7.1	17.0	31.4	0.8	..	..	..
53 Kuwait	445	41	11	27.4	..	22.6	71.3	1.7	4.9	7.3	..
54 Grenada	595	16	..	0.8	..	22.8	80.4	..	0.4	..	..
55 Qatar	428	43	69	3.7	..	21.5	116.8	1.5	1.8	..	..
56 Saint Lucia	764	25	..	7.5	..	17.2	102.3	..	0.4	..	..
57 Saint Vincent	667	23	..	0.8	..	15.5	21.1	0.6	..	..	..
59 Thailand	190	25	13	11.3	7.3	4.7	3.3	0.1	1.1	1.6	1.2
60 Malaysia	432	23	21	27.5	12.4	14.7	9.5	0.3	2.9	4.5	3.3
61 Mauritius	367	19	8	11.2	9.4	11.7	17.1	1.6	0.5	..	..
63 Belize	581	17	34	1.9	..	13.4	24.7	..	0.4	..	..
64 Libyan Arab Jamahiriya	226	10	..	0.9	..	5.1	4.8	..	..	..	..
Medium human development	207	19	8	6.9	..	3.5	1.9	(.)	0.2	0.9	..
Excluding China	234	15	8	5.8	..	5.0	3.0	0.1	0.2	2.3	..
65 Lebanon	889	26	..	16.9	..	8.4	3.2	..	..	..	..
66 Suriname	680	15	..	1.6	..	12.0	15.4	..	0.3	..	0.1
68 Brazil	393	25	14	11.6	7.9	7.4	1.1	..	0.4	0.3	0.9
70 Iran, Islamic Rep. of	237	12	16	2.5	..	6.6	3.2	(.)	(.)	(.)	..
72 Ecuador	327	13	(.)	6.0	4.9	5.9	3.2	..	0.2	1.6	..
73 Saudi Arabia	294	25	..	5.9	..	9.6	27.3	..	0.1	(.)	2.5
74 Turkey	162	27	8	6.1	..	20.0	4.6	0.2	0.3	2.4	0.9
75 Korea, Dem. People's Rep. of	126	12	..	0.4	..	4.7	0.1	(.)	..	..	..
78 Syrian Arab Rep.	257	8	4	2.6	..	4.8	2.8	(.)	..	..	..
81 Tunisia	199	9	6	7.3	..	5.4	7.3	0.2	(.)	0.4	0.5
82 Algeria	236	7	1	2.9	10.6	4.1	4.5	(.)	..	(.)	..
83 Jamaica	436	30	..	6.9	..	10.0	20.3	..	1.1	1.7	..
84 Jordan	243	16	10	6.9	..	7.2	15.9	0.6	(.)	..	..
86 Cuba	347	19	9	1.4	..	3.2	1.1	..	(.)	..	..
87 Dominican Rep.	173	9	..	4.9	..	7.9	8.3	..	0.3	..	..
88 Oman	583	73	1	6.4	..	7.6	23.9	..	0.3	..	..
89 Peru	255	10	9	9.0	..	3.3	2.2	(.)	0.2	0.4	..
90 South Africa	314	10	11	20.0	..	9.1	6.3	0.2	0.8	36.7	2.2
91 Sri Lanka	201	7	17	5.0	23.0	1.0	1.2	0.1	0.2	..	..
94 Paraguay	172	7	3	6.9	7.2	3.1	3.3	..	0.3	..	..
96 Samoa (Western)	462	..	..	1.5	..	..	43.3	0.3	..	..	..
97 Botswana	125	2	..	..	12.8	3.5	21.0	0.2	..	..	..
98 Philippines	144	12	2	4.5	4.0	1.7	2.5	0.1	0.3	0.3	0.5
99 Indonesia	148	15	3	4.3	5.4	1.3	1.0	(.)	(.)	0.1	0.3
101 Mongolia	136	6	12	0.2	..	2.9	0.5	(.)	..	..	(.)
104 Guyana	491	4	4	1.6	..	5.3	22.3	..	0.2	..	..
108 China	184	23	8	7.8	..	2.3	1.0	(.)	0.1	(.)	..
109 Egypt	307	9	5	5.0	12.4	4.3	1.4	(.)	(.)	0.2	..
111 Maldives	118	4	..	0.9	..	4.8	12.3	0.2	..	..	..
112 El Salvador	443	23	..	6.7	5.2	4.4	11.1	..	0.1	..	..
113 Bolivia	670	14	..	3.2	2.8	3.5	2.2	..	0.1	..	..
114 Swaziland	163	7	..	..	8.3	2.0	25.5	0.1	..	..	..
116 Honduras	408	8	(.)	3.0	..	2.4	6.7	..	..	..	..
117 Guatemala	68	5	..	4.8	6.5	2.4	5.5	0.1	0.1	..	..
118 Namibia	139	3	..	..	..	4.7	2.0	..	..	..	..

HDI rank	Radios (per 1,000 people) 1994	Televisions (per 100 people) 1994	Book titles published (per 100,000 people) 1992-94	Printing and writing paper consumed (metric tons per 1,000 people) 1994	Post offices (per 100,000 people) 1991	Main telephone lines (per 100 people) 1994	International telephone calls (minutes per person) 1994	Fax machines (per 100 people) 1994	Mobile cellular telephone subscribers (per 100 people) 1992	Internet users (per 10,000 people) 1994	Personal computers (per 100 people) 1994
119 Morocco	219	7	1	3.0	..	3.8	4.9	..	0.1	..	..
120 Gabon	147	5	..	..	8.5	3.0	15.3	..	0.3	..	..
121 Viet Nam	104	11	8	1.4	..	0.6	0.3	(.)	(.)	..	..
122 Solomon Islands	122	2	..	0.6	..	1.5	5.0	0.2	(.)	..	..
123 Cape Verde	176	..	..	0.1	16.8	4.9	8.5	0.1	..	..	..
124 Vanuatu	294	1	..	0.3	..	2.7	..	0.3	(.)	..	..
125 São Tomé and Principe	270	..	..	0.1	9.1	2.0	3.6	0.1	..	..	..
126 Iraq	218	7	..	0.4	..	3.4	..	..	..	..	..
127 Nicaragua	262	15	..	1.7	..	2.0	5.2	..	0.1	0.6	..
128 Papua New Guinea	76	17	..	1.1	..	0.9	5.0	(.)	..	..	..
129 Zimbabwe	86	3	2	2.2	2.8	1.2	3.9	0.1	..	0.1	..
130 Congo	115	1	..	0.1	..	0.8	2.0	..	..	..	..
Low human development	96	4	1	1.3	13.8	0.8	0.5	..	..	..	..
Excluding India	111	3	..	0.7	..	0.5	0.6	..	..	..	..
131 Myanmar	82	8	8	0.4	..	0.3	0.1	..	..	..	..
132 Ghana	229	2	(.)	0.4	6.5	0.3	0.7	(.)	(.)	..	..
133 Cameroon	148	8	..	0.5	..	0.4	1.4	..	(.)	..	..
134 Kenya	88	2	..	2.2	..	0.9	0.8	(.)	(.)	..	..
135 Equatorial Guinea	424	9	..	..	..	0.6	1.4	(.)	..	..	..
136 Lao People's Dem. Rep.	127	1	1	0.1	4.9	0.4	0.4	(.)	(.)	..	..
137 Lesotho	33	1	..	..	..	0.8	5.8	..	..	..	..
138 India	81	6	1	1.8	17.6	1.1	0.4	(.)	..	(.)	0.1
139 Pakistan	88	2	(.)	1.2	11.5	1.5	0.5	0.1	(.)	..	..
140 Comoros	129	1	..	0.7	..	0.9	2.7	..	..	..	..
141 Nigeria	196	4	1	0.6	4.0	0.3	0.6	..	(.)	..	0.4
142 Zaire	98	(.)	(.)	0.2	1.3	0.1	..	..	..	..	..
143 Zambia	83	3	..	0.4	..	0.9	1.2	(.)	..	0.4	..
144 Bangladesh	47	1	..	1.2	..	0.2	0.2	..	..	..	..
145 Côte d'Ivoire	143	6	..	0.8	3.0	..	2.0	..	..	..	..
146 Benin	91	2	2	0.1	3.9	0.5	0.9	(.)	..	..	..
147 Togo	212	1	..	0.2	..	0.5	2.2	0.1	..	..	..
148 Yemen	32	27	..	0.5	..	1.2	1.6	(.)	0.1	..	..
149 Tanzania, U. Rep. of	26	(.)	..	0.6	3.7	0.3	0.2	..	..	..	..
150 Mauritania	147	4	..	0.4	..	0.4	2.2	..	..	..	..
151 Central African Rep.	73	1	..	..	..	0.2	0.7	..	..	..	..
152 Madagascar	192	2	1	0.4	8.0	0.3	0.3	..	..	..	..
153 Cambodia	108	1	..	0.3	..	0.1	..	..	0.1	..	..
154 Nepal	35	(.)	..	..	..	0.4	0.6	..	..	..	..
155 Bhutan	17	..	..	..	5.5	0.7	0.6	(.)	..	..	..
156 Haiti	50	1	..	0.4	2.0	0.7	2.8	..	..	..	..
157 Angola	30	3	..	0.2	0.7	..	1.4	(.)	..	..	..
158 Sudan	258	8	..	0.2	..	0.2	0.4	(.)	..	..	..
159 Uganda	107	2	2	0.1	..	0.2	0.2	..	..	..	..
160 Senegal	117	4	..	0.6	1.9	0.9	2.2	..	..	..	0.6
161 Malawi	226	..	3	(.)	..	0.3	0.8	(.)	..	..	..
162 Djibouti	81	5	..	0.1	..	1.3	8.0	(.)	..	..	..
163 Guinea-Bissau	40	..	..	0.1	..	0.9	1.9	0.1	..	..	..
164 Chad	246	(.)	..	..	0.6	0.1	0.3	..	..	..	..
165 Gambia	163	..	2	0.2	..	1.7	3.9	0.1	0.1	..	..
166 Mozambique	37	(.)	..	(.)	1.6	0.3	0.7	(.)	..	..	..
167 Guinea	43	1	..	(.)	..	0.1	0.6	..	(.)	(.)	..
168 Eritrea	87	1	3	..	..	0.4	0.3	(.)	..	..	..
169 Burundi	64	1	..	..	0.6	0.3	0.4	..	(.)	..	..
170 Ethiopia	197	(.)	..	0.2	..	0.3	0.2	..	..	..	..
171 Mali	44	1	..	0.1	..	0.2	0.6	..	..	..	..
172 Burkina Faso	28	1	..	..	..	0.3	0.6	..	..	..	..
173 Niger	61	2	..	0.1	0.8	0.1	0.4	..	..	..	..
174 Rwanda	67	(.)	..	(.)	..	0.2	0.2	..	..	..	..
175 Sierra Leone	233	1	..	0.2	2.0	0.3	0.3	(.)	..	..	..
All developing countries	178	14	7	5.8	..	3.3	2.5	0.1	0.3	1.5	..
Least developed countries	96	2	..	0.5	..	0.3	0.5	..	..	..	..
Sub-Saharan Africa	149	3	..	2.3	..	1.1	1.4	..	..	..	..
Industrial countries	1,018	50	52	74.0	..	40.1	35.1	2.8	4.1	223.2	14.2
World	361	22	18	20.6	..	11.5	9.4	0.7	1.4	60.9	..

Source: Column 1: calculated on the basis of estimates from UNESCO 1995a; *columns 2 and 6-11:* ITU 1996; *columns 3 and 4:* calculated on the basis of estimates from UNESCO 1996d; *column 5:* UNDP 1994.

18 Social investment

HDI rank	Social security benefits expenditure (as % of GDP) 1993	Social security and welfare		Housing and community amenities		Health		Education	
		1980[a]	1992-95	1980[a]	1992-95	1980[a]	1992-95	1980[a]	1992-95
High human development	..	..	..	..	..	..	..	..	..
22 Hong Kong	..	..	..	..	..	..	..	..	..
24 Cyprus	..	16.4	23.0	9.3	3.6	6.8	6.1	12.2	11.1
25 Barbados	..	14.3	..	6.0	..	10.8	..	19.5	..
26 Singapore	7.2	1.4	3.8	7.1	7.0	7.2	6.0	19.2	24.8
28 Bahamas	..	6.7	4.1	0.1	1.3	13.8	14.6	20.8	18.7
29 Antigua and Barbuda	..	..	..	..	..	..	..	..	..
30 Chile	..	36.6	33.3	4.7	5.6	6.5	12.2	14.7	13.9
32 Korea, Rep. of	2.3	6.0	10.2	0.8	2.1	1.3	0.7	18.0	20.2
33 Costa Rica	..	10.3	17.7	2.3	0.4	29.7	20.5	23.7	22.9
36 Argentina	4.5	33.9	45.8	0.3	0.4	1.4	2.8	7.3	9.4
37 Uruguay	14.8	..	60.6	..	0.2	..	5.8	..	6.5
38 Brunei Darussalam	..	..	..	..	..	..	..	..	..
40 Trinidad and Tobago	..	6.4	..	11.4	..	5.9	..	11.2	..
41 Dominica	..	..	..	..	..	..	..	..	..
43 Bahrain	..	2.3	4.5	12.8	1.6	7.6	8.6	9.7	12.0
44 United Arab Emirates	..	2.5	3.4	1.3	2.0	6.2	7.3	7.6	17.1
45 Panama	..	9.3	22.2	3.5	5.5	13.2	20.0	12.8	20.2
46 Fiji	..	2.7	4.8	1.4	5.4	7.7	8.7	19.9	19.1
47 Venezuela	..	7.0	..	2.1	..	7.6	..	16.0	..
49 Saint Kitts and Nevis	..	..	..	..	..	..	..	..	..
50 Mexico	2.8	14.7	12.4	4.1	0.6	1.9	1.9	18.2	13.9
51 Colombia	2.4	..	7.8	..	1.4	..	5.4	..	19.0
52 Seychelles	..	..	..	..	..	..	..	..	..
53 Kuwait	..	..	16.6	6.2	4.8	4.9	5.7	9.0	10.9
54 Grenada	..	..	..	..	..	..	..	..	..
55 Qatar	..	..	..	..	..	..	..	..	..
56 Saint Lucia	..	..	..	..	..	..	..	..	..
57 Saint Vincent	..	..	6.4	..	1.9	10.0	12.5	15.6	15.9
59 Thailand	0.1	2.5	4.0	2.9	2.7	4.2	8.1	18.9	21.1
60 Malaysia	2.3	4.0	5.7	6.5	6.1	4.4	5.6	15.9	21.8
61 Mauritius	3.6	..	16.5	3.4	6.9	7.0	8.8	15.8	17.0
63 Belize	..	..	3.5	3.1	9.5	8.9	15.9	15.8	16.4
64 Libyan Arab Jamahiriya	..	..	..	..	..	..	..	..	..
Medium human development	..	..	..	..	..	..	..	..	..
Excluding China	..	..	..	..	..	..	..	..	..
65 Lebanon	..	..	..	..	..	..	..	..	..
66 Suriname	..	..	..	..	..	..	..	..	..
68 Brazil	..	34.6	29.5	0.2	0.5	7.4	5.2	3.8	3.6
70 Iran, Islamic Rep. of	1.5	9.0	10.3	2.5	2.4	5.4	8.9	15.9	15.9
72 Ecuador	..	..	1.9	..	0.6	..	11.2	..	18.4
73 Saudi Arabia	..	..	..	..	..	..	..	..	..
74 Turkey	4.9	..	3.9	8.4	1.2	2.1	3.0	16.8	13.6
75 Korea, Dem. People's Rep. of	..	..	..	..	..	..	..	..	..
78 Syrian Arab Rep.	..	8.2	2.3	3.2	..	1.1	2.3	7.1	9.8
81 Tunisia	4.1	8.3	14.3	5.4	4.4	7.7	6.6	15.3	17.5
82 Algeria	..	..	..	..	..	..	..	..	..
83 Jamaica	..	..	..	..	..	..	..	..	..
84 Jordan	0.6	13.7	15.3	0.8	..	3.8	7.1	7.6	16.3
86 Cuba	..	..	..	..	..	..	..	..	..
87 Dominican Rep.	..	7.5	4.2	6.1	14.9	9.7	11.3	13.9	9.6
88 Oman	..	..	3.2	1.6	7.8	3.0	6.4	5.3	12.5
89 Peru	..	..	..	0.9	..	5.3	..	11.4	..
90 South Africa	..	..	..	..	..	..	..	..	..
91 Sri Lanka	2.5	12.1	16.7	4.8	1.4	3.9	5.8	8.2	11.2
94 Paraguay	..	19.0	16.2	3.7	0.4	4.5	7.3	11.8	22.1
96 Samoa (Western)	..	..	..	..	..	..	..	..	..
97 Botswana	..	0.3	2.6	6.6	13.5	5.9	4.9	21.2	20.3
98 Philippines	1.2	..	3.1	4.6	1.9	5.0	3.0	15.9	15.9
99 Indonesia	..	..	0.0	1.2	1.6	2.5	2.7	7.9	10.0
101 Mongolia	..	..	21.6	..	0.9	..	3.8	..	6.6
104 Guyana	..	3.0	..	0.3	..	5.7	..	10.2	..
108 China	..	..	0.1	..	0.1	..	0.4	..	2.9
109 Egypt	..	12.1	11.0	2.9	..	2.2	2.4	8.6	12.3
111 Maldives	..	3.9	..	11.2	..	4.5	..	8.2	..
112 El Salvador	..	..	7.3	1.6	7.8	8.4	8.3	17.9	13.2
113 Bolivia	1.6	..	14.6	1.9	0.6	7.1	7.1	24.5	18.5
114 Swaziland	..	..	..	10.5	..	5.4	..	21.2	..
116 Honduras	..	..	..	..	..	..	..	..	..
117 Guatemala	..	..	..	..	..	..	10.6	..	19.0
118 Namibia	..	..	..	..	..	..	..	..	..

HDI rank	Social security benefits expenditures (as % of GDP) 1993	Percentage of central government expenditure on							
		Social security and welfare		Housing and community amenities		Health		Education	
		1980[a]	1992-95	1980[a]	1992-95	1980[a]	1992-95	1980[a]	1992-95
119 Morocco	1.8	4.6	5.9	1.0	0.5	3.0	3.0	16.6	17.9
120 Gabon	..	..	..	..	..	..	..	..	..
121 Viet Nam	..	..	..	..	..	..	..	..	..
122 Solomon Islands	..	2.7	..	8.1	..	10.2	..	14.7	..
123 Cape Verde	..	..	..	..	..	..	..	..	..
124 Vanuatu	..	0.9	..	..	..	10.9	..	23.3	..
125 São Tomé and Principe	..	..	..	..	..	..	..	..	..
126 Iraq	..	..	..	..	..	..	..	..	..
127 Nicaragua	..	..	14.7	..	3.3	..	13.4	..	15.5
128 Papua New Guinea	..	0.2	0.7	2.1	3.5	9.0	8.9	16.1	17.6
129 Zimbabwe	..	6.7	..	1.1	..	7.1	..	20.0	..
130 Congo	..	4.9	..	2.1	..	..	..	..	..
Low human development	..	..	..	..	..	..	..	..	..
Excluding India	..	..	..	..	..	..	..	..	..
131 Myanmar	..	5.8	4.1	3.4	0.4	6.1	4.7	10.1	15.3
132 Ghana	0.1	7.2	7.1	1.7	2.8	6.4	7.0	17.1	22.0
133 Cameroon	..	3.7	1.0	1.4	1.8	2.7	4.8	7.5	18.0
134 Kenya	0.7	0.1	0.1	4.8	1.8	7.8	5.4	20.6	18.9
135 Equatorial Guinea	..	..	..	..	..	..	..	..	..
136 Lao People's Dem. Rep.	..	..	..	..	..	..	..	..	..
137 Lesotho	..	..	1.5	..	3.9	..	11.5	..	21.9
138 India	0.3	..	..	..	7.3	2.0	1.8	1.9	1.9
139 Pakistan	..	3.4	..	3.8	..	1.6	..	3.1	..
140 Comoros	..	..	..	..	..	..	..	..	..
141 Nigeria	..	..	..	..	..	..	..	..	..
142 Zaire	..	0.7	(.)	..	2.8	2.6	0.7	20.2	0.6
143 Zambia	..	2.2	3.2	0.4	5.1	6.1	14.2	11.9	15.0
144 Bangladesh	..	1.7	..	1.2	..	5.7	..	8.8	..
145 Côte d'Ivoire	..	..	..	..	..	..	..	..	..
146 Benin	..	..	..	..	..	..	..	..	..
147 Togo	1.1	8.8	..	3.2	..	5.3	..	16.7	..
148 Yemen	..	..	0.0	..	2.4	3.6	4.7	14.8	20.7
149 Tanzania, U. Rep. of	..	..	..	..	..	..	..	..	..
150 Mauritania	0.9	..	..	..	..	..	..	..	..
151 Central African Rep.	..	6.5	..	0.2	..	5.1	..	17.6	..
152 Madagascar	..	..	1.5	..	0.0	..	6.6	..	17.1
153 Cambodia	..	..	..	..	..	..	..	..	..
154 Nepal	..	0.6	..	1.0	6.7	4.1	4.6	9.7	10.9
155 Bhutan	..	..	0.0	..	11.5	..	8.0	..	10.5
156 Haiti	..	..	..	..	..	..	..	..	..
157 Angola	0.2	..	..	..	..	..	..	..	..
158 Sudan	0.7	..	..	..	..	..	..	..	..
159 Uganda	..	..	..	2.9	..	5.9	..	12.6	..
160 Senegal	..	5.9	..	3.9	..	4.6	..	22.4	..
161 Malawi	..	1.2	..	1.6	..	5.2	..	11.1	..
162 Djibouti	..	..	..	..	..	..	..	..	..
163 Guinea-Bissau	..	..	..	..	..	..	..	..	..
164 Chad	..	..	..	..	..	..	..	..	..
165 Gambia	..	0.8	3.0	3.4	4.6	7.2	6.9	14.6	12.3
166 Mozambique	..	..	..	..	..	..	..	..	..
167 Guinea	..	..	..	..	..	..	..	..	..
168 Eritrea	..	..	..	..	..	..	..	..	..
169 Burundi	0.4	..	..	..	..	..	..	..	..
170 Ethiopia	1.7	4.6	4.7	1.3	4.5	3.7	3.2	9.8	10.6
171 Mali	..	..	..	..	..	..	..	..	..
172 Burkina Faso	0.6	6.7	0.0	0.2	0.8	5.8	6.9	15.8	17.3
173 Niger	0.4	..	..	..	..	..	..	..	..
174 Rwanda	..	..	..	..	..	..	..	..	..
175 Sierra Leone	..	..	..	..	0.8	..	9.6	..	13.3
All developing countries	..	..	..	..	..	..	..	..	..
Least developed countries	..	..	..	..	..	..	..	..	..
Sub-Saharan Africa	..	..	..	..	..	..	..	..	..
Industrial countries	..	..	..	..	..	..	..	..	..
World	..	..	..	..	..	..	..	..	..

a. Data refer to 1980 or a year around 1980.
Source: Column 1: ILO 1995a; *columns 2-9:* IMF, *Government Finance Statistics Yearbook,* various editions.

		Defence expenditure					Military expenditure (as % of combined education and health expenditure)		Imports of conventional weapons (1990 prices)[a]		Total armed forces	
		US$ millions (1995 prices)		As % of GDP		Per capita (US$; 1995 prices)				US$ millions	Index (1990=100)	Thous-ands	Index (1985=100)
HDI rank		1985	1995	1985	1995	1985	1995	1960	1990-91	1995	1995	1995	1995
High human development		33,889 T	44,220 T	3.7	2.5	116	131	65	44	..	..	1,832 T	112
22	Hong Kong	..	..	..	..	..	..	..	10	..	..	..	..
24	Cyprus	119	354	3.6	4.5	179	477	..	17	..	..	10.0	100
25	Barbados	16	13	0.9	0.7	62	50	..	5	..	..	0.6	60
26	Singapore	1,622	3,970	6.7	5.9	634	1,349	11	129	91	23	53.9	98
28	Bahamas	13	19	0.5	0.6	59	70	..	..	..	..	0.9	180
29	Antigua and Barbuda	3	3	0.5	0.8	32	48	..	..	..	..	0.2	200
30	Chile	1,696	1,936	7.8	3.8	140	136	60	68	386	190	99.0	98
32	Korea, Rep. of	8,592	14,359	5.1	3.4	209	320	273	60	1,677	244	633.0	106
33	Costa Rica	40	21	0.7	0.3	16	6	17	5	..	..	..	..
36	Argentina	4,945	3,732	3.8	1.7	162	109	62	51	515	..	67.3	62
37	Uruguay	232	320	2.5	2.6	58	101	40	38	..	..	25.6	80
38	Brunei Darussalam	280	268	6.0	6.0	1,250	909	..	125	..	..	4.9	120
40	Trinidad and Tobago	100	82	1.4	1.3	84	63	..	9	..	..	2.1	100
41	Dominica	..	..	..	..	..	..	..	..	..	..	..	..
43	Bahrain	206	261	3.5	5.2	494	456	..	41	353	88	10.7	382
44	United Arab Emirates	2,790	1,880	7.6	4.8	2,031	1,044	..	44	427	46	70.0	163
45	Panama	123	95	2.0	1.3	61	36	2	34	..	..	..	..
46	Fiji	19	27	1.2	1.5	27	35	..	37	..	..	3.9	144
47	Venezuela	1,125	683	1.3	1.1	65	31	40	33	..	..	46.0	94
49	Saint Kitts and Nevis	..	..	..	..	..	..	..	..	..	..	..	..
50	Mexico	1,695	2,676	0.7	0.9	22	30	23	5	..	..	175.0	136
51	Colombia	579	1,195	1.6	2.0	20	34	57	57	..	..	146.4	221
52	Seychelles	11	14	2.1	3.9	168	192	..	..	..	..	0.3	25
53	Kuwait	2,453	3,147	9.1	11.8	1,434	2,091	..	88	1,117	396	16.6	138
54	Grenada	..	..	..	..	..	..	..	..	..	..	..	..
55	Qatar	410	326	6.0	4.4	1,301	600	..	192	..	..	11.1	185
56	Saint Lucia	..	..	..	..	..	..	..	..	..	..	..	..
57	Saint Vincent	..	..	..	..	..	..	..	..	..	..	..	..
59	Thailand	2,559	3,896	5.0	2.5	49	64	96	71	888	203	259.0	110
60	Malaysia	2,409	3,514	5.6	4.5	155	177	48	38	1,120	..	114.5	104
61	Mauritius	3	14	1.7	0.5	25	12	4	4	..	..	1.3	130
63	Belize	5	14	1.4	2.6	30	65	..	..	..	..	..	..
64	Libyan Arab Jamahiriya	1,844	1,401	6.2	5.5	490	259	29	71	..	..	80.0	110
Medium human development		132,948 T	90,685 T	10.1	3.6	72	40	140	72	..	118	9,101 T	91
Excluding China		105,841 T	58,954 T	10.5	2.8	131	57	84	61	..	..	6,171 T	101
65	Lebanon	273	407	9.0	5.3	102	102	..	..	..	..	44.3	255
66	Suriname	11	14	2.4	3.9	16	34	..	27	..	..	1.8	90
68	Brazil	3,209	6,890	0.8	1.5	24	43	72	23	237	118	295.0	107
70	Iran, Islamic Rep. of	19,423	2,460	36.0	3.9	435	38	141	38	187	24	513.0	168
72	Ecuador	388	550	1.8	3.4	41	47	104	26	..	..	57.1	134
73	Saudi Arabia	24,530	13,215	19.6	10.6	2,125	699	150	151	961	39	162.5	260
74	Turkey	3,134	6,004	4.5	3.6	62	98	153	87	1,125	140	507.8	81
75	Korea, Dem. People's Rep. of	5,675	5,232	23.0	25.2	278	219	..	..	..	..	1,128.0	135
78	Syrian Arab Rep.	4,756	2,026	16.4	6.8	453	142	329	373	185	661	423.0	105
81	Tunisia	569	369	5.0	2.0	80	41	45	31	..	..	35.5	101
82	Algeria	1,301	1,234	1.7	2.5	59	44	31	11	165	43	121.7	72
83	Jamaica	27	27	0.9	0.6	11	11	..	8	..	..	3.3	157
84	Jordan	822	440	15.9	6.7	235	100	464	138	..	..	98.6	140
86	Cuba	2,181	335	9.6	2.8	216	30	64	125	..	..	105.0	65
87	Dominican Rep.	70	111	1.1	1.3	11	14	147	22	..	..	24.5	110
88	Oman	2,946	1,840	20.8	15.1	1,841	978	..	293	..	..	43.5	1,740
89	Peru	875	817	4.5	1.6	47	35	59	39	..	..	115.0	90
90	South Africa	3,922	3,720	2.7	2.9	117	88	26	41	39	..	136.9	129
91	Sri Lanka	311	624	3.8	4.9	20	35	17	107	..	..	125.3	580
94	Paraguay	82	107	1.3	1.4	22	22	94	42	..	..	20.3	141
96	Samoa (Western)	..	..	..	..	..	..	..	..	..	..	..	..
97	Botswana	51	225	1.1	7.1	47	152	..	22	..	..	7.5	188
98	Philippines	647	1,151	1.4	1.6	12	17	44	41	..	..	106.5	93
99	Indonesia	3,197	2,751	2.8	1.6	20	14	207	49	711	352	274.5	99
101	Mongolia	47	19	9.0	2.4	24	9	..	..	..	..	21.1	64
104	Guyana	27	7	9.7	1.1	78	9	..	21	..	..	1.6	24
108	China	27,107	31,731	7.9	5.7	26	26	387	114	1,696	1,357	2,930.0	75
109	Egypt	3,527	2,417	7.2	4.3	73	42	117	52	1,555	206	436.0	98
111	Maldives	..	..	..	..	..	..	..	..	..	..	..	..
112	El Salvador	344	126	4.4	1.8	72	22	34	66	..	..	30.5	73
113	Bolivia	173	146	2.0	2.6	27	18	105	57	..	..	33.5	121
114	Swaziland	..	..	..	..	..	..	..	11	..	..	..	..
116	Honduras	98	47	2.1	1.3	22	8	38	92	..	..	18.8	113
117	Guatemala	160	140	1.8	1.4	21	13	45	31	..	..	44.2	139
118	Namibia	..	65	..	2.7	..	39	..	23	..	..	8.0	..

HDI rank	Defence expenditure US$ millions (1995 prices) 1985	1995	As % of GDP 1985	1995	Per capita (US$; 1995 prices) 1985	1995	Military expenditure (as % of combined education and health expenditure) 1960	1990-91	Imports of conventional weapons (1990 prices)[a] US$ millions (1990=100) 1995	Index 1995	Total armed forces Thousands 1995	Index (1985=100) 1995
119 Morocco	875	1,347	5.4	4.3	40	49	49	72	50	45	195.5	131
120 Gabon	108	95	1.8	1.7	108	73	..	51	..	..	4.7	196
121 Viet Nam	3,277	910	19.4	4.3	53	12	..	..	..	..	572.0	56
122 Solomon Islands	..	..	..	..	..	..	..	..	..	..	..	..
123 Cape Verde	5	4	0.9	1.8	15	9	..	..	..	..	1.1	14
124 Vanuatu	..	..	..	..	..	..	..	..	..	..	..	..
125 São Tomé and Principe	..	..	..	..	..	..	..	..	..	..	..	..
126 Iraq	17,573	2,700	25.9	14.8	1,105	128	128	271	..	..	382.5	74
127 Nicaragua	870	34	14.2	1.8	94	8	100	97	..	..	12.0	19
128 Papua New Guinea	49	66	1.5	1.3	14	15	..	41	..	..	3.8	119
129 Zimbabwe	232	233	3.1	4.2	28	21	..	66	..	..	45.0	110
130 Congo	76	49	1.9	1.7	41	18	7	37	..	..	10.0	115
Low human development	20,080 T	18,723 T	3.4	2.8	13	11	76	66	..	..	3,191 T	107
Excluding India	11,527 T	10,434 T	3.9	3.4	15	12	..	67	..	..	2,046 T	120
131 Myanmar	1,645	1,880	7.0	6.2	18	40	241	222	310	157	286.0	154
132 Ghana	86	92	1.0	1.2	7	5	22	12	..	..	7.0	46
133 Cameroon	217	158	1.4	1.8	21	12	63	48	..	..	14.6	200
134 Kenya	350	206	3.1	2.3	17	7	8	24	..	..	24.2	177
135 Equatorial Guinea	4	2	2.0	1.3	11	5	..	..	..	..	1.3	59
136 Lao People's Dem. Rep.	75	73	7.8	4.2	21	15	..	..	..	..	37.0	69
137 Lesotho	63	33	4.6	5.5	41	17	..	48	..	..	2.0	100
138 India	8,553	8,289	3.0	2.5	11	9	68	65	770	48	1,145.0	91
139 Pakistan	2,835	3,642	6.9	6.5	29	28	393	125	391	53	587.0	122
140 Comoros	..	..	..	..	..	..	..	..	..	..	..	..
141 Nigeria	1,709	1,233	4.0	2.9	5	12	11	33	..	..	77.1	82
142 Zaire	111	125	0.9	2.0	4	3	..	71	..	..	28.1	59
143 Zambia	55	62	1.1	1.9	8	7	42	63	..	..	21.6	133
144 Bangladesh	341	500	1.4	1.8	3	4	..	41	118	73	115.5	127
145 Côte d'Ivoire	104	98	0.8	1.0	10	7	8	14	..	..	8.4	64
146 Benin	29	24	1.1	1.3	7	4	28	..	..	..	4.8	107
147 Togo	26	28	1.3	2.5	9	7	..	39	..	..	7.0	194
148 Yemen	668	345	9.9	3.9	67	24	..	197	..	..	39.5	62
149 Tanzania, U. Rep. of	191	87	4.4	2.7	9	3	4	77	..	..	34.6	86
150 Mauritania	71	28	6.5	1.9	42	12	..	40	..	..	15.7	185
151 Central African Rep.	24	24	1.4	1.8	9	7	..	33	..	..	2.7	117
152 Madagascar	74	49	2.0	1.1	7	4	8	37	..	..	21.0	100
153 Cambodia	..	126	..	4.7	..	13	..	..	..	..	88.5	253
154 Nepal	49	44	1.5	1.0	3	2	67	35	..	..	35.0	140
155 Bhutan	..	..	..	..	..	..	..	..	..	..	..	..
156 Haiti	42	35	1.5	2.1	7	5	100	30	..	..	..	..
157 Angola	883	300	225.0	4.8	179	28	..	208	..	..	82.0	166
158 Sudan	365	389	3.2	4.3	17	14	52	44	..	..	118.5	209
159 Uganda	72	126	1.8	2.6	5	7	..	18	..	..	50.0	250
160 Senegal	86	74	1.1	1.9	13	9	13	33	..	..	13.4	133
161 Malawi	29	21	1.0	1.2	4	2	..	24	..	..	8.0	151
162 Djibouti	44	22	7.9	5.3	129	35	..	..	..	..	8.4	280
163 Guinea-Bissau	15	8	5.7	3.0	17	7	..	..	..	..	7.2	84
164 Chad	51	34	2.9	2.6	10	5	..	74	..	..	25.4	208
165 Gambia	3	15	1.5	3.8	4	14	..	11	..	..	0.8	160
166 Mozambique	326	58	22.5	3.7	24	3	..	121	..	..	12.0	76
167 Guinea	71	52	1.8	1.4	12	8	52	37	..	..	9.7	98
168 Eritrea	..	40	..	5.7	..	11	..	..	55.0	..	..	..
169 Burundi	48	47	3.0	5.3	10	7	..	42	..	..	12.6	242
170 Ethiopia	610	111	17.9	2.1	14	2	107	190	..	..	120.0	55
171 Mali	41	56	1.4	2.4	5	6	57	53	..	..	7.4	151
172 Burkina Faso	46	68	1.1	2.4	6	6	29	30	..	..	5.8	145
173 Niger	16	21	0.5	0.9	3	2	43	11	..	..	5.3	241
174 Rwanda	45	57	1.9	4.4	7	7	..	25	..	..	40.0	769
175 Sierra Leone	7	41	1.0	5.7	2	9	..	23	..	..	6.2	200
All developing countries	186,917 T	153,628 T	7.1	3.1	52	35	102	63	..	113	14,125 T	96
Least developed countries	6,145 T	4,935 T	3.9	2.7	14	9	..	71	..	..	1,316 T	122
Sub-Saharan Africa	9,909 T	7,842 T	3.0	2.6	22	14	..	44	..	..	967 T	107
Industrial countries	636,637 T	643,515 T	4.1	2.7	742	526	110	33	..	..	7,555 T	80
World	823,554 T	797,143 T	4.6	2.8	185	143	109	38	..	..	21,680 T	92

a. Figures are trend indicator values.
Source: Columns 1-6, 9 and 11: IISS 1996; columns 7 and 8: IISS 1993; columns 10 and 12: calculated on the basis of estimates from IISS 1996.

HDI rank		Total external debt		Debt service ratio (debt service as % of exports of goods and services)		Total net official development assistance received, 1995 (net disbursements)			Net foreign direct investment (as % of GNP)	Export-import ratio (exports as % of imports)	Terms of trade (1987 =100)	Current account balance before official transfers (US$ millions)
		US$ billions 1994	As % of GNP 1994	1980	1994	US$ millions	As % of 1994 GNP	Per capita (US$)	1993	1994	1994	1994
High human development		445 T	31	28	17	2,650 T	0.2	8	1.7	90	96	-51,999 T
22	Hong Kong	..	..	..	..	14	(.)	2	..	..	87	..
24	Cyprus	..	..	..	..	22	..	30	..	..	..	..
25	Barbados	..	..	..	..	-1	-0.1	-4	0.4	..	..	..
26	Singapore	..	..	..	..	16	(.)	6	10.8	103	91	2,253
28	Bahamas	..	..	..	..	4	0.1	15	0.9	..	..	..
29	Antigua and Barbuda	..	..	..	..	2	2.7	200	2.2	..	..	..
30	Chile	22.9	46	45	20	159	0.3	11	0.9	93	94	-1,045
32	Korea, Rep. of	54.5	15	20	7	58	(.)	1	-0.2	96	102	-4,304
33	Costa Rica	3.8	48	30	15	25	0.3	8	3.9	85	92	-516
36	Argentina	77.4	28	42	35	222	0.1	7	2.6	67	120	-10,074
37	Uruguay	5.1	33	20	16	81	0.5	26	0.8	88	112	-416
38	Brunei Darussalam	..	..	..	..	4	0.1	133	..	..	..	..
40	Trinidad and Tobago	2.2	50	7	32	26	0.6	20	7.7	111	86	213
41	Dominica	..	..	..	..	24	12.1	343	5.0	..	..	..
43	Bahrain	..	..	..	..	49	1.2	89	..	..	..	..
44	United Arab Emirates	..	..	..	..	8	..	4	..	..	93	..
45	Panama	7.1	107	14	..	50	0.8	19	-0.6	99	86	-136
46	Fiji	..	..	..	..	43	2.5	56	1.4	..	..	..
47	Venezuela	36.8	66	30	21	81	0.1	4	-0.1	120	82	2,450
49	Saint Kitts and Nevis	..	..	..	..	4	2.1	100	5.0	..	..	..
50	Mexico	128.3	35	51	35	379	0.1	4	1.3	62	92	-28,878
51	Colombia	19.4	30	18	30	231	3.7	6	1.6	76	71	-2,993
52	Seychelles	..	..	..	..	13	2.8	186	7.7	..	..	..
53	Kuwait	..	..	..	..	6	(.)	4	-2.4	146	88	4,221
54	Grenada	..	..	..	..	10	4.2	111	9.2	..	..	..
55	Qatar	..	..	..	..	3	(.)	6	..	..	..	..
56	Saint Lucia	..	..	..	..	47	9.6	313	7.1	..	..	..
57	Saint Vincent	..	..	..	..	47	20.5	427	13.4	..	..	..
59	Thailand	61.0	43	20	16	863	0.6	15	0.9	87	105	-8,282
60	Malaysia	24.8	37	7	8	114	0.2	6	8.7	94	92	-4,262
61	Mauritius	1.4	40	9	7	23	0.7	21	-0.6	88	121	-230
63	Belize	..	..	..	..	16	3.0	76	1.8	..	..	..
64	Libyan Arab Jamahiriya	..	..	..	..	7	..	1	..	..	..	..
Medium human development		706 T	38	25	22	18,394 T	1.9	11	1.6	94	98	-23,118 T
Excluding China		605 T	48	28	28	14,873 T	2.5	21	0.5	91	96	-30,275 T
65	Lebanon	..	..	..	..	188	2.0	48	..	..	..	..
66	Suriname	..	..	..	..	77	27.6	183	-10.4	..	..	..
68	Brazil	151.1	28	68	36	366	0.1	2	-0.1	93	101	-1,203
70	Iran, Islamic Rep. of	22.7	37	7	22	183	0.2	3	..	121	90	4,581
72	Ecuador	15.0	97	35	22	235	1.5	21	0.9	83	82	-962
73	Saudi Arabia	..	..	..	..	21	(.)	1	..	105	92	-13,278
74	Turkey	66.3	51	28	33	303	0.2	5	0.4	98	109	2,248
75	Korea, Dem. People's Rep. of	..	..	..	..	14	..	1	..	..	..	..
78	Syrian Arab Rep.	..	..	..	..	347	..	25	..	..	..	..
81	Tunisia	9.3	61	15	19	69	0.4	8	1.6	86	93	-419
82	Algeria	29.9	74	28	56	310	0.8	11	(.)	75	83	-1,821
83	Jamaica	4.3	110	20	21	108	2.7	43	2.3	86	105	15
84	Jordan	7.1	122	9	12	536	9.3	127	0.4	64	118	-723
86	Cuba	..	..	..	..	64	..	6	..	..	..	..
87	Dominican Rep.	4.3	42	26	17	124	1.2	16	2.0	80	144	-232
88	Oman	3.1	31	7	..	59	0.6	29	0.9	104	77	-1,087
89	Peru	22.6	46	46	18	428	0.9	18	1.0	65	86	-2,935
90	South Africa	..	..	..	..	384	..	10	(.)	98	102	-654
91	Sri Lanka	7.8	68	12	9	553	48.0	31	1.8	72	88	-933
94	Paraguay	2.0	25	21	10	146	1.9	30	2.0	67	101	-1,282
96	Samoa (Western)	..	..	..	..	43	24.3	253	..	..	..	..
97	Botswana	0.7	17	2	4	92	2.3	64	..	112	152	174
98	Philippines	39.3	60	29	22	884	23.8	109	1.4	86	114	-3,316
99	Indonesia	96.5	57	14	32	1,389	0.8	7	1.4	93	79	-2,960
101	Mongolia	0.4	61	..	10	208	28.8	88	1.0	88	..	-59
104	Guyana	..	..	..	..	88	19.2	106	7.1	..	..	..
108	China	100.5	19	4	9	3,521	0.7	3	4.0	105	105	7,157
109	Egypt	33.4	79	14	16	2,017	4.8	35	1.2	65	95	-536
111	Maldives	..	..	..	..	55	22.1	220	3.5	..	..	..
112	El Salvador	2.2	27	8	13	304	3.7	54	0.2	56	89	-303
113	Bolivia	4.7	89	36	28	692	13.0	96	2.2	73	69	-419
114	Swaziland	..	..	..	..	54	5.6	59	2.8	..	..	..
116	Honduras	4.4	..	22	34	411	14.1	75	1.1	74	73	-394
117	Guatemala	3.0	23	8	11	213	1.6	21	1.3	69	93	-770
118	Namibia	..	..	..	..	188	6.4	125	-0.3	97	..	-19

HDI rank	Total external debt US$ billions 1994	As % of GNP 1994	Debt service ratio (debt service as % of exports of goods and services) 1980	1994	Total net official development assistance received, 1995 (net disbursements) US$ millions	As % of 1994 GNP	Per capita (US$)	Net foreign direct investment (as % of GNP) 1993	Export-import ratio (exports as % of imports) 1994	Terms of trade (1987 =100) 1994	Current account balance before official transfers (US$ millions) 1994
119 Morocco	22.5	76	33	33	494	1.7	19	1.9	71	107	-750
120 Gabon	4.0	122	18	10	143	4.4	138	1.8	106	90	71
121 Viet Nam	25.1	161	..	6	826	5.3	(.)	2.5	79	..	-1,130
122 Solomon Islands	..	..	..	..	47	15.1	127	..	..	..	..
123 Cape Verde	..	..	..	..	111	33.6	292	0.9	..	..	..
124 Vanuatu	..	..	..	..	46	24.5	288	14.4	..	..	..
125 São Tomé and Principe	..	..	..	..	78	339.1	600	9.9	..	..	..
126 Iraq	..	..	..	..	326	1.6	16	..	..	..	..
127 Nicaragua	11.0	801	23	38	662	48.1	155	2.7	32	95	-940
128 Papua New Guinea	2.9	58	15	30	372	7.4	88	(.)	124	90	402
129 Zimbabwe	4.4	86	4	..	490	9.6	45	0.5	86	84	-295
130 Congo	5.3	454	11	52	125	10.8	50	..	77	93	-346
Low human development	293 T	61	12	25	21,945 T	4.2	13	0.7	73	94	-15,460 T
Excluding India	194 T	100	12	23	20,207 T	9.6	24	1.5	69	90	-12,987 T
131 Myanmar	6.5	9	26	15	152	0.2	3	..	63	107	-339
132 Ghana	5.4	102	13	25	644	12.1	38	1.8	65	64	-466
133 Cameroon	7.3	107	15	17	444	6.5	35	2.1	89	79	-257
134 Kenya	7.3	112	22	34	707	3.9	42	..	94	80	-30
135 Equatorial Guinea	..	..	..	..	33	20.5	85	-7.7	..	..	..
136 Lao People's Dem. Rep.	2.1	136	..	8	311	20.3	66	2.3	65	..	-131
137 Lesotho	0.6	44	6	17	114	8.4	57	1.2	60	..	-360
138 India	99.0	34	10	27	1,738	0.6	2	0.2	80	100	-2,473
139 Pakistan	29.6	57	18	35	805	1.5	6	0.6	66	101	-2,020
140 Comoros	..	..	..	..	43	20.4	88	0.2	..	..	..
141 Nigeria	33.5	102	4	18	208	0.6	2	2.2	79	86	-2,079
142 Zaire	..	..	..	..	189	..	4	..	..	..	..
143 Zambia	6.6	204	26	32	2,029	62.9	221	0.1	74	85	-427
144 Bangladesh	16.6	63	26	16	1,269	4.8	11	0.1	67	94	-336
145 Côte d'Ivoire	18.5	339	39	40	1,200	22.0	87	0.4	89	81	-726
146 Benin	1.6	109	7	10	276	18.6	53	..	78	110	-48
147 Togo	1.5	157	9	8	188	20.2	47	..	89	90	-31
148 Yemen	6.0	..	..	5	173	4.7	13	24.4	63	84	-124
149 Tanzania, U. Rep. of	7.4	230	22	20	875	..	30	0.8	41	83	-762
150 Mauritania	2.3	240	18	23	220	22.6	99	1.5	75	106	-140
151 Central African Rep.	0.9	104	5	13	161	18.4	50	..	66	91	-95
152 Madagascar	4.1	225	20	10	301	16.4	23	0.8	64	82	-327
153 Cambodia	..	..	..	..	567	24.4	57	..	..	..	..
154 Nepal	2.3	56	3	8	430	..	21	..	76	85	-250
155 Bhutan	..	..	..	..	73	26.8	107	..	..	..	..
156 Haiti	0.7	44	6	1	733	45.5	104	..	30	52	-109
157 Angola	..	..	..	..	423	..	40	..	..	..	..
158 Sudan	..	..	..	..	225	..	8	..	..	..	..
159 Uganda	3.5	88	17	46	805	20.4	43	0.1	37	58	-264
160 Senegal	3.7	99	29	15	663	17.9	82	..	78	107	-350
161 Malawi	2.0	160	28	17	429	34.1	40	..	61	87	-230
162 Djibouti	..	..	..	..	103	..	181	0.6	..	..	..
163 Guinea-Bissau	0.8	341	..	15	119	49.6	113	..	54	92	-37
164 Chad	0.8	91	8	8	237	26.4	38	..	54	103	-163
165 Gambia	0.4	117	6	14	46	12.3	43	3.0	87	111	-20
166 Mozambique	5.5	450	..	23	1,102	90.4	66	2.4	24	124	-870
167 Guinea	3.1	95	20	14	392	12.0	62	0.1	71	91	-315
168 Eritrea	..	..	..	..	145	..	42	..	..	..	..
169 Burundi	1.1	114	..	42	288	32.1	46	(.)	35	52	-171
170 Ethiopia	5.1	110	8	12	876	18.7	16	..	47	74	-317
171 Mali	2.8	152	5	28	542	29.6	57	..	48	103	-194
172 Burkina Faso	1.1	61	6	..	483	16.6	48	..	37	103	-493
173 Niger	1.6	104	23	26	268	17.8	30	..	70	101	-106
174 Rwanda	0.5	165	5	15	711	122.8	92	0.2	10	75	-400
175 Sierra Leone	1.4	187	23	..	205	27.7	45	1.0	..	89	..
All developing countries	1,444 T	38	24	20	59,876 T	1.4	11	1.5	90	97	-90,577 T
Least developed countries	89 T	106	18	16	16,467 T	17.5	29	2.0	58	91	-7,059 T
Sub-Saharan Africa	213 T	79 a	10	14	18,299 T	12.6	32	0.6	84	95	-10,977 T
Industrial countries	..	..	..	..	..	..	..	-0.4	101	104	40,659 T
World	..	..	..	..	..	..	..	-0.1	99	102	..

a. World Bank 1996g.
Source: Columns 1, 2 and 8: calculated on the basis of estimates from World Bank 1996g; *columns 3, 4, 9,10 and 11:* World Bank 1996g; *columns 5-7:* OECD 1996a.

21 Growing urbanization

HDI rank		Urban population (as % of total)			Urban population annual growth rate (%)		Population in cities of more than 750,000		Largest city		Growth rate (%)	
		1960	1994	2000	1960-1994	1994-2000	As % of total population 1990	As % of urban population 1990	City	Population (thousands) 1995	1970-75	1990-95
High human development		45	68	71	3.8	2.2	32	48	–	–	–	–
22	Hong Kong	85	95	96	2.3	0.5	94	100	Hong Kong	5,574	2.6	0.8
24	Cyprus	36	54	57	1.9	2.0	..	..	..	..	..	..
25	Barbados	35	47	50	1.2	1.7	..	..	..	..	..	..
26	Singapore	100	100	100	1.6	0.9	100	100	Singapore	2,848	1.7	1.0
28	Bahamas	74	86	89	3.2	1.9	..	..	..	..	..	..
29	Antigua and Barbuda	40	36	37	0.3	1.2	..	..	..	..	..	..
30	Chile	68	84	85	2.5	1.6	35	42	Santiago	5,065	2.7	2.0
32	Korea, Rep. of	28	80	86	5.0	2.3	48	65	Seoul	11,641	4.9	2.0
33	Costa Rica	37	49	53	3.9	3.3	25	53	San Jose	760	3.5	2.9
36	Argentina	74	88	89	2.0	1.5	42	48	Buenos Aires	10,990	1.6	0.7
37	Uruguay	80	90	91	1.0	0.8	42	47	Montevideo	1,326	0.1	0.6
38	Brunei Darussalam	43	58	59	4.7	2.2	..	..	..	..	..	..
40	Trinidad and Tobago	65	71	74	1.6	1.8	..	..	..	..	..	..
41	Dominica	..	..	..	..	..	..	..	..	..	..	..
43	Bahrain	82	90	92	4.1	2.9	..	..	..	..	..	..
44	United Arab Emirates	40	84	86	12.0	2.7	..	..	..	..	..	..
45	Panama	41	53	55	3.3	2.4	34	67	Panama City	948	2.3	2.8
46	Fiji	30	40	43	3.0	2.5	..	..	..	..	..	..
47	Venezuela	67	92	94	4.1	2.5	30	34	Caracas	2,959	2.2	1.3
49	Saint Kitts and Nevis	28	42	46	0.6	0.8	..	..	..	..	..	..
50	Mexico	51	75	78	3.9	2.5	30	41	Mexico City	15,643	4.3	0.7
51	Colombia	48	72	75	3.6	2.2	28	40	Bogota	5,614	4.8	2.9
52	Seychelles	25	54	59	4.1	2.4	..	..	..	..	..	..
53	Kuwait	72	97	98	6.7	0.5	51	53	Kuwait City	1,090	4.0	0.0
54	Grenada	..	..	..	..	..	..	..	..	..	..	..
55	Qatar	72	91	93	8.6	2.2	..	..	..	..	..	..
56	Saint Lucia	39	48	51	1.6	2.0	..	..	..	..	..	..
57	Saint Vincent	14	46	52	4.9	2.9	..	..	..	..	..	..
59	Thailand	13	20	22	3.8	2.8	11	57	Bangkok	6,566	4.2	2.2
60	Malaysia	27	53	58	4.8	3.6	6	13	Kuala Lumpur	1,238	7.1	2.0
61	Mauritius	33	41	42	2.2	1.5	..	..	..	..	..	..
63	Belize	54	47	47	2.0	2.5	..	..	..	..	..	..
64	Libyan Arab Jamahiriya	23	85	88	8.3	4.0	77	93	Tripoli	3,272	10.5	4.6
Medium human development		24	40	45	3.6	3.6	14	38	–	–	–	–
	Excluding China	30	52	56	4.2	3.4	19	38	–	–	–	–
65	Lebanon	40	87	90	3.7	2.9	..	..	..	..	..	..
66	Suriname	47	50	54	1.2	2.5	..	..	..	..	..	..
68	Brazil	45	78	81	4.0	2.4	32	42	São Paulo	16,417	4.1	2.0
70	Iran, Islamic Rep. of	34	59	62	5.0	3.1	20	35	Teheran	6,830	5.2	1.5
72	Ecuador	34	58	62	4.4	3.3	25	46	Guayaquil	1,717	4.2	2.8
73	Saudi Arabia	30	80	82	7.6	3.6	20	26	Riyadh	2,576	11.0	5.3
74	Turkey	30	67	75	4.9	3.7	22	37	Istanbul	7,817	5.1	3.7
75	Korea, Dem. People's Rep. of	40	61	63	3.6	2.3	10	17	Pyongyang	2,470	6.0	2.0
78	Syrian Arab Rep.	37	52	55	4.4	4.4	27	54	Damascus	2,052	4.1	2.7
81	Tunisia	36	57	60	3.6	2.7	22	39	Tunis	2,037	3.2	3.1
82	Algeria	30	55	60	4.6	3.6	12	24	Algiers	3,702	4.2	4.0
83	Jamaica	34	53	56	2.6	1.7	..	..	..	..	..	..
84	Jordan	43	71	75	4.9	4.7	22	33	Amman	1,187	5.1	4.3
86	Cuba	55	76	78	2.3	1.2	20	27	Havana	2,241	0.9	1.1
87	Dominican Rep.	30	64	68	4.9	2.9	43	71	Santo Domingo	2,580	5.1	3.2
88	Oman	4	13	16	8.0	7.7	..	..	..	..	..	..
89	Peru	46	72	75	3.9	2.5	30	43	Lima	7,452	4.5	2.8
90	South Africa	47	50	53	2.8	3.1	21	43	Cape Town	2,671	3.7	3.1
91	Sri Lanka	18	22	24	2.4	2.7	..	..	..	..	..	..
94	Paraguay	36	52	56	4.1	4.0	..	..	..	..	..	..
96	Samoa (Western)	19	21	22	1.6	1.9	..	..	..	..	..	..
97	Botswana	2	27	33	12.3	6.6	..	..	..	..	..	..
98	Philippines	30	53	59	4.3	3.9	15	30	Metro Manila	9,280	6.9	3.1
99	Indonesia	15	34	40	4.7	4.2	12	38	Jakarta	11,500	4.1	4.4
101	Mongolia	36	60	64	4.3	3.0	..	..	..	..	..	..
104	Guyana	29	36	40	1.7	2.9	..	..	..	..	..	..
108	China	19	29	35	3.1	3.8	10	38	Shanghai	15,082	0.5	2.3
109	Egypt	38	45	46	2.9	2.6	23	51	Cairo	9,665	2.6	2.2
111	Maldives	11	27	28	5.4	4.2	..	..	..	..	..	..
112	El Salvador	38	45	47	2.8	2.9	..	..	..	..	..	..
113	Bolivia	39	60	65	3.5	3.9	16	28	La Paz	1,246	3.3	3.6
114	Swaziland	4	30	36	9.5	5.9	..	..	..	..	..	..
116	Honduras	23	43	47	5.2	4.4	..	..	..	..	..	..
117	Guatemala	32	41	44	3.6	4.1	9	23	Guatemala City	946	1.6	2.3
118	Namibia	15	36	43	5.3	5.6	..	..	..	..	..	..

HDI rank	Urban population (as % of total)			Urban population annual growth rate (%)		Population in cities of more than 750,000		Largest city			
						As % of total population 1990	As % of urban population 1990		Population (thousands)	Growth rate (%)	
	1960	1994	2000	1960-1994	1994-2000			City	1995	1970-75	1990-95
119 Morocco	29	48	51	4.0	3.0	17	36	Casablanca	3,289	3.4	3.1
120 Gabon	17	49	54	6.2	4.4	..	..	..	..	..	..
121 Viet Nam	15	21	22	3.2	3.5	7	33	Ho Chi Minh City	3,555	3.3	1.9
122 Solomon Islands	9	17	20	5.4	6.4	..	..	..	..	..	..
123 Cape Verde	16	53	63	5.6	5.9	..	..	..	..	..	..
124 Vanuatu	9	19	21	5.6	3.8	..	..	..	..	..	..
125 São Tomé and Principe	16	46	51	5.4	3.6	..	..	..	..	..	..
126 Iraq	43	74	77	4.9	3.6	22	31	Baghdad	4,478	6.5	2.0
127 Nicaragua	40	62	66	4.5	4.3	26	44	Managua	1,195	5.3	4.3
128 Papua New Guinea	3	16	18	8.0	4.0	..	..	..	..	..	..
129 Zimbabwe	13	31	36	6.0	4.6	9	30	Harare	854	5.5	4.0
130 Congo	32	58	63	4.6	4.4	36	66	Brazzaville	1,009	2.8	4.8
Low human development	15	27	30	4.4	4.0	10	37	—	—	—	—
Excluding India	12	27	31	5.5	5.2	10	39	—	—	—	—
131 Myanmar	19	26	28	3.1	3.7	8	32	Yangon	3,851	4.3	3.1
132 Ghana	23	36	39	4.0	4.5	9	28	Accra	1,687	3.3	3.7
133 Cameroon	14	44	49	6.2	4.9	16	22	Douala	1,322	5.3	5.6
134 Kenya	7	27	32	7.6	6.0	6	27	Nairobi	2,079	4.9	6.3
135 Equatorial Guinea	26	41	48	2.6	5.5	..	..	..	..	..	..
136 Lao People's Dem. Rep.	8	21	25	5.3	5.9	..	..	..	..	..	..
137 Lesotho	3	22	27	8.4	6.0	..	..	..	..	..	..
138 India	18	27	29	3.4	3.0	9	36	Mumbai	15,093	3.3	4.2
139 Pakistan	22	34	38	4.3	4.6	16	49	Karachi	9,863	4.9	4.3
140 Comoros	10	30	34	6.7	5.8	..	..	..	..	..	..
141 Nigeria	14	39	43	5.8	5.0	9	27	Lagos	10,287	9.8	5.7
142 Zaire	22	29	31	3.8	4.4	9	33	Kinshasa	4,214	4.7	4.0
143 Zambia	17	43	45	6.1	3.4	12	29	Lusaka	1,327	6.5	6.1
144 Bangladesh	5	18	21	6.3	5.4	8	52	Dhaka	7,832	7.9	5.7
145 Côte d'Ivoire	19	43	47	6.4	4.9	18	45	Abidjan	2,797	11.0	5.1
146 Benin	9	31	34	6.3	4.7	..	..	..	..	..	..
147 Togo	10	30	34	6.4	4.9	..	..	..	..	..	..
148 Yemen	9	33	38	6.8	6.6	..	..	..	..	..	..
149 Tanzania, U. Rep. of	5	24	28	8.2	5.9	6	27	Dar es Salaam	..	9.8	3.8
150 Mauritania	6	53	59	9.4	4.6	..	..	..	..	..	..
151 Central African Rep.	23	39	42	3.9	3.6	..	..	..	..	..	..
152 Madagascar	11	26	31	5.7	5.8	..	..	..	..	..	..
153 Cambodia	10	20	24	3.7	5.8	..	..	..	..	..	..
154 Nepal	3	13	17	6.8	6.9	..	..	..	..	..	..
155 Bhutan	3	6	8	4.7	6.0	..	..	..	..	..	..
156 Haiti	16	31	35	3.9	4.1	16	56	Port-au-Prince	1,266	4.4	3.9
157 Angola	10	32	36	5.7	6.0	18	63	Luanda	2,207	7.5	5.9
158 Sudan	10	24	27	5.3	4.7	8	35	Khartoum	2,492	6.0	4.5
159 Uganda	5	12	14	6.2	5.6	4	38	Kampala	954	3.2	4.7
160 Senegal	32	42	45	3.6	4.0	22	55	Dakar	1,986	5.0	4.2
161 Malawi	4	13	16	6.8	5.0	..	..	..	..	..	..
162 Djibouti	50	83	84	7.6	2.5	..	..	..	..	..	..
163 Guinea-Bissau	14	22	25	3.4	4.6	..	..	..	..	..	..
164 Chad	7	21	23	5.6	4.1	..	..	..	..	..	..
165 Gambia	12	25	29	5.5	5.6	..	..	..	..	..	..
166 Mozambique	4	33	41	9.0	7.4	11	41	Maputo	2,227	7.2	7.1
167 Guinea	10	29	34	5.4	5.7	20	76	Conakry	1,508	8.0	5.8
168 Eritrea	..	17	..	..	..	..	..	..	..	..	..
169 Burundi	2	7	9	6.1	6.7	..	..	..	..	..	..
170 Ethiopia	6	13	15	4.7	5.2	4	31	Addis Ababa	2,209	4.8	4.0
171 Mali	11	26	30	5.2	5.7	..	..	..	..	..	..
172 Burkina Faso	5	25	38	7.5	9.8	..	..	..	..	..	..
173 Niger	6	17	19	6.5	5.9	..	..	..	..	..	..
174 Rwanda	2	6	7	6.0	4.7	..	..	..	..	..	..
175 Sierra Leone	13	35	40	5.1	4.6	..	..	..	..	..	..
All developing countries	22	37	41	3.9	3.7	14	39	—	—	—	—
Least developed countries	9	22	26	5.7	5.4	8	47	—	—	—	—
Sub-Saharan Africa	15	31	35	5.6	5.1	10	34	—	—	—	—
Industrial countries	61	74	75	1.4	0.8	29	39	—	—	—	—
World	34	45	47	3.3	2.5	17	39	—	—	—	—

Source: Columns 1, 3, 8, 10 and 11: UN 1994c; columns 2, 4-7 and 9: calculated on the basis of estimates from UN 1994c.

22 Demographic profile

HDI rank	Estimated population (millions)			Annual population growth rate (%)		Population doubling date (at current growth rate) 1994	Crude birth rate 1994	Crude death rate 1994	Total fertility rate 1994	Contraceptive prevalence rate, any method (%) 1987-94
	1960	1994	2000	1960-1994	1994-2000					
High human development	163 T	351 T	382 T	2.3	1.4	2043	22.8	5.9	2.5	67
22 Hong Kong	3.1	6.0	6.4	2.0	0.9	2072	11.8	5.8	1.3	86
24 Cyprus	0.6	0.7	0.8	0.7	1.3	2045	16.9	7.5	2.4	..
25 Barbados	0.2	0.3	0.3	0.3	0.2	2266	15.1	9.2	1.8	55
26 Singapore	1.6	3.3	3.6	2.1	1.6	2038	18.5	4.8	1.8	74
28 Bahamas	0.1	0.3	0.3	2.7	1.6	2036	18.0	4.9	1.9	62
29 Antigua and Barbuda	0.1	0.1	0.1	0.5	0.8	2086	..	..	..	53
30 Chile	7.6	14.0	15.2	1.8	1.4	2043	21.4	5.4	2.5	..
32 Korea, Rep. of	25.0	44.5	46.9	1.7	0.9	2073	15.3	6.3	1.6	79
33 Costa Rica	1.2	3.3	3.8	3.0	2.1	2026	25.5	3.7	3.1	75
36 Argentina	20.6	34.3	37.0	1.5	1.3	2048	20.5	8.1	2.8	..
37 Uruguay	2.5	3.2	3.3	0.6	0.6	2119	16.9	10.4	2.3	..
38 Brunei Darussalam	0.1	0.3	0.3	3.7	2.2	2025	25.5	3.0	2.9	..
40 Trinidad and Tobago	0.8	1.3	1.3	1.2	0.8	2079	16.3	5.9	2.1	53
41 Dominica	0.1	0.1	0.1	0.5	(.)	..	..	..	..	50
43 Bahrain	0.2	0.5	0.6	3.7	2.2	2026	23.8	3.7	3.2	53
44 United Arab Emirates	0.1	2.2	2.4	9.8	2.1	2027	18.9	2.6	3.6	..
45 Panama	1.1	2.6	2.9	2.5	1.7	2035	24.3	5.2	2.8	64
46 Fiji	0.4	0.8	0.8	2.0	1.6	2037	23.0	4.5	2.9	41
47 Venezuela	7.6	21.4	24.2	3.1	2.1	2027	26.5	4.7	3.2	..
49 Saint Kitts and Nevis	0.1	(.)	(.)	-0.6	(.)	..	..	..	..	41
50 Mexico	36.9	89.6	98.9	2.6	1.7	2036	26.4	5.1	3.0	53
51 Colombia	15.9	35.2	38.9	2.4	1.7	2035	25.4	5.8	2.8	72
52 Seychelles	(.)	0.1	0.1	1.6	0.9	2071	..	..	..	..
53 Kuwait	0.3	1.8	2.0	5.6	1.9	2030	22.9	2.0	2.8	35
54 Grenada	0.1	0.1	0.1	0.1	0.4	2187	..	..	..	54
55 Qatar	(.)	0.5	0.6	7.6	1.8	2032	18.1	3.3	3.9	32
56 Saint Lucia	0.1	0.1	0.2	1.5	1.3	2049	..	..	..	47
57 Saint Vincent	0.1	0.1	0.1	1.0	0.9	2073	..	..	..	58
59 Thailand	26.4	57.8	60.5	2.3	0.8	2084	16.6	6.1	1.8	74
60 Malaysia	8.1	19.7	22.3	2.6	2.1	2027	27.8	5.0	3.5	..
61 Mauritius	0.7	1.1	1.2	1.5	1.1	2057	21.1	6.8	2.4	75
63 Belize	0.1	0.2	0.2	2.4	2.6	2021	34.0	4.6	4.0	47
64 Libyan Arab Jamahiriya	1.3	5.2	6.4	4.1	3.4	2014	41.3	7.6	6.2	..
Medium human development	1,102 T	2,210 T	2,392 T	2.1	1.3	2046	22.5	7.4	2.4	72
Excluding China	445 T	1,002 T	1,116 T	2.4	1.8	2033	27.7	7.5	3.3	56
65 Lebanon	1.9	2.9	3.3	1.3	2.0	2028	26.6	6.9	3.0	53
66 Suriname	0.3	0.4	0.5	1.1	1.1	2054	24.8	5.7	2.6	..
68 Brazil	72.8	156.9	169.2	2.3	1.3	2049	20.4	7.2	2.3	66
70 Iran, Islamic Rep. of	21.6	66.7	76.4	3.4	2.3	2024	36.4	6.4	5.1	65
72 Ecuador	4.4	11.2	12.6	2.8	2.0	2028	27.4	6.0	3.4	57
73 Saudi Arabia	4.1	17.8	21.7	4.4	3.4	2014	34.6	4.4	6.2	..
74 Turkey	27.5	59.9	65.7	2.3	1.6	2038	21.0	6.4	2.4	63
75 Korea, Dem. People's Rep. of	10.5	21.7	23.9	2.2	1.6	2037	22.4	5.5	2.1	62
78 Syrian Arab Rep.	4.6	13.8	16.1	3.3	2.6	2021	30.3	5.1	4.1	36
81 Tunisia	4.2	8.8	9.8	2.2	1.8	2032	24.4	6.1	3.0	60
82 Algeria	10.8	27.4	31.6	2.8	2.4	2023	29.9	6.1	4.1	52
83 Jamaica	1.6	2.4	2.6	1.2	0.9	2067	24.2	6.1	2.6	62
84 Jordan	1.7	5.1	6.3	3.3	3.5	2014	39.0	5.2	5.4	35
86 Cuba	7.0	10.9	11.2	1.3	0.4	2150	14.2	6.9	1.5	70
87 Dominican Rep.	3.2	7.7	8.5	2.6	1.7	2035	26.1	5.4	3.0	56
88 Oman	0.6	2.1	2.7	4.0	4.2	2010	43.6	4.5	7.2	9
89 Peru	9.9	23.1	25.7	2.5	1.8	2034	26.6	6.6	3.3	59
90 South Africa	17.4	40.6	46.3	2.5	2.2	2025	30.7	8.6	4.0	50
91 Sri Lanka	9.9	17.8	18.8	1.7	1.0	2065	17.8	5.8	2.1	66
94 Paraguay	1.8	4.7	5.5	2.8	2.6	2020	33.3	5.8	4.4	56
96 Samoa (Western)	0.1	0.2	0.2	1.1	1.1	2057	25.4	6.0	4.1	..
97 Botswana	0.5	1.4	1.6	3.2	2.3	2025	36.6	11.8	4.7	33
98 Philippines	27.6	66.4	75.0	2.6	2.1	2027	30.7	6.2	3.9	40
99 Indonesia	96.2	194.5	212.6	2.1	1.5	2040	23.5	8.0	2.8	55
101 Mongolia	1.0	2.4	2.7	2.8	2.1	2027	27.0	7.6	3.2	61
104 Guyana	0.6	0.8	0.9	1.1	1.0	2060	24.8	7.9	2.5	..
108 China	657.5	1,208.3	1,276.3	1.8	0.9	2069	17.2	7.4	1.8	83
109 Egypt	27.8	60.9	68.1	2.3	1.9	2031	26.8	7.6	3.6	47
111 Maldives	0.1	0.2	0.3	2.7	3.5	2014	41.5	8.2	6.8	..
112 El Salvador	2.6	5.5	6.3	2.3	2.2	2025	29.5	5.8	3.3	53
113 Bolivia	3.4	7.2	8.3	2.3	2.4	2023	35.4	9.8	4.7	45
114 Swaziland	0.3	0.8	1.0	2.8	2.8	2018	38.5	10.1	4.7	20
116 Honduras	1.9	5.5	6.5	3.2	2.8	2019	36.4	5.9	4.8	47
117 Guatemala	4.0	10.3	12.2	2.8	2.9	2018	38.0	7.3	5.2	32
118 Namibia	0.6	1.5	1.7	2.6	2.5	2022	37.0	11.9	5.1	29

HDI rank	Estimated population (millions)			Annual population growth rate (%)		Population doubling date (at current growth rate)	Crude birth rate	Crude death rate	Total fertility rate	Contraceptive prevalence rate, any method (%)
	1960	1994	2000	1960-1994	1994-2000	1994	1994	1994	1994	1987-94
119 Morocco	11.6	26.0	29.0	2.4	1.8	2032	28.0	7.3	3.5	50
120 Gabon	0.5	1.0	1.2	2.3	2.8	2019	35.3	15.0	5.0	..
121 Viet Nam	34.7	72.4	80.5	2.2	1.8	2032	28.0	7.4	3.2	65
122 Solomon Islands	0.1	0.4	0.4	3.4	3.3	2015	37.1	4.3	5.3	..
123 Cape Verde	0.2	0.4	0.4	1.9	2.5	2022	33.0	8.0	3.6	..
124 Vanuatu	0.1	0.2	0.2	2.8	2.6	2021	34.8	7.1	4.6	..
125 São Tomé and Principe	0.1	0.1	0.1	2.1	2.0	2029	..	..	..	14
126 Iraq	6.8	19.6	23.1	3.2	2.7	2019	37.8	11.4	5.6	..
127 Nicaragua	1.5	4.0	4.7	3.0	2.7	2020	35.0	5.9	4.2	49
128 Papua New Guinea	1.9	4.2	4.8	2.3	2.3	2024	33.4	10.4	5.0	..
129 Zimbabwe	3.8	10.9	12.4	3.2	2.2	2026	40.5	14.4	5.1	48
130 Congo	1.0	2.5	3.0	2.8	2.9	2018	44.8	14.9	6.3	..
Low human development	788T	1,765T	2,000T	2.4	2.1	2027	33.7	11.8	4.2	30
Excluding India	346T	852T	993T	2.7	2.6	2021	40.5	14.0	5.5	17
131 Myanmar	21.7	44.3	49.3	2.1	1.8	2032	27.9	10.5	3.4	17
132 Ghana	6.8	16.9	19.9	2.7	2.8	2018	39.1	11.2	5.5	20
133 Cameroon	5.3	12.8	15.1	2.6	2.8	2019	40.1	12.5	5.6	16
134 Kenya	8.3	26.5	30.3	3.5	2.3	2024	35.3	11.6	5.0	33
135 Equatorial Guinea	0.3	0.4	0.5	1.3	2.5	2021	43.4	17.5	5.9	..
136 Lao People's Dem. Rep.	2.2	4.7	5.7	2.3	3.1	2016	45.2	14.7	6.7	19
137 Lesotho	0.9	2.0	2.3	2.4	2.5	2021	36.5	11.1	5.1	23
138 India	442.3	913.5	1,006.8	2.2	1.6	2036	26.3	9.4	3.2	41
139 Pakistan	50.0	132.7	156.0	2.9	2.7	2019	38.6	8.7	5.4	12
140 Comoros	0.2	0.6	0.7	3.0	3.1	2016	42.4	11.1	5.8	..
141 Nigeria	42.3	108.5	128.8	2.8	2.9	2018	45.2	15.0	6.4	6
142 Zaire	15.3	43.9	51.7	3.1	2.8	2019	48.2	14.4	6.7	8
143 Zambia	3.1	7.9	9.1	2.8	2.5	2022	43.4	18.5	5.8	15
144 Bangladesh	51.4	116.5	128.3	2.4	1.6	2037	23.7	10.2	3.0	47
145 Côte d'Ivoire	3.8	13.3	15.1	3.8	2.2	2026	36.9	12.9	5.3	11
146 Benin	2.2	5.3	6.2	2.5	2.8	2018	44.0	13.1	6.2	9
147 Togo	1.5	4.0	4.7	2.9	2.8	2019	44.4	15.1	6.6	..
148 Yemen	5.2	14.3	18.1	3.0	4.0	2011	48.4	11.5	7.6	7
149 Tanzania, U. Rep. of	10.2	29.2	33.7	3.1	2.4	2022	42.6	14.4	5.8	20
150 Mauritania	1.0	2.2	2.6	2.4	2.6	2021	39.4	13.9	5.3	3
151 Central African Rep.	1.5	3.2	3.6	2.2	2.2	2026	38.5	16.9	5.2	24
152 Madagascar	5.4	14.4	17.4	3.0	3.2	2016	42.7	10.7	5.9	17
153 Cambodia	5.4	9.8	11.2	1.7	2.3	2024	36.4	13.4	4.9	..
154 Nepal	9.3	20.9	24.3	2.4	2.6	2021	39.6	12.6	5.3	29
155 Bhutan	0.9	1.7	2.0	2.1	2.6	2020	41.5	14.7	5.9	..
156 Haiti	3.8	7.0	7.8	1.8	1.9	2031	35.0	12.9	4.7	18
157 Angola	4.8	10.5	12.8	2.3	3.4	2014	50.7	18.5	7.2	..
158 Sudan	11.2	26.1	29.8	2.5	2.2	2025	34.0	13.8	4.9	8
159 Uganda	6.6	19.1	22.5	3.2	2.8	2019	51.1	22.3	7.1	15
160 Senegal	3.2	8.1	9.5	2.8	2.7	2020	42.2	15.5	5.9	7
161 Malawi	3.5	9.6	11.0	3.0	2.3	2024	50.2	22.7	7.1	13
162 Djibouti	0.1	0.6	0.7	5.9	2.7	2019	38.0	15.8	5.7	..
163 Guinea-Bissau	0.5	1.0	1.2	2.0	2.0	2028	42.3	21.4	5.8	..
164 Chad	3.1	6.2	7.3	2.1	2.8	2019	43.4	18.2	5.9	..
165 Gambia	0.4	1.1	1.2	3.3	2.4	2022	42.3	18.6	5.4	12
166 Mozambique	7.5	16.6	19.6	2.4	2.7	2019	45.0	18.6	6.5	..
167 Guinea	3.1	7.1	7.9	2.4	1.7	2034	50.5	19.8	7.0	2
168 Eritrea	1.4	3.1	3.8	2.3	3.6	2013	42.5	15.4	5.7	5
169 Burundi	2.9	5.9	7.0	2.1	2.7	2019	45.6	20.3	6.8	9
170 Ethiopia	22.8	54.6	66.2	2.6	3.2	2015	48.9	17.5	7.0	4
171 Mali	4.4	10.5	12.6	2.6	3.1	2016	50.7	18.6	7.1	7
172 Burkina Faso	4.5	10.2	12.1	2.5	2.8	2018	47.3	18.0	7.0	8
173 Niger	3.0	8.8	10.8	3.2	3.4	2014	51.5	18.5	7.3	4
174 Rwanda	2.7	5.3	7.7	2.0	6.4	2005	43.5	52.7	6.4	21
175 Sierra Leone	2.2	4.1	4.9	1.8	2.8	2019	49.0	30.3	6.5	..
All developing countries	2,054T	4,326T	4,774T	2.2	1.7	2036	27.1	9.0	3.1	56
Least developed countries	227T	534T	620T	2.5	2.5	2022	39.8	15.0	5.3	21
Sub-Saharan Africa	211T	535T	632T	2.8	2.8	2019	44.2	15.8	6.1	16
Industrial countries	941T	1,228T	1,252T	0.8	0.3	2212	13.1	10.0	1.7	71
World	2,994T	5,554T	6,026T	1.8	1.4	2045	24.0	9.2	2.8	58

Source: Columns 1-3 and 7-9: UN 1996b; columns 4-6: calculated on the basis of estimates from UN 1996b; column 10: UN 1997.

		Electricity consumption			Traditional fuel consumption (as % of total consumption)		House-hold energy from fuel-wood[a] (%)	Commercial energy use (oil equivalent)						Net commercial energy imports (as % of energy consumption)	
		Total (millions of kilowatt-hours)	Index (1970 =100)	Per capita (kilowatt-hours)				Total (1,000 metric tons)		Per capita (kg)		GDP output per kilogram (US$)			
HDI rank		1994	1994	1970	1994	1973	1993	1990	1980	1994	1980	1994	1980	1994	1980	1994
High human development		803,876T	695	545	2,310	..	..	..	294,052T	564,968T	1,122	1,681	2.4	3.6	-48	-41
22	Hong Kong	33,236	652	1,287	5,693	..	..	..	5,628	13,822	1,117	2,280	5.1	9.5	100	100
24	Cyprus	2,681	440	1,010	3,653	..	..	..	..	..	..	..	..	..	..	..
25	Barbados	571	391	613	2,188	..	..	..	..	..	..	..	..	..	..	..
26	Singapore	20,585	934	1,063	7,297	(.)	(.)	..	6,049	19,210	2,651	6,556	1.9	3.6	100	100
28	Bahamas	985	201	2,860	3,621	..	..	..	..	..	..	..	..	..	..	..
29	Antigua and Barbuda	355	646	733	5,145	..	..	..	..	..	..	..	..	..	..	..
30	Chile	25,250	334	806	1,798	13	13	..	7,743	13,200	695	943	3.6	3.9	50	66
32	Korea, Rep. of	185,993	1,938	298	4,174	16	1	..	41,426	133,374	1,087	3,000	1.5	2.8	77	85
33	Costa Rica	4,766	464	595	1,424	61	36	..	..	1,843	..	558	..	4.5	..	41
36	Argentina	67,162	309	915	1,965	8	5	43	39,669	47,850	1,411	1,399	1.9	5.9	8	-21
37	Uruguay	5,957	267	772	1,881	15	27	..	2,208	1,971	758	623	4.6	7.9	89	68
38	Brunei Darussalam	1,315	953	1,062	4,696	..	..	..	..	..	..	..	..	..	..	..
40	Trinidad and Tobago	3,978	331	1,170	3,079	4	1	..	3,863	5,891	3,570	4,549	1.6	0.8	-240	-89
41	Dominica	34	378	127	479	..	..	..	..	..	..	..	..	..	..	..
43	Bahrain	4,550	1,086	1,949	8,288	..	..	..	..	..	..	..	..	..	..	..
44	United Arab Emirates	18,870	13,479	617	10,140	(.)	(.)	..	8,558	24,017	8,205	12,795	3.5	..	-996	-470
45	Panama	3,533	421	585	1,367	98	21	..	1,376	1,479	703	566	2.6	4.7	97	83
46	Fiji	520	329	304	674	48	52	..	..	..	..	..	..	..	..	..
47	Venezuela	72,796	573	1,237	3,405	2	1	..	35,011	49,355	2,354	2,331	2.0	1.2	-280	-245
49	Saint Kitts and Nevis	86	538	246	2,098	..	..	..	..	..	..	..	..	..	..	..
50	Mexico	143,447	497	569	1,562	8	5	23	97,434	139,600	1,453	1,577	2.0	2.7	-49	-55
51	Colombia	43,617	499	426	1,263	23	22	60	13,972	22,271	501	613	2.4	3.0	7	-103
52	Seychelles	126	1,800	135	1,726	..	..	..	..	..	..	..	..	..	..	..
53	Kuwait	23,152	870	3,577	14,178	(.)	(.)	..	9,500	12,337	6,909	7,615	3.0	2.0	-739	-711
54	Grenada	70	467	160	761	..	..	..	..	..	..	..	..	..	..	..
55	Qatar	5,850	2,075	2,541	10,833	..	..	..	..	..	..	..	..	..	..	..
56	Saint Lucia	112	622	178	794	..	..	..	..	..	..	..	..	..	..	..
57	Saint Vincent	64	533	129	577	..	..	..	..	..	..	..	..	..	..	..
59	Thailand	75,278	1,670	124	1,294	49	24	77	12,093	44,655	259	770	2.7	3.2	96	59
60	Malaysia	40,027	1,130	338	2,032	22	8	..	9,522	33,662	692	1,711	2.6	2.1	-58	-66
61	Mauritius	1,000	455	273	906	67	44	60	..	431	..	387	..	7.9	..	92
63	Belize	110	478	192	524	55	49	..	..	..	..	..	..	..	..	..
64	Libyan Arab Jamahiriya	17,800	4,178	214	3,407	7	1	..	..	..	..	..	..	..	..	..
Medium human development		1,988,669T	739	180	895	..	..	..	755,169T	1,444,186T	463	685	2.6	2.6	-65	-28
Excluding China		1,062,632T	641	254	1,035	..	..	..	342,039T	674,186T	526	735	2.9	3.4	-125	-53
65	Lebanon	5,150	419	498	1,767	5	4	32	..	..	..	..	..	..	..	..
66	Suriname	1,683	127	3,563	4,026	1	5	..	..	..	..	..	..	..	..	..
68	Brazil	292,339	643	491	1,837	49	35	32	72,141	110,000	595	691	3.3	5.0	65	38
70	Iran, Islamic Rep. of	79,128	1,171	236	1,203	1	1	..	38,347	97,891	980	1,565	2.4	0.7	-118	-127
72	Ecuador	8,163	860	159	728	42	23	65	4,209	5,807	529	517	2.8	2.9	-156	-223
73	Saudi Arabia	66,760	6,298	171	3,826	(.)	(.)	..	35,496	85,326	3,787	4,744	4.4	1.4	-1,361	-435
74	Turkey	77,783	902	247	1,280	27	5	48	31,314	58,100	705	955	1.8	2.3	45	56
75	Korea, Dem.People's Rep. of	37,000	224	1,179	1,576	3	1	..	..	..	..	..	..	..	..	..
78	Syrian Arab Rep.	14,800	1,563	151	1,044	(.)	(.)	33	..	..	..	..	..	..	..	..
81	Tunisia	6,486	817	155	743	25	12	37	3,083	5,204	483	590	2.8	3.0	-99	-7
82	Algeria	18,764	948	138	687	5	2	29	12,078	28,244	647	1,030	3.5	1.5	-452	-273
83	Jamaica	3,927	255	825	1,617	7	5	61	2,169	2,776	1,017	1,112	1.2	1.5	99	100
84	Jordan	5,075	2,236	99	976	(.)	(.)	20	1,710	4,024	784	997	..	1.5	100	97
86	Cuba	10,982	225	572	1,002	35	36	25	..	..	..	..	..	..	..	..
87	Dominican Rep.	6,182	616	247	805	32	15	55	..	2,591	..	340	..	4.0	..	89
88	Oman	7,856	7,482	161	3,782	(.)	(.)	..	1,346	4,924	1,223	2,347	4.4	2.4	-1,024	-801
89	Peru	15,163	274	411	650	25	22	76	8,139	8,159	471	351	2.5	6.1	-36	1
90	South Africa	181,290	..	..	3,913	100	4	..	60,511	91,349	2,074	2,253	1.3	1.3	-14	-33
91	Sri Lanka	4,386	538	65	242	58	53	85	1,411	1,979	96	111	2.9	5.9	91	83
94	Paraguay	3,090	1,417	95	640	75	52	68	550	1,251	175	261	8.3	6.3	88	-141
96	Samoa (Western)	64	582	77	379	..	..	..	..	..	..	..	..	..	..	..
97	Botswana	..	..	..	..	100	100	57	..	549	..	380	..	7.3	..	55
98	Philippines	26,425	305	235	399	40	33	81	13,406	24,428	277	364	2.4	2.6	79	70
99	Indonesia	61,370	2,668	19	315	64	36	86	25,028	74,794	169	393	3.1	2.3	-275	-101
101	Mongolia	3,472	634	439	1,469	25	11	..	..	2,550	..	1,079	..	0.3	..	15
104	Guyana	254	79	456	308	23	23	..	..	..	..	..	..	..	..	..
108	China	926,037	866	132	780	11	6	80	413,130	770,000	421	647	0.5	0.7	-4	-1
109	Egypt	47,920	631	228	777	9	4	..	15,176	34,538	371	608	1.5	1.2	-120	-67
111	Maldives	46	4,600	9	187	..	..	..	..	..	..	..	..	..	..	..
112	El Salvador	3,415	509	190	605	58	35	71	..	1,236	..	219	..	6.6	..	58
113	Bolivia	2,892	368	184	400	26	18	81	1,713	2,220	320	307	1.8	2.5	-107	-90
114	Swaziland	..	..	..	..	66	100	..	..	..	..	..	..	..	..	..
116	Honduras	2,672	848	119	486	61	57	..	..	969	..	169	..	3.4	..	71
117	Guatemala	3,161	417	144	306	59	59	73	1,443	1,921	209	186	5.5	6.7	84	70
118	Namibia	..	..	..	..	..	..	..	..	..	..	..	..	..	..	..

HDI rank	Electricity consumption — Total (millions of kilowatt-hours) 1994	Index (1970=100) 1994	Per capita (kilowatt-hours) 1970	Per capita 1994	Traditional fuel consumption (as % of total consumption) 1973	Traditional fuel 1993	House-hold energy from fuelwood[a] (%) 1990	Commercial energy use (oil equivalent) — Total (1,000 metric tons) 1980	Total 1994	Per capita (kg) 1980	Per capita 1994	GDP output per kilogram (US$) 1980	GDP output per kg 1994	Net commercial energy imports (as % of energy consumption) 1980	Net commercial energy imports 1994
119 Morocco	11,693	605	125	441	5	4	67	4,927	8,107	254	307	3.8	3.8	87	95
120 Gabon	933	962	194	727	24	45	..	759	676	942	520	5.6	5.8	-1,106	-2,268
121 Viet Nam	12,020	334	70	165	33	44	88	4,024	7,549	75	105	..	2.1	32	-55
122 Solomon Islands	30	333	55	82	61	62	..	..	..	..	..	..	..	..	..
123 Cape Verde	39	557	26	102	..	..	..	..	..	..	..	..	..	..	..
124 Vanuatu	29	322	108	176	..	..	..	..	..	..	..	..	..	..	..
125 São Tomé and Principe	16	229	95	123	..	..	..	..	..	..	..	..	..	..	..
126 Iraq	27,060	984	291	1,358	1	(.)	60	..	1,001	..	241	..	1.8	..	84
127 Nicaragua	1,727	275	342	404	47	43	..	..	990	..	236	..	5.5	..	-150
128 Papua New Guinea	1,790	937	77	426	70	64	..	..	..	..	..	..	..	..	..
129 Zimbabwe	9,050	142	1,203	823	26	25	..	2,797	4,654	399	432	1.9	1.2	28	26
130 Congo	547	720	63	217	69	48	..	262	379	157	147	6.5	4.2	-1,193	-2,492
Low human development	512,878T	556	95	289	..	..	..	130,813T	300,320T	122	185	3.4	2.3	-5	5
Excluding India	126,976T	399	67	147	..	..	..	..	78,058T	..	112	..	3.6	..	-45
131 Myanmar	3,500	583	22	77	76	73	89	..	..	..	..	..	..	..	..
132 Ghana	5,857	201	339	346	64	69	86	1,303	1,511	121	91	3.4	3.6	57	64
133 Cameroon	2,740	236	172	213	81	76	74	774	1,077	89	83	9.7	6.9	-269	-525
134 Kenya	3,802	458	74	139	80	79	79	1,991	2,792	120	107	3.6	2.5	95	82
135 Equatorial Guinea	20	125	55	51	84	69	..	..	..	..	..	..	..	..	..
136 Lao People's Dem. Rep.	294	338	29	62	79	89	..	..	182	..	38	..	8.4	..	-19
137 Lesotho	..	..	..	..	100	100	..	..	..	..	..	..	..	..	..
138 India	385,902	630	114	420	41	23	84	93,907	222,262	137	243	1.8	1.3	21	20
139 Pakistan	57,147	655	67	418	33	21	72	11,698	32,247	142	255	2.0	1.6	38	38
140 Comoros	17	850	7	27	..	..	..	..	..	..	..	..	..	..	..
141 Nigeria	14,790	954	28	136	80	59	74	9,879	17,503	139	162	9.4	2.0	-968	-484
142 Zaire	4,523	148	141	106	81	83	94	..	..	..	..	..	..	..	..
143 Zambia	6,305	158	941	686	52	72	86	1,685	1,292	294	140	2.3	2.7	32	29
144 Bangladesh	10,010	..	..	85	78	47	83	2,809	7,700	32	65	4.6	3.4	60	31
145 Côte d'Ivoire	1,917	371	97	139	57	49	70	1,435	2,350	175	170	7.1	2.9	87	82
146 Benin	248	752	12	47	84	87	84	149	97	43	18	9.4	15.7	93	-239
147 Togo	408	600	35	102	48	53	83	..	183	..	46	..	5.4	..	100
148 Yemen	1,958	8	..	141	..	..	75	1,364	3,165	160	214	..	..	100	-406
149 Tanzania, U. Rep. of	912	190	36	32	79	92	89	1,023	957	55	34	..	3.5	92	83
150 Mauritania	148	203	59	67	1	(.)	80	..	229	..	103	..	4.5	..	100
151 Central African Rep.	101	215	26	31	89	92	..	..	93	..	29	..	9.4	..	76
152 Madagascar	605	246	36	42	77	84	84	..	479	..	37	..	4.0	..	83
153 Cambodia	187	141	19	19	97	88	..	..	..	..	..	..	..	..	..
154 Nepal	940	1,237	7	44	95	92	84	174	486	12	23	11.2	8.3	91	84
155 Bhutan	230	..	..	143	99	85	..	..	..	..	..	..	..	..	..
156 Haiti	362	307	28	51	88	86	72	..	326	..	47	..	5.0	..	70
157 Angola	1,865	290	115	175	63	68	85	..	..	..	..	..	..	..	..
158 Sudan	1,333	340	28	49	61	82	82	..	..	..	..	..	..	..	..
159 Uganda	681	128	54	33	81	90	86	..	425	..	23	..	9.4	..	58
160 Senegal	769	233	77	95	61	57	82	875	840	158	102	3.4	4.6	100	100
161 Malawi	802	557	32	74	86	92	89	..	370	..	39	..	3.5	..	59
162 Djibouti	185	430	453	327	..	..	..	..	..	..	..	..	..	..	..
163 Guinea-Bissau	45	450	21	43	72	58	..	..	39	..	37	..	6.2	..	100
164 Chad	85	202	12	14	91	97	82	..	100	..	16	..	9.1	..	100
165 Gambia	75	577	28	69	89	75	..	..	60	..	56	..	6.0	..	100
166 Mozambique	815	147	68	52	71	91	83	1,123	614	93	40	1.8	2.4	-15	74
167 Guinea	530	137	99	82	69	70	87	..	418	..	65	..	8.1	..	87
168 Eritrea	..	..	..	..	..	..	..	..	..	..	..	..	..	..	..
169 Burundi	192	873	6	31	97	94	77	..	143	..	23	..	7.0	..	97
170 Ethiopia	1,284	247	21	24	91	90	86	624	1,156	17	21	..	4.1	91	86
171 Mali	289	507	11	28	90	88	81	..	205	..	22	..	9.1	..	80
172 Burkina Faso	216	..	..	22	96	91	85	..	160	..	16	..	11.6	..	100
173 Niger	375	1,250	10	42	86	76	71	..	327	..	37	..	4.7	..	83
174 Rwanda	177	224	21	23	97	88	84	..	209	..	27	..	2.8	..	78
175 Sierra Leone	237	120	73	54	64	83	..	..	323	..	73	..	2.6	..	100
All developing countries	3,305,423T	691	180	763	..	..	..	1,180,034T	2,309,474T	397	570	2.7	3.0	-52	-26
Least developed countries	40,178T	218	61	74	..	..	..	..	19,738T	..	50	..	5.6	..	14
Sub-Saharan Africa	244,316T	243	107	418	..	..	..	..	131,990T	..	281	..	2.9	..	-68
Industrial countries	9,176,061T	212	4,933	7,514	..	..	..	4,936,667T	5,461,707T	4,615	4,499	..	5.4	30	13
World	12,481,484T	277	1,088	2,258	..	..	..	6,116,701T	7,771,181T	1,509	1,471	..	5.0	7	3

a. Countries deriving less than 20% of household energy from fuelwood have been excluded.
Source: Columns 1-4: UN 1996a; columns 5-6: WRI 1996b; column 7: UN 1995d; columns 8-15: World Bank 1996g.

HDI rank	Land area (1,000 ha) 1993	Forest and woodland (as % of land area) 1993	Arable land (as % of land area) 1993	Irrigated land (as % of arable land area) 1993	Gini coefficient for land distribution[a] 1985-93	Annual rate of deforestation (%) 1981-90	Annual rate of reforestation (%) 1981-90	Internal renewable water resources per capita (1,000 m³ per capita) 1995	Urban population in coastal cities (1980=100) 2000	Annual marine catch (% change since 1981-83)[b] 1991-93
High human development	1,073,441 T	23.5	7.8	19.9	..	..	..	15.4	168	..
22 Hong Kong	104	21.2	5.8	33.3	..	..	..	..	132	..
24 Cyprus	925	13.3	11.9	35.5	0.36	..	..	..	157	..
25 Barbados	43	11.6	37.2	..	0.92	..	..	..	146	..
26 Singapore	62	4.8	1.6	..	..	(.)	..	0.2	122	..
28 Bahamas	1,388	23.3	0.6	..	0.88	..	..	..	122	-32
29 Antigua and Barbuda	44	11.4	18.2	..	..	..	..	..	..	..
30 Chile	75,695	21.8	5.3	31.8	..	-0.8	12	32.8	151	67
32 Korea, Rep. of	9,902	65.2	19.0	71.1	..	(.)	..	1.5	173	12
33 Costa Rica	5,110	30.7	5.6	42.1	..	-2.6	133	27.7	215	20
36 Argentina	276,689	18.4	9.0	6.8	0.79	-0.6	1	28.7	136	85
37 Uruguay	17,741	5.2	7.1	11.1	..	-0.2	1	38.9	123	-5
38 Brunei Darussalam	577	78.0	0.5	33.3	..	..	..	..	..	..
40 Trinidad and Tobago	513	45.8	14.6	29.3	..	-1.9	1	3.9	178	199
41 Dominica	75	66.7	9.3	..	..	..	..	..	..	..
43 Bahrain	68	..	1.5	100.0	..	..	..	..	209	..
44 United Arab Emirates	8,360	..	0.3	17.2	..	..	..	1.0	184	33
45 Panama	7,552	43.2	6.6	6.4	0.88	-1.7	14	54.7	177	7
46 Fiji	1,827	64.9	9.9	0.6	0.74	-0.4	18	36.4	173	8
47 Venezuela	91,250	32.9	3.5	5.9	..	-1.2	19	60.3	181	74
49 Saint Kitts and Nevis	36	16.7	22.2	..	..	..	..	..	..	..
50 Mexico	195,820	24.9	11.8	26.3	..	-1.2	9	3.8	146	-10
51 Colombia	113,891	43.9	3.4	13.5	0.71	-0.6	24	30.5	134	260
52 Seychelles	45	11.1	2.2	..	..	..	..	..	..	..
53 Kuwait	1,782	0.1	0.3	40.0	..	..	..	0.1	..	..
54 Grenada	(.)	8.8	32.4	..	..	..	..	..	..	-3
55 Qatar	1,100	..	0.6	..	..	..	..	..	231	..
56 Saint Lucia	62	12.9	8.1	20.0	..	..	..	..	..	..
57 Saint Vincent	39	35.9	10.3	25.0	0.71	..	..	..	..	..
59 Thailand	51,312	26.3	34.3	25.0	0.13	-2.9	13	3.0	238	52
60 Malaysia	32,975	67.6	3.2	32.7	..	-1.8	35	22.6	229	-13
61 Mauritius	204	21.6	49.0	17.0	..	(.)	2	2.0	138	124
63 Belize	2,296	91.5	2.0	4.4	..	-0.2	(.)	74.4	..	42
64 Libyan Arab Jamahiriya	175,954	0.5	1.0	25.9	..	..	11	0.1	289	-28
Medium human development	4,001,980 T	30.7	7.0	31.2	..	..	..	7.7	193	..
Excluding China	3,045,880 T	36.4	6.2	20.2	..	..	..	14.3	199	..
65 Lebanon	1,040	7.7	20.8	39.8	..	-0.9	(.)	1.9	156	29
66 Suriname	16,327	91.9	0.3	..	..	-0.1	4	472.8	154	182
68 Brazil	851,197	57.3	4.9	6.7	..	-0.6	7	43.0	192	-10
70 Iran, Islamic Rep. of	164,800	6.9	10.1	56.5	..	-1.6	16	1.7	170	219
72 Ecuador	28,356	55.0	5.7	34.1	..	-1.7	5	27.4	254	-31
73 Saudi Arabia	214,969	0.8	1.7	11.9	..	-1.9	(.)	0.3	..	36
74 Turkey	77,945	25.9	31.4	15.0	0.40	..	..	3.1	172	-14
75 Korea, Dem. People's Rep. of	12,054	61.1	14.1	85.9	..	(.)	11	2.8	238	13
78 Syrian Arab Rep.	18,518	3.5	27.6	17.7	..	-2.8	36	3.7	321	48
81 Tunisia	16,361	4.1	18.3	12.9	..	-1.5	13	0.4	183	35
82 Algeria	238,174	1.7	3.1	7.6	..	-2.0	6	0.5	218	43
83 Jamaica	1,099	16.8	14.1	22.6	..	-5.3	6	3.4	166	-8
84 Jordan	8,921	0.8	3.5	20.0	..	-2.0	6	0.3	209	-92
86 Cuba	11,086	23.5	23.5	34.9	..	-0.9	12	3.1	135	-40
87 Dominican Rep.	4,873	12.3	20.5	23.0	..	-2.5	8	2.6	208	25
88 Oman	21,246	..	0.1	..	..	..	..	0.9	487	23
89 Peru	128,522	66.0	2.6	37.6	..	-0.4	9	1.7	206	187
90 South Africa	122,104	6.7	10.1	10.3	..	-0.8	2	1.2	194	-33
91 Sri Lanka	6,561	32.0	14.2	59.1	..	-1.3	8	2.4	144	4
94 Paraguay	40,675	31.6	5.4	3.1	0.91	-2.4	35	63.3	..	..
96 Samoa (Western)	284	47.2	19.4	..	..	..	..	..	..	..
97 Botswana	58,173	45.6	0.7	0.5	..	-0.5	(.)	9.9	..	..
98 Philippines	30,000	45.3	18.4	28.6	..	-2.9	(.)	4.8	210	34
99 Indonesia	190,457	58.7	9.9	24.3	..	-1.0	12	12.8	200	71
101 Mongolia	156,650	8.8	0.9	5.7	..	(.)	..	10.2	..	..
104 Guyana	21,497	76.8	2.2	27.1	..	-0.1	172	288.6	200	21
108 China	956,100	13.5	9.6	53.6	..	-0.4	6	2.3	171	168
109 Egypt	100,145	..	2.4	..	..	..	2	0.9	189	207
111 Maldives	30	3.3	10.0	..	..	..	..	..	..	..
112 El Salvador	2,104	4.9	26.9	21.2	..	-2.1	37	3.3	181	-42
113 Bolivia	109,858	52.8	1.9	8.3	..	-1.1	5	40.5	..	..
114 Swaziland	1,736	6.9	10.8	35.8	..	(.)	0	5.3	..	..
116 Honduras	11,209	53.5	15.0	4.4	0.73	-2.0	101	11.2	330	153
117 Guatemala	10,889	53.4	12.2	9.4	..	-1.6	17	10.9	119	2
118 Namibia	82,429	21.8	0.8	0.9	..	-0.3	..	29.5	382	2,305

HDI rank	Land area (1,000 ha) 1993	Forest and woodland (as % of land area) 1993	Arable land (as % of land area) 1993	Irrigated land (as % of arable land area) 1993	Gini coefficient for land distribution[a] 1985-93	Annual rate of deforestation (%) 1981-90	Annual rate of reforestation (%) 1981-90	Internal renewable water resources per capita (1,000 m³ per year) 1995	Urban population in coastal cities (1980=100) 2000	Annual marine catch (% change since 1981-83)[b] 1991-93
119 Morocco	44,655	20.1	20.7	13.6	..	-0.7	4	1.1	207	46
120 Gabon	26,767	74.3	1.1	1.4	..	-0.6	6	124.2	321	24
121 Viet Nam	33,169	29.1	16.6	33.8	..	-1.4	5	5.0	256	65
122 Solomon Islands	2,890	84.8	1.4	..	..	-0.2	2	118.3	..	36
123 Cape Verde	403	0.2	10.7	7.0	..	..	..	..	288	..
124 Vanuatu	1,219	75.0	1.6	..	..	..	..	..	..	..
125 São Tomé and Principe	96	..	2.1	..	..	..	..	..	..	..
126 Iraq	43,832	0.4	12.0	48.6	..	..	..	5.3	..	-47
127 Nicaragua	13,000	24.6	8.5	8.0	..	-1.7	144	39.5	243	39
128 Papua New Guinea	46,284	90.7	0.1	..	..	-0.3	10	186.2	298	-12
129 Zimbabwe	39,076	22.5	7.0	7.0	..	-0.6	2	1.8	..	..
130 Congo	34,200	61.7	0.4	0.7	..	-0.2	22	321.2	263	2
Low human development	2,582,787 T	29.7	13.1	22.6	..	..	..	6.0	244	..
Excluding India	2,254,028 T	31.0	7.7	16.4	..	..	..	10.1	285	..
131 Myanmar	67,658	47.9	14.2	11.1	0.25	-1.2	50	23.3	196	37
132 Ghana	23,854	33.1	11.7	0.2	..	-1.3	2	3.0	235	64
133 Cameroon	47,544	75.5	12.5	0.4	..	-0.6	29	20.3	328	-18
134 Kenya	58,037	28.9	6.9	1.7	..	-0.6	2	1.1	413	-11
135 Equatorial Guinea	2,805	46.3	4.6	..	..	-0.4	0	75.0	217	44
136 Lao People's Dem. Rep.	23,680	52.8	3.3	16.0	..	-0.9	5	55.3	..	..
137 Lesotho	3,035	..	10.5	0.9	..	..	..	2.6	..	..
138 India	328,759	20.8	50.5	28.9	0.43	-0.6	32	2.2	210	68
139 Pakistan	79,610	4.4	26.1	82.3	0.37	-2.9	3	3.3	237	62
140 Comoros	223	17.9	35.0	..	..	..	..	..	270	..
141 Nigeria	92,377	12.2	32.3	3.2	..	-0.7	3	2.5	323	15
142 Zaire	234,486	74.1	3.1	0.1	0.39	-0.6	17	23.2	271	167
143 Zambia	75,261	38.1	7.0	0.9	..	-1.0	8	12.3	..	..
144 Bangladesh	14,400	13.2	65.6	32.8	..	-3.3	11	19.6	279	115
145 Côte d'Ivoire	32,246	22.0	7.6	2.8	..	-1.0	10	5.5	276	-13
146 Benin	11,262	30.2	12.7	0.7	..	-1.2	7	4.8	432	147
147 Togo	5,679	15.8	36.5	0.3	..	-1.4	23	2.9	303	107
148 Yemen	52,797	3.8	2.6	26.2	..	(.)	..	0.4	..	31
149 Tanzania, U. Rep. of	94,509	35.4	3.2	5.0	..	-1.1	13	3.0	397	55
150 Mauritania	102,552	4.3	0.2	23.9	..	(.)	101	5.0	495	42
151 Central African Rep.	62,298	75.0	3.1	..	..	-0.4	..	42.5	..	..
152 Madagascar	58,704	39.5	4.4	42.1	..	-0.8	2	22.8	356	306
153 Cambodia	18,104	64.1	13.0	3.9	..	-1.0	0	48.6	574	678
154 Nepal	14,080	40.8	16.5	36.6	0.33	-1.0	32	7.8	..	..
155 Bhutan	4,700	66.0	2.4	29.6	..	-0.6	11	58.0	..	..
156 Haiti	2,775	5.0	20.2	13.4	..	-4.0	257	1.5	234	-16
157 Angola	124,670	41.6	2.4	2.5	..	-0.7	1	16.6	318	-37
158 Sudan	250,581	17.7	5.1	15.1	..	-1.0	8	5.5	335	-29
159 Uganda	23,588	23.3	21.4	0.2	0.62	-0.9	0	3.1	..	..
160 Senegal	19,672	53.1	11.8	3.0	..	-0.6	118	4.7	223	48
61 Malawi	11,848	31.2	14.1	1.7	..	-1.3	12	1.7	..	..
162 Djibouti	2,320	0.3	..	..	..	..	..	..	216	..
163 Guinea-Bissau	3,612	29.6	8.3	5.7	..	-0.7	0	25.2	203	46
164 Chad	128,400	25.2	2.5	0.4	..	-0.7	8	6.8	..	..
165 Gambia	1,130	24.8	15.9	8.3	..	-0.8	0	7.2	269	122
166 Mozambique	80,159	17.5	3.7	4.0	..	-0.7	5	13.0	473	-28
167 Guinea	24,586	58.8	2.5	15.2	0.19	1.1	6	33.7	291	56
168 Eritrea	10,100	..	..	..	..	..	..	2.5	..	..
169 Burundi	2,783	3.1	40.8	1.2	..	-0.6	59	0.6	..	..
170 Ethiopia	110,076	22.7	10.9	1.6	0.32	-0.3	17	2.0	251	-70
171 Mali	124,019	5.6	2.0	3.1	..	0.8	144	6.2	..	..
172 Burkina Faso	27,400	50.4	13.0	0.6	..	-0.7	13	2.7	..	..
173 Niger	126,700	2.0	2.8	1.8	..	(.)	18	3.6	..	..
174 Rwanda	2,634	20.9	32.5	0.5	..	-0.2	9	0.8	..	..
175 Sierra Leone	7,174	28.4	6.8	6.0	..	-0.6	3	35.5	259	35
All developing countries	7,658,208 T	29.3	9.2	25.7	..	..	..	7.6	198	..
Least developed countries	1,905,610 T	31.9	5.5	9.5	..	..	..	14.0	295	..
Sub-Saharan Africa	2,098,331 T	32.6	6.2	3.8	..	..	..	9.1	294	..
Industrial countries	5,503,009 T	35.1	11.3	9.9	..	..	..	12.2	..	..
World	13,161,217 T	31.8	10.1	18.3	..	..	..	8.6	..	..

a. The Gini coefficient is a measure of inequality in the distribution of landholdings. It ranges from zero to 1: the closer the value to 1, the greater the inequality.
b. Figures are based on national totals averaged over a three-year period and represent nominal catch (that is, landings converted to a live-weight basis).
Source: Column 1: FAO 1994; columns 2-4: calculated on the basis of data from FAO 1994; column 5: WRI 1996a; columns 6-10: WRI 1996b.

National income accounts

HDI rank	GDP (US$ billions) 1994	Agriculture (as % of GDP) 1994	Industry (as % of GDP) 1994	Services (as % of GDP) 1994	Consumption Private (as % of GDP) 1994	Consumption Government (as % of GDP) 1994	Gross domestic investment (as % of GDP)[a] 1994	Gross domestic savings (as % of GDP)[a] 1994	Tax revenue (as % of GNP) 1994	Central government expenditure (as % of GNP) 1994	Exports (as % of GDP) 1994	Imports (as % of GDP) 1994
High human development	1,726T	8	34	59	64	11	28	28	..	..	32	36
22 Hong Kong	131.9	(..)	18	82	59	8	31	33	..	..	..	..
24 Cyprus	..	..	..	..	..	..	..	..	..	..	..	..
25 Barbados	..	..	..	..	..	..	..	..	..	..	..	..
26 Singapore	68.9	(..)[b]	36[b]	64[b]	40	8	32	51	17	18	148	144
28 Bahamas	..	..	..	..	..	..	..	..	..	..	..	..
29 Antigua and Barbuda	..	..	..	..	..	..	..	..	..	..	..	..
30 Chile	52.0	..	..	..	63	9	27	28	19	21	29	31
32 Korea, Rep. of	376.5	7[b]	43[b]	50[b]	53	10	38	39	18	19	31	32
33 Costa Rica	8.3	15[b]	24[b]	61[b]	60	17	28	23	23	32	41	48
36 Argentina	281.9	5	30	65	82	..	20	18	..	..	8	11
37 Uruguay	15.5	8[b]	23[b]	69[b]	79	10	13	12	32	37	22	25
38 Brunei Darussalam	..	..	..	..	..	..	..	..	..	..	..	..
40 Trinidad and Tobago	4.8	3	46	51	63	12	14	24	..	..	45	41
41 Dominica	..	..	..	..	..	..	..	..	..	..	..	..
43 Bahrain	..	..	..	..	..	..	..	..	..	..	..	..
44 United Arab Emirates	35.4	2	57	40	49	18	25	33	1	11	..	..
45 Panama	7.0	11[b]	16[b]	73[b]	61	16	25	23	22	29	110	111
46 Fiji	..	..	..	..	..	..	..	..	..	..	..	..
47 Venezuela	58.3	5[b]	42[b]	53[b]	72	7	13	22	15	20	33	28
49 Saint Kitts and Nevis	..	..	..	..	..	..	..	..	..	..	..	..
50 Mexico	377.1	8[b]	28[b]	64[b]	70	12	23	18	..	..	14	23
51 Colombia	67.3	14	32	54	75	9	20	15	14	15	19	24
52 Seychelles	..	..	..	..	..	..	..	..	..	..	..	..
53 Kuwait	24.3	(.)[b]	53[b]	47[b]	41	37	11	22	1	50	74	51
54 Grenada	..	..	..	..	..	..	..	..	..	..	..	..
55 Qatar	..	..	..	..	..	..	..	..	..	..	..	..
56 Saint Lucia	..	..	..	..	..	..	..	..	..	..	..	..
57 Saint Vincent	..	..	..	..	..	..	..	..	..	..	..	..
59 Thailand	143.2	10[b]	39[b]	50[b]	55	9	40	35	17	15	41	48
60 Malaysia	70.6	14[b]	43[b]	42[b]	53	10	39	37	23	26	93	99
61 Mauritius	3.4	9	33	58	64	13	32	23	20	23	62	71
63 Belize	..	..	..	..	..	..	..	..	..	..	..	..
64 Libyan Arab Jamahiriya	..	..	..	..	..	..	..	..	..	..	..	..
Medium human development	2,071T	16	39	45	57	15	27	28	13	..	23	24
Excluding China	1,549T	14	36	50	62	16	22	23	18	29	22	25
65 Lebanon	..	..	..	..	..	..	..	..	..	..	..	..
66 Suriname	..	..	..	..	..	..	..	..	..	..	..	..
68 Brazil	554.6	13	39	49	61	17	21	22	18	35	9	10
70 Iran, Islamic Rep. of	63.7	21	37	42	54	15	23	31	8	26	31	26
72 Ecuador	16.6	12[b]	38[b]	50[b]	70	7	21	23	15	17	27	33
73 Saudi Arabia	117.2	..	..	..	44	29	24	28	..	..	47	45
74 Turkey	131.0	16	31	52	67	11	22	23	15	24	23	23
75 Korea, Dem. People's Rep. of	..	..	..	..	..	..	..	..	..	..	..	..
78 Syrian Arab Rep.	..	..	..	..	..	..	..	..	..	..	..	..
81 Tunisia	15.8	15	32	53	62	16	24	22	24	33	44	51
82 Algeria	41.9	12	44	44	57	17	32	27	..	..	23	31
83 Jamaica	4.2	8[b]	37[b]	54[b]	69	12	22	19	..	..	63	73
84 Jordan	6.1	8	27	65	75	22	26	3	22	34	50	78
86 Cuba	..	..	..	..	..	..	..	..	..	..	..	..
87 Dominican Rep.	10.4	15[b]	22[b]	63[b]	80	4	20	16	16	18	25	31
88 Oman	11.6	3	53	44	33	39	17	27	9	50	50	48
89 Peru	50.1	7[b]	37[b]	56[b]	70	10	24	20	14	16	12	18
90 South Africa	121.9	5	31	65	59	21	18	20	25	36	24	25
91 Sri Lanka	11.7	24[b]	25[b]	51[b]	76	9	27	15	17	28	35	48
94 Paraguay	7.8	24	22	54	79	7	23	14	9	13	34	51
96 Samoa (Western)	..	..	..	..	..	..	..	..	..	..	..	..
97 Botswana	4.0	5[b]	49[b]	46[b]	44	32	25	25	31	40	59	52
98 Philippines	64.2	22[b]	33[b]	45[b]	71	11	24	18	15	18	38	43
99 Indonesia	174.6	17[b]	41[b]	42[b]	61	8	29	30	16	17	27	29
101 Mongolia	0.7	21	45	34	71	14	21	15	17	21	57	65
104 Guyana	..	..	..	..	..	..	..	..	..	..	..	..
108 China	522.2	21[b]	47[b]	32[b]	43	13	42	44	3	..	24	23
109 Egypt	42.9	20	21	59	81	14	18	6	26	43	25	38
111 Maldives	..	..	..	..	..	..	..	..	..	..	..	..
112 El Salvador	8.1	14[b]	24[b]	62[b]	88	8	19	4	11	15	20	37
113 Bolivia	5.5	..	..	..	79	13	15	8	12	26	22	30
114 Swaziland	..	..	..	..	..	..	..	..	..	..	..	..
116 Honduras	3.3	20	32	38	73	13	26	14	..	..	41	56
117 Guatemala	12.9	25[b]	19[b]	56[b]	86	6	17	8	7	9	20	29
118 Namibia	2.9	14	29	56	52	31	20	17	31	40	61	63

HDI rank	GDP (US$ billions) 1994	Agriculture (as % of GDP) 1994	Industry (as % of GDP) 1994	Services (as % of GDP) 1994	Consumption Private (as % of GDP) 1994	Consumption Government (as % of GDP) 1994	Gross domestic investment (as % of GDP)[a] 1994	Gross domestic savings (as % of GDP)[a] 1994	Tax revenue (as % of GNP) 1994	Central government expenditure (as % of GNP) 1994	Exports (as % of GDP) 1994	Imports (as % of GDP) 1994
119 Morocco	30.8	21 [b]	30 [b]	49 [b]	68	17	21	16	27	31	23	32
120 Gabon	3.9	8 [b]	52 [b]	40 [b]	40	13	25	47	..	..	61	58
121 Viet Nam	15.6	28 [b]	30 [b]	43 [b]	77	9	24	13	..	..	32	40
122 Solomon Islands	..	..	..	..	..	..	..	..	..	..	..	..
123 Cape Verde	..	..	..	..	..	..	..	..	..	..	..	..
124 Vanuatu	..	..	..	..	..	..	..	..	..	..	..	..
125 São Tomé and Principe	..	..	..	..	..	..	..	..	..	..	..	..
126 Iraq	..	..	..	..	..	..	..	..	..	..	..	..
127 Nicaragua	1.8	33 [b]	20 [b]	46 [b]	95	14	18	-9	29	42	25	78
128 Papua New Guinea	5.4	28 [b]	38 [b]	33 [b]	53	15	15	32	21	32	54	44
129 Zimbabwe	5.4	15	36	48	64	19	22	17	..	..	37	43
130 Congo	1.6	10 [b]	44 [b]	46 [b]	54	23	16	23	..	..	68	89
Low human development	483T	32	26	42	72	11	20	17	..	..	16	22
Excluding India	189T	34	24	42	78	11	16	12	..	..	22	32
131 Myanmar	..	63	9	28	89	..	12	11	5	10	..	..
132 Ghana	5.4	46 [b]	16 [b]	39 [b]	84	12	16	4	13	21	26	39
133 Cameroon	7.5	32 [b]	28 [b]	41 [b]	73	8	14	20	11	18	30	33
134 Kenya	6.9	29	17	54	62	15	21	24	22	31	39	42
135 Equatorial Guinea	..	..	..	..	..	..	..	..	..	..	..	..
136 Lao People's Dem. Rep.	1.5	51 [b]	18 [b]	31 [b]	..	..	..	..	..	..	17	26
137 Lesotho	0.9	14	46	40	86	28	86	-14	..	..	62	103
138 India	293.6	30	28	42	68	11	23	21	10	17	12	15
139 Pakistan	52.0	25	25	50	71	12	20	17	13	24	16	25
140 Comoros	..	..	..	..	..	..	..	..	..	..	..	..
141 Nigeria	35.2	43	32	25	79	10	10	11	..	..	28	36
142 Zaire	..	..	..	..	..	..	..	..	..	..	..	..
143 Zambia	3.5	31 [b]	35 [b]	34 [b]	84	13	7	4	11	21	34	46
144 Bangladesh	26.2	30 [b]	18 [b]	52 [b]	85	7	14	8	..	..	12	19
145 Côte d'Ivoire	6.7	41	26	32	58	17	13	25	..	..	47	54
146 Benin	1.5	34 [b]	12 [b]	53 [b]	82	9	20	9	..	..	27	34
147 Togo	1.0	38	21	41	78	15	11	7	..	..	31	35
148 Yemen	..	..	..	..	..	..	..	..	..	..	..	..
149 Tanzania, U. Rep. of	3.4	57	17	26	88	8	31	3	..	..	25	61
150 Mauritania	1.0	27	30	43	80	10	17	10	..	..	42	55
151 Central African Rep.	0.9	44	13	43	78	15	14	7	..	..	21	32
152 Madagascar	1.9	35	13	52	91	7	12	2	9	20	33	52
153 Cambodia	..	..	..	..	..	..	..	..	..	..	..	..
154 Nepal	4.0	44	21	35	78	9	21	12	..	..	25	33
155 Bhutan	..	..	..	..	..	..	..	..	..	..	..	..
156 Haiti	1.6	44	12	44	101	6	2	-7	..	..	4	13
157 Angola	..	..	..	..	..	..	..	..	..	..	..	..
158 Sudan	..	..	..	..	..	..	..	..	..	..	..	..
159 Uganda	4.0	49	14	37	85	10	14	4	..	..	8	23
160 Senegal	3.9	17 [b]	20 [b]	63 [b]	79	12	16	10	..	..	35	45
161 Malawi	1.3	31	21	47	79	22	16	-1	..	..	30	48
162 Djibouti	..	..	..	..	..	..	..	..	..	..	..	..
163 Guinea-Bissau	0.2	45	18	37	90	8	20	2	..	..	23	42
164 Chad	0.9	44 [b]	22 [b]	35 [b]	93	17	9	-10	..	..	20	37
165 Gambia	0.4	28	15	58	76	18	21	5	22	21	61	70
166 Mozambique	1.5	33	12	55	75	20	60	5	..	..	23	96
167 Guinea	3.4	24	31	45	82	9	14	9	13	22	20	28
168 Eritrea	..	..	..	..	..	..	..	..	..	..	..	..
169 Burundi	1.0	53	18	29	99	11	9	-10	..	..	11	31
170 Ethiopia	4.7	57 [b]	10 [b]	32 [b]	85	12	15	3	12	..	12	25
171 Mali	1.9	42 [b]	15 [b]	42 [b]	82	12	26	6	..	..	21	44
172 Burkina Faso	1.9	34	27	39	78	16	22	6	9	16	19	50
173 Niger	1.5	39 [b]	18 [b]	44 [b]	82	17	6	1	..	..	16	23
174 Rwanda	0.6	51	9	40	158	11	6	-69	12	25	9	85
175 Sierra Leone	0.8	47	18	35	83	12	9	4	15	25	..	..
All developing countries	4,280T	15	36	50	61	13	27	27	14	..	26	28
Least developed countries	72T	37	19	44	85	10	17	5	..	..	18	32
Sub-Saharan Africa	247T	20	29	51	67	17	17	16	24	33	29	34
Industrial countries	20,744T	3	35	62	62	17	21	21	24	33	22	22
World	25,024T	6	35	58	62	16	22	22	23	..	23	23

Note: The percentage shares of agriculture, industry and services may not necessarily add to 100 because of rounding.
a. Includes public and private investment and savings.
b. GDP and its components are at purchaser values.
Source: Columns 1-9: World Bank 1996g; *columns 10-12:* calculated on the basis of data from World Bank 1996g.

26 Trends in economic performance

HDI rank	GNP (US$ billions) 1994	GNP annual growth rate (%) 1980-93	GNP per capita annual growth rate (%)		Average annual rate of inflation (%)		Exports as % of GDP (% annual growth rate) 1980-93	Tax revenue as % of GNP (% annual growth rate) 1980-92	Overall budget surplus/deficit (as % of GNP)	
			1965-80	1980-93	1984-94	1993			1980	1994
High human development	1,947T	3.7	2.8	1.7	89.6	9.8	3.2	..	0.9	..
22 Hong Kong	126.3	..	6.2	5.4	9.0	8.8	7.0		..	..
24 Cyprus	..	5.7	..	4.9	..	2.9	1.4	..	..	..
25 Barbados	1.7	-0.1	3.5	0.5	..	1.9	..	..	..	..
26 Singapore	65.8	7.6	8.3	6.1	3.9	4.0	2.9	0.3	2.2	15.7
28 Bahamas	3.2	2.3	1.0	1.4	..	-1.8	..	..	..	..
29 Antigua and Barbuda	0.5	5.4	-1.4	5.2	..	1.5	..	..	..	..
30 Chile	50.1	4.6	(.)	3.6	18.5	12.1	2.2	-1.8	5.6	1.7
32 Korea, Rep. of	366.5	8.7	7.3	8.2	6.8	4.6	2.3	0.2	-2.3	0.3
33 Costa Rica	7.9	3.3	3.3	1.1	18.2	11.6	4.3	1.4	-7.8	-5.9
36 Argentina	275.7	1.0	1.7	-0.5	317.2	7.2	2.5	..	-2.6	..
37 Uruguay	14.7	-0.4	2.5	-0.1	73.8	45.2	4.1	2.2	0	-3.0
38 Brunei Darussalam	4.0	..	..	..	..	..	..	..	..	..
40 Trinidad and Tobago	4.8	-0.8	3.1	-2.8	6.5	9.9	9.7	..	7.6	..
41 Dominica	0.2	4.6	-0.8	4.6	..	1.6	..	..	..	..
43 Bahrain	4.1	0.8	..	-2.9	..	-1.1	..	..	..	..
44 United Arab Emirates	..	0.2	0.6	-4.4	..	..	..	..	2.0	-0.2
45 Panama	6.9	2.5	2.8	-0.7	1.6	3.5	0.5	0.6	-5.4	4.6
46 Fiji	1.8	1.8	4.2	0.5	..	8.8	..	..	..	..
47 Venezuela	59.0	1.6	2.3	-0.7	36.4	32.4	1.0	-2.1	0	-4.3
49 Saint Kitts and Nevis	0.2	4.7	4.0	5.4	..	2.3	..	..	..	..
50 Mexico	368.7	1.9	3.6	-0.5	40.0	9.7	4.4	-0.8	-3.1	..
51 Colombia	58.9	3.2	3.7	1.5	25.6	21.9	2.8	..	-1.8	-0.6
52 Seychelles	0.5	3.9	4.6	3.4	..	-0.1	..	..	..	..
53 Kuwait	314.3	-0.1	0.6	-4.3	..	..	..	..	50.2	..
54 Grenada	0.2	..	0.1	3.8	..	1.6	..	..	..	..
55 Qatar	7.8	1.4	..	-7.2	..	..	..	..	..	..
56 Saint Lucia	0.5	..	2.7	4.4	..	(.)	..	..	..	..
57 Saint Vincent	0.2	6.0	0.2	5.0	..	-0.7	..	..	..	..
59 Thailand	129.9	7.9	4.4	6.4	5.0	3.4	5.4	1.7	-4.9	1.9
60 Malaysia	68.7	6.4	4.7	3.5	3.1	1.8	4.2	..	-6.2	4.1
61 Mauritius	3.5	5.9	3.7	5.5	8.8	9.0	1.6	1.2	-10.4	-0.3
63 Belize	0.5	4.9	3.4	2.9	..	5.2	4.5	..	..	..
64 Libyan Arab Jamahiriya	..	..	0.6	..	..	..	..	..	..	..
Medium human development	2,111T	4.2	4.4	2.4	251.0	548.9	3.7	..	..	-2.7
Excluding China	1,480T	2.8	4.0	0.5	288.9	696.1	4.0	-0.2	-4.9	-3.1
65 Lebanon	..	..	0.6	..	..	..	..	..	..	..
66 Suriname	0.4	8.7	5.5	-2.0	..	136.3	..	..	..	..
68 Brazil	536.3	1.6	6.3	0.3	900.3	2,207.9	5.7	-1.3	-2.5	-4.0
70 Iran, Islamic Rep. of	..	3.3	2.9	..	23.4	37.5	6.8	1.0	-13.7	-0.1
72 Ecuador	14.7	2.6	5.4	..	47.5	38.4	3.3	2.7	-1.5	0
73 Saudi Arabia	126.6	..	0.6	-3.6	2.8	..	..	..	..	..
74 Turkey	149.0	5.5	3.6	2.4	65.8	67.7	9.7	0.4	-3.8	-4.0
75 Korea, Dem. People's Rep. of	..	..	0.6	..	..	..	..	..	..	..
78 Syrian Arab Rep.	..	..	5.1	..	..	..	..	5.5	..	..
81 Tunisia	15.9	3.8	4.7	1.2	6.3	4.5	0.9	-0.4	-2.9	-2.6
82 Algeria	46.1	2.0	4.2	-0.8	22.0	13.9	1.2	..	..	..
83 Jamaica	3.6	1.4	-0.1	-0.3	27.6	34.6	1.0	..	-16.9	..
84 Jordan	5.8	..	5.8	..	9.2	4.9	..	..	..	1.9
86 Cuba	..	..	0.6	..	..	..	..	..	..	..
87 Dominican Rep.	10.1	3.0	3.8	0.7	28.9	4.2	1.8	(.)	-2.7	0
88 Oman	10.8	9.3	9.0	3.4	0.1	-7.1	..	-3.0	0.5	-12.6
89 Peru	44.1	0.1	0.8	-2.7	492.2	46.5	0.1	-4.9	-2.5	3.1
90 South Africa	125.2	1.1	3.2	-0.2	14.3	11.2	0.8	2.0	-2.5	9.2
91 Sri Lanka	11.6	4.6	2.8	2.7	11.0	8.2	1.3	-0.5	-18.4	-8.7
94 Paraguay	7.6	2.6	4.1	-0.7	26.2	18.7	5.4	-0.5	0.3	1.2
96 Samoa (Western)	..	..	..	..	..	..	..	..	..	..
97 Botswana	4.0	9.5	9.9	6.2	11.7	9.0	..	1.1	-0.2	11.2
98 Philippines	63.3	1.7	3.2	-0.6	10.0	6.8	2.5	1.6	-1.4	-1.4
99 Indonesia	167.6	6.0	5.2	4.2	8.9	19.3	-1.9	-1.2	-2.3	0.6
101 Mongolia	0.8	2.3	0.6	0.2	46.0	332.4	-6.6	..	..	-1.8
104 Guyana	0.4	-1.8	0.7	-3.0	..	16.8	0.1	..	..	..
108 China	630.2	9.6	4.1	8.2	8.4	12.3	2.9	..	..	-2.1
109 Egypt	41.0	4.6	2.8	2.8	16.4	10.4	0.5	..	-6.8	2.1
111 Maldives	0.2	..	1.8	7.2	..	14.9	..	..	..	..
112 El Salvador	8.4	1.3	1.5	0.2	15.5	14.1	-0.4	-1.7	-5.9	-0.8
113 Bolivia	5.6	1.3	1.7	-0.7	20.0	7.6	2.9	..	..	-3.7
114 Swaziland	1.0	4.1	3.7	2.3	..	11.7	..	..	..	..
116 Honduras	3.2	2.7	1.1	-0.3	13.0	8.9	-1.8	..	..	..
117 Guatemala	12.2	1.5	3.0	-1.2	19.5	13.8	-2.3	..	-3.5	-1.2
118 Namibia	3.0	1.7	0.6	0.7	10.6	7.4	..	..	..	-4.7

HDI rank	GNP (US$ billions) 1994	GNP annual growth rate (%) 1980-93	GNP per capita annual growth rate (%) 1965-80	GNP per capita annual growth rate (%) 1980-93	Average annual rate of inflation (%) 1984-94	Average annual rate of inflation (%) 1993	Exports as % of GDP (% annual growth rate) 1980-93	Tax revenue as % of GNP (% annual growth rate) 1980-92	Overall budget surplus/deficit (as % of GNP) 1980	Overall budget surplus/deficit (as % of GNP) 1994
119 Morocco	30.3	2.9	2.7	1.2	5.0	3.8	1.5	1.0	-10	-1.4
120 Gabon	3.7	0.1	5.6	-1.6	3.3	1.0	2.3	-1.3	6.8	..
121 Viet Nam	13.8	..	0.6	..	102.6	14.3	..	..	..	..
122 Solomon Islands	0.3	6.6	5.0	2.6	..	..	..	..	..	..
123 Cape Verde	0.3	4.9	..	3.0	..	5.9	-1.1	..	..	..
124 Vanuatu	0.2	..	..	0.5	..	0.5	..	..	..	..
125 São Tomé and Principe	..	-2.6	3.3	-3.6	..	20.1	1.4	..	..	..
126 Iraq	..	..	0.6	..	..	..	..	..	..	..
127 Nicaragua	1.4	-2.1	-0.7	-5.7	1,311.2	20.2	1.7	-1.6	-7.3	-5.7
128 Papua New Guinea	4.9	3.7	0.6	0.6	3.9	3.2	2.7	-0.1	-2.0	-4.5
129 Zimbabwe	5.4	3.1	1.7	-0.3	19.7	36.2	0.6	3.0	-11.1	..
130 Congo	1.6	4.0	2.7	-0.3	-0.3	-4.3	1.4	..	-5.8	..
Low human development	478T	4.2	1.2	1.8	12.4	10.7	2.0	..	-5.6	..
Excluding India	200T	2.8	0.9	0.1	16.2	14.7	1.4	..	..	..
131 Myanmar	..	2.1	1.6	..	26.5	29.2	4.0	-4.1	1.2	-2.2
132 Ghana	7.3	2.7	-0.8	0.1	28.6	25.2	0.9	..	-4.2	-2.5
133 Cameroon	8.7	1.1	2.4	-2.2	1.3	1.1	4.7	-1.9	0.5	-2.0
134 Kenya	6.6	..	3.1	0.3	11.7	24.5	2.5	1.4	-4.6	-3.6
135 Equatorial Guinea	0.2	..	..	1.2	..	-1.5	..	..	..	..
136 Lao People's Dem. Rep.	1.5	..	0.6	..	24.2	6.3	..	..	..	..
137 Lesotho	1.4	2.7	6.8	-0.5	14.0	10.6	-1.0	4.1	..	..
138 India	278.7	5.0	1.5	3.0	9.7	8.1	2.4	1.1	-6.5	-6.0
139 Pakistan	55.6	6.1	1.8	3.1	8.8	8.6	3.5	-0.8	-5.8	-6.9
140 Comoros	0.2	2.5	0.6	-0.4	..	1.4	9.5	..	..	..
141 Nigeria	30.0	1.8	4.2	-0.1	29.6	24.9	-3.2	..	..	..
142 Zaire	..	..	-1.3	..	..	..	..	..	..	..
143 Zambia	3.2	1.0	-1.2	-3.1	92.0	180.0	-0.4	..	-20	-7.3
144 Bangladesh	26.6	4.5	-0.3	2.1	6.6	0.2	3.9	..	2.5	..
145 Côte d'Ivoire	7.1	-1.0	2.8	-4.6	0.2	-0.4	0.3	1.1	-11.4	..
146 Benin	2.0	3.0	-0.3	-0.4	2.9	1.6	-4.6	..	..	..
147 Togo	1.3	-0.5	1.7	-2.1	3.3	-2.8	-3.3	..	-2.0	..
148 Yemen	3.9	..	5.1	..	..	..	..	..	..	..
149 Tanzania, U. Rep. of	..	2.7	0.8	0.1	33.3	22.5	..	..	-7.0	..
150 Mauritania	1.1	1.8	-0.1	-0.8	7.2	4.9	0.6	..	..	..
151 Central African Rep.	1.2	0.3	0.8	-1.6	2.6	1.5	-3.5	..	-3.5	..
152 Madagascar	3.1	-0.1	-0.4	-2.6	15.8	13.0	-1.4	-4.7	..	-5.0
153 Cambodia	..	..	0.6	..	..	108.3	..	..	..	..
154 Nepal	4.2	4.6	(.)	2.0	12.1	10.3	..	1.7	-3.0	..
155 Bhutan	0.3	7.6	0.6	..	..	9.7	..	-2.6	..	..
156 Haiti	1.5	-1.9	0.9	..	13.2	19.6	-0.5	..	-4.7	..
157 Angola	..	..	0.6	..	..	..	..	..	..	..
158 Sudan	..	..	0.8	..	..	..	..	..	..	..
159 Uganda	3.7	..	-2.2	..	75.4	30.7	..	..	-3.1	..
160 Senegal	5.0	2.3	-0.5	..	2.9	0.4	0.4	..	0.9	..
161 Malawi	1.6	2.9	3.2	-1.2	18.8	21.8	-1.7	..	-17.3	..
162 Djibouti	..	..	..	..	..	3.0	..	..	..	..
163 Guinea-Bissau	0.3	4.6	-2.7	2.8	65.7	53.5	-10.3	..	..	..
164 Chad	1.2	5.0	-1.9	3.2	1.7	0.6	-4.6	..	..	..
165 Gambia	0.4	4.0	2.3	-0.2	10.1	-1.5	-0.3	..	-4.7	3.6
166 Mozambique	1.3	-0.2	0.6	-1.5	53.2	46.5	-2.6	..	..	..
167 Guinea	3.3	..	1.3	..	18.6	8.1	..	..	..	-3.3
168 Eritrea	..	..	..	..	..	..	..	..	..	..
169 Burundi	0.9	3.6	2.4	0.9	5.4	7.7	1.3	..	-3.9	..
170 Ethiopia	6.9	..	0.4	..	..	13.3	..	..	..	..
171 Mali	2.4	1.5	2.1	-1.0	3.4	3.0	3.6	..	-4.7	..
172 Burkina Faso	3.0	3.4	1.7	0.8	1.6	2.0	-1.5	..	0.2	..
173 Niger	2.0	-1.4	-2.5	-4.1	0.2	-0.1	-4.1	..	-4.8	..
174 Rwanda	..	1.4	1.6	-1.2	4.5	9.7	0.4	0.8	-1.7	-6.9
175 Sierra Leone	0.7	0.6	0.7	-1.5	67.3	32.9	-6.6	-1.3	-13.2	-6.1
All developing countries	4,536T	4.0	3.2	2.0	164.6	298.2	3.2	..	..	-1.9
Least developed countries	80T	2.5	(.)	(.)	17.6	17.9	1.4	..	..	..
Sub-Saharan Africa	254T	1.5	1.2	-1.4	16.1	14.9	0.3	..	-3.7	..
Industrial countries	20,849T	2.3	3.0	1.7	12.5	70.9	2.1	..	..	-3.9
World	25,385T	2.6	2.0	0.9	34.9	103.0	2.3	..	..	-3.6

Source: Column 1: World Bank 1996e; *columns 2, 5, 9 and 10:* World Bank 1996g; *columns 3-4 and 6-8:* calculated on the basis of data from World Bank 1995d.

HDI rank	Life expectancy at birth (years) 1994	Maternal mortality rate (per 100,000 live births) 1990	Population per doctor 1988-91	R & D scientists and technicians (per 1,000 people) 1988-95	Combined first-, second- and third-level gross enrolment ratio (%) 1994	Tertiary students (per 100,000 people) 1992	Female tertiary students (per 100,000 women) 1992	Daily newspapers (copies per 100 people) 1994	Televisions (per 100 people) 1994	Real GDP per capita (PPP$) 1994	GNP per capita (US$) 1994
High human development	76.7	14	341	3	87	3,554	3,562	29	58	20,357	22,532
1 Canada	79.0	6	446	2	100[a]	6,903	7,424	19	65	21,459	19,510
2 France	78.7	15	333	3	89	3,409	3,605	24	58	20,510	23,420
3 Norway	77.5	6	309	..	92	3,890	4,120	61	43	21,346	26,390
4 USA	76.2	12	..	4	96	5,486	5,834	23	78	26,397	25,880
5 Iceland	79.1	..	..	3	83	2,393	2,812	52	32	20,566	24,630
6 Netherlands	77.3	12	398	3	91	3,339	3,038	33	49	19,238	22,010
7 Japan	79.8	18	..	6	78	2,340	1,861	58	62	21,581	34,630
8 Finland	76.3	11	405	4	97	3,739	3,856	47	50	17,417	18,850
9 New Zealand	76.4	25	521	2	94	4,251	4,512	30	51	16,851	13,350
10 Sweden	78.3	7	395	4	82	2,622	2,783	48	47	18,540	23,530
11 Spain	77.6	7	262	1	90	3,306	3,328	10	43	14,324	13,440
12 Austria	76.6	10	..	2	87	2,836	2,560	47	48	20,667	24,630
13 Belgium	76.8	10	298	2	86	2,776	2,621	32	46	20,985	22,870
14 Australia	78.1	9	..	2	79	3,219	3,435	26	48	19,285	18,000
15 United Kingdom	76.7	9	..	2	86	2,405	2,291	35	45	18,620	18,340
16 Switzerland	78.1	6	585	..	76	2,095	1,490	41	40	24,967	37,930
17 Ireland	76.3	10	633	2	88	3,087	3,195	17	32	16,061	13,530
18 Denmark	75.2	9	360	3	89	3,045	3,147	36	54	21,341	27,970
19 Germany	76.3	22	..	3	81	2,319	1,813	32	55	19,675[b]	25,580
20 Greece	77.8	10	313	1	82	1,907	1,884	16	21	11,265	7,700
21 Italy	77.8	12	211	1	73	2,829	2,782	10	43	19,363	19,300
23 Israel	77.5	7	..	4	75	3,208	3,131	28	30	16,023	14,530
27 Luxembourg	75.9	..	..	..	58	..	..	38	34	34,155	39,600
31 Portugal	74.6	15	352	1	81	1,936	2,264	4	23	12,326	9,320
34 Malta	76.4	..	..	(.)	76	1,300	1,236	18	41	13,009[c,d]	..
35 Slovenia	73.1	13	..	3	74	2,033	2,143	18	30	10,404[c]	7,040
39 Czech Rep.	72.2	15	..	1	70	1,132	974	22	38	9,201	3,200
42 Slovakia	70.8	..	..	2	72	1,247	1,173	26	28	6,389	2,250
48 Hungary	68.8	30	312	1	67	1,145	1,113	23	52	6,437	3,840
58 Poland	71.2	19	467	1	79	1,527	1,680	14	30	5,002	2,410
62 Belarus	69.2	37	282	3	80	3,317	3,060	19	26	4,713	2,160
Medium human development	67.5	70	..	4	74	2,850	2,869	20	30	3,791	1,966
67 Russian Federation	65.7	75	..	4	78	3,174	3,307	27	38	4,828	2,650
69 Bulgaria	71.1	27	315	4	66	2,085	2,189	21	26	4,533	1,250
71 Estonia	69.2	41	..	3	72	2,603	2,475	24	36	4,294	2,820
76 Lithuania	70.1	36	..	1	70	2,802	3,097	14	34	4,011	1,350
77 Croatia	71.3	..	..	2	67	1,720	1,603	58	23	3,960[b]	2,560
79 Romania	69.5	130	552	1	62	1,019	939	30	20	4,037	1,270
80 Macedonia, FYR	71.7	..	..	1	60	1,260	1,313	2	16	3,965[c,d]	820
85 Turkmenistan	64.7	55	..	..	90	2,078	..	..	22	3,469[c]	..
92 Latvia	67.9	40	..	1	67	2,786	2,775	23	47	3,332	2,320
93 Kazakstan	67.5	80	..	..	73	3,433	..	..	26	3,284	1,160
95 Ukraine	68.4	50	259	7	76	3,152	2,954	12	23	2,718	1,910
100 Uzbekistan	67.5	55	..	2	73	3,054	..	1	18	2,438	960
102 Albania	70.5	65	730	..	59	679	722	5	9	2,788[c,d]	380
103 Armenia	70.8	50	..	..	78	3,711	..	2	24	1,737	680
105 Georgia	73.1	33	..	..	69	2,710	..	..	22	1,585	..
106 Azerbaijan	71.0	22	..	..	72	2,323	2,453	3	21	1,670	500
107 Kyrgyzstan	67.8	110	..	..	73	1,837	..	1	24	1,930	630
110 Moldova, Rep. of	67.7	60	..	..	67	2,665	..	2	28	1,576[b]	870
115 Tajikistan	66.8	130	..	1	69	2,298	..	1	19	1,117	360
All developing countries	61.8	471	5,833	(.)	56	748	559	4	14	2,908	1,053
Industrial countries	74.1	31	..	3	83	3,367	3,407	27	50	15,986	17,221
World	63.2	416	..	1	60	1,489	1,377	10	22	5,806	4,797
North America	76.4	12	..	4	96	5,626	5,991	23	77	25,908	25,249
Eastern Europe and CIS	68.1	63	..	4	75	2,622	2,595	20	30	4,203	2,125
Western and Southern Europe	77.3	14	310	2	84	2,840	2,726	24	48	18,739	21,304
OECD	75.4	46	498	3	82	3,352	3,255	26	54	18,621	20,152
European Union	77.2	13	301	2	84	2,776	2,666	25	48	18,575	20,460
Nordic countries	77.1	8	373	3	89	3,185	3,339	48	48	19,451	24,036

a. Capped at 100.
b. UNECE estimate based on data from the 1993 European Comparison Programme.
c. Preliminary update of the Penn World Tables using an expanded set of international comparisons, as described in Summers and Heston 1991.
d. Provisional.
Source: Column 1: UN 1996b; column 2: UNICEF 1997; column 3: WHO 1993; columns 4 and 8: calculated on the basis of estimates from UNESCO 1996d; column 5: UNESCO 1996b; columns 6 and 7: UNESCO 1995b; column 9: ITU 1996; column 10: calculated on the basis of estimates from World Bank 1997a; column 11: World Bank 1996g.

28 Women and capabilities

	Female net enrolment				Female tertiary students		Female life expectancy at birth		Total fertility	
	Primary		Secondary							
	Ratio	Index (1980=100)	Ratio	Index (1980=100)	Per 100,000 women	Index (1980=100)	Years	Index (1970=100)	Rate	Index (1970=100)
HDI rank	1992	1992	1992	1992	1992	1992	1994	1994	1994	1994
High human development	98	101	88	111	3,562	145	80	107	1.8	77
1 Canada	97	101	90	107	7,424	141	82	107	1.8	78
2 France	99	100	89	109	3,605	..	83	109	1.7	68
3 Norway	99	100	90	105	4,120	224	80	104	1.9	77
4 USA	100	103	90	..	5,834	110	80	107	2.1	92
5 Iceland	..	..	..	..	2,812	146	81	105	2.2	74
6 Netherlands	96	102	87	106	3,038	151	80	105	1.6	68
7 Japan	100	100	..	..	1,861	140	83	110	1.4	70
8 Finland	..	..	94		3,856	160	80	108	1.9	102
9 New Zealand	98	98	89	107	4,512	227	79	106	2.1	71
10 Sweden	100	103	91	107	2,783	128	81	105	2.0	102
11 Spain	100	100	92	124	3,328	209	81	108	1.2	42
12 Austria	91	103	91	..	2,560	177	80	108	1.5	65
13 Belgium	97	99	90	106	2,621	147	80	108	1.6	77
14 Australia	99	99	82	116	3,435	171	81	108	1.9	70
15 United Kingdom	100	103	84	104	2,291	218	79	106	1.8	78
16 Switzerland	95	..	77	..	1,490	188	81	107	1.5	75
17 Ireland	90	99	84	105	3,195	243	79	107	1.9	50
18 Denmark	98	103	88	99	3,147	157	78	103	1.8	86
19 Germany	83	..	86	..	1,813	..	79	108	1.3	64
20 Greece	94	97	89	119	1,884	184	80	109	1.3	57
21 Italy	..	..	..	..	2,782	169	81	108	1.2	51
23 Israel	..	..	..	..	3,131	122	79	109	2.9	77
27 Luxembourg	..	..	..	..	..	..	79	107	1.7	82
31 Portugal	100	100	..	..	2,264	256	78	111	1.5	53
34 Malta	99	101	82	119	1,236	889	79	109	2.1	99
35 Slovenia	..	..	..	..	2,143	..	78	106	1.3	56
39 Czech Rep.	..	..	..	..	974	..	75	102	1.6	77
42 Slovakia	..	..	..	..	1,173	..	75	103	1.8	70
48 Hungary	92	97	77	171	1,113	122	74	102	1.6	81
58 Poland	95	97	81	110	1,680	93	76	103	1.8	80
62 Belarus	..	..	..	..	3,060	92	75	99	1.6	68
Medium human development	..	..	..	..	2,869	..	72	102	2.1	66
67 Russian Federation	96	..	..	..	3,307	77	72	98	1.4	68
69 Bulgaria	79	82	62	86	2,189	171	75	102	1.4	65
71 Estonia	80	..	77	..	2,475	..	75	101	1.4	67
76 Lithuania	..	..	..	..	3,097	..	76	101	1.7	74
77 Croatia	80	..	70	..	1,603	..	76	105	1.6	79
79 Romania	76	..	73	..	939	129	73	104	1.3	45
80 Macedonia, FYR	84	..	..	..	1,313	..	74	110	2.0	64
85 Turkmenistan	..	..	..	..	..	..	68	108	3.8	60
92 Latvia	80	..	..	..	2,775	..	74	100	1.5	79
93 Kazakstan	..	..	..	..	..	..	72	105	2.3	66
95 Ukraine	..	..	..	..	2,954	..	74	100	1.5	76
100 Uzbekistan	..	..	..	..	..	..	71	106	3.7	60
102 Albania	..	..	..	..	722	129	74	108	2.8	57
103 Armenia	..	..	..	..	..	..	75	100	2.0	63
105 Georgia	..	..	..	..	..	..	77	107	2.0	79
106 Azerbaijan	..	..	..	..	2,453	..	75	104	2.5	55
107 Kyrgyzstan	..	..	..	..	..	..	72	108	3.4	71
110 Moldova, Rep. of	..	..	..	..	..	..	72	105	2.0	77
115 Tajikistan	..	..	..	..	..	..	70	107	4.0	59
All developing countries	86	..	..	..	559	..	63	121	3.6	60
Industrial countries	96	..	..	..	3,407	134	78	106	1.8	73
World	89	..	..	..	1,377	212	65	119	3.4	61
North America	100	103	90	..	5,991	113	80	107	2.1	91
Eastern Europe and CIS	..	..	..	..	2,595	..	73	102	2.0	68
Western and Southern Europe	94	100	88	112	2,726	186	81	108	1.5	63
OECD	98	102	88	112	3,255	184	78	111	2.0	68
European Union	95	101	88	110	2,666	191	80	108	1.5	65
Nordic countries	99	102	91	104	3,339	160	80	105	1.9	93

Source: Columns 1, 3 and 5: UNESCO 1995b; *columns 2, 4 and 6:* calculated on the basis of data from UNESCO 1995b; *columns 7-10:* UN 1996b.

HDI rank	Administrators and managers		Professional and technical workers		Clerical and sales workers		Service workers		Women in government		
	Female (%) 1990	Female as % of male 1990	Female (%) 1990	Female as % of male 1990	Female (%) 1990	Female as % of male 1990	Female (%) 1990	Female as % of male 1990	Total[a] (%) 1995	At ministerial level[a] (%) 1995	At sub-ministerial level[a] (%) 1995
High human development	27	44	48	94	59	161	60	159	15.8	14.2	15.9
1 Canada	42	73	56	128	68	209	57	133	19.1	19.2	19.1
2 France	9	10	41	71	..	..	..	..	8.8	6.5	9.3
3 Norway	31	45	58	135	66	192	75	301	44.1	40.9	45.7
4 USA	42	72	53	111	67	201	60	150	30.1	21.1	30.7
5 Iceland	..	..	..	..	..	..	..	..	8.1	13.3	6.4
6 Netherlands	15	18	44	79	52	109	70	238	19.7	26.3	17.0
7 Japan	9	9	42	72	50	101	54	118	8.3	6.7	8.8
8 Finland	26	36	62	166	67	207	71	250	16.3	35.0	10.0
9 New Zealand	32	122	48	43	76	325	67	207	16.8	7.4	20.0
10 Sweden	39	64	64	181	77	335	77	333	33.3	47.8	25.6
11 Spain	12	14	48	93	47	90	59	141	9.7	15.0	7.1
12 Austria	19	24	49	95	64	178	71	243	6.8	21.1	4.0
13 Belgium	19	23	51	102	..	..	..	..	8.3	10.5	7.3
14 Australia	43	76	25	33	19	24	77	339	23.7	13.3	26.7
15 United Kingdom	33	49	44	78	..	..	..	..	8.4	9.1	8.3
16 Switzerland	28	39	24	31	..	..	..	..	7.0	16.7	4.4
17 Ireland	17	21	48	92	52	107	52	106	11.1	18.2	8.5
18 Denmark	20	25	63	169	61	155	73	263	19.0	30.4	17.4
19 Germany	19	24	43	75	..	..	..	..	6.8	16.0	5.4
20 Greece	12	14	44	79	44	79	44	77	6.3	0	10.4
21 Italy	38	60	46	86	..	..	..	..	9.6	3.4	11.8
23 Israel	19	23	54	118	55	121	57	135	9.8	13.0	9.0
27 Luxembourg	9	9	38	61	48	93	72	256	7.7	16.7	3.7
31 Portugal	37	58	52	110	48	91	66	190	17.5	9.1	19.1
34 Malta	..	..	..	..	..	..	..	..	1.5	0	1.9
35 Slovenia	..	..	..	..	..	..	..	..	..	..	..
39 Czech Rep.	..	..	..	..	..	..	..	..	1.2	0	1.6
42 Slovakia	..	..	..	..	..	..	..	..	12.8	13.6	12.5
48 Hungary	58	139	49	96	75	307	75	306	7.7	5.3	8.1
58 Poland	16	18	60	152	..	..	..	..	8.0	6.3	8.8
62 Belarus	..	..	..	..	..	..	..	..	4.4	8.1	3.1
Medium human development	..	..	..	..	..	..	..	..	2.7	3.3	3.0
67 Russian Federation	..	..	..	..	..	..	..	..	2.1	2.8	2.0
69 Bulgaria	29	41	57	132	79	373	76	320	8.5	9.1	8.3
71 Estonia	..	..	..	..	..	..	..	..	10.4	6.3	11.8
76 Lithuania	..	..	..	..	..	..	..	..	8.6	0	11.8
77 Croatia	..	..	..	..	..	..	..	..	..	..	..
79 Romania	..	..	..	..	..	..	..	..	3.3	0	4.0
80 Macedonia, FYR	..	..	..	..	..	..	..	..	..	..	..
85 Turkmenistan	..	..	..	..	..	..	..	..	3.9	4.3	3.6
92 Latvia	..	..	..	..	..	..	..	..	15.5	5.6	17.3
93 Kazakstan	..	..	..	..	..	..	..	..	1.1	2.7	0
95 Ukraine	..	..	..	..	..	..	..	..	1.0	0	1.3
100 Uzbekistan	..	..	..	..	..	..	..	..	2.9	2.8	2.9
102 Albania	..	..	..	..	..	..	..	..	12.3	0	16.1
103 Armenia	..	..	..	..	..	..	..	..	2.0	0	3.1
105 Georgia	..	..	..	..	..	..	..	..	3.3	0	4.7
106 Azerbaijan	..	..	..	..	..	..	..	..	5.3	4.0	6.0
107 Kyrgyzstan	..	..	..	..	..	..	..	..	8.0	4.3	11.1
110 Moldova, Rep. of	..	..	..	..	..	..	..	..	3.5	0	5.3
115 Tajikistan	..	..	..	..	..	..	..	..	4.0	6.9	2.9
All developing countries	10	12	36	64	..	..	..	..	5.5	5.8	5.6
Industrial countries	27	44	48	95	..	..	..	..	12.5	12.1	12.7
World	14	19	39	71	..	..	..	..	7.4	7.4	7.5
North America	42	72	53	113	67	202	60	148	29.0	20.9	29.5
Eastern Europe and CIS	..	..	..	..	..	..	..	..	3.5	4.1	3.9
Western and Southern Europe	21	29	46	87	54	130	63	191	10.5	13.8	9.9
OECD	26	41	46	88	54	142	55	140	15.1	14.0	15.0
European Union	23	32	46	86	53	128	63	187	9.9	12.7	9.4
Nordic countries	30	45	62	167	69	240	74	293	28.1	39.5	23.8

a. Including elected heads of state and governors of central banks. For countries for which the value is zero, no women ministers were reported by the United Nations Division for the Advancement of Women; this information could not be reconfirmed by the Human Development Report Office.
Source: Columns 1-8: UN 1994b; columns 9-11: calculations by the United Nations Division for the Advancement of Women based on data from Worldwide Government Directories 1995.

30 Health profile

| | Adults who smoke (%) | | Alcohol consumption per capita (litres) | Likelihood of dying after age 65 of | | | | AIDS cases (per 100,000 people)[a] | People with disabilities (as % of total population) | Public expenditure on health (as % of total public expenditure) | Private expenditure on health (as % of total health expenditure) | Total expenditure on health (as % of GDP) | |
| | | | | Heart disease (per 1,000 people) | | Cancer (per 1,000 people) | | | | | | | |
HDI rank	Male 1986-94	Female 1986-94	1991	Male 1990-93	Female 1990-93	Male 1990-93	Female 1990-93	1995	1985-92	1989-91	1989-91	1960	1991
High human development	38	23	8.1	270	291	245	163	7.2	9.9	13.4	33.6	4.5	9.7
1 Canada	31[b]	28[b]	7.1	..	..	..	..	4.0	15.5	14.6	27.8	5.3	9.9
2 France	49[b]	26[b]	11.9	220	244	289	179	8.4	..	13.2	26.1	4.3	9.1
3 Norway	42[b]	32[b]	4.1	340	314	222	160	1.5	..	13.0	3.4	3.2	8.4
4 USA	30[b]	24[b]	7.0	..	..	..	..	15.2	12.0	14.8	56.1	5.3	13.3
5 Iceland	39[b]	32[b]	3.9	..	..	..	..	1.1	..	19.3	13.0	3.4	8.3
6 Netherlands	41[b]	33[b]	8.2	279	285	291	191	3.1	11.5	10.4	26.9	4.0	8.7
7 Japan	66	14	6.3	212	264	247	156	0.2	2.3	30.7	28.0	3.0	6.8
8 Finland	35[b]	17[b]	7.4	366	351	212	151	0.8	17.0	14.7	19.1	3.8	8.9
9 New Zealand	35[b]	29[b]	7.8	347	337	248	183	1.4	13.0	..	21.1	4.2	7.7
10 Sweden	26	30	5.5	388	357	208	165	2.1	12.0	11.1	22.0	4.7	8.8
11 Spain	58	27	10.4	235	277	238	139	15.7	15.0	11.8	17.8	1.6	6.5
12 Austria	33[b]	22[b]	10.3	378	403	247	180	2.4	22.7	11.2	32.9	4.4	8.5
13 Belgium	35	21	9.4	..	..	..	..	2.1	..	12.2	11.1	3.4	8.1
14 Australia	37[b]	30[b]	7.7	342	370	252	174	3.8	15.6	15.4	32.2	4.8	8.6
15 United Kingdom	36	32	7.4	..	..	..	..	2.6	14.2	12.2	16.7	3.9	6.6
16 Switzerland	46[b]	29	10.7	322	346	281	188	6.2	..	15.7	31.7	3.3	8.0
17 Ireland	..	..	7.4	349	324	235	186	1.2	3.5	12.0	24.2	3.8	8.0
18 Denmark	49	38	9.9	320	305	252	202	4.1	12.0	9.0	18.5	3.6	7.0
19 Germany	..	..	10.9	350	359	242	184	1.7	8.4	12.3	28.2	4.9	9.1
20 Greece	54[b]	13[b]	8.6	294	310	219	122	1.7	..	12.2	23.0	2.6	4.8
21 Italy	46[b]	18[b]	8.4	256	280	263	174	9.6	2.7	14.8	22.5	3.6	8.3
23 Israel	38	25	0.9	340	324	183	156	1.0	..	..	..	1.0	4.2
27 Luxembourg	..	..	12.3	448	502	180	109	3.7	..	10.3	8.6	..	6.6
31 Portugal	37[b]	10[b]	11.6	182	187	181	124	6.6	11.0	9.8	38.3	2.3	6.2
34 Malta	..	..	..	..	..	..	..	0.8	..	..	..	..	..
35 Slovenia	..	..	..	..	..	..	..	0.8	..	..	..	..	..
39 Czech Rep.	..	..	..	331	313	233	171	0.1	..	..	..	2.9	5.9
42 Slovakia	..	..	..	..	..	..	..	(.)	..	..	..	..	..
48 Hungary	50	25	10.5	283	283	221	168	0.3	15.7	..	..	2.6	6.0
58 Poland	63[b]	29[b]	7.1	240	201	188	124	0.3	9.9	..	..	3.5	5.1
62 Belarus	..	..	..	394	399	151	82	(.)	..	..	..	..	3.2
Medium human development	..	..	..	363	352	150	89	0.3	..	..	..	..	3.4
67 Russian Federation	..	..	..	365	359	164	97	(.)	..	..	..	..	3.0
69 Bulgaria	..	..	7.8	349	351	119	82	(.)	0.4	..	..	2.0	5.4
71 Estonia	..	..	..	422	453	..	..	0.2	..	..	..	..	3.6
76 Lithuania	..	..	..	..	..	..	..	0.1	..	..	..	..	..
77 Croatia	..	..	..	..	..	..	..	0.3	..	..	..	..	..
79 Romania	48[b]	13[b]	6.4	..	..	..	..	2.8	..	..	..	2.0	3.9
80 Macedonia, FYR	..	..	..	..	..	..	..	0.8	..	..	..	..	..
85 Turkmenistan	..	..	..	..	..	..	..	..	..	..	..	..	5.0
92 Latvia	..	..	..	398	393	164	99	0.1	..	..	..	..	..
93 Kazakstan	..	..	..	..	..	..	..	..	..	..	..	..	4.4
95 Ukraine	..	..	..	304	297	133	75	0.1	..	..	..	..	3.3
100 Uzbekistan	..	..	..	508	538	89	60	..	..	..	..	..	5.9
102 Albania	..	..	..	304	307	102	51	0.1	..	..	..	..	4.0
103 Armenia	..	..	..	475	524	105	69	..	..	..	..	..	4.2
105 Georgia	..	..	..	..	..	..	..	(.)	..	..	..	..	4.5
106 Azerbaijan	..	..	..	..	..	..	..	(.)	..	..	..	..	4.3
107 Kyrgyzstan	..	..	..	364	404	163	103	..	..	..	..	..	5.0
110 Moldova, Rep. of	..	..	..	..	..	..	..	0.1	..	..	..	..	3.9
115 Tajikistan	..	..	..	364	378	102	60	..	..	..	..	..	6.0
All developing countries	49	8	..	..	..	..	..	4.8	2.6	..	..	..	..
Industrial countries	42	24	8.0	298	308	219	143	5.6	..	..	..	..	9.4
World	47	12	..	..	..	..	..	5.0	..	..	..	..	..
North America	28	24	7.0	..	..	..	..	14.1	12.3	14.8	56.1	5.3	13.0
Eastern Europe and CIS	..	..	..	345	332	160	99	0.3	..	..	..	..	3.7
Western and Southern Europe	39	25	10.0	285	302	253	171	6.4	9.2	12.7	24.2	4.1	8.5
OECD	39	23	8.1	267	290	247	165	6.7	9.3	13.4	33.6	4.5	9.7
European Union	37	25	9.6	283	301	253	171	5.8	10.2	12.6	23.5	4.1	8.2
Nordic countries	29	28	6.6	359	337	221	169	2.1	13.3	11.6	16.8	4.0	8.3

a. The number of reported cases in adults and children.
b. Data refer to years before 1986.
Source: Columns 1 and 2: UN 1994b; *column 3:* ARF 1994; *columns 4-7:* WHO 1994; *column 8:* WHO and UNAIDS 1996; *column 9:* UN 1993a; *columns 10-14:* World Bank 1993.

HDI rank	Full-time students per 100 people (age 5-29) 1994	Secondary full-time net enrolment ratio (%) 1994	Upper-secondary technical enrolment (as % of total upper secondary) 1992	Tertiary net enrolment ratio (as % of ages 18-21) 1994	Tertiary natural and applied science enrolment (as % of total tertiary) 1992	Public expenditure on higher education (as % of all levels) 1990-94	Public expenditure per tertiary student (PPP$)[a] 1994	Public expenditure on education (as % of GNP) 1993-94	Total expenditure on education (as % of GDP) 1960	Total expenditure on education (as % of GDP) 1991
High human development	55	94	54	28	24	21.2	9,547	5.4	4.4	5.9
1 Canada	58	94	..	40	16	27.9	11,132	7.6	4.6	7.4
2 France	60	96	54	33	19	16.7	6,033	5.8	3.6	6.0
3 Norway	58	94	60	24 [b]	20	25.9	8,343	9.2	4.6	7.6
4 USA	57	95	..	35	17	25.2	14,607	5.5	5.3	7.0
5 Iceland	..	86	..	19	16	24.6	5,059	5.4	..	6.0
6 Netherlands	56	98	70	22	24	32.1	8,665	5.5	4.9	5.8
7 Japan	53	96	28	..	22	..	7,556	4.7	4.9	5.0
8 Finland	63	96	54	27 [b]	38	28.7	7,295	8.4	4.9	6.6
9 New Zealand	60	94	19	31	20	36.7	7,337	7.3	2.2	5.8
10 Sweden	51	96	..	15 [b]	29	15.8	12,693	8.4	5.9	6.5
11 Spain	58	82	41	25	26	15.3	3,835	4.7	1.1	5.6
12 Austria	50	92	76	12	29	18.6	8,642	5.5	2.9	5.4
13 Belgium	..	104	59	37	24	17.3	6,380	5.6	4.8	5.4
14 Australia	54	96	24	29	26	26.6	9,036	6.0	..	5.5
15 United Kingdom	55	87	58	24	28	22.3	8,241	5.4	3.4	5.3
16 Switzerland	50	87	73	14 [b]	32	20.3	15,731	5.6	3.3	5.4
17 Ireland	57	93	..	31	31	21.5	7,076	6.4	3.0	5.9
18 Denmark	56	94	56	22 [b]	27	25.0	8,045	8.5	4.0	6.1
19 Germany	54	96	80	17 [b]	39	21.4	7,902	4.8	2.4	5.4
20 Greece	..	82	..	37	37	19.6	2,502	3.0	2.0	3.0
21 Italy	50	..	67	..	28	13.7	5,169	5.2	4.2	4.1
23 Israel	..	..	..	..	27	17.6	..	6.0	..	6.0
27 Luxembourg	..	..	..	..	..	3.3	..	3.1	..	5.8
31 Portugal	..	74	..	19	31	14.2	5,667	5.4	1.8	5.5
34 Malta	..	..	..	..	13	17.9	..	5.1	..	4.4
35 Slovenia	..	..	..	..	..	18.9	..	6.2	..	..
39 Czech Rep.	..	88	54	15	42	17.9	4,788	5.9	..	..
42 Slovakia	..	..	..	..	47	14.3	..	4.9	..	..
48 Hungary	..	86	75	11	29	17.8	5,189	6.7	..	6.7
58 Poland	..	..	75	15	28	16.0	..	5.5	3.8	4.9
62 Belarus	..	..	..	..	40	11.1	..	6.1	..	..
Medium human development	..	..	..	..	49	..	..	5.3	..	..
67 Russian Federation	..	..	44	..	51	12.4	..	4.4	..	..
69 Bulgaria	..	..	..	..	37	15.5	..	4.5	..	5.4
71 Estonia	..	..	..	..	36	14.0	..	5.8	..	..
76 Lithuania	..	..	..	..	..	19.0	..	4.5	..	..
77 Croatia	..	..	..	..	..	..	..	..	..	..
79 Romania	..	..	..	..	57	15.9	..	3.1	2.9	3.1
80 Macedonia, FYR	..	..	..	..	..	21.7	..	5.6	..	..
85 Turkmenistan	..	..	..	..	..	..	..	7.9	..	..
92 Latvia	..	..	..	..	46	13.3	..	6.5	..	..
93 Kazakstan	..	..	..	..	26	..	..	5.4	..	..
95 Ukraine	..	..	..	..	52	9.8	..	8.2	..	..
100 Uzbekistan	..	..	..	..	..	9.7	..	11.0	..	..
102 Albania	..	..	..	..	30	10.3	..	3.0	..	..
103 Armenia	..	..	..	..	..	22.6	..	..	..	..
105 Georgia	..	..	..	..	..	18.5	..	1.9	..	..
106 Azerbaijan	..	..	..	..	51	10.4	..	5.5	..	..
107 Kyrgyzstan	..	..	..	..	..	10.8	..	6.8	..	..
110 Moldova, Rep. of	..	..	..	..	..	..	..	5.5	..	..
115 Tajikistan	..	..	..	..	..	9.8	..	9.5	..	..
All developing countries	..	..	..	..	33	..	..	3.6	..	..
Industrial countries	..	..	..	..	30	21.0	..	5.4	..	5.9
World	..	..	..	..	32	..	..	5.1	..	..
North America	57	95	..	36	17	25.2	14,263	5.7	5.3	7.0
Eastern Europe and CIS	..	..	..	..	45	..	..	5.4	..	..
Western and Southern Europe	55	92	63	23	29	18.8	6,638	5.5	3.4	5.4
OECD	53	85	53	28	25	21.3	9,044	5.4	4.4	5.9
European Union	55	91	62	23	29	19.2	6,698	5.4	3.4	5.4
Nordic countries	56	95	56	21	28	22.3	9,626	8.6	5.0	6.6

a. US dollars converted using purchasing power parity (PPP) rates. See OECD 1996c.
b. Age 22-25.
Source: Columns 1-4 and 7: OECD 1996c; *column 5:* UNESCO 1995b; *columns 6 and 8:* calculated on the basis of estimates from UNESCO 1996d; *columns 9 and 10:* UNESCO 1993.

HDI rank	Labour force (as % of total population) 1990	Women's share of adult labour force (aged 15 and above) 1970	Women's share of adult labour force (aged 15 and above) 1990	Percentage of labour force in Agriculture 1990	Industry 1990	Services 1990	Future labour force replacement ratio 1994	Real earnings per employee annual growth rate (%) 1980-92	Labour force unionized (%) 1970	Labour force unionized (%) 1990	Weekly hours of work (per person in manufacturing) 1993	Expenditure on labour market programmes (as % of GDP) 1994-95
High human development	49	36	42	7	31	63	94	1.3	..	26	39	1.6
1 Canada	53	32	44	3	25	71	97	0.1	31	36	39	2.1
2 France	44	36	43	5	29	66	97	..	22	10	39	3.1
3 Norway	50	29	45	6	25	68	95	2.3	51	56	37	2.5
4 USA	50	37	45	3	26	71	108	0.4	23	16	41	0.6
5 Iceland	55	34	44	11	27	62	119	..	68	78	..	..
6 Netherlands	46	26	39	5	26	70	86	1.7	38	26	40	4.1
7 Japan	52	39	40	7	34	59	78	1.9	35	25	38	0.5
8 Finland	52	44	47	8	31	61	92	2.6	51	72	38	5.6
9 New Zealand	48	29	43	10	25	65	113	0.1	..	45	42	2.0
10 Sweden	54	36	48	4	30	66	94	1.2	68	83	37	5.5
11 Spain	41	24	35	12	33	55	82	1.2	27	11	36	3.3
12 Austria	46	38	41	8	38	55	84	2.0	62	46	35	1.8
13 Belgium	40	30	39	3	28	70	88	0.5	46	51	32	4.3
14 Australia	50	31	41	6	26	68	103	0.5	50	40	38	2.4
15 United Kingdom	50	36	42	2	29	69	96	2.5	45	39	43	1.9
16 Switzerland	53	34	39	6	35	60	82	..	30	27	32	1.7
17 Ireland	37	26	32	14	29	57	124	2.0	53	50	40	4.7
18 Denmark	57	36	46	6	28	66	82	-0.3	60	71	32	6.9
19 Germany	50	39	42	4	38	58	76	..	33	33	38	3.5
20 Greece	42	26	35	23	27	50	85	0.8	36	34	41	0.9
21 Italy	43	29	37	9	31	60	72	5.8	36	39	..	2.0
23 Israel	39	30	38	4	29	67	154	-1.6	..	..	41	..
27 Luxembourg	43	27	37	4	27	69	82	..	47	50	41	1.0
31 Portugal	49	25	43	18	34	48	88	0.5	61	32	38	2.0
34 Malta	37	21	25	3	35	63	107	..	..	..	..	..
35 Slovenia	49	36	46	6	46	48	88	..	..	..	..	..
39 Czech Rep.	53	46	47	11	45	43	92	..	..	..	40	0.3
42 Slovakia	51	41	48	12	33	55	113	..	..	..	..	..
48 Hungary	46	40	44	15	38	47	89	1.7	..	..	36	..
58 Poland	49	45	45	27	36	37	115	-0.8	..	..	34	..
62 Belarus	52	51	49	20	40	40	110	..	..	..	..	..
Medium human development	49	49	48	19	39	42	119	..	..	..	..	..
67 Russian Federation	52	51	48	14	42	45	105	..	..	..	..	..
69 Bulgaria	51	44	48	13	48	38	93	..	..	..	..	..
71 Estonia	54	51	49	14	41	44	103	..	..	..	34	..
76 Lithuania	52	49	48	18	41	41	108	..	..	..	..	..
77 Croatia	47	38	43	16	34	50	94	..	..	..	..	..
79 Romania	46	44	44	24	47	29	102	..	..	..	8	..
80 Macedonia, FYR	45	30	10	22	40	38	120	..	..	..	..	..
85 Turkmenistan	41	46	45	37	23	40	220	..	..	..	..	..
92 Latvia	55	51	50	16	40	44	103	..	..	..	..	..
93 Kazakstan	47	47	46	22	32	46	151	..	..	..	34	..
95 Ukraine	50	51	49	20	40	40	101	..	..	..	..	..
100 Uzbekistan	39	48	46	35	25	40	226	..	..	..	..	..
102 Albania	48	40	40	55	23	22	158	..	..	..	..	..
103 Armenia	48	46	47	18	43	39	146	..	..	..	..	..
105 Georgia	49	48	46	26	31	43	120	..	..	..	..	..
106 Azerbaijan	42	45	43	31	29	40	166	..	..	..	..	..
107 Kyrgyzstan	41	49	46	32	27	41	205	..	..	..	..	..
110 Moldova, Rep. of	49	52	49	33	30	37	135	..	..	..	28	..
115 Tajikistan	36	45	42	41	23	36	248	..	..	..	..	..
All developing countries	47	37	39	61	16	23	177	..	..	..	..	..
Industrial countries	49	40	44	10	33	57	100	..	..	..	38	..
World	48	38	40	49	20	31	157	..	..	..	..	..
North America	51	36	45	3	26	71	107	0.4	..	18	41	0.7
Eastern Europe and CIS	49	48	47	19	39	42	117	..	..	..	..	..
Western and Southern Europe	46	33	40	7	33	60	83	2.7	..	31	37	3.2
OECD	48	35	41	10	29	61	103	1.6	..	26	39	1.6
European Union	46	34	41	6	32	62	85	2.7	..	32	39	3.1
Nordic countries	53	37	47	6	29	65	92	1.4	..	73	36	5.3

Note: Percentage shares of labour force in agriculture, industry and services may not necessarily add to 100 because of rounding.
Source: Columns 1-6: ILO 1996b; *column 7:* calculated on the basis of estimates from UN 1996b; *column 8:* World Bank 1995e; *columns 9 and 10:* OECD 1994b; *column 11:* OECD 1995a; *column 12:* OECD 1996d.

HDI rank	Un-employed people (thousands) 1993	Total unemploy-ment rate (%) 1995	Unemployment rate (%) Male 1993	Female 1993	Youth unemployment rate (%) Male (age 15-24) 1991-93	Female (age 15-24) 1991-93	Incidence of long-term unemployment (%) More than 6 months Male 1995	Female 1995	More than 12 months Male 1995	Female 1995	Dis-couraged workers (as % of total labour force) 1993	Involuntary part-time workers (as % of total labour force) 1993	Unemployment benefits expenditure (as % of total government expenditure) 1991
High human development	34,589T	8.0	7.9	8.9	16	17	46	40	30	25	1.2	3.6	2.1
1 Canada	1,649	9.5	11.8	10.6	20	15	29	25	16	12	0.9	5.5	8.1
2 France	2,929	11.6	10.0	13.7	22	28	67	71	45	47	0.2	4.8	3.2
3 Norway	127	4.9	6.6	5.2	13	10	44	31	29	17	1.2	..	2.2
4 USA	8,734	5.5	7.1	6.5	14	12	19	16	11	8	0.9	5.0	1.5
5 Iceland	6	..	3.6	5.4	..	..	27	32	11	14	..	..	..
6 Netherlands	415	6.5	6.0	7.3	10	10	73	75	49	38	0.6	5.6	4.5
7 Japan	1,660	3.1	2.4	2.6	5	5	44	28	24	10	2.2	1.9	0.7
8 Finland	444	17.1	19.5	15.7	31	29	49	45	35	29	1.5	2.9	3.6
9 New Zealand	157	6.3	10.0	8.9	18	16	44	33	27	18	1.0	6.3	..
10 Sweden	326	9.2	..	..	22	15	37	32	17	14	2.0	6.2	0.8
11 Spain	2,260	22.7	9.9	23.8	40	47	67	77	51	62	0.2	1.0	7.0
12 Austria	222	..	6.7	6.9	4	3	29	32	17	17	..	..	1.8
13 Belgium	550	9.5	9.7	17.4	17	20	76	79	61	63	1.5	3.8	5.8
14 Australia	939	8.5	11.5	10.1	20	17	54	47	34	26	1.6	6.9	4.0
15 United Kingdom	2,891	8.7	12.4	7.5	21	13	66	51	50	32	0.6	3.2	1.7
16 Switzerland	163	..	4.4	4.7	7	7	48	54	32	35	..	..	0.4
17 Ireland	294	12.9	18.8	19.5	27	23	..	..	..	..	0.5	3.3	6.3
18 Denmark	349	..	11.3	13.7	14	15	52	42	32	25	1.6	4.8	5.5
19 Germany	2,720	8.2	8.0	8.4	8	8	63	68	46	51	..	1.5	3.0
20 Greece	398	..	6.4	15.2	20[a]	39[a]	64	78	42	57	0.3	3.1	..
21 Italy	2,799	12.2	8.1	17.3	27	36	78	81	62	64	2.6	2.3	1.0
23 Israel	195	..	8.5	12.1	21	25	..	..	..	..	..	..	..
27 Luxembourg	4	..	1.5	1.9	5	4	48	47	25	21	..	..	..
31 Portugal	258	7.1	4.6	6.5	10	15	60	64	46	51	0.1	1.8	..
34 Malta	6	..	5.2	2.5	..	..	..	..	..	..	..	..	..
35 Slovenia	..	14.5[b]	..	..	..	..	..	..	..	..	..	..	..
39 Czech Rep.	200	2.9	3.1	4.6	..	..	52	53	30	31	..	..	..
42 Slovakia	306	13.1	12.7	11.7	..	..	..	..	..	..	..	..	..
48 Hungary	632	10.4	14.2	10.1	..	..	..	..	..	..	..	..	..
58 Poland	2,890	14.9	15.0	17.9	25[a]	32[a]	..	..	..	..	..	..	..
62 Belarus	66	2.7[b]	..	..	..	..	..	..	..	..	..	..	..
Medium human development	2,782T	3.4	..	..	..	..	..	..	..	..	..	..	..
67 Russian Federation	578	3.2[b]	0.4	1.1	..	..	..	..	..	..	..	..	..
69 Bulgaria	626	11.1[b]	..	..	..	..	..	..	..	..	..	..	..
71 Estonia	16	4.9[b]	1.7	2.1	..	..	..	..	..	..	..	..	..
76 Lithuania	66	7.3[b]	3.8	3.3	..	..	..	..	..	..	..	..	..
77 Croatia	..	17.6[b]	..	..	..	..	..	..	..	..	..	..	..
79 Romania	1,165	8.9[b]	8.1	12.6	..	..	..	..	..	..	..	..	..
80 Macedonia, FYR	..	37.2[b]	..	..	..	..	..	..	..	..	..	..	..
85 Turkmenistan	..	..	..	..	..	..	..	..	..	..	..	..	..
92 Latvia	77	6.6	5.2	6.4	..	..	..	..	..	..	..	..	..
93 Kazakstan	78	2.1[b]	..	..	..	..	..	..	..	..	..	..	..
95 Ukraine	..	0.6[b]	..	..	..	..	..	..	..	..	..	..	..
100 Uzbekistan	..	0.3[b]	..	..	..	..	..	..	..	..	..	..	..
102 Albania	140	13.0[b]	..	..	..	..	..	..	..	..	..	..	..
103 Armenia	..	8.1[b]	..	..	..	..	..	..	..	..	..	..	..
105 Georgia	..	3.4[b]	..	..	..	..	..	..	..	..	..	..	..
106 Azerbaijan	19	1.1[b]	..	..	..	..	..	..	..	..	..	..	..
107 Kyrgyzstan	3	3.0[b]	..	..	..	..	..	..	..	..	..	..	..
110 Moldova, Rep. of	14	1.4[b]	..	..	..	..	..	..	..	..	..	..	..
115 Tajikistan	..	1.8[b]	..	..	..	..	..	..	..	..	..	..	..
All developing countries	..	..	..	..	..	..	..	..	..	..	..	..	..
Industrial countries	37,371T	6.6	6.9	7.7	16	17	..	..	..	..	..	..	..
World	..	..	..	..	..	..	..	..	..	..	..	..	..
North America	10,383T	5.9	7.6	6.9	15	13	20	17	12	9	0.9	5.1	2.0
Eastern Europe and CIS	6,876T	4.8	..	..	..	..	..	..	..	..	..	..	..
Western and Southern Europe	14,270T	11.6	8.6	12.9	20	24	65	68	47	49	1.1	2.8	3.0
OECD	34,016T	7.5[c]	7.8	8.8	16	17	43	40	28	25	1.2	3.8	2.1
European Union	16,859T	11.1	9.3	12.2	20	23	66	66	48	47	0.9	2.9	2.9
Nordic countries	1,252T	10.2	12.4	11.9	21	18	44	37	26	20	1.7	5.0	2.7

a. ILO 1995a.
b. Official unemployment rate. Registered unemployment only.
c. OECD 1996b.
Source: Columns 1 and 13: ILO 1995a; column 2: OECD 1996d and UNECE 1996; columns 3-6: OECD 1995a and ILO 1995a; columns 7-10: OECD 1996d; columns 11 and 12: OECD 1995a.

34 Communication profile

HDI rank	Radios (per 1,000 people) 1994	Televisions (per 100 people) 1994	Book titles published (per 100,000 people) 1992-94	Printing and writing paper consumed (metric tons per 1,000 people) 1994	Main telephone lines (per 100 people) 1994	International telephone calls (minutes per person) 1994	Fax machines (per 100 people) 1994	Mobile cellular telephone subscribers (per 100 people) 1992	Internet users (per 100,000 people) 1994	Personal computers (per 100 people) 1994
High human development	1,221	58	65	95.8	49.2	43.7	3.6	5.2	291.2	17.3
1 Canada	1,051	65	76	96.3	59.0	28.3	..	6.5	352.7	17.5
2 France	891	58	78	79.1	54.7	43.3	2.8	1.5	88.7	14.0
3 Norway	799	43	159	98.0	55.0	93.4	..	13.5	633.4	19.0
4 USA	2,122	78	20	141.1	60.2	50.4	5.3	9.1	671.2	29.8
5 Iceland	793	32	537	52.8	55.7	97.5	..	8.2	978.5	..
6 Netherlands	909	49	222	93.2	51.1	87.4	2.9	2.1	318.9	15.6
7 Japan	912	62	28	105.8	48.0	11.3	4.8	3.5	42.6	12.0
8 Finland	1,003	50	247	166.4	55.1	46.9	2.4	12.8	772.3	15.9
9 New Zealand	991	51	..	53.9	46.8	77.9	1.4	6.5	486.2	19.0
10 Sweden	879	47	158	93.4	68.3	79.8	..	15.8	488.5	17.2
11 Spain	312	43	112	51.0	37.5	24.0	..	1.0	39.6	7.0
12 Austria	619	48	100	71.2	46.5	102.4	3.0	3.5	206.4	10.7
13 Belgium	774	46	..	105.3	44.9	104.1	..	1.3	102.0	12.9
14 Australia	1,291	48	61	87.5	49.6	36.4	2.5	6.9	486.8	21.7
15 United Kingdom	1,429	45	164	104.5	48.8	55.5	2.6	6.8	228.4	15.2
16 Switzerland	841	40	217	120.8	59.7	231.4	2.5	4.7	397.5	28.8
17 Ireland	636	32	..	54.2	35.0	107.6	..	2.5	96.5	13.8
18 Denmark	1,036	54	230	74.3	60.0	93.7	4.0	9.7	275.7	19.3
19 Germany	935	55	87	102.9	48.3	61.1	1.8	3.1	140.8	14.4
20 Greece	418	21	..	33.6	47.8	40.6	..	1.6	21.1	2.9
21 Italy	802	43	57	16.1	42.8	30.8	..	3.9	29.5	7.2
23 Israel	478	30	86	48.7	39.4	33.2	2.0	2.6	134.5	7.8
27 Luxembourg	636	34	169	..	55.3	532.5	..	3.2	84.2	..
31 Portugal	233	23	68	33.2	34.8	31.0	..	1.8	33.6	5.0
34 Malta	530	41	115	69.2	44.8	74.4	..	2.1	..	..
35 Slovenia	378	30	151	32.7	28.7	46.7	0.7	0.9	50.2	..
39 Czech Rep.	631	38	91	17.8	21.2	15.2	0.6	0.3	61.9	2.9
42 Slovakia	568	28	65	12.8	18.7	9.8	0.7	0.1	14.6	..
48 Hungary	625	52	100	17.5	16.9	23.3	0.4	1.4	46.0	3.4
58 Poland	441	30	28	12.3	13.1	9.3	0.1	0.1	16.5	2.2
62 Belarus	285	26	32	(.)	18.6	..	0.1	..	(.)	..
Medium human development	406	30	19	3.9	14.7	3.8	0.1	(.)	1.3	..
67 Russian Federation	339	38	20	5.3	16.2	1.5	(.)	(.)	0.7	0.8
69 Bulgaria	454	26	69	4.6	29.5	9.5	0.1	0.1	0.9	..
71 Estonia	467	36	152	13.5	25.2	31.2	0.7	0.9	49.8	..
76 Lithuania	387	34	77	2.3	24.1	14.8	0.1	0.1	1.8	..
77 Croatia	261	23	59	11.7	25.2	40.3	0.6	0.5	13.3	..
79 Romania	204	20	18	4.0	12.3	3.2	0.1	(.)	1.4	..
80 Macedonia, FYR	182	16	31	6.7	16.1	26.4	0.1	..	..	..
85 Turkmenistan	..	22	14	..	7.6	1.3	..	(.)	..	..
92 Latvia	662	47	65	17.0	25.8	15.2	(.)	0.3	13.0	..
93 Kazakstan	376	26	7	(.)	11.7	0.6	(.)	..	(.)	..
95 Ukraine	812	23	10	0.1	15.7	..	..	(.)	0.6	0.3
100 Uzbekistan	81	18	6	0.3	6.9	..	..	..	..	..
102 Albania	190	9	..	3.8	1.2	6.3	..	..	..	..
103 Armenia	..	24	6	..	15.6	14.3	(.)	..	0.3	..
105 Georgia	550	22	6	(.)	9.6	0.3	(.)	..	..	..
106 Azerbaijan	..	21	5	..	8.5	..	(.)	(.)	(.)	..
107 Kyrgyzstan	..	24	7	(.)	7.3	0.3	..	..	..	..
110 Moldova, Rep. of	679	28	18	1.1	12.6	14.9	(.)	..	(.)	..
115 Tajikistan	..	19	4	..	4.5	0.1	(.)	..	..	..
All developing countries	178	14	7	5.8	3.3	2.5	0.1	0.3	1.5	..
Industrial countries	1,018	50	52	74.0	40.1	35.1	2.8	4.1	223.2	14.2
World	361	22	18	20.6	11.5	9.4	0.7	1.4	60.9	..
North America	2,016	77	25	136.7	60.1	48.2	5.3	8.9	639.6	28.6
Eastern Europe and CIS	420	30	25	6.0	15.0	5.9	0.1	0.1	6.4	..
Western and Southern Europe	769	48	101	71.5	47.8	56.2	..	3.3	135.0	12.0
OECD	1,094	53	61	84.0	44.6	38.5	3.5	4.6	255.0	15.1
European Union	871	48	108	75.4	47.6	52.2	..	3.7	138.2	12.1
Nordic countries	925	48	197	105.3	61.1	78.5	..	13.3	534.7	17.7

Source: Columns 1, 3 and 4: calculated on the basis of estimates from UNESCO 1996d; *columns 2 and 5-10:* ITU 1996.

	Social security benefits expenditure (as % of GDP) 1993	Percentage of central government expenditure on							
		Social security and welfare		Housing and community amenities		Health		Education	
HDI rank		1980[a]	1992-95	1980[a]	1992-95	1980[a]	1992-95	1980[a]	1992-95
High human development	14.3	38.1	34.7	2.1	2.1	11.8	15.1	5.4	4.0
1 Canada	21.7	31.7	41.3	2.4	1.4	6.2	5.6	3.5	3.0
2 France	..	43.9	45.0	3.2	1.2	14.7	15.5	8.3	7.0
3 Norway	19.6	33.5	39.5	1.8	1.5	10.3	10.2	8.5	9.7
4 USA	10.5	34.2	29.6	2.6	2.7	10.7	18.3	2.5	1.6
5 Iceland	..	15.9	24.3	2.7	1.1	21.2	23.6	12.9	12.2
6 Netherlands	..	37.0	37.2	2.9	3.2	11.7	14.3	12.5	10.1
7 Japan	11.5	..	36.8	..	13.8	..	1.6	..	6.0
8 Finland	30.5	26.0	45.6	2.8	2.7	11.2	11.2	14.5	11.3
9 New Zealand	20.2	27.9	36.9	1.2	0.2	14.2	15.6	13.5	15.2
10 Sweden	38.3	46.4	48.2	3.1	5.4	2.0	0.2	10.5	5.0
11 Spain	..	59.0	39.0	1.5	0.5	0.6	6.2	7.7	4.4
12 Austria	24.5	45.1	45.8	3.3	2.7	13.2	13.2	9.6	9.5
13 Belgium	..	41.6	..	1.6	..	1.7	..	14.4	..
14 Australia	..	27.4	33.8	0.7	1.4	10.1	13.1	8.1	7.6
15 United Kingdom	..	28.3	29.6	2.5	2.9	13.2	14.0	2.2	3.3
16 Switzerland	14.0	48.3	..	0.8	..	12.7	..	3.3	..
17 Ireland	19.4	..	28.2	..	2.0	..	14.0	..	12.8
18 Denmark	29.5	41.2	39.9	2.1	1.8	1.4	1.1	10.0	10.6
19 Germany	24.7	49.5	..	0.4	0.6	19.2	16.8	0.8	0.8
20 Greece	..	30.6	13.4	2.5	1.3	10.5	7.4	9.6	8.5
21 Italy	..	31.4	..	1.0	..	10.8	..	9.1	..
23 Israel	11.8	13.7	24.5	0.2	5.8	3.5	5.7	8.5	13.6
27 Luxembourg	..	51.7	50.8	1.7	4.1	2.4	2.9	8.5	8.6
31 Portugal	9.0	24.6	..	0.7	..	10.4	..	10.3	..
34 Malta	..	35.6	34.0	1.2	7.4	9.7	12.1	8.0	12.4
35 Slovenia	..	..	..	..	..	..	..	..	..
39 Czech Rep.	11.1	..	28.1	..	1.2	..	16.7	..	11.2
42 Slovakia	13.3	..	..	..	..	..	..	..	..
48 Hungary	17.3	20.7	28.7	1.7	..	2.7	7.9	1.8	3.3
58 Poland	17.0	..	..	..	..	..	..	..	..
62 Belarus	12.0	..	36.5	..	1.2	..	2.5	..	17.6
Medium human development	..	..	..	..	..	..	..	..	..
67 Russian Federation	..	..	28.5	..	..	..	1.4	..	3.2
69 Bulgaria	19.8	..	28.0	..	1.9	..	2.8	..	3.3
71 Estonia	..	..	30.0	..	3.9	..	16.9	..	8.8
76 Lithuania	..	..	37.5	..	(.)	..	4.7	..	7.0
77 Croatia	..	32.4	..	3.2	..	..	13.9	..	6.7
79 Romania	16.9	16.2	28.8	1.3	0.9	0.7	8.1	3.0	9.7
80 Macedonia, FYR	..	..	..	..	..	..	..	..	..
85 Turkmenistan	..	..	..	..	..	..	..	..	..
92 Latvia	9.1	..	36.7	..	(.)	..	6.1	..	14.5
93 Kazakstan	..	..	..	..	..	..	..	..	..
95 Ukraine	..	..	..	..	..	..	..	..	..
100 Uzbekistan	..	..	..	..	..	..	..	..	..
102 Albania	..	..	..	..	..	..	..	..	..
103 Armenia	..	..	..	..	..	..	..	..	..
105 Georgia	5.5	..	..	..	..	..	..	..	..
106 Azerbaijan	3.1	..	..	..	..	..	..	..	..
107 Kyrgyzstan	..	..	..	..	..	..	..	..	..
110 Moldova, Rep. of	..	..	..	..	..	..	..	..	..
115 Tajikistan	..	..	..	..	..	..	..	..	..
All developing countries	..	..	..	..	..	..	..	..	..
Industrial countries	..	..	..	..	..	..	..	..	..
World	..	..	..	..	..	..	..	..	..
North America	11.4	34.2	29.6	2.6	2.7	10.7	18.3	2.5	1.6
Eastern Europe and CIS	..	..	..	..	..	..	..	..	..
Western and Southern Europe	..	42.5	42.1	1.8	1.5	12.3	13.3	7.4	5.4
OECD	14.0	38.2	34.4	2.1	2.0	11.8	15.1	5.5	4.0
European Union	..	40.6	39.0	1.9	1.7	12.5	13.5	6.6	4.9
Nordic countries	30.8	39.1	43.9	2.5	3.3	5.1	4.3	10.6	8.4

a. Data refer to 1980 or a year around 1980.
Source: Column 1: ILO 1995a; *columns 2-9:* IMF, *Government Finance Statistics Yearbook,* various editions.

HDI rank	Prisoners (per 100,000 people)		Young adult prisoners (as % of total prisoners)		Intentional homicides by men (per 100,000 people)	Drug crimes (per 100,000 people)	Reported adult rapes (thousands)	Injuries and deaths from road accidents (per 100,000 people)	Suicides (per 100,000 people) Male	Female	Divorces (per 1,000 couples)	Single-female-parent homes (%)	Live births per 1,000 women aged 15-19	One-person-households headed by women aged 65 and above (as % of all households)
	1987	1993	1987	1990	1985-90	1980-86	1986	1990-93	1989-93	1989-93	1987-91	1985-91	1989-93	1992[a]
High human development	77	93	..	..	4.8	..	129T	1,062	22	7	34	..	33	..
1 Canada	..	45	..	..	2.7	225	20.5	..	21	6	43	..	26	6
2 France	89	86	13	11	1.4	..	2.9	239	30	11	39	7	9	20
3 Norway	46	60	8	6	1.6	116	0.3	201	21	8	45	..	16	12
4 USA	..	..	..	..	12.4	234	90.4	2,367	20	5	48	8	64	8
5 Iceland	28	39	9	5	0.6	..	..	381	..	..	19	6	23	..
6 Netherlands	37	51	18	28	1.2	38	1.2	73	14	7	30	5	7	8
7 Japan	..	..	..	..	0.9	31	1.8	..	22	11	22	5	4	..
8 Finland	..	62	..	7	4.1	..	0.3	122	45	11	58	10	12	10
9 New Zealand	..	..	..	..	2.6	..	0.5	..	24	6	38	8	34	..
10 Sweden	51	66	4	5	1.7	..	1.0	159	22	10	48	6	11	11
11 Spain	70	115	10	6	1.7	15	1.5	202	11	4	11	3	11	..
12 Austria	98	91	1	3	1.4	77	0.5	532	32	11	36	..	23	12
13 Belgium	67	72	..	..	2.3	40	..	547	..	..	32	7	..	9
14 Australia	..	..	..	..	2.5	..	2.3	..	20	5	35	..	21	..
15 United Kingdom	96	92	25	21	1.6	..	..	395	..	..	42	10	31	12
16 Switzerland	..	81	2	..	1.1	129	0.4	324	30	11	33	4	7	9
17 Ireland	55	60	28	..	1.2	..	(.)	181	17	3	..	..	17	6
18 Denmark	62	71	..	..	1.4	176	0.6	165	29	16	49	6	10	11
19 Germany	85	81	..	..	1.2	..	..	477	23	9	33	8	11	12
20 Greece	41	68	6	..	1.2	..	0.6	214	6	2	14	..	15	..
21 Italy	61	89	2	1	2.5	6	0.7	299	12	4	8	2	8	9
23 Israel	..	..	..	..	0.5	25	0.4	..	11	4	19	..	19	..
27 Luxembourg	96	108	7	6	1.6	..	..	1,180	..	..	39	3	12	8
31 Portugal	84	111	10	8	2.3	13	0.2	517	12	4	13	6	23	..
34 Malta	15	..	..	..	0.6	..	(.)	2,868	..	..	..	..	12	..
35 Slovenia	..	..	..	..	..	..	..	..	..	..	..	..	22	..
39 Czech Rep.	..	165	..	..	1.3	..	..	244	28	10	32	..	43	10
42 Slovakia	..	136	..	..	..	..	..	..	..	..	..	..	51	8
48 Hungary	..	132	..	6	3.5	..	1.1	191	55	18	37	..	35	10
58 Poland	..	160	..	..	2.5	..	1.9	128	25	5	17	..	29	6
62 Belarus	..	..	..	..	..	..	..	72	49	10	35	8	46	10
Medium human development	..	..	..	..	..	..	..	106	50	11	38	..	48	..
67 Russian Federation	..	..	..	..	9.0	..	..	121	66	13	42	35	47	..
69 Bulgaria	..	99	..	..	4.0	..	0.7	83	25	10	20	..	71	7
71 Estonia	..	..	..	..	..	..	..	85	64	15	47	..	43	12
76 Lithuania	..	..	..	..	..	..	..	116	74	14	36	..	42	..
77 Croatia	..	..	..	..	..	..	..	..	..	..	..	..	25	..
79 Romania	..	200	..	..	..	..	..	..	..	..	20	..	48	6
80 Macedonia, FYR	..	..	..	..	..	..	..	..	..	..	..	..	44	..
85 Turkmenistan	..	..	..	..	..	..	..	..	..	..	..	..	22	..
92 Latvia	..	..	..	..	..	..	..	130	72	17	46	..	48	7
93 Kazakstan	..	..	..	..	..	..	..	93	38	9	..	..	54	..
95 Ukraine	..	..	..	..	..	..	..	79	38	9	40	..	60	..
100 Uzbekistan	..	..	..	..	..	..	..	..	9	3	..	..	42	..
102 Albania	..	..	..	..	..	..	..	..	2	1	10	..	..	..
103 Armenia	..	..	..	..	..	..	..	26	4	1	..	..	83	..
105 Georgia	..	..	..	..	..	..	..	..	..	..	..	..	58	..
106 Azerbaijan	..	..	..	..	..	..	..	..	..	..	..	..	28	3
107 Kyrgyzstan	..	..	..	..	..	..	..	..	..	..	..	..	55	16
110 Moldova, Rep. of	..	..	..	..	..	..	..	55	..	..	31	..	62	..
115 Tajikistan	..	..	..	..	..	..	..	..	5	2	..	..	39	..
All developing countries	..	..	..	..	..	..	..	..	..	..	..	..	..	..
Industrial countries	..	..	..	..	5.4	..	..	820	28	8	35	..	38	..
World														
North America	..	..	..	..	11.4	233	111T	2,367	20	5	48	..	60	..
Eastern Europe and CIS	..	..	..	..	..	..	..	115	47	10	36	..	46	..
Western and Southern Europe	73	85	..	..	1.7	..	10T	321	20	8	27	..	11	..
OECD	80	88	..	..	4.8	..	129T	1,020	21	7	34	..	33	..
European Union	77	87	..	..	1.7	..	10T	331	20	7	29	..	15	..
Nordic countries	53	65	..	..	2.1	..	2T	162	28	11	50	..	12	..

a. Data refer to 1992 or a year around 1992.
Source: Columns 1-4 and 11-13: UNECE 1995b; columns 5-7: UNDP 1994; column 8: UNECE 1995a; columns 9 and 10: WHO 1994; column 14: Eurostat and UN 1995.

HDI rank	Net official development assistance (ODA) disbursed US$ millions 1995	As % of GNP Average 1984/85	As % of GNP 1995	ODA as % of central government budget 1992/93	ODA per capita of donor country (1994 US$) 1984/85	ODA per capita 1994/95	Multilateral ODA as % of GNP 1994-95	Government subsidies to NGOs (US$ millions; 1993-94 prices) 1993-94	Aid by NGOs as % of GNP 1984-85	Aid by NGOs as % of GNP 1994-95	Aid to least developed countries (as % of GNP) 1994-95
High human development	58,894T	0.35	0.26	..	74	74	-0.01	..	0.03	0.04	0.06
1 Canada	2,067	0.50	0.38	1.63	82	73	0.14	207	0.05	0.05	0.09
2 France	8,443	0.62	0.55	..	120	137	-0.13	..	0.01	0.02	0.12
3 Norway	1,244	1.02	0.87	1.70	210	255	0.26	..	0.09	0.09	0.37
4 USA	7,367	0.24	0.10	1.82	51	33	0.03	..	0.04	0.04	0.03
5 Iceland	..	..	..	..	..	..	..	..	..	..	..
6 Netherlands	3,226	0.97	0.81	..	172	172	-0.25	256	0.08	0.09	0.22
7 Japan	14,489	0.31	0.28	1.35	88	106	0.08	136	0.01	..	0.05
8 Finland	388	0.38	0.32	1.51	67	59	-0.11	4	0.03	..	0.09
9 New Zealand	123	0.25	0.23	0.36	31	31	0.05	1	0.03	0.03	0.05
10 Sweden	1,704	0.83	0.77	..	172	189	-0.23	..	0.07	0.04	0.24
11 Spain	1,348	0.09	0.24	0.97	..	31	-0.10	..	..	0.02	0.03
12 Austria	767	0.33	0.33	0.73	69	82	-0.08	3	0.02	0.05	0.05
13 Belgium	1,034	0.56	0.38	..	107	81	-0.16	2	0.02	0.02	0.10
14 Australia	1,194	0.47	0.36	1.27	68	62	0.08	19	0.03	0.02	0.07
15 United Kingdom	3,157	0.33	0.28	..	48	53	-0.14	54	0.03	0.05	0.08
16 Switzerland	1,084	0.30	0.34	3.13	108	135	0.10	120	0.05	0.06	0.11
17 Ireland	153	0.23	0.29	..	19	35	-0.12	..	0.14	0.10	0.10
18 Denmark	1,623	0.83	0.96	2.51	191	273	-0.44	6	0.03	0.02	0.31
19 Germany	7,524	0.46	0.31	..	85	81	-0.12	98	0.06	0.05	0.08
20 Greece	..	..	..	..	..	..	..	..	..	..	..
21 Italy	1,623	0.27	0.15	0.64	39	37	-0.08	43	..	..	0.04
23 Israel	..	..	..	..	..	..	..	..	..	..	..
27 Luxembourg	65	0.16	0.36	..	..	148	-0.13	..	..	0.03	0.05
31 Portugal	271	0.05	0.27	..	..	27	-0.10	..	..	..	0.19
34 Malta	..	..	..	..	..	..	..	..	..	..	..
35 Slovenia	..	..	..	..	..	..	..	..	..	..	..
39 Czech Rep.	..	..	..	..	..	..	..	..	..	..	..
42 Slovakia	..	..	..	..	..	..	..	..	..	..	..
48 Hungary	..	..	..	..	..	..	..	..	..	..	..
58 Poland	..	..	..	..	..	..	..	..	..	..	..
62 Belarus	..	..	..	..	..	..	..	..	..	..	..
Medium human development	..	..	..	..	..	..	..	..	..	..	..
67 Russian Federation	..	..	..	..	..	..	..	..	..	..	..
69 Bulgaria	..	..	..	..	..	..	..	..	..	..	..
71 Estonia	..	..	..	..	..	..	..	..	..	..	..
76 Lithuania	..	..	..	..	..	..	..	..	..	..	..
77 Croatia	..	..	..	..	..	..	..	..	..	..	..
79 Romania	..	..	..	..	..	..	..	..	..	..	..
80 Macedonia, FYR	..	..	..	..	..	..	..	..	..	..	..
85 Turkmenistan	..	..	..	..	..	..	..	..	..	..	..
92 Latvia	..	..	..	..	..	..	..	..	..	..	..
93 Kazakstan	..	..	..	..	..	..	..	..	..	..	..
95 Ukraine	..	..	..	..	..	..	..	..	..	..	..
100 Uzbekistan	..	..	..	..	..	..	..	..	..	..	..
102 Albania	..	..	..	..	..	..	..	..	..	..	..
103 Armenia	..	..	..	..	..	..	..	..	..	..	..
105 Georgia	..	..	..	..	..	..	..	..	..	..	..
106 Azerbaijan	..	..	..	..	..	..	..	..	..	..	..
107 Kyrgyzstan	..	..	..	..	..	..	..	..	..	..	..
110 Moldova, Rep. of	..	..	..	..	..	..	..	..	..	..	..
115 Tajikistan	..	..	..	..	..	..	..	..	..	..	..
All developing countries	..	..	..	..	..	..	..	..	..	..	..
Industrial countries	..	..	..	..	..	..	..	..	..	..	..
World	..	..	..	..	..	..	..	..	..	..	..
North America	9,434T	0.26	0.12	1.80	54	36	0.40	..	0.04	0.04	0.03
Eastern Europe and CIS	..	..	..	..	..	..	..	..	..	..	..
Western and Southern Europe	30,497T	0.47	0.39	..	94	97	-0.12	..	0.04	0.04	0.10
OECD	58,894T	0.35	0.26	..	74	74	-0.01	..	0.03	0.03	0.06
European Union	31,326T	0.45	0.37	..	83	87	-0.13	75T	0.04	0.04	0.09
Nordic countries	4,959T	0.79	0.76	2.00	161	202	-0.16	..	0.06	0.05	0.26

Source: Columns 1-3 and 5-11: OECD 1996a; *column 4:* OECD 1994a.

		Defence expenditure						Military expenditure (as % of combined education and health expenditure)		ODA disbursed (as % of defence expenditure)	Exports of conventional weapons (1990 prices)[a]		Total armed forces	
		US$ millions (1995 prices)		As % of GDP		Per capita (US$; 1995 prices)					US$ millions	Share[b] (%)	Thousands	Index (1985 =100)
HDI rank		1985	1995	1985	1995	1985	1995	1960	1990-91	1995	1995	1991-95	1995	1995
High human development		626,543T	555,661T	4.1	2.6	761	616	110	30	11	17,096T	79	4,816T	79
1	Canada	10,688	9,004	2.2	1.6	421	320	66	15	23	301	1	71	85
2	France	44,604	48,002	4.0	3.1	808	826	131	29	18	815	5	409	88
3	Norway	2,862	3,755	3.1	2.6	681	863	48	22	33	35	..	30	81
4	USA	352,551	277,834	6.5	3.8	1,473	1,056	173	46	3	9,894	51	1,547	72
5	Iceland	..	..	..	..	..	..	(.)	(.)	..	..	..	..	..
6	Netherlands	8,121	8,520	3.1	2.2	561	552	67	22	38	448	2	74	71
7	Japan	29,350	50,219	1.0	1.1	243	401	17	12	29	..	..	240	99
8	Finland	2,051	2,113	2.8	2.0	418	414	25	15	18	..	..	31	85
9	New Zealand	882	918	2.9	1.7	271	260	29	16	13	..	..	10	81
10	Sweden	4,359	6,035	3.3	2.9	522	687	30	16	28	221	1	64	97
11	Spain	10,289	8,460	2.4	1.5	267	216	126	18	16	62	(.)	206	64
12	Austria	1,763	2,106	1.2	1.0	233	264	20	9	36	33	(.)	56	102
13	Belgium	5,621	4,570	3.0	1.7	570	454	49	20	23	168	(.)	47	52
14	Australia	7,436	8,544	3.4	2.5	472	468	46	24	14	14	(.)	56	80
15	United Kingdom	43,536	34,154	5.2	3.1	770	586	96	40	9	1,663	6	240	73
16	Switzerland	2,636	5,093	2.1	1.9	408	720	45	14	21	132	1	31	157
17	Ireland	437	688	1.8	1.2	123	191	24	12	22	..	..	13	94
18	Denmark	2,855	3,124	2.2	1.8	558	599	37	18	52	..	..	33	112
19	Germany	48,149	41,815	3.2	2.0	634	509	67	29	18	1,964	8	340	71
20	Greece	3,180	5,056	7.0	4.6	320	484	145	71	..	..	..	171	85
21	Italy	23,462	20,042	2.3	1.8	411	346	39	21	8	324	2	329	85
23	Israel	6,899	7,197	21.2	9.2	1,630	1,279	85	106	..	317	1	172	121
27	Luxembourg	87	141	0.9	0.9	238	348	19	10	46	..	..	1	114
31	Portugal	1,674	2,797	3.1	2.9	164	283	156	32	10	..	..	54	74
34	Malta	22	31	1.4	1.1	61	85	..	10	..	..	..	2	238
35	Slovenia	..	279	..	1.5	..	139	..	..	..	..	..	8	..
39	Czech Rep.	..	1,108	..	2.8	..	107	60	17	..	326	1	86	..
42	Slovakia	..	434	..	2.8	..	80	..	..	..	178	(.)	47	..
48	Hungary	5,165	612	7.2	1.4	485	60	31	18	..	..	..	71	67
58	Poland	7,864	2,551	8.1	2.5	211	66	41	30	..	201	(.)	279	87
62	Belarus	..	459	..	3.3	..	44	..	..	..	..	..	98	..
Medium human development		..	87,854T	..	5.8	..	272	..	..	..	..	..	2,739T	..
67	Russian Federation	..	82,000	..	7.4	..	551	134	132	..	3,905	13	1,520	..
69	Bulgaria	7,931	387	14.1	3.3	886	46	70	29	..	0	(.)	102	69
71	Estonia	..	101	..	5.3	..	68	..	..	..	..	..	4	..
76	Lithuania	..	68	..	2.4	..	18	..	..	..	..	..	5	..
77	Croatia	..	1,894	..	12.6	..	406	..	..	..	..	..	105	..
79	Romania	1,905	872	4.5	3.1	84	38	47	25	..	..	..	217	115
80	Macedonia, FYR	..	..	..	..	..	..	..	..	..	..	..	..	..
85	Turkmenistan	..	96	..	1.9	..	21	..	..	..	..	..	11	..
92	Latvia	..	121	..	3.2	..	46	..	..	..	..	..	7	..
93	Kazakstan	..	426	..	3.0	..	26	..	..	..	..	..	40	..
95	Ukraine	..	1,005	..	3.0	..	19	..	..	..	74	1	453	..
100	Uzbekistan	..	385	..	3.6	..	17	..	..	..	464	1	25	..
102	Albania	258	49	5.3	2.8	87	14	..	51	..	..	..	73	181
103	Armenia	..	79	..	4.4	..	22	..	..	..	..	..	60	..
105	Georgia	..	92	..	3.4	..	17	..	..	..	..	..	9	..
106	Azerbaijan	..	109	..	5.0	..	14	..	..	..	..	..	87	..
107	Kyrgyzstan	..	56	..	3.5	..	13	..	..	..	..	..	7	..
110	Moldova, Rep. of	..	45	..	3.7	..	10	..	..	..	..	..	12	..
115	Tajikistan	..	69	..	6.9	..	11	..	..	..	..	..	3	..
All developing countries		186,917T	153,628T	7.1	3.1	52	35	102	63	..	..	..	14,125T	96
Industrial countries		636,637T	643,515T	4.1	2.7	742	526	110	33	..	21,539T	94	7,555T	80
World		823,554T	797,143T	4.6	2.8	185	143	109	38	..	..	..	21,680T	92
North America		363,239T	286,838T	6.1	3.6	1,371	983	166	43	3	10,195T	52	1,618T	72
Eastern Europe and CIS		..	93,297T	..	5.0	..	233	..	..	..	..	..	3,328T	..
Western and Southern Europe		162,172T	162,348T	3.0	2.2	521	498	72	24	19	4,202T	17	1,892T	80
OECD		624,451T	555,941T	4.0	2.6	662	540	110	30	11	16,601T	77	5,171T	80
European Union		200,188T	187,623T	3.4	2.3	561	504	78	27	17	5,698T	23	2,068T	78
Nordic countries		12,127T	15,027T	2.9	2.4	537	641	34	17	33	..	..	158T	94

a. Figures are trend indicator values.
b. Calculated using the 1991-95 total for the 30 leading suppliers of major conventional weapons as defined by SIPRI 1996 (excluding the former Yugoslavia).
Source: Columns 1-6 and 10-12: IISS 1996; *columns 7 and 8:* IISS 1993; *column 9:* calculated on the basis of estimates from IISS 1996 and OECD 1996a; *column 13:* calculated on the basis of estimates from IISS 1996.

HDI rank	Export-import ratio (exports as % of imports) 1994	Export growth rate as % of import growth rate 1980-94	Trade dependency (exports plus imports as % of GDP) 1994	Terms of trade (1987=100) 1994	Net foreign direct investment (as % of GNP) 1993	Net workers' remittances from abroad (US$ millions) 1994	Gross international reserves (months of import coverage) 1994	Current account balance before official transfers (US$ millions) 1994
High human development	101	105	45	104	-0.4	..	2.6	45,676T
1 Canada	91	92	74	97	-0.2	..	0.8	-18,153
2 France	104	105	63	106	(.)	-1,290	1.7	15,043
3 Norway	112	110	88	97	1.0	-236	5.1	4,813
4 USA	87	84	27	101	-0.6	-7,680	2.0	-136,484
5 Iceland	..	..	..	..	0.1	..	..	..
6 Netherlands	109	114	115	101	-1.4	-395	3.1	14,707
7 Japan	130	133	23	128	-0.3	..	3.5	133,900
8 Finland	104	119	73	94	-1.3	..	3.9	1,402
9 New Zealand	88	103	67	108	..	177	2.4	-1,123
10 Sweden	103	117	84	105	1.1	91	3.8	2,513
11 Spain	92	111	48	112	0.8	1,780	4.7	-7,667
12 Austria	98	112	85	93	-0.3	33	3.4	-1,858
13 Belgium	107	114	191	101	..	-360	1.2	14,576
14 Australia	84	96	38	98	0.5	..	2.5	-9,955
15 United Kingdom	102	94	75	105	-1.1	..	1.5	5,414
16 Switzerland	120	131	85	64	-2.3	-2,007	7.7	17,329
17 Ireland	102	130	154	92	0.2	..	1.9	911
18 Denmark	108	119	96	102	0.2	..	2.0	5,086
19 Germany	102	103	55	97	-0.8	-4,634	2.5	2,327
20 Greece	69	94	49	99	1.3	2,576	8.2	-4,453
21 Italy	108	125	52	104	-0.3	242	2.7	21,453
23 Israel	72	99	75	113	-0.5	..	2.4	-6,111
27 Luxembourg	..	..	..	..	..	..	..	..
31 Portugal	81	126	63	104	1.3	3,844	8.8	-1,926
34 Malta	..	..	..	..	2.4	..	..	..
35 Slovenia	105	..	120	..	..	56	2.2	532
39 Czech Rep.	99	..	109	..	3.9	..	4.2	-16
42 Slovakia	108	..	143	..	1.3	..	3.1	706
48 Hungary	70	34	67	99	6.5	..	5.1	-4,067
58 Poland	86	131	52	109	2.0	..	2.8	-2,718
62 Belarus	83	..	30	..	0.1	..	..	-505
Medium human development	95	..	37	..	0.3	..	..	-5,017T
67 Russian Federation	100	..	31	..	0.1	..	1.5	-202
69 Bulgaria	100	123	108	..	0.5	..	..	146
71 Estonia	95	..	53	..	3.8	..	3.8	-68
76 Lithuania	87	..	88	..	1.2	..	2.9	-279
77 Croatia	97	..	97	..	..	340	2.5	7
79 Romania	93	83	49	111	0.3	..	4.9	-352
80 Macedonia, FYR	71	..	176	..	..	..	1.2	-370
85 Turkmenistan	..	..	..	..	..	..	..	..
92 Latvia	87	..	47	..	0.8	..	5.3	-158
93 Kazakstan	80	..	39	..	2.0	..	..	-722
95 Ukraine	91	..	33	..	(.)	..	..	-1,977
100 Uzbekistan	100	..	33	..	0.1	..	..	-8
102 Albania	36	45	58	..	5.0	265	..	-238
103 Armenia	49	..	30	..	..	..	..	-232
105 Georgia	..	..	..	..	0.2	..	..	..
106 Azerbaijan	75	..	42	..	1.2	..	..	-179
107 Kyrgyzstan	69	..	31	..	0.3	..	..	-202
110 Moldova, Rep. of	75	..	39	..	0.3	..	2.6	-183
115 Tajikistan	..	..	..	..	..	..	..	..
All developing countries	90	87	54	97	1.5	9,791T	4.3	-90,577T
Industrial countries	101	105	44	104	-0.4	..	2.6	40,659T
World	99	100	46	102	-0.1	2,593T	2.9	-49,918T
North America	88	84	31	100	-0.5	-7,680T	1.8	-154,637T
Eastern Europe and CIS	93	..	46	..	0.9	..	2.8	-11,085T
Western and Southern Europe	104	112	69	100	-0.3	-356T	2.9	84,256T
OECD	101	105	44	103	-0.4	-1,527T	2.5	27,142T
European Union	103	109	69	102	-0.4	1,887T	2.5	67,528T
Nordic countries	106	116	86	101	0.5	..	3.5	13,814T

Source: Columns 1-3: calculated on the basis of estimates from World Bank 1996g; *columns 4 and 6-8:* World Bank 1996g; *column 5:* World Bank 1995d.

HDI rank		Urban population (as % of total)			Urban population annual growth rate (%)		Population in cities of more than 750,000		Largest city			
							As % of total population 1990	As % of urban population 1990	City	Population (thousands) 1995	Growth rate (%)	
		1960	1994	2000	1960-1994	1994-2000					1970-75	1990-95
High human development		66	76	77	1.2	1.8	33	43	–	–	–	–
1	Canada	69	77	77	1.8	1.2	36	48	Toronto	4,483	1.8	3.5
2	France	62	73	73	1.2	0.5	23	31	Paris	9,469	0.9	0.3
3	Norway	50	73	74	1.7	0.7	..	..	..	..	..	..
4	USA	70	76	78	1.3	1.2	41	55	New York	16,329	-0.4	0.3
5	Iceland	80	91	92	1.6	1.2	..	..	..	..	..	..
6	Netherlands	85	89	90	1.0	0.7	14	16	Amsterdam	1,109	-1.0	1.0
7	Japan	63	78	78	1.5	0.4	37	48	Tokyo	25,013	3.7	1.4
8	Finland	38	63	65	1.9	1.0	18	28	Helsinki	1,059	2.2	3.9
9	New Zealand	76	86	87	1.5	1.4	26	31	Auckland	945	2.8	1.5
10	Sweden	73	83	83	0.9	0.5	17	21	Stockholm	1,545	2.2	0.7
11	Spain	57	76	78	1.7	0.4	18	24	Madrid	4,072	2.5	-0.5
12	Austria	50	56	56	0.6	0.8	27	48	Vienna	2,060	0.5	0.1
13	Belgium	93	97	97	0.4	0.4	12	12	Brussels	1,122	1.0	-0.5
14	Australia	81	85	85	1.8	1.2	59	69	Sydney	3,590	2.1	0.4
15	United Kingdom	86	89	90	0.4	0.4	23	26	London	7,335	..	..
16	Switzerland	51	61	62	1.3	1.4	12	20	Zurich	897	0.1	1.6
17	Ireland	46	57	59	1.3	0.7	26	46	Dublin	911	1.6	-0.1
18	Denmark	74	85	86	0.8	0.2	26	31	Copenhagen	1,326	..	-0.3
19	Germany	76	86	88	0.7	0.4	43	51	Essen	6,481	-0.4	0.4
20	Greece	43	65	68	1.9	1.1	43	68	Athens	3,693	1.7	1.1
21	Italy	59	67	67	0.7	0.1	24	37	Milan	4,603	0.2	-1.3
23	Israel	77	91	91	3.3	2.1	38	43	Tel Aviv-Yafa	1,921	3.2	1.4
27	Luxembourg	62	89	91	1.8	1.5	..	..	..	..	..	..
31	Portugal	22	35	38	1.7	1.3	19	50	Lisbon	1,863	2.3	2.3
34	Malta	70	89	91	1.2	0.9	..	..	..	..	..	..
35	Slovenia	..	63	..	..	..	..	..	..	..	..	..
39	Czech Rep.	46	65	66	1.3	0.3	12	18	Prague	1,225	0.9	0.2
42	Slovakia	34	58	61	2.4	1.2	..	..	..	..	..	..
48	Hungary	43	64	67	1.3	0.4	20	31	Budapest	2,017	0.6	..
58	Poland	48	64	67	1.7	0.9	22	35	Katowice	3,552	1.8	0.6
62	Belarus	32	70	75	3.0	0.9	16	24	Minsk	1,788	3.7	1.4
Medium human development		48	66	68	2.0	0.8	18	26	–	–	–	–
67	Russian Federation	54	76	78	1.7	0.3	20	27	Moscow	9,233	1.4	0.4
69	Bulgaria	39	70	73	2.2	0.3	15	22	Sofia	1,384	1.7	1.1
71	Estonia	58	73	75	1.5	-0.2	..	..	..	..	..	..
76	Lithuania	40	71	75	2.6	0.7	..	..	..	..	..	..
77	Croatia	..	64	..	..	..	..	..	..	..	..	..
79	Romania	34	55	58	2.1	0.6	9	17	Bucharest	2,090	2.3	0.4
80	Macedonia, FYR	..	59	..	..	..	..	..	..	..	..	..
85	Turkmenistan	46	45	46	2.7	2.5	..	..	..	..	..	..
92	Latvia	57	73	75	1.4	-0.3	35	48	Riga	924	1.6	0.1
93	Kazakstan	45	59	62	2.5	1.4	7	12	Alma-Ata	1,262	2.5	1.7
95	Ukraine	47	70	73	1.8	0.6	18	27	Kiev	2,809	3.0	1.3
100	Uzbekistan	34	41	43	3.4	2.8	10	25	Tashkent	2,288	2.8	1.6
102	Albania	31	37	40	2.8	2.1	..	..	..	..	..	..
103	Armenia	51	68	70	2.8	1.7	36	54	Yerevan	1,305	3.2	1.5
105	Georgia	43	58	61	1.7	1.1	24	42	Tbilisi	1,353	2.0	1.2
106	Azerbaijan	48	56	58	2.4	1.7	25	45	Baku	1,853	2.3	1.1
107	Kyrgyzstan	34	39	41	2.7	2.4	..	..	..	..	..	..
110	Moldova, Rep. of	23	51	56	3.5	1.8	..	..	..	..	..	..
115	Tajikistan	33	32	33	3.0	3.2	..	..	..	..	..	..
All developing countries		22	37	41	3.9	3.7	14	39	–	–	–	–
Industrial countries		61	74	75	1.4	0.8	29	41	–	–	–	–
World		34	45	48	3.3	3.0	17	39	–	–	–	–
North America		70	76	78	1.3	1.2	41	54	–	–	–	–
Eastern Europe and CIS		47	66	68	2.0	0.8	18	27	–	–	–	–
Western and Southern Europe		64	75	76	1.0	0.5	27	36	–	–	–	–
OECD		64	76	77	1.6	1.1	32	44	–	–	–	–
European Union		68	78	79	0.9	0.4	27	35	–	–	–	–
Nordic countries		61	77	78	1.2	0.6	20	25	–	–	–	–

Source: Columns 1, 3, 8, 10 and 11: UN 1995c; *columns 2, 4-7 and 9:* calculated on the basis of data from UN 1995c.

HDI rank	Estimated population (millions)			Annual population growth rate (%)		Total fertility rate	Contraceptive prevalence rate, any method (%)	Dependency ratio (%)	Population aged 65 and above (as % of total population)
	1960	1994	2000	1960-1994	1994-2000	1994	1987-94	1994	1994
High human development	701T	904T	928T	0.8	0.4	1.7	71	49.5	13.7
1 Canada	18	29	31	1.4	0.9	1.8	..	47.9	11.9
2 France	46	58	59	0.7	0.3	1.7	77	52.8	14.9
3 Norway	4	4	4	0.6	0.4	1.9	76	54.4	16.0
4 USA	186	265	278	1.0	0.8	2.1	71	53.2	12.6
5 Iceland	0	0	0	1.2	1.0	2.2	..	54.7	11.3
6 Netherlands	12	15	16	0.9	0.5	1.6	78	45.8	13.1
7 Japan	94	125	126	0.8	0.2	1.4	59	43.4	13.7
8 Finland	4	5	5	0.4	0.3	1.9	80	49.4	14.0
9 New Zealand	2	4	4	1.2	1.1	2.1	..	52.9	11.4
10 Sweden	8	9	9	0.5	0.3	2.0	78	56.3	17.4
11 Spain	31	40	40	0.8	0.1	1.2	59	46.6	14.6
12 Austria	7	8	8	0.4	0.6	1.5	71	48.2	14.8
13 Belgium	9	10	10	0.3	0.3	1.6	79	50.4	15.7
14 Australia	10	18	19	1.6	1.1	1.9	76	49.8	11.7
15 United Kingdom	52	58	58	0.3	0.1	1.8	82	54.1	15.8
16 Switzerland	5	7	7	0.8	0.7	1.5	..	46.3	14.3
17 Ireland	3	4	4	0.6	0.2	1.9	..	56.7	11.3
18 Denmark	5	5	5	0.4	0.2	1.8	78	48.1	15.2
19 Germany	73	81	83	0.3	0.3	1.3	75	45.6	15.2
20 Greece	8	10	11	0.7	0.3	1.3	..	48.6	15.5
21 Italy	50	57	57	0.4	(.)	1.2	78	44.9	15.7
23 Israel	2	5	6	2.8	2.1	2.9	..	64.1	9.4
27 Luxembourg	0	0	0	0.7	1.1	1.7	..	45.1	13.7
31 Portugal	9	10	10	0.3	-0.1	1.5	66[a]	48.4	14.5
34 Malta	0	0	0	0.4	0.6	2.1	..	49.8	11.0
35 Slovenia	2	2	2	0.6	-0.1	1.3	..	44.5	12.2
39 Czech Rep.	10	10	10	0.2	-0.1	1.6	69	47.1	12.6
42 Slovakia	4	5	5	0.7	0.2	1.8	74	51.3	10.7
48 Hungary	10	10	10	0.1	-0.6	1.6	73	47.8	13.9
58 Poland	30	39	39	0.8	0.1	1.8	75	52.0	10.8
62 Belarus	8	10	10	0.7	-0.1	1.6	50	52.2	12.2
Medium human development	240T	324T	324T	0.9	..	1.8	..	54.0	10.7
67 Russian Federation	120	149	146	0.6	-0.3	1.4	..	49.8	11.7
69 Bulgaria	8	9	8	0.2	-0.5	1.4	76	49.4	14.2
71 Estonia	1	2	1	0.6	-1.0	1.4	70	50.5	12.6
76 Lithuania	3	4	4	0.9	-0.2	1.7	..	51.3	11.9
77 Croatia	4	5	5	0.3	-0.1	1.6	..	46.7	12.4
79 Romania	18	23	23	0.6	-0.2	1.3	57	48.3	11.5
80 Macedonia, FYR	1	2	2	1.3	0.7	2.0	..	49.2	7.9
85 Turkmenistan	2	4	5	2.7	1.9	3.8	..	78.0	4.1
92 Latvia	2	3	2	0.6	-1.2	1.5	..	51.3	13.0
93 Kazakstan	10	17	17	1.5	0.1	2.3	59	58.8	6.8
95 Ukraine	43	52	51	0.6	-0.3	1.5	..	51.9	13.7
100 Uzbekistan	9	22	25	2.9	1.9	3.7	..	80.2	4.3
102 Albania	2	3	4	2.2	0.6	2.8	..	59.0	5.5
103 Armenia	2	4	4	2.0	0.2	2.0	..	56.9	7.1
105 Georgia	4	6	5	0.8	-0.1	2.0	..	53.9	11.1
106 Azerbaijan	4	8	8	1.9	0.8	2.5	..	61.5	5.6
107 Kyrgyzstan	2	5	5	2.1	0.3	3.4	..	74.9	5.7
110 Moldova, Rep. of	3	4	5	1.1	0.1	2.0	..	56.2	9.1
115 Tajikistan	2	6	6	3.0	1.9	4.0	..	87.2	4.2
All developing countries	2,054T	4,326T	4,774T	2.2	1.7	3.1	56	64.5	4.6
Industrial countries	941T	1,228T	1,252T	0.8	0.3	1.7	71	50.6	12.9
World	2,994T	5,554T	6,026T	1.8	1.4	2.8	58	61.2	6.5
North America	204T	294T	309T	1.1	0.8	2.1	71	52.6	12.5
Eastern Europe and CIS	303T	401T	401T	0.8	..	1.8	..	53.3	10.9
Western and Southern Europe	273T	325T	329T	0.5	0.2	1.4	74	47.8	15.0
OECD	720T	992T	1,030T	0.9	0.6	1.8	69	51.3	12.5
European Union	316T	371T	375T	0.5	0.2	1.5	75	48.7	15.2
Nordic countries	20T	24T	24T	0.5	0.3	1.9	78	52.6	15.9

a. Data refer to 1979-80.
Source: Columns 1-5 and 8-9: calculated on the basis of estimates from UN 1996b; *column 6:* UN 1996b; *column 7:* UN 1997.

42 Energy use

HDI rank	Electricity consumption Total (millions of kilowatt-hours) 1994	Index (1970=100) 1994	Per capita (kilowatt-hours) 1970	1994	Commercial energy use (oil equivalent) Total (1,000 metric tons) 1980	1994	Per capita (kg) 1980	1994	GDP output per kilogram (US$) 1980	1994	Net commercial energy imports (as % of energy consumption) 1980	1994	CO$_2$ emissions (per unit of real GDP) 1980	1992
High human development	7,769,158T	213	5,110	8,645	3,865,244T	4,458,242T	4,766	4,995	2.4	5.6	31	20	0.9	0.8
1 Canada	510,272	252	9,489	17,510	193,170	228,000	7,854	7,795	1.4	2.4	-7	-46	1.3	0.9
2 France	412,454	282	2,885	7,139	190,660	222,400	3,539	3,839	3.5	6.0	75	47	0.6	0.4
3 Norway	113,256	..	..	26,205	18,865	23,100	4,611	5,326	3.1	4.7	-195	-636	0.5	0.6
4 USA	3,312,888	202	8,015	12,711	1,801,000	2,060,400	7,908	7,905	1.5	3.2	14	19	1.2	1.0
5 Iceland	4,780	325	7,206	17,970	..	..	..	..	..	..	..	..	..	..
6 Netherlands	90,239	223	3,109	5,861	65,106	70,100	4,601	4,558	2.6	4.7	-10	9	0.8	0.5
7 Japan	964,328	..	..	7,726	347,120	478,000	2,972	3,825	3.1	9.6	88	82	0.5	0.4
8 Finland	72,087	332	4,714	14,182	24,998	30,300	5,230	5,954	2.1	3.2	72	62	0.8	0.5
9 New Zealand	32,416	183	4,876	9,180	9,202	15,200	2,956	4,352	2.4	3.3	39	5	0.6	0.7
10 Sweden	143,150	221	8,045	16,382	40,992	49,200	4,933	5,603	3.1	4.0	61	36	0.5	0.3
11 Spain	163,357T	297	1,628	4,129	68,692	94,500	1,837	2,414	3.1	5.1	77	69	0.8	0.6
12 Austria	52,536	213	3,316	6,635	23,449	26,300	3,105	3,276	3.3	7.5	67	65	0.5	0.4
13 Belgium	76,219	247	3,200	7,561	46,122	51,500	4,684	5,091	2.6	4.4	83	77	1.0	0.6
14 Australia	167,151	310	4,309	9,363	70,399	92,300	4,792	5,173	2.3	3.6	-22	-91	1.2	1.2
15 United Kingdom	342,270	137	4,504	5,870	201,200	219,200	3,572	3,754	2.7	4.6	2	-9	1.0	0.8
16 Switzerland	53,793	189	4,534	7,512	20,840	25,200	3,298	3,603	4.9	10.3	66	59	0.3	0.2
17 Ireland	17,105	281	2,069	4,833	8,485	11,200	2,495	3,136	2.4	4.6	78	70	0.9	0.8
18 Denmark	36,252	229	3,197	7,008	19,488	20,800	3,804	3,996	3.4	7.0	97	27	0.7	0.5
19 Germany	530,558	..	..	6,528	359,170	334,000	4,587	4,097	..	6.1	49	58	..	..
20 Greece	41,005	417	1,119	3,937	15,973	23,300	1,656	2,235	2.5	3.3	77	63	1.2	1.4
21 Italy	269,382	222	2,262	4,711	139,190	154,800	2,466	2,710	3.3	6.6	86	81	0.6	0.5
23 Israel	27,985	408	2,306	5,127	8,616	15,151	2,222	2,815	2.6	5.1	98	96	0.7	0.9
27 Luxembourg	5,645	153	10,894	14,077	..	..	..	..	..	..	..	..	..	..
31 Portugal	32,268	430	830	3,283	10,291	18,100	1,054	1,828	2.8	4.8	86	90	0.7	0.9
34 Malta	1,500	526	874	4,121	..	..	..	..	..	..	..	..	..	..
35 Slovenia	10,696	..	..	5,508	..	2,995	..	1,506	..	4.7	..	19	..	..
39 Czech Rep.	58,260	..	..	5,659	29,394	40,324	2,873	3,902	1.0	0.9	-29	13	..	4.4
42 Slovakia	23,901	..	..	4,482	..	..	..	..	..	..	..	..	..	2.5
48 Hungary	35,520	198	1,735	3,496	28,322	25,191	2,645	2,455	0.8	1.6	49	44	3.7	2.6
58 Poland	132,668	205	1,986	3,460	124,500	98,800	3,499	2,563	0.5	0.9	3	5	7.7	6.0
62 Belarus	35,217	..	..	3,465	..	27,881	..	2,692	..	0.7	..	89	..	4.0
Medium human development	1,406,903T	..	..	4,360	1,071,423T	1,003,465T	4,138	3,118	..	0.6	..	-20	..	5.9
67 Russian Federation	855,418	..	..	5,805	750,240	599,027	5,397	4,038	..	0.6	(.)	-52	..	5.5
69 Bulgaria	38,061	..	2,286	4,316	28,476	23,500	3,213	2,786	0.7	0.4	74	63	3.6	2.4
71 Estonia	10,879	..	..	7,060	..	5,325	..	3,552	..	0.9	..	42	0.1	4.9
76 Lithuania	11,199	..	..	3,022	11,353	8,164	3,326	2,194	..	0.6	-2	80	..	3.1
77 Croatia	11,840	..	..	2,629	..	5,051	..	1,057	..	2.8	..	28	..	..
79 Romania	55,861	171	1,615	2,437	63,846	39,782	2,876	1,750	..	0.8	19	27	5.7	4.5
80 Macedonia, FYR	5,678	..	..	2,651	..	..	..	..	..	..	..	..	..	..
85 Turkmenistan	7,846	..	..	1,957	7,948	14,090	2,778	3,198	..	..	-101	-116	..	..
92 Latvia	6,258	..	..	2,423	..	4,469	..	1,755	..	1.3	..	88	..	2.6
93 Kazakstan	78,277	..	..	4,597	76,799	62,368	5,153	3,710	..	0.3	(.)	-16	..	12.6
95 Ukraine	208,100	..	..	4,044	108,290	170,910	2,164	3,292	..	0.5	-1	43	..	6.9
100 Uzbekistan	47,400	..	..	2,121	..	42,209	..	1,886	..	0.5	..	3	..	8.5
102 Albania	3,903	414	442	1,143	3,058	1,350	1,145	422	0.5	1.3	(.)	28	40.0	18.0
103 Armenia	5,674	..	..	1,599	..	2,500	..	667	..	1.0	..	87	..	1.8
105 Georgia	7,603	..	..	1,395	4,474	3,098	882	572	..	0.7	-5	81	..	3.0
106 Azerbaijan	17,800	..	..	2,382	15,001	10,545	2,433	1,414	..	0.3	1	-41	..	13.6
107 Kyrgyzstan	10,427	..	..	2,234	1,938	3,197	534	715	..	0.9	-113	76	..	4.3
110 Moldova, Rep. of	8,579	..	..	1,941	..	4,185	..	962	..	0.9	..	99	..	..
115 Tajikistan	16,100	..	..	2,714	..	3,695	..	642	..	0.6	..	55	..	1.6
All developing countries	3,305,423T	691	180	763	1,180,034T	2,309,474T	397	570	2.7	3.0	-52	-26	1.9	2.2
Industrial countries	9,176,061T	212	4,933	7,514	4,936,667T	5,461,707T	4,615	4,499	..	5.4	30	13	1.0	0.9
World	12,481,484T	277	1,088	2,258	6,116,701T	7,771,181T	1,509	1,471	..	5.0	7	3	1.1	1.2
North America	3,823,160T	207	8,151	13,187	1,994,170T	2,288,400T	7,903	7,894	1.5	3.1	11	10	1.2	1.0
Eastern Europe and CIS	1,703,165T	..	..	4,269	1,253,639T	1,198,656T	3,974	3,048	..	0.8	..	-13	..	5.6
Western and Southern Europe	2,115,586T	254	2,704	6,520	1,052,321T	1,154,800T	3,405	3,567	3.3	6.0	51	20	0.6	0.5
OECD	7,891,089T	217	4,502	7,701	3,985,376T	4,609,915T	4,339	4,503	2.4	5.5	29	18	1.0	0.8
European Union	2,284,527T	220	3,041	6,164	1,213,816T	1,325,700T	3,419	3,575	3.1	5.7	56	47	0.7	0.6
Nordic countries	369,525T	247	5,829	15,654	104,343T	123,400T	4,678	5,270	3.0	4.8	-13	-168	0.6	0.4

Source: Columns 1-4: UN 1996a; columns 5-12: World Bank 1996g.

43 Natural resource use

HDI rank	Land area (1,000 ha) 1993	Forest and woodland (as % of land area) 1993	Arable land (as % of land area) 1993	Irrigated land (as % of arable land area) 1993	Wooded area (km² per 1,000 inhabitants; 1980=100) 1993	Imports of tropical products (as % of total imports of wood and cork) 1992	Internal renewable water resources per capita (1,000 m³ per year) 1995
High human development	3,258,483T	33.8	12.0	9.9	89.0	16.7	9.9
1 Canada	997,614	49.5	4.6	1.6	81.7	2.3	98.5
2 France	55,150	27.1	33.1	8.1	92.9	38.3	3.4
3 Norway	32,390	25.7	2.7	10.9	94.5	7.3	90.4
4 USA	980,943	29.2	18.9	11.1	87.9	8.9	9.4
5 Iceland	10,300	1.2	0.1	..	91.4	2.3	624.5
6 Netherlands	3,733	9.4	24.3	61.8	100.0	27.2	5.8
7 Japan	37,780	66.4	10.7	69.1	90.9	27.3	4.4
8 Finland	33,813	68.6	7.6	2.5	94.1	4.4	22.1
9 New Zealand	27,099	27.2	9.0	11.6	96.0	34.3	91.5
10 Sweden	44,996	62.2	6.2	4.1	97.6	2.6	20.5
11 Spain	50,478	32.0	29.7	23.0	97.6	28.3	2.8
12 Austria	8,385	38.6	16.9	0.3	98.0	1.9	11.3
13 Belgium	..	..	..	..	100.0	15.1	1.2
14 Australia	771,336	18.8	6.0	4.6	85.1	30.7	19.0
15 United Kingdom	24,488	10.0	24.8	1.8	100.0	12.2	1.2
16 Switzerland	4,129	30.3	9.6	6.3	94.7	2.2	6.9
17 Ireland	7,028	4.6	13.1	..	110.0	24.3	14.1
18 Denmark	4,309	10.3	58.9	17.1	90.0	3.3	2.5
19 Germany	35,691	30.0	32.7	3.9	100.0	13.4	2.1
20 Greece	13,199	19.8	18.3	54.4	92.6	18.3	5.6
21 Italy	30,127	22.5	30.0	30.0	109.1	16.6	2.9
23 Israel	2,106	6.0	16.6	51.4	..	..	0.4
27 Luxembourg	..	..	..	..	100.0	..	..
31 Portugal	9,239	35.7	25.5	26.7	110.0	58.2	7.1
34 Malta	32	..	37.5	8.3	..	..	..
35 Slovenia	..	..	..	..	..	..	..
39 Czech Rep.	7,886	33.3	40.2	0.8	..	..	5.7
42 Slovakia	4,901	40.6	30.3	5.4	..	..	5.8
48 Hungary	9,303	19.0	51.0	4.3	106.3	..	11.9
58 Poland	31,268	28.1	45.7	0.7	92.0	..	1.5
62 Belarus	20,760	33.7	29.4	1.6	..	..	7.3
Medium human development	2,244,526T	37.0	10.2	10.0	..	..	18.7
67 Russian Federation	1,707,540	45.6	7.6	3.1	..	..	30.6
69 Bulgaria	11,091	35.0	36.6	30.4	..	..	23.4
71 Estonia	4,510	44.8	25.0	..	..	..	11.5
76 Lithuania	6,520	30.7	34.6	..	..	..	6.5
77 Croatia	..	..	..	..	..	..	..
79 Romania	23,750	28.1	39.3	33.2	..	..	9.1
80 Macedonia, FYR	..	..	..	..	..	..	..
85 Turkmenistan	48,810	8.2	2.9	92.9	..	..	17.6
92 Latvia	6,450	44.0	26.2	..	..	..	13.3
93 Kazakstan	271,730	3.5	12.7	6.4	..	..	9.9
95 Ukraine	60,370	17.1	55.2	7.8	..	..	4.5
100 Uzbekistan	44,740	2.9	9.2	97.6	..	..	5.7
102 Albania	2,875	36.5	20.1	59.1	..	..	6.2
103 Armenia	2,980	14.1	16.2	59.4	..	..	3.7
105 Georgia	6,970	38.7	10.0	57.1	..	..	11.9
106 Azerbaijan	8,660	11.0	18.5	62.5	..	..	4.4
107 Kyrgyzstan	19,850	3.5	7.1	64.3	..	..	13.0
110 Moldova, Rep. of	3,370	12.5	51.8	17.8	..	..	3.1
115 Tajikistan	14,310	3.8	5.7	78.9	..	..	16.6
All developing countries	7,658,208T	29.3	9.2	25.7	..	..	7.6
Industrial countries	5,503,009T	35.1	11.3	9.9	89.0	..	12.2
World	13,161,217T	31.7	10.1	18.3	..	..	8.6
North America	1,978,557T	39.4	11.7	9.2	84.3	7.7	18.2
Eastern Europe and CIS	2,318,644T	36.7	11.2	9.0	..	..	16.0
Western and Southern Europe	342,999T	34.9	20.7	16.1	94.0	19.4	5.9
OECD	3,504,449T	33.2	12.3	11.2	88.7	16.7	9.1
European Union	320,636T	35.1	23.7	15.1	94.4	19.2	3.8
Nordic countries	125,808T	47.8	7.0	8.1	94.4	4.0	36.5

Source: Column 1: FAO 1994; *columns 2-4:* calculated on the basis of data from FAO 1994; *columns 5-7:* WRI 1996b.

44 Environment and pollution

		Greenhouse gas emissions (CO$_2$ emissions)		Major protected areas (as % of national territory) 1993[b]	Spent fuel produced (metric tons of heavy metal) 1993	Hazardous waste produced (1,000 metric tons) 1991-94	Municipal waste generated (kg per person) 1992	Population served by municipal waste services (%) 1993[a]	Waste recycling (as % of apparent consumption)	
HDI rank		Thousands of tons 1980	Share of world total (%) 1993[a]						Paper and cardboard 1990-93	Glass 1990-93
High human development		10,852,283T	50.00	11.7	8,424T	337,777T	519	97	42	42
1	Canada	459,390	2.10	8.9	1,690	7,786	660	100	32	75
2	France	416,140	1.91	9.7	1,250	4,000	470	100	42	46
3	Norway	38,490	0.18	17.1	..	151	510	97	32	67
4	USA	5,128,734	23.50	10.6	2,400	276,000	730	100	34	22
5	Iceland	2,763	(.)	8.8	..	6	560	95	30	75
6	Netherlands	178,950	0.82	10.2	15	1,430	500	100	53	76
7	Japan	1,146,360	5.25	7.3	876	..	410	100	51	56
8	Finland	56,330	0.26	8.1	68	560	620[c]	..	45	46
9	New Zealand	30,220	0.14	22.8	..	110	..	..	..	..
10	Sweden	55,440	0.25	6.6	230	..	370[c]	100	50	59
11	Spain	258,034	1.18	8.4	156	..	360	90	78	29
12	Austria	62,580	0.29	23.9	..	668	430[c]	99	78	68
13	Belgium	116,782	0.54	2.5	84	27,529	400	100	11	55
14	Australia	286,283	1.30	7.7	..	426	690	..	50	36
15	United Kingdom	564,351	2.59	20.3	1,080	1,957	..	100	32	29
16	Switzerland	49,295	0.23	17.7	85	837	400	99	54	78
17	Ireland	34,360	0.16	0.7	..	66	..	..	3	29
18	Denmark	61,190	0.28	32.2	..	91	460	100	36	62
19	Germany	921,740	4.22	25.8	490[d]	6,633[d]	360[c]	100	46	70
20	Greece	80,320	0.37	1.7	..	450	310	100	30	20
21	Italy	435,281	1.99	7.6	..	3,387	350	..	47	52
23	Israel	..	..	..	..	..	..	..	..	..
27	Luxembourg	11,815	0.05	13.9	..	86	490	100	..	..
31	Portugal	49,900	0.23	6.3	..	1,365	330	89	41	29
34	Malta	..	..	..	..	..	..	..	..	..
35	Slovenia	..	..	..	..	..	..	..	..	..
39	Czech Rep.	..	..	13.5	..	..	..	..	..	..
42	Slovakia	..	..	20.7	..	..	..	..	..	..
48	Hungary	64,325	0.29	6.2	..	795	390	63	..	..
58	Poland	343,210	1.57	9.8	..	3,444	340	55	..	..
62	Belarus	..	..	..	..	..	..	..	..	..
Medium human development		..	..	..	..	..	..	..	..	..
67	Russian Federation	..	..	..	..	..	..	..	..	..
69	Bulgaria	..	..	..	..	..	..	..	..	..
71	Estonia	..	..	..	..	..	..	..	..	..
76	Lithuania	..	..	..	..	..	..	..	..	..
77	Croatia	..	..	..	..	..	..	..	..	..
79	Romania	..	..	..	..	..	..	..	..	..
80	Macedonia, FYR	..	..	..	..	..	..	..	..	..
85	Turkmenistan	..	..	..	..	..	..	..	..	..
92	Latvia	..	..	..	..	..	..	..	..	..
93	Kazakstan	..	..	..	..	..	..	..	..	..
95	Ukraine	..	..	..	..	..	..	..	..	..
100	Uzbekistan	..	..	..	..	..	..	..	..	..
102	Albania	..	..	..	..	..	..	..	..	..
103	Armenia	..	..	..	..	..	..	..	..	..
105	Georgia	..	..	..	..	..	..	..	..	..
106	Azerbaijan	..	..	..	..	..	..	..	..	..
107	Kyrgyzstan	..	..	..	..	..	..	..	..	..
110	Moldova, Rep. of	..	..	..	..	..	..	..	..	..
115	Tajikistan	..	..	..	..	..	..	..	..	..
All developing countries		..	..	..	..	..	..	..	..	..
Industrial countries		10,852,283T	50.00	11.7	..	..	..	..	..	..
World		..	..	..	..	..	..	..	..	..
North America		5,588,124T	26.00	10.4	4,090T	283,786T	723	100	34	27
Eastern Europe and CIS		..	..	..	..	..	..	..	..	..
Western and Southern Europe		2,829,410T	13.00	13.4	..	47,259T	394	98	48	53
OECD		10,852,283T	50.00	11.7	..	337,777T	519	97	42	42
European Union		3,303,213T	15.00	14.4	3,373T	48,222T	393	98	46	49
Nordic countries		214,213T	1.00	14.5	..	808T	471	99	42	59

a. Data refer to 1993 or latest year available from 1990 on.
b. National classifications may differ. Includes only areas greater than 10 square kilometres except for islands.
c. Data refer to 1990.
d. Data refer to former territory of the Federal Republic of Germany.
Source: Columns 1-3 and 6-9: OECD 1995b; columns 4 and 5: calculated on the basis of data from OECD 1995b.

45 National income accounts

HDI rank	GDP (US$ billions) 1994	Agri-culture (as % of GDP) 1994	Industry (as % of GDP) 1994	Services (as % of GDP) 1994	Consumption Private (as % of GDP) 1994	Consumption Government (as % of GDP) 1994	Gross domestic investment (as % of GDP)a 1994	Gross domestic savings (as % of GDP)a 1994	Tax revenue (as % of GNP) 1994	Central government expenditure (as % of GNP) 1994	Exports (as % of GDP) 1994	Imports (as % of GDP) 1994
High human development	20,142T	2	35	63	62	16	20	21	25	34	22	22
1 Canada	543	..	..	..	61	22	18	18	20	..	35	39
2 France	1,330	2	28	70	61	19	18	20	38	47	32	31
3 Norway	110	..	..	..	52	22	20	26	37	50	46	42
4 USA	6,648	..	..	..	68	17	16	15	19	23	13	14
5 Iceland	..	..	..	..	..	..	..	..	..	..	..	..
6 Netherlands	330	3	27	70	61	15	19	24	45	53	60	55
7 Japan	4,591	2	40	58	58	10	30	32	18	..	13	10
8 Finland	98	5	32	63	57	23	14	20	30	48	37	36
9 New Zealand	51	..	..	..	60	15	21	24	34	36	32	36
10 Sweden	196	2	30	68	55	28	13	17	32	51	43	41
11 Spain	483	3	..	..	63	18	20	19	30	37	23	25
12 Austria	197	2	34	64	55	19	25	26	34	42	42	43
13 Belgium	228	2	..	..	62	15	18	23	43	50	99	92
14 Australia	332	3	30	67	63	18	20	19	21	28	18	21
15 United Kingdom	1,017	2	32	66	64	22	15	14	32	43	38	37
16 Switzerland	260	..	..	..	59	14	22	27	20	..	46	39
17 Ireland	52	8	9	83	56	16	14	28	39	47	78	76
18 Denmark	146	4	27	69	52	26	14	21	33	46	50	46
19 Germany	2,046	1	..	..	58	20	22	22	30	34	28	27
20 Greece	78	16	31	53	73	19	18	8	26	43	20	29
21 Italy	1,025	3	31	66	62	18	17	20	39	50	27	25
23 Israel	78	..	..	..	61	26	23	13	34	44	32	44
27 Luxembourg	..	..	..	..	..	..	..	..	..	..	..	..
31 Portugal	87	..	..	..	66	17	26	17	29	43	28	35
34 Malta	..	..	..	..	..	..	..	..	..	..	..	..
35 Slovenia	14	5	38	57	55	21	21	25	..	..	62	58
39 Czech Rep.	36	6	39	55	58	22	20	20	38	43	54	55
42 Slovakia	12	7	36	57	53	24	17	23	..	..	74	69
48 Hungary	41	7	33	60	72	13	21	15	..	..	28	40
58 Poland	93	6	40	54	64	19	16	17	38	45	24	28
62 Belarus	20	17	54	29	51	22	35	27	31	38	14	17
Medium human development	603T	13	39	48	53	20	26	27	..	..	18	19
67 Russian Federation	377	7	38	55	50	21	27	29	19	28	16	16
69 Bulgaria	10	13	35	53	64	15	21	21	29	44	54	54
71 Estonia	5	10	36	55	48	24	32	28	29	..	26	27
76 Lithuania	5	21	41	38	76	13	18	11	18	21	41	47
77 Croatia	14	13	25	62	60	28	14	12	42	42	48	49
79 Romania	30	21	33	46	62	13	27	25	27	32	24	26
80 Macedonia, FYR	2	..	..	..	89	7	18	4	..	..	73	103
85 Turkmenistan	5	..	..	..	..	..	..	..	..	..	..	..
92 Latvia	6	9	34	57	53	22	9	25	25	29	22	25
93 Kazakhstan	18	44	35	21	60	20	24	20	..	..	17	22
95 Ukraine	91	19	50	31	..	..	..	..	..	..	16	17
100 Uzbekistan	22	33	34	34	51	25	23	24	..	..	17	17
102 Albania	2	55	22	23	100	15	13	-15	..	..	15	43
103 Armenia	3	49	30	26	101	18	10	-19	..	..	10	20
105 Georgia	2	61	23	16	..	..	..	..	..	..	..	..
106 Azerbaijan	4	27	32	41	96	..	23	4	..	..	18	24
107 Kyrgyzstan	3	37	30	33	74	11	30	14	..	..	13	18
110 Moldova, Rep. of	4	48	28	25	79	21	8	..	..	..	17	22
115 Tajikistan	2	..	..	..	..	..	..	..	..	..	..	..
All developing countries	4,280T	15	36	50	61	13	27	27	14	..	26	28
Industrial countries	20,744T	3	35	62	62	17	21	21	24	33	22	22
World	25,024T	6	35	58	62	16	22	22	23	..	23	23
North America	7,191T	..	..	..	68	17	16	15	19	23	14	16
Eastern Europe and CIS	819T	12	39	50	56	20	24	24	..	..	22	24
Western and Southern Europe	6,665T	2	..	..	..	19	19	21	34	43	35	34
OECD	20,525T	2	..	63	63	16	20	21	24	33	22	22
European Union	7,313T	2	30	68	60	20	19	20	34	43	35	34
Nordic countries	550T	3	29	67	54	25	15	20	33	49	44	42

Note: The percentage shares of agriculture, industry and services may not necessarily add to 100 because of rounding.
a. Includes public and private investment and savings.
Source: Columns 1-12: World Bank 1996g.

Trends in economic performance

HDI rank	GNP (US$ billions) 1994	GNP annual growth rate (%) 1980-93	GNP per capita annual growth rate (%)		Average annual rate of inflation (%)		Exports as % of GDP (% annual growth rate) 1980-93	Tax revenue as % of GNP (% annual growth rate) 1980-92	Overall budget surplus/deficit (as % of GNP)	
			1965-80	1980-93	1984-94	1993			1980	1994
High human development	20,252T	2.5	3.0	1.9	4.3	5.2	2.2	1.4	-4.4	-3.8
1 Canada	570	2.2	3.3	1.4	3.1	1.1	3.2	1.2	-3.6	-4.5
2 France	1,355	1.8	3.7	1.6	2.9	2.2	1.9	0.4	-0.1	-5.5
3 Norway	114	2.6	3.6	2.2	3.0	1.0	2.9	-0.5	-2.0	-7.5
4 USA	6,737	2.4	1.8	1.7	3.3	2.0	2.8	(.)	-2.8	-3.0
5 Iceland	7	2.0	..	1.2	..	2.9	-0.2		..	..
6 Netherlands	338	1.9	2.7	1.7	1.6	1.6	2.2	0.3	-4.5	-0.5
7 Japan	4,321	3.6	5.1	3.4	1.3	0.8	1.6	2.0	-7.0	-1.6
8 Finland	96	1.1	3.6	1.5	4.2	2.3	1.7	0.9	-2.2	-14.1
9 New Zealand	47	1.8	1.7	0.7	4.6	0.9	2.3	0.9	-6.8	0.8
10 Sweden	206	0.9	2.0	1.3	5.8	2.6	2.5	2.0	-8.1	-13.4
11 Spain	525	2.4	4.1	2.7	6.5	4.4	3.6	2.9	-4.2	-4.8
12 Austria	198	2.0	4.0	2.0	3.2	3.6	2.4	0.1	-3.4	-5.1
13 Belgium	231	1.7	3.6	1.9	3.2	4.4	2.4	0.2	-8.2	-6.1
14 Australia	321	2.7	2.2	1.6	4.1	1.1	3.9	2.1	-1.5	-2.9
15 United Kingdom	1,070	2.0	2.0	2.3	5.4	3.4	1.1	1.0	-4.6	-6.6
16 Switzerland	265	1.5	1.5	1.1	3.7	2.1	1.3	..	-0.2	..
17 Ireland	48	3.1	2.8	3.6	2.0	3.6	4.7	1.6	-12.9	-2.3
18 Denmark	145	1.8	2.2	2.0	2.9	1.2	2.4	0.7	-2.7	-5.7
19 Germany	2,076	2.8	3.0	2.1	..	3.9	-0.1	0.4	..	-2.5
20 Greece	80	1.3	4.8	0.9	15.5	12.6	4.8	0.8	-4.8	-15.6
21 Italy	1,101	1.7	3.2	2.1	6.2	4.4	2.8	2.8	-10.7	-10.6
23 Israel	78	4.4	3.7	2.0	18.0	11.0	1.1	-5.4	-16.1	-3.0
27 Luxembourg	16	3.2	..	2.8	..	6.2	1.0	..	..	..
31 Portugal	92	2.6	4.6	3.3	12.0	7.4	3.7	1.4	-8.7	-2.2
34 Malta	..	3.8	..	3.2	..	3.3	-0.3	..	..	..
35 Slovenia	14	..	..	..	..	..	..	..	..	..
39 Czech Rep.	33	..	..	..	11.8	15.6	..	..	..	0.9
42 Slovakia	12	..	..	..	9.8	15.2	..	..	..	..
48 Hungary	39	0.4	5.1	1.2	19.4	21.5	-0.3	0.1	-2.9	-2.4
58 Poland	95	0.7	..	0.4	97.8	31.1	3.2	..	..	-2.4
62 Belarus	22	1.8	..	2.4	136.7	1,428.7	..	..	..	-5.2
Medium human development	597T	-1.8	..	-2.5	141.7	1,208.0	..	..	..	..
67 Russian Federation	393	-1.8	..	-1.0	124.3	873.5	..	..	..	-10.7
69 Bulgaria	10	0.2	..	0.5	42.2	57.5	-11.0	..	..	-4.5
71 Estonia	4	-3.9	..	-2.2	77.3	81.2	..	..	..	1.2
76 Lithuania	5	-3.9	..	-2.8	102.3	342.7	..	..	..	1.7
77 Croatia	12	..	..	..	..	..	..	..	..	..
79 Romania	28	-2.3	..	-2.4	62.0	225.9	-1.2	..	0.5	-2.5
80 Macedonia, FYR	2	..	..	..	..	..	..	..	..	..
85 Turkmenistan	..	..	..	..	58.6	..	..	..	..	..
92 Latvia	6	-2.7	..	-0.6	69.8	74.2	..	..	..	-4.4
93 Kazakhstan	19	-2.0	..	-1.6	150.2	1,255.5	..	..	..	..
95 Ukraine	81	-0.5	..	0.2	297.0	3,691.2	..	..	..	..
100 Uzbekistan	21	1.7	..	-0.2	109.1	914.5	..	..	..	..
102 Albania	1	-1.5	..	-3.2	32.7	105.7	-2.7	..	..	..
103 Armenia	3	-14.8	..	-4.2	138.6	1,480.7	..	..	..	..
105 Georgia	..	-9.4	..	-6.6	228.3	..	..	..	..	..
106 Azerbaijan	4	-4.5	..	-3.5	122.8	714.5	..	..	..	..
107 Kyrgyzstan	3	0.2	..	0.1	100.9	792.2	..	..	..	..
110 Moldova, Rep. of	4	..	..	-2.0	..	..	..	..	..	..
115 Tajikistan	2	-4.0	..	-3.6	104.3	1,251.7	..	..	..	..
All developing countries	4,536T	4.0	3.2	2.0	164.6	298.2	3.2	..	..	-1.9
Industrial countries	20,849T	2.3	3.0	1.7	12.5	70.9	2.1	..	..	-3.9
World	25,385T	2.6	2.0	0.9	34.9	103.0	2.3	..	..	-3.6
North America	7,307T	2.4	1.9	1.4	3.3	1.9	2.8	..	-2.9	-3.1
Eastern Europe and CIS	812T	-1.4	..	-2.0	134.4	1,072.8	..	..	..	..
Western and Southern Europe	6,894T	2.1	3.2	1.7	4.5	3.4	1.8	1.1	-4.8	-5.6
OECD	20,643T	2.5	2.8	1.7	4.8	3.0	2.2	1.3	-4.3	-3.8
European Union	7,577T	2.1	3.0	1.8	4.7	3.5	1.7	1.1	-5.0	-5.7
Nordic countries	568T	1.5	2.6	1.2	4.3	1.9	2.4	1.0	-4.6	-10.3

Source: Column 1: World Bank 1996e; columns 2, 5, 9 and 10: World Bank 1996g; columns 6-8: calculated on the basis of data from World Bank 1995d.

47 Regional aggregates of human development indicators

	Sub-Saharan Africa	Arab States	South Asia	East Asia	East Asia excl. China	South-East Asia and Pacific	Latin America and the Caribbean	Least developed countries	All developing countries	Eastern Europe and CIS	Industrial countries[a]	World
Table 1: Human development index												
Life expectancy (years)	50.0	62.9	61.4	69.0	71.5	64.3	69.0	50.4	61.8	68.1	74.1	63.2
Adult literacy rate	55.9	54.7	49.7	81.8	96.2	86.3	86.2	48.1	69.7	98.1	98.5	77.1
Combined 1st, 2nd and 3rd level gross enrolment ratio	42	58	53	59	78	61	69	36	56	75	83	60
Real GDP per capita (PPP$)	1,377	4,450	1,686	3,001	9,429	3,638	5,873	965	2,904	4,203	15,986	5,798
Human development index	0.380	0.636	0.459	0.652	0.881	0.672	0.829	0.336	0.576	0.760	0.911	0.764
Table 2: Gender-related development index												
Life expectancy (years)												
Female	51.5	64.8	61.2	71.3	74.9	66.5	72.1	51.2	63.5	72.9	77.8	65.4
Male	48.5	62.0	60.7	66.9	68.0	62.7	65.9	49.1	60.6	63.2	70.2	61.8
Adult literacy rate												
Female	44.4	40.6	34.3	72.0	95.1	82.7	84.9	34.7	60.3	98.1	98.5	70.8
Male	64.3	66.9	61.6	90.0	98.2	91.6	87.3	56.6	78.4	98.1	98.5	83.5
Combined primary, secondary and tertiary gross enrolment ratio												
Female	38.4	53.7	43.2	55.9	76.4	58.9	68.6	30.7	51.6	76.5	83.9	57.1
Male	46.6	63.3	59.6	61.9	82.2	61.8	69.0	40.0	60.3	73.3	81.5	63.9
Earned income share												
Female	35.5	21.7	25.3	37.7	28.1	34.9	26.9	33.1	31.7	40.2	37.7	33.3
Male	64.6	78.9	74.8	62.3	72.0	65.2	73.1	67.2	68.4	59.9	62.4	66.9
Gender-related development index	0.374	0.537	0.412	0.626	0.823	0.641	0.729	0.323	0.555	0.749	0.856	0.637
Table 3: Gender empowerment measure (% women)												
Seats held in parliament	..	..	6.9	20.3	..	11.1	9.6	..	12.7	..	13.6	12.9
Administrators and managers	..	..	2.9	11.3	..	14.7	20.0	..	10.0	..	27.4	14.1
Professional and technical workers	..	..	21.3	45.1	..	46.5	49.5	..	36.7	..	47.8	39.3
Earned income share	..	..	30	40	..	30	40	..	30	..	40	40
Gender empowerment measure	..	..	0.231	0.474	..	0.399	0.418	..	0.367	..	0.586	0.418
Table 5: Trends in human development and per capita income												
GDP per capita (1987 US$)												
1960	495	989	193	98	..	282	1,122	247	330	658	6,448	2,049
1970	598	1,893	229	135	..	370	1,435	259	461	1,108	9,546	2,756
1980	634	2,757	363	230	2,379	575	1,965	252	671	1,701	11,562	3,205
1990	514	1,740	462	455	4,674	756	1,793	242	723	1,954	14,119	3,470
1994	507	1,595	514	659	5,759	935	1,931	254	823	1,370	14,473	3,402
Table 7: Profile of human development												
Life expectancy (years)	50.0	62.9	61.4	69.0	71.5	64.3	69.0	50.4	61.8	68.1	74.1	63.2
Access to health services (%)	53	87	78	88	..	85	..	49	80	..	..	..
Access to safe water (%)	51	76	82	68	93	66	75	57	71	..	..	..
Access to sanitation (%)	45	52	35	27	..	56	61	36	39	..	..	..
Daily calorie supply per capita	2,096	2,874	2,367	2,751	3,107	2,541	2,756	2,054	2,553	..	..	..
Adult literacy rate	56.2	55.7	49.7	81.6	96.7	86.3	86.2	48.4	69.7	..	..	..
Combined 1st and 2nd level gross enrolment ratio	53	73	67	88	95	78	89	46	74	91	98	78
Daily newspapers (copies per 100)	1.1	4.5	..	4.3	36.4	3.6	7.3	0.8	4.0	19.5	26.4	9.8
Televisions (per 100)	3	12	5	23	26	14	21	2	14	30	50	22
Real GDP per capita (PPP$)	1,373	4,450	1,686	3,001	9,429	3,638	5,873	951	2,908	4,203	15,986	5,806
GNP per capita (US$)	539	1,978	325	904	9,425	1,279	3,188	210	1,053	2,125	17,221	4,797
Table 8: Trends in human development[b]												
Life expectancy (years)												
1960	39.9	45.5	43.9	47.5	54.5	45.3	55.3	39.1	46.0	66.6	68.6	50.2
1994	49.9	63.0	61.3	69.0	71.5	64.3	69.0	50.6	62.1	68.0	73.8	63.7
Infant mortality rate												
1960	166	166	163	146	84	127	107	170	149	55	39	129
1994	97	67	73	41	17	50	38	103	64	25	14	58
Access to safe water (%)												
1975-80	24	71	30[c]	..	70	15	60	..	41	..	..	..
1990-96	42	83	76[c]	..	94	67	75	..	69	..	..	..
Underweight children under five (%)												
1975	31	20	69	26	..	46	18	..	41	..	..	..
1990-96	32	14	50	16	..	35	11	..	32	..	..	..
Adult literacy rate												
1970	27	30	32	..	..	65	72	..	43	..	..	..
1994	56	57	49	..	..	87	86	..	64	..	..	..
Gross enrolment ratio, all levels (age 6-23)												
1980	39	47	37	51	65	51	59	32	46	..	..	..
1994	39	58	53	59	79	61	70	36	56	..	..	..
Real GDP per capita (PPP$)												
1960	990	..	698	729	..	732	2,137	561	915	..	..	..
1994	1,460	..	1,687	2,983	..	4,149	5,933	974	2,923	..	..	..

	Sub-Saharan Africa	Arab States	South Asia	East Asia	East Asia excl. China	South-East Asia and Pacific	Latin America and the Caribbean	Least developed countries	All developing countries	Eastern Europe and CIS	Industrial countries[a]	World
Table 9: South-North gaps (Index: North=100)												
Life expectancy												
1960	58	66	64	70	80	66	81	57	67	97	100	73
1994	68	85	83	93	97	87	94	68	84	92	100	86
Adult literacy												
1970	27	30	32	..	..	66	73	..	43	..	100	..
1994	56	57	50	..	..	87	87	..	64	..	100	..
Daily calorie supply per capita												
1965	75	71	71	70	78	70	83	71	72	..	100	..
1992	67	91	76	88	96	81	88	66	82	..	100	..
Access to safe water												
1975-80	..	..	..	..	..	..	60	..	..	..	100	..
1990-96	..	..	..	..	..	..	76	..	..	..	100	..
Under-five mortality												
1960	17	18	17	21	36	24	30	15	21	..	100	..
1995	12	34	18	44	148	35	49	12	29	..	100	..
Table 10: Women and capabilities												
Female net enrolment ratio												
Primary												
1992	54	78	..	95	..	..	..	..	86	..	96	89
Index (1980=100)	..	118	..	..	..	..	..	..	..	..	..	..
Secondary												
1992	..	44	..	..	..	..	..	..	..	..	..	..
Index (1980=100)	..	..	..	..	..	..	..	..	..	..	..	..
Female tertiary students												
1992	222	916	..	235	..	1,429	..	109	559	2,595	3,407	1,377
Index (1980=100)	227	222	..	239	..	..	..	..	..	..	134	212
Female life expectancy												
1994	52	64	62	71	75	66	72	52	63	73	78	65
Index (1970=100)	114	125	128	115	120	127	117	118	121	102	106	119
Total fertility rate												
1994	6.2	4.7	3.6	1.8	1.8	3.2	3.0	5.6	3.6	2.0	1.8	3.4
Index (1970=100)	93	67	60	32	35	56	54	84	60	68	73	61
Table 11: Women and political and economic participation												
Administrators and managers												
Female (%)	10	13	3	11	..	15	20	9	10	..	27	14
Female as % of male	12	16	3	13	..	19	26	10	12	..	44	19
Professional and technical workers												
Female (%)	28	30	21	45	..	47	50	24	36	..	48	39
Female as % of male	43	44	27	82	..	94	102	33	64	..	95	71
Clerical and sales workers												
Female (%)	..	..	..	40	..	..	..	..	..	..	..	..
Female as % of male	..	..	..	66	..	..	..	..	..	..	..	..
Service workers												
Female (%)	..	..	..	52	..	57	..	..	..	..	..	..
Female as % of male	..	..	..	109	..	133	..	..	..	..	..	..
Share of women												
in government	6.6	2.0	5.2	3.9	1.4	5.9	11.3	6.0	5.5	3.5	12.5	7.4
at ministerial level	7.4	..	4.3	6.2	2.7	5.0	8.0	7.8	5.8	4.1	12.1	7.4
at sub-ministerial level	7.4	2.2	5.3	3.4	1.2	5.9	12.0	6.2	5.6	3.9	12.7	7.5
Table 12: Child survival and development												
Pregnant women with anaemia (%)	..	..	85	..	..	62	..	..	..	..	..	..
Births attended by trained health personnel (%)	38	58	33	85	99	57	76	30	54	..	99	58
Low-birth-weight infants (%)	16	11	32	9	9	15	10	23	18	..	6	17
Maternal mortality rate	971	380	554	95	99	447	190	1,030	471	63	31	416
Infant mortality rate	97	67	73	41	17	50	38	103	64	25	14	58
Under-five mortality rate	174	65	112	46	20	71	46	169	95	35	18	85
Mothers breast-feeding at six months (%)	94	..	79	60	..	91	50	..	72	..	..	..
Oral rehydration therapy use rate (%)	73	55	44	85	..	92	..	82	67	..	..	..
Underweight children under five (%)	31	16	50	16	..	36	11	42	31	..	..	..
Table 13: Health profile												
One-year-olds fully immunized												
against tuberculosis (%)	69	93	92	92	96	89	96	74	87	94	91	87
against measles (%)	53	83	75	93	93	79	84	59	76	91	85	77
AIDS cases (per 100,000)	22	..	..	..	..	4	5	14	5	0	6	5
Tuberculosis cases (per 100,000)	94	41	111	32	..	80	50	85	69	49	27	60
Malaria cases (per 100,000)	..	89	228	6	..	178	220	..	206	..	..	..
Cigarette consumption (1970-72=100)	120	153	134	141	116	108	94	133	113	..	93	103
Population per doctor	18,514	1,516	3,704	..	..	6,193	1,042	19,035	5,833	..	..	..
Population per nurse	6,548	..	5,468	..	..	..	..	13,842	4,691	..	..	..
People with disabilities (%)	..	2.0	0.8	4.9	..	1.7	..	..	2.6	..	..	..
Public expenditure on health												
as % of GNP (1960)	0.7	0.9	0.6	0.9	..	1.7	..	..	0.9	..	..	..
as % of GDP (1990)	2.5	2.9	1.4	2.3	..	1.0	2.4	1.8	2.1	..	..	..

	Sub-Saharan Africa	Arab States	South Asia	East Asia	East Asia excl. China	South-East Asia and Pacific	Latin America and the Caribbean	Least developed countries	All developing countries	Eastern Europe and CIS	Industrial countries[a]	World
Table 14: Food security												
Food production per capita (1979-81=100)	97	121	120	142	87	128	104	94	123	..	96	118
Agricultural production (as % of GDP)	20	..	28	15	..	16	10	37	15	12	3	6
Food consumption (as % of total household consumption)	45	..	51	60	..	44	34	..	51			
Daily calorie supply per capita	2,096	2,874	2,367	2,751	3,107	2,541	2,756	2,054	2,553	..	..	..
Per capita food supply from fish and seafood												
Total (kg)	8	5	4	13	52	19	8	7	9	..	29	13
% change since 1980-82	-8	-6	34	103	30	18	-4	12	44	..	19	39
Food imports (as % of merchandise imports)												
1980	11	..	12	..	..	10	13	15	13	..	11	11
1994	10	..	9	4	..	4	9	16	7	11	6	6
Cereal imports (1,000 metric tons; total)	10,162	34,873	9,319	29,292	12,961	13,148	31,571	7,651	129,243	12,916	90,212	219,455
Food aid in cereals (1,000 metric tons; total)	2,752	705	1,672	..	..	205	1,079	3,752	6,427	2,799	..	..
Table 15: Education imbalances												
Secondary technical enrolment (as % of total secondary)	..	8.7	..	..	..	..	..	..	..	..	..	..
Tertiary natural and applied science enrolment (as % of total tertiary)	31	25	26	47	..	23	27	26	33	45	30	32
Tertiary students abroad (as % of those at home)	..	..	..	..	..	..	..	..	..	..	..	..
R & D scientists and technicians (per 1,000)	..	..	0.1	0.4	..	0.2	0.2	..	0.3	3.6	3.3	1.0
Public expenditure on education as % of GNP												
1980	5.1	4.1	4.3	2.9	..	2.7	3.7	3.1	3.8	4.1	5.8	5.5
1993-94	5.5	..	3.5	3.3	..	2.9	3.6	2.8	3.6	5.4	5.4	5.1
as % of total government expenditure	..	..	..	..	..	..	..	..	..	..	..	..
Public expenditure (as % of all levels)												
on primary and secondary education	..	..	..	..	..	..	..	..	..	..	..	..
on higher education	..	..	..	..	..	..	..	..	..	..	..	..
Table 16: Employment												
Labour force (as % of population)	45	33	42	59	47	47	40	47	47	49	49	48
Women's share of labour force												
1970	43	23	34	42	37	38	24	43	37	48	40	38
1990	42	24	32	45	41	42	32	43	39	47	44	40
Labour force in agriculture (%)												
1960	81	71	76	82	58	76	50	86	77	42	27	61
1990	66	37	62	70	23	58	26	74	61	19	10	49
Labour force in industry (%)												
1960	7	11	11	7	17	7	20	5	9	30	35	17
1990	9	22	16	16	34	14	24	10	16	39	33	20
Labour force in services (%)												
1960	12	18	14	11	25	17	30	9	14	28	38	22
1990	25	42	21	14	43	28	50	17	23	42	57	31
Real earnings per employee growth rate												
1970-80	..	..	..	..	..	..	..	..	..	..	..	..
1980-92	..	..	1.6	..	..	..	..	..	..	..	..	..
Table 17: Communication profile												
Radios (per 1,000)	149	259	88	214	702	154	349	96	178	420	1,018	361
Televisions (per 100)	3	12	5	23	26	14	21	2	14	30	50	22
Book titles published (per 100,000)	..	4	2	11	..	6	..	..	7	25	52	18
Printing and writing paper consumed (metric tons per 1,000)	2.3	3.9	1.8	9.4	34.6	6.0	10.7	0.5	5.8	6.0	74.0	20.6
Post offices (per 100,000)	..	..	16.9	..	..	6.0	..	..	..	..	..	..
Main telephone lines (per 100)	1.1	4.6	1.3	3.9	29.4	2.4	8.1	0.3	3.3	15.0	40.1	11.5
International telephone calls (minutes per person)	1.4	8.8	0.6	2.5	26.8	3.2	4.7	0.5	2.5	5.9	35.1	9.4
Fax machines (per 100)	..	0.1	(.)	0.1	0.8	0.1	..	..	0.1	0.1	2.8	0.7
Mobile cellular telephone subscribers (per 100)	..	0.2	..	0.2	..	0.4	0.5	..	0.3	0.1	4.1	1.4
Internet users (per 10,000)	..	..	(.)	1.4	..	1.6	2.0	..	1.5	6.4	223.2	60.9
Personal computers (per 100)	..	..	0.1	..	..	0.8	..	..	..	..	14.2	..

	Sub-Saharan Africa	Arab States	South Asia	East Asia	East Asia excl. China	South-East Asia and Pacific	Latin America and the Caribbean	Least developed countries	All developing countries	Eastern Europe and CIS	Industrial countries[a]	World
Table 18: Social investment												
Social security benefits expenditure (as % of GDP)	..	..	0.7	..	..	..	..	..	..	..	..	..
Share of central government expenditure on social security and welfare												
1980	..	..	..	..	..	..	..	..	..	..	..	..
1992-95	..	..	..	..	..	..	..	..	..	..	..	..
on housing and community amenities												
1980	..	..	..	..	..	3.8	..	..	..	..	..	..
1992-95	..	..	6.9	..	..	3.5	..	..	..	..	..	..
on health												
1980	..	..	2.0	..	..	4.3	..	..	..	..	..	..
1992-95	..	..	2.5	..	..	17.5	..	..	..	..	..	..
on education												
1980	..	..	2.5	..	..	14.5	..	..	..	..	..	..
1992-95	..	..	2.0	..	..	5.0	..	..	..	..	..	..
Table 19: Military expenditure and resource use imbalances												
Defence expenditure												
US$ millions (total)												
1985	9,909	65,952	31,512	41,421	14,314	15,779	19,129	6,145	186,917	..	636,637	823,554
1995	7,842	33,766	15,559	51,341	19,610	18,632	20,175	4,935	153,628	93,297	643,515	797,143
as % of GDP												
1985	3	12	15	7	..	6	2	4	7	..	4	5
1995	3	..	3	5	..	3	2	3	3	5	3	3
per capita (US$)												
1985	22	365	32	37	225	38	47	14	52	..	742	185
1995	14	143	12	40	277	39	43	9	35	233	526	143
Military expenditure (as % of education and health expenditure)												
1960	..	75	89	363	..	127	56	..	102	..	110	109
1990-91	44	108	61	85	..	66	29	71	63	..	33	38
Imports of conventional weapons												
US$ millions (total)	..	..	..	..	..	..	..	..	..	..	..	..
Index (1990=100)	..	..	45	416	..	..	..	..	113	..	..	..
Armed forces												
Thousands (total)	967	2,298	2,521	4,712	1,782	1,805	1,326	1,316	14,125	3,328	7,555	21,680
Index (1985=100)	107	108	115	88	121	86	100	122	96	..	80	92
Table 20: Resource flows												
External debt												
US$ billions (total)	213[d]	..	178	156	..	258	529	89	1,444	217	..	..
as % of GNP	79[d]	..	41	18	..	54	35	106	38	27	..	..
Debt service ratio												
1980	10[d]	..	10	13	..	15	40	18	24	..	..	..
1994	14[d]	..	25	8	..	18	30	16	20	11	..	..
Net ODA received (US$ millions; total)	18,299[e]	4,941	5,106	3,815	294	5,677	6,058	16,467[e]	59,876[e]	..	..	..
as % of 1994 GNP	12.6[e]	0.6	2.6	0.4	0.1	3.6	0.5	17.5[e]	1.4	..	..	..
per capita (US$)	31.7	21.7	4.1	3.0	4.0	23.5	12.9	29.2	11.3	..	..	..
Net foreign direct investment (as % of GNP)	0.6	..	0.3	2.5	..	3.4	1.0	2.0	1.5	0.9	-0.4	-0.1
Export-import ratio	84	..	84	101	..	94	78	58	90	93	101	99
Terms of trade (1987=100)	95	..	97	104	..	94	96	91	97	..	104	102
Current account balance (US$ millions; total)	-10,977	..	-1,431	2,794	..	-17,765	-50,929	-7,059	-90,577	-11,085	40,659	..
Table 21: Growing urbanization												
Urban population (% of total)												
1960	15	31	18	20	36	18	50	9	22	47	61	34
1994	31	52	28	32	75	33	74	22	37	66	74	45
2000	35	55	31	37	79	37	77	26	41	68	75	47
Urban population growth rate												
1960-94	5.6	4.6	3.9	3.2	4.4	4.2	3.6	5.7	3.9	2.0	1.4	3.3
1994-2000	5.1	3.6	3.5	3.7	2.2	3.8	2.5	5.4	3.7	0.8	0.8	2.5
Population in cities of more than 750,000												
as % of total population	10	20	10	12	41	12	31	8	14	18	29	17
as % of urban population	34	40	39	39	54	37	42	47	39	27	39	39
Table 22: Demographic profile												
Estimated population (millions; total)												
1960	210.9	92.5	585.4	697.1	39.6	226.7	214.0	226.9	2,053.6	302.5	940.7	2,994.3
1994	535.4	236.0	1,270.0	1,283.0	74.7	478.8	463.9	534.2	4,325.5	400.6	1,228.3	5,553.8
2000	632.0	272.4	1,413.0	1,356.2	79.9	527.6	509.3	619.9	4,773.7	400.6	1,251.9	6,025.6
Population growth rate												
1960-94	2.8	2.8	2.3	1.8	1.9	2.2	2.3	2.5	2.2	0.8	0.8	1.8
1994-2000	2.8	2.4	1.8	0.9	1.1	1.6	1.6	2.5	1.7	..	0.3	1.4
Population doubling date	2019	2023	2033	2069	2056	2037	2039	2022	2036	..	2212	2045
Crude birth rate	44	33	29	18	18	26	25	40	27	14	13	24
Crude death rate	16	8	10	7	6	8	7	15	9	12	10	9
Total fertility rate	6.1	4.5	3.5	1.8	1.8	3.0	2.8	5.3	3.1	1.8	1.7	2.8
Contraceptive prevalence rate	15.9	37.1	40.1	82.5	74.0	53.2	60.2	20.9	55.5	..	70.5	58.2

	Sub-Saharan Africa	Arab States	South Asia	East Asia	East Asia excl. China	South-East Asia and Pacific	Latin America and the Caribbean	Least developed countries	All developing countries	Eastern Europe and CIS	Industrial countries[a]	World
Table 23: Energy use												
Electricity consumption												
Total (millions of kilowatt-hours)	244,316	285,262	537,789	1,185,738	259,701	243,434	728,905	40,178	3,305,423	1,703,165	9,176,061	12,481,484
Index (1970=100)	243	1,233	680	855	818	931	485	218	691	..	212	277
Per capita (kilowatt-hours)												
1970	107	205	112	161	622	89	547	61	180	..	4,933	1,088
1994	418	1,229	421	936	3,454	514	1,556	74	763	4,269	7,514	2,258
Traditional fuels (as % of total consumption)												
1973	..	..	..	..	..	..	..	..	..	..	..	..
1993	..	..	..	..	..	..	..	..	..	..	..	..
Household energy from fuelwood (%)	..											
Commercial energy use												
Total (millions of metric tons)												
1980	..	93	148	460	..	70	292	..	1,180	1,254	493	6,117
1994	132	210	363	920	150	205	422	20	2,309	1,199	5,462	7,771
Per capita (kg)												
1980	..	849	161	449	..	225	917	..	397	3,974	4,615	1,509
1994	281	1,303	292	739	2,830	494	936	50	570	3,048	4,499	1,471
GDP per kg (US$)												
1980	..	..	2.2	1.4	..	2.7	2.7	..	3.1	..	..	..
1994	2.9	..	1.7	2.4	4.5	2.7	4.4	5.6	3.0	0.8	5.4	5.0
Commercial energy imports (as % of energy consumption)												
1980	..	-710	4	12	..	-32	-11	..	-52	..	30	7
1994	-68	-327	1	16	86	-6	-27	14	-26	-13	13	3
Table 24: Natural resource use												
Land area (millions of hectares; total)	2,098	1,201	613	1,135	179	500	2,042	1,906	7,658	2,319	5,503	13,161
Forest and woodland (as % of land area)	32.6	5.9	15.7	13.8	15.5	54.8	44.8	31.9	29.3	36.7	35.1	31.8
Arable land (as % of land area)	6.2	4.4	35.3	8.5	2.8	12.3	6.0	5.5	9.2	11.2	11.3	10.1
Irrigated land (as % of arable land area)	3.8	18.0	36.5	53.8	57.6	22.9	13.7	9.5	25.7	9.0	9.9	18.3
Gini coefficient for land distribution	..	..	..	..	..	..	..	..	..	..	..	..
Annual rate of deforestation	..	..	..	..	..	..	..	..	..	..	..	..
Annual rate of reforestation	..	..	..	..	..	..	..	..	..	..	..	..
Internal renewable water resources per capita (1,000 m³)	9.1	1.8	4.1	2.3	2.2	13.4	28.2	14.0	7.6	16.0	12.2	8.6
Urban population in coastal cities, 2000 (1980=100)	294	207	211	175	180	210	174	295	198			
Annual marine catch (% change since 1981-83)	..	..	..	..	..	..	..	..	..	..	..	..
Table 25: National income accounts												
GDP (US$ billions; total)	247	..	451	1,031	509	544	1,549	72	4,280	819	20,744	25,024
Agriculture (as % of GDP)	20	..	28	15	..	16	10	37	15	12	3	6
Industry (as % of GDP)	29	..	28	42	36	39	33	19	36	39	35	35
Services (as % of GDP)	51	..	44	45	58	47	57	44	50	50	62	58
Consumption (as % of GDP)												
Private	67	..	68	49	55	57	69	85	61	56	62	62
Government	17	..	11	11	10	9	13	10	13	20	17	16
Gross domestic investment (as % of GDP)	17	..	22	39	36	33	21	17	27	24	21	22
Gross domestic savings (as % of GDP)	16	..	21	41	37	33	20	5	27	24	21	22
Tax revenue (as % of GNP)	..	..	10	9	..	17	..	..	14	..	24	23
Central government expenditure (as % of GNP)	..	..	19	..	..	18	..	..	..	..	33	..
Exports (as % of GDP)	29	..	16	27	..	56	14	18	26	22	22	23
Imports (as % of GDP)	34	..	19	27	..	60	18	32	28	24	22	23
Table 26: Trends in economic performance												
GNP (US$ billions; total)	254	607	377	1,124	494	522	1,503	80	4,536	812	20,849	25,385
GNP growth rate	1.5	2.0	4.5	9.2	8.5	5.7	1.7	2.5	4.0	-1.4	2.3	2.6
GNP per capita growth rate												
1965-80	1.2	3.8	1.3	6.4	..	4.0	2.8	(.)	3.2	..	3.0	2.0
1980-93	-1.4	-0.4	2.2	7.7	..	3.8	-0.4	(.)	2.0	-2.0	1.7	0.9
Average annual rate of inflation												
1984-94	16.1	..	14.3	8.2	..	8.0	422.3	17.6	164.6	134.4	12.5	34.9
1993	14.9	..	16.8	12.4	..	10.2	878.3	17.9	298.2	1,072.8	70.9	103.0
Exports as % of GDP, growth rate	0.3	..	3.9	2.6	..	2.1	3.9	1.4	3.2	..	2.1	2.3
Tax revenue as % of GNP, growth rate	..	..	0.9	..	..	0.1	-1.3	..	..	..	..	..
Overall budget surplus/deficit (as % of GNP)												
1980	-3.7	..	-8.8	..	..	-2.6	-2.5	..	..	..	..	..
1994	..	..	-6.2	-1.2	..	3.2	..	..	-1.9	..	-3.9	-3.6

Note: Columns 1-9 are for developing countries only. Aggregates for table 1 differ from those for other tables because table 1 includes a number of Human Development Report Office estimates that are presented and used only in the calculation of the HDI. These estimates are not used in other indicator tables.
a. Includes Eastern Europe and the CIS countries.
b. Aggregates are for countries for which data are available for both 1960 and 1994.
c. Excluding India.
d. World Bank 1996f.
e. OECD 1996a.

	International covenant on economic, social and cultural rights 1966	International covenant on civil and political rights 1966	International convention on the elimination of all forms of racial discrimination 1969	Convention on the prevention and punishment of the crime of genocide 1948	Convention on the rights of the child 1989	Convention on the elimination of all forms of discrimination against women 1979	Convention against torture and other cruel, inhuman or degrading treatment or punishment 1984	Convention relating to the status of refugees 1951
Afghanistan	●	●	●	●	●	○	●	
Albania	●	●a	●b	●	●	●	●c	●
Algeria	●	●a	●b	●	●	●	●	●
Andorra					●			
Angola	●	●			●	●		●
Antigua and Barbuda			●	●	●	●	●	●
Argentina	●	●a	●	●	●	●	●	
Armenia	●	●a	●b	●	●	●	●	
Australia	●	●a	●	●	●	●	●c	
Austria	●	●a	●	●	●	●	●c	●
Azerbaijan	●	●	●	●	●	●	●	●
Bahamas			●	●	●	●		
Bahrain			●	●	●			
Bangladesh			●	●	●	●		
Barbados	●	●		●	●	●		
Belarus	●	●a	●	●	●	●	●	
Belgium	●	●a	●	●	●	●	○	●
Belize		●	●		●	●	●	●
Benin	●	●	○		●	●	●	●
Bhutan			○		●	●		
Bolivia	●	●	●	○	●	●	○	●
Bosnia Herzegovina	●	●a	●	●	●	●	●	●
Botswana			●	●	●	●	●	
Brazil	●	●	●	●	●	●	●	●
Brunei Darussalam					●			
Bulgaria	●	●a	●b	●	●	●	●c	
Burkina Faso			●		●	●	●	●
Burundi	●	●	●	●	●	●	●	●
Cambodia	●	●	●	●	●	●	●	
Cameroon	●	●	●		●	●	●	●
Canada	●	●a	●	●	●	●	●c	●
Cape Verde	●	●	●		●	●	●	
Central African Rep.	●	●	●		●	●		●
Chad	●	●	●		●	●	●	●
Chile	●	●a	●b		●	●	●	●
China			●	●	●	●	●	●
Colombia	●	●			●	●	●	●
Comoros					●	●		
Congo	●	●a	●		●	●		●
Costa Rica	●	●	●b	●	●	●	●	●
Côte d'Ivoire	●	●	●		●	●	●	●
Croatia	●	●a	●	●	●	●	●c	●
Cuba			●	●	●	●	●c	
Cyprus	●	●	●b	●	●	●	●	●
Czech Rep.	●	●a	●	●	●	●	●	●
Denmark	●	●a	●b	●	●	●	●	●
Djibouti					●			
Dominica	●	●			●	●		
Dominican Rep.	●	●	●	○	●	●	○	●
Ecuador	●	●a	●b	●	●	●	●	●
Egypt	●	●	●	●	●	●	●	●
El Salvador	●	●	●	●	●	●		●
Equatorial Guinea	●	●			●	●		
Eritrea					●	●		
Estonia	●	●		●	●	●	●	
Ethiopia	●	●	●	●	●	●	●	
Fiji			●b		●	●	...c	
Finland	●	●a	●b	●	●	●	●c	●
France	●	●	●b	●	●	●	●c	●
Gabon	●	●	●	●	●	●	○	●
Gambia	●	●a	●	●	●	●	○	●
Georgia	●	●	●	●	●	●	●	
Germany	●	●a	●	●	●	●	●	●
Ghana			●	●	●	●	●	●
Greece	●		●	●	●	●	●c	●
Grenada	●	●	○		●	●		
Guatemala	●	●	●	●	●	●	●	●
Guinea	●	●	●		●	●	●	
Guinea-Bissau	●		●		●	●		
Guyana	●	●a	●		●	●	●	

	International covenant on economic, social and cultural rights 1966	International covenant on civil and political rights 1966	International convention on the elimination of all forms of racial discrimination 1969	Convention on the prevention and punishment of the crime of genocide 1948	Convention on the rights of the child 1989	Convention on the elimination of all forms of discrimination against women 1979	Convention against torture and other cruel, inhuman or degrading treatment or punishment 1984	Convention relating to the status of refugees 1951
Haiti		●	●	●	●	●		●
Holy See			●	●				●
Honduras	●	○		●	●	●	●	●
Hungary	●	●[a]	●[b]	●	●	●	●[c]	●
Iceland	●	●[a]	●[b]	●	●	●	●	●
India	●	●	●	●	●	●		
Indonesia					●	●	○	
Iran, Islamic Rep. of	●	●	●	●	●			●
Iraq	●	●	●	●	●	●		
Ireland	●	●[a]	○	●	●	●	●	●
Israel	●	●	●	●	●	●	●	●
Italy	●	●[a]	●[b]	●	●	●	●[c]	●
Jamaica	●	●	●	●	●	●		●
Japan	●	●	●		●	●		●
Jordan	●	●	●	●	●	●	●	
Kazakhstan					●			
Kenya	●	●			●	●		●
Kiribati					●			
Korea, Dem. People's Rep. of	●	●		●	●	●		
Korea, Rep. of	●	●[a]	●	●	●	●	●	●
Kuwait	●	●	●	●	●	●	●	
Kyrgyzstan	●				●	●		●
Lao People's Dem. Rep.			●	●	●	●		
Latvia	●	●	●	●	●	●	●	
Lebanon	●	●	●	●	●	●		
Lesotho	●	●	●	●	●	●		●
Liberia	○	○	●	●	●	●		●
Libyan Arab Jamahiriya	●	●	●	●	●	●	●	
Liechtenstein				●	●	●	●[c]	●
Lithuania	●	●		●	●	●	●[c]	
Luxembourg	●	●[a]	●	●	●	●	●[c]	●
Macedonia, FYR	●	●	●		●	●	●	●
Madagascar	●	●	●		●	●		
Malawi	●	●	●		●	●	●	●
Malaysia				●	●	●		●
Maldives			●	●	●	●		
Mali	●	●[a]	●	●	●	●		●
Malta	●	●[a]	●		●	●	●[c]	●
Marshall Islands					●			
Mauritania				●	●			●
Mauritius	●	●	●		●	●	●	●
Mexico	●	●	●	●	●	●	●	
Micronesia, Federal States of					●			
Moldova, Rep. of	●	●	●	●	●	●	●[c]	
Monaco			●	●	●		●[c]	●
Mongolia	●	●	●	●	●	●		
Morocco	●	●	●	●	●	●	●	●
Mozambique		●	●	●	●		●	●
Myanmar				●	●	●		
Namibia	●	●	●	●	●	●	●	
Nauru					●			
Nepal	●	●	●	●	●	●	●	
Netherlands	●	●[a]	●[b]	●	●	●	●[c]	●
New Zealand	●	●[a]	●	●	●	●	●[c]	●
Nicaragua	●	●	●	●	●	●	○	●
Niger	●	●	●		●			●
Nigeria	●	●	●		●	●	○	
Niue					●			
Norway	●	●[a]	●[b]	●	●	●	●[c]	●
Oman					●			
Pakistan			●	●	●	●		
Palau								
Panama	●	●	●	●	●	●	●	●
Papua New Guinea			●		●	●		●
Paraguay	●	●		○	●	●	●	●
Peru	●	●[a]	●[b]	●	●	●	●	●
Philippines	●	●[a]	●	●	●	●	●	●
Poland	●	●[a]	●	●	●	●	●[c]	●
Portugal	●	●	●		●	●	●[c]	●
Qatar			●		●		●	

	International covenant on economic, social and cultural rights 1966	International covenant on civil and political rights 1966	International convention on the elimination of all forms of racial discrimination 1969	Convention on the prevention and punishment of the crime of genocide 1948	Convention on the rights of the child 1989	Convention on the elimination of all forms of discrimination against women 1979	Convention against torture and other cruel, inhuman or degrading treatment or punishment 1984	Convention relating to the status of refugees 1951
Romania	●	●	●	●	●	●	●c	●
Russian Federation	●	●a	●b	●	●	●	●c	●
Rwanda	●	●	●	●	●	●		
Saint Kitts and Nevis					●	●		
Saint Lucia			●		●	●		
Saint Vincent	●	●	●	●	●	●		●
Samoa (Western)					●	●		
San Marino	●	●			●			●
São Tomé and Principe	○	○			●	○		●
Saudi Arabia				●	●			
Senegal	●	●a	●b	●	●	●	●	●
Seychelles	●	●	●	●	●	●	●	●
Sierra Leone	●	●	●		●	●	○	●
Singapore				●	●	●		●
Slovakia	●	●a	●b	●	●	●	●c	●
Slovenia	●	●a	●	●	●	●	●c	●
Solomon Islands	●		●		●			●
Somalia	●	●	●				●	●
South Africa	○	○	○		●	●	○	●
Spain	●	●a	●	●	●	●	●c	●
Sri Lanka	●	●a	●	●	●	●	●	
Sudan	●	●	●		●		○	●
Suriname	●	●	●		●	●		●
Swaziland			●		●			●
Sweden	●	●a	●b	●	●	●	●c	●
Switzerland	●	●a	●	●	●	○	●c	●
Syrian Arab Rep.	●	●	●	●	●		●	●
Tajikistan					●			
Tanzania, U. Rep. of	●	●	●		●	●		●
Thailand		●			●	●		
Togo	●	●	●	●	●	●	●c	●
Tonga			●	●	●			
Trinidad and Tobago	●	●	●		●	●	●c	●
Tunisia	●	●a	●	●	●	●	●c	●
Turkey			○	●	●	●	●c	●
Turkmenistan			●		●			
Tuvalu					●			●
Uganda	●	●	●b	●	●	●	●	●
Ukraine	●	●a	●b	●	●	●	●	
United Arab Emirates			●		●			
United Kingdom	●	●a	●	●	●	●	●d	●
USA	○	●a	●	●	○	○	●c	
Uruguay	●	●	●b	●	●	●	●c	●
Uzbekistan	●	●	●		●	●	●	
Vanuatu					●	●		
Venezuela	●	●	●	●	●	●	●c	
Viet Nam	●	●	●	●	●	●		
Yemen	●	●	●	●	●	●	●	●e
Yugoslavia	●	●	●	●	●	●	●c	●
Zaire	●	●	●	●	●	●	●	●
Zambia	●	●	●		●	●		●
Zimbabwe	●	●	●	●	●	●		●
Total states parties	135	136	148	120	190	153	102	125
Signatures not followed by ratification	4	4	6	3	1	4	11	0
States that have not ratified and not signed	53	52	38	69	1	35	79	67

● Ratification, accession, approval, notification or succession, acceptance or definitive signature.
○ Signature not yet followed by ratification.
Note: Status is as of 1 March 1997.
a. Declaration recognizing the competence of the Human Rights Committee under Article 41 of the International Convenant on Civil and Political Rights.
b. Declaration recognizing the competence of the Committee on the Elimination of Racial Discrimination under Article 41 of the International Convention on the Elimination of All Forms of Racial Discrimination.
c. Declaration recognizing the competence of the Committee against Torture under Articles 21 and 22 of the Convention against Torture and other Cruel, Inhuman or Degrading Treatment or Punishment.
d. Declaration under Article 21 only.
e. Ratification, accession, approval, notification or succession, acceptance or definitive signature only by the former Republic of Yemen.
Source: United Nations Centre for Human Rights 1997.

Primary statistical references

ARF (Addiction Research Foundation). 1994. "Statistical Information, International Profile 1994." Ontario, Canada.

Eurostat and UN (United Nations). 1995. *Women and Men in Europe and North America.* Geneva.

FAO (Food and Agriculture Organization of the United Nations). 1994. *1994 Country Tables: Basic Data on the Agricultural Sector.* Economic and Social Policy Department. Rome.

IISS (International Institute for Strategic Studies). 1993. *The Military Balance 1993–94.* London: Brasseys.

———. 1996. *The Military Balance 1996–97.* Oxford: Oxford University Press.

ILO (International Labour Office). 1994. *Yearbook of Labour Statistics 1994.* Geneva.

———. 1995a. *World Labour Report 1995.* Geneva.

———. 1995b. *Yearbook of Labour Statistics 1995.* Geneva.

———. 1996b. *Estimates and Projections of the Economically Active Population, 1950–2010.* 4th ed. Diskette. Geneva.

IMF (International Monetary Fund). Various editions. *Government Finance Statistics Yearbook.* Washington, DC.

IPU (Inter-Parliamentary Union). 1997. *Democracy Still in the Making.* Geneva.

ITU (International Telecommunication Union). 1996. *World Telecommunication Indicators.* Diskette. Geneva.

OECD (Organisation for Economic Co-operation and Development). 1994a. *Development Co-operation: Development Assistance Committee Report 1994.* Paris.

———. 1994b. *Employment Outlook.* Paris.

———. 1995a. *Employment Outlook.* Paris.

———. 1995b. *Environmental Data: Compendium 1995.* Paris.

———. 1996a. *Development Co-operation: Development Assistance Committee Report 1996.* Paris.

———. 1996b. *Economic Outlook.* 60th issue. Paris.

———. 1996c. *Education at a Glance 1996.* Paris.

———. 1996d. *Employment Outlook.* Paris.

Psacharopoulos, George, and Zafiris Tzannatos, eds. 1992. *Case Studies on Women's Employment and Pay in Latin America.* Washington, DC: World Bank.

SIPRI (Stockholm International Peace Research Institute). 1996. *SIPRI Yearbook 1996.* New York: Oxford University Press.

Summers, Robert, and Alan Heston. 1991. "Penn World Tables (Mark 5): An Expanded Set of International Comparisons, 1950–1988." *Quarterly Journal of Economics* 106: 327–68.

UN (United Nations). 1993a. "Statistical Chart on World Families." Statistical Division and the Secretariat for the International Year of the Family. New York.

———. 1993b. *Statistical Yearbook 1990/91.* 38th issue. Statistical Division. New York. ST/ESA/STAT/SER.S/14.E/F/93.XVII.1.

———. 1994a. *Statistical Yearbook 1992.* 39th issue. Statistical Division. New York. ST/ESA/STAT/SER.S/15.E/F/94.XVII.1.

———. 1994b. *Women's Indicators and Statistics Database.* Version 3. CD-ROM. Statistical Division. New York.

———. 1995b. *Statistical Yearbook 1993.* 40th issue. Statistical Division. New York.

———. 1995c. "World Urbanization Prospects: The 1994 Revision." Database. Population Division. New York.

———. 1995d. *The World's Women 1970–95: Trends and Statistics.* New York.

———. 1996a. *Energy Statistics Yearbook 1994.* New York.

———. 1996b. "World Population Prospects 1950–2050." Database. Population Division. New York.

———. 1997. "World Population Monitoring—Issues of International Migration and Development: Selected Aspects." Population Division. New York. Draft.

UNAIDS (Joint United Nations Programme on HIV/AIDS). 1996. *The Current Global Situation of AIDS.* Geneva.

———. 1997. Correspondence on AIDS cases reported to the WHO by country/territory through 20 November 1996. Received January. Geneva.

UNCSDHA (United Nations Centre for Social Development and Humanitarian Affairs). 1995. "Results of the Fourth United Nations Survey of Crime Trends and Operations of the Criminal Justice System (1986–90)—Interim Report by the Secretariat." Vienna.

UNDP (United Nations Development Programme). 1994. *Human Development Report 1994.* New York: Oxford University Press.

———. 1995a. *Human Development Report 1995.* New York: Oxford University Press.

———. 1996d. *Human Development Report 1996.* New York: Oxford University Press.

UNECE (United Nations Economic Commission for Europe). 1995a. *Statistics of Traffic Accidents in Europe and North America.* New York and Geneva.

———. 1995b. *Trends in Europe and North America: The Statistical Yearbook of the Economic Commission for Europe.* New York and Geneva.

———. 1996. Database. Geneva.

———. 1997. Correspondence on GNP per capita. Received January.

UNESCO (United Nations Educational, Scientific and Cultural Organization). 1993. *World Education Report 1993.* Paris.

———. 1995a. *Statistical Yearbook 1995.* Paris.

———. 1995b. *World Education Report 1995.* Paris.

———. 1996a. Correspondence on adult literacy. Received November. Division of Statistics. Paris.

———. 1996b. Correspondence on adult literacy and combined primary, secondary and tertiary enrolment. Received December. Division of Statistics. Paris.

———. 1996d. *Statistical Yearbook 1996.* Paris.

UNICEF (United Nations Children's Fund). 1997. *The State of the World's Children 1997.* New York: Oxford University Press.

United Nations Centre for Human Rights. 1997. "Human Rights: International Instruments—Chart of Ratifications as of 31 December 1996." Geneva. ST/HR/4/Rev.13.

WHO (World Health Organization). 1993. *World Health Statistics Annual 1993.* Geneva.

———. 1994. *World Health Statistics Annual 1994.* Geneva.

———. 1996a. *Tabac Alerte.* Special issue. Geneva.

———. 1996b. *World Health Report 1996.* Geneva.

World Bank. 1993. *World Development Report 1993.* New York: Oxford University Press.

———. 1995c. *Social Indicators of Development.* Baltimore: Johns Hopkins University Press.

———. 1995d. *World Data 1995.* CD-ROM. Washington, DC.

———. 1995e. *World Development Report 1995.* New York: Oxford University Press.

———. 1996a. Correspondence on GDP. Received May. Washington, DC.

———. 1996e. *World Bank Atlas 1996.* Washington, DC.

———. 1996f. *World Debt Tables 1995–96.* Washington, DC.

———. 1996g. *World Development Report 1996.* New York: Oxford University Press.

———. 1997a. Correspondence on unpublished World Bank data on GNP per capita estimates using the GDP/GNP ratio for 1994. Received January. Washington, DC.

———. 1997b. *World Development Indicators 1997.* Washington, DC.

Worldwide Government Directories. 1995. *Worldwide Government Directory with International Organizations.* Bethesda, Md.

WRI (World Resources Institute). 1996a. Correspondence on the Gini coefficient. Received December. Washington, DC.

———. 1996b. *World Resources 1996–97.* New York: Oxford University Press.

Selected definitions

Administrators and managers Includes legislators, senior government administrators, traditional chiefs and heads of villages and administrators of special interest organizations. It also includes corporate managers such as chief executives and general managers as well as specialized managers and managing supervisors, according to the International Standard Classification of Occupations (ISCO-1968).

Alcohol consumption per capita Derived from sales data for beer, wine and spirits, each of which is converted to absolute alcohol based on its alcohol content. The total absolute alcohol is then divided by the population to get per capita consumption.

Births attended The percentage of births attended by physicians, nurses, midwives, trained primary health care workers or trained traditional birth attendants.

Budget surplus/deficit (overall surplus/deficit) Central government current and capital revenue and official grants received, less expenditure and net government lending.

Central government expenditures Expenditures, both current and capital, by all government offices, departments, establishments and other bodies that are agencies or instruments of the central authority of a country.

Cereal imports All cereals in the Standard International Trade Classification (SITC), Revision 2, Groups 041–046. This includes wheat and flour in wheat equivalent, rice, maize, sorghum, barley, oats, rye, millet and other minor grains. Grain trade data include both commercial and food aid shipments but exclude trade between the member states of the European Union and within the Commonwealth of Independent States. Cereal imports are based on calendar-year data reported by recipient countries.

Children reaching grade 5 Percentage of children starting primary school who eventually attain grade 5 (grade 4 if the duration of primary school is four years). The estimate is based on the Reconstructed Cohort Method, which uses data on enrolment and repeaters for two consecutive years.

Cigarette consumption per adult Estimated by the World Health Organization (WHO) according to this formula: the sum of production and imports minus exports divided by the population aged 15 years and older. This measure of apparent consumption has been adjusted for consumption of bidis and rolled tobacco as well as smuggling, but not for stocks kept by the trade.

CO_2 emissions by source Anthropogenic (human-originated) carbon dioxide (CO_2) emissions from energy use only. It includes oil held in international marine bunkers, with quantities assigned to the countries in which bunker deliveries were made. It also includes peat, but it excludes oil and gas for non-energy purposes and the use of biomass fuels.

Coastal cities Coastal area is defined as a zone no more than 60 kilometres inland.

Commercial energy Commercial forms of primary energy—petroleum (crude oil, natural gas liquids and oil from nonconventional sources), natural gas, solid fuels (coal, lignite and other derived fuels) and primary electricity (nuclear, hydroelectric, geothermal and other)—all converted into oil equivalents.

Commercial energy consumption Refers to domestic primary commercial energy supply before transformation to other end-use fuels (such as electricity and refined petroleum product) and is calculated as indigenous production plus imports and stock changes, minus exports and international marine bunkers. Energy consumption also includes products consumed for non-energy uses, mainly derived from petroleum. The use of firewood, dried animal manure and other traditional fuels, although substantial in some developing countries, is not taken into account because reliable and comprehensive data are not available.

Commercial energy production Refers to the first stage of commercial production. Thus for hard coal the data refer to mine production; for briquettes, to the output of briquetting plants; for crude petroleum and natural gas, to production at oil and gas wells; for natural gas liquids, to production at wells and processing plants; for refined petroleum products, to gross refinery output; for cokes and coke-oven gas, to the output of ovens; for other manufactured gas, to production at gas works, blast furnaces or refineries; and for electricity, to the gross production of generating plants.

Compulsory education The existence of laws that stipulate that children, unless exempted, must attend a certain number of grades between designated ages. For example, regulations may specify that the duration of compulsory education is six grades between ages 6 and 14. This means that a child ceases to be subject to the regulations either on his or her 14th birthday or on completion of six years of schooling (though he or she might then be only 12 or 13 years old). However, in many countries and territories where the urgent problem is to provide a sufficient number of schools for all children, the existence of compulsory education laws may be of only academic interest since almost all such regulations exempt a child from attending if there is no suitable school within a reasonable distance from his or her home.

Contraceptive prevalence rate The percentage of married women of child-bearing age who are using, or whose husbands are using, any form of contraception, whether modern or traditional.

Crude birth rate Annual number of births per thousand population.

Crude death rate Annual number of deaths per thousand population.

Current account balance The difference between (a) exports of goods and services (factor and non-factor) as well as inflows of unrequited transfers but exclusive of foreign aid and (b) imports of goods and services as well as all unrequited transfers to the rest of the world.

Daily calorie supply per capita The calorie equivalent of the net food supplies in a country, divided by the population, per day.

Debt service The sum of principal repayments and interest payments on total external debt.

Defence expenditure All expenditure, whether by defence or other departments, on the maintenance of military forces, including the purchase of military supplies and equipment, construction, recruitment, training and military aid programmes.

Deforestation The permanent clearing of forest lands for shifting cultivation, permanent agriculture or settlements; it does not include other alterations such as selective logging.

Dependency ratio The ratio of the population defined as dependent—those under 15 and over 64—to the working-age population, aged 15–64.

Disability As defined by the International Classification of Impairments, Disabilities and Handicaps (ICIDH) issued by the World Health Organization (WHO), disability is a restriction or lack of ability (resulting from impairment) to perform an activity in the manner or within the range considered normal for a human being. Impairment is defined as any loss of psychological, physiological or anatomical structure and function. The World Programme of Action concerning disabled persons monitors the implementation of national action to enhance the socio-economic opportunities and integration of disabled persons.

Disbursement The release of funds to, or the purchase of goods or services for, a recipient; by extension, the amount thus spent. Disbursements record the actual international transfer of financial resources or of goods or services, valued at the cost to the donor. For activities carried out in donor countries, such as training, administration or public awareness programmes, disbursement is taken to have occurred when the funds have been transferred to the service provider or the recipient. They may be recorded as gross (the total amount disbursed over a given accounting period) or net (less any repayments of loan principal during the same period).

Discouraged workers Individuals who would like to work and who are available for work, but are not actively seeking work because of a stated belief that no suitable job is available or because they do not know where to get work. The number of discouraged workers is used as an additional measure of labour market slack by the OECD.

Doctors Refers to physicians and includes all graduates of any faculty or school of medicine in any medical field (including practice, teaching, administration and research).

Earnings per employee All remuneration to employees expressed in constant prices, derived by deflating nominal earnings per employee by the country's consumer price index.

Economically active population All men or women who supply labour for the production of economic goods and services, as defined by the UN System of National Accounts, during a specified time period. According to this system, the production of economic goods and services should include all production and processing of primary products (whether for the market, for barter or for own-consumption), the production of all other goods and services for the market and, in the case of households that produce such goods and services for the market, the corresponding production for own-consumption.

Education expenditure Expenditure on the provision, management, inspection and support of pre-primary, primary and secondary schools; universities and colleges; vocational, technical and other training institutions; and general administration and subsidiary services.

Employees Includes regular employees, working proprietors, active business partners and unpaid family workers, but excludes homemakers.

Enrolment ratio (gross and net) The gross enrolment ratio is the number of students enrolled in a level of education—whether or not they belong in the relevant age group for that level—as a percentage of the population in the relevant age group for that level. The net enrolment ratio is the number of students enrolled in a level of education who belong in the relevant age group, as a percentage of the population in that age group.

Exports of goods and services The value of all goods and non-factor services provided to the rest of the world, including merchandise, freight, insurance, travel and other non-factor services.

Female-male gap A set of national, regional and other estimates in which all the figures for females are expressed in relation to the corresponding figures for males, which are indexed to equal 100.

Fertility rate (total) The average number of children that would be born alive to a woman during her lifetime, if she were to bear children at each age in accord with prevailing age-specific fertility rates.

Food aid in cereals Cereals provided by donor countries and international organizations, including the World Food Programme and the International Wheat Council, as reported for that particular crop year. Cereals include wheat, flour, bulgur, rice, coarse grain and the cereal components of blended foods.

Food consumption as a percentage of total household consumption Computed from details of GDP (expenditure at national market prices) defined in the UN System of National Accounts, mostly as collected from the International Comparison Programme phases IV (1980) and V (1985).

Food production per capita index The average annual quantity of food produced per capita in relation to that produced in the indexed year. Food comprises nuts, pulses, fruit, cereals, vegetables, sugar cane, sugar beets,

starchy roots, edible oils, livestock and livestock products.

Food supply from fish and seafood The quantity of both freshwater and marine fish products available for human consumption. Data on aquatic plants and whale meat are excluded. Consumption levels are given exclusive of discarding and loss during storage, preparation and cooking.

Future labour force replacement ratio The population under 15 divided by a third of the population aged 15–59.

Government consumption Includes all current expenditure for purchases of goods and services by all levels of government. Capital expenditure on national defence and security is regarded as consumption expenditure.

Greenhouse index Net emissions of three major greenhouse gases (carbon dioxide, methane and chlorofluorocarbons), with each gas weighted according to its heat-trapping quality (in carbon dioxide equivalents) and expressed in metric tons of carbon per capita.

Gross domestic investment Outlays on additions to the fixed assets of the economy plus net changes in the level of inventories.

Gross domestic product (GDP) The total output of goods and services for final use produced by an economy, by both residents and non-residents, regardless of the allocation to domestic and foreign claims. It does not include deductions for depreciation of physical capital or depletion and degradation of natural resources.

Gross national product (GNP) Comprises GDP plus net factor income from abroad, which is the income residents receive from abroad for factor services (labour and capital), less similar payments made to non-residents who contribute to the domestic economy.

Gross national product (GNP) per capita growth rates Annual GNP per capita is expressed in current US dollars, and GNP per capita growth rates are average annual growth rates computed by fitting trend lines to the logarithmic values of GNP per capita at constant market prices for each year in the period.

Health expenditure Public expenditure on health comprises the expenditure, both current and capital, by all government offices, departments, establishments and other bodies that are agencies or instruments of the central authority of a country on hospitals, clinics and maternity and dental centers with a major medical component; on national health and medical insurance schemes; and on family planning and preventive care. The data on health expenditure are not comparable across countries. In many economies private health services are substantial; in others public services represent the major component of total expenditure but may be financed by lower levels of government. Caution should therefore be exercised in using the data for cross-country comparisons.

Health services access The percentage of the population that can reach appropriate local health services on foot or by local means of transport in no more than one hour.

Homicides Includes intentional deaths (purposely inflicted by another person, including infanticide), non-intentional deaths (not purposely inflicted by another person) and manslaughter but excludes traffic accidents resulting in death.

Housing and community amenities expenditure Expenditures on housing (excluding interest subsidies) such as income-related schemes, on provision and support of housing and slum clearance activities, on community development and on sanitation services. Expenditures on environmental defence, such as pollution abatement, are also included in this category.

Human priority areas Basic education, primary health care, safe drinking water, adequate sanitation, family planning and nutrition.

Immunized The average vaccination coverage of children under one year of age for the antigens used in the Universal Child Immunization (UCI) Programme.

Income share The distribution of income or expenditure (or share of expenditure) accruing to percentile groups of households ranked by total household income, by per capita income or by expenditure. Shares of population quintiles and the top decile in total income or consumption expenditure are used in calculating income shares. The data sets for these countries are drawn mostly from nationally representative household surveys conducted in different years during 1978–92. Data for the high-income OECD economies are based on information from the Statistical Office of the European Union (Eurostat), the Luxembourg Income Study and the OECD. Data should be interpreted with caution owing to differences between income studies in the use of income and consumption expenditure to estimate living standards.

Infant mortality rate The annual number of deaths of infants under one year of age per thousand live births. More specifically, the probability of dying between birth and exactly one year of age times 1,000.

Inflation rate Measured by the growth rate of the GDP implicit deflator for each of the periods shown. The GDP deflator is first calculated by dividing, for each year of the period, the value of GDP at current values by the value of GDP at constant values, both in national currency. This measure of inflation, like others, has limitations, but it is used because it shows annual price movements for all goods and services produced in an economy.

International reserves (gross) Holdings of monetary gold, Special Drawing Rights (SDRs), the reserve positions of members in the IMF and holdings of foreign exchange under the control of monetary authorities expressed in terms of the number of months of imports of goods and services these could pay for at the current level of imports.

Involuntary part-time workers Refers directly to the International Labour Organisation (ILO) concept of visible underemployment and includes three groups of workers: those who usually work full-time but are working part-time because of economic slack; those who usually work part-time but are working fewer hours in their part-time job because of economic slack; and those working part-time because full-time work could not be found. The number of involuntary part-time workers is used as an additional measure of labour market slack by the OECD.

Labour force See *Economically active population*.

Least developed countries The least developed countries are those recognized by the United Nations as low-income countries encountering long-term impediments to economic growth, particularly low levels of human resource development and severe structural weaknesses. The main purpose of constructing a list of such countries is to give guidance to donor agencies and countries for allocation of foreign assistance.

Life expectancy at birth The number of years a newborn infant would live if prevailing patterns of mortality at the time of birth were to stay the same throughout the child's life.

Literacy rate (adult) The percentage of people aged 15 and above who can, with understanding, both read and write a short, simple statement on their everyday life.

Low-birth-weight infants The percentage of babies born weighing less than 2,500 grams.

Marine catch Marine fish killed, caught, trapped, collected, bred or cultivated for commercial, industrial and subsistence use, including crustaceans, molluscs, miscellaneous aquatic animals (excluding whales and other mammals) and quantities taken in recreational activities. Figures include fish caught by a country's fleet anywhere in the world.

Maternal mortality rate The annual number of deaths of women from pregnancy-related causes per 100,000 live births. According to the Tenth International Classification of Diseases, a maternal death is defined as the death of a woman while pregnant or within 42 days of termination of pregnancy, irrespective of the duration and the site of the pregnancy, from any causes related to or aggravated by the pregnancy or its management, but not from accidental or incidental causes. This complicated definition and the relative infrequency of maternal deaths in a short period (such as 1–2 years), except in very large population samples, led to misclassification and underreporting in many countries. To address the problem, a new set of estimates for 1990 was developed by the World Health Organization (WHO) and the United Nations Children's Fund (UNICEF) that adjusted available data for underreporting and misclassification and included a model to predict values for countries with no reliable national data. These estimates should be seen as a recalculation of the previous (1991) revision rather than as indicative of trends since then. They cannot be used to monitor trends on a year-to-year basis, but rather provide a baseline estimate against which it will be possible to assess progress by 2003.

Military expenditure See *Defence expenditure*.

Multilateral official development assistance (ODA) Funds contributed in the form of ODA to an international institution with governmental membership that conducts all or a significant part of its activities in favour of development and aid recipient countries. A contribution by a donor to such an agency is deemed to be multilateral if it is pooled with other contributions and disbursed at the discretion of the agency. ODA received by aid recipient countries is considered multilateral if it comes from multilateral agencies such as multilateral development banks (the World Bank, regional development banks), UN agencies and regional groupings (certain European Union and Arab agencies).

Municipal waste Waste collected by municipalities or by their order, including waste originating from households, commercial activities, office buildings, schools, government buildings and small businesses that dispose of waste at the same facilities used for waste collected by municipalities.

Nurses All persons who have completed a programme of basic nursing education and are qualified and registered or authorized by the country to provide responsible and competent service for the promotion of health, prevention of illness, care of the sick and rehabilitation.

Occupation The classification of occupations brings together individuals doing similar work, irrespective of where the work is performed. Most countries have supplied data on the basis of the International Standard Classification of Occupations (ISCO). The actual content of occupational groups may differ from one country to another owing to variations in definitions and methods of data collection.

Official development assistance (ODA) Grants or loans to countries and territories on Part I of the OECD Development Assistance Committee (DAC) List of Aid Recipients (developing countries) that are undertaken by the official sector, with promotion of economic development and welfare as the main objective— and at concessional financial terms (if a loan, at least 25% grant element). Figures for total net ODA disbursed are based on OECD data for DAC member countries, multilateral organizations and Arab states.

Oral rehydration therapy use rate The percentage of all cases of diarrhoea in children under age five treated with oral rehydration salts or an appropriate household solution.

Population density The total number of inhabitants divided by the surface area.

Population served by waste water treatment plants National population connected to public sewage networks with treatment.

Poverty line Based on the concept of an absolute poverty line, expressed in monetary terms: the income or expenditure level below which a minimum, nutritionally adequate diet plus essential non-food requirements are not affordable. National estimates that rely on a relative poverty line (such as share of food in total expenditures) are excluded, as are those that rely on a poverty line defined exclusively in relation to another variable (such as the minimum wage) rather than the satisfaction of the food and non-food needs at a minimally acceptable level. Poverty estimates are based on data from an actual household budget, income or expenditure survey. Exceptions include some African and small island countries or territories for which otherwise virtually no observations would have been available.

Primary education Education at the first level (International Standard Classification of Education—ISCED—level 1), the main function of which is to provide the basic elements of education, such as elementary schools.

Primary intake rate Number of new entrants into first grade, regardless of age, expressed as a percentage of the population of official admission age for the first level of education.

Primary school completion rate The proportion of children entering the first grade of primary school who successfully complete that level in due course.

Private consumption The market value of all goods and services, including durable products (such as cars, washing machines and home computers), purchased or received as income in kind by households and non-profit institutions. It excludes purchases of dwellings but includes imputed rent for owner-occupied dwellings.

Production as a percentage of national energy reserves The data on production of energy refer to the first stage of production; thus for hard coal and lignite the data refer to mine production, and for crude oil and natural gas, to production at oil and gas wells. The data for reserves refer to proved recoverable reserves of coal, crude oil and natural gas—that is, the tonnage of the proved amount in place that can be recovered (extracted from the earth in raw form) in the future under present and expected economic conditions and existing technological limits. The ratio of production to reserves is the annual production of energy commodities as a percentage of the total proved recoverable reserves.

Professional and technical workers Physical scientists and related technicians; architects, engineers and related technicians; aircraft and ships' officers; life scientists and related technicians; medical, dental, veterinary and related workers; statisticians, mathematicians, systems analysts and related technicians; economists; accountants; jurists; teachers; workers in religion; authors, journalists and related writers; sculptors, painters, photographers and related creative artists; composers and performing artists; athletes, sportsmen and related workers; and professional, technical and related workers not elsewhere classified, according to the International Standard Classification of Occupations (ISCO-1968).

Purchasing power parity (PPP$) The purchasing power of a country's currency: the number of units of that currency required to purchase the same representative basket of goods and services (or a similar basket of goods and services) that a US dollar (the reference currency) would buy in the United States. Purchasing power parity could also be expressed in other national currencies or in Special Drawing Rights (SDRs).

Real GDP per capita (PPP$) The GDP per capita of a country converted into US dollars on the basis of the purchasing power parity of the country's currency. The system of purchasing power parities has been developed by the United Nations International Comparison Programme (ICP) to make more accurate international comparisons of GDP and its components than those based on official exchange rates, which can be subject to considerable fluctuation.

Reforestation The establishment of plantations for industrial and non-industrial uses; it does not, in general, include regeneration of old tree crops, although some countries may report regeneration as reforestation.

Refugees According to the United Nations Convention Relating to the Status of Refugees and its 1967 Protocol, refugees are persons who—owing to a well-founded fear of being persecuted for reasons of race, religion, nationality, membership in a particular social group or political opinion—are outside their country of nationality and are unable or, owing to such fear, unwilling to avail themselves of the protection of that country; or who, not having a nationality and being outside the country of their former habitual residence, are unable or, owing to such fear, unwilling to return to it. According to the United Nations High Commissioner for Refugees (UNHCR), refugees also include selected groups of internally displaced persons, returnees and others of concern to or assisted by the UNHCR.

Rural-urban disparity A set of national, regional and other estimates in which all the rural figures are expressed in relation to the corresponding urban figures, which are indexed to equal 100.

Safe water access The percentage of the population with reasonable access to safe water supply, including treated surface water or untreated but uncontaminated water such as that from springs, sanitary wells and protected boreholes.

Sanitation access The percentage of the population with reasonable access to sanitary means of excreta and waste disposal, including outdoor latrines and composting.

Science graduates Tertiary education graduates in the natural and applied sciences, including medicine.

Scientists and technicians Scientists refers to scientists and engineers with scientific or technological training (usually completion of third-level education) in any field of science who are engaged in professional work in research and development activities, including administrators and other high-level personnel who direct the execution of research and development activities. Technicians refers to persons engaged in scientific research and development activities who have received vocational or technical training for at least three years after the first stage of second-level education.

Secondary education Education at the second level (International Standard Classification of Education—ISCED—levels 2 and 3), based on at least four years of previous instruction at the first level and providing general or specialized instruction or both, such as middle school, secondary school, high school, teacher training school at this level and vocational or technical school.

Secondary technical education Education provided in second-level schools aimed at preparing the pupils directly for a trade or occupation other than teaching.

Social protection Refers to OECD member countries' provision of social welfare in the areas of health, pensions, unemployment benefits and other income support schemes. This provision is intended not just to assist those in need, but also to meet economic goals by covering the social costs of economic restructuring.

Social security benefits expenditure Compensation for loss of income for persons who are ill and temporarily disabled; payments to the elderly, persons with permanent disability and the unemployed; family, maternity and child allowances; and the cost of welfare services.

Social security expenditure Transfer payments (including payments in kind) to compensate for reduction or loss of income or inadequate earning capacity.

South-North gap A set of national, regional and other estimates in which all figures for developing countries are expressed in relation to the corresponding average figures for all the industrial countries, indexed to equal 100.

Sulfur and nitrogen emissions Emissions of sulfur in the form of sulfur oxides and of nitrogen in the form of its various oxides, which together contribute to acid rain and adversely affect agriculture, forests, aquatic habitats and the weathering of building materials.

Tax revenue Compulsory, unrequited, non-repayable receipts for public purposes—including interest collected on tax arrears and penalties collected for non-payment or late payment of taxes—shown net of refunds and other corrective transactions.

Terms of trade The ratio of a country's index of average export prices to its index of average import prices.

Tertiary education Education at the third level (International Standard Classification of Education—ISCED—levels 5, 6 and 7), such as universities, teachers colleges and higher professional schools—requiring as a minimum condition of admission the successful completion of education at the second level or evidence of the attainment of an equivalent level of knowledge.

Total external debt The sum of public, publicly guaranteed and private non-guaranteed long-term external obligations, short-term debt and use of IMF credit. The data on debt are from the World Bank's Debtor Reporting System, supplemented by World Bank estimates. The system is concerned solely with developing economies and does not collect data on external debt for other groups of borrowers or from economies that are not members of the World Bank. Dollar figures for debt are in US dollars converted at official exchange rates.

Traditional fuels Includes fuelwood, charcoal, bagasse and animal and vegetable wastes.

Transition from first- to second-level education Number of new entrants into secondary general education, expressed as a percentage of the total number of pupils in the last grade of primary education in the previous year.

Under-five mortality rate The annual number of deaths of children under age five per 1,000 live births averaged over the previous five years. More specifically, the probability of dying between birth and exactly five years of age expressed per 1,000 live births.

Underweight (moderate and severe child malnutrition) The percentage of children under age five who are below minus two standard deviations from the median birth weight for age of the reference population.

Unemployment All persons above a specified age who are not in paid employment or self-employed, but are available and have taken specific steps to seek paid employment or self-employment.

Urban population Percentage of the population living in urban areas as defined according to the national definition used in the most recent population census.

Waste recycling The reuse of material that diverts it from the waste stream, except for recycling within industrial plants and the reuse of material as fuel. The recycling rate is the ratio of the quantity recycled to the apparent consumption.

Water resources, internal renewable The average annual flow of rivers and aquifers generated from endogenous precipitation.

Water withdrawals Includes those from non-renewable aquifers and desalting plants but does not include losses from evaporation.

Welfare expenditure Expenditures on assistance delivered to persons or groups with special needs, such as the young, the old or the handicapped.

Classification of countries

Countries in the human development aggregates

High human development
(HDI 0.800 and above)

Antigua and
  Barbuda
Argentina
Australia
Austria
Bahamas
Bahrain
Barbados
Belarus
Belgium
Belize
Brunei
  Darussalam
Canada
Chile
Colombia
Costa Rica
Cyprus
Czech Rep.
Denmark
Dominica
Fiji
Finland
France
Germany
Greece
Grenada
Hong Kong
Hungary
Iceland
Ireland
Israel
Italy
Japan
Korea, Rep. of
Kuwait
Libyan Arab
  Jamahiriya
Luxembourg

Malaysia
Malta
Mauritius
Mexico
Netherlands
New Zealand
Norway
Panama
Poland
Portugal
Qatar
Saint Kitts and
  Nevis
Saint Lucia
Saint Vincent
Seychelles
Singapore
Slovakia
Slovenia
Spain
Sweden
Switzerland
Thailand
Trinidad and
  Tobago
United Arab
  Emirates
United Kingdom
Uruguay
USA
Venezuela

Medium human development
(HDI 0.500 to 0.799)

Albania
Algeria
Armenia
Azerbaijan
Bolivia
Botswana
Brazil
Bulgaria
Cape Verde
China
Congo
Croatia
Cuba
Dominican Rep.
Ecuador
Egypt
El Salvador
Estonia
Gabon
Georgia
Guatemala
Guyana
Honduras
Indonesia
Iran, Islamic Rep. of
Iraq
Jamaica
Jordan
Kazakstan
Korea, Dem.
  People's Rep. of
Kyrgyzstan
Latvia
Lebanon
Lithuania
Macedonia, FYR
Maldives
Moldova, Rep. of
Mongolia

Morocco
Namibia
Nicaragua
Oman
Papua New Guinea
Paraguay
Peru
Philippines
Romania
Russian Federation
Samoa (Western)
São Tomé and Principe
Saudi Arabia
Solomon Islands
South Africa
Sri Lanka
Suriname
Swaziland
Syrian Arab Rep.
Tajikistan
Tunisia
Turkey
Turkmenistan
Ukraine
Uzbekistan
Vanuatu
Viet Nam
Zimbabwe

Low human development
(HDI below 0.500)

Angola
Bangladesh
Benin
Bhutan
Burkina Faso
Burundi
Cambodia
Cameroon
Central African Rep.
Chad
Comoros
Côte d'Ivoire
Djibouti
Equatorial Guinea
Eritrea
Ethiopia
Gambia
Ghana
Guinea
Guinea-Bissau
Haiti
India
Kenya
Lao People's Dem. Rep.
Lesotho
Madagascar
Malawi
Mali
Mauritania
Mozambique
Myanmar
Nepal
Niger
Nigeria
Pakistan
Rwanda
Senegal
Sierra Leone
Sudan
Tanzania, U. Rep. of
Togo
Uganda
Yemen
Zaire
Zambia

Countries in the income aggregates

High income (GNP per capita above $8,955 in 1994)	Middle income (GNP per capita $726 to $8,955 in 1994)		Low income (GNP per capita $725 and below in 1994)	
Andorra	Algeria	Martinique	Afghanistan	Tajikistan
Aruba	American Samoa	Mauritius	Albania	Tanzania
Australia	Angola	Mayotte	Armenia	Togo
Austria	Antigua and Barbuda	Mexico	Azerbaijan	Uganda
Bahamas	Argentina	Micronesia Fed.	Bangladesh	Viet Nam
Belgium	Bahrain	States	Benin	Yemen
Bermuda	Barbados	Moldova, Rep. of	Bhutan	Zaire
Brunei Darussalam	Belarus	Morocco	Bosnia and Herzegovina	Zambia
Canada	Belize	Namibia	Burkina Faso	Zimbabwe
Cayman Islands	Bolivia	New Caledonia	Burundi	
Channel Islands	Botswana	N. Mariana Islands	Cambodia	
Cyprus	Brazil	Oman	Cameroon	
Denmark	Bulgaria	Panama	Central African Rep.	
Faeroe Islands	Cape Verde	Papua New Guinea	Chad	
Finland	Chile	Paraguay	China	
France	Colombia	Peru	Comoros	
French Polynesia	Costa Rica	Philippines	Congo	
Germany	Croatia	Poland	Côte d'Ivoire	
Greenland	Cuba	Puerto Rico	Egypt	
Hong Kong	Czech Rep.	Réunion	Equatorial Guinea	
Iceland	Djibouti	Romania	Eritrea	
Ireland	Dominica	Russian Federation	Ethiopia	
Israel	Dominican Rep.	Saint Kitts and Nevis	Gambia	
Italy	Ecuador	Saint Lucia	Georgia	
Japan	El Salvador	Saint Vincent	Ghana	
Kuwait	Estonia	Samoa (Western)	Guinea	
Liechtenstein	Fiji	Saudi Arabia	Guinea-Bissau	
Luxembourg	French Guiana	Seychelles	Guyana	
Macao	Gabon	Slovakia	Haiti	
Monaco	Greece	Slovenia	Honduras	
Netherlands	Grenada	Solomon Islands	India	
Netherlands Antilles	Guadeloupe	South Africa	Kenya	
New Zealand	Guam	Suriname	Kyrgyzstan	
Norway	Guatemala	Swaziland	Lao People's Dem. Rep.	
Portugal	Hungary	Syrian Arab Rep.	Lesotho	
Qatar	Indonesia	Thailand	Liberia	
Singapore	Iran, Islamic Rep. of	Tonga	Madagascar	
Spain	Iraq	Trinidad and Tobago	Malawi	
Sweden	Isle of Man	Tunisia	Mali	
Switzerland	Jamaica	Turkey	Mauritania	
United Arab Emirates	Jordan	Turkmenistan	Mongolia	
United Kingdom	Kazakstan	Ukraine	Mozambique	
USA	Kiribati	Uruguay	Myanmar	
Virgin Islands (U.S.)	Korea, Dem. People's	Uzbekistan	Nepal	
	Rep. of	Vanuatu	Nicaragua	
	Korea, Rep. of	Venezuela	Niger	
	Latvia	West Bank and Gaza	Nigeria	
	Lebanon	Yugoslavia	Pakistan	
	Libyan Arab Jamahiriya		Rwanda	
	Lithuania		São Tomé and Principe	
	Macedonia, FYR		Senegal	
	Malaysia		Sierra Leone	
	Maldives		Somalia	
	Malta		Sri Lanka	
	Marshall Islands		Sudan	

Least developed countries

Afghanistan
Angola
Bangladesh
Benin
Bhutan
Burkina Faso
Burundi
Cambodia
Cape Verde
Central African Rep.
Chad
Comoros
Djibouti
Equatorial Guinea
Eritrea
Ethiopia
Gambia
Guinea
Guinea-Bissau
Haiti
Kiribati
Lao People's Dem. Rep.
Lesotho
Liberia
Madagascar
Malawi
Maldives
Mali
Mauritania
Mozambique
Myanmar
Nepal
Niger
Rwanda
Samoa (Western)
São Tomé and Principe
Sierra Leone
Solomon Islands
Somalia
Sudan
Tanzania, U. Rep. of
Togo
Tuvalu
Uganda
Vanuatu
Yemen
Zaire
Zambia

All developing countries

Afghanistan
Algeria
Angola
Antigua and Barbuda
Argentina
Bahamas
Bahrain
Bangladesh
Barbados
Belize
Benin
Bhutan
Bolivia
Botswana
Brazil
Brunei Darussalam
Burkina Faso
Burundi
Cambodia
Cameroon
Cape Verde
Central African Rep.
Chad
Chile
China
Colombia
Comoros
Congo
Costa Rica
Côte d'Ivoire
Cuba
Cyprus
Djibouti
Dominica
Dominican Rep.
Ecuador
Egypt
El Salvador
Equatorial Guinea
Eritrea
Ethiopia
Fiji
Gabon

Gambia
Ghana
Grenada
Guatemala
Guinea
Guinea-Bissau
Guyana
Haiti
Honduras
Hong Kong
India
Indonesia
Iran, Islamic Rep. of
Iraq
Jamaica
Jordan
Kenya
Korea, Dem. People's Rep. of
Korea, Rep. of
Kuwait
Lao People's Dem. Rep.
Lebanon
Lesotho
Liberia
Libyan Arab Jamahiriya
Madagascar
Malawi
Malaysia
Maldives
Mali
Mauritania
Mauritius
Mexico
Mongolia
Morocco
Mozambique
Myanmar
Namibia
Nepal
Nicaragua
Niger
Nigeria

Oman
Pakistan
Panama
Papua New Guinea
Paraguay
Peru
Philippines
Qatar
Rwanda
Saint Kitts and Nevis
Saint Lucia
Saint Vincent
Samoa (Western)
São Tomé and Principe
Saudi Arabia
Senegal
Seychelles
Sierra Leone
Singapore
Solomon Islands
Somalia
South Africa
Sri Lanka
Sudan
Suriname
Swaziland
Syrian Arab Rep.
Tanzania, U. Rep. of
Thailand
Togo
Trinidad and Tobago
Tunisia
Turkey
Uganda
United Arab Emirates
Uruguay
Vanuatu
Venezuela
Viet Nam
Yemen
Zaire
Zambia
Zimbabwe

Industrial countries

Albania
Armenia
Australia
Austria
Azerbaijan
Belarus
Belgium
Bulgaria
Canada
Croatia
Czech Rep.
Denmark
Estonia
Finland
France
Georgia
Germany
Greece
Hungary
Iceland
Ireland
Israel
Italy
Japan
Kazakstan
Kyrgyzstan
Latvia
Lithuania
Luxembourg
Macedonia, FYR
Malta
Moldova, Rep. of
Netherlands
New Zealand
Norway
Poland
Portugal
Romania
Russian Federation
Slovakia
Slovenia
Spain
Sweden
Switzerland
Tajikistan
Turkmenistan
Ukraine
United Kingdom
USA
Uzbekistan

Countries in the regional aggregates

		Asia and the Pacific and Oceania	*Latin America, the Caribbean and North America*	
Sub-Saharan Africa	*Arab States*			*Europe*

DEVELOPING COUNTRIES

Sub-Saharan Africa	Arab States	Asia and the Pacific and Oceania	Latin America, the Caribbean and North America	Europe
Angola	Algeria	**East Asia**	**Latin America**	**Southern Europe**
Benin	Bahrain	China	**and the Caribbean**	Cyprus
Botswana	Djibouti	Hong Kong	Antigua and Barbuda	Turkey
Burkina Faso	Egypt	Korea, Dem. People's	Argentina	
Burundi	Iraq	Rep. of	Bahamas	
Cameroon	Jordan	Korea, Rep. of	Barbados	INDUSTRIAL
Cape Verde	Kuwait	Mongolia	Belize	COUNTRIES
Central African Rep.	Lebanon		Bolivia	
Chad	Libyan Arab Jamahiriya	**South-East Asia**	Brazil	**Eastern Europe and**
Comoros	Morocco	**and the Pacific**	Chile	**the Commonwealth of**
Congo	Oman	Brunei Darussalam	Colombia	**Independent States**
Côte d'Ivoire	Qatar	Cambodia	Costa Rica	Albania
Equatorial Guinea	Saudi Arabia	Fiji	Cuba	Armenia
Eritrea	Somalia	Indonesia	Dominica	Azerbaijan
Ethiopia	Sudan	Lao People's Dem. Rep.	Dominican Rep.	Belarus
Gabon	Syrian Arab Rep.	Malaysia	Ecuador	Bulgaria
Gambia	Tunisia	Myanmar	El Salvador	Croatia
Ghana	United Arab Emirates	Papua New Guinea	Grenada	Czech Rep.
Guinea	Yemen	Philippines	Guatemala	Estonia
Guinea-Bissau		Samoa (Western)	Guyana	Georgia
Kenya		Singapore	Haiti	Hungary
Lesotho		Solomon Islands	Honduras	Kazakstan
Liberia		Thailand	Jamaica	Kyrgyzstan
Madagascar		Vanuatu	Mexico	Latvia
Malawi		Viet Nam	Nicaragua	Lithuania
Mali			Panama	Macedonia, FYR
Mauritania		**South Asia**	Paraguay	Moldova, Rep. of
Mauritius		Afghanistan	Peru	Poland
Mozambique		Bangladesh	Saint Kitts and Nevis	Romania
Namibia		Bhutan	Saint Lucia	Russian Federation
Niger		India	Saint Vincent	Slovakia
Nigeria		Iran, Islamic Rep. of	Suriname	Slovenia
Rwanda		Maldives	Trinidad and Tobago	Tajikistan
São Tomé and Principe		Nepal	Uruguay	Turkmenistan
Senegal		Pakistan	Venezuela	Ukraine
Seychelles		Sri Lanka		Uzbekistan
Sierra Leone				
South Africa				**Western and**
Swaziland		INDUSTRIAL COUNTRIES		**Southern Europe**
Tanzania, U. Rep. of				Austria
Togo		Australia	**North America**	Belgium
Uganda		Israel	Canada	Denmark
Zaire		Japan	USA	Finland
Zambia		New Zealand		France
Zimbabwe				Germany
				Greece
				Iceland
				Ireland
				Italy
				Luxembourg
				Malta
				Netherlands
				Norway
				Portugal
				Spain
				Sweden

Other aggregates

European Union

Austria
Belgium
Denmark
Finland
France
Germany
Greece
Ireland
Italy
Luxembourg
Netherlands
Portugal
Spain
Sweden
United Kingdom

OECD

Australia
Austria
Belgium
Canada
Czech Rep.
Denmark
Finland
France
Germany
Greece
Hungary
Iceland
Ireland
Italy
Japan
Luxembourg
Mexico
Netherlands
New Zealand
Norway
Poland
Portugal
Spain
Sweden
Switzerland
Turkey
United Kingdom
USA

Nordic countries

Denmark
Finland
Iceland
Norway
Sweden